Health, Tourism and Hospitality

Health, Tourism and Hospitality: Spas, Wellness and Medical Travel, Second Edition takes an in-depth and comprehensive look at the growing health, wellness and medical tourism sectors in a global context. The book analyses the history and development of the industries, the way in which they are managed and organised, the expanding range of new and innovative products and trends, and the marketing of destinations, products and services.

The only book to offer a complete overview and introduction to health, tourism and hospitality, this second edition has been updated to include:

- Expanded coverage of the hospitality sector with a particular focus on spa management.
- New content on medical tourism throughout the book, to reflect the worldwide growth in medical travel with more and more countries entering this competitive market.
- Updated content to reflect recent issues and trends including ageing population, governments encouraging preventative health, consumer use of contemporary and alternative therapies, self-help market, impacts of economic recession, spa management and customer loyalty.
- New case studies taken from a range of different countries and contexts, and focusing on established or new destinations, products and services, such as conventional medicine, complementary and alternative therapies, lifestyle-based wellness, beauty and cosmetics, healthy nutrition, longevity and anti- (or active-)ageing, amongst others.

Written in a user-friendly style, this is essential reading for students studying health, tourism and hospitality.

Melanie Smith has worked for more than ten years on issues relating to health, wellness and spa tourism, including research and consultancy projects and the publication of several journal articles and book chapters. She has also lectured on health tourism in Hungary, Germany and Estonia. She has been an international Advisor in Health Tourism for the Global Spa Summit as well as the ETC and UNWTO, amongst others. She has been an invited Keynote Speaker at international Health and Wellness Conferences in numerous countries.

László Puczkó founded The Tourism Observatory for Health, Wellness and Spa (2012). He is currently the Head of the Tourism and Catering Institute at the BKF University of Applied Sciences in Budapest and Head of Tourism at Xellum Advisory Ltd. He has participated in more than a hundred projects, many of which were for international clients such as the Global Spa Summit, ETC and UNWTO. He is an internationally known expert in health tourism and he lectures at various international professional and academic conferences.

'Like their pioneering first edition, the second edition by Smith and Puczkó will become the standard reference text for anyone who is interested in wellness tourism. Large parts of this book are completely rewritten and updated, retracing the significant diversification and growth of this tourism sector. Particularly noteworthy new material includes a more extensive discussion on lifestyle issues contributing to the growth of wellness tourism. There are numerous "mini" and 41 extended case studies, boxes and figures, many written by many well-known industry practitioners and tourism academics and covering a rich array of content. These will facilitate students' comprehension of the topic in faster and more enjoyable ways.'

Cornelia Voight, Adjunct Research Fellow, School of Marketing,
Curtin University, Perth, Australia

'Smith and Puczkó's first edition, *Health and Wellness Tourism*, offered us a much-needed look into the rapidly growing field of health and wellness tourism. Their second edition, *Health, Tourism and Hospitality: Spas, Wellness and Medical Travel*, is more than a facelift. Anyone studying or working in the field of hospitality and tourism should read this book. Besides the wide array of case studies from different countries and contexts, the book also takes a strong management and marketing stand.'

Mário Passos Ascenção, Principal Lecturer, HAAGA-HELIA
University of Applied Sciences, Helsinki, Finland

 A range of further resources for this book are available on the Companion Website: www.routledge.com/cw/puczko

Health, Tourism and Hospitality

Spas, wellness and medical travel

Second edition

Melanie Smith and László Puczkó

Routledge
Taylor & Francis Group

LONDON AND NEW YORK

First published 2014
by Routledge
2 Park Square, Milton Park, Abingdon, Oxon OX14 4RN

and by Routledge
711 Third Avenue, New York, NY 10017

Routledge is an imprint of the Taylor & Francis Group, an informa business

British Library Cataloguing in Publication Data
A catalogue record for this book is available from the British Library

Library of Congress Cataloging in Publication Data
Smith, Melanie K.
 Health, tourism and hospitality : spas, wellness and medical travel / Melanie Smith and
 László Puczkó.—Second edition.
 pages cm
 ISBN 978–0–415–63864–7 (hardback) — ISBN 978–0–415–63865–4 (pbk.)—
 ISBN 978–0–203–08377–2 (ebook) 1. Medical tourism. 2. Hospitality industry.
 3. Travel–Health aspects. 4. Tourists–Health and hygiene. 5. Health resorts. I. Title.
 RA793.5.S65 2013
 338.4'791—dc23

                                                            2013016047

ISBN: 978–0–415–63864–7 (hbk)
ISBN: 978–0–415–63865– 4(pbk)
ISBN: 978–0–203–08377–2(ebk)

Typeset in Helvetica Neue
by RefineCatch Limited, Bungay, Suffolk

Printed and bound in Great Britain by
CPI Group (UK) Ltd, Croydon, CR0 4YY

For our lovely boys, Levi and Ferdi

Contents

List of figures   xi
List of tables   xiii
List of case studies   xv
Notes on authors   xvii
Notes on contributors   xix
Preface   xxxi
Acknowledgements   xxxv

Part I: History and development of health, wellness and medical tourism   **1**

1   Definitions and concepts   3
2   A historical overview   29
3   A geographical and regional analysis   49
4   Leisure, lifestyle and society   79

Part II: Managing and marketing health, wellness and medical tourism   **107**

5   Demand and motivation of tourists   109
6   Targeting and branding   137
7   Planning and management   169
8   Future trends and predictions   203

Part III: The international context for health, wellness and medical tourism: case studies   **229**

Spa developments   235

9   SpaFinder Wellness trends: what they teach us and why they are important   237
    Susie Ellis

10 Spa lifestyle resort communities and staycations   243
    Mick Matheusik

11 The rise of destination spas in emerging economies: a case study of
    GOCO Hospitality's Qatar and China destination spa projects   249
    Ingo Schweder

12 The Russian spa market: diverse and maturing   255
    Elena Bogacheva

13 Italian spas today: demand and offer evolution and trends   259
    Sonia Ferrari

14 Traditional spas – between health and wellness tourism: the Trentino
    strategy to face the challenge of the market   265
    Geradine Parisi

15 Day spa revenue management: some examples from Italy   269
    Patrizia Modica and Elisa Scanu

16 A multipurpose wellness park: the case study of Hamat Gader, Israel   275
    Yechezkel Israeli

17 Benchmarking pilot study for Hungarian wellness and spa hotels   281
    Andrea Vermesi

18 Comparative analysis of health tourism products and online
    communication of selected Hungarian spas and hotels   285
    Krisztina Priszinger and Katalin Formádi

19 Sleep therapy: a case study from Tervis Medical Spa, Estonia   291
    Inna Bentsalo

20 Benefits of higher education to the international spa industry: a UK
    perspective   295
    Kathryn Dowthwaite and Sarah Rawlinson

21 Labour and compensation structure of the spa industry in Canada   299
    Marion Joppe

22 Joining together and shaping the future of the global spa and
    wellness industry   305
    Susie Ellis

Health tourism destinations   313

23 Wellness tourism development in Slovenia in the last two decades   315
    Sonja Sibila Lebe

24 Wellness and spa provision in the Silesian health resorts of Poland   321
    Andrzej Hadzik, Dorota Ujma and Sean Gammon

25 History, traditions and the recent trends in the spa industry in the
    Czech Republic   329
    Alexey Kondrashov

26 Special health tourism products in the Bükk and Mátra regions   335
    Lóránt Dávid, Bulcsú Remenyik and Csaba Szűcs

27 Health tourism and horse milk therapy in Kyrgyzstan   341
    Ingeborg Nordbø and Elvira Sagyntay Kyzy

28 Well-being tourism in Finland   345
    Henna Konu, Anja Tuohino and Peter Björk

29 Health leisure market: the evolution in Portugal   351
    Nuno Gustavo and Fernando Completo

30 The holy Himalayas: an adobe to wellness   357
    Parikshat Singh Manhas

31 Te Aroha wellness tourism: yesterday and today   361
    Maria Hyde-Smith and John S. Hull

32 Revitalising the healing tradition: thermal springs in the
    Western Cape   369
    Mark Simon Boekstein

33 Opportunities and barriers to sustainable health tourism development
    in the Israeli Dead Sea region   373
    Dalit Gasul

34 Heritage and the renaissance of Domburg as a health resort   379
    Peter Kruizinga

35 Health cuisine: a new health destination marketing tool   383
    Nico Dingemans

Well-being, holistic and spiritual tourism   389

36 The social construction of travelling for well-being in Australia   391
    Alison van den Eynde and Adrian Fisher

37 Building tourism and well-being policy: engaging with the public
    health agenda in the UK   397
    *Heather Hartwell, Ann Hemingway, Alan Fyall, Viachaslau Filimonau,
    Stacy Wall and Neil Short*

38 Activities as a component of a social tourism holiday experience   403
    Riikka Ilves and Raija Komppula

39 Research on preventive wellness in the Netherlands   407
    Jacques Vork and Angelique Lombarts

40 Natural wellness: the case of Icelandic wilderness landscapes for
    health and wellness tourism   413
    Edward H. Huijbens

41 Global wellness in Sedona, Arizona   417
    Mia Mackman

42 A new age in tourism: a case study of New Age centres in Costa Rica 421
    Marinus C. Gisolf

43 The holistic approach of Ayurveda-based wellness tourism offered
    in Kerala   425
    Ramesh Unnikrishnan

44 Meditation tourism: exploring the meditation flow experience
    and well-being   429
    Tzuhui A. Tseng and Ching-Cheng Shen
45 The propensity for yoga practitioners to become tourists: a case study
    of Budapest   435
    Ivett Sziva, Noémi Kulcsár and Melanie Smith

Medical tourism and medical wellness   *443*

46 Apollo Hospitals group: a key player in the Indian medical tourism industry   445
    Anita Medhekar
47 The UK National Health Service and international patients   451
    Neil Lunt, Johanna Hanefeld, Daniel Horsfall and Richard D. Smith
48 Kurotel – turning a dream into reality: milestones and keys to success   455
    Victoria Winter
49 The Gawler Foundation in Australia: wellness and lifestyle-based
    therapeutic retreats for people with serious illnesses   461
    Cornelia Voigt
50 Challenges of balneotherapy development in Oyoun Moussa, Egypt   467
    Islam Elgammal and Heba Elakras

    References   *473*
    Index   *503*

Figures

1.1	Global health tourism services grid	26
3.1	Typology of global health and wellness facilities	76
4.1	Internal and external factors affecting lifestyle	104
5.1	GFK Roper lifestyles (2010)	119
6.1	Product levels in health and wellness tourism	138
6.2	Positioning health and wellness tourism facilities	167
7.1	Experience mapping	193
8.1	Some new trends in health and wellness travel	216
8.2	Characterising wellness tourism	220
8.3	Characterising medical tourism	222
8.4	Tour of wellness and spa	224
10.1	Comparative size of US spa industry	244
14.1	Location of Trentino spas	266
17.1	Effectiveness of marketing channels	284
22.1	The spa industry cluster	306
22.2	The wellness cluster	307
22.3	The wellness tourism and medical tourism market spectrum	309
22.4	Spa industry stakeholders	310
29.1	Thermal facilities demand in Portugal since 1927 – evolution	352
29.2	Motivations for thermal facilities demand in Portugal, 2006–10	354
37.1	The policy determinants of well-being at tourist destinations	401
39.1	Preventative wellness model	409
44.1	The causal relationship between meditation flow experience and well-being	434
45.1	The distribution of sample by age	437
45.2	Evaluation of the motivations for doing yoga	437
45.3	The benefits of doing yoga	437
45.4	Yoga travel according to age	438

45.5   The destinations for yoga trips   439

45.6   The factors influencing yoga trips   439

45.7   The importance of other activities   440

45.8   The preferred locations for yoga trips   440

Tables

1.1	Medical tourists' and wellness tourists' activities in spas	11
1.2	ISPA's changing categorisation of spas	12
3.1	Regional differences and trends in Europe	50
3.2	Spas in Sarein	64
4.1	Tribal versus urban living	80
4.2	Saudi patients in Germany	86
4.3	Three lifestyle trends in the UK	101
5.1	How customers see wellness and health care	110
5.2	Types of health and wellness products and typical visitors	110
5.3	Push and pull factors for health and wellness tourists	114
5.4	Well-being travel motivations in Australia	115
6.1	Multi-level marketing messages	140
6.2	Online sources of spa and wellness information	142
6.3	Branding considerations in health and wellness tourism	147
6.4	Country communication and positioning messages for health and wellness tourism	149
7.1	Economic impacts of health and wellness tourism	173
7.2	Environmental impacts of health and wellness tourism	176
7.3	Social and cultural impacts of health and wellness tourism	177
7.4	Feng Shui colour basics	194
8.1	What is wellness and medical tourism and what is not	226
14.1	Resources and specialisations of Trentino spas	267
18.1	Analysis of Hungarian spas and wellness hotels	286
18.2	The spectrum of health tourism in the examined hotels	288
18.3	The spectrum of health tourism in the examined spas	289
21.1	Hours and salaries of spa employees	301
24.1	Pre-delivery importance and post-delivery assessment of the quality of the health-resort tourism services offered in the Silesian health resorts of Ustroń and Goczałkowice	324

28.1 Finnish well-being tourism characteristics and well-being in
      South Ostrobothnia   348
29.1 Evolution of thermal facilities offer, 1926–2010   352
31.1 Wellness dimensions   364
32.1 Distribution of thermal spring resorts among the provinces of South Africa   370
33.1 Tourism statistics for the Dead Sea region (2000, 2005, 2011)   376
39.1 Strengths and weaknesses of the wellness sector in the Netherlands   408
44.1 Meditation flow activity analysis   431
44.2 Well-being analysis of meditation   432
46.1 Cost comparison for selected surgeries ($US – 2009 prices)   448
50.1 Benefits and effects of balneotherapy/hydrotherapy (includes
      exercising in water)   468
50.2 A comparison between the components of Oyoun Moussa water and
      Dead Sea water   470

Case studies

1.1	Thalassotherapy spas in France	14
1.2	Surgeon and Safari, South Africa	18
1.3	Confusing the religious and the spiritual? Ananda, Assisi	20
1.4	New Age community: Findhorn Foundation, Scotland	23
2.1	Spa in Belgium	33
2.2	Kumbha Mela festival in India	40
2.3	Rancho La Puerta	45
2.4	The Spa of Colonial Williamsburg	46
3.1	Wine spas in France by Jennifer Laing and Warwick Frost	51
3.2	City spa 'SLADO'™ – a new concept of a Russian spa by Elena Bogacheva	53
3.3	Karlovy Vary by Alexey Kondrashov	55
3.4	Health-consciousness in the background: conscious or trendy? by Katalin Formádi and Krisztina Priszinger	56
3.5	Pärnu in Estonia by Heli Tooman and Kai Tomasberg	58
3.6	Skyros Holistic Holiday Centres	61
3.7	Sarein, the Spa town in Iran by Hamid Zargham and Mehrnaz Salimi	64
3.8	Hot springs in Uganda by Eddy Tukamushaba	66
3.9	Wildfitness, Kenya	67
3.10	ASEAN Spa Standard by Andrew Jacka	68
3.11	Byron Bay, Australia	71
3.12	The success of Baños, Ecuador by Tamás Várhelyi	74
3.13	Adventure Spas in South America	75
4.1	Pritikin Longevity Center	82
4.2	Therapeutic recreation: experience therapy	85
4.3	Promises Malibu Luxury Rehab Retreats	87
4.4	Detox retreats in Austria	90
4.5	Patients using the internet for medical tourism by David G. Vequist, Michael Guiry and Emre Bolatkale	93

4.6	Ecotherapy: the green agenda for mental health (UK, 2007)	97
4.7	Ashram tourism	99
5.1	Children's spas	113
5.2	Spas and camping in France by Véronique Campion	124
5.3	Spas for men	124
5.4	Gay spas	126
5.5	Yoga in Rishikesh, India	133
5.6	Different nationality guests in Pärnu, Estonia	135
6.1	Royal Spas of Europe	140
6.2	Healing Hotels of the World	145
6.3	Switzerland's marketing of wellness and spa tourism	148
6.4	Alpine Wellness	152
6.5	Starwood Hotels and Resorts	154
6.6	Danubius Hotels	155
6.7	Lanserhof Health Spa	156
6.8	Speaking health German	158
6.9	Techniker Krankenkasse	162
6.10	Spa holidays by Kuoni	165
7.1	Operational issues: retaining staff in a seasonal environment by Su Gibson	171
7.2	Therapeutic tourism on the Dead Sea of Jordan is in danger by Salem Harahsheh	174
7.3	Management challenges in Pamukkale, Turkey	175
7.4	The Green Spa Network	180
7.5	A sustainably managed natural resource: the Blue Lagoon, Iceland	180
7.6	A unique cultural experience: Botanique Hotel and Spa, Brazil	183
7.7	Health-care cluster: Medellin Health City (Colombia)	186
7.8	South Korea: Healience Zen Town by Timothy Jeonglyeol Lee and Ji-Sook Han	188
7.9	Bath: regeneration of a historic spa	190
8.1	Wellness in the countryside by Corné de Regt	209
8.2	Helsinki Airport Spa	211
8.3	Product development: smart and intelligent versus plain unappealing!	225

Notes on authors

Melanie Smith is co-author of the book *Health and Wellness Tourism* (2009) with Dr László Puczkó. She has also worked for ten years on issues relating to holistic wellness, including research projects and the publication of several journal articles and book chapters. She was founder of the ATLAS (Association for Tourism and Leisure Education) Spa and Wellness Special Interest Research Group in 2007. Since 2009 she has been Curriculum Development Advisor and Visiting Lecturer for Pärnu College (University of Tartu, Estonia) for MA Wellness and Spa Service Design and Management, where she has also run workshops on health and wellness for the Estonian Tourist Board. She has also lectured on spas and wellness in Hungary and Germany. In 2011 she was an advisor and researcher for the Global Spa Summit research report *Wellness Tourism and Medical Tourism: Where Do Spas Fit?* and a researcher for the Gifts of Health project on Islamic Wellness Traditions. She has been an invited keynote speaker at international health and wellness conferences in Belgium, Estonia, Finland, Hungary, Iceland, Israel, South Korea, the Netherlands and Slovenia.

László Puczkó is co-author of the book *Health and Wellness Tourism* with Dr Melanie Smith. He is a Certified Management Consultant (CMC) and since 2006 he has been the President of the Association of Tourism Consultants, and founded The Tourism Observatory for Health, Wellness and Spa (2012). He is currently the Head of the Institute of Tourism, Leisure and Hospitality, BKF University of Applied Sciences, Budapest. He has participated in more than a hundred projects, many of which were for international clients such as the Global Spa Summit, in various fields: research, strategic and tactical planning, product development, experience mapping and design, impact assessment; and marketing in health-, wellness- and spa-tourism, transport, heritage and cultural tourism, eco-tourism and some specialised or themed tourism products. He has also lectured at various international professional and academic conferences and congresses, and is a member of the Global Speakers' Network.

Notes on contributors

Inna Bentsalo works at the University of Tartu Pärnu College as an Assistant of Spa Management and has a Master's in Wellness and Spa Service Design and Management. Her Master's thesis focused on sleep therapy and she has also lectured on this subject. She is currently continuing her research in spas and wellness.

Peter Björk is Associate Marketing Professor at HANKEN School of Economics, Vaasa, Finland. He is associate editor for the *Scandinavian Journal of Hospitality and Tourism* and *Finnish Journal of Tourism Research*. He has a special passion for new service development, destination branding and tourism innovations. Furthermore, his area of expertise is policy and management issues of well-being tourism development.

Mark Simon Boekstein lectures in tourism at Cape Peninsula University of Technology, Cape Town, South Africa. His main research interest is in the medicinal value of natural thermal springs, and he is author of *Hot Spring Holidays* (1998), a visitors' guide to hot-spring resorts in southern Africa.

Elena Bogacheva is founder and President of SWIC, a non-profit organisation for the spa and wellness industry in Russia and CIS. With 18 years of experience in the spa business, she is the author of many publications, including the first manual in Russian devoted to spas, organises conferences and seminars, and acts as a consultant for spa facilities.

Emre Bolatkale is a Consultant and Management Assistant with 21st Century Strategies. He also works for the University of the Incarnate Word in San Antonio, Texas.

Véronique Campion has worked in the tourism and wellness industry for over 15 years with experience in Germany, Ireland and France. She completed her Master's thesis on spa and wellness tourism in France in 2012. She runs her own travel agency in France specialising in spa and wellness holidays. Her credo is to democratise wellness tourism and make it more accessible to the younger generation.

Fernando Completo is Professor at Estoril Higher Institute for Tourism and Hotel Studies (Portugal). He is a member of the Tourism Planning Area and a Tourism Studies Association (CESTUR) Researcher. He completed his PhD in Tourism at the Institute of Geography and Regional Planning, University of Lisbon. He is an expert in nature and adventure tourism, sport tourism, geotourism and leisure management.

Lóránt Dávid is co-author of the *Basis of Health Tourism* textbook (2012) with Dr Csilla Molnár. He has been researching health tourism for more than six years, lectures in the field of spa and wellness in Transylvania, and is the author of a number of publications in this field.

Nico Dingemans is an international hotelier by origin, graduating from the Hotel Management School Leeuwarden of Stenden University of Applied Sciences, with ten years of work experience in 4 and 5 star hotels in Asia, the USA, the Middle East and Europe. Based in the Netherlands, he has owned two boutique hospitality consultancy brands since 2007, serving luxury hotels and resorts with hospitality perspectives, and world-class hospitals and healthcare providers with hospitality in health (HIH). One of the cornerstones in the mission of HIH to bring hospitality, wellness and healthcare closer together is healthy gastronomy. Under the motto 'Good food should simply be tasteful, healthy and pleasing to the eye', he is in the process of writing a wellness-based book entitled *Health Cuisine. 12 Chefs. 12 Destinations*, and he published his first book *From Farm to Fork in Twente* in 2012.

Kathryn Dowthwaite, Higher Education Spa Degree Programme Leader at the University of Derby, UK, has worked in the spa and wellness industry for over 15 years with international experience ranging from therapy to management. In more recent years she has specialised in training, lecturing and research in spa and wellness.

Heba Elakhras is a Lecturer in the Tourism Management Department at Suez Canal University, Egypt. Her PhD focused on wellness tourism and she is currently lecturing and supervising a number of postgraduates.

Islam Elgammal is a Lecturer at the Suez Canal University, Department of Tourism and Hotels.

Susie Ellis is Chairman and CEO of the Global Spa and Wellness Summit and President of SpaFinder Wellness. A spa/wellness trends expert, she is the author of SpaFinder Wellness Trends' 'What They Teach Us and Why They're Important' and co-author of the GSWS research report 'Wellness Tourism and Medical Tourism: Where Do Spas Fit?' (2011). She received ISPA's 2012 Visionary Award.

Sonia Ferrari is Associate Professor of Tourism Marketing, Event Marketing and Place Marketing at the University of Calabria, Italy. She is President of Tourism Science Degree Course in the University of Calabria and President of Valorizzazione dei Sistemi Turistico Culturali Degree Course in the University of Calabria since 2007. Her main fields of study and research are tourism and place marketing, event marketing, spa and wellness tourism.

Viachaslau Filimonau is a Research Fellow at Bournemouth University. His research interests include sustainable tourism, tourism environmental impact appraisal and use of information and communication technologies with tourism and travel purposes.

Adrian Fisher is an Associate Professor in Community Psychology at Victoria University, Australia. He has expertise in qualitative and quantitative research methods, with a strong focus on community involvement and community change. His work is applied psychology, often with a policy focus. Adrian has published extensively in areas of psychological sense of community and community development. He has held grants in health promotion, sense of community and social support. More recently, he has been researching people's perceptions of water quality and alternative sources of drinking water.

Katalin Formádi is an Associate Professor at the Tourism Department, University of Pannonia, Hungary. She holds a Bachelor's degree in tourism economics and a Master's degree in economics and sociology from the Corvinus University in Budapest. She finished her PhD in 2010 in the sociology of professions from Corvinus University. She has been researching the process of professionalisation, careers and tourism employment in the area of health and wellness tourism and the event tourism for several years and lately has been involved in disabled tourism. She is the author of several publications in these fields.

Warwick Frost is a Lecturer at La Trobe University's School of Management. Dr Frost has authored and edited many books on tourism and event management for various publishers.

Alan Fyall is Visiting Professor at the Rosen College of Hospitality Management, University of Central Florida. Prior to arriving in the USA, Alan was Professor in Tourism and Deputy Dean Research and Enterprise in the School of Tourism, Bournemouth University. He has published widely in his fields of expertise and is the author of over 100 articles, book chapters and conference papers as well as 14 books including *Tourism Principles and Practice*, one of the leading international textbooks on the subject, published by Pearson.

Sean Gammon is a Senior Lecturer at the School of Sport, Tourism and the Outdoors, University of Central Lancashire. He has written extensively in the area of sport-related tourism; predominantly focusing on exploring sport-tourist motives, experiences and behaviour. His current research interest involves determining the interaction between sport places and visitors, using environmental psychological perspectives. He is an Associate Editor of the *Journal of Sport and Tourism* and is a member of the Leisure Studies Association. He is currently co-editing a book entitled *Contemporary Perspectives in Leisure: Meanings, Motives and Lifelong Learning*.

Dalit Gasul is a Lecturer and Researcher at the Department of Tourism and Hospitality Management, Kinneret College on the Sea of Galilee in Israel. She wrote her PhD about sustainable tourism by the Dead Sea in Israel.

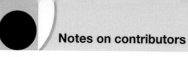

Su Gibson is the Spa Management lecturer at the Conrad N. Hilton College at the University of Houston and organiser of the Houston Spa Association. With an MBA in International Business and more than ten years of experience within the spa industry, she enjoys writing and learning about all topics in health and wellness. She has worked for spas in the US and UK in various roles from massage therapist to spa director, and conducted numerous related classes and workshops. Completely dedicated to the pursuit of wellness and life-in-balance, she is a long-term vegetarian, nature-lover and yoga enthusiast.

Marinus C. Gisolf has been running a receptive tourism agency in Latin America for nearly 20 years and received the highest standard of 5 green leaves granted in Costa Rica. For the past three years he has been heading a consultancy in sustainable tourism called Tourism Theories and has published various books and articles on the subject. His research in wellness tourism started five years ago in Costa Rica.

Michael Guiry is an Associate Professor of Marketing at the University of the Incarnate Word and a Senior Fellow at the Center for Medical Tourism Research. He has a PhD in Marketing from the University of Florida, an MBA from Duke University, and a BSc in Agricultural Business Management and Marketing from Cornell University. His current research interests include medical tourism service quality and brand positioning, retirement tourism, recreational shopping and cross-cultural consumer behaviour.

Nuno Gustavo has focused his academic research career on health and wellness tourism since 2003. Besides several publications, his PhD, MSc and BSc theses were in this field of studies.

Andrzej Hadzik is an Assistant Professor in the Faculty of Sport and Tourism Management at the Akademia Wychowania Fizycznego w Katowicach (University of Physical Education in Katowice), he has also chaired the Tourism and Recreation Department at the same institution. He completed three programmes of studies: economics, physical education and physiotherapy. He has a PhD in economics. His research interests revolve around health tourism and sport tourism and he has published over 120 reviewed articles in these areas, both in Poland and internationally.

Johanna Hanefeld is from the London School of Hygiene and Tropical Medicine. She is co-author of a UK study focused on inward and outward medical tourism.

Salem Harahsheh is Assistant Professor of Tourism Marketing, Department of Travel and Tourism, Faculty of Tourism and Hotel Management of Yarmouk University, Irbid-Jordan. He gained his MA in tourism management in 2002 and his PhD in tourism marketing from Bournemouth University, UK, in 2009. His research interests include: destination marketing, destination image, health tourism, social media marketing, religious tourism, tourist behaviour and motivation, voluntourism, museum studies, tourism and the media, policing tourism, culture and communication in tourism.

Heather Hartwell is an Associate Professor at Bournemouth University, UK, in the field of public health. She is editor of *Perspectives in Public Health* and a trustee of the Royal Society for Public Health. Her current research on well-being and tourism was featured in the Research Councils UK 'Big Ideas for the Future' identifying the relationship between recreation, leisure and well-being as a key theme for the next twenty-year time period.

Ann Hemingway is Deputy Director at the Centre for Wellbeing at Bournemouth University, UK. She is public health research lead within the Academic Centre for Health and Wellbeing where her interests have focused on the promotion of sustainable well-being through resident involvement in planning and providing services; and capacity building particularly in deprived areas.

Daniel Horsfall is based at the University of York. He is co-author of a UK study focused on inward and outward medical tourism.

Edward H. Huijbens is a geographer and the director of the Icelandic Tourism Research Centre. He also holds an Associate Professor's Chair in the Department of Business at the University of Akureyri. He has researched landspaces and spatial conceptions for over a decade and in recent years has devoted himself to tourism and well-being research.

John S. Hull has been involved with the health and wellness industry in Iceland, New Zealand, Indonesia and Canada. In 2006–7, he was director of a wellness strategy for Northeast Iceland. In 2008 he was a keynote speaker at the New Zealand Wellness Tourism Symposium and in 2011 he presented a joint keynote address with Maria Hyde-Smith at the Bali International Spa and Wellness Expo. He has taught courses in spa and wellness in New Zealand and Canada, and is presently researching wellness and aboriginal tourism in British Columbia.

Maria Hyde-Smith is a programme leader and Senior Lecturer at Auckland University of Technology, New Zealand. She leads the spa and wellness discipline in the School of Hospitality and Tourism and is currently researching quality control in the wellness spa industry. Her professional background includes working at some of the UK's leading spa and health facilities as a therapist, and managing and teaching at a variety of beauty and spa training organisations both in the UK and New Zealand.

Riikka Ilves wrote her thesis about social tourism and the case study was her first research on well-being tourism.

Yechezkel Israeli is an expert in tourism management at the Department of Tourism and Hotel Management, Kinneret College on the Sea of Galilee in Israel. For many years he has been involved in academic research and in planning works in the field of medical and wellness tourism. He holds a position on the board of directors of the largest wellness site in Israel, and has an active role in consulting.

Andrew Jacka has a background in hospitality but later moved into the spa industry. His work at both local and international levels and his affiliations with spa-industry organisations, together with the knowledge gained from practical operational spa management, ensures an up-to-date knowledge suited to those operators/developers seeking to establish or re-establish their own spa operation.

Marion Joppe is a Professor in the School of Hospitality and Tourism Management, University of Guelph, Canada. She specialises in destination planning, development and marketing, and the experiences upon which destinations build, including spa and wellness tourism.

Raija Komppula is Professor of Tourism Business at the University of Eastern Finland. She has been researching well-being tourism together with her students especially in rural and nature based contexts in Finland.

Alexey Kondrashov is a teaching and research assistant at the Department of Tourism, University of Economics, Prague, Czech Republic. He has been researching the main indicators for measurement of spa hotels and facilities economic performances in the Czech Republic, Slovakia and Slovenia since 2010. He is the author of several research publications in this field.

Henna Konu is project manager at the Centre for Tourism Studies at the University of Eastern Finland. She has worked in several well-being and wellness research and development projects and she has published academic papers in that field. Currently she is writing her PhD dissertation on the customer's role in experience service development in a well-being tourism context.

Peter Kruizinga is project manager, Senior Lecturer and researcher in the field of Vitality and Tourism Management, at HZ University of Applied Sciences, the Netherlands. He is doing his PhD research on well-being and the coast.

Noémi Kulcsár is a Lecturer and Researcher with a PhD in rural tourism development in Hungary. She has recently been researching the role of yoga in well-being in Budapest.

Elvira Sagyntay Kyzy is the head of the Science and International Relations Department and a Senior Lecturer in the Tourism Department of Issykkul State University in Kyrgyzstan. Elvira's main field of teaching and research are within tourism economy, the management of tourism businesses and ecology. Her publications are on tourism education and diverse aspects of mountain tourism. She is a co-author of the report 'Mountain Research and Development (MRD) Special Issue: Central Asian Mountain Societies in Transition'. Elvira also has extensive experience in working on Tempus and Erasmus Mundus Projects.

Jennifer Laing is a Senior Lecturer in the Department of Marketing, Tourism and Hospitality at La Trobe University. She has been researching health and wellness tourism for many years now, including extensive research on health tourism in Australia, a case study of Byron Bay and, more recently, wine therapy in France.

Sonja Sibila Lebe was leader of the cross-border European Wellness Project for Slovenia (2004–6); she contributed a presentation on ITB Wellness Day in 2008, and has been researching and publishing on wellness for more than a decade. She was a contributor to *Health and Wellness Tourism* (2009).

Timothy Jeonglyeol Lee works at the Department of Tourism and Hospitality Management, Ritsumeikan Asia Pacific University (APU), Beppu, Japan. He has been researching medical, health and wellness tourism, and thalassotherapy, and is currently focusing on 'zen' towns.

Angelique Lombarts is co-author of a research project on preventive wellness in the Netherlands. She is a Professor in city marketing and leisure management at Inholland University in the Netherlands and she has her own consultancy firm in tourism. She has a lot of marketing and sales experience in the international tourism industry.

Neil Lunt is based at the University of York (Lunt and Horsfall). He is co-author of a UK study focused on inward and outward medical tourism. He has also published other articles and chapters on medical tourism.

Mia Mackman is the founder and President of the Arizona Spa and Wellness Association. She has been in the spa industry for 18 years. She has spent the last ten years as a consultant creating innovative programmes, marketing strategies and adding new layers to spa and wellness development.

Mick Matheusik is President of TREC International Inc., a management consulting office specialising in tourism, retail, spas, health and wellness, resorts, and leisure-based real estate and businesses located in West Vancouver, BC and Vice President of Resort and Leisure Commercial with NAI Commercial brokerage Vancouver office Canada. Mick advises clients on markets, concepts, strategic planning, development and marketing of these types of real-estate projects and businesses worldwide.

Anita Medhekar is a Senior Lecturer in Economics at Central Queensland University, Australia. She has been teaching and researching in economics of Asia-Pacific countries, development economics, international trade, spiritual tourism, health and tourism economics, and medical tourism, and is the author of several publications in this field.

Patrizia Modica is Associate Professor at the University of Cagliari, Department of Economics and Business Studies. Her research interests and conference presentations cover the areas of tourism management and revenue management, and specifically pricing policies in the tourism wellness industry.

Ingeborg Nordbø holds a PhD in tourism and entrepreneurship and works as an Associate Professor in Tourism Management at Telemark University College, Norway. Nordbø has published and specialised in tourism development in rural and remote areas, including health and wellness aspects. She has worked as a consultant and researcher in a number of international projects, mainly in Scandinavia, Latin America and Central Asia.

Geradine Parisi is a consultant in local development in Trentino in Italy. Her specialities include local development, destination management, tourism marketing and business management.

Krisztina Priszinger is a Lecturer at the University of Pannonia, Hungary. Her research focus is on health and wellness tourism; she has been writing her thesis on risk factors in Hungarian health-and-wellness-oriented hotels and has published in this field. She lectures on Health Tourism and Health Tourism Management at BA and MA levels. She is a member of the international research project called WelDest.

Sarah Rawlinson is Assistant Director (Academic), University of Derby, Buxton. Her recent research focuses on the experience of spa graduates entering the spa industry and the value their employers place on them. The results of her research are used to further develop the vocational degrees offered at the University of Derby.

Corné de Regt is a farmer's son who went to the Hoge Hotelschool Maastricht (hotel-management school) and then worked as a manager for companies such as ABN Amro Bank, Novotel Amsterdam, Randstad Uitzendbureau, PNO Consultants and Stimuland (for developing farmers' entrepreneurship in the countryside in areas such as bed and breakfast, healthcare, jobs, municipal strategy). After that he started his own company, Rode Wangen.

Bulcsú Remenyik is an Associate Professor at the Budapest Business School in Hungary. He holds a BA in History, Geography and Tourism, and a PhD in Geography, both from the University of Pécs. He has a long-standing research interest in tourism and regional development, and a lengthy publishing record. He was responsible for the administration of more than 20 regional and local projects and initiatives involving development of tourism destinations.

Mehrnaz Salimi has a BA in English Literature, is an English teacher and has been a Master's student in Tourism Management majoring in planning at the Allame Tabatabai' University of Tehran since 2010. She is currently working on her Master's thesis entitled 'Wellness Tourism in Chosen Countries with an Emphasis on Developing Ones'. She has chosen five foreign countries to compare their wellness and spa tourism (Australia, Austria, Hungary, Thailand and India), and her final results will also be applied to her Iranian case study of Sarein, one of the most important spa towns in Iran.

Elisa Scanu is a PhD candidate at the School of Management and Accounting, University of Cagliari, Italy. Her research is directed towards tourism issues and her interests include revenue and demand management in the tourism wellness industry.

Ingo Schweder is CEO and founder of GOCO with more than 20 years of experience from the fields of spa and hospitality. Working with and managing some of the world's most prestigious hotel groups, he has been involved with the design, development and worldwide operation of iconic properties and spas. He has been recognised with many industry awards including 'Spa Personality of the Year', 'Excellence in Hospitality Design', 'Most Distinguished Industry Motivator' and 'Best Spa Company'. He sits on the board of the Spa India Association and the China Spa Symposium.

Ching-Cheng Shen is an Associate Professor in the Graduate Institute of Travel and Tourism Management in National Kaohsiung University of Hospitality and Tourism, Taiwan. He has been researching health tourism and rural tourism for many years, and has published in this field.

Neil Short is a Policy Development Manager in Environmental Services at Bournemouth Borough Council, UK. He co-ordinates projects that link environmental and health issues, such as fuel poverty alleviation, and works with partners to help achieve the town's Earth Charter commitments.

Parikshat Singh Manhas is an Associate Professor at School of Hospitality and Tourism Management and the Business School, University of Jammu. He is the author or co-author of five books on destination marketing and branding, and has done extensive research in the field of destination management, with about 60 publications in this field.

Richard D. Smith is a Professor at the London School of Hygiene and Tropical Medicine. He has been a Health Economist for over 20 years. From 2008–2011 he served as Head of the Department of Global Health & Development, and since 2011 has been Dean of Faculty of Public Health & Policy. His recent work focuses on developing the application of macro-economics to health, the economics of globalization and health, and aspects of trade in health goods, services, people and ideas.

Ivett Sziva is Associate Professor, Budapest College of Communication and Business. She takes part in academic and consulting research, and is mostly committed to qualitative methods. She lectures and has published on the topics of destination management, competitiveness, health and clinical tourism, and e-tourism. At present, she is focusing her research work on the newest trends of health tourism – clinical and spiritual health tourism.

Csaba Szűcs is a Lecturer, Researcher and translator from the Károly Róbert Főiskola in Budapest, Hungary.

Kai Tomasberg is currently working as Programme Manager of the International Master's programme Wellness and Spa Service Design and Management in the Department of Tourism Studies of the University of Tartu Pärnu College in Estonia and as a project manager of international summer courses on nature, culture and spa tourism. She focuses on the topics of resort history as well as bathing culture and spa treatments, providing lecturers and practical study visits. She has studied cosmetics and skin care in France and worked as a freelancer for several cosmetics brands and magazines.

Heli Tooman is Senior Lecturer of Tourism Management, Department of Tourism Studies at Pärnu College of the University of Tartu. Her research and teaching focuses on quality in tourism and customer service, health, wellness and spa tourism, as well as sustainable tourism destination development. She has published six tourism textbooks and more than 40 articles. She has participated in many tourism-related projects as an expert and consultant on the development of Estonian and regional tourism plans and participated in the development of the categorisation system for Estonian spas. She also has practical working experience as a hotel manager.

Tzuhui A. Tseng is an Associate Professor in the Department of Environmental and Cultural Resources of National Hsinchu University of Education, Taiwan, and is also the Chief of the International Programme and Exchange. Her research interests are about therapeutic landscape and healthy leisure behaviour.

Eddy Tukamushaba has a PhD in Hotel and Tourism Management from the Hong Kong Polytechnic University. He worked in the tourism and hospitality industry for close to seven years before joining academia in 2001. He has been Head of the Department of Leisure and Hospitality at Makerere University Business School in Uganda.

Anja Tuohino is Development Manager at the Centre for Tourism Studies at the University of Eastern Finland and a member of the national well-being tourism strategy working group. She has extensive experience with several well-being and wellness tourism research and development projects. She has also published academic papers in the field.

Dorota Ujma is a Course Leader for Undergraduate Hospitality Courses at the University of Central Lancashire, UK. Dorota's research interests are focused upon tourism marketing and events tourism, specifically distribution in tourism and hospitality, but also health resorts. Recently she has been involved in a project to translate eminent tourism research into Polish for *Folia Turistica*, an academic journal for tourism research, as well as a collaborative research project in the Silesian health resorts of Poland.

Ramesh Unnikrishnan is presently employed as the Director of the All India Council for Technical Education, New Delhi, India. He has published several articles in reputed journals on wellness tourism and his area of interest includes Ayurveda, wellness, tourism education and holistic therapies.

Alison van den Eynde is a PhD candidate researching the social construction of well-being travel in Australia. She is from a sociology background and currently teaches sociology and tourism.

Tamás Várhelyi graduated as a medical doctor and as a computer programmer, and he has an MBA, PhD and CMC. He was deputy state secretary of Ministry of Environment, Hungary and senior manager of KPMG. Now he is a professor of a tourism college and general manager of Compudoc Plc. He has published six books and travelled to more than 110 countries. His current focus is on the collaboration between spa and wellness and the health-care industry.

David Vequist is the founder and Director of the Center for Medical Tourism Research (CMTR). He has done extensive research on the business of medical travel. His experience includes: keynote speaker at conferences worldwide; a featured author with many papers and articles about medical tourism trends; interviews in a variety of media around the world; founder and co-editor of the first academic journal devoted to the business of medical tourism (starting this year); chair of the first ever Medical Tourism Research conferences; and leading researcher on several projects for countries, regions, facilities and providers. In the past, he was an executive with HCA managing the human resources for a large subsidiary (Methodist Healthcare) in San Antonio, Texas, USA and prior to that was a consultant with Ernst and Young LLP. He is currently expanding his research on the impact of health, wellness, dental, medical and retirement tourism.

Andrea Vermesi is the Operations Manager of International Wellness Institute, an adult learning training provider in Hungary specialising in health tourism, wellness and fitness education. She has an MSc in Health Policy Planning, a BSc in Health Promotion and leads the Wellness and Spa Management course. She initiated the first industrial spa benchmarking study in Hungary. Her main research area is the prevention of health problems through fitness and recreational activities and their implementation in health-care policies and protocols.

Cornelia Voigt is Adjunct Research Fellow at the Tourism Research Cluster, Curtin University, Perth, Australia. Her PhD was entitled 'Understanding Wellness Tourism: An Analysis of Benefits Sought, Health-Promoting Behaviours and Positive Psychological Well Being' (2010), and she is co-author with Christoph Pforr of the book *Wellness Tourism* (Routledge, 2013).

Jacques Vork is Associate Professor in City Marketing and Leisure Management at Inholland University and has his own consultancy firm in destination marketing. His expertise is focused on incoming tourism.

Stacy Wall is a PhD student at Bournemouth University, UK. Her research is investigating well-being as a boundary object between public health and tourism communities of practice.

Victoria Winter is Commercial Manager of Kurotel. She specialises in international health-care legislation, Brazilian health-care marketing and promotion legislation, private and public sector cooperative initiatives, the impact of global economics on the health-care sector, client-driven service design, health-care branding and marketing, international trade fare networking and international health-care corporate branding.

Hamid Zargham has been a Professor at the Allameh Tabataba'i University in Iran for more than 30 years. He is a national Tourism Development Consultant and Advisor, as well as a data analyst and planner.

Preface

Confrontation with other cultures and customs is central to the idea of tourism. To travel is to embark upon a voyage of discovery: self-discovery . . .

(Smith, 2010: 150)

The second edition of this book was written quite soon after the first one, just because the field of health, wellness and spa tourism has moved on so quickly. It is exciting to see such growing interest in academic and industry circles as well as in education. I now teach a Health and Wellness Tourism course which is popular with Hungarian students and Erasmus students alike. I have also taught Spa and Wellness Management to very receptive students in Germany. László and I both teach on the MA Wellness and Spa Service Design and Management at Pärnu College, University of Tartu in Estonia, where we have had the chance to meet some fantastic students from around the world with a great enthusiasm for wellness and spas. Many of my students have started to focus on spas and wellness for their Dissertation research at both BA and MA level, and I have started a Live Group Project working with spa and wellness hotels in Budapest, as well as doing research with students and colleagues on yoga and retreat tourism here. I have examined PhDs recently in thermal tourism and medical tourism. I have also been lucky enough to be invited to speak in more than ten countries on the subject of wellness, including Belgium, Estonia, Finland, Germany, Hungary, Iceland, Israel, the Netherlands, South Korea and Slovenia.

My own wellness journey has continued with an almost daily yoga practice, meditation when I need it, a weekly Pilates session with a trainer (for 'medical wellness' reasons) and a weekly back massage, plus learning some Tai Chi and Chi Kung. I am a big fan of 'living room' and 'DVD' wellness, being a busy working mum. I try to remember to practise at home what I preach in my work, especially when I am stressed with work or juggling everyday life with two little boys (both of whom are fascinated by yoga and Tai Chi – our six-year-old Levi has even invented his own form of massage!).

My feelings about wellness are changing. I used to believe that evidence-based research, scientific studies and regulation of the industry were essential to its future being taken seriously. However, seeing the exponential growth of all aspects of health and wellness activities and tourism, I can't help thinking that the most important thing is that we take full advantage and do whatever makes us feel as healthy and as happy as we possibly can. We don't need a doctor's prescription for this or 'permission' from the latest scientific study. As stated by Louise Hay (in Hay and Richardson, 2011: 45):

> The real goal in life is to feel good. We want money because we want to feel better. We want good health because we want to feel better. We want a nice relationship because we think we will feel better. And if we could just make feeling better our goal, we would eliminate a lot of extra work.

We hope you enjoy the new edition of this book and wish you happiness on your own wellness journey!

Melanie Smith

Associate Professor, Budapest College of Communication and Business, Budapest (Hungary)

Visiting Associate Professor, Parnü College, University of Tartu (Estonia), March, 2013

> Some people feel more alive when they travel and visit unfamiliar places or foreign countries because at those times sense perception – experiencing – takes up more of their consciousness than thinking. They become more present.
>
> (Tolle, 2005: 239)

Travelling for health and searching for healing: having participated in numerous professional events and congresses on health, medical, wellness and spa-related issues in the USA, Brazil, China, South Korea, Bali, Iran and Turkey, as well as in several European countries, I have not only discussed various topics, but more importantly I have learned a great deal too. It is absolutely fascinating how wide the list of those resources and assets are that either already have been or could be used for health purposes. I have observed the proliferation of the market. Almost every country, region or destination would like to define, develop or create some services that can serve the needs of the health-oriented traveller. This includes medical, wellness or spa tourism services and facilities. This is especially interesting, since many developments used no site-specific resources and started to compete based on existing price differences (especially in medical tourism). In wellness and spa tourism, the architecture, the interior design and the location became the influential factors. Not only destinations, but self-made experts also entered the field both in medical and in wellness tourism and many of them even became 'celebrities' in the field, too. I myself learned the hard way about the unethical and even illegal practices of one of them.

I also found out a lot about the existing differences between countries and cultures regarding health travel. Ever since the first edition of the book there has been no clear development in the terminologies and definitions used. Rather, the opposite can be seen!

Heated discussions exist about the (perceived?) differences between medical travel and medical tourism, for example. We can also observe the competition between the terms 'wellness' and 'spa'. And we should not forget the evergreen discussion about what medical tourism actually means: does it have to have a surgical intervention or can non-invasive therapies also form medical tourism services? It was an eye opener to see how little tourism is understood or even discussed in wellness and spa circles.

In the last couple of years we could also see how overused and even tired several terminologies become. I especially refer here to 'wellness' and 'spa'. If you are lucky and live in a good area, you can even send your car to a 'car wellness weekend' or to a 'car spa'. No surprise that more and more new terminologies have been introduced, such as the recent buzzword 'hideaway'.

I agree with Melanie that happiness, which is probably one of the fundamental factors of both physical and mental health, does not need certifications or highly sophisticated (and consequently expensive) brands. I would like to see the democratisation of health-oriented services and travel. Travelling can heal. Tourism can improve quality of life and it does not need a scalpel to do so. However, I do not mean that as of now simply enjoying the sunset on a beach should be relabelled as health tourism! The industry is way more complex and complicated than that.

I have not become a very active practitioner of wellness techniques and practices, quite sadly. Still, I could really enjoy the best ever massage in a jimjilbang (in Seoul) or the thermal facilities and sauna worlds in Austria and Germany or an impromptu meditation session on a low tide sandbank on the beach in Bali.

László Puczkó
The Tourism Observatory for Health, Wellness and Spa (an initiative of Xellum Ltd),
Budapest
Head of Institute of Tourism and Catering, Budapest College of Communication and
Business (Hungary)
Associate Professor, Parnü College, University of Tartu (Estonia)

Acknowledgements

Thank you very much to our editors Emma Travis and Pippa Mullins at Routledge for their help and support with this second edition.

Thank you also to all of our case study authors for their diverse and interesting contributions to this book. It has been great working with you all!

History and development of health, wellness and medical tourism

Definitions and concepts

Much of wellness tourism is based on getting in touch with what is (inside or outside us) without reasoning it through or even having the words to express what is going on. This makes wellness tourism a manifestation of phenomenological 'letting be', which Heidegger . . . actually claims is our most natural way of encountering and dealing with the world. We have lost our natural way and seek it in wellness tourism.

(Steiner and Reisinger, 2006: 9)

This chapter defines some of the main concepts and terms that are used throughout this book. It is important to note that there are major debates about the precise meanings of certain words or concepts, but the increasing research in the field has led to more focused definitions, especially those relating to tourism. What is offered here are definitions based on a combination of academic theory and industry research, which are certainly not definitive or entirely comprehensive, but they provide a firm foundation for our discussions in this book and research in this field.

Defining key terms: health, wellness, well-being, happiness and quality of life

Health is the umbrella term for many of the other terms used in this book, especially the broad definition of the World Health Organization (WHO) from 1984:

> The extent to which an individual or a group is able to realize aspirations and satisfy needs, and to change or cope with the environment. Health is a resource for everyday life, not the objective of living; it is a positive concept, emphasizing social and personal resources as well as physical capabilities.
>
> (WHO, 1984)

In addition to freedom from the risk of disease and untimely death, the WHO also refers to people's abilities to perform family, work and community roles; their ability to deal with physical, biological, psychological and social stress; the extent to which they experience feelings of well-being; and their state of equilibrium with their environment.

Quality of life is an even broader and more complex concept than health and combines both objective and subjective elements. Rahman et al. (2005) include the domains of health, work and productivity, material well-being, feeling part of one's local community, personal safety, quality of environment, emotional well-being, and relationship with family and friends. Puczkó and Smith (2012) apply Rahman's quality of life domains to tourism and they also add spiritual well-being and social and cultural well-being to this list. They argue that tourism can contribute to most of the domains, but in particular health, work and productivity, emotional and spiritual well-being and relationship with family and friends. Tourists may also feel part of a temporary community when they are travelling, and may pay more attention to the environment, especially if they are ecotourists or travelling in beautiful or fragile locations.

Happiness is a somewhat elusive term, although considerable research is now devoted to producing global indices of happiness for numerous countries. As stated by Gilbert (2007: 238), 'There is no simple formula for finding happiness'. Martin Seligman (2003), one of the founders of positive psychology, defines happiness as both positive feelings such as ecstasy and comfort and positive activities that have no feeling component at all such as absorption and engagement. In his happy life formula, Seligman defines a happy life as a life filled with positive feelings and activities. Haidt (2006) suggests that happiness comes from within and without; however, the Dalai Lama (1999), who believes that the very purpose of life is to seek happiness, suggests that happiness is determined more by the state of one's mind than by one's external conditions, circumstances or events – at least once one's basic survival needs are met. Haidt (2006: 242) analyses different approaches to happiness: 'The East stresses acceptance and collectivism; the West encourages striving and individualism . . . both perspectives are valuable. Happiness requires changing yourself and changing your world. It requires pursuing your own goals and fitting in with others.' It is interesting to note that Buddhists are often considered to be some of the happiest people in the world, partly because of their practice of meditation and mindfulness (Connor, 2003). The Vietnamese Buddhist monk Thich Nhat Hanh emphasises the importance of mindfulness in being happy. However, even the Dalai Lama (1999) recognises the importance of achieving material stability or comfort first in these four factors of fulfilment:

1   wealth;
2   worldly satisfaction;
3   spirituality;
4   enlightenment.

Seligman uses the words happiness and well-being interchangeably, but the New Economics Foundation (NEF, 2004) makes a distinction between happiness and well-being as follows: 'Well-being is more than just happiness. As well as feeling satisfied and

happy, well-being means developing as a person, being fulfilled, and making a contribution to the community.' This definition takes the discussion beyond the transformation of the individual through self-development and personal fulfilment towards a sense of social responsibility. Alison van den Eynde and Adrian Fisher discuss the concept of well-being in more depth in Part III based on their research in Australia. The concept of wellness takes this idea even further and includes domains such as physical, mental and spiritual health, self-responsibility, social harmony, environmental sensitivity, intellectual development, emotional well-being, and occupational satisfaction (Müller and Kaufmann, 2001; National Wellness Institute, 2007). Wellness has stronger ties with changing lifestyle or doing something healthy than with curing a specific disease. People consuming wellness services tend to show higher health awareness than others. They are eager to do something for a healthier lifestyle, they are conscious about their nutrition and often do physical exercise. Wellness addresses human health in a holistic or comprehensive sense and assumes that each person will actively participate in protecting their health, in preventing diseases and will not leave all this to medication. Myers et al. (2000) define wellness as being 'a way of life oriented toward optimal health and well-being in which the body, mind, and spirit are integrated by the individual to live more fully within the human and natural community'. GSS (2010: ii) describes wellness using the following dimensions:

- wellness is multi-dimensional;
- wellness is holistic;
- wellness changes over time and along a continuum;
- wellness is individual, but also influenced by the environment;
- wellness is self-responsibility.

It seems to be the case that the concept of health and wellness are increasingly being used inter-changeably, but it should still be emphasised that health tourism includes medical or cure aspects, and that wellness is more preventative than curative. In recent years the term 'medical wellness' has been used, especially in German-speaking environments. The Deutscher Wellness Verband (2008) suggests that the term 'medical wellness' can be used to integrate the concepts of health and wellness, in the sense that there is a medically supervised programme that enhances wellness for clients. This involves making specific changes to lifestyle which can help to achieve optimum wellness. However, Nahrstedt (2008) argues that this does not meet the goal of complete well-being, whereas the concept of 'cultural wellness' combined with 'wellness education' takes us to a form of 'high level wellness'. The US-based Medical Wellness Association defines medical wellness as 'the practice of health and medical care relating to proven wellness outcomes'. A more specific definition of medical wellness by AMWA is an approach to delivering care that considers multiple influences on a person's health and consequently multiple modalities for treating and preventing disease as well as promoting optimal well-being (Breuleux, 2013). Several industry representatives also argue, based on their experiences, that the term 'medical wellness' confuses not only the customers but also creates tension between the medical and wellness professionals. Probably another term, such as structured wellness, can provide a solution to the debate.

Cultural differences in understandings of health and wellness

There are clearly different historic, cultural and linguistic understandings of health and wellness. In some languages (e.g. Hebrew) there is no word for 'wellness', and it is merely translated as 'health'. However, it seems to be increasingly common that the term 'wellness' is used internationally, even in those countries where the language is very different from English (e.g. Hungary) or in countries which are protectionist about language (e.g. France). Translating the term for the purposes of marketing or carrying out research can create a few problems. For example, in Finnish, there is not an easy direct translation of the word 'wellness' and the Finnish version corresponds more closely to 'well-being'. Well-being seems to be used increasingly in many English-speaking countries, also in the context of tourism. For example, the term 'well-being' tourism is quite common in Australia, as well as in Finland. In Slovenian, the translation is more like 'well-feeling'. In German-speaking countries, not only is the term wellness (in English) fully embraced, but it has even been taken a stage further with the concepts of 'selfness' and 'mindness' being developed. 'Selfness' and 'mindness' imply that people are taking responsibility for their own lifestyle and making relevant physical, emotional, psychological and social changes. Interestingly, as noted by the BMWA (2002), some Anglicisms like the term 'wellness' (and even less, 'selfness' and 'mindness') are not so well understood in the UK, neither is the term 'health tourism', mainly because of the lack of a *kur* (sometimes translated as 'resort medical therapy') or medical wellness tradition. In Spanish or Portuguese Latin-based expressions are common, such as *saúde* (health) and *bem-estar* (well-being). In German tourists can find terms such as *wohlbefinden, wohlfülen* (well-feeling) or vitality as an alternative to wellness.

Irrespective of terminology, health and wellness as a concept clearly means different things in different countries and cultures. In Central and Eastern Europe and the Baltic States, the term health is closely related to physical and medical therapeutic healing. The existence of medical waters and other natural assets (such as muds, peloid or caves) means that the main association for people in the region is with these forms of activity. Treatments tend to be curative for specific physical conditions. Visitors from these regions may seek out a medical practitioner for a consultation, or expect some kind of medical supervision during their stay. Many Western Europeans are familiar with the concept of historic, thermal spa tourism as well as thalassotherapy (cures based on sea elements), especially on the Atlantic coast. However, to most cultures, hydrotherapy (healing with water) or balneotherapy (healing based on medicinal thermal water) is not known or understood and tourists would be surprised and even put off to find a hospital or clinic-like atmosphere within these medical baths or sanatoria since often these are translated as spas. They are unlikely to seek out medical services and may instead look for pampering, relaxation, body–mind–spirit or stress-management programmes.

In Southern Europe, there is an emphasis on seaside wellness, where sunshine, sea air and thalassotherapies are used to enhance well-being. In addition, the pace of life is relaxed and siestas are common, and the Mediterranean diet is considered to be one of

the healthiest in the world. Turkish baths are used in Turkey and similar facilities exist in some parts of Spain (e.g. Andalucia) where the legacy of the Moors is dominant and in several North African countries, too. Visitors from Nordic countries may be more attracted to outdoor recreation and nature, and simple, functional, but clean facilities. In Scandinavia, there is a large emphasis on outdoor recreation such as Nordic walking, cross-country skiing and lake swimming, even in winter. In Finland especially, almost all people have a sauna in their house or in the close vicinity as this is seen as an integral part of everyday wellness. In Germany, Austria and Switzerland, physical fitness is also seen as being extremely important, but this is combined with other principles of optimum wellness, including healthy eating, rest and relaxation, and some forms of spiritual activity such as yoga and meditation. There is an increasing shift towards self-responsibility and a balanced approach to life.

In Asian countries, many spiritual activities such as yoga, meditation and massage are more integrated into everyday life than they are in most Western countries. The use of energy flows is a more accepted form of healing (e.g. Reiki, Shiatsu) and balance creation for living space (e.g. Feng Shui, Vasati). Water also plays an important role in some parts of Asia. Japanese Onsen or South Korean jimjilbang culture has a long tradition both within spiritual and secular society. Water is also used for ritual purification by Hindus in India. Some parts of China are rich in mineral springs many of which are currently being developed for tourism. In Middle Eastern and North African countries where religion is a much more central focus of life, spirituality is not seen as an 'optional extra'. For example, all Muslims are expected to undertake the Haj pilgrimage to Mecca at least once during their lifetime. Enhanced physical wellness may come from physical healing (e.g. using spas) or medical intervention (e.g. medical trips to India). Several Asian countries (e.g. Thailand) and Arabic Gulf cities (e.g. Dubai) have become famous for their recent developments in medical tourism facilities.

In the UK, USA, Canada and Australasia, the use of day spas or health and beauty farms is fairly widespread. Emphasis is more on cosmetic treatments, relaxation and pampering than it is about medical treatments. However, there are also clear growth trends in occupational wellness (e.g. work–life balance, stress management) as well as the need for enhanced spirituality as organised religion declines. Especially in North America the concept of MediSpa, which is most of the time an outpatient beauty clinic often located in malls has become popular.

Chapter 2 explains in more detail about the history of health and wellness and some of the reasons why these cultural differences in understandings and perceptions exist.

The role of tourism and travel in health

Tourism has always been seen as a process of self-regeneration as well as relaxation, education or indulgence (Ryan, 1997). The majority of tourists in the past have tended to prefer escapist and diversionary forms of tourism which manifest themselves in hedonistic activities (e.g. sun, sea, sand). However, it is not easy to escape from normativity and the baggage of everyday life, which may be a major barrier to enjoyment of travel (Edensor, 2001; de Botton, 2002). Nevertheless, Filep's work on the relationship between tourism and happiness (Filep and Deery, 2010; Pearce et al., 2011; Filep, 2012) has provided a sound academic basis for concluding that travel does have a positive impact on people's happiness and even their quality of life. He suggests that holidays provide the three main elements of happiness: positive emotions, such as joy, interest, contentment and love; meaning, which gives people a sense of purpose; and engagement, which gives people a sense of involvement.

Although the idea of 'getting away from it all' in tourism is important, so too is the process of self-discovery or self-development. Graburn (2002) discusses how the inner and outer journey – that is, the inner world of consciousness and the outer world of experience – can be reconciled through travel. As stated by the contemporary philosopher and author Alain de Botton (2002: 59): 'At the end of hours of train-dreaming, we may feel we have been returned to ourselves – that is, brought back into contact with emotions and ideas of importance to us. It is not necessarily at home that we best encounter our true selves.'

There are debates in this book as to whether wellness tourism is concerned with escapism *from* the self and the world to environments that offer pure relaxation, or, whether it is about *confrontation* of the self and re-negotiation of one's place in the world and relationships to others. Several authors and researchers have analysed the concept of existential authenticity within a tourism context (e.g. Wang, 1999), but Steiner and Reisinger (2006) have also applied this concept in a wellness tourism context. They suggest that existential authenticity is about one's essential nature and being true to oneself, but note that the self is always changing and fluctuating. Although existential authenticity can be about finding meaning and happiness, it may also involve the confrontation of anxiety. Working through difficult and painful issues in one's life may be done more easily in a setting away from home and this is an important part of self-development and moving forward. Most forms of tourism offer us a 'flight', but few equip us with a 'fight' mechanism. One exception to this may be wellness through the guidance and support of doctors, teachers, guides or counsellors.

If wellness tourism were merely about relaxation, then one might argue that the traditional beach holiday with its emphasis on sunbathing is the ultimate form of meditation! Similarly, spa tourism sometimes offers little more than a soak in warm thermal or medicinal waters.

In order to qualify as a wellness tourism experience, we would contend that some deliberate or (pro)active contribution has to be made to psychological, spiritual or emotional well-being in addition to healing or resting the physical body. This takes wellness tourism from the realm of being merely a passive form of tourism with a focus on escapism to one where tourists are purposefully driven by the desire to actively improve their health or change their lives.

Although Singh and Singh (2009: 137) state that 'Travel, for its own sake, can be a spiritual experience – if it obliterates the significance of the destination', the destination often still matters even if an 'inner journey' is the main focus of a wellness trip. Tourists frequently seek locations and activities that are transcendent. For example, de Botton (2002: 159) describes how travellers are attracted to 'sublime' landscapes that benefit their soul by making them feel small, yet part of an infinite and universal cycle. He describes how the

English poet Wordsworth 'had urged us to travel through landscapes to feel emotions that would benefit our souls'. It is no coincidence then that many wellness centres and holistic retreats are located beside the ocean or on a mountain top.

Wellness tourists (perhaps ironically) need to be in good enough physical health to embark on a journey, as well as being materially affluent (as stated by Hall (2013) there appears to be little consideration of those who cannot afford spa and wellness in the general literature on this subject). As with all forms of tourism, the flows of tourists are predominantly from more developed Western to less developed non-Western countries. This is usually the case with medical travel and tourism, but sometimes it is the other way around, that is when affluent citizens of non-Western countries travel for medical intervention, such as Russian patients travelling to Switzerland or Arabic patients to the UK). The pursuit of wellness is time-consuming and expensive. Indulgence in wellness activities is therefore largely the premise of the middle classes, except in countries where governments subsidise medical activities in the form of social tourism (e.g. spas in Central and Eastern Europe during the socialist era) or where yoga and/or meditation are integrated into everyday life (e.g. India, Thailand).

Definitions and typologies of health tourism

In recent years the health, wellness and medical tourism has grown exponentially (Bushell and Sheldon, 2009; Erfurt-Cooper and Cooper, 2009; Smith and Puczkó, 2009; Connell, 2011; Voigt and Pforr, 2013). This includes visits to spas, thermal springs, spa and wellness hotels, hospitals and clinics for surgery and medical procedures, and spiritual or holistic retreats. We might differentiate between health, wellness and medical tourism, with health tourism generally being seen as an umbrella term for wellness tourism and medical tourism (Smith and Puczkó, 2009), although health tourism is used by many governments as being synonymous with medical tourism (GSS, 2011). Henderson (2004) differentiates between travel for reasons of wellness (e.g. leisure and beauty spas) and travel for reasons of illness (e.g. medical interventions and health check-ups). Illness or disease is one of the key motivations for those people who travel to hospitals, clinics and dental surgeries. Many travel to medical spas, and they often have a prescription from their doctor confirming that they need a specific treatment for an illness, disease or debilitating condition. Although some sick visitors may just enjoy the chance to relax and recuperate in a spa or by the sea, the motivations are somewhat different from those visitors who are in good health and simply want to enhance well-being and live better. It is also rare that mental and psychological problems are given the same consideration as physical illnesses, and treatment is rarely state-subsidised. An exception might be where occupational or work-based wellness is encouraged through incentive trips to spas or stress relief workshops. Usually those people with non-diagnosed mental troubles are forced to pay high prices for a wellness-enhancing holiday. However, this situation may change in the future as it becomes even more economically sound for governments to encourage preventative wellness (i.e. preserving good health rather than curing illness) through, for example, physical exercise, healthy nutrition, stress management and spa visits.

It is important to focus on sub-sectors or niches or health tourism, because not all health tourists are seeking the same thing. A typical spa visitor may not expect nor want to receive a medical treatment; a medical tourist may not want to or be able to visit a spa; a spiritual tourist may not want medical or spa activities. There is little connection between a spa which deals specifically with physical or medical problems using water treatments and a spiritual retreat which focuses on meditation for the mind and soul. Depending on motivation, life-stage and interests, tourists will select the form of wellness they require, and this could be purely physical with a focus on sports and fitness; medical with a focus on the treatment of disease or surgery; mental or psychological with a focus on life-coaching or mind-control; relaxing and pampering in a luxury spa; entertaining and recreational in a purpose-built water-park; or meditational and spiritual in a retreat. Although the medical and wellness fields are arguably converging in the areas of mental and psychological health, stress management, fit-living, active ageing and longevity, distinctions are still necessary for understanding product development, segmentation and marketing.

The following section defines and discusses the main sub-sectors of health and wellness tourism, as well as some of the smaller niches within these sub-sectors.

Spa tourism

> Tourism which focuses on the relaxation, healing or beautifying of the body in spas using preventative wellness and/or curative medical techniques

ISPA (2013a) defines spas as 'places devoted to overall well-being through a variety of professional services that encourage the renewal of mind, body and spirit'. Spa tourism is arguably the best known form of health tourism. It should be noted that the spa industry has not traditionally considered itself to be part of tourism (except perhaps some destination and resort spas and hotels). However, in 2011, the Global Spa Summit (now the Global Spa and Wellness Summit) commissioned the authors of this book along with SRI to analyse the role that spas play in medical tourism and wellness tourism. So it may not be entirely accurate to refer to 'spa tourism', especially as many tourists stay in spa or wellness hotels, but their primary motivation for the trip may be a very different activity (i.e. business, culture, sightseeing, shopping, etc.).

GSS (2011) shows that around 67 per cent of respondents from the spa industry feel that spas play an important or very important role in wellness tourism, whereas only 24 per cent thought the same for medical tourism (globally, this did not vary much either). However, many practitioners were also confused about definitions, which is not surprising (this is complicated by the fact that many European spas offer medical tourism in healing waters, as discussed later in this section). The top treatments that the industry believes tourists are interested in include the ones listed in Table 1.1 (in order of preference).

Interestingly, water-based treatments only come in at number 6 in the Wellness Tourists list and not at all for Medical Tourists (of course, many post-operative bodies cannot be

TABLE 1.1 Medical tourists' and wellness tourists' activities in spas	
Medical tourists	Wellness tourists
Massage	Massage
Health assessments and consultations	Body treatments
Recovery from surgery	Meditation/spiritual/mind–body programmes
Medical testing	Facial treatments
Body treatments	Exercise facilities and programmes
Source: GSS (2011).	

submerged in water). About 85 per cent of spa respondents were planning to make investments to pursue wellness tourism opportunities in the future, whereas only 54 per cent were planning to do the same for medical tourism. 97 per cent of respondents believed that spas should increase their role in wellness tourism and about 66 per cent said the same for medical tourism. The report recommends the need for greater collaboration between spas and other key players in medical and wellness tourism sectors, as it was estimated that only about a quarter of respondents were collaborating effectively with public and private health or medical agencies and tourism companies.

Within ISPA's (2013a) categorisation of spas, the ones listed in Table 1.2 tend to play a role in the tourism industry (day spas and club spas are excluded). ISPA represents the North American approach to spas and we can see the development and streamlining of the terminologies if we look at the changes in the official ISPA terms since 2007 (Smith and Puczkó, 2009).

It should be noted that SpaFinder (2013) differentiates between a medical spa (cosmetic) and medical spa (wellness). In the former, medical personnel work alongside spa therapists in an atmosphere that integrates clinical-grade aesthetic enhancement and spa treatments/concepts. However, there may not be any accommodation. In the latter, traditional Western medical concepts and complementary/alternative philosophies may be used separately or in combination for preventative wellness and stress management programmes.

SpaFinder (2013) adds two more categories which are relevant to tourism:

Airport spa: Airport spas provide passengers with pre- or post-flight pampering, and spa treatments are sometimes abbreviated to accommodate travellers' schedules. Options include quick chair massages and express facials, although some spas feature extensive menus. Spa treatments may be found in some airport lounges, as well, though access is sometimes restricted.

Cruise-ship spa: Spas on cruise ships provide travellers a chance to indulge in spa experiences amid the high seas. Accessible to all (though age restrictions may apply), most spas feature salons, full-service fitness facilities and extensive menus, with treatments offered on deck, on shore or in the water. Some speciality themed cruises or voyages offer special wellness programming.

TABLE 1.2 ISPA's changing categorisation of spas

ISPA spa types (2013a)	ISPA spa types (2007)
Destination spa A destination spa is a facility with the primary purpose of guiding individual spa-goers to develop healthy habits. This lifestyle transformation can be accomplished by providing a comprehensive programme that includes spa services, physical fitness activities, wellness education, healthful cuisine and special interest programming	**Structured spa** An establishment operating by strict rules which offers guests the chance to attain a specific objective (e.g. weight loss)
Medical spa A facility that operates under the supervision of a licensed medical doctor whose primary purpose is to provide medical and wellness care in an environment that integrates spa services	**Medical spa** A facility that offers traditional and complementary therapeutic and health protection treatment as well as other spa services, and may also include health institutions
Mineral springs spa A spa offering an on-site source of natural mineral, thermal or sea-water used in hydrotherapy treatments	**Bath** A spa constructed to utilise natural mineral, medicinal or sea-water located on site by offering hydrotherapy to guests
Resort/hotel spa A spa located within a resort or hotel providing professionally administered spa services, fitness and wellness components	**Resort spa** A resort in a remote location of beautiful natural setting normally detached from civilisation, offering a wide array of wellness services and programmes in an all inclusive arrangement to guests
	Spa hotel A spa offering hotel accommodation and normally several days of all inclusive programmes designed to ensure physical, spiritual and mental balance
	Holistic spa A spa that offers alternative therapy and diet (for instance, vegetarian or macro-biotic cuisine) in an effort to make positive adjustments to the mindset of guests
	Sport spa An establishment offering spa services and special sports programmes (the latter could range from golf through skiing and angling to training for running a marathon)

Source: ISPA 2007, 2013.

In Europe the same name 'spa' has a very different meaning. Perceptions differ greatly, for example, tourists in Central and Eastern Europe are very familiar with the concept of historic medical spas, whereas visitors from the USA or UK might expect something similar to a beauty salon. The European Spa Association (ESPA, 2013) declares that: 'The European Spa Association's objective is to promote spas and balneology in Europe and to take care that the natural remedies based on mineral water, landscape and climate will be available to as great a number of citizens and visitors as possible.' This objective is very much based on natural healing assets, especially healing waters, while the North American concept is closer to wellness and may not involve water at all. Many spas in Europe traditionally had some form of water-based treatments and wet-areas. However, there is a difference between mineral, thermal and healing waters which many visitors may not be familiar with, especially if their country does not have a water-based healing tradition:

- Mineral waters: these have at least the set amount of dissolved mineral content which is minimum 500mg/1 or 1000mg/l.
- Thermal waters: natural waters that are at least 30 or 32C at source (this can vary country by country).
- Healing waters: the medical effects have to be proven, i.e. evidence-based.

ESPA (2013) estimates that there are more than 1,200 spas and health resorts in Europe, many of which are medically respected health centres and provide physical healing to visitors who are often called patients. For example, historical medical spas in Central and Eastern Europe have a medical practitioner who oversees the care given to guests and tourists many of whose visit is based on a prescription from their doctor, and whose trip may then be funded by holiday vouchers or so-called 'social tourism' systems. Many European spas have natural, medical waters which are used for treating certain conditions such as locomotion or circulatory disorders. ESPA emphasises the fact that balneology and health-resort medicine is part of a scientific medicine and has to be based on scientific evidence. However, many European spas offer other curative assets, such as:

- springs with medicinal water for therapeutic use;
- healing gases;
- spas, spa facilities and health resorts at the seaside;
- peloids in spas, health resorts and spa facilities;
- bioclimatic/healing climate;
- kneipp therapy.

Thalassotherapy spas also have a long history in Europe, especially in France.

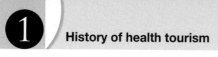

CASE STUDY 1.1
Thalassotherapy spas in France

The first thalassotherapy centre was opened in Roscoff in 1899. With 1,600 miles of coast-line, France is a perfect location for the seaside spas that practise thalassotherapy.

There are around 55 Thalasso resorts along the Channel, the Atlantic and the Mediterranean.

Thalassa Sea and Spa, a division of the French multinational Accor Group, introduced the practice of thalassotherapy to European spa-goers more than 20 years ago. A survey of spas in France estimated that 200,000 people would have thalassotherapy in French spas in 2009.

Since 1986 France Thalasso has helped to guarantee the quality of thalassotherapy in France.

There are currently 38 accredited centres. They recommend at least six days of treatment for maximum health benefits. France Thalasso's Quality Charter guarantees the following:

- *An exceptional seaside location, a protected environment*: Thalassotherapies are exclusively in a prime location by the sea.

- *The use of natural sea-water*: Fresh sea-water heated to a comfortable temperature recharges the body by transferring minerals and trace elements through the skin. It is never kept more than 24 hours.

- *Medical surveillance for a serene cure*: A medical check-up is advised when starting a cure. The doctor will work with you to create your schedule and to respond to your need for advice.

- *A qualified and attentive team of professionals*: Treatments carried out and supervised by experienced staff, trained in different treatment techniques: physiotherapist, hydro-therapist, dietician, sports instructors, beauticians, etc.

- *An optimal hygiene and security guarantee*: Thalassotherapy centres are subjected to very rigorous regulatory constraints especially controlling sea-water quality and marine products used during treatments.

- *Standardised and well-maintained systems*: Accredited centres have specially designed, top-quality high-tech equipment, that is constantly serviced to comply with the quality standards and to optimise the use of sea-water.

Increasingly, purpose-built spas are becoming more popular in Europe as they are in the USA, Asia and elsewhere. These are mainly recreational or leisure-orientated (leisure complexes and water-parks) and may combine water-based treatments with fitness and nutritional programmes, even including occupational wellness workshops. European spas are becoming more globalised. Bodeker and Burford (2008: 426) suggest that 'most

regions of Europe now are also influenced by other cultures (e.g. Thai, Chinese, Ayurvedic), which contribute to the eclectic mix of indigenous or traditional therapies on offer'. However, it is still important to note that medical tourism and medical wellness traditions in spas (e.g. *kur*) in Europe are still strong in German-speaking countries, Central and Eastern Europe, the Baltic States and Russia. GSS (2010: 53) suggests that, 'The European medi-spa model presents an interesting potential model for spas in other regions that are interested in serving medical tourists'. Nevertheless, even medical spas are not always included in definitions of medical tourism!

Medical tourism

Medical tourism involves a trip to a place outside a person's normal place of residence for the purpose of receiving medical treatments, interventions or therapies. The patient and whoever accompanies them also make use of the destination's tourist infrastructure, attractions and facilities.

Medical travel means travelling for the *sole* purpose of having medical treatments, interventions or therapies. The touristic qualities of the destination are secondary and may not even be used, but that is rather unlikely since medical travellers use transport services, accommodation and several other services, but may not visit attraction sites.

Patient mobility refers to those people who travel for medical procedures to a bordering country, within their own country (i.e. another state in the USA), or within their geographical region (i.e. the EU) because the treatment is cheaper or more readily available.

The field of medical tourism has been extensively and intensively researched in recent years. There are several definitions of medical tourism which have been used within an industry context, for example the Medical Tourism Association (2013) definition:

People who live in one country travel to another country or travel within their country to receive medical, dental and surgical care while at the same time receiving equal to or greater care than they would have in their own country, and are travelling for medical care because of affordability, better access to care or a higher level of quality of care.

The Global Spa Summit (2011) definition does not differ much, except to emphasise that medical tourists as opposed to wellness tourists tend to be ill:

Medical tourism involves people who travel to a different place to receive treatment for a disease, ailment, or condition, and who are seeking lower cost of care, higher quality of care, better access to care, or different care than what they could receive at home.

Bottom line: Undertaken by people who are sick.

Hall (2013) reiterates the idea that medical tourism is usually curative and that the traveller tends to be ill. However, the common inclusion of cosmetic surgery and (cosmetic) dentistry in the category of medical tourism means that it is debatable that medical tourists are necessarily ill (unless the need for cosmetic surgery is diagnosed as a serious psychological issue). For example, in Brazil, medical tourism statistics does not include plastic surgery, although it is considered to be the largest medical intervention by volumes! Voigt et al. (2011: 36) add the notion that medical tourists combine their use of medical intervention services with 'a vacation or tourism elements in the conventional sense'. Cook et al. (2013: 64) write that medical tourism definitions are becoming fuzzy around the edges because 'medical treatment is merging with the tourist experience, and also because it is sometimes hard to see the boundary between body modification and medical treatment'.

Connell (2012: 10) discusses in depth the definitional problems within the field of medical tourism: 'Medical tourism is difficult to define, the effort is usually unproductive.' One of the major discussions within the field of medical tourism is whether people who travel for medical reasons will actually be in a fit state to enjoy any tourism experiences or indeed want to. Kangas (2010) suggests using 'medical travel', 'medical care abroad' or 'treatment abroad'. Munro (2012: 17) states that, 'Medical travel is a phrase much preferred over medical tourism by health care leaders, hospital executives, doctors and other medical professionals'. Medical travel is therefore used by the Medical Travel Quality Alliance, of which Munro is the President. Connell also prefers the term 'medical travel' for cross-border mobility for medical care, stating that a lot of medical tourism is regional rather than global as it is just to neighbouring countries. There is also a great deal of diasporic medical tourism, where immigrants go back to their country of origin. In the European Union the latest terminology that has been introduced for medical tourism is cross-border patient mobility.

Cohen (2008) created a categorisation based on his research in Thailand:

- medicated tourists (who receive treatments for accidents or health problems while on holiday);
- medical tourists proper (who visit a country for some medical treatment, or who may decide on a procedure once in a country);
- vacationing patients (who visit mainly for medical treatment, but make incidental use of holiday opportunities);
- mere patients (who visit solely for medical treatment and make no use of holiday opportunities).

Connell (2012) suggests that it would be interesting to research whether medical tourists see themselves as patients, travellers or tourists. He shows that many medical trips do indeed include some leisure or tourism activities; for example, medical tourists in China, India, Jordan and Thailand do some sightseeing, shopping or cultural activities, and accompanying friends or relatives certainly do: 'Some recuperation is usually possible, and a journey with a serious purpose can have a frivolous, pleasurable and celebratory ending. Tourism offers added value' (Connell, 2012: 3).

It is hard to estimate the size of the medical tourism industry. Munro (2012) questions whether medical tourists and medical travellers should be counted separately. She also notes that wellness travellers seek non-invasive medical procedures such as dental treatments and dermatology procedures. Youngman (2012) states that many make the mistake of equating 'international patients' with 'medical tourists'. The usual trick is to include some or all of the following in the counting of medical tourists:

- holidaymakers;
- diplomats;
- military personnel;
- business travellers;
- non-nationals who are residents but not citizens of the country;
- temporary expatriates;
- long-term expatriates;
- overseas students;
- health/spa tourists.

Connell (2012: 2) notes that statistics for medical tourism are notoriously unreliable and that no countries produce official data on medical tourism as they have no means: 'By definition every official figure is flawed. They are often badly collected, imperfectly collated and spun to infinity.' For example, some hospitals count the number of patient visits rather than the number of patients. Numbers of Western tourists tend to be fewer than intimated but, as mentioned earlier, cross-border and diasporic medical tourism tends to be greater. Glinos (2012) also states that patient mobility is over-rated within the EU, and that it is common to confuse planned treatment with emergency needs for health care while abroad. She identifies several kinds of medical travel:

- residents of cross-border regions for whom special cross-border schemes are in place;
- those with time to travel and generous insurance cover;
- those who are cost-aware with no cover looking for affordable options;
- patients with rare diseases;
- impatient, wealthy patients on waiting lists;
- those seeking care not available at home (included outlawed practices);
- expatriates returning home for care.

Sometimes certain countries are perceived as being 'expert' in medical techniques (e.g. dentistry in Hungary or sex-change operations in Thailand), or treatment is not available or illegal in the tourists' own country (e.g. abortion, euthanasia). In South America, countries such as Argentina, Bolivia, Brazil and Colombia lead on plastic surgery medical skills as their surgeons have a wide experience of treating domestic patients. It is estimated that one in 30 Argentineans have had plastic surgery procedures and 70 per cent of middle- and upper-class women in Bolivia and Colombia (Balch, 2006).

There is clearly a spectrum of medical tourism which ranges from necessary surgery for life-threatening conditions (e.g. cancer), to more aesthetic but sometimes necessary practices (e.g. orthodontic dentistry), to physically non-essential but psychologically boosting cosmetic surgery. Many people are only just discovering medical tourism as there were frequently concerns about safety, sanitation, professionalism and insurance in countries like India or Africa. However, increasingly patients are being reassured that many of the institutions (e.g. hospitals and clinics) and the techniques and equipment used are of an even higher standard than they are at home. For example, in the UK where dangerous 'superbugs' are spreading through hospitals and waiting lists are at an all-time peak, many people are more than happy to take their money and their health problems elsewhere.

There are naturally concerns about destinations where medical tourism is taking place, as it is inevitably becoming a private-sector-dominated practice. This often means that the best doctors and surgeons are lured away from the public health-care system as they can make more money from medical tourism. The most beautiful or accessible locations are being developed for medical tourism, therefore there might also be a 'brain drain' from rural and remote areas where medical facilities for local people are often the most needed. Ethical approaches to the development of medical tourism are therefore needed and governments should carefully regulate the practice. Medical tourism services remain largely unregulated, including the safeguarding of medical tourists (Cross et al., 2013; Lunt et al., 2013).

CASE STUDY 1.2
Surgeon and Safari, South Africa

Surgeon and Safari, whose slogan is 'Privacy in Paradise', first opened its doors in 1999 and had just one client from California. Clientele had increased to ten by the following year, and the company has enjoyed growth of almost 100 per cent every year since. Lorraine Melville, founder of Surgeon and Safari, a company that specialises in facilitating medical tours, reports that her company services up to 30 clients a month. The majority of her clients come from the United Kingdom and the United States. The average client is aged between 45 and 65 and is usually single. The most requested procedures are face and eyelifts, tummy tucks, breast reductions and dental rehabilitation, including implants, crowns and periodontic work. Clients can also choose from hair transplants, liposuction, chin or calf augmentations, ear surgery, brow lifts, botox, ophthalmic procedures (such as cataract surgery), and orthopaedic procedures like knee and hip replacements. Melville argues that the quality and professionalism of the services offered, from the surgeons to the hotels, are amongst the very best in the world, and the prices are highly competitive. The internet is used to create communication between client and surgeon on an ongoing basis. High medical standards are combined with true business ethics. When clients want to recuperate, they have the option of doing so on safari or going to the sea. Although many need to rest instead, some excursions take up most of the average ten-day visit, such as trips to the Waterberg or Pilanesberg Game Reserve. There are also day trips to Sandton City, cultural villages, Soweto, the Apartheid Museum and other touristic experiences. Some of the medical tourists' testimonies on the website refer to the experience as 'fun', which refutes the idea that medical tourism is always a serious business!

(Surgeon and Safari, 2013)

Little is yet known about how medical tourists choose destinations (Connell, 2012; Lunt, 2013). Hall (2013: 210) is probably right to conclude that medical tourism is probably 'more of a reflection of the policy debates and economic difficulties that exist in the health and medical services of the tourist generating countries as it is in the attractiveness of the medical tourism destination'.

Spiritual tourism

> Tourism which focuses on the secular (non-religious) spiritual domain of wellness using body–mind–spirit activities, retreat and ashram visits, and connection to nature and landscapes

Some authors have argued that spirituality is at the core of wellness (e.g. Devereux and Carnegie, 2006; Johnston and Pernecky, 2006; Steiner and Reisinger, 2006). This represents a shift away from orthodox religion towards a kind of transcendent spirituality, where one aims to develop beyond the self and the ego. Heelas and Woodhead (2005) suggest that a slow but steady spiritual revolution is taking place in which secular spirituality is taking over from traditional religion. Some Western psychologists such as Freud believed that religion was detrimental to the emotional health of the individual. Others like Jung believed that spirituality was the essence of what it meant to be human. Indeed, the word 'spirituality' comes from the Latin *spiritualitas*, an abstract word, related to the Greek word *pneuma* meaning breath, the essence of life.

Some researchers have developed 'wheels of wellness' (denoting an ideal balance of activities in life) some of which place spirituality at the centre (e.g. Myers et al., 2000). Spirituality is a holistic discipline which is not limited to the 'explorations of the explicitly religious' but considers all aspects of the spiritual experience, namely 'the psychological, bodily, historical, political, aesthetic, intellectual and other dimensions of the human subject' (Schneiders, 1989: 693). Davie (1994) described spirituality as 'believing without belonging', which arguably suits more individualistic societies. Sociological research has suggested that the development of more individualistic cultures and societies has increased social alienation, rendering a greater need for seeking spiritual solace.

Cohen (1996) describes how the quest for a 'spiritual centre' is an integral part of tourism, especially when people feel socially alienated. Traditional aspects of spiritual retreats have often been in the form of pilgrimages for religious tourists (Carrasco, 1996; Devereux and Carnegie, 2006; Timothy and Olsen, 2006), but the secular tourist may seek other forms of spiritual enlightenment. Spiritual tourism can include visiting religious sites or buildings, spiritual landscapes, pilgrimage centres, ashrams, retreats or gurus. However, the spiritual quest is seen as more abstract than a specifically religious one, focusing on the balance of body, mind and spirit. It can even include contemplation of landscape, as discussed by Edward Huijbens in his case study in Part III.

Magyar (2008: 24–5) compiled the most popular spiritual destinations around the world by collecting information from major spiritual travel oriented websites. We can see that there are some destinations which seem surprising, such as Alaska, which is mainly visited because of their untouched nature and spiritual atmosphere rather than for any religious associations.

- Jerusalem (Israel);
- Mecca (Saudi Arabia);
- The Vatican and Rome (Italy);
- Tibet, Nepal and Mount Everest;
- Goa and Benares (India);
- Machu Picchu (Peru);
- Egypt;
- Mount Fuji (Japan);
- Navaho Region (USA);
- Rio de Janeiro (Brazil);
- Alaska (USA).

CASE STUDY 1.3
Confusing the religious and the spiritual? Ananda, Assisi

Ananda was founded in 1968 by Swami Kriyananda, a direct disciple of the Indian yoga guru Paramhansa Yogananda (author of the influential *Autobiography of a Yogi* first published in 1946). Paramhansa Yogananda was the first great Indian master to live most of his life in the Western world. Yogananda emphasised the universality of religion. The inner essence of all religions, he said, is one and the same: the way to union with the Infinite, known as 'Self-realisation', which will be the religion of the future.

Ananda is a network of seven spiritual communities, with hundreds of centres and meditation groups in the United States and in Europe. The teaching at Ananda blends Western and Eastern spiritual disciplines with special emphasis being given to both the teachings of Christ and to India's scientific and ancient gift of yoga and meditation.

Ananda Europa was founded in Italy in 1983 and has been flourishing at its present location near Assisi since 1986. There are about 80 residents at Ananda, some living within the community and others, including families and children, in homes nearby. Ananda specialises in community living and in applying spiritual principles to every aspect of life: work, family, relationships, educating children, religion, how to solve problems and overcome crises, healing, creativity, and much more. Open all year round, Ananda offers residential weekend, week-long and intensive programmes on a variety of subjects, for example:

- Meditation and self-realisation;

- Ananda yoga;

- Ananda yoga teacher training;

- Ananda raja yoga teacher training;

- Material success;

- Spiritual self-healing;

- Vegetarian cooking;

- Kriya yoga;

- Vedic astrology;

- Spirituality in daily life;

- Pilgrimages in Italy: 'Spirit Walk' and 'In the Footsteps of St Francis'.

They also lead pilgrimages, Himalayan adventures and Ayurveda vacations in India.

For many visitors, the blend of Western religion and Eastern spirituality may work; however, it is a controversial juxtaposition, especially with the religious town of Assisi nearby. As a result, Assisi has been investigated and even raided by police in the past and accused of being a cult and brainwashing weak and vulnerable people, and being involved in criminal activities or sex scandals. There is some debate about the accuracy of the charges, but this perhaps demonstrates the difficulties of trying to blend conventional religion with 'universal' spirituality.

(Ananda Retreats, 2013)

Holistic, alternative and 'New Age' tourism

Tourism which focuses on the balance of body, mind and spirit through alternative, complementary, 'New Age' or esoteric therapies which take place in retreats, wellness centres or at festivals

New Age teachings started in England in the 1960s and became globally popular in the 1970s; therefore they are often associated with the hippy era and 'baby boomers'. They were largely a reaction to the failure of organised religion to meet the spiritual needs of all people. Heelas (1996) asserts that the essence of the New Age movement is self-spirituality, that is the notion that the self is sacred and that spirituality lies within the individual person. Miller (1994) discussed the New Age movement and its commercial dimensions. According to her, people want to believe in something, to have some hope and faith, and the selling of spirituality offers divine dividends. New Age products have become very lucrative, with a wild boom in the 1990s when spirituality was the buzzword in the merchandising business (Green and Aldred, 2002: 61). Marinus Gisolf discusses the continuing popularity of the New Age movement in his case study in Part III, especially as it focuses on lifestyle issues which are (still) important today, such as environmentalism, community values, constructive host–guest interactions and social responsibility.

However, by the 1980s and 1990s the movement came under criticism because healing methods were seen as unscientific (e.g. crystals, tarot), many New Age leaders were accused of being charlatans, and some rituals were confused with the occult or satanism. Harrison (2006) describes Professor Dwakin's attack on all New Age therapies, stating that 'alternative remedies constitute little more than a money-spinning, multi-million pound industry that impoverishes our culture and throws up new age gurus who exhort us to run away from reality'. His research included faith healers, psychic mediums, angel therapists, aura photographers, astrologers, tarot card readers and water diviners. However, one might argue that if a therapy or activity makes people feel better and more balanced, unless it does physical or psychological harm, it is a key element of wellness.

Johnston and Pernecky (2006) categorised New Age tourism activities in the following way:

- *Power/sacred places*: sacred sites/stones, temples, pilgrimages, holy sites, visiting tribes, rituals, etc.
- *Wellness and holistic health*: reflexology, Bach flower therapy, aromatherapy, reiki, acupuncture, homeopathy, etc.
- *Divination*: visiting places to foretell future, I ching, runes, scrying, tarot cards, pendulum movements, etc.
- *Greenery and eco-spirit*: spirituality related visits to nature, deep ecology, Mother Earth, Goddess, etc.
- *Workshops/seminars/festivals*: visualisation, feng shui, karma, reincarnation, auras, sacred dance/song, self-development, gurus, etc.
- *Other*: retreat centres, New Age accommodation, spas, UFOs, purchase of crystals or other Goods, etc.

Holistic approaches can also be interpreted as 'New Age' or esoteric depending on the treatments that are offered under this label. The American Holistic Health Association (AHHA) (2007) suggests that there are two standard definitions that are used for 'holistic':

1   Holistic as a whole made up of interdependent parts. You are most likely to hear these parts referred to as the mind/body connection; mind/body/spirit, or physical/mental/ emotional/spiritual aspects. When this meaning is applied to illness, it is called holistic medicine and includes a number of factors, such as dealing with the root cause of an illness; increasing patient involvement; and considering both conventional (allopathic) and complementary (alternative) therapies.

2 Holistic as a synonym for alternative therapies. By this definition, 'going holistic' means turning away from any conventional medical options and using alternative treatment exclusively. This meaning mainly relates to illness situations, and some-times is used for controversial therapies.

Holistic tourism tends to be mainly offered at 'retreat centres' which are usually purpose built (as opposed to temporary venues that can be hired for multiple purposes by multiple users) and owner-run. A retreat centre has multiple meanings; it can be a place for quiet reflection and rejuvenation, an opportunity to regain good health, and/or it can mean a time for spiritual reassessment and renewal, either alone, in silence or in a group (Retreats Online, 2006). For example, many holistic centres such as Skyros in Greece or Cortijo Romero in Spain include such activities:

- physical (e.g. massage, dance, Pilates, Alexander technique);
- therapeutic (e.g. massage, aromatherapy, acupuncture, kinesiology);
- medicinal (e.g. Ayurveda, herbalism, Chinese medicine, Bach flower remedies);
- mental (e.g. NLP, dream workshops, psycho-drama);
- spiritual (e.g. meditation, yoga, Tai Chi, Shamanism);
- healing (e.g. reiki, aurasoma, colour therapy);
- creative (e.g. painting, photography, cookery);
- expressive (e.g. singing, drama, comedy);
- esoteric/New Age (e.g. tarot, crystals, angels, astrology);
- personal development (e.g. counselling, stress management, life coaching).

(Adapted from Kelly and Smith, 2008)

In some cases, whole centres are devoted to the practices and visitors come specifically to meet or join like-minded communities as the following case study of Findhorn shows.

CASE STUDY 1.4
New Age community: Findhorn Foundation, Scotland

The Findhorn Foundation in Inverness, Scotland welcomes more than 14,000 visitors every year, from more than 70 countries. The Findhorn Community was established in 1962 by Peter and Eileen Caddy and Dorothy Maclean, who began by cultivating a world-famous garden which attracted more and more people seeking to join a nature-based, self-sufficient community. In the late 1960s the Park Sanctuary for meditation and a Community Centre were built by Peter and community members in accordance with Eileen's guidance (she used the guidance from spirits to influence both the cultivation of the garden and the construction of the centre).

In 1970 a young American spiritual teacher named David Spangler arrived in the community and with his partner Myrtle Glines helped to develop the spiritual education programmes of the Findhorn Community. Today the Centre runs almost 200 week-long courses every year. There are also conferences, trainings, worldwide pilgrimages and an outreach programme of educational workshops which are taken round the world. Those who wish to take a course are asked to attend Experience Week first, which introduces the main principles of life in the community, including love in action, meditation, sacred dance and nature outings. Examples of courses include Ecovillage Training, a month-long programme which has an ecological focus; or Essence of the Arts in Community, a three-month programme focusing on visual and performing arts. There are also shorter workshops on Healing, Meditation, Dance, Enlightened Leadership, Conflict Resolution, Shamanism, Manifestation, Energy Management, Yoga and many more. Retreat weeks also exist, including vegetarian cookery courses, pilgrimages, even gay and lesbian retreats.

By the 1990s the Findhorn Foundation became the heart of a diverse community of hundreds of people who spanned dozens of holistic businesses and initiatives. They were all linked by a commitment to non-doctrinal spirituality and a shared positive vision for humanity and the earth. In 1997 the Foundation was recognised as an official United Nations NGO. Findhorn also founded an Ecovillage in 1985 in accordance with principles of sustainability.

(Findhorn, 2013; Findhorn Ecovillage, 2013)

New Age tourism destinations often have a spiritual dimension. Even some of the world's major monuments and World Heritage Sites such as Stonehenge in the UK, the Pyramids in Egypt and Machu Picchu in Peru are sometimes sold as being New Age destinations. New Agers tend to visit sites and events belonging to different cultures and religions.

Yoga and meditation could be said to be sub-sectors of holistic tourism, but also of spiritual tourism. Iyengar (1989) once said that yoga is not a religion but is meant for individual growth and for physical, emotional, intellectual and spiritual balance. Yoga and meditation are practices which are ideally integrated into everyday life, but many people first discover them as part of a holistic holiday. It is sometimes difficult for many Westerners to grasp that yoga is not a fitness routine, but instead a spiritual practice which can lead to self-knowledge and create harmony with others and the world around us. It is also considered to be a form of meditation. However, it is sometimes difficult to distinguish between a holistic or spiritual retreat and a yoga holiday. According to Yoga Holidays (2008):

> A yoga holiday is primarily an activity holiday. The time devoted daily to yoga usually won't exceed four hours, in one, or possibly two daily classes, and you will have time for other activities or just to relax and chill out. The location should reflect this, with a beach or other notable attractions nearby. The atmosphere is often relaxed, and it is usually a great opportunity to meet other like-minded people. On a retreat, on the other hand, the yoga schedule is likely to be more intense, possibly including some meditation, times of silence, etc. The main focus is no longer to enjoy yourself on holiday, but to deepen your yoga practice. Again, the choice of location should reflect

this, with a quiet, possibly remote location. Retreats should be fully residential, the food vegetarian, and meal times carefully thought out to fit smoothly within the daily yoga routine. You will find more 'hard core' yogis and yoginis on retreats, and the overall atmosphere can be quite serious, with much less 'free' time.

It is recommended that beginners or those who are not so serious about yoga should opt for a yoga holiday rather than a retreat. Whereas yoga works for some people, others need a different type of activity to clear or control their minds. It is possible to learn meditation on a holiday, but it is usually recommended that beginners spend several days learning the basic techniques. One rather extreme version of a meditation retreat (at least for many uninitiated Westerners) is a Vipassana silent meditation retreat offered in countries like India and Thailand. Tai Chi and Chi Kung and other mind–body philosophies are growing in popularity within the wellness tourism sector, with some medical evidence to support their health benefits (e.g. Harvard Health Publications, 2009). There is clearly a growth of interest in both yoga and meditation retreats, as shown by Tzuhui Tseng and Ching-Cheng Shen (meditation in Taiwan) and Ivett Sziva, Noémi Kulcsár and Melanie Smith (yoga tourism in Budapest) in their case studies in Part III.

Wellness tourism

> Trips aiming at a state of health where the main domains of wellness are harmonised or balanced (e.g. physical, mental, psychological, social). There is an emphasis on prevention rather than cure, but some medical treatments may be used in addition to lifestyle-based therapies.

Voigt et al. (2011: 17) suggest that it is difficult to define or distinguish wellness travel as most tourism activities promote health and well-being in some way. Their definition takes into consideration beauty spa visitors, lifestyle resort visitors and spiritual retreat visitors:

> . . . the sum of all the relationships resulting from a journey by people whose motive, in whole or in part, is to maintain or promote their health and well-being, and who stay at least one night at a facility that is specifically designed to enable and enhance people's physical, psychological, spiritual and/or social well-being.

The Global Spa Summit (2011) used the following definition for research purposes:

> Wellness tourism involves people who travel to a different place to proactively pursue activities that maintain or enhance their personal health and well-being, and who are seeking unique, authentic, or location-based experiences that are not available at home.
>   **Bottom line: Undertaken by people who are healthy.**

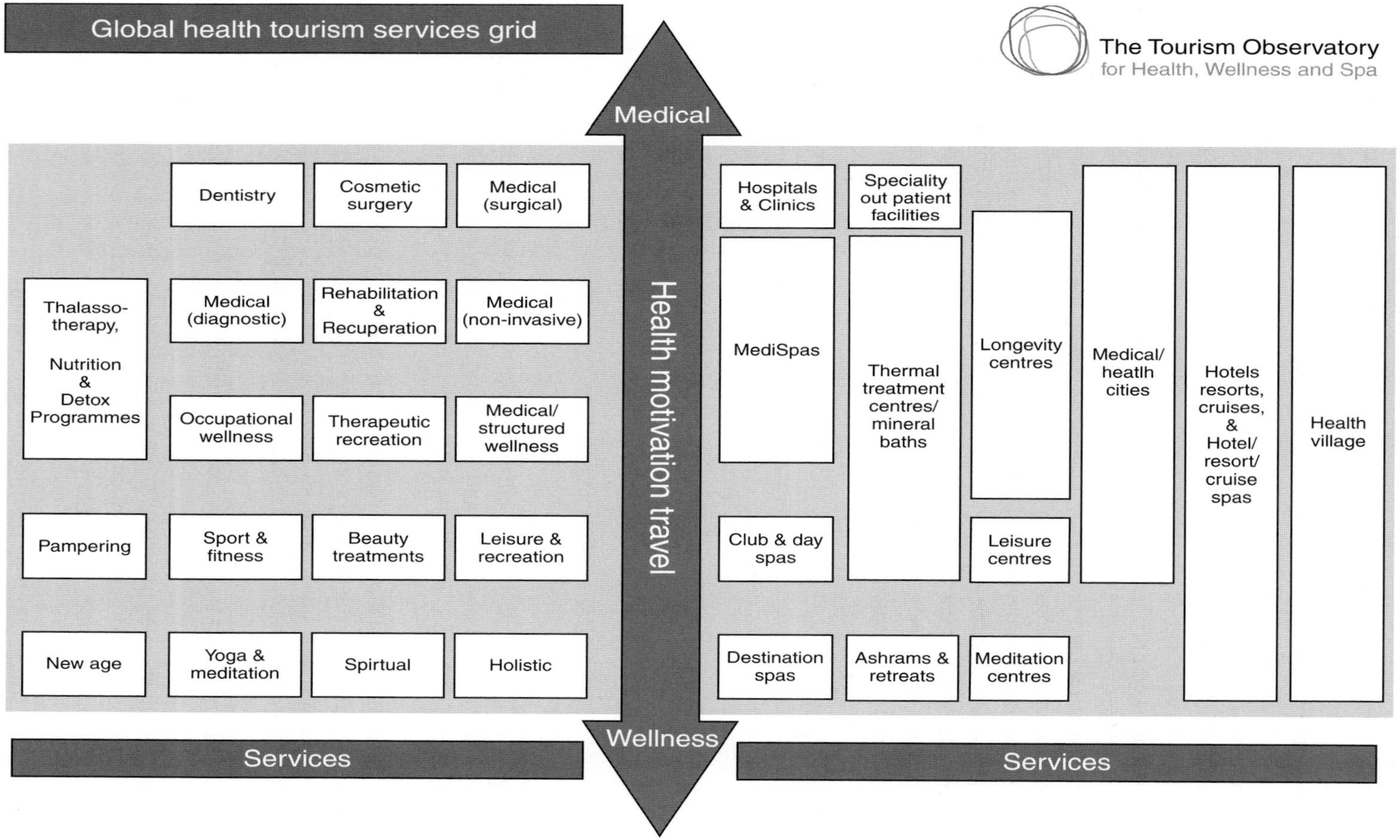

FIGURE 1.1 Global health tourism services grid

Here, the notion of authenticity is emphasised. Within a wellness context, authentic treatments may be said to be those which are undertaken ideally in the 'home' location or country of a tradition or practice and which follow prescribed steps or procedures. However, these may have been changed or modified over the centuries and may be further adapted when practices are shifted from one context to another (i.e. Thai massage being practised in countries outside Thailand, for example).

Connell (2012: 3) suggests that, 'Health and wellness tourism are usually differentiated as too "soft" and trivial to be MT (medical tourism)'. This is true to a certain extent, but the boundaries between medical and wellness tourism are becoming more blurred, especially if mental and psychological health eventually start to become included in medical tourism statistics. As discussed earlier, many European spas also include medical healing treatments in thermal water, and there are now officially defined 'medical spas'. We also argue in this book that medical tourism is a sub-sector of health tourism.

Of course, wellness tourism could be said to incorporate many of the other forms of tourism mentioned here. According to GSS (2010) customers tend to associate 'mental health' and 'medical health' with wellness and industry members associate 'holistic health' and 'spiritual health' with this term. The wellness industry tends to be proactive and preventative (rather than reactive and curative like the medical industry), so lifestyle-based habits and self-responsibility are important elements. Wellness tourism can include spas, retreats, wellness hotels, even sport and fitness holidays. According to GSS (2010) 90 per cent of spa industry respondents use the term 'wellness' in their business and a GSS (2011) report shows that 43 per cent of spa industry stakeholders associate wellness tourism with visiting a spa. It is noted here too that it is almost impossible (at present) to quantify the wellness tourism sector, mainly because of confusions over definitions.

The focus of wellness tourism may be on the physical body (e.g. nutrition, sleep, fitness, relaxation); the mind and psychology (e.g. stress management, mindfulness, positive thinking); or the spirit (e.g. connecting to oneself and the universe through yoga, Tai Chi, meditation or nature). Improving health, fitness, quality of life, balance and happiness, increasing relaxation and reducing stress are many of the main aims of wellness tourism.

Conclusion

This chapter has demonstrated that the health tourism sector is diverse and consists of a number of sub-sectors. It should be noted that several wellness approaches have very close links with mental and psychological health, and that many spas start to focus on medical procedures. Travellers in search of mental balance or a better psychological state often look for complementary or alternative approaches (e.g. Ayurveda, massage, yoga, meditation). However, most of these are not yet 'evidence based' and are therefore not always accepted officially by the medical industry or counted in official health tourism statistics.

A historical overview

The new phase in human evolution represents a culmination of thousands of years of human history during which many different cultures, philosophies, traditions and technologies have attempted to address the questions of life, ageing, illness and death. It seems that all people have tried to tackle with the question of: How to live well in the world?

(Cohen, 2008: 5)

This chapter provides an overview of the history and development of health and wellness, emphasising the different ways in which health has traditionally been understood in various regions and countries of the world. As health becomes more globalised as a result of international travel and increased mobility through immigration and guest working, there is a chance that products and services will become more homogenised and ubiquitous (i.e. the same or similar products will be available all over the world). However, in historical terms, health and wellness practices have been very much embedded in regional and local traditions and cultures, with available natural resources also determining the forms of wellness that were developed. Clearly, the concept of travelling for health reasons is a relatively late addition to the history of health so the emphasis on tourism is fairly minimal in this chapter. However, later chapters (e.g. Chapter 3) show just how these regions have developed their tourism facilities and resources over the past few decades using their unique traditions as described here.

A brief international overview of health and wellness

Many visitors to modern day health and wellness centres are often unaware of the cultural origins of the treatments they enjoy. Visitors may not realise that Indian Ayurvedic practices go back as far as 5000 BC, or that Egyptian women in 3000 BC used similar cosmetics to the ones that are sometimes used today. Loh (2008) notes that Ancient Babylonian and Chinese men indulged in manicures and pedicures as far back as three millennia. The earliest known writings about Chinese medicine go back to 1000 BC (Crebbin-Bailey et al., 2005), yet Chinese medicine in Western societies is often viewed as something 'new' and exotic. Erfurt-Cooper and Cooper (2009) give a very comprehensive timeline of the history and development of hot springs around the world from 3000 BC.The earliest reference to magical healing waters according to the Spas Research Fellowship (2008) is about 1700 BC. Hippocrates, the classic philosopher and physician of the Hellenistic age, and a prophet of natural healing methods, said: '. . . water is still, after all, the best'. The most ancient evidence of bathing culture was found in the valleys beside the river Indus where an ancient culture with water ducts, bathrooms and bath pools existed. Crebbin Bailey et al. (2005) provide an interesting timeline showing how ancient Greek civilisations from 700 BC introduced cold water bathing for warriors, Persians (600–300 BC) already used steam and mud baths, Hebrews introduced ritual purification by water through immersion in the Dead Sea in 200 BC and Thais (then Siamese) practised massage as far back as 100 BC. The Roman Empire left an incredible legacy of baths, one of the principal ones being in Bath in Britain in AD 76, as well as the discovery of thermal springs in destinations like Spa in Belgium before AD 100 and Baden-Baden in Germany in AD 211. The term *therme* was used for elegant leisure facilities whereas the term *balnea* was used for simple and mainly healing oriented bathing establishments.

The Baths of Caracalla near Rome were in use for three centuries before they lost their aqueduct water supply in the siege of Rome AD 537. The baths could accommodate between 6,000 and 8,000 bathers a day (Spas Research Fellowship, 2008). Lomine (2005) describes how Augustan Society in Rome during the Roman Empire (44 BC–AD 69) travelled fairly extensively for health reasons to relaxing landscapes, seaside resorts and hot springs. Medicine was not very developed and the average lifespan was about 40 years, so wealthy citizens would travel in the hope of finding treatment or recovering in a healthier climate. Typical trips would include sea voyages from Italy to Alexandria in Egypt or visits to mineral springs in what are now Vichy, Aix-en-Provence, Bath and Wiesbaden. Augustans would also travel to consult oracles or 'fortune tellers', for example in Delphi (Greece), Delos (Aegean Sea) or Claros (Asia Minor). Health and religion were combined in the case of visits to the sanctuaries of Asclepius (the Greek god of medicine), where visitors entered the sanctuary, took a bath to get purified, entered the god's temple, prayed, and laid down to sleep where the god would visit them and magically cure them or give advice about what treatment to take.

The Ottoman Empire built Turkish baths in AD 800 and knights from Britain experienced them during crusades in AD 1200. Saunas began appearing along the Baltic in Finland as early as AD 1000. The fourteenth century saw the development of the first shower in the baths of Bormie in Italy, as well as the discovery of warm springs in Central Europe (e.g. Buda – now Budapest in Hungary – and Carlsbad in Germany – now Karlovy Vary in the Czech Republic).

Unfortunately, in some parts of Europe (e.g. Britain) by the fifteenth century there were concerns about public bathing in warm waters because of the spread of diseases like syphilis, leprosy and plague. Naked, mixed bathing was also deemed immoral by the Bishop of Bath and Wells (which may explain the tendency in Britain today to still bathe in spas partly clothed!). Ellis (2008: 68) describes European spa visitors as traditionally 'being in pursuit of health, beauty, inspiration and even sexual pleasures'.

The Renaissance in Europe (sixteenth century) witnessed a boost to balneotherapy (water therapy treatments) as a medical practice, especially in Italy where there were famous sulphurous springs in Abano, mud baths in Padua, Lucca and Caldiero. In 1553 the first European Spa Directory was printed in Venice listing more than 200 spas. Elizabeth I popularised public bathing in 1571 in Britain to discourage the British from travelling to Spa in Belgium. The chemical and mineral properties of spa water were discovered in the mid-seventeenth century (for drinking and douching as well as bathing) and their effects were gradually listed and understood, and the effects of different temperatures were also researched. Many European kings and queens supported the visiting of spas. The late eighteenth century saw the recognition of the benefits of sea-water, the beginning of thalas-sotherapy, which was particularly popular in France. Tabacchi (2008) states that European spas were originally of two types: 1) mineral springs spas or therme, and 2) thalassotherapy spas (sea-water based). Modern massage techniques began to be developed in the early nineteenth century, particularly in Sweden. In the United States, the spiritual value of indig-enous (Native American Indian) landscapes started to be appreciated, and spas were built around springs there. In Germany, the first modern hydrotherapy spa was developed in the early nineteenth century offering health packages of treatments, such as fresh air, cold water and diet. This started a trend in both Europe and America. In 1880 Father Sebastian Kneipp started practising hydrotherapy for the poor, and his ideas still continue today. By the turn of the nineteenth century, travel guides were promoting the health treatments of air and sun cures all over the world, including the resorts of the Caribbean and spas in North Africa as well as Europe or Russia. There was an increased enthusiasm for health and exer-cise amongst the upper classes, and active tourism became popular (MacKenzie, 2005). By the early twentieth century, the benefits of spas for the war-wounded was well recognised all over Europe, and visits to the seaside were recommended for industrial workers.

We clearly see a growing awareness of the health-giving properties of water, whether sea, thermal or mineral water. Greeks and Romans focused on both cleanliness and fitness and understood the health benefits of various types of water treatments. The Japanese also had their own spas known as *onsens*, which are based on natural thermal springs. In AD 737, Japan's first onsen (hot spring) opened near Izumo, and centuries later the first *ryoken* (inns) were built, offering fine food, accommodation, Zen gardens, outdoor baths and indoor soaking tubs called cypress *ofuro* (SpaFinder, 2008).

However, it should also be remembered that the ancient civilisations of Asia and the Middle East and indigenous peoples all over the world have been aware of the benefits of massage, yoga, meditation, herbal medicines, and other forms of healing and spiritual practice for many more centuries than in Europe. Although the standard of living and quality of life of many people throughout the world is still deemed low by Western standards (e.g. in India, Africa or amongst indigenous tribal groups), those people have found their own ways of preserving health and maintaining well-being. As stated by Loh (2008: 43): 'Long before the science and mysteries of the mind became the subject of study in the West, sages of the East recognised the connection between breathing, stillness, silence and optimum functioning of the mind and body.' Some indigenous traditions and techniques, especially from Asia, are becoming more and more valued in modern day spas. Tourists are also keen to visit the 'homes' of certain practices and traditions like Ayurveda and Thai massage, for example. However, Bodeker and Burford (2008: 417) note that, 'Current spa programmes offer Ayurvedic packages in well designed luxury settings, a far cry from the original clinic in which they would have been performed in rural villages of India'.

The following sections provide a more comprehensive overview of the way in which health and wellness traditions have developed over time in different regions of the world. Although it is impossible to be fully representative of the whole world, these sections give a good understanding of the available resources, cultures and traditions of several regions, in which the individual countries tend to have much in common with each other. Much of the analysis is resource-based but with some reference to the influence of cultural traditions too.

Europe

The history of health tourism in Europe has tended to be based around spas and sea-water treatments, mainly because of the large numbers of thermal and mineral springs and sea coasts. The word spa is thought maybe to have originated from Latin and phrases such as *sanitas per aqua*, or from the Walloon word *espa* for fountain. The town of Spa in Belgium was one of the first, so it is sometimes thought that the term comes from this name. Hydrotherapy or water-based treatments are the cornerstone of what European spas have traditionally had to offer with a focus on health and physical well-being. It is only in recent years that cosmetic or beauty treatments have become more popular, as well as more spiritual or psychological activities. However, historically they were viewed as places to rehabilitate and 'take the waters' or 'take the cure'. Mineral water, thermal water, sea-water, muds, climate therapy, oxygen therapy, and sometimes special diets were the main focus.

The Romans built very sophisticated baths all over Europe which were integral to their way of life, and would consist of a series of cool to hot baths and a final cold plunge pool. Roman (Latin) terms like *frigidarium* (cool), *tepidarium* (lukewarm), *caldarium* (warm), *laconium* (hot), and so on, are still used in spas today. Baths or spas as they were later called were places where people met to discuss issues, like politics and philosophy, and they were the centres of social life for soldiers and administrators (Crebbin-Bailey et al., 2005).

The Roman bath experience

- Ideally undertake sports or a workout.
- Enter a *tepidarium* (lukewarm room of 35°C) and treatment begins.
- Receive an oil massage to soften the skin and then relax for a while.
- Enter the *laconium* (a hot, dry room of 80°C like a sauna) to initiate the detoxifying process.
- Receive a body scrub to remove dead skin in preparation for a vigorous massage.
- Enter the *caldarium* (a warm, damp room like a steam bath) and relax.
- Plunge into a cold pool to close the pores of the skin and invigorate the body.
- Rest and read in a library or quiet room.

The Romans travelled to different spas for healing purposes, with Spa in Belgium being one of the best known at that time, as well as destinations like Bath in the UK, Baden-Baden in Germany, Budapest in Hungary and Gerona in Spain. The Roman baths in Gerona were later used by the Arab occupiers in the twelfth century.

CASE STUDY 2.1
Spa in Belgium

The town of Spa is one of the oldest and most famous thermal resorts in the world. It is situated in French-speaking Belgium (Walloon region) on the fringes of the Ardennes. It was already known and appreciated by the Romans, it received famous guests such as Peter the Great, and it became so internationally renowned that in the sixteenth century the English language started to use the word 'spa' to refer to other thermal resorts. Specific geological conditions helped to create this resort development, namely the mineral and curative qualities of the waters, as well as the peaceful and green surroundings which were considered particularly conducive to health improvement and enhancement. From the mid-sixteenth century onwards, the healing effects of the spring were confirmed (before that it was little more than a village in the woods), and this attracted numerous illustrious visitors. The first private spa institute was founded in 1764 and the first public one in 1820. Spa's heyday came in the eighteenth century when it was referred to as the 'Café of Europe' (de Groote, 2008). 'Les Thermes de Spa' were constructed in 1868, encouraged by King Leopold II. The mineral springs were combined with entertainment, namely the casino, as well as cafés and organised events. The architecture of the resort became distinctive, with the neo-classical building of the casino, impressive gardens, the Pouhon Pierre-le-Grand (the most important source in Spa) and its beautiful winter garden, the Galerie Léopold II and the Parc de Sept Heures.

After World War I, Spa started to lose its former grandeur as a destination well known to the international elite, and gradually attracted more of a mass market. In 1921 the Spa Monopole Company started to export its mineral water in order to create revenue for the town and promote its image. After World War II, the traditional focus on health tourism was broadened to include more general aspects of leisure. Although there was a growth in the number of spa visitors from 1950 to 1970, this was mainly due to the financial support offered by the social security system. Visitation declined again from 1987 when the social security system no longer funded thermal treatments, thus the emphasis on leisure rather than medical thermalism started to grow. An agreement between Spa Monopole, Aqualis (association of local authorities), and the Walloon Region was signed for the building of a new complex in 2001. The project was completed three years later on 30 March 2004, and was a successful public–private partnership. The thermal centre's management was entrusted to the French Group Ebrard Thermes, which specialises in the business of spas and health centres (de Groote, 2008). The nineteenth-century 'Thermes de Spa' were therefore no longer used.

The Moors also left a legacy of baths or hammams in Spain, for example in Granada, Córdoba, Seville, Jerez and Cadiz (although some of these baths are built on the site of the original hammam). The hammam of Córdoba (or Cordova) is a UNESCO-designated World Heritage Site. Robinson (1996) describes how the city of Córdoba alone could boast 600 public baths in its eleventh-century heyday. When the Moorish cities fell to the Christians, the baths were not used or were demolished, but now 500 years later, many have been or are being regenerated.

Many of Europe's historic spa towns were built around healing springs between the fourteenth and sixteenth centuries, such as Vichy in France. Since Roman times Vichy waters have been famous for their health benefits. Today, Vichy waters can be taken for different therapeutic reasons, such as rheumatology and gastro-enterology, and for dermatological or dermo-cosmetic problems or beauty. Under Louis XIV, or Napoleon III the town and thermal spa were renovated and Vichy was not only a resort for taking the waters, but also a place of pleasure and elegance (it was called 'the second Paris') and Vichy became 'the queen of spa towns' (the king was Baden-Baden in Germany). Originally, travel to such destinations was common for royalty or nobility, but this later declined as domestic bathing conditions improved. From the sixteenth to the twentieth centuries, religion flourished and the church became more of a centre for social activities than spas. However, in the late twentieth and early twentieth centuries, as traditional religion once again declined, spas became one of the most desirable public spaces in which to congregate. Andrzej Hadzik and his co-authors provide a brief but interesting history of thermal spas in Poland from the twelfth century in their case study in Part III.

By the end of the eighteenth century, spa treatments and sea bathing seemed to develop concomitantly. Peter Kruizinga's case study in Part III gives a detailed history of Domburg in the Netherlands, which became a seaside bathing resort in 1834. Hydrotherapy was studied as a scientific way as another form of medicine, and confidence in the curative properties of water, both as bathing and drinking spread throughout Europe in the first half of the nineteenth century. Numerous mountain climatic resorts were built in the Alps, the Carpathians or around the Mediterranean. By 1889 there were 188 spas in Spain, for example (Larrinaga, 2005). However, gradually the motivation for coming to spas changed from being predominantly about health and cures to a desire for leisure, so many spas started to develop casinos and dance halls, as well as other entertainment facilities. The first International Balneological Congress was organised in Budapest (the world's only spa capital city) in 1937.

After World War II, many spa resorts in Western Europe went into stagnation, and sometimes even earlier. For example, Bacon (1998) describes how spas in the UK tended to be eclipsed by seaside resorts in the nineteenth century. Whereas in the mid-nineteenth century there were around 200 operational spas in the UK, by 1919 this number had declined to around 60, by 1946 there were only ten, and in 1978 only one (Leamington Spa). Only Bath spa has continued to be an important tourist attraction.

In communist Central and Eastern Europe and in the Soviet Union the spas or thermal baths entered a new phase of development just as many Western European spas were declining, with non-invasive treatment mainly sponsored by the state or the trade unions in their specialised facilities. The democratisation of access to the spas was coupled with

a narrow specialisation in medical treatment. A profound change occurred in the appearance of the spas. A dominating feature of their physical planning became the trade-union rest houses, hotels and sanatoria. Spas became 'healing combinats' for the people, based on mineral waters, climate and other local natural resources. The accommodation facilities were typically large buildings with mineral water basins and healing devices, with a residential part, dining facilities and meeting halls. Other services were almost absent.

The first bath of the North was initiated in Stockholm by medical doctor Carl Curman Sturebadet in 1885 to meet the '. . . desperately needed swimming, exercise, and a road to better health . . . In 1899 there were 63 treatment areas with 43 bathtubs for soaking' (Sturebadet, 2008). The facility in 1902 was extended with a swimming pool in Art Nouveau with Old Norse and Moorish features. Interestingly, the use of the term 'Swedish massage' is a misnomer, and although it is often attributed to Peter Henry Ling (1776–1837), he in fact developed a system of movements and gymnastics.

The Finnish 'golden spa age' had been in the 1800s, and the density of spas was the highest in Europe from the early 1890s, even though there were only a few natural spas (i.e. thermal/mineral waters). The Yrjönkatu Bath in Helsinki opened in 1928 and has ever since been a must-see attraction of the city. In Finland, one of the compensations offered to wounded Finnish soldiers after World War II was veteran spa rehabilitation. A system of regular periods (usually one–three weeks) of physical rehabilitation was created and the state paid the costs. From the 1960s onwards, war veterans were given good-quality professional medical care in these spas, as well as some leisure/wellness activities and facilities. In the future when the war veterans are no longer alive, a new use for such spas will need to be created, which may be based on wellness rather than medical tourism (Aho, 2007).

Lee (2004) suggests that the European health and wellness model has been based around the four elements: water, fire, earth and air (Indian Ayurveda and Chinese philosophy do this too, but in a slightly different way as discussed later in the chapter). The balance or harmonisation of these elements was considered essential to wellness by Greek philosophers. Water therapies help to heal and soothe the body; heat treatments induce sweating and accelerate circulation of the blood; earth offers numerous natural herbs, flowers, plants, muds and fruit; and fresh air and oxygen are the essence of life. Greeks and other ancient civilisations believed that thermal and mineral springs were a gift from the Gods and built temples for various deities near to them. There is often a connection between spas and spirituality; for example, Lourdes in France is both a healing spring and a pilgrimage destination. Diet, exercise and massage along with water were seen by the Greeks and Romans as being essential for combating disease and preserving good health. Bathing in the sea or rivers was always considered to be health-giving, a process akin to baptism or re-birth in which individuals were symbolically purified and cleansed. Cleanliness and hygiene were considered essential, a philosophy which was later forgotten in mediaeval and Renaissance Europe, when public diseases in spas became rife. Thalassotherapy or the use of sea-water in health and wellness was practised by ancient Egyptians, but the Greeks added more treatments, such as the use of mud to this tradition (pelotherapy). Later, this expanded to include salt scrubs, seaweed wraps and salt inhalation, amongst others. Roscoff in France and Varberg in Sweden became popular destinations for sea-water cures.

The principle of fire was first developed in the context of health and wellness in Roman baths (where thousands could congregate at once in heated rooms), Turkish hamams or steam baths, Russian 'white' or 'black' banias (a steam room and sauna, respectively), and Finnish saunas. Some farmers in Germany in the eighteenth century also used dry heated rooms where flax or hemp was stored, and Austrian farmers used hay-storing barns with a stove. Sweat bathing was thought to ease aching muscles after a long day in the fields as it could draw toxins out of the body, such as lactic acid. Finns and Russians used the sauna as an integral part of everyday life and one in which to celebrate special occasions (e.g. birth, weddings, death). Russian banias were traditionally more vigorous than Finnish saunas, and whipping with twigs was not uncommon. The air was generally wetter and special oils were used such as eucalyptus or mint (a common practice in spas today). Although it is recommended that alcohol should not be drunk before, during or immediately after a sauna, it was not unusual in Russia or Finland to consume vodka or other alcoholic beverages like beer as part of the social experience!

Air is another integral part of health and wellness everywhere, but in Europe this usually meant (and still does) going to the seaside or to mountain regions to escape heavily polluted cities. Pure air therapy is sometimes known as climatotherapy, which harnesses facets of the environment such as air, climate, atmosphere, temperature, humidity and light. The movement from one climate to another is well known in European wellness tourism, for example Northern Europeans going to Southern Europe for warmer, drier climates and more sunshine, or city dwellers going to the mountains or the sea to recharge and relax. Those with tuberculosis or blood problems traditionally convalesced in the mountains, and those with bronchitis or rheumatism went to the seaside. Regular exercise and fitness programmes were also known to assist better respiration. Beckerson and Walton (2005) describe how from the mid-eighteenth century onwards, resort visiting in Britain (and later in Belgium) was based mainly on the healthy qualities of the seaside air, and by the late nineteenth century, it was even more important than sea bathing. It was much later in the twentieth century when sunshine started to become even more popular. Publicists promoted 'ozone' as being fresh, revitalising and invigorating. Mountain and countryside air was also thought to have numerous health benefits, especially for workers from industrial cities. Increasingly in European spas, breathing work is being done as part of yoga or meditation, but this is usually derived from Asian traditions. Oxygen therapy is also sometimes used to improve skin damage. Ozone treatment in medical spas was traditionally used with oxygen and injected into the body to inactivate bacteria, oxidise certain poisons, increase blood circulation and strengthen the immune system, but its usage is a bit more controversial these days.

Finally, earth elements in Europe mainly consisted of muds, which were derived from a number of sources (e.g. moors, bogs, volcanoes, sea-beds), herbs or plant extracts used in medicines, flower essences use in remedies (e.g. Bach flower remedies), essential oils most commonly used in aromatherapy or caves used in climatotherapy. The use of medical mud originated in France as a way of treating war wounds in World War II, and was then used in massage by the mid-1950s. Farmers in Europe sometimes fell asleep in the hay

and this was thought to have a therapeutic effect and now forms the basis of some Alpine wellness techniques. Phytotherapy (the use of plants for healing or theraputic uses) and Western herbalism is still treated with some scepticism by medical practitioners as it is unscientifically proven for the most part. However, the ancient Egyptians, Greeks, Romans and Indians all used essential oils as perfumes or for massage. Vinotherapy – the therapeutic use of wine and grapes in beauty and health treatments is believed to date back to Egypt in 3200 BC but became widespread in France in the Bordeaux region only recently when grape seeds were found to have healing properties for the skin. The first vinotherapy spa did not open in Caudalie until 1999, where elements from grapes and wine were combined with warm spring water for baths, massages, masks, scrubs and wraps. Caves with special climatic conditions are used for medical healing, especially in pulmonology.

In terms of balancing the elements, the nineteenth-century priest Kneipp prescribed alternating hot and cold baths, compresses, steam baths, showers, wraps, footbaths (Kneipp footbaths can be found in numerous spas around the world today) as well as herbal therapies, nutrition, fresh air, sunshine and rest. Kneipp's legacy continues in healing traditions today, especially in the German *kur* system, with the national health programme sometimes paying for stays in a Kneipp Kurhaus if prescribed by a doctor. This represents an early form of holistic or integrated wellness, which is preventative as well as curative.

Middle East and North Africa

Gifts of Health (2011) produced a beautiful publication based on extensive research analysing how Islamic traditions from the Middle East, Asia, Africa and Europe could be used to create unique and authentic spa experiences. Much of this focuses on the way in which nature has been harnessed to enhance human health and well-being. This includes the use of herbs, spices and fruits in creating nutrition, cosmetics, massage oils and aromas. Hammam traditions are also omnipresent. The work of the Arab physician Ibn Sina (known in Europe as Avicenna) was particularly influential, including in Europe. His *The Canon of Medicine* (1025) lists 800 tested drugs, plants and minerals. He is also credited with the discovery of the steam distillation, which farther facilitated the extraction of essential oils (the first of which was rose oil). Musk and floral women's perfumes were brought to Europe in the eleventh and twelfth centuries from Arabia.

Arabian medicine was originally influenced by that of Greeks and Romans; however, by the Dark Ages in Europe, medical developments in Arabia were far superior and even today the Middle East is one of the major growth regions for medical tourism. Egyptians were particularly focused on diseases of the eye, and it is thought that kohl eyeliner pencils were originally used to disinfect the eye rather than for cosmetic purposes. However, beauty cosmetics were used in ancient Egypt as far back as 1400 BC including skin oils, face creams, deodorants, toothpaste, henna and hair dyes, red ochre lip gloss and perfumes. Sunburn and prickly heat treatments were developed throughout the region as the desert sun was so intense (an even more major issue for tourists today). Egyptians and

Babylonians used bathing to heal the spirit and treat the body. Whereas European bathing focused on medical or physical health-giving properties, Egyptians believed that they should be clean and beautiful to reach a higher spirituality. Cleansing involved exfoliating and massaging the skin in a warm bath using yoghurt and honey. It was said that Queen Cleopatra (69–30 BC) bathed in milk to keep her skin soft, hence the modern day spa's 'Cleopatra Bath' treatment. Egyptians used thermal baths, whereas Arabian hammams or Turkish steam baths played a fundamental role in Ottoman culture (around 600 AD), and were places of social gathering and ritual. There were separate quarters for men and women, and like Roman baths there was a graduating sequence of heat, as well as scrub massages, followed by cooling and resting.

Since the time of Aristotle (304–322 BC) people also visited the Dead Sea to experience its healing waters and therapeutic climate, as well as mud wraps. The Rasul is a traditional Arabian cleansing ritual that is administered in an elaborately tiled steam chamber that has a domed starlit ceiling. A steam injector infuses a mixture of aromatic dried herbs which cleanse and detoxify. Visitors take a short shower, medicinal muds are applied to the skin to cleanse and exfoliate, and the mud is then massaged until it hardens. The mud starts to liquefy as the humidity increases, and after about 20 minutes a tropical rain shower falls from the dome of the rasul and washes away the mud. Nowadays, more and more luxury spas where the Arabic architecture and traditions blend with Western-style spa resorts are opening along the coastline in Qatar, Saudi Arabia, Oman or Dubai.

Arabian medicine tends to use Hippocrates' idea of the 'four humours' (yellow bile, black bile, phlegm and blood), their respective qualities (choleric, melancholic, phlegmatic and sanguineous), and their natures (hot, dry, humid and cold), and the seasons. It is these elements that needed to be in harmony or balance to attain optimal health. Astrological influence was also considered important, as well as the will of Allah. Diet and bathing were both considered important, as well as herbal and natural medicines, such as cassia (cinnamon), cloves, myrrh, nutmeg, sienna and sandalwood, as well as drugs like opium, cannabis and camphor to balance body and mind. The rose and its oils were considered to be the most important flower and it was used for a range of health problems as well as for its scent. Although not only indigenous to Arabia and the Middle East (many of the traditions are Indian), other therapies were used to help balance energies within the body. These include crystal and gem therapy, aura readings, colour therapy and chakra cleansing. Gold was also commonly used, as it is believed to ease tension, feelings of inferiority and anger as well as encouraging the realisation of one's innate potential (Van der Meulen and O'Brien, 2006).

Alexander (2001) describes the holistic system of medicine known as 'Tibb', which was mainly practised in Persia and Turkey in the past, but increasingly in the Middle East, India, Pakistan, Bangladesh, Afganistan and Malaysia. It combines elements of ancient Egyptian and Greek medicine, Chinese and Indian traditions, and the healing wisdom of Persia and the Middle East. It recognises the vital energy known as *qawa* in Arabic, and shares the concept that medicine needs to be holistic, to look at the whole person, balance the elements and use herbal remedies to heal the body. Tibb focuses on lifestyle rather than just diet alone (the traditional Chinese starting point), including breathing, emotions (counselling or psychotherapy is deemed valuable), sleeping patterns, eating patterns, a

person's working life, their ability to relax and, finally, their spiritual state. This appears to be one of the precursors of holistic wellness, for which many people travel to retreats or special workshops to experience.

The key principles of Tibb

- Get up early before sunrise and certainly before 7 a.m.
- Eat a good breakfast, a reasonable-sized lunch but a small dinner at least two hours before bedtime.
- Take regular exercise to keep you healthy in body and mind.
- Make sure you get enough exercise, as people in the West tend to be over-stimulated.
- Take a siesta in the afternoon for 30 minutes. Take a day off work if you are tired. Have a warm bath with essential oils.
- Incorporate spirituality into your life, e.g. prayer, meditation or simple contemplation of the beauty in the world.
- Don't go to bed too late, 11 p.m. at the latest.
- Cultivate good sleep. Try meditating or gentle massage before bed.

(Alexander, 2001)

Jews also take part in ritual bathing, since traditionally orthodox Jews have to go to the *mikveh*. The water comes from a barrel in which they collect rain water. This then has to be purified to become *kosher*, in which women and men can bathe separately.

Of course, one of the main natural resources in this region is the Dead Sea, which has attracted visitors from around the Mediterranean basin for thousands of years. Biblically, it was a place of refuge for King David, and it was one of the world's first health resorts (e.g. for Herod the Great).

Asia-Pacific

Asia's wellness traditions take a holistic approach of treating the body, mind and spirit as one, trying to identify the root cause of a problem and encouraging the body to heal itself. The natural healing approach in Asia is therefore usually rooted in tradition and spirituality rather than based on natural assets. This is, however, a little different in Japan, where onsens (traditional bathing establishments) are often visited by locals looking for relaxation or meditation and increasingly by tourists. An onsen is a Japanese hot spring. As it is a volcanically active country, Japan has thousands of onsen, and they were traditionally thought to have spiritual beings living in them which gave vision and guidance. The Balneotherapy Institute was founded by Kyushu University in 1931 and by 1955 there were over 90 medical facilities in the mineral spring locations in Japan. Like European spas or Arabic hammams, onsens are social spaces as well as sites of purification and ritual. Therapies like shiatsu massage or reiki have also emerged from Japan and are commonly used in Western spas nowadays.

India's cultural and historical legacy predates even that of Ancient Egypt, and Ayurveda ('the science of life') is regarded by scholars as the oldest healing system in the world. It is the prime healing tradition in India, Sri Lanka and Nepal. Ramesh Unnikrishnan provides a detailed and interesting analysis of the Ayurvedic tradition in his case study in Part III. It is interesting therefore that it has only been in recent years that Ayurveda has started to be used in modern spas. It is a long-term lifestyle choice, but can increasingly be experienced in small doses whilst on holiday in the form of massage or diet. Balance should be achieved in the three universal governing forces or *doshas: vata* (air), *pitta* (fire) and *kapha* (earth). One of these forces tends to dominate in most individuals and the task of Ayurveda is to redress the balance through appropriate diet, oil and massage therapies, herbal remedies, yoga and meditation. Spirituality is an important and inherent part of most Asian traditions, and this is particularly true in India. There are close connections to religion and pilgrimage in some cases, for example the world famous 'Kumbha Mela', which also includes ritual bathing.

CASE STUDY 2.2
Kumbha Mela festival in India

Sacred festivals in India are called 'Melas' and they are an important part of the Hindu pilgrimage tradition. The greatest of these is the Kumbha Mela, which is a riverside festival held four times every twelve years in different locations, such as Allahabad at the confluence of the river Ganges and Yamuna. Bathing in these sacred waters is thought to be cleansing for body, mind and spirit and is said to purge pilgrims of all their sins.

In theory the Kumbha Mela festivals are supposed to occur every three years, rotating between four cities, but this is dependent on astrological factors. Such festivals can attract up to five million pilgrims or more. It is thought that not only is the Kumbha Mela the largest religious gathering in the world, it may also be the oldest. Although historical research on this festival is not conclusive, it is thought that its origins date back to the 9th century, when a philosopher called Sankaracharaya organised the Kumbha Mela in Prayaga (Allahabad) so that yogis, sadhus and sages from all corners of India could meet in a central location. One of the reasons to meet was to create an environment of mutual understanding between different religious sects. Another was to give ordinary householders the chance to interact with normally reclusive holy men.

At the most auspicious hour on the most auspicious day of the festival many thousands of holy men from various sects will bathe in the river. Following the ceremonial bathing of the sadhus, millions of other people rush to enter the river. For a devout Hindu, to bathe at the Kumbha Mela sites at this auspicious time is considered an event of immeasurable spiritual significance. Unfortunately, this great religious fervour has often resulted in hundreds of pilgrims being crushed to death as the masses race towards the river banks. Furthermore, many Hindus consider the Kumbha Mela sites to be the most favoured places to die, and ritual suicide, though discouraged by the government, is still practised.

(Sacred Sites, 2008)

Traditional or Chinese medicine (TCM) forms the basis of many Asian therapies, although therapies vary from one country to another. Originally, medicine was based on ancestral worship, shamanism and magic, but these principles became more philosophical, scientific and rational over time. Chinese practices focus on the individual and provide a unique combination of therapies based on the 'Three Treasures' listed below:

- *energy* – or life force, called qi or chi;
- *jing* – the essence which governs vitality and longevity;
- *shen* – the mind or spirit, responsible for consciousness and mental ability.

There is always an attempt to balance yin (feminine, cold, static) and yang (masculine, warm, dynamic), the opposing but complementary forces which govern chi. The philosophy of yin and yang is further refined into the theory of five elements of earth, fire, metal, water and wood, where each nurtures and supports the others. This balance of energy and elements forms the basis of Feng Shui philosophy. Chinese medicine, like Indian Ayurveda, tends to be a holistic and preventative approach to health including diet, movement, spiritual and emotional well-being. A number of therapies are offered such as herbal medicine, acupuncture, reflexology, Chi Kung or Tai Chi, as well as massages which focus on meridians or energy lines in the body. Bodeker and Burford (2008) discuss how Chinese-themed treatments and products are now very much globalised in the spa world, including Chinese medicine, Tai Chi and acupuncture.

Thailand is famous for Thai massage which is exported to wellness centres all over the world. It is given clothed and involves a system of stretching, loosening joints and easing muscle tension through a sequence of yoga-like movements, as well as manipulating meridian or sen lines. The technique is around 2,500 years old and was developed by an Ayurvedic doctor, Shivago Komarpaj. The massage has a spiritual as well as a physical dimension, and it is common for masseurs to say a short prayer before they begin wishing improved health to their patient. Other countries in Asia have developed their own approaches to health and wellness, like Jamu in Indonesia which is a blend of a selection out of 150 possible ingredients to make health-giving drinks, cosmetics, medicines and remedies.

The indigenous peoples in the Asia-Pacific region (including Australian Aborigines and New Zealand Maori) have always used traditional herbal remedies, massages and deep spiritual beliefs in holistic ways to preserve good health and enhance well-being. Many of the products found in modern-day spas in Australia, for example, have been used for more than 40,000 years by Aboriginal Australians (e.g. the Li'Tya range). Rotorua in New Zealand has numerous hot springs in its vicinity because of its volcanic landscape. Maori people were originally attracted to the springs and built whole villages in the area. The British found the modern town of Rotorua in the 1830s and soon discovered the curative effects of the hot springs. The Maori Te Arawa people were instrumental in bringing the tourism industry into the town and they formed a guild of hospitable tour guides who showed Europeans around the place. Word got around and curious tourists from Europe and America visited Rotorua. Since the early twentieth century, the town has developed a tourism industry that revolves around the hot springs and millions of people have been drawn to the place because of the curative power of its mineral-enriched water. The Rotorua Baths complex was built in mock Tudor style during the 1920s. Maria Hyde-Smith and John Hull provide an interesting case study of Te Aroha in Part III of this book. This was already a booming spa tourism destination in the 1880s.

Africa

Africa has a wide range of indigenous herbs and plants which have been used for centuries for health and healing. Different tribes in Africa have traditionally drawn on the natural world for all kinds of remedies, using sand from the deserts, mud or clay from the soil, salt from the oceans, and plant and herbs from the jungles. Masai tribes people in Kenya and Tanzania administered massage to each other to ease backs and shoulders after carrying heavy loads or hunting all day. Zulu warriors had different ways of preparing for the fight ahead, using physical, psychological and spiritual techniques to do so. Ancient bushmen in countries like Botswana used a combination of drumming and trance dance to heal sickness.

MacKenzie (2005) describes some of the guidebooks which promoted Africa in the late 1nineteenth and early twentieth centuries, especially in southern Africa where railway lines had spread to support the gold rush. Cruises were seen as being a health-giving experience because of the healthy air on the sea and the warm climate. Putative health resorts with hotels and sanatoria in the mountains and drier areas of the region were promoted. Lung diseases were particularly thought to benefit from a stay in Africa. Sulphur and hot springs were also discovered around the Cape. South Africa is particularly rich in thermal spring resorts, as discussed by Mark Boekstein in his case study in Part III of this book. Erfurt-Cooper and Cooper (2009) note that most African countries have hot springs, but that they have had very little development. Usually, they were used by the local population or tribal groups, with the exception of hot springs in Namibia and Cameroon. The former were used by white settlers in the 1800s and a few safari tourists visited the latter in the 1930s.

However, the main evidence of health and wellness tourism in Africa is in the development of European colonial hill stations, spas and seaside resorts, and other enclaves that catered to the health and welfare of the expatriate community. Jennings (2007) describes a 1924 advertisement for one of France's spas: 'Beware! Against the poison that is Africa, there is but one antidote: Vichy.' His book describes how throughout the French Empire, water cures and high-altitude resorts were widely believed to serve important therapeutic and even prophylactic functions against tropical disease and the tropics themselves. Although colonisers sometimes frequented spas back home as the advertisement suggested, it was more common to build spa retreats in the colonies. The Ministry of the Colonies published bulletins accrediting a number of spas thought to treat tropical diseases ranging from malaria to yellow fever and

specialist guidebooks gave advice on the best spas for colonial ills. Treatments were based on acclimatisation theory and the development of a science of hydrotherapy. Many spas and hill stations served as a refuge from disease, heat, insects and wildlife, and other perceived 'dangers', including contact with indigenous peoples! Crossette (1998) notes that the age of the hill station mirrored the period when seaside resorts, spas, and great mountains lodges were being built in Europe and the United States, and how in some cases, the style and atmosphere of these European or American mountain retreats were copied in the colonies. Hill stations usually had to be around 5,000 to 8,000 feet above sea level beyond the reach of mosquitoes, and had to be more than just resorts. They were also a medical centre of sorts used for recovery and recuperation, as well as a retreat from reality for homesick Europeans. Although more common in Asia, they were also built in Kenya, Uganda and elsewhere in Africa where Europeans had colonised.

The Americas

Clearly, when we talk about the Americas we have to make a distinction between the modern spas of the past 100 years or so in the USA and Canada, Central and South America, and the traditions of indigenous peoples throughout the region which pre-date those spas by thousands of years. South America has thousands of hot springs, volcanic thermal waterfalls (e.g. Costa Rica, Ecuador or the Caribbean), some of which were traditionally used by indigenous peoples such as the Incas. The hot springs of Brazil and Peru were documented by the Spanish conquerors in the sixteenth century.

Influences of ancient civilisations are pervasive throughout the region, especially in modern-day spas. In Maroma Spa (Mexico) the orientation of the rooms follow the ancient Maya traditions. This will apparently allow the positive energy from planets and stars to come to the rooms. According to Mayan spirituality this has a good impact both on the soul and body of those who stay in the rooms. Guests at the Ikal del Mar on the Mexican Riviera can enjoy facials and massages influenced by Mayan traditions such as the Mayan Bath, the Mayan Massage, the Hammock Massage where the colour hammock is chosen according to the guest's desired energy and the Temazcal Spiritual Mayan Sauna. The word Temazcal, in the Nahuatl language, is a combination of the words Temaz, meaning bath, and Calli, meaning home. The ceremony was practised by the Mayans and other indigenous groups as a therapeutic and purifying ritual. Mexico's Mayan Riviera also boasts one of the world's most extensive varieties of native herbs. Therefore, spa treatments tend to offer a combination of natural marine elements with native herbs and aromas. The One&Only resorts offer an 'Aztec Aromatic Ritual', where the spiciness of the wrap was traditionally used as a curative treatment to heal headaches, arthritis and muscular aches. An ancient village recipe of aromatic spices provides a warm and stimulating sensation.

Traditionally, Native Americans viewed mineral and healing springs as inherently spiritual. They also used other rituals for preserving health and well-being, such as 'sweat lodges'. There are several styles of Native American Indian (e.g. Navaho) sweat lodges that include a domed or oblong hut similar to a wickiup, a teepee, or even a simple hole dug into the ground and covered with planks or tree trunks. Stones are heated in an exterior fire and then placed in a central pit in the ground. Often the stones are granite and they glow red in the dark lodge. Rituals and traditions vary from region to region and tribe to tribe. They often include prayers, drumming, and offerings to the spirit world. In Mexico the Temazcal is a ritual ceremony that has been practised by indigenous people for hundreds of years. It is similar to a Sweat Lodge, and is a thanksgiving to the four elements, and a healing for the body, mind and spirit. Participants are often asked to fast the day before and the experience (traditionally led by a medicine man) can be intense. Other typical Native American Indian traditions and tools, which are increasingly being used in retreats and holistic centres, include animal totems or spirit guides; dream catchers, which can protect from nightmares; smudge sticks or smoking wands for purification; and talking sticks which are passed from speaker to speaker to encourage the respectful sharing of opinions.

The year 1806 saw the first coming together of indigenous traditions and modern spa culture when John Arnold of Rhode Island opened the US's first European-style spa in Saratoga (New York), a Native American Indian word for the 'place of the medicine waters of the great spirit'. Native Americans had been frequenting the mineral springs since the fourteenth century, and they believed the springs had healing powers, and that they were also sacred. In the late 1700s, Sir William Johnson, a friend of the Native Americans, became ill and he was transported to the springs to drink the water and to bathe. He is believed to be the first white man to visit the springs. By the 1800s, Saratoga was already a very popular tourist attraction, and water was being bottled and shipped around the world (Saratoga State Park, 2008).

The American Hydropathic Institute opened in New York in 1851 and was said to be the first medical school based on water cure principles. The concept of 'naturotherapy' also originated in New York. It focuses on the vital curative force within the body (Alexander, 2001). As well as water-based treatments, natural cures are derived from diet and fasting, fresh air and sunlight, relaxation and psychological counselling. Remedial exercises in water were developed in the early 1920s for those with mobility problems. The Boyes Hot Spring near Calistoga dated from 1895 and was re-developed and re-named in 1928 as the Sonoma Mission inn and Spa. Towards the end of the twentieth century, it started to offer additional services such as massage, beauty treatments and fitness activities.

However, generally spas in America tended to be more social than therapeutic, and demanded little from patients (Crebbin-Bailey et al., 2005). The first day spa, Manhattan's Red Door Salon, was introduced by Elizabeth Arden in 1910, offering manicures, facials and the signature 'Arden Wax' (in addition to serving as a finishing school). Tabacchi (2008) suggested that the spa 'cure' almost disappeared in the USA with the development of antibiotics and mood-modulating drugs. However, the personal health concept was not forgotten and a second-generation American, Deborah Szekely, created the first destination spa, Rancho La Puerta, located just south of the border in Baja California.

CASE STUDY 2.3
Rancho La Puerta

Ranch La Puerta was founded by Edmond and Deborah Szekely in 1940 and has always been a family-owned and operated business. It is probably the first destination fitness and resort spa. The motto has always been 'Siempre Mejor' which means 'Always Better', which is described by the founder as meaning 'Always changing'. Edmond Szekely was a Professor and one of the main highlights for the first guests of Rancho La Puerta was listening to his talks about good health and long life that recognized the interdependence of mind, body, and spirit. He also wrote and talked about herb uses at a time when they had been nearly forgotten; and about vitamins and minerals before their recommended daily allowances were well known. He also followed the hydrotherapy recommendations of Sebastian Kneipp and adapted his herbal wrap as a signature Ranch treatment to ease sore muscles after exercise. The spa has always followed Edward Szekely's essential philosophy, which was:

> To survive in this increasingly artificial world, mankind must reprise old ways of eating nutritiously and moving naturally, and in so doing establish new ways of achieving balance and realizing one's entire potential. So we can lead a useful, long, healthful life.

In the meantime, Deborah developed a programme of exercises including calisthenics and yoga (before it was popular in the West), dance and exercise to music, especially jazz, which was very popular. Participants in their first Ranch camps joined them at dawn for a meditation hike up the mountain to greet the morning sun, and at sundown they paid a similar tribute to the evening star.

The Rancho La Puerta menu was simple but revolutionary, consisting of vegetarian foods and fresh ingredients from the local area or grown on the ranch. For example, fresh raw milk from their goats, whole-grain bread from wheat that was grown and germinated there, and wild-sage honey. Everyone who stayed performed farm chores and kitchen duties. They then went to eat alone in a chosen nature spot free from interruption where they could experience oneness with nature, something like an eating meditation.

To inspire positive thoughts, guests were given cards printed with Communions for the day, which included simple thanksgiving, celebration or supplications.

A newsletter was established to inform, educate, and celebrate all that was going on. Subscribers received a monthly mind–body fitness bulletin as well as individual advice in response to their write-in questions. By the end of WWII, there were over a hundred members in a half-dozen countries who ensured that the annual six-week summer school was over-subscribed.

Deborah Szekely still gives lectures at the age of more than 90. She talks about self-responsibility for the body, listening to the body and paying respect to the body. Rancho La Puerta has always been about self-reliance and knowledge sharing, even today. Deborah's new mission is to promote health-care education and prevention, something that she started with her husband more than 70 years ago.

(Rancho La Puerta, 2013; Terry, 2013)

In 1958, Szekely also opened the pioneering Golden Door spa in California, offering individualised weight loss and fitness programmes (and purportedly introducing Jane Fonda to aerobics). The first fitness spa, The Ashram, also debuted in California, in 1974, brandishing a gruelling weight loss/fitness regimen that was toned down and popularised by Tucson's Canyon Ranch in 1979. Tabacchi (2008) states that in 1993 Deepak Chopra was urging spa operators to examine alternative medicine. By 1997, innovative U.S. doctors began to introduce 'medical spas', combining Western and holistic medicine in a luxurious, spa-inspired environment alongside spa services (SpaFinder, 2007). Overall, in the past 40 years or so, numerous so-called 'super spas' have emerged in America which preserve the privacy of individuals and shelter them from the outside world so that they can relax, be pampered and rejuvenate (e.g. vine-spas or spa and golf, or ski and spa products). Tabacchi (2008) quotes an ISPA study from 2004 which showed that American spa-goers liked yoga and pilates-type activities in addition to massage, and they were starting to prefer clothed massage such as Thai. She also predicts that the European hydrotherapy tradition is likely to continue to expand in the USA as guests are starting to appreciate more and more the benefits of water therapy.

To finish this chapter, the following case study gives an example of a spa which draws on a number of historic traditions from America and the rest of the world to create a unique experience.

CASE STUDY 2.4
The Spa of Colonial Williamsburg

The Spa of Colonial Williamsburg in the USA was opened in spring 2007 and it adopted a unique approach. It uses a 21st-century interpretation of five centuries of health and healing practices from European, African and American Indian cultures in a so-called 'continuum of wellness'. The menu of services are in keeping with the Foundation's mission of learning from the past:

17th century: Cleansing Hot Stones Experience: the Powhatan Indians employed wellness tactics involving heating their bodies with hot stones in sweathouses followed by cold water plunges. In this modern-day interpretation, the body is warmed by hot stones, and then wrapped in herb-infused, steaming linen to encourage the natural release of toxins. During the heated wrap, cool aromatherapy cloths are applied to refresh the brow. The experience concludes with full-body, hot stone massage using oil containing lavender, cypress, juniper and rosemary.

18th century: Colonial Herbal Spa Experience: the 18th century marked the beginning of the assimilation between cleanliness and health, with doctors realizing that dirt on the skin prevented the essential process of perspiration. Thus, individuals began mixing baths of herbal and apothecary ingredients, a ritual adapted for the modern spa patron with a cleansing foot bath, followed by an orange-ginger body scrub, herbal body wrap and signa-

ture Williamsburg massage. Historic-inspired components of the experience include a variety of colonial herbs.

19th century: Root and Herbal Spa Experience: African traditions during the 1800s focused on the use of herbs for healing purposes. The Spa translates this into the experience by incorporating body exfoliation and an herbal bath with a 'strengthening' full-body massage. The exfoliating High Road Powder helps to boost spirit and energy before guests soak in an invigorating herbal bath steeped in Ritual Bath Tea and undergo an invigorating massage.

20th century: Williamsburg Water Cures Spa Experience: Developments in medicine, health care, fitness and wellness in the last century highlight the importance of the 20th century in the continuum of wellness. The development of technologically advanced spa equipment, coupled with the history of bathing rituals inspired this experience. The Williamsburg Water Cures consists of a full-body, dry-brush exfoliation, followed by a hydrotherapy Vichy shower 'rain' massage and concluding with a traditional Aqua Latte bath to seal in the skin's moisture.

21st century: Skin Rejuvenation Spa Experience: Late in the 20th century and into today, the popularity in laser treatments and microdermabrasion has grown significantly, so this experience draws on new technology and products geared for anti-ageing to address rejuvenation on two fronts. A deep pore cleansing and skin analysis prepares the face for a particle-free, ultrasonic exfoliation. This is followed by an enzyme-rich mask specific to skin type and an oxygen treatment to brighten the skin. Finally, an antioxidant serum and vitamin-rich moisturizer conclude the Skin Rejuvenation for results similar to, but more gentle than, microdermabrasion, with immediate results.

The Spa's designer Sylvia Sepielli, who is recognized worldwide as a spa visionary, assisted in the facility design concept and was retained to create signature treatments and amenities. She is known for creating a completely unique look for each spa she designs, making it an expression of its location. She creates a signature for each spa that reflects the personality and culture of the area, and is known for doing extensive research into each location to create treatments that reflect that area, fitting perfectly into their settings. This spa represents a blend of the history and heritage of America, with its indigenous traditions and colonial influences, as well as contemporary features of modern global living and technology.

(Spa of Colonial Williamsburg, 2013)

Conclusion

This chapter has demonstrated the diversity of health and wellness traditions which exist in different regions of world, providing an overview of their origins and their continuity over time. Although the degree of travel within most regions was somewhat limited by transport until the latter part of the twentieth century, there was nevertheless some movement to spa or thermal destinations as early as Roman times, if not before. Medical travel in its surgical sense, however, is more like a modern phenomenon based on price differences and shorter waiting lists and availability.

The influence of the most ancient cultures on subsequent cultures is clearly widespread, whether it is the indigenous peoples of the Americas, Africa or Australasia, Indian traditions in Arabic countries, or Chinese medicine in Asian ones. As time goes on, we see an even greater degree of cross-over and hybridisation as indigenous and traditional cultures increasingly influence Western ones (e.g. Feng Shui sauna or Aquaveda) and vice versa (e.g. spa resorts in the Middle East). It seems that the globalisation of health and wellness can only be a positive development as the whole world starts to share in practices that often remained within one small region or locality for thousands of years. It seems that the route to optimum wellness is one in which ideas are shared, especially through travel, tourism and increased mobility of practitioners from one region of the world to another. Although many wellness systems have much in common with one another (i.e. the tendency towards holistic and lifestyle-based approaches), the tools and techniques that are used can vary greatly, so an increased choice for consumers and tourists alike is one of the most welcome developments of the twenty-first century.

A geographical and regional analysis

> Earth is a beautiful green-and-blue jewel hung upon the tapestry of eternity. However long we stay here to drink the pure water and breathe the life-giving air, eternity is more truly our home.
>
> (Chopra, 1993: 315)

Following on from the previous chapter which focused on the history of global health and wellness traditions, this chapter examines in more detail not only contemporary developments in health and wellness, but also in tourism. It is useful to consider the geography as well as the history of health and wellness tourism, especially when developing regional initiatives based on indigenous resources (e.g. Alpine wellness, Nordic well-being). There are also social and cultural traditions which tend to be rooted in geographical locations as much as historical traditions. The emphasis in this chapter is mainly on the supply side of tourism in different regions and countries of the world with later chapters focusing on demand.

Europe

According to ESPA (2013) in Europe there are more than 1,200 spas and health resorts, which are medically respected health (thermal) centres. Although regional divisions can be made in Europe, it is important to note that these are not definitive or clear-cut. There are many similarities between Western and Northern countries, for example those which do not have much of a thermal bath tradition (e.g. UK, Netherlands, Scandinavia). The Baltic States, Central and Eastern Europe and Russia have much in common in terms of their traditions of medical thermal tourism, sanatoria and rehabilitation. Croatia and Bulgaria have coastal tourism in common with many Southern European countries, as well as thermal traditions (e.g. similar to Italy or Portugal). Nevertheless, some regional trends can be identified and distinctions can be made between some of the traditions, resources, attitudes and activities in different regions of Europe. A summary is provided in Table 3.1.

TABLE 3.1 Regional differences and trends in Europe

Region(s)/countries	Typical focus	Typical products/services
Western Europe (Austria, Belgium, France, Germany, Luxembourg, Netherlands, Northern France, Switzerland, UK)	• Beauty • Weight loss • Lifestyle improvements (e.g. mental well-being, stress relief) • Leisure and recreation • Private clinics specializing in certain treatments	• Day/beauty spas • Spa and wellness hotels • Thermal leisure spas • Holistic activities (e.g. yoga, meditation) • Vinotherapy • Occupational wellness • Alpine wellness • Selfness and mindness • Balneotherapy
Northern Europe (Scandinavia, Baltic States)	• Physical recreation • Leisure and relaxation • Lifestyle improvements (e.g. diet, exercise, fresh air)	• Nordic well-being • Saunas • Outdoor recreation (e.g. Nordic walking) • Cold therapies (e.g. cryotherapy, ice swimming) • Hot geysers (Iceland) • Thermal, medical and seaside spas (Estonia, Latvia, Lithuania)
Central and Eastern Europe (Bosnia, Bulgaria, Croatia, Czech Republic, Hungary, Moldova, Poland, Romania, Russia, Serbia, Slovakia, Slovenia)	• Curative rather than preventative health care • Therapy and rehabilitation for the body • Medical tourism • Water-based leisure	• Medical and thermal baths • Spa hotels • Caves • Aquaparks • Wellness hotels
Southern Europe (Cyprus, Greece, Italy, Malta, Portugal, Southern France, Spain, Turkey)	• Physical recuperation and relaxation • Sea-water-based wellness • Lifestyle elements (e.g. climate, healthy cuisine, pace of life) • Medical tourism	• Thalassotherapy • Traditional thermal and medical spas • Holistic retreats (often run by non-locals) • Religious and spiritual tourism (e.g. Lourdes, Fatima, Santiago de Compostela)

Source: Adapted from Smith and Puczkó, 2010.

Western Europe

Austria has a highly developed wellness tourism industry with large numbers of high-quality thermal baths and wellness hotels (around 892 in 2009) and about 12 per cent of all tourists take health-oriented holidays, so Austria is the European leader in this segment (ABA, 2011). Austria shares many characteristics with other Alpine countries as it uses its climate, fresh air, mountains and lakes as an inherent part of the wellness tourism product. Other German-speaking countries like Germany and Switzerland are also very advanced in terms of their development of high-quality thermal resorts, spas and baths. The emphasis is more on wellness tourism than medical tourism, but the tradition of *kur* and the concept of medical wellness are also widespread. The German health insurance system still supports some treatments in medical spas which is a fundamental element of domestic health tourism. On the other hand, Austrian and German wellness hotels and spas are now reaching saturation point and there is a need to limit the number of new developments or to diversify existing products.

Switzerland or several cities (e.g. Berlin Health Care City) and regions (e.g. Bavaria) in Germany have established themselves as key destinations for medical tourists looking for high quality (and expensive) surgical interventions, especially from Russian-speaking countries and Arabic countries. Switzerland has also become known as a country to perform euthanasia.

Thalassotherapy (or marine medical tourism) has a long history in Western Europe, especially in resorts on the Atlantic Ocean. It is especially popular in France. SpaFinder predicted a revival of interest in thalassotherapy in 2006. The II International Thalasso Congress in 2008 organised by the European Spas Association encouraged tourism players in seaside spas and resorts to start providing thalassotherapy again and to highlight the various ways in which it can be applied. Still, the revival or the spread of thalassotherapy is still to come.

Vinotherapy also has its roots in Europe, especially in France.

CASE STUDY 3.1
Wine spas in France
Jennifer Laing and Warwick Frost

The Burgundy and Champagne wine regions are currently seeking World Heritage listing. Each is arguably pre-eminent in terms of global wine production and reputation, with their appellations subject to protection, based on a distinctive *terroir* combining soil, climate, aspect and a long history of wine-making. Tourism is also important to these regions. Several of their towns, notably Beaune in Burgundy and Epernay in Champagne, have begun to promote spa visits, alongside traditional activities such as tours of wineries and gastronomic experiences. This case study exemplifies the trend for wine regions to broaden their offerings to incorporate wellness tourism. It is seen as having a strong appeal to their traditional market segments (older, wealthy visitors) as well as encouraging a new, younger demographic to visit and experience a package of culture and indulgence.

In some destinations, the ready availability of ingredients associated with good health has led to the development of *vinotherapy*. This creation of spa treatments incorporating grapes or wine leverages off the image of red wine or grape juice as high in antioxidants, contributing to healthy hearts and protecting against or preventing certain cancers. Applying the seeds, pulp or juice to the skin, during facials, massages and baths might have anti-ageing benefits, with the polyphenols extracted from grape seeds said to fight free-radicals. The Caudalíe range of beauty products was developed with this philosophy in mind, and the company later branched out into spas, notably their flagship property in Bordeaux, which offer vinotherapy experiences to visitors. Many spas in Beaune and Epernay however have not fully embraced this phenomenon. Instead, the tendency is for a more generic wellness product to be promoted to visitors, which arguably could be experienced in many spas across France, and indeed around the globe.

In Beaune, a few spa businesses are leading the way in using local grapes and wine in their treatments and therapies. This might be argued to lend their experiences a sense of authenticity in the minds of visitors and reference the brand heritage (Urde et al., 2007) associated with burgundy wine. The La Cueillette spa, for example, offers *fruititherapy*®, treatments based on grapes and local berries such as blackcurrants, which are normally used to make the traditional local liquor *crème de cassis*. At the Spa Bourgogne Vignes and Bien-Être à Beaune, visitors can soak in a barrel of red wine, be massaged with grape-seed oil, exfoliated with a grape seed scrub or wrapped up in grape pulp. While the Hotel le Richebourg proffers a few treatments using grapes and grape-seeds, they proudly boast their globalised product on their website: 'De l'Asie aux îles des Caraïbes en passant par l'Egypte, parcourez le monde!' ('From Asia to the Caribbean Islands and passing through Egypt, go around the world!'). Others avoid any overt association with local winemaking. The Shambali spa offers Thai, Singaporean and Bengali massages, as well as lomi lomi, which originated in Hawaii. There is an emphasis on exotica, epitomised by the Orient, rather than taking advantage of the link between local vines and well-being.

In Epernay, spa experiences are also burgeoning, but with far less emphasis on vinotherapy than in Beaune. For example, L'Hostellerie la Briqueterie uses French spa products (Carita and Decleor) but these are international brands and not destination-specific. The Jean Moët Hotel offers clients treatments such as a facial 'adapted [from] an ancestral rite of Balinese princesses', rather than therapies based on champagne or the local grapes. This is perhaps due to the high cost of champagne compared to other wines, or alternatively their use in spa treatments may not be the image champagne houses and accommodation providers wish to promote to visitors. Thus, the opportunity to provide a distinctive local product has been passed over by these spa providers, although the association between drinking wine, health and pampering/luxury is clearly being made through their promotion of experiences to visitors.

Holistic tourism is growing quickly in Western Europe, especially in the UK and the Netherlands. This includes yoga and meditation retreats and workshops, trade shows (e.g. two–three-day body–mind–spirit or yoga shows), and holistic festivals and events.

Occupational or corporate wellness (or health) programmes incorporating some travel component are to become more and more widespread, especially in the mid to top management benefit packages at financial and business hubs, such as London.

Central and Eastern Europe

Some governments (e.g. Hungary, Czech Republic, Slovakia and Slovenia) have invested large sums in the development and upgrade of traditional medical resorts. Sonia Sibila Lebe discusses recent developments in Slovenia in her case study in Part III of this book, Alexey Kondrashov writes about the Czech Republic and Elena Bogacheva discusses Russia. Russia has been investing in the upgrade and modernisation of its medical tourism facilities (especially in and around Sochi, the host of the Winter Olympics in 2014). Several countries, especially Hungary and Poland, have become popular destinations for dental tourists. In Hungary special European Union and government co-funded schemes (approximately 15 million euros) were available for the improvement of dental technology and communication.

CASE STUDY 3.2
City Spa 'SLADO'™ – a new concept of a Russian spa
Elena Bogacheva

Russians, living in a country with severe climate conditions, always had to take adaptation measures to enable their bodies to survive in coldest winters and unpredictable summers.

The methods used by generations of Russian people are:

- Russian steam bath (banya);

- phytotherapy and honey treatments;

- special massage.

The Russian banya

This is a combination of mild humidity (70 per cent) generated by a fragrant steam, and a comfortable temperature (up to 70°C). This proportion is the most favourable for a human body, providing optimal conditions for deep detoxification.

'SLADO' banyas located in towns employ two types of steam rooms: a wooden one, made of cedar, and a 'Scythyan' steam bath. The cedar wood is well known for its healing properties – the aromatic substances of cedar wood produce a rejuvenating and anti-bacterial effect. When the wood is heated these properties become even stronger. The Scythians used a different method of heat therapy. They created a cloth tent, and inside it they produced heated steam, saturated with healing herbs.

In modern banyas the client is diagnosed prior to the treatment and the dosage of heat therapy is chosen individually.

Phytotherapy

Local herbs, honey and berries are also chosen to accompany banya treatments. Herbal wraps and special drinks are offered to clients. The ingredients employed in Slavic phyto-therapy are numerous: peppermint leaves, rosehip, origan, chamomile, buckwheat, linden, blackcurrant, raspberry, wild strawberry, blackberry, etc. Nowadays all herbs and berries are subject to a radiation control before being used in treatments.

Special Slavic massage

This is a combination of unique methods routed in the history of ancient Slavic tribes.

In 'SLADO' spa the following massage techniques are employed:

- The Russian spa massage;

- The Slavic buckwheat massage;

- The Slavic herbal massage.

The above-mentioned treatments are performed by massage therapists with a medical education and background, to ensure careful diagnostics, monitoring and tangible results. Slavic massage therapies are perceived as comfortable and mild by clients. In some massage treatments linden honey is applied on the skin of a client, and the massage tech-nique resembles lymphatic drainage. In Slavic buckwheat massage linen bags filled with heated buckwheat are employed by a massage therapist. Slavic massage techniques are aimed at deep tissues of a human body.

The above-mentioned therapies have been restored and introduced by the Russian spa expert Andrey Syrchenko in the new concept 'City Spa SLADO', created for urban day spas.

Through social and health policy the governments in CEE are still providing large subsidies for medical treatments and trips in the form of social tourism and prescribed therapeutic cure trips.

Poland enjoys a long history of health tourism and destinations have been attracting health tourists since the thirteenth century. Visitors can find thermal waters, salt caves, medical muds and even oxygen bars in Poland. Andrzej Hadzik, Dorota Ujma and Sean Gammon discuss the development of Polish resorts in more detail in their case study in

Part III. Most countries on the Balkan Peninsula (i.e. Slovenia, Croatia, Serbia, Romania, Macedonia, Bosnia and Hercegovina, and Bulgaria) have natural healing resources, such as thermal water springs, healing climates or caves, and the price levels are relatively cheap. Wellness facilities are also growing in popularity.

CASE STUDY 3.3
Karlovy Vary
Alexey Kondrashov

Carlsbad (Karlovy Vary), which means the 'the baths of King Charles', is the largest and most famous spa town in the Czech Republic. The town was established around 1350 by Charles IV (King of Bohemia). It is situated in a beautiful valley surrounded by wooded hills, and 79 springs are found in this locality, 12 of which are used for drinking cures and are located in five colonnades. The most famous colonnades are Park, Mill and Market which were built in the 1880s. The most frequently visited colonnade is also a Hot Spring built in 1975. The healing effects of the waters are related to their temperature; for example, laxative effects are attributed to colder springs, whereas warmer springs have a calming effect, slowing down the secretion of bile and gastric juices. Carlsbad spa facilities traditionally specialised in the treatment of digestive disorders, metabolic diseases and problems of locomotion.

The town has 50,000 inhabitants and in 2011 more than 270,000 visitors stayed in accommodation facilities there. The majority of visitors (about 158,000 stayed in spa hotels). In fact, all of the Czech five star spa hotels located in Carlsbad were opened in the past ten years. As a response to the growing demand, new spa hotels are constantly being opened. For the third consecutive year since 2009 the number of visitors has increased, reaching a growth of 12 per cent per year on average. In addition to the spas, cultural events like the Karlovy Vary film festival help to fill the hotels and encourage growth in the accommodation sector. Hotel-room occupancy rates are at the same level as in Prague and were above 65 per cent in 2011. The main guest groups in spa facilities are visitors aged 50+, coming mostly from Russia and Germany.

(Statistical Office of the Czech Republic, 2011)

Despite the relatively large numbers of thermal spas in Central and Eastern Europe and Russia, the emphasis has traditionally been and is still mainly on curative medical thermal tourism. As shown in Case Study 3.3, those Hungarian visitors who go to spa and wellness facilities do not use those spas for health (i.e. medical thermal tourism is better understood than preventative wellness).

CASE STUDY 3.4
Health-consciousness in the background: conscious or trendy?
Katalin Formádi and Krisztina Priszinger

Central and Eastern European countries are behind with health-consciousness. On the one hand, a spa-goer can choose from countless wellness services but, on the other hand, most spa-goers are not aware of the effects of a therapy or of the needs of their own body. CEE wellness spa-goers have not developed a health-conscious attitude; they are visiting spas because they seek enjoyment, fun and recreation but not for health reasons (even medical spa visitors in this region are usually told by their doctor what they need).

Health-consciousness can be defined according to various aspects, such as the number and the composition of used services while visiting a spa and also the duration of spa services. Another is the number of services in different wellness categories (like beauty, therapy or lifestyle). Before undertaking research, our main assumption was that 'entertaining water' is more popular with Hungarian spa-goers than regenerating or healing water. According to a 330 sample size research carried out among Hungarian wellness guests, we discovered the following.

Generally visitors experience four to five services (with 2.5 st. deviation) during a spa visit. The list of services includes four types of pools. Most of the visitors use the wellness pool (75 per cent) and the thermal water/medical pool (50 per cent). As the proportion of families is high among the visitors, the use of the children's pool is very high (57.5 per cent). Using the pools seems to be obvious in the case of a spa visit, but saunas (49.1 per cent) and massage (12.1 per cent) are also clearly the most popular services offered by spas. Beauty treatments are less frequently used by the spa-goers in the sample: only a small percentage of the visitors purchased a manicure, pedicure or facial treatment or body scrub service. Other healing elements such as acupuncture or medical treatment are rarely used by the respondents.

The research showed that visiting a spa has become a trendy way of spending leisure time for lots of people. Regardless of the age of the visitors and their health conditions, most visitors had only experienced the spa in general (the thermal part and wellness pools), with just a few wellness services. The full range of wellness services are not really used in this Hungarian spa. The spiritual services are completely missing: no guided meditation or lifestyle classes or Ayurvedic treatments are available. The latter exist in only a few high-quality hotels. Nevertheless the sign of a health-conscious attitude can be found in the preferences for healthy cuisine expressed by the visitors (although this is not always available in many Hungarian spas).

Nevertheless, there are also other factors which should be kept in mind when interpreting the results. First, the wellness services raise the prices of a wellness holiday or a spa visit so the cost of the wellness services can be prohibitive. Second, among families the presence

of kids can also influence the purchase of wellness services, as some of the services exclude children and without a babysitting service or a kindergarten parents' consumption of wellness services will be limited.

Nordic and Scandinavian countries

In much of Northern Europe, because of the lack of natural healing assets and traditions, people do not tend to know about or believe in the beneficial impacts of medical waters (the Baltic States and Russia are exceptions). This results in health and wellness (tourism) being based on relaxation and mainly includes fitness services, massages, (fun) baths with hot water and saunas. In Nordic countries, the sauna often represents an integral part of everyday life (especially in Finland) rather than being a luxury that is associated with wellness programmes (there are three forms of saunas: smoke, wood and electricity heated). It is well known that Nordic people have a generally healthy attitude to life, and many of the fitness activities which are part of everyday life (e.g. Nordic walking) have now been exported to wellness centres and spas all over the world. Nordic Well (2007) describes how:

> The cold North is home to many traditions that are warming and soothing. Underpinning them are the ideas that relaxation and cleansing are every person's right, and that relaxation therapies can contribute to a better society. These traditions – some of them, a thousand years old – include sauna, water therapies, massage and herbal treatments.

They also describe how design is modern, simple, clean, airy, light, calm, uncluttered, in harmony with nature, inviting, functional and inclusive, as well as being combined with three influences: a Zen-like belief in the power of nature; a tradition of linking design to the well-being of all people; and a skill for choosing appropriate technology (e.g. the Serena Water Amusement Park in Korpilamp (Espoo, Finland) combines these factors, since it was carved into the rocks, so guests can enjoy the pools, the slides as well as the sauna areas – all within the hill overlooking the ski slopes on the other side of the valley).

Julie Lindahl, a wellness expert, social entrepreneur and author of several books, including *On My Swedish Island: Discovering the Secrets of Scandinavian Well-being*, was the first to use the term 'Nordic well-being', which focuses on five lifestyle areas: design, food, gardens and herbs, outdoor life and relaxation. She advocates fitness and nature meditation; gathering and preparing food from nature; detoxing and relaxation techniques including sauna, herbal baths and massage; and a quiet opportunity to write, paint or do needlework in an inspirational natural environment. Since then, the term has been used by groups of Nordic academics and researchers. For example Henna Konu, Anja Tuohino and Peter Björk analyse the Nordic well-being concept in their case study in Part III. It is generally agreed that Nordic well-being is typically oriented towards nature and outdoor recreation combined with healthy gastronomy and cleanliness of air, landscape and water

(Tuohino, 2008). Northern seas are usually too cold to be used extensively in health tourism, although the concept of Lake Wellness is being developed in Finland (Kangas and Tuohino, 2008). Remedios (2008: 285) describes Scandinavian spas as being based around the sauna and 'the vacillation between hot and cold experiences'. There are several hotels in Nordic countries and regions which offer a treatment known as cryotherapy, which means natural treatment of human skin with extremely cold air (−80 up to −110 degrees centigrade or less) with numerous benefits to cell production, pain killing, treatment of injuries and inflammatory diseases and improving general health. By contrast, people in Iceland recognise the benefits of hydrotherapy in hot water. The average Reykjaviker goes to a thermal pool about 15 times a year (Nordic Well, 2007). One of the ultimate Nordic spa experiences is the Blue Lagoon or the Fontana of Iceland. Edward Huijbens also discusses the significance of Icelandic landscapes in Part III of this book. Erfurt-Cooper and Cooper (2009) also describe the unique possibility of bathing in thermal springs in Greenland in the middle of the wilderness with icebergs floating in the sea nearby or the fascination of cruise ship visitors in Antarctica with bathing in the volcanic hot springs.

The Baltic countries (Estonia, Latvia and Lithuania) all have a long tradition of health and wellness tourism which is closer to that of Central and Eastern Europe and Russia than to Scandinavia. There are many traditional thermal baths, rehabilitation centres and sanatoria, many of which are located on the Baltic sea coast (e.g. Pärnu in Estonia and Jūrmala in Latvia). These were and still are used for healing as well as leisure, with an increasing number of Russian and Russian-speaking guests visiting the resorts but also buying properties in the towns. Estonia also attracts many Finnish and Norwegian tourists, although the numbers have declined slightly in recent years. Apparently, no other country has as many spa hotels per capita than Estonia at more than 40 and still growing. The Estonian SPA Association implemented a quality system for medical spa hotels in 2008 which was extended to wellness spas and centres in 2012 (Estonian spas, 2011). Inna Bentsalo discusses how sleep therapy is becoming a popular treatment in one Estonia spa in Pärnu in Part III of this book.

CASE STUDY 3.5
Pärnu in Estonia
Heli Tooman and Kai Tomasberg

Pärnu is a beautiful seaside resort on the Baltic sea coast of Estonia located two hours from Tallinn the capital city, and two hours from Riga in Latvia. In 1838 the first bathing house in Pärnu was opened, and its health resort status was established in 1890, when the town was placed on the official list of imperial health resorts of Russia. World War I put a temporary end to the activities of the resort as well as a fire in 1915 which destroyed the bathing houses. However, interest in Pärnu between World War I and II grew quickly, especially amongst Swedish tourists. From 1946 to 1948 Pärnu developed into an all-year-round sanatorial health resort supported by the unions and the number of Estonians undergoing

treatments as well as visitors from all over the Soviet Union grew quickly. Scientific research work in balneology started in Estonia in 1957 and from 1960 there were three specialised balneo mud treatment sanatoria in the resort. In 1971 the new sanatorium Tervis was opened, and by the 1980s the Pärnu sanatoria received about 25,000 health visitors out of a total number of about 300,000 tourists per year (Veinpalu and Veinpalu, 1988; Kask, 2007). In 1990–1 the eastern spa tourists and holidaymakers mainly from the former Soviet Union decreased due to political circumstances. Therefore it was necessary to re-orientate to new foreign markets, especially those from the region nearby such as Finland, Sweden and Latvia.

In 1996 Pärnu was granted the prestigious title of the summer capital of Estonia. Today Pärnu is the largest and most visited resort in Estonia. There are several modern spa hotels such as Tervis Medical Spa, Tervise Paradiis Spa Hotel and Water Park, Estonia Medical Spa Hotel, Strand SPA and Conference Hotel, Viiking SPA Hotel, and Sõprus Medical SPA and Hotel. These spa hotels provide all year round jobs for more than 600 people from Pärnu and can accommodate more than 2,000 visitors per day (Spa Holidays, 2012). The largest number of guests to the spas comes from Finland and different regions of Estonia but also the number of visitors from Russia and Latvia is rising. There are also some visitors from other European countries, the USA, Australia and even China, as the traditional therapeutic mud is gaining fame there.

Pärnu College, University of Tartu, has been running a MA Wellness and Spa Service Design and Management course for several years which attracts students from all over the world. Because of its variety of spa and wellness resorts and facilities, it is an excellent place to study spa management in context.

Latvia's current tourism slogan 'Best Enjoyed Slowly' implies connections to the slow movement as discussed in Chapter 4. Its natural cosmetics ranges (e.g. Madara) are becoming world famous, and like the other Baltic States, green and ecotourism are an inherent part of the tourism product. 'Pirts' or Latvian wood saunas can be accessed almost everywhere. Unlike Finnish saunas which are dry, water is used to create steam. They are heated to 100°C ideally and the body is usually thrashed with branches of broom (Olte, 2013). According to the IMTJ (2013) Latvia is becoming famous for its cancer treatments and has established its own health tourism organisation which will focus mainly on marketing, regulation and developing health tourism packages. The organisation includes a wide spectrum of health tourism entrepreneurs, ranging from surgical, medical rehabilitation, resort rehabilitation, health restoration, spa and wellness, to the organic cosmetic industry and higher medical education institutions. Latvian health tourism is mainly promoted in Northern Europe, Russia and Israel. Jūrmala City Council is working with the Latvian Resorts Association to develop a health tourism strategy until 2020 and helped to establish the Latvian Wellness Tourism Cluster. The aim is to increase the number of medical, wellness and spa tourists to Latvia and develop the local health tourism industry.

Latvia is already seeing an increase in the number of medical and wellness tourists due to competitive prices and high service quality.

Lithuania has a relatively rich wellness culture. According to the Lithuanian Association of Hotels and Resorts research from 2011 quoted by Hood (2013) 26 per cent of tourists stayed in a spa resort or old sanitorium. The National Spa Association was founded in 2007 and has more than 20 members. The spa culture is medically orientated and 95 per cent of spa visitors have therapeutic experiences or come to prevent or treat illnesses. The country has numerous famous mineral waters and therapeutic mud baths and treatments. The southern town of Druskininkai is thought to be the spa capital of Lithuania with its many spa and wellness venues. Foreign tourists come mainly from Russia, Poland, Germany, Belarus and Latvia. A feasibility study of a proposed medical tourism cluster was prepared in 2012 and is expected to be implemented.

Southern Europe

There are also a number of traditional historic spas in Southern Europe. Erfurt-Cooper and Cooper (2009) discuss the importance of hot springs in the Mediterranean region. Italy has one of the longest recorded histories of usage, as does Greece. Spain and Portugal also have numerous mineral-medicinal thermal sources, but the therapeutic qualities of the waters in Portugal were not recognised until the eighteenth century. Gustavo (2009) counted 37 Portuguese thermal centres, and many of the spas are being regenerated, diversifying into wellness as opposed to medical tourism, or are developing parallel facilities for medical and wellness tourism (Gustavo, 2009). The same is true of Italian spas (Ferrari, 2009). Both Nuno Gustavo and Sonia Ferrari provide case studies of the current spa and wellness tourism developments in Portugal and Italy respectively in their case studies in Part III of this book.

Some modern spas also exist, especially in mountain resorts which are used by skiers (e.g. in Andorra). In addition to historic and thermal spas, the lifestyle and diet in the Mediterranean is one of the healthiest in the world. The existence of a good climate and the seaside has benefited residents and tourists for centuries. Thalassotherapy is offered throughout the region, for example in Greece, Spain, France and Italy. Islands like Cyprus and Malta are increasingly positioning themselves as medical tourism destinations, capitalising on their English language skills as well as their high-quality clinics. Wellness hotels in the region are proliferating extensively and there are few countries which do not have a large number of spa and wellness hotels. One of the very first longevity centres in Europe was established in the Algarve (Portugal).

Although some parts of Turkey are technically in Asia, many visitors consider the country (especially the seaside) to be an extension of Southern Europe. Turkey is located on top of a major geothermal belt, therefore it is among the top seven countries in the world for quality and quantity of thermal springs with over 1,000, with temperatures ranging from 20°C to 110°C. Most are in the Aegean regions and because of their proximity to popular tourism destinations such as Izmir, Pamukkale and Marmaris, public transport is easy. Many of Turkey's historical places developed because of their springs like the ancient city of Hieropolis which was built upon the rich mineral springs of Pamukkale, and the ancient

Lydian city of Kaunos, whose people took baths in the rich mineral mud of Lake Koycegiz. In Kangal Hot Spings the carbon-dioxide rich water is the home to small fish that actually bite the infected skin off the guests sitting in the water. These so-called Turkish carp are now being used increasingly in spas all over the world. Turkey with the sound support from the Turkish government has been developing its medical tourism facilities and offers in a rather fast pace with over 30 JCI-accredited hospitals by 2013.

Many yoga and holistic centres are located in Southern Europe (for example, Skyros and Yoga Plus in Greece, and Cortijo Romero in Spain). This is largely because the landscapes and climate are so attractive to visitors and course tutors alike. Although such centres could technically be located anywhere, many of the lifestyle practitioners who choose to re-locate (especially from the UK) go to Spain or Greece. Turkey is becoming increasingly popular with yoga centres and retreats being located there (e.g. Huzur Vadisi).

CASE STUDY 3.6
Skyros Holistic Holiday Centres

The two Skyros Centres in Greece were set up in 1979. Visitors stay for one or two weeks at a time and undertake a number of self-selected courses and workshops that are designed to balance body, mind and spirit. Participants can take a range of psychological, thera-peutic, creative, communicative or active courses, usually two per day for five days. Participants are also encouraged to engage in morning *Demos* – a community meeting led by a different participant each day; *Oekos* – an open group discussion/listening forum, co-listening with one other participant; work groups based on different collective tasks; and evening and weekend social activities. The aim of this structure is to create strong bonds between the community members, and to encourage an atmosphere of support, trust and openness. None of the activities are compulsory, however, and participants have the freedom to plan their own time.

Skyros attracts a wide range of people. The majority are professionals (e.g. teachers, lecturers, doctors, nurses, business and media people). Approximately 70 per cent of partic-ipants are in their thirties or forties. Many also have 'life issues' to resolve or may be on the brink of burnout. Glouberman (2004) describes the intention of Skyros to create a world that heals and to create a healthy culture: 'This culture must be one that encourages us to come home to ourselves, to honour our true selves in relation to others, and to commit ourselves to the most universal values we can find.' Thus, the ethos behind Skyros is to create more than just a holiday, which explains why many participants claim to find it so life-changing, and repeat visitation is more than 30 per cent. Skyros 'aftercare' is excellent, including a letter to all participants, invitations to reunions and social events, and website chat rooms and notice boards.

(Skyros, 2008)

The province around Granada in Spain has Arabic baths, the remains of thermal baths dating from the Roman period, water cisterns, fountains, natural swimming pools and irrigation channels, all of which are evidence of the great importance that water had for the area. The typical atmosphere of traditional hammans has been re-created, which in the Andalusi period were the centres of social life. Visitors alternate between pools with waters at different temperatures. The baths include a Warm Room, with a pool at a temperature of approximately 36°C, a Cold Room, in which the water is at 16°C, and a Massage Room. They are beautifully decorated with mosaics, arches with fine lattice work, and exotic scents, music and warm light help to create atmosphere.

There have also been some new developments in the Canary Islands and in the Balearics. The Canary Islands have an all-year-round climate which is ideal for certain medical conditions and healing. Islas Canarias Wellness Delight (2013) state that the Canary Islands are healthy by nature because of the climate, sunshine, sea, natural beauty and the most prestigious mineral-medicinal waters in Spain, calling the environment 'A spa in the open air'. They promote several spa hotels and resorts, including those offering thalassotherapy.

Middle East and North Africa

In terms of natural resources in the Middle East and North Africa, there is mainly desert and sea, although as far as 3000 BC people with eye problems could make a pilgrimage to Tell Brak (Syria) hoping that deities would perform miracles. Some wellness hotels offer products and services that are unique to the region, such as the Desert Sand-Herb Rasoul Scrub offered in Dubai. The Gulf countries and cities (such as Dubai, Doha or Muscat) have some of the most spectacular and luxurious spas facilities built in the last few years (e.g. spas in the Jumeirah chain). Hammams are indigenous to the region and consist of a process of sweating, exfoliation and cleansing of the skin, and massage administered by therapists. Special hammam hotels exist in countries like Morocco. Thalassotherapy is also offered in several hotels in Morocco and Tunisia, as well as Egypt and the United Arab Emirates. Indeed, large numbers of high-quality spa hotels are being developed in the region, especially in the United Arab Emirates, or Oman where the distinctive local architectural features are particularly stunning. However, it is perhaps the Dead Sea which attracts the majority of wellness tourists to the region. The Dead Sea is sometimes described as the world's largest 'natural spa'. Dalit Gasul discusses the Dead Sea resources and their management in their case study in Part III.

One spa in northern Israel (Ada Barak's beauty spa) is becoming famous for its snake massage. California and Florida king snakes, corn snakes and milk snakes (all non-venomous) are used for the massage and sometimes as many as six at once. The size of the snake determines the kind of massage. Large ones are said to alleviate deep muscle tensions whereas small ones create a 'fluttering' effect. Physical contact with snakes is thought to be stress-relieving, once guests get over their initial horror! This snake massage is included with a further nine 'weird spa treatments' around the world as shown below.

Top ten weird spa treatments around the world

1 Snake massage in Israel

2 Cryotherapy in Finland (Haikko spa in Porvoo, Finland has a super-cold chamber of −110°C)

3 Beer bathing in the Czech Republic (dark beer is mixed with mineral water at the Chodovar Brewery in Chodová Planá and is said to have medicinal effects)

4 Orgasm Hotel, Sweden (Venusgarden is a 'love hotel' in Scania owned by an orgasm coach. All rooms come equipped with sex toys and erotic pictures, plus a copy of the owner's best-selling book, *Orgasming More*)

5 Chocolate facial, Pennsylvania (Hershey's hotel and spa offers an edible facial treatment)

6 Sake Spa, Japan (The Hakone Kowakien Yunessun hot springs amusement park and spa resort has pools for bathing in sake, green tea, wine and coffee – and occasionally even ramen noodle soup!)

7 Solitary retreat, Egypt (Sinai desert retreat where visitors trek across the desert, sleep under the stars, wash with a Bedouin herbal treatment and spend a few days alone in self-reflection)

8 Sound Bath, California (The Integratron is described as 'an acoustically perfect tabernacle and energy machine sited on a powerful geomagnetic vortex in the magical Mojave desert'. Visitors can have 'sound baths', relaxing yet energising 30-minute sonic sessions which are said to align with their chakras or energy centres)

9 Fire cupping, Beijing (Cupping is an extreme massage technique involving suction. Fire cupping is similar, but with added flames)

10 Waterfall massage, Canada (the Willow Stream Spa at the Fairmont Hotel in Banff Springs has three indoor waterfalls used for reviving tired muscles after a day's skiing in the Rockies)

(Dixon, 2012)

Increasingly, the Middle East is gaining a reputation for medical tourism, especially in the United Arab Emirates (e.g. Dubai) and Jordan, which for years positioned itself as the 'mecca' of medical tourism in the Middle East. Dubai has also become a hub for medical services, since over 120 medical facilities and 3,700 health-care professionals have chosen the Dubai Healthcare City. Foreign medical/health-care (tourism) brands, such the Cleveland Clinic in Abu Dhabi have also become established in the region. Jordan was recognised by the World Bank as the leading regional destination for health care, and the fifth medical tourism destination worldwide in 2010 (Stefano, 2010). Most Jordanian health-care facilities are accredited by both domestic and international organisations. Dental tourism is one of the fastest growing sectors within medical tourism in Jordan (Al-Hammouri, 2010). The spa business in Jordan is currently growing at 12 to 15 per cent per year, with 11 per cent of room nights at the Dead Sea currently derived from spa and wellness visits. That market is expected to grow 10 per cent per year over the next ten years (USAID, 2009). Other countries like Iran are also boasting excellent doctors, high-quality facilities and cheap health care. However, Iran also has potential for thermal spa development, as the following case study shows.

CASE STUDY 3.7
Sarein, the Spa town in Iran
Hamid Zargham and Mehrnaz Salimi

Sarein (meaning 'spring' in Persian), one of the most famous spa and hot spring cities in Iran, is located in Ardabil Province. Eleven major hot springs and spas in Sarein beside Alvares ski resort, the second standardised ski resort in Iran, have attracted a lot of tourists to this city even in winter. Each spring has its own specific healing power which can be used to cure certain diseases:

TABLE 3.2 Spas in Sarein

Spa centre	Establishment	Location	Best time to visit	Good for . . .	Temperature
Sabalan	Modern and Developed	Sarein	All seasons	Blood circulation, chronic pains of the leg, and good for skin	38
Besh Bajilar	Modern	Sarein	All seasons	Blood circulation through vessels, chronic pains of the leg	41
Gavmish Goli	Traditional	Sarein	All seasons	Joint pains, meditation, bulge	46
Sari Sou	Traditional	Sarein	All seasons	Joint pains, meditation, bulge	46
Qare Sou	Traditional	Sarein	All seasons	Meditation and relaxing, Insomnia	42.5
Pahn lou/ sou	Traditional	Sarein	All seasons	Blood circulation, Skin vessels	43.5
General	Traditional	Sarein	All seasons	Dermatitis	43
Qahve sou (1 and 2)	Traditional	Sarein	All seasons	Joint pains, meditation, bulge	43
Yel sou	Traditional	Sarein	All seasons	Joint pains, Gastrointestinal problems	40
Vila Darre	Traditional	5 km from Sarein	Spring and Summer	Renal and Gastrointestinal problems, malnutrition, Trachoma	15.5

Climate is another important factor in Sarein and every year thousands of people enjoy its elegant and favourable weather in summer. Beside the natural beauties of this city, traditional food is served in the centres, such as Ayren pottage, local yoghurt and hot milk, special honey and qeimaq (top milk), Special Kebab and Dizi (special food made in Cruse), make the experience unique. In winter experiencing the spas outdoors while it is snowing is a unique experience.

Unfortunately despite the potential for becoming a major spa and hot spring destination not only in Iran but also worldwide, people are losing interest in going to the spas and hot springs because the waters are not properly managed. There is a lack of awareness about how to use the waters. The government plays the most important role in Sarein's development and because of this the private sector cannot invest and start new projects there. There have been some investments by the government which led to the building of Laleh Hotel, Sabalan and Besh Bajilar Spa center in Sarein, but still private investment and activity is needed. The infrastructure of the city would also need to be upgraded if it were to host international tourists.

(Ghafouri, 2006; Nemat, 2002)

Yoga holidays are offered almost anywhere in the world, but increasingly in the Middle East and North Africa (e.g. in Dahab on the Red Sea, Egypt). Doing yoga in a desert setting, for example, can add to the spiritual experience. Sometimes yoga holidays are combined with belly dancing (e.g. in Hammamet, Tunisia). One yoga holiday in Morocco includes a Jimi Hendrix experience in Essouira or trekking with Bedouins in Egypt (Yoga Travel, 2007). Spiritual tourism does not tend to be combined with religious tourism in the Middle East, even though it is a major centre for pilgrimage tourism (with all Muslims being expected to complete the Haj to Mecca in Saudi Arabia). Spiritual and religious tourism are also common in Israel, but usually for different/separate religious groups rather than secular spiritualists. However, recently there has been a growth of spiritual or holistic festivals which appeal to younger residents and tourists.

Africa

Although luxury spas exist in Africa, this is largely in South Africa and on some of the islands, for example in the Seychelles or Mauritius. South Africa is the leading destination in Africa for spa tourism and use is made of the mountains and sea as well as the bush. Increasing use is also being made of the thermal springs. The South African Tourist Board (2008) describes how the African spa has taken on a whole new meaning from the European concept, as nature is almost always used in products and treatments, as well as centuries of indigenous and tribal traditions of healing. South Africa has developed a number of luxury safari or bush spas which are located near to national parks where visitors can go on safari. Some spas or wellness centres also specialise in vinotherapy or wine therapy. Many of the spas offer global and especially Asian treatments, but a few specialise in African traditions, such as African wood massage and African raindrop treatment. The African Day Spa has become almost a brand name (e.g. for product ranges) and the Bush Spa is a common phenomenon, where tourists stay in a lodge in the African bush, experiencing natural and herbal treatments, often combined with safaris. The spa at Cape Grace in South Africa uses healing techniques and traditional remedies of the region's native San and Khoi tribes, who used massage, indigenous plants and the spices introduced by the Indian Ocean traders en route from Asia to Europe. The South African Tourist Board also promotes the Spiritual South where guests can participate in 'wholistic' tourism, such as: animal or eco-therapies like 'Mingling with Meerkats', 'Horse-labyrinth' or eco-psychology. Medical tourism is also a big industry in South Africa, especially cosmetic surgery.

The following case study shows the potential for other African destinations which have hot springs, for example Uganda.

CASE STUDY 3.8
Hot springs in Uganda
Eddy Tukamushaba

Kitagata springs are found in Sheema south, Bushenyi district, around 350 km west of the Ugandan capital Kampala. The patients use the water from Kitagata twice a day to drink and to bathe. Here, you witness patients taking turns to lie in the water for treatment. The official schedule is four hours in the morning and up to seven hours in the evening. It is as busy as a hospital. Kabasekye says that they get around 800 visitors (patients) every week, people of all ages and from all corners of the country. Many illnesses which the medical people have failed to treat can be cured by the Kitagata hot springs.

The Sempaya hot springs at Semliki National Park in Bundibugyo are capable of boiling eggs and are too hot for some. The tribesmen and women, in the past, believing that the springs had healing powers, would carry goats and sacrifice them to be cured. Others would bathe in the salty waters to achieve health.

The Ihimba hot springs derive their name from the Bahimba people who live near these springs. The Ihimba hot springs are muddy but pleasant pools on the side of the highway. They are well known by local residents for their healing properties. Many of the Bakiga of Kigezi and the people of Rwanda, suffering from rheumatism, backache and other ailments use the healing properties of the Ihimba hot springs.

Amoropii hot spring is found in northern Uganda and it is believed to do miracles for its visitors. It is believed to have divine powers and is worshipped by people just like Sempaya hot springs found in Semuliki National Park. Before visiting these hot springs, one must first get permission from the Prime Minister.

Rwagimba Hot Springs is where people, cows, sheep and goats go for healing.

Kenya offers opportunities to combine safaris and spas, as well as centres like Wildfitness, where visitors can get fitter using natural habitats (e.g. sprinting in sand dunes, swimming in creeks, jogging through jungles).

CASE STUDY 3.9
Wildfitness, Kenya

Wildfitness is a special kind of health holiday – more like an open-air fitness retreat than a spa (although massages and therapies are offered). It aims to help people rediscover their natural physical potential which they would have needed to survive in the wild. The concept is based on the fact that humans used to be hunter-gatherers in wild savannahs, nature provided everything they needed, and they were tall, lean, agile, fast and fertile. These days, most people tend to resemble 'zoo humans' who live in an environment which is very different to the one they evolved for. As a result, physical, mental, psychological and spiritual health has suffered. Activities take place on the beach and in its forest surrounds, where inmates spend their days swinging from trees, canoeing along mangrove swamps, running, jumping, weight-training and diving. Other activities include five-mile runs on the sand, swims across the creek, hikes into the bush, yoga, Tai Chi and aerobics.

Expert fitness coaches cater for all ages and levels of ability. A typical programme lasts from nine days to three and a half weeks, and group size is limited to eleven people. Emphasis is placed on three main elements, which are:

- **Wild Movement** e.g. learning proper techniques for physical activities like running and swimming, challenging oneself, enhancing performance, preventing injuries, strength training.

- **Wild Eating** e.g. locally-sourced raw and organic produce to ease digestive and other problems. Two menus are available: The Primate Menu (e.g. eggs, seeds, nuts, fruit, non-starchy vegetables) and the Hunter-Gatherer Menu (the same but with the addition of meat and fish). There may also be cookery lessons and nutritional workshops.

- **Wild Living** e.g. learning how to control stress through breathing, sleeping, relaxing, being in nature and studying physiological responses to these aspects of life. This also includes having fun and bonding with the small group as tribes would have done.

Wildfitness aims to be eco-friendly by employing local people wherever possible, making donations to national park and turtle conservation, using local produce, paying a fee to local communities if they are used in any way, and use of energy saving devices and biodegradable products.

(Wildfitness, 2013)

Increasingly, Kenya is also offering medical tourism, for example, cardiology, dentistry, dermatology, endoscopic, general and spinal surgery, obstetrics and gynaecology. The Kenyan government also supports herbal practice and has registered and licensed herbalists to practise in public and private hospitals. Medical tourists tend to come from Uganda, Tanzania, Rwanda, Burundi and the Democratic Republic of Congo (DRC), among others (Softkenya.com, 2013). In South Africa, medical tourists besides the plastic or dental surgery can enjoy wine, bush, wilderness or train safaris.

Asia

Spa and wellness are gaining unprecedented growth and popularity across Asia. SpaFinder (2013) stated that in 2011 Asia-Pacific had the largest number of spas and hotels under development of any region in the world, with 77 per cent of that regional hotel expansion earmarked for China and India (56 per cent and 21 per cent, respectively). Luxury spas and spa hotels are being built throughout the region with some of the world's best being located in places like Bali, Phuket, Langkawi and the Maldives. New and well-established brands such as the Oberoi, the Peninsula, Sanghri-La or the Lux Island Resorts all invested significant sums in the development and improvement of their spa and wellness services. Even some of the less visited destinations such as Laos, Cambodia or Vietnam have an emergent spa industry. China and South Korea have just been discovering the medical tourism opportunities on their healing traditions (Traditional Chinese and Traditional Korean Medicine, respectively). Some of the former Soviet Union countries, for example Kyrgizstan, offer traditional, natural asset-based healing services, such as treatments in salt mines.

Most of the Asia spas, even if they are located in chain hotels, include local signature treatments which can be very special and luxurious (e.g. Balinese coffee-peeling ritual).

CASE STUDY 3.10
ASEAN Spa Standard
Andrew Jacka

The following is a list of local and traditional treatments that are being recognised through the development of an ASEAN Spa Standard by the Tourism Ministries of the ASEAN member states under the ASEAN Secretariat. They are included in the standard as an acknowledgement to increase the knowledge of some of these traditional practices and for spa operators to be respectful of them accordingly. The ASEAN Spa Standard is due for implementation in 2015.

Brunei Darussalam

1 Lulut (as a ritual)
2 Mandi Daun (as a healing tradition)
3 Hirup-Hirupan (a herbal coffee) (as a natural asset)

Cambodia

4 Chab Sor Shai (as a healing tradition)
5 Khmer J'pong (as a healing tradition)
6 S'Ahm (as a healing tradition)

Indonesia

7 Lulur (as a ritual)
8 Javanese Lulur (as a healing tradition)
9 Javanese Massage (as a healing tradition)

Malaysia

10 Bertungku (as a healing tradition)
11 Tangas (as a healing tradition)
12 Urutan Melayu (as a healing tradition)

Philippines

13 Hilot (as a healing tradition)
14 Dagdagay (as a healing tradition)
15 Bentosa (as a healing tradition)

Thailand

16 Nuad Rachasamnak (as a healing tradition)
17 Nuad Chalueysak (as a healing tradition)
18 Ao Maan (as a healing tradition)

In Japan, onsens (ritual bathing establishments that can be individual facilities or as part of a ryokan, i.e. inn) are representative of tradition and heritage. Japan is very rich in hot thermal and volcanic waters and visiting an onsen is a must for almost any visitor (in Jigokudani Monkey Park, snow monkeys are sitting in the hot spring!). Japan is one of the biggest spa-going nations in the world, it has the largest number of spas in Asia currently and is the number one country in Asia in terms of spa revenue (Demetriou, 2008). In South

Korea, which is rich in thermal springs a very special facility and tradition was developed known as the jimjilbang. In these bathing complexes guests can not only bath, have a massage but also can rest and sleep as long as they wish (in a common resting room).

Asia remains the key medical tourism region in the world with India, Thailand and Singapore in particular attracting growing numbers of tourists because of cheap prices as well as good service and extensive expertise. According to some reports, Thailand holds a 38 per cent stake in the world's medical tourism market, the largest of any country in the world (GSS, 2011). Bangkok is the homeland of probably the most globally acclaimed hospital treating over 400,000 international patients every year. The Bumrungrad International Hospital has over 30 speciality centres, hotel and suite accommodation and even a small shopping arcade. Malaysia is also growing fast as a medical tourism destination (Mun and Musa, 2013). The South Korean government together with leading industry representatives (e.g. LG and SAMSUNG) have been working hard to develop the medical tourism supply in the country (having several centres in Seoul, Daejeon or Jeju), partially building on the large Korean population in the West Coast of the USA.

In Asia, the traditional health approaches and techniques (e.g. Thai massage, Chinese medicine, yoga, Ayurveda) have become globally exportable. However, for many tourists, especially holistic or spiritual tourists, an authentic experience can only really be gained in the country of origin. Thai massage is available everywhere in Thailand, but visitors can also learn the technique in massage schools which offer special training programmes. The path-making facilities providing integrative health solutions to guests, such as the Chiva Som International Health Resort and Destination Spa (Hua Hin) or the Kamalaya Wellness Sanctuary, Luxury Detox Resort and Holistic Spa (in Koh Samiu), are also in Thailand.

It is possible to experience yoga and meditation in numerous ashrams and retreats throughout India. Ayurvedic treatments are on offer throughout India, but most especially in Kerala where the practice originates. India has a long history of spiritual tourism and the Ministry of Tourism (2011) has invested in the development of infrastructure for spiritual destinations such as Leh-Ladakh in Jammu and Kashmir, Chitrakoot in Madhya Pradesh, Haridwar-Rishikesh and Puducherry.

The Philippines government has been promoting health tourism since the early 2000s, which includes spas, wellness, leisure and, more recently, medical tourism. The Philippines is rich in natural springs, famous for Hilot massage, as well as being known as the healing centre of the Far East because of its herbal and non-traditional medicine, pranic and reiki healing, hypnosis, acupuncture, faith healing, massage, herbal medicine, reflexology and so-called psychic surgery.

Australasia and the South Pacific

Australia has much in common with many other Western developed countries, for example the UK and the USA as well as much of Europe. The emphasis is mainly on wellness tourism and day spas, and holistic retreats also play an important role. Voigt et al. (2010) show that medical tourism is not yet developed in any kind of organised way, but that the number of spas has grown significantly in the last ten years (by 129 per cent) and the most

popular kinds of wellness facilities are beauty spas (including water-based treatments such as the Peninsula Hot Springs in Melbourne), lifestyle resorts (including fitness, nutrition, counselling, weight and stress management), and spiritual retreats (including meditation, yoga, Tai Chi or reiki, for example). Some spas are exploring opportunities to source and include products that are indigenous to the area, for example Hepburn Springs and Daylesford Naturals products, which is located in the most visited spa region in Australia. This can include raw products used in treatments that are sourced in the local area, or those that have been or are currently being used by Australia's indigenous Aboriginal communities. For example, the spa menu at the Daintree Eco Lodge and Spa in Queensland has been collated out of respect and with approval of the local tribal Kuku Yalanji Elders and aims to integrate the wisdom of ancient cultures, medicines, spirituality and healing. Australia also has a growing number of holistic retreats, especially around Byron Bay.

CASE STUDY 3.11
Byron Bay, Australia

Byron Bay is often described as 'the alternative and spiritual capital of Australia'. Located in New South Wales just south of the Queensland border, Byron Bay is a small town which for years has been seen as the place for alternative lifestyles. From the 1960s onwards, surfers enjoyed a nature-based lifestyle here and at the same time many different therapies began to emerge – for example, massage, tarot readings and astrology. In the early 1970s, a group of festival organisers (of the Aquarious Festival) approached the local Aboriginal elders to seek their permission to hold a festival in Nimbin. It signified an important step. The new thinkers' respect for the indigenous people, their land and their culture was not only fundamental to the value systems of these people but to the genesis of reconciliation. Students and hippies flocked to the area for the festival in 1973 and many just never left. Two decades of new settlers and alternative lifestylers began to repopulate the area. A consultancy study undertaken for Byron Shire Council in 1983 showed that the 'relaxing lifestyle' was the most valued feature about living in the area.

Byron Bay became an important Australian tourism destination during the 1990s and the accommodation stocks diversified from 1950s/1960s-style beach houses to backpacker hostels, luxury guesthouses and apartments. Many entertainment venues and nightclubs were also developed. Many of the hostels in the area function as communes with a number of long-staying residents, and there are options of staying in tents, tepees and wagons as well as dorms and rooms. There are many alternative New Age shops, including spiritual services and New Age therapies such as meditation classes, tarot card reading, energy therapies and healing centres. The weekly roving markets of the Byron area are famous for their range of new age and holistic products. There are daily programmes of yoga, dance and hula-hoop classes, as well as fire-juggling, drumming, or making your own didgeridoo.

Some spa and wellness resorts and retreats were built in the mid-2000s, such as the Gaia Retreat and Spa which was developed in 2005 by Australian celebrity Olivia Newton-John. The retreat offers health, fitness, detox and yoga packages, day spa services and daily activities such as yoga, Tai Chi, Chi Kung, meditation and Pilates. Byron Bay is also well known for its detoxification and rehabilitation retreats for addicts (e.g. the Sanctuary). Wray, Laing and Voigt (2010) estimate that there are 144 operations offering beauty, spa, health, wellness and spiritual services in Byron Bay.

(Wray et al., 2010; Virtual Byron, 2013)

New Zealand is a destination where spa services are based on the assets of the natural environment making bathing in natural hot springs a key attraction. The Polynesian Spa in Rotorua is perhaps the best known, as it combines a geothermal, cultural and health and spa experience. Another is Hell's Gate Wai Ora Spa, which is home to New Zealand's most active geothermal field, including a large variety of volcanic features including exploding waters, steaming fumaroles, pools of boiling mud, the only accessible mud volcano and the largest hot waterfall in the Southern Hemisphere. Within this active geothermal reserve is the Wai Ora Spa and Wellness Centre, where visitors can experience the unique geothermal muds and sulphurous geothermal waters in a traditionally Maori-themed environment. Maori have been bathing in the geothermal muds and sulphurous waters for over 700 years for healing. The mud can be used to enhance the skin and sulphurous spas with hot water falls are used for relaxation. The traditional Wai Ora massage is also offered, which is based on the concepts of Miri Miri, the traditional Maori massage regime that has been practiced for hundreds of years (New Zealand Tourism, 2007).

Several hotels in the South Pacific already have spa facilities which are combined with other packages (e.g. beach tourism, business tourism, honeymoons and weddings). Fiji in particular has several spa and wellness hotels. Fox (2012) reports that spa and wellness tourism have been one of the key growth segments in this region recently with many world class spas being developed.

Americas and the Caribbean

In the USA and Canada there are large numbers of day-spas catering for mainly urban dwellers who are looking for relaxation, pampering and stress relief. However, the number of destination, resort and hotel or speciality spas (e.g. wine spas) is growing. Canada's spa health and wellness tourism sector is relatively young by global standards, given that most spa facilities are just over a decade old. In the USA and Canada, the concept of 'therapeutic recreation' is well established. It is defined by the Canadian Therapeutic Recreation Association (2007) as:

A profession which recognizes leisure, recreation and play as integral components of quality of life. Service is provided to individuals who have physical, mental, social or emotional limitations which impact their ability to engage in meaningful leisure experiences. Therapeutic Recreation is directed toward functional interventions, leisure education and participation opportunities. These processes support the goal of assisting the individual to maximize the independence in leisure, optimal health and the highest possible quality of life. Spa vacations are ideal for people who are living with lifelong disabilities or debilitating conditions.

Apart from the abundant supply of resort and hotel spas, and well-established destinations spas (e.g. Golden Door) there are several new services emerging in the North American market. MediSpas, health villages or 'health care plazas' have been developed recently, along with the wellness services in strip malls (e.g. Massage Envy). Medical services in the USA are popular for affluent patients from Central and South America, and intra-USA medical travel is also on the rise. In Part III of this book, Mia Mackman discusses the importance of Sedona in Arizona as one of the country's most unique wellness destinations, especially for holistic healing.

Several South American cities (Medellin, Colombia or Santa Cruz, Ecuador) or destinations (e.g. Venezuela, Argentina or Brazil) have entered in the international medical tourism market, targeting primarily North American patients.

Many indigenous traditions are derived from the Americas and are being exported to spas all over the world. One of the best known is Lomi Lomi massage from Hawaii, which is usually offered as a two-hour treatment in European spas and is a gentle wave-like or rocking technique. Native American Indian rituals are also used increasingly in holistic and spiritual retreat centres. These are now quite globalised, but in the USA, Canada and Mexico, some more 'authentic' experiences can be found in holistic or spiritual retreats. 'Sweat Lodges' (Native Indian ceremonial saunas) are becoming more popular in spas and retreat centres. In Mexico, Temazcals are similar, and they are also offered in other Central and South American retreats and spas. Goldsmith (2008) gives numerous examples of how indigenous American traditions are being used in spas and retreat centres. In countries like Peru, the consultation of local Shamans can be offered to visitors, for example a ceremony involving drinking shamanic medicine which is said to expand consciousness (Sylge, 2007).

In South America there is a long tradition of baños, which are similar to historic baths or spas in Europe. Erfurt-Cooper and Cooper (2009) describe how Brazil, Argentina, Uruguay, Peru and Chile (and Cuba) have numerous thermal spring areas which are used for health, wellness or leisure tourism. As stated earlier in the book, plastic surgery and other forms of cosmetic tourism are extremely popular in Central and South America, especially in Argentina, Columbia, Brazil and Bolivia. Apparently, Brazil has 4,500 licensed cosmetic surgeons, the highest per capita in the world (Discover Medical Tourism, 2011). Certain forms of dance that are indigenous to Central or South America are frequently offered as core products, such as salsa dancing in Cuba or capoeira in Brazil (an Afro-Brazilian dance-like martial art, first practised by African slaves in the sixteenth century during Portuguese colonial rule). Although there is a growth in the number of spas, these countries are tending to focus more on medical tourism at present.

CASE STUDY 3.12
The success of Baños, Ecuador
Tamás Várhelyi

Probably Baños is the most successful spa city in South America. It is a small city in the eastern slopes of the Andean highlands at 1800m elevation. It is not far from the Amazon Basin. The town is a popular tourist area with both Ecuadorian and foreign visitors. They come for the famous hot springs, the wonderful scenery and the interesting Basilica of the Virgin of the Holy Water.

With these resources, Baños could have become a famous spa but instead became world famous when Tungurahua volcano erupted above the town in 1999. Later the town was not in real danger but tourists coming to Ecuador wanted to observe the phenomenon. Since then a number of hotels and spas have been built, which are regularly full at the weekends. During the week the town is not empty, but guests are mainly foreigners. Although the activity of the volcano has reduced, maintaining popularity succeeded by offering new services (rafting, mountain bike rental, climbing, jungle tours, volcano hiking, tours and adventure activities in the Valley of the Waterfalls). Due to the new services tourists who are not especially interested in spas can spend four to five days in the town. Evening massage services also can be used by tourists after participating in a cycling tour or an adventure tour.

Ecuador has another famous destination spa town, Papallacta at 3300m above sea level, probably the highest spa town in the world. Baños is much farther from the capital than Papallacta. But this disadvantage became an advantage as tourists come here because of the diverse services not only for a one-day visit but at least for two days or even for a week.

There is a realisation in Baños that success is not just about becoming well known; it is also important to utilise local features in tourism developments and attractions.

One interesting trend in Central and South America is the development of adventure spas. By definition, an adventure spa offers spa treatments, healthy gourmet food and an abundance of outdoor activity. Guests typically want to combine adventurous, outdoors activities by day (e.g. rock climbing, kayaking, hiking, biking) with pampering spa services and luxury treatments by night (Pascarella, 2008). Central and South America have the perfect landscapes for adventure spas, from the wildlife-rich jungles, to the rugged mountain chains, to the numerous hot springs, beaches, lakes and rivers. There is also a keen emphasis on ecospas which aim to preserve and protect these natural resources. Marinus Gisolf also discusses the growing number of eco-friendly New Age retreats in Costa Rica in Part III of this book.

CASE STUDY 3.13
Adventure Spas in South America

The Island Experience Adventure Spa in Brazil is located on the island of Ilha Grande and promises a unique adventure spa, yoga retreat and fitness vacation programme in one. The seven-day programme offers a sequence of yoga, rainforest hiking, sea kayaking, snorkelling, daily massage, spa treatments and Brazilian spa cuisine specially designed to detox the body. Groups are small with no more than 12 people.

The day starts with outdoor yoga followed by a healthy organic breakfast. Next, there may be a hike through the rainforest down to a quiet cove, where guests kayak near a secluded beach. Snorkelling is also possible. After a vegetarian lunch there may be a rest and later a massage or an optional second yoga class. Creative activities may also be offered, such as painting or learning the basics of Brazilian rhythms, e.g. samba, bossa nova or capoeira. A special detox dinner is followed by Brazilan cultural events and entertainment.

A typical package includes:

- six nights of lodging;

- private room and bath overlooking ocean;

- all meals, juices, mineral water and snacks everyday (natural spa cuisine developed by on-site nutritionist);

- more than six hours per day of supervised activities (trekking, kayaking and snorkelling);

- daily yoga classes (two per day);

- daily one-hour full body massages (three in total for each person);

- various cultural activities (capoeira, Brazilian dance, painting).

The Adventure Spa in Brazil believes that people can change their life in just one week. Facing their own limits, beating whatever challenge is waiting for them, learning to manage their fears and frustrations, opening themselves to new cultures, thoughts and beliefs.

Their motto is: 'Breathe, disconnect and go for the experience!'

(Island Experience, 2013)

The Caribbean Spa and Wellness Association was established in 2006 and provides help, guidelines and coordination for those interested in health tourism development. There is a focus on wellness and spas rather than medical tourism, although Cuba is an exception (its developed medical services are popular among patients from Central America). One of the mottos of the Caribbean Spa and Wellness Association (2013) is 'there are lots of spas in the Caribbean, but not enough of the Caribbean in our spas'. The

Regions	Main Sending Markets		Prominent Approach to Health Tourism			Notes
	Domestic	International	Advanced	Traditional	Under-developed/minimal	
Europe						
Northern Europe	✓	✓	✓		✓	Mainly Leisure and Recreation Innovative solutions Medical services in the Baltic states
Western Europe	✓✓✓	✓✓	✓	✓		All forms available
Central and Eastern Europe	✓✓✓	✓✓✓	✓	✓		Medical therapeutic orientation Introduction of global wellness treatments and leisure and recreation Specialty medical services (e.g. dentistry)
Southern Europe	✓	✓	✓	✓		Traditional and new approaches and services co-exist (e.g. historic spas and resort spas)
Americas						
North	✓✓✓	✓✓	✓			(Re)discovering medical services as well as proliferation of products and segments Wellness centres and spas
Central	✓✓	✓✓✓	✓		✓	New approaches and services capitalise on local resources (especially resort or eco-spas) Developing medical tourism supply
South	✓✓	✓✓	✓			New approaches and services capitalise on local resources (especially resort or adventure spas) Developing medical tourism supply
Africa						
	✓	✓	✓		✓	New approaches and services capitalise on local resources (e.g. traditions) Sporadic medical tourism supply

FIGURE 3.1 Typology of global health and wellness facilities

Asia						
Middle East	✓✓	✓✓✓	✓	✓		Traditional and new approaches and services co-exist (e.g. hotel spas and hammams; and medical services)
South-East	✓	✓✓✓	✓	✓		Traditional and new approaches and services co-exist and blend Global medical tourism destinations
Far East	✓✓✓	✓✓	✓	✓		Medical services attract foreign tourists, domestic tourism builds on local traditions Rapid development in spas and wellness centres
Australia, New Zealand and South Pacific						
	✓✓	✓	✓	✓		New approaches and services capitalise on local resources (e.g. traditions)

Key: the number of ✓ refers to the relative role of the given market; and indicates the most prominent approach(es)

FIGURE 3.1 Continued

group is therefore aiming to create a single brand which builds on the natural attributes of the region, which they already describe as 'the world's largest spa and wellness centre'. Much of this concept is based on the beautiful and relaxing environment such as beaches, mountains and rainforests, as well as the chilled out atmosphere. Treatments make use of local ingredients, such as coconut, tropical fruit, ginger, bamboo, aloe vera, coffee, allspice, sea salt and sugar cane.

Conclusion

This chapter has demonstrated the regional diversity of health and wellness tourism, indicating that despite trends towards globalisation and standardisation of facilities and services, there are unique products in different areas of the world which are worth travelling for. This might mean natural resources, for example medical and mineral waters in CEE or hot springs in New Zealand or Iceland, spiritual traditions in Asia (e.g. massage, yoga or meditation), thalassotherapy treatments in a specific location (e.g. by the Dead Sea), real Turkish baths in Turkey, traditional Arab baths in Spain, Finnish saunas and lakes. Even in cases where the surroundings seem irrelevant (e.g. for yoga or holistic holidays, fitness-based or nutritional programmes, medical and beauty tourism), it seems that place, geography and traditions still matter in health and wellness tourism.

Acknowledgement

This chapter was based on the research entitled 'The adaptation and ICT-supported development opportunities of regional wellbeing and wellness concepts to the Balkans' (ref: KTIA_AIK_12-1-2013-0043).

Leisure, lifestyle and society

The world has never been as divided as it is now, with religious wars, genocides, a lack of respect for the planet, economic crises, depression, poverty, with everyone wanting instant solutions to at least some of the world's problems or their own. And things only look bleaker as we head into the future.

(Coelho, 2011: 1)

This chapter focuses on some of the current trends in modern living which have led to an increased need for health and wellness products and trips. It is argued that the world which human beings have created for themselves in most developed countries is less than ideal for developing lifestyles of optimum well-being and quality of life. There are numerous reasons for this which are discussed here, including the breakdown of traditional communities, loss of religion, the obsession with self and celebrities, increasing working hours and stress, and the growth of new technology which should (technically) have made life better. Although travel is only one means of improving the quality of people's lives, it is often only away from their place of residence that they can really start to assess their lives and engage in self-development.

Trends in modern living

Since humans began the process of exploration and travel, the assumption has generally been that the travelling societies are somehow superior to those who are visited. Explorers, settlers, conquerors, anthropologists and Christian missionaries alike often seemed surprised by the 'primitive' way in which tribal or indigenous peoples were living in the countries that they visited. Several strategies were adopted to transform or convert those societies to more modern ways, often using force and cruelty. Table 4.1 offers a comparison (albeit a simplistic one) of traditional tribal living and typical urban living in a so-called developed country. Questions could be asked about which way of life is truly superior!

TABLE 4.1 Tribal versus urban living	
Tribal	Urban
• Working as much as is needed to sustain families and communities • Walking to fetch water • Exhausted from physical activity • Hunting and gathering food which is available locally • Considerable time spent with families and community • Herbal and traditional medicines gathered from nature • Living in harmony with nature and natural cycles • Relatively short life expectancy	• Working minimum eight hours per day regardless of family commitments • Commuting twice a day • Mentally and emotionally exhausted • Mainly buying processed, artificial, non-local foods • Little time to see family and friends, but more virtual communities • Chemical medicine prescribed by doctors • Little time spent in nature or green spaces • Relatively long life expectancy but lifestyle-related illnesses increasing

Most Western people live in permanent settlements and aspire to a materialistic life-style. Many developing countries are now aspiring to emulate the patterns of capitalist countries, with many Asian societies achieving phenomenal educational and economic success, for example. But with what cost to well-being and life satisfaction? Capitalism encourages accumulation, profit maximisation and prosperity is measured in economic terms. However, research has shown time and again that there is little correlation between material gain and happiness after a certain standard of living has been reached. Until recently, the environment was seen as a resource which was unlimited and was there to be exploited for maximum profit. Half the world is starving, the other half have more than they could ever need and are even stressed out by too many choices and opportunities!

However, according to proponents of the Age of Aquarius (often Kundalini Yoga spiritual leaders and practitioners), we are witnessing the dawn of a new age. It is generally agreed that the actual time that we entered the Age of Aquarius was 2012, but turbulent times were predicted up until this transition. Indeed, as indicated in the Paolo Coelho quotation at the start of this chapter, the new millennium has so far brought an unprecedented number of environmental, political, social and economic crises. In response to this, the new age will supposedly lead to an increased rate of change in our society and ourselves and a major review of our world-views and our consciousness. As stated by Yogi Bajan (2000: 24):

Each action we take must be considered ecologically and globally because each person does affect, directly or indirectly, vast networks of people and other living beings and places. In the Aquarian Age we will enjoy union with all humankind, elitism will break down and a sense of connection between all men and women will be experienced. There will also be a need for responsibility, both individually and collectively to create the environment that truly reflects our ideals.

One of the most urgent actions is clearly that of creating more sustainable activities which support and prolong the life of the planet rather than squandering or diminishing it. This is discussed further in a practical context in Chapters 5 and 7. However, it is fundamental to the health and well-being of all human beings, so it is also inextricably linked to lifestyle habits and changes.

Health tourism trends in Germany

The Institut für Freizeitwissenschaften published a report in 2008 about the health tourism trends until 2020 in Germany (Sydow, 2011). According to the forecasts on target segments and the factors influencing holiday choice:

- Leisure time: time to recover, recharge batteries to maintain health status, possibility to compensate daily deficits
- Demographic change
  - strong increase of leisure time of the elderly until 2020: women + 9%, men: + 18%
  - risk of having chronic diseases increase
  - elderly people have to adapt to increasing physical weakness
- Wish to spend leisure time appropriately
  - You can only enjoy your leisure time when you are in a good physical condition
- Employment
  - increasing retirement age, increasing stress
  - feeling under pressure
  - maintaining good physical condition is a must
- General lifestyle
  - living at high speed
  - unhealthy nutrition
  - physical inactivity
  - being overweight
  - subject to stress
  - alcohol and cigarette consumption

Source: Sydow, 2011

Active ageing and longevity

People are living longer but not necessarily better. The World Health Organization (2012) statistics show that the number of people today aged 60 and over has doubled since 1980, and that the number of people aged 80 years will almost quadruple to 395 million between now and 2050. Within the next few years, the number of adults aged 65 and over will outnumber children under the age of five. Much of this is due to improvements in public health; however, how well human beings age is also a result of the lifestyle choices they make (at least, for those who have a choice). Even in poorer countries heart disease, cancer and diabetes tend to be the most common causes of death.

The World Health Organization also warns of the dangers of neglecting or stereotyping the elderly, forcing them to retire early, implying they are no longer useful or physically or mentally incompetent. The health and wellness industries arguably provide a kind of 'counter-revolution' to these attitudes. The term 'anti-ageing' is no longer even seen as appropriate and has often been replaced by 'active ageing', 'fit ageing' or even 'youth building'. However, as discussed by McCarthy (2012), the idea is not to fight against age but to accept and embrace it, and to improve the quantity and quality of life while ageing. He suggests why not use the term 'happy ageing' instead, not reversing ageing but enjoying each moment regardless of age. Deepak Chopra's (1993) seminal work *Ageless Body, Timeless Mind* argues that longevity is an individual achievement which comes primarily to those whose expectations are high enough to want it and that it involves a lifelong commitment to oneself every day. This includes eating moderately, getting regular (but not necessarily excessive) exercise, sleeping and resting enough, fresh air, having a congenial occupation, ideally being married, keeping the intellect active, moderate alcohol consumption, and not worrying too much. Much of this seems fairly simple and not out of the reach of the majority of the populations of developed countries. Increasing numbers of longevity centres around the world are guiding people in how to lead the optimum healthy and long life, for example the Pritikin Longevity Center. Victoria Winter provides a detailed case study of the Kurotel longevity centre in Brazil in her case study in Part III of this book.

CASE STUDY 4.1
Pritikin Longevity Center

The Pritikin Program was established in Florida in 1958 and was based on an effective combination of diet, exercise and lifestyle changes. It is thought to be the longest running and most scientifically documented (there have been more than a 100 studies) food, fitness and healthy living programme. Nathan Pritikin founded the first Pritikin Longevity Center in 1976 as well as launching a book about diet and exercise. The programme and centre were credited with reversing conditions like high cholesterol, heart disease, high blood pressure, diabetes and obesity.

The four-pillar approach is based on natural whole foods, daily exercise, lifestyle education, and stress management for mental and emotional health. Specialist doctors consult guests on their personal health and lifestyle goals and carry out tests before and after the programme. A team of specialists is present including medical doctors, dieticians, physio-therapists, exercise physiologists, cosmetologists and dermatologists. Guests can be any age from 18 to 80, but special segments include working executives, women over 35, post-natal women and senior citizens. It is mainly a residential model. A typical week includes stretching exercises every morning, cardio-vascular work after breakfast, yoga and relaxation or aquatics, talks about healthy nutrition and cookery classes, dinner and then a movie.

(Pritikin, 2013)

It is still important to note that longevity is not the only indicator of a successful life; it should ideally be a happy one too with a high perceived quality of life. Seligman (2011) even suggested that positive psychologists like himself had placed too much emphasis on happiness in the past, and that well-being should be measured instead by the degree of 'flourishing'. He defines flourishing in his PERMA model:

- positive emotions;
- engagement;
- relationships;
- meaning;
- accomplishment (or achievement).

The remainder of this chapter will demonstrate that there are unfortunately many barriers to creating a long, happy, flourishing life, but that these can be addressed through health and wellness activities, many of which may also include travel to participate in them.

Psychology

Psychological wellness focuses mainly on control of the mind and emotions. This could include tools and techniques such as the development of mindfulness, meditation, building self-esteem, becoming a better communicator, reducing stress, managing anxiety and overcoming depression. Smalley and Winston (2010) suggest that a more mindful society would be a kinder one, and that 'In the midst of our techno-savvy yet anxiety-producing culture, scientific investigation has become increasingly interested in the ancient practice of mindfulness as an antidote of sorts to the ills of the modern world and as a tool for skilfully examining our lives' (p. xv). McCarthy (2012: 2) refers to positive psychology about being 'the science of human flourishing'. There is a large and growing self-help industry based on the books, TV and radio programmes and workshops of famous gurus such as Deepak Chopra. Individuals can begin to diagnose and solve their own psychological problems using books about relationships, stress, depression, anger, and so on, or they can attend a workshop or training programme. The reference to popular or 'pop' psychology which is used most frequently in wellness circles (as opposed to medical ones) is often used in a derogatory way, as many of the theories are said to be scientifically unproven. However, Hay and Richardson (2011) feel that they no longer have to 'prove' themselves scientifically, as they know that what they do works. As a spiritual teacher and self-help guru, Louise Hay says that she is not a salesperson but a teacher and that she is happy to teach people who want to learn and change, but not to force others. They also note the importance of anecdotal evidence from people who have experienced healing and the leaps of consciousness they make. In many ways, it is no different from those people who make a leap of faith in conventional religion. Many holistic holidays, hideaways and retreat centres focus on self-help, usually in the form of group workshops. Some have a firmer basis in traditional psychology than others. For example, life coaching has been growing fast, but it is neither counselling nor therapy; instead it is described as 'a practical, forward-looking way to gain clarity on what you don't like and what you can do about it. It's also a powerful support system to keep people moving in the right direction. It provides an external perspective on your life' (UK Life Coaching, 2007). Life coaches tend to focus on a number of domains within a person's life such as work, home, finances, social life, partner, health, dreams, spiritual and work/life balance.

Complementary and alternative medicine and therapy

In addition to conventional medicine, there is also a growing market for complementary and alternative medicine (CAM). This can be used as an alternative to conventional medicine or in combination (sometimes called 'integrative medicine'). Often CAM medical systems developed and evolved much earlier than conventional medical systems. Examples in Western cultures include homeopathic or naturopathic medicine, and in non-Western cultures Traditional Chinese Medicine, Traditional Korean Medicine or Indian Ayurveda. Mind–body medicine is also an important part of CAM, although techniques like support groups or cognitive-behavioural therapy have become mainstream. Others such as meditation, prayer, mental healing and therapies that use creative outlets like art, music and dance are still being researched. Biologically based practices use substances found in food, herbs or vitamins. Manipulative or body-based practices use movement or manipulation such as chiropractic or osteopathic techniques, as well as massage. Energy therapies involve the use of energy fields, for example through therapeutic touch, qi gong or reiki (National Center for Alternative and Complementary Medicine, 2007). Many conventional medical practitioners remain sceptical about the impacts of CAM, as there is too little scientific evidence to prove its medical or health benefits. However, it should be emphasised that as long as people are doing themselves no harm, the effects of CAM are beneficial if people believe they are. The only problem is that the sector is largely unregulated so that people tend to self-medicate and so-called 'experts' may not be properly qualified to advise. Many alternative and complementary medicine practices are used in holistic centres and retreats, whereas manipulative treatments are used in medical baths and conventional medicine is used in medical spas and in destinations which provide specific medical services. Even some leisure and recreational spas offer visitors health checks with a doctor, for example measuring their fitness levels, weight, body fat, blood pressure, cholesterol, and so on, and making recommendations for a healthier life.

Therapy and healing

If something is therapeutic (non-invasive), it has healing powers. We can talk about psychological therapy, sex therapy, beauty therapy, diet therapy, detox therapy, trauma therapy, stress therapy, and so on. Most therapies are administered by a qualified practitioner on a regular basis, for a set time period and with specified outcomes. For example, therapeutic recreation organisations (e.g. the American Therapeutic Recreation Association) focus on rehabilitating people with illnesses or disabling conditions. Cornelia Voigt discusses a therapeutic lifestyle retreat run by the Gawler Foundation in Australia in Part III of this book.

CASE STUDY 4.2
Therapeutic recreation: experience therapy

SeriousFun (or as formerly known Hole in the Wall) Camps are the world's largest family of camps for children with serious illnesses and life-threatening conditions. To date, more than 253,000 children from over 50 countries have attended free of charge, since 1988. The philosophy of the chain of camps can be summarised as follows: 'to create opportunities for children and their families to reach beyond serious illness and discover joy, confidence and a new world of possibilities; always free of charge'. Children served through various initiatives (such as the Global Parnership Program) running camps in every continent suffer from HIV, AIDS or cancer.

Today, as the network continues to grow globally, they have changed the name from the Association of Hole in the Wall Camps to SeriousFun Children's Network. The new identity embodies the root of their work – highlighting Paul Newman's belief that taking fun seriously can make a real difference in the lives of children who need it most. As they plan to move forward, they remain committed to the cherished Hole in the Wall history that brought the network here today. And those core values that all of their camps and programs share remain the same. Because they believe, as Paul did, that every kid deserves the chance to simply be a kid.

- More and more it's been shown that for children with serious illnesses, laughter really is the best medicine. In addition to the contagious laughter found at each Camp and Program, there is 24-hour, high quality medical care provided for each camper. Each facility is staffed by trained medical professionals. The medical presence at Camp is carefully kept in the background so that the children can fully concentrate on the fun activities.

- Children with cancer or HIV, and other serious illnesses can feel safe and cared for. Doctors and nurses volunteer their time and talents, and attend to every child's needs. Each medical facility accommodates the full array of treatments for the medical conditions they serve, whether it's a chemotherapy treatment, a dialysis procedure, or daily infusions. Our medical facilities are designed to be as welcoming as possible. They are friendly, brightly-painted places that blend in with the look and feel of other camp structures. And their catchy names reflect the distinct charm and personality of each camp.

(Hole in the Wall Camps, 2008; SeriousFun, 2013)

Many baths/spas are thought to have therapeutic properties because of the mineral content of the waters, mud or even climate. Patients can benefit from internal therapy such as drinking the waters, inhalation therapy (e.g. inhaling droplets or fumes of water), lavages (oral, nasal, gynaecological), as well as external therapy which can include baths and showers, hydromassaging, balneotherapy (using thermal and healing waters for bathing, drinking or inhalation), or fangotherapy (applying mud to those parts of the body that suffer from various disorders). Many visitors choose their spa destination and hotel carefully according to which therapies are offered; for example, thalassotherapy which makes use of sea-water, mud, seaweed, and so on. One of the most attractive offers in recent years has been aromatherapy where essential oils are blended to create different effects and are used for massage or inhalation. Many holistic centres and retreats offer a range of healing techniques and therapies, and tend to be more creative and experimental than medically proven. This might include colour or sound therapy, bach flower remedies, angel or animal medicine therapies, amongst others.

Rehabilitation

The Spas Research Fellowship (2008) describes how spa treatments are increasingly being perceived as a potential tool in the rehabilitation of people with alcohol and drug problems. Even back in the mid-nineteenth century, hydrotherapy was being used to treat alcoholics who would detoxify by drinking the mineral waters, bathing in hot, warm and cold baths, applying wet packs and taking showers. Immersion and flotation were also deemed important treatments for detoxification. Rehabilitation can refer to the process of enabling people with disabilities, serious or long-term illnesses to reach and maintain their optimal physical, sensory, intellectual, psychological and social functional levels.

However, the term 'rehab' is these days more commonly associated with recovering alcoholics, drug or sex addicts, especially famous celebrities. An unusual form of tourism maybe, but one which is becoming increasingly familiar to those who have drink and drug problems is to rehabilitate in luxury surroundings. In Southern California, a number of rehab centres with enticing names such as 'Harmony Place' and 'Renaissance' offer ocean views, massage and horse riding. Celebrities must pay for the privilege of rehabilitating, however, with a month's stay costing as much as 80,000 US dollars (Reuters, 2006). We Care Holistic Spa even offers pre-Oscar detox for strung-out celebrities in Palm Springs!

TABLE 4.2 Saudi patients in Germany

According to Yasen (2012), 86 per cent of Saudi patients chose Germany for medical treatments, and France had some 10 per cent of Saudi patients. Most treatments were performed in orthopaedics, oncology and in rehabilitation, although they spent the most on rehabilitation. Saudi patients find that the most important obstacles are:

- visa regulations;
- organizing appointments;
- the treatment plan and the medical reports;
- treating professionals.

Source: Yasen, 2012.

CASE STUDY 4.3
Promises Malibu Luxury Rehab Retreats

Since 1988, Promises has been a provider of (drug) addiction treatment. The Malibu model is based on treatments which are tailored to each individual in a private, home-like retreat instead of a hospital-like environment. It is one of the world's most exclusive and luxury settings for rehabilitation. The website claims that, 'At Promises, recovery is not only an exercise in physical rehabilitation, but also emotional, social and spiritual healing'. The number of clients in each estate at one time is limited to six and guidance is received from some of America's leading addiction specialists, many of whom have experienced recovery in their own lives.

The programme is based on the pillars of: detox, residential, outpatient, extended care and sober living. A broad range of traditional and alternative therapies are used, including:

- comprehensive assessments;
- medically monitored detox;
- individual, group and family therapy;
- 12-step meetings;
- equine therapy;
- art therapy;
- neurofeedback;
- yoga, acupuncture and massage;
- fitness and nutritional counselling;
- life coaching;
- psycho-educational groups;
- SPECT brain imaging and DESA testing;
- Eye Movement Desensitization and Reprocessing (EMDR);
- psychiatric care;
- relapse prevention planning;
- alumni groups and aftercare.

The programme also aims to assess and treat the complex issues that can contribute to addictive patterns, such as depression, anxiety, sex and intimacy issues, and other disorders.

(Promises Malibu, 2013)

The Search for Community

Communities are becoming increasingly dislocated and fragmented in modern society. Growing international mobility has resulted in many people leaving their home town or even home country and spending long periods of their life far away from family or friends. The number of single people has increased with larger numbers of women choosing to pursue a career before settling down. As a result, the birth rate or number of children per family in many Western countries is decreasing. Divorce rates are also high with up to 50 per cent in many European countries. Unlike Asia where collectivity is valued highly, European societies tend to value individuality and independence. The decreasing importance of organised religion has also exacerbated this phenomenon.

The increasing need for 'community' as part of the wellness quest is noted by many authors (e.g. Devereux and Carnegie, 2006; Smith and Kelly, 2006). Holistic retreats and ashrams tend to create communities around collective, 'karmic' activities. For example, Dina Glouberman (2002) describes how her desire to establish the well-known holistic holiday centre Skyros was partly based on her own yearning for community. Edmond and Deborah Szekely did the same even earlier with their Golden Door in Southern California (1958). Many wellness tourists are seeking a sense of community, perhaps within a holistic centre, a yoga retreat, at a New Age festival, or on a pilgrimage. Although their primary focus may be on self-development, they wish to enter into a kind of psychological, emotional or spiritual communion with others. Marinus Gisolf mentions the importance of communities in New Age retreats in his case study in Part III.

Temporary communities are formed during a medical holiday, where guests or patients tend to spend at least a week (but three–four weeks are not unknown either). During these weeks the days are spent with very similar activities, guests eat with the same people day-by-day. This gives the opportunity to talk and to socialise. Many ill and especially older people are looking for understanding and sympathy, which they may not have from healthy people, but can expect it from people in a similar situation. In countries, where medical trips are at least partially financed by the state health insurance, an unknown, but supposedly significant, percentage of the trips are motivated by looking for company.

Obsession with the self and celebrity

As concepts of community become increasingly blurred and diminished, obsession with the self is reaching an all-time high thanks to new media, technology and consumer-orientated services. This is often played out in terms of fixations on body image, clothing, consumerism and a growing fascination with celebrity and its supposed set of ideal existence characteristics. At one end of the spectrum lies an engagement with the outer self – 'the physical body' – and at the other, a search for the inner self, or spirit. However, the route to creating individual identities is often based on a superficial obsession with celebrity figures who appear to embody the characteristics that many people are aspiring to. The quest for the body beautiful can lead women in particular to diet endlessly in an attempt to be an elusive size zero after their favourite Hollywood stars. Men, on the other hand, struggle to pump up or tone their bodies to an artificial and usually

unretainable level using steroids, proteins or other aids which can irreparably harm the body in the long term.

Harrison (2006) describes how around one third of Americans are suffering from 'celebrity-worship syndrome' or CWS. Social psychologists seem to think that people alleviate boredom through celebrity obsession, as well as searching for identity. Fame appears to be like a new religion and celebrities are the new gods! Series like *Big Brother* or The *X Factor* transform unknown people into stardom, a dream for many people leading humdrum, ordinary or poverty-stricken lives. Although celebrity worship can be harmless escapism, it can also lead to fanaticism and unhealthy self-image (e.g. inducing anorexia, promoting the need for cosmetic surgery).

Nutrition

Unfortunately, the cult of celebrity and obsession with physical perfection has led to a worldwide increase in eating disorders such as anorexia and bulimia. The Eating Disorders Coalition (2013) secured state funding for more research into eating disorders arguing that most eating disorders are illnesses, not choices. Much of this is related to the striving for perfection fuelled by media. They show that anorexia is now diagnosed in boys as young as eight, a full 40 per cent of those with binge-eating disorders are male, and it is affecting more and more women over 30. Geneen Roth who regularly runs retreats for those with eating disorders states that 'our relationship to food is an exact microcosm of our relationship to life itself' (2010: 2) and that problems with food are almost never about the food but about the emotional and psychological issues which lie behind under- or over-eating.

The subject of healthier nutrition has become something of a public education campaign in recent years in many countries. It is hard to turn a corner without seeing a book, magazine or a TV programme about diets, healthy eating or detoxing. 'Boot camps' to which overweight people are sent for a diet and fitness programme are becoming more common. In the UK celebrity chefs like Jamie Oliver have tried to revolutionise school dinners and home-cooking (not always with great success because of public resistance!), and pseudo-doctors like Gillian McKeith have encouraged the nation into making healthier diet choices. Diets like the Atkins, Weight Watchers and Paleo have become world-famous. However, Roth (2010) notes that studies have shown that 83 per cent of those who diet have tended to gain back more weight than they lost in the long term.

Numerous celebrities are promoting the need to 'detox', even though it has been medically proven not to be necessary, or it can even be dangerous (e.g. being physically and/ or mentally unprepared giving an unexpected shock to the body and mind). Although detox used to be primarily thought of as a treatment for alcohol or drug dependence, the term is also used to refer to diets, herbs, and other methods of removing environmental and dietary toxins from the body for optimum health. There are numerous retreat centres which now offer special dietary and detox programmes, not only vegetarian but also vegan, organic, 'live' and raw food. Some clinics focus specifically on digestive health (e.g. the Mayr Centre in Austria), but here it is medically supervised.

CASE STUDY 4.4
Detox retreats in Austria

The Viva Mayr Health Resort in Southern Austria runs detox holidays under the supervision of doctors who follow Mayr therapy, the belief that the reduction of food is the best stimulator for the body's self-healing powers. A typical day starts at 7 a.m. with an Epsom salt drink followed by body brushing with alternating hot and cold showers, 7.30 a.m. breakfast, then a consultation with a detox specialist doctor using kinesiology and a breath test to check imbalances. Lectures are given about digestive disorders and their causes, as well as nutritional advice – for example, eating little in the evenings, no liquid with food, no raw foods after 2 p.m., chewing properly, etc. As well as a strictly controlled, customised diet, Kneipp therapies are used (water treatments which dissolve and remove matter-containing disease from the body), Nasal Reflex Therapy (acupuncture combined with aromatherapy to unblock nasal passages), Phytomer detox algen packs for de-toxing the body, hydroxeur herbal baths and Elektrolyse foot baths to increase circulation, rebalance and stimulate different organs, and allow tissues to eliminate acidity, toxic burdens and other pollutants. Patients are given massages, reflexology, manipulation of digestive organs, and are asked to apply a liver pack every evening to allow the liver to detoxify. Yoga and relaxation are an important part of the package as detoxing can make participants feel depressed, angry, tired, high or induce headaches depending on what dietary changes are required.

(Mayr Centre, 2008)

Spas and wellness hotels are starting to recognise the need to provide healthier food for visitors (those in Central and Eastern Europe, for example, traditionally offered high calorie, fatty foods with little consideration of the health consequences). Visitors may be able to choose from certain menus (e.g. vegetarian, gluten and wheat-free, low calorie) or there may be a diverse buffet with clearly labelled dishes. There have been considerable developments in spa cuisine in recent years with the aim of offering healthy, balanced, nutritional but tasty food. One of the key challenges is still to make healthy foods taste and look nicer! Many travellers may happily choose a healthy or healthier option from a menu if it tasted less 'healthy', that is less different or odd (e.g. grass-shoot juice). Nico Dingemans discusses the growing importance of health cuisine in spas and wellness centres in his case study in Part III of this book.

Cosmetics

The use of make-up by women is an ancient concept, but never before has its usage been so intensive and commercialised. Whole magazines are devoted to the subject of beauty and hair-care. Women who choose *not* to wear make-up in Western societies are the exception rather than the norm. This places considerable pressure on the majority of women to invest in expensive skin and haircare products in the attempt to look naturally

younger and more beautiful. This is the major focus of day spas and many hotel spas too, which offer facials, manicures, pedicures, hair-care, and so on. The admittance, even advocating, of plastic surgery by many celebrities has led to the increasing demand for such services, with many women choosing to go on holiday for cosmetic surgery.

However, McCarthy (2012) suggests that the beauty element in spas goes far beyond mere vanity and has a lot to do with making clients feel nurtured, cared for, loved and ultimately more confident. In addition, one positive outcome of the sustainability and green movement is that the most recent trend is towards organic or mineral cosmetics which contain as few chemicals as possible. Euromonitor (2012) suggests that the idea of 'beauty from within' becoming more important. Interest is especially growing in some of the newer products, such as:

- Cosmeceuticals – beauty products combining cosmetics and pharmaceutical properties and containing biologically active ingredients which have a cosmetic effect on the user.
- Nutricosmetic – ingestible beauty products (dietary supplements, food and drink) that have been developed to promote healthy skin, nails, hair and general beauty.

Fitness and sports

Statistics show that worldwide obesity is at an all-time high with up to half of the population in countries like the US and Britain being technically obese. Excess body weight is pandemic therefore there is a need not only to advocate good diet but also to encourage fitness and sports. In most Western societies life expectancy is increasing, therefore there are growing numbers of older people who want and should be encouraged to remain fit and healthy. However, awareness of the close relationship between exercise and a healthy lifestyle needs to be integrated into the education of young children if it is to succeed in later life. There is a growing awareness of the connection between fitness, sports, lifestyle, quality of life and wellness. This includes the mental and emotional balance that can come from more spiritual activities such as yoga and Pilates or the need to follow certain exercise and diet programmes to boost health.

Well+GOODNYC (2012) compiled 14 trends (specific to the USA) in wellness and fitness some of which are rather interesting globally, such as:

1. yoga for jocks, i.e. those who want to have a workout;
2. CrossFit from specialist workout becomes mainstream;
3. fitness studios go online;
4. appearance of wellness evangelists;
5. non-GMO becomes the new organic;
6. the health coach revolution.

However, many nations are actually becoming less active rather than more so. Britain is a good example, where it is predicted that half the population do no sport or active recreation at all (BBC News Online, 2006). The 2012 London Olympics may have changed all that for the better, however! Finland turned itself around from being one of the world's unhealthiest nations to one of the fittest with an emphasis on outdoor pursuits like Nordic walking, cycling, cross-country skiing (*Guardian Unlimited*, 2005). Many people in Western countries have decreasing leisure time as a result of long working hours and use their lack of time or energy as an excuse for not exercising. Slumping in front of the TV with a takeaway meal after a long day in the office can seem far more appealing! However, public education campaigns are starting to suggest ways in which fitness can be integrated into everyday life (e.g. walking to work, using stairs instead of lifts, taking a short walk in the lunch break). Fitness and sport programmes are also a very common feature in wellness hotels, resorts and destinations. Some world class spas like LeSport are specifically focused on sports and fitness. Sport focused hotels and resorts are emerging, such as the Vitalclass Lanzarote Sport and Wellness Resort (Lanzarote, Canary Islands) or the Hotel Cala del Sol (Fuerteventura, Canary Islands).

New media and technology

The amount of time that the majority of individuals spend watching television, surfing the net or playing computer games has increased exponentially in recent years. Television watching is one of the few leisure activities that continues to increase. The health problems of watching too much television, especially for young children have been researched and documented for several years. Donnolly (2012) writes about a poll of those using social media technology, half of whom said their lives had been altered for the worse with falling confidence levels, inability to relax completely and to sleep, as well as relationship problems. Research quoted in Quigley (2011) demonstrated the addictive powers of internet, with 55 per cent of people saying they felt 'worried or uncomfortable' when they could not access their Facebook or email accounts. Scientists asked volunteers from 12 universities around the world to stay away from computers, mobile phones, iPods, television and radio for 24 hours. They found that the participants began to develop symptoms typically seen in smokers attempting to give up. The majority of those who enrolled in the study failed to last the full 24 hours without demanding their gadgets back.

Most people cannot easily be parted from their laptop, tablet or mobile phone, even on holiday. An American Express survey of top online activities of 2,000 people while on holiday also quoted in Quigley (2011) found that 79 per cent of travellers remain connected almost all or at least some of the time on their holiday. For example:

- 72 per cent read personal email.
- 49 per cent utilized internet sites to find trip-related information.
- 41 per cent did online banking.
- 27 per cent checked/updated their social-media profiles.
- 25 per cent stayed abreast of the news.
- 17 per cent checked work email.

One of the latest trends is 'Digital Detox Retreats'. As suggested by McCarthy (2012: 42), 'Spas and churches may be the only two places left in our society where we

are forced to separate from technology and spend some time in silent reflection'. In some cases, if travellers promise to leave all their digital devices behind, or check them in at front desk for the duration of the stay, they are rewarded with extra amenities, freebies or discounts of up to 20 per cent. Guests at the Renaissance Pittsburgh Hotel can book 'Zen and the Art of Detox' on some summer weekends. The Hotel Monaco in Chicago offers anyone who reserves its 'tranquility suite' the option to add a 'Technology Break'. Staff may offer guests who take the 'unplugged option' alternatives like board games and books. Some even unplug the TV and take out telephones. Several (smaller) hotels and resorts use as a unique selling proposition that they do *not* have wi-fi, and retreats ask guests to lock their mobile equipment upon arrival! The first internet addiction disorder clinic in the USA, the Heavensfield Retreat Center, was opened in 2009 offering a 45-day (reSTART) plan for internet-addicted youngsters. 'Tech-free tourism' is growing, but it might not be long before special rehabilitation programmes are needed for technology addicts!

On the positive side, there has been an increase in connectedness of people around the world in wellness communities on social media such as Facebook, even online retreats, workshops and classes (e.g. Deepak Chopra meditations or Kundalini yoga retreats). The following case study also shows how important the internet can be for medical tourism.

CASE STUDY 4.5
Patients using the internet for medical tourism
David G. Vequist, Michael Guiry and Emre Bolatkale

It is well documented that a very important driver behind the 'modern' medical tourism trend is the vast amount of information available on the internet (Vequist et al., 2011). Supporting this, Jotikasthira (2010) found that contemporary tourists 'now tend to rely more heavily on information from brochures or Internet websites'. In 2010, the Center for Medical Tourism Research (CMTR) surveyed over 2,000 potential medical tourists in the US and asked them, 'What sources have you used to research medical tourism countries/facilities/providers?'; the vast majority (75.3 per cent) of respondents choose the internet (Vequist, 2012). In Hungary, Árpási (2011) also found that 76 per cent of Europeans engaging in wellness tourism choose the internet as the most valuable source of information about destinations.

This would be particularly expected for medical tourists because of the critical decision to travel for health care. As Jotikasthira (2010) suggests, information-seeking behaviours can facilitate decision-making thus reducing the perceptions of risk. This author states: 'Given the high involvement and perceptions of risk associated with medical tourism . . . it is therefore reasonable to expect that medical tourists will engage in extensive information-search activities.' In the modern age, this is now probably the usual case for most health-care decision making. Pew, the research firm, found in 2011 that 80 per cent of internet users in the US (59 per cent of all adults) now look online for health information. This is the third most popular online activity, behind email and social media (Anonymous, 2011), in the survey. Thus, medical tourism service providers, such as the promotion agency CzechTourism, are launching internet campaigns targeting specific countries to attract more medical tourists (Johnstone, 2012).

A fascinating opportunity for the researchers was to analyse one month's (January, 2011) worth of searches from the medical tourism portal AllMedicalTourism (Bolatkale, 2012). This data yielded 1,783 observations across ten variables collected from potential medical tourists searching worldwide. The researchers found that 58 per cent of searchers were women, 43 per cent of searchers were between the ages of 40 to 59 years old (37 per cent were 18 to 39 years old), and the most common procedures requested were dental and cosmetic (41.2 per cent and 38.6 per cent respectively). Most searchers came from the US, the UK and Canada (1,087, 281, and 119 searches respectively).

Therefore, it is suggested that searching the internet for medical tourism is part of a growing and healthy trend of consumerism in health care. This is described by Scher (2013) in her touching piece describing her personal medical tourism experience to India: '. . . embryonic stem cell therapy, the most promising for my condition, is not available in the [US]. I have researched many types of stem cell therapies . . . but (I found that I had) to have an "approved" condition to use them.'

As consumers continue to grow more comfortable searching for possible health-care solutions (and overcoming boundaries) it appears that the medical tourism industry will probably grow as well.

The need or desire to downsize

Employment stability is a thing of the past these days and it is not uncommon for people to be suddenly made redundant and take time to find a new job. Sometimes, substantial financial compensation means that the individual concerned has the money to re-think what he or she would like to do in the future with regards to a career. In other cases, consequent financial hardship means a radical downsizing in terms of expenditure and lifestyle. However, in some cases, the desire to downsize comes from a need to escape from the 'rat race' of constant working, long hours, excessive stress and too much focus on material living. There are a surprising number of blogs and websites established by enthusiasts of 'voluntary simplicity'. The Trends Research Institute, a think-tank of educators and specialists that predict social trends, estimated that by 2010, 15 per cent of American adults would be living 'the simple life', the main reason being that they want to improve the quality of their life (Humphreys, 2007). The tendency of the over 30s to simplify their lives has led to the increased use of labels such as 'downsizers', 'downshifters' and 'simple livers'. Such people voluntarily give up stressful, high-paying jobs in favour of other kinds of 'luxuries' – a job that helps others, for example, or free time to enjoy hobbies, family and friends. Some people simply opt for a less stressful, time-consuming job and

subsequently spend less, whereas others change location completely and purchase a smaller home in a more natural, calmer environment. In some cases, people may decide to follow their dream of running a small retreat or yoga centre. Many of the holistic practitioners running retreat centres questioned by Kelly and Smith (2008) were motivated by the desire to simplify their lives.

Another reason to downsize might be to avoid 'burnout'. In her influential book *The Joy of Burnout*, Dina Glouberman describes the characteristics of burnout and how victims can rediscover the joy of living and this has always been one of the main aims of Skyros retreat holidays. Spas may also focus on this, for example the Alpina Dolomites Spa launched a Burnout Prevention course in 2012 which aims to improve sleep patterns, reduce exhaustion and stress-related problems in everyday life. Each guest receives a personally tailored treatment and activity plan for three, four, seven or 14 days in the hotel's spa and medical centre. Another way of improving life may be to de-clutter. There is even an Association of Professional Declutterers and Organisers in the UK. There are now many life coaching and lifestyle gurus who advocate clearing out any unwanted material possessions. The terms feng shui or zen are frequently used in the context of de-cluttering as it is thought that dealing with physical clutter can help to make way for a better emotional and spiritual life. De-cluttering is now even described as a therapy and workshops are becoming more and more mainstream and are starting to feature in holistic retreat programmes.

The slow movement

There is no doubt that modern living is fast, stressful, exhausting and that time has become a more precious commodity than almost any other. Ralph Keyes (1991) coined the word 'rushaholism' which is the compulsive need to be quick and to fill every spare minute with activity. This was followed a decade later by Carl Honoré's (2005) *In Praise of Slow*, which is not just about slowing down; it is about enjoying what we are doing and creating quality experiences. It can affect every area of our life, including work, education, food, parenting and travel. The slow food movement is closely connected to organic and sustainable farming, and slow travel aims to create more meaningful and authentic experiences in local places, such as so-called 'slow cities'. Slow travellers prefer to rent an apartment rather than staying in a hotel and enjoy activities such as walking, cycling, tasting local cuisine and visiting cafes in their neighbourhood which encourages interaction with local communities. There are several books devoted to slow tourism and travel (e.g. Dickinson and Lumsdon, 2010; Fullagar et al., 2012).

The idea of 'slow working' may seem undesirable, especially for employers! However, research shows that working less can mean working better. The Institute for Work and Technology (IAT) proved that long working hours are counter-productive, diminish motivation and efficiency, and cause mental health problems. With their 35–38 hour week, the French are actually some of the world's most productive workers per hour. Norway, Denmark, Finland and Sweden all work relatively short hours yet their economies are highly competitive. Americans work up to 12 weeks per year more than Europeans but are not as productive. Those who work long hours are more stressed, exercise less, are more inclined to eat junk food, spend less time with their families and friends, do not socialise, and devote fewer hours to their hobbies and recreation (Haw, 2011). Studies have shown that businesses that implement health and wellness programmes see improvements in productivity as well as staff morale, which decreases absenteeism, insurance costs and internal conflicts. A wellness diagnostic may be needed which analyses the health of the organisation, not just of its employees. This includes job satisfaction, workload balance, communications, and causes of stress in the workplace (Loszach, 2011). Companies may offer their employees incentive trips to spas, occupational wellness or stress management workshops in addition to improving general working conditions. GSS (2010) quotes a Harvard study which estimated that medical costs fall for every 3.27 dollars spent on workplace wellness programmes, while absenteeism costs fall by about 2.73 dollars for every dollar spent. One- to three-day executive physicals may also take place in a spa setting and can include massage, personal training, nutrition, meditation and psycho-therapy as well as medical assessments. However, it is not proven that these costly phys-icals can prevent disease. Delivering spa services to the workplace (e.g. massage, life coaching) may be more (cost) effective.

Environmental psychology and ecotherapy

Environmental psychologists try to determine what makes humans comfortable and how we can adjust our surroundings to reduce stress and enhance quality of life for as many people as possible. A great deal of the environmental psychology discipline is devoted to how environments affect society, believing that unspoiled nature can provide one of the best backdrops for human life. Unfortunately, most urban dwellers spend very little of their time in nature or green spaces. Research shows that when human beings are surrounded by parks and trees and flowers, their minds function more efficiently and their moods become more positive. In Part III of this book, Lóránt Dávid, Bulcsú Remenyik and Csaba Szűcs provide an overview of the diversity of wellness experiences that can be gained in the mountain areas of Hungary, and Parikshat Manhas Singh does the same for the Himalayas. Despite the significant geographical differences between these regions, they are both notable for their climate, herbal and spiritual healing possibilities.

Caroll (2004) argues that true sustainability must be based in spirituality and looks at religious communities dedicated to the environment. Taylor (2009) also believes that a good deal of the global sustainability movement has become like a religion, which he terms 'dark green religion'. Although this can become fanatical like all religions, it is also about a fervent recognition of the importance of belonging to and connecting to nature. In modern societies which have lost many of their traditional markers of stability (i.e. religion), there is arguably a need for returning to the spirituality of nature. Numerous articles are devoted to the benefits of tree-hugging, for example.

Howard Clinebell (1996) wrote a book about ecotherapy which he defines as healing and growth nurtured by healthy interaction with the earth. He also called it 'green therapy' and 'earth-centered therapy'. Ecotherapeutic work as Clinebell conceived it takes guidance from an Ecological Circle of three mutually interacting operations or dynamics:

- Inreach: receiving and being nurtured by the healing presence of nature, place, Earth.
- Upreach: the actual experience of this more-than-human vitality as we relocate our place within the natural world.
- Outreach: activities with other people that care for the planet.

Ecotherapy uses a range of practices in order to help us connect with nature and ultimately with our 'inner' nature. The principles behind ecotherapy are not new. In the past, mental health institutions were often situated in pleasant gardens and natural landscapes. Activities in nature can be extremely therapeutic, even contributing to the reduction of stress and depression. Richard Louv, an author who is part of the so-called 'New Nature Movement', first used the term 'nature deficit disorder', claiming that access to a healthy natural environment is essential for children and adults alike and that it should be a basic human right.

CASE STUDY 4.6
Ecotherapy: the green agenda for mental health (UK, 2007)

Three of the UK government's six key priorities set out in a 2007 Public Health White Paper were to increase exercise, improve mental health and reduce obesity believing that implementing a green agenda would go some way to achieving all three. For the first study, 108 people involved in green exercise activities with local Mind groups were surveyed. The activities included gardening projects (52 per cent), walking groups (37 per cent), conservation work (7 per cent), running (3 per cent) and cycling groups (1 per cent).

90 per cent of people who took part in Mind green exercise activities said that the combination of nature and exercise is most important in determining how they feel. 94 per cent of people commented that green exercise activities had benefited their mental health. Some of their comments included:

- 'I feel better about myself and have a sense of achievement.'

- 'I am more relaxed, have better focus of mind, greater coordination and greater self-esteem.'

- 'It improves my depression, helps me be more motivated and gives me satisfaction in doing things. Since starting the project I have been able to improve on my quality of life. Coming here has helped me overcome most of my problems.'

90 per cent of those surveyed commented that taking part in green exercise activities had benefited their physical health. Comments included:

- 'My fitness has improved, I feel refreshed and alive.'

- 'I feel as though I can do things without being tired. I am more active, I want to join in things and my body is looser and more agile.'

The second study looked at the role the environment plays in the effectiveness of exercise for mental wellbeing. Twenty members of local Mind associations took part in two walks in contrasting environments to test the impact on self-esteem, mood and enjoyment.

The green, outdoor walk was around Belhus Woods Country Park in Essex (south-east England), which has a varied landscape of woodlands, grasslands and lakes. The indoor walk was around a shopping centre in Essex.

- Self-esteem: outdoors improved 70 per cent; indoors 17 per cent.

- Depression: outdoors 71 per cent improved; indoors 45 per cent.

- Tension: outdoors 71 per cent improved; indoors 28 per cent.

(Mind, 2013)

Modern-day spas and retreats tend to be located in natural surroundings whenever possible. Susie Ellis mentions getting back to nature and 'earthing' as major new trends in spas and wellness in Part III of this book. This means promoting direct contact with the earth's electron-rich surface, such as walking or hiking barefoot. More classes (e.g. yoga, Tai Chi) are being held outside in natural surroundings. Spa design is becoming more focused on views of nature and some are even being built in remote wildernesses (e.g. 'pop-up' spas).

Towards a new spirituality

The role of religion in health and wellness is quite significant, as many of the rituals and traditions to do with bathing were a way of purifying the body and washing away sins. Ancient cultures also believed that spirits lived in certain springs and mineral waters and were responsible for healing sickness. Religion can dictate certain aspects of diet and other lifestyle factors, such as the daily routine. Many monks and nuns practise regular meditation (or prayer), fasting, and tend to rise and go to bed early. However, many Western capitalist societies have moved towards increasing secularisation, its citizens either disillusioned with, or alienated from, the faith that they were brought up with (if any). Relationships between religion and spirituality are notoriously difficult to define. The latter, however, appears to have gained strength in recent times and new explorations of the relationship between Western psychology and Eastern spiritualism have been gaining increased interest among researchers and practitioners for many years (e.g. Kowalski, 2001). Fosarelli (2002: 207) describes how, 'In addition to taking better care of their bodies, many people are searching for new ways to make themselves healthier by paying more attention to their emotional and spiritual lives'. As stated by Cohen (2008: 8):

Wellness now defines a form of secular spirituality that transcends formal religion. Spas and wellness resorts may therefore be conceptualised in cultural/sociological terms as modern day temples where people can experience rituals, learn to deepen

their personal wellness practices, raise their consciousness, become open to enhanced ways of being and deepen their experience of being alive.

Many people aspire towards finding their spiritual centre within another society and culture through travel. Many of these are using tourism as a means of visiting locations which are viewed as more spiritual than home (India and Thailand being good examples). In such locations, spiritual activities such as yoga, massage or meditation may be an integral part of everyday life, and many tourists want to learn how to change their whole philosophy of or approach to life. Brown (1998) explores the various engagements that a so-called 'spiritual tourist' may be involved in (e.g. visiting retreats, ashrams, gurus). Although there has been concern about the exploitative nature of spiritual tourism with its sometimes fake or charlatan gurus, the majority of tourists appear to find what they are looking for, and many find themselves staying longer than they intended to or returning periodically throughout their lives.

CASE STUDY 4.7
Ashram tourism

The Osho Commune International in Pune, India is a well-known ashram. Osho was an inspirational (sometimes controversial) guru who died in 1990 but left the legacy of his ashram as well as many publications. Up to 200,000 visitors from every religion come to visit the ashram every year and take part in the meditation programmes, other courses and everyday life in the Commune. The average age of visitors is 35 to 45 years old and 34 per cent have university degrees. 40 per cent of these visitors are Indian, but visitors from over 100 countries can be found visiting at any one time, either for a short visit or for many months. The religious backgrounds of Osho's disciples are as follows: 20 per cent are Jewish, 40 per cent are Christian, about 30 per cent Hindu, 5 per cent Shinto/Buddhist, and 5 per cent from other religious beliefs (Indiatravelite, 2007). In accordance with Osho's wishes participants in the Osho Commune International wear maroon most of the time and for evening meditation they wear white. They have to take AIDS tests before entering the Commune, which has unsurprisingly created speculation about the nature of activities within the centre!

As well as meditation auditoria, the facilities at the ashram include beautiful landscaped zen gardens, a large swimming lagoon and a sports facility. The Commune also runs an organic farming project. The ashram attracts many artists and musicians who provide cultural performances. Many meditations take place every day starting at sunrise, and other courses includes Western therapy approaches, healing arts, esoteric sciences, creative arts, martial arts, tantra, zen and sufism. One unique therapy designed by Osho is the Mystic Rose, a three-week course, in which the participant laughs for three hours a day the first week, cries for the same period the next week and sinks into silence the third week.

The Commune has sometimes been referred to as a 'Spiritual Disney Land' with Osho described as 'a guru of hedonism' or 'an impresario of spiritual Mardi Gras'. Osho was frequently criticised for his materialistic practices (saying that material poverty was not a spiritual value), for example, acquiring 93 Rolls-Royces, and was also accused of sex scandals (he attracted thousands of followers in the 1970s and 1980s with talk about sex as a path to super-consciousness). He and his followers set up a commune in Oregon before he was arrested and deported for immigration violations in 1985. Soon after, he returned to India and founded the still-flourishing Pune Commune. Despite the controversies his legacy lives on and there are still thousands of people who are subscribing to his philosophy of life, visiting his ashram and reading his numerous publications with translations published in 55 languages.

(Osho, 2008; Pune Commune, 2008)

Self-development trends

Although working hours seem to have increased in recent years, research by the Future Foundation in the UK (2007) showed that women participate, on average, in ten different leisure pursuits a year, compared to around six 20 years before that. They also suggest that the determination to fit in so many hobbies on top of work might be stoking the belief that people have less free time nowadays. Although watching television and surfing the net are the main pastimes for many people, the Foundation's research also showed a growing desire for self-improvement: around half of British adults believed that free time should be spent on worthy pastimes, such as visiting art galleries, rather than on frivolous activities. 'Personal fulfilment' was the top priority for 50 per cent of British adults, compared with 25 per cent in 1983.

> There's this emerging idea of ourselves as projects — we are no longer labelled by our education or gender, or born into a social situation that we then play out for the rest of our lives. We can do new things, pick up new skills, learn a new language. Because we're living longer, we have more time to think about who we really want to be. We are all asking ourselves, 'How can I get more out of my life?'

This has important implications for the wellness industry and might explain why there are growing numbers of people who are willing to spend their hard-earned cash on the pursuit of self-development, even on holiday. People may have less time to travel for leisure purposes, but they want to ensure that their trips create a memorable experience which they can savour for a long time. In many cases, there will be more trips but of a shorter duration (e.g. long weekends). In particular, women have more and more spending power. For example, Marks & Spencer (2005) showed how the 'Bridget Jones Generation's' spending power has increased by as much as 50 per cent in the last 20 years with an increase in women working full-time and earning 75 per cent of what men earn. They are

more likely to purchase 'Me' items such as spa days and beauty treatments, as well as joining gyms and consuming diet products. They may also take several holidays per year. Grainger (2007) describes how many 'time-poor, cash-rich' women are booking themselves on 'therapy holidays' complete with life coaches, nutritionists, psychologists and fitness instructors. Such holidays involve people getting away for a relatively long period of time (e.g. three weeks) and re-assessing their life using professional help. Such trips are expensive – as much as 6,000 pounds! Grainger (2007) describes how:

> A decade ago therapy holidays in five-star settings were rare. Alternative magazines and festivals advertised dozens of retreats offering courses in yoga, meditation, nutrition, art, dancing or self-improvement, but most were set in old, rambling country houses with shared rooms, basic vegetarian food and group tuition.

Although such holidays still exist, there is a definite shift towards the luxury market. The biggest boom seems to have been at the top end of the market, where counsellors are flown around the world to cater for rich clients and provide therapies for the famous.

However, Grainger (2007) also questions the extent to which a holiday can have long-lasting effects on people's lives, suggesting they create a 'geographic fallacy' that by changing location people can change what they are unhappy about. There is also a debate about whether holidays should be pleasurable or painful (e.g. retreats which use extreme emotional counselling such as the Hoffmann Process are exhausting, even traumatic). People often need post-holiday counselling when they return just to deal with the impacts of their trip! Some holistic holiday companies such as Skyros advise people not to make any major decisions about their life until at least two months after their return, and Cortijo Romero aims to send people away stronger and more in control of their lives, rather than weaker and more vulnerable.

TABLE 4.3 Three lifestyle trends in the UK

According to a national lifestyle survey the following three lifestyle trends can become influential (Mintel UK, 2011):

- Show It All Down: The faster life's pace, the greater the need to slow it all down (at least once in a while) and they may partner to 'Switch Off' trend where people seek a degree of disconnection. For this segment facilities should promote slowness: conveying superior quality of an experience, product or service, as well as the therapeutic value of the journey.

- Alpha Mothers: Mothers are being redefined as empowered individuals who happen to have children. Marketing should streamline their life: using technology (e.g. smartphones, e-readers) to reduce the (house)workload and create niche communities.

- Girly Men: Men have become more comfortable defining masculinity on their own terms. Avoid pigeonholing men! Marketers should encourage the kind of identity fluidity women have been enjoying for decades.

Source: Mintel UK, 2011.

Government and social tourism

Governments approach travel and tourism very differently. Some support by funded schemes, such as the so-called holiday vouchers, fall under this approach. Companies, trade unions, associations and even NGOs can apply for state (co-)funded schemes from which their employees or members can receive holiday vouchers. These vouchers can be redeemed during holidays (in hotels, restaurants, etc.). Among other beneficiaries, baths, spas or spa hotels can also benefit from this funded spending. Furthermore, governments through the state and enterprises, through private health insurance funds and companies can also finance health treatments and even trips. These could aim at prevention, healing or recuperation. Health treatments based on natural assets can be heavily subsidised, so a whole trip can cost relatively little. This is one of the main problems medical destinations face: the guest mix is dominated by segments with low-spending capacities. This leaves very little room for raising funds for reconstruction or upgrading. Some governments support social tourism, as discussed by Riikka Ilves and Raija Komppula in their case study in Part III of this book.

As prices can differ from country to country, operators in a cheaper country try to attract patients from other countries. This is the issue which the European Union faces. In its Eastern European member countries health related services are much cheaper, but this does not necessarily mean that patients should then go to a cheaper country. Political and economic interests are competing with each other, since state health insurance funds do not tend to finance treatments in another country. It could have a negative effect on the home countries' health sector.

The Eastern Mediterranean Regional Health System Observatory (EMRHSO, 2013), for example, provides information and support about the outsourcing of medical services to the countries in the region. Several governments, for example Lebanon, has schemes for interested health-care providers. Through these initiatives patients can be sent to third countries for medical treatment. The process for outsourcing of non-clinical support services is supported by bid prices and the value of technical proposal.

At supranational level probably one of the most influential decisions was the approval of the European Union's Cross-border Healthcare Directive (EU, 2011), which states as a general rule patients will be allowed to receive health care in another member state and be reimbursed up to the level of costs that would have been assumed by the member state of affiliation. If this health care had been provided on its territory, instead of reimbursing the patient, member states of affiliation may also decide to pay the health-care provider directly.

How to live better?

This chapter has suggested that modern living is less than ideal, so how should people live better? ISPA (2013b) provides a list of 'Ten Things You Can Do To Live Well', only one of which includes a spa visit!

1   Get eight hours of sleep.
2   Eat and drink healthy – organic fruits and veggies and water.

3   Exercise – yoga, tai chi, walking.

4   Meditate/breathe.

5   Enjoy nature and beautiful things.

6   Nurture your body with a spa visit – massage, facials, body wraps.

7   Learn or teach someone else.

8   Volunteer – give back to your community and your Earth.

9   Avoid negativity – from yourself or from others.

10   Love – yourself and others around you.

The New Economics Foundation in 2008 suggested the following 'Five Ways to Wellbeing':

1   Connect (with people, not technology): 'social isolation increases ill health and death rates'.

2   Be active: 'not being active makes us depressed because we are evolved to be active'.

3   Take notice: 'the more you relate to nature, the more positive your emotions and the greater your life satisfaction'.

4   Keep learning: 'Those with more open minds are happier, not only because they stay mentally vigorous but also because they gain a renewed sense of mastery'.

5   Give: 'It can be about thinking ahead and how to give a healthy planet to future generations, as yet unborn'.

Euromonitor (2012) assumes that global consumers became so concerned with health because:

- An ageing population perpetuates an increasing interest in general well-being, or preventive care, providing some important pockets of opportunity.
- Anti-ageing products are an example of this; defying the recession.
- Consumer interest in wellness is no longer just about looking good and exercising, but about holistic and preventative health.
- Brands have a lot to gain by catering to ageing consumers around the world.

This summarises many of the issues mentioned in this chapter relating to sustainability, nature, community, fitness, technology, as well as keeping the intellect alive, an essential part of increasing longevity according to Deepak Chopra (1993).

Finally, an Australian nurse working in palliative care called Bonnie Ware recorded the most common regrets of the dying. These are her findings as quoted by Steiner (2012):

1   **I wish I'd had the courage to live a life true to myself, not the life others expected of me.**
   'This was the most common regret of all. When people realise that their life is almost over and look back clearly on it, it is easy to see how many dreams have gone unfulfilled. Most people had not honoured even a half of their dreams and

had to die knowing that it was due to choices they had made, or not made. Health brings a freedom very few realise, until they no longer have it.'

2   **I wish I hadn't worked so hard.**

'This came from every male patient that I nursed. They missed their children's youth and their partner's companionship. Women also spoke of this regret, but as most were from an older generation, many of the female patients had not been breadwinners. All of the men I nursed deeply regretted spending so much of their lives on the treadmill of a work existence.'

3   **I wish I'd had the courage to express my feelings.**

'Many people suppressed their feelings in order to keep peace with others. As a result, they settled for a mediocre existence and never became who they were truly capable of becoming. Many developed illnesses relating to the bitterness and resentment they carried as a result.'

4   **I wish I had stayed in touch with my friends.**

'Often they would not truly realise the full benefits of old friends until their dying weeks and it was not always possible to track them down. Many had become so caught up in their own lives that they had let golden friendships slip by over the years. There were many deep regrets about not giving friendships the time and effort that they deserved. Everyone misses their friends when they are dying.'

5   **I wish that I had let myself be happier.**

'This is a surprisingly common one. Many did not realise until the end that happiness is a choice. They had stayed stuck in old patterns and habits. The so-called "comfort" of familiarity overflowed into their emotions, as well as their physical lives. Fear of change had them pretending to others, and to their selves, that they were content, when deep within, they longed to laugh properly and have silliness in their life again.'

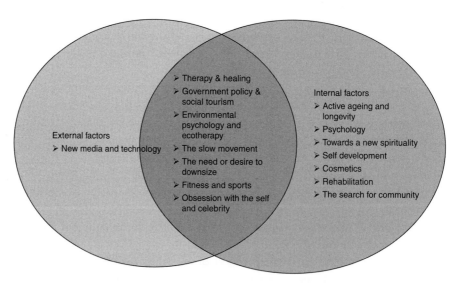

FIGURE 4.1 Internal and external factors affecting lifestyle

One of the latest indices of a long, healthy and happy life is the Happy Planet Index (New Economics Foundation, 2012). However, this research emphasises that it is not enough for nations to focus on the life expectancy and experienced well-being of their citizens. Their carbon footprint is also an important indicator of their contribution to a happy planet. Perhaps not unsurprisingly, many of those countries which have the longest life expectancy and the highest levels of experienced well-being are also those with the biggest carbon footprint. Later chapters (e.g. Chapter 7) focus in more detail on the issue of sustainability, but as mentioned at the start of this chapter, Western, capitalist and materialistic models of living are arguably not the most beneficial for the future of the planet and its people.

Conclusion

The health, wellness and travel industries cannot be expected to deliver the perfect life to individuals who have no desire to increase their longevity, enhance their quality of life and happiness or to flourish more. As stated by Chopra (1993), this requires individual determination, and as said by McCarthy (2012: 130), 'self-change is possible and some people are clearly better at it than others'. However, this chapter has shown that there are numerous tools that can be used to enhance wellness if people should want to avail themselves of it, including travel. As societies become more sceptical about traditional forms of medicine, they are turning to alternative sources of wellness, such as popular psychology or self-help books. In some cases, this may lead to downsizing, voluntary simplicity, and slower living and travelling. In others, it may mean the integration of more spiritual practices into their life. Some may seek community to alleviate feelings of isolation or alienation in society. Travel experiences are an integral part of this process, especially in cases where people need to engage in intensive programmes and workshops to change their lives (e.g. psychological or spiritual retreats), to rest and relax (e.g. spas), or to deal with stress away from the workplace (e.g. occupational therapy, life coaching).

Managing and marketing health, wellness and medical tourism

Demand and motivation of tourists

Instead of an ecstatic high, people want meditative tranquility and spiritual experiences. People are exhausted by life in the experience society. Opportunities for relaxation will become more important than entertainment.

(Schweder, 2008: 171)

Relatively little research has been undertaken about the profiles and motivations of health and wellness tourists. It is generally easier to look at the motivations of tourists and patterns of behaviour or type of activity than to identify specific segments or target markets. However, there are some distinctive patterns and segments which have been established, such as the large number of women and baby boomers who engage in health and wellness activities and tourism. It is important to understand the latest lifestyle trends as discussed in Chapter 4 in order to comprehend current leisure and actual or potential tourism trends. General consumer segmentation models are often useful when identifying the possible markets for health and wellness tourism. This chapter will also consider new and growth markets in health and wellness tourism and suggest ways in which they can be targeted more effectively. Finally, the chapter focuses on cross-cultural issues and some of the challenges of attracting and satisfying guests of different nationalities.

Profiling health and wellness visitors

Nolen (2012) provides an interesting introduction to how customers may see the differences between wellness and health care. This comparison gives some background information to the difficulties of how the profiling of visitors can take place.

Table 5.2 gives a general indication of the types of visitors who use the current range of health and wellness products and services. This is by no means definitive, but it shows some of the trends in different regions of the world.

TABLE 5.1 How customers see wellness and health care

Wellness	Health care
• Healthy	• Sick or in decline
• Emotional	• Rational
• 'I want to . . .'	• 'You need to . . .'
• Two-way	• One-way
• Carrots	• Sticks
• Means to an end	• An end in itself

TABLE 5.2 Types of health and wellness products and typical visitors

Type of wellness product/location	Typical activities	Health domain(s)	Typical visitors
Traditional spas and hot springs (e.g. Central and Eastern Europe, Japan, Italy)	Sitting in thermal and healing waters	Physical, curative, medical	Older people (55+) with specific diseases or complaints
Spa and wellness hotels and day spas (e.g. UK, US, Caribbean, South East Asia)	Beauty treatments, relaxing massage, steam rooms, saunas, jacuzzi	Cosmetic, leisure, relaxation	High income visitors, business and leisure tourists
Purpose built recreational spas (e.g. Austria, Germany, Netherlands)	Swimming pools, thermal but not medical waters, themed saunas and steam rooms, jacuzzis, fitness activities	Physical, relaxation, fun	Active visitors, couples, younger visitors (18–30), families with children
Seaside resorts and thalassotherapy centres (e.g. France, Israel, Greece)	Hydrotherapy, salt inhalations, salt scrubs, seaweed wraps, tanning	Physical, curative, cosmetic	High-income hotel guests, older visitors
Holistic retreat centres (e.g. Greece, Spain, USA, Australia)	Yoga, massage, creative, spiritual and psychological workshops	Physical, mental, psychological, social, creative, spiritual	Average age 35–55, more likely to be women
Yoga centres (e.g. India, US, Canada, Europe)	Yoga, meditation, chanting	Physical, mental, spiritual	Mainly professional women aged 25–55

Meditation retreats (e.g. Thailand, India)	Meditation, fasting, chanting	Mental, spiritual	'Baby boomers' (aged 40–70), hippies, backpackers
Pilgrimage centres (e.g. Spain, France)	Visiting spiritual landscapes, religious buildings, walking pilgrimage routes	Physical, spiritual	All ages but increasingly under 30, not necessarily religious
Medical centres and clinics (e.g. Hungary, South Africa, India)	Operations, cosmetic surgery, dentistry, special treatments	Physical, cosmetic	Affluent segments usually aged 30+ travelling for medical treatments or interventions
Destination spas (global)	Lifestyle oriented services (both physical and psychological)	Total (holistic) health	Affluent segments usually aged 30+ singles and couples

Sources: ISPA data 2003–8; Monteson and Singer, 2004; Devereux and Carnegie, 2006; Lehto et al., 2006; Puczkó and Bachvarov, 2006; Smith and Kelly, 2006; Connell, 2012; Kelly, 2012.

From this table, we can see that there are a high number of women and people over 30 involved in wellness activities, but relatively few men and young people. The reasons for this have not been explored in great depth, but of course women have always been far more interested in physical appearance, weight issues, make-up and hair-care than men. This is partly due to social expectation, fashion, media pressure, and so forth, but it has meant that day spas and beauty salons are more regularly frequented by women. Women are also more open to discussing their feelings and emotions in a public forum, according to popular psychological research (e.g. Gray, 2002). Women traditionally played the role of carer in many families and therefore took primary responsibility for the health and well-being of family members, for example, medication and nutrition, even encouraging exercise and relaxation. Although many women now work full-time and cannot devote as much time to supporting husbands and children, it is still often expected that women should somehow hold families together and play a nurturing role. It is well documented that working mothers have very little time to themselves for leisure activities and relaxation, as they still tend to do the majority of domestic work and childcare. It is not surprising therefore that more women crave or need specialist wellness services and time out from busy schedules to look and feel better. The 2012–13 Global Wellness and Spa Tourism Monitor data, however, shows that couples became the number one segment for wellness and spa services followed by women, and families (The Tourism Observatory for Health, Wellness and Spa, 2013).

In comparison to women, men may prefer different modes of relaxation, some of which have a wellness dimension such as sports or fitness activities. The labelling that is used to target men needs to take a different form, as it is unlikely that beauty or pampering would sound appealing. For example, spas can sell their services to men, but as tools for relaxation, stress relief or adventure. Popular activities include massage, saunas, steam rooms and gym facilities. Young people (e.g. 18–30), on the other hand, might not see the need for wellness when they are often in peak physical condition, suffer relatively little stress and have few responsibilities compared to the over-30s. They would not be attracted by any kind of services that imply sickness or disease and which primarily attract elderly visitors (e.g. medical spas), and luxury spas or beauty salons are usually too expensive for them, but male grooming and skin-care have been growing at exponential rate. However, there are rising levels of depression in young people aged 18–25 especially men in many Western countries (Mullholland, 2005). This could be attributed to many factors, such as peer pressure or media pressure to be attractive, rich and successful; the loss of a clear gender role with the increasing emancipation of women; or too much stress and competition within education or the workplace. For marketing purposes, words like 'fitness', 'chilling', 'escape' or 'fun' can be more attractive than wellness for young people, and even 'rehab' which has become trendy amongst celebrities who need to detox after indulging in party lifestyles for too long!

Typical consumer research focuses on a number of factors, some of which have already been discussed in Chapter 4. Demographic segments are clearly important such as age, gender, income level, life stage, geography, religion or education. In addition, psycho-graphic segments become even more important for wellness tourism analysis such as lifestyle, values, occupation, personality and hobbies. The life-stage of individuals or the aspiration to be part of 'tribes' makes a difference to their needs. For example, young people may have relatively few physical health problems, will be unencumbered by family responsibilities, tend to have more free time but will have less spending power. They are most likely to travel with friends seeking fun (e.g. in aqua parks or fun waters), to enjoy music festivals perhaps with chill-out zones, or in some cases to backpack in spiritual destinations (e.g. India) and try out yoga, meditation or other practices which are associ-ated with a 'cool', hippie-like identity. Busy middle-aged executives tend to have very little spare time because of long working hours and family responsibilities, but have high spending power and a willingness to pay for short-term pampering and luxury (e.g. day or weekend spas and massage) or work/life balance courses and stress management (e.g. life coaching). Elderly travellers will have less spending power but more time, and they may suffer from more physical health problems. Therefore medical spas or wellness cruises may provide the best form of relaxation, although physical mobility problems may hinder their ability to travel.

Motivations for visiting spas or fitness centres can differ greatly as the research by Mintel/Toluna (Mintel, 2011) showed. Whereas in Germany the (rather rich) supply of saunas and steam rooms in spas counts for 16 per cent of the market, in the UK it is only 8 per cent. The reasons for having a massage, however, is mainly to relax and de-stress, regardless of the country in question.

Euromonitor (2012) sees the ageing populations of the world as having untapped potential for health and wellness products and services. It is believed that the highest revenue from anti-agers will come from China, despite the country's relatively low disposable income levels. As well as targeting ageing consumers, new market strategies aim to target younger females, men and mid to low income segments. The following case study gives examples of children's spas.

CASE STUDY 5.1
Children's spas

Many popular spas around the world have started to offer treatments to children. One example is the Hello Kitty Spa in Dubai which has some special treatments for kids and their mums too, such as the 'Princess' and 'Queen' treatments. This includes manicures and nail painting, as well as hand and foot massages and facials.

Children aged four to fourteen can use the Vanya Kids Spa in Delhi, and newborns are even welcome in the Leonia Holistic Destination in Hyderabad. Treatments are offered which pamper both mums and babies, although parents are usually present during all treatments. The treatments have interesting names to attract the children, such as 'Bookworm' for a head and neck massage and 'Backpack' for a back massage. The spa also offers Fun Yoga.

Little Lambs was awarded the best kids' spa in 2010 and 2011 as it has a holistic approach combining paediatric and alternative medicine. The spa offers everything from massage to reflexology to body scrubs. The spa also organises birthday parties and graduation parties, when the kids can try different massages and salon services.

Other examples include the Karma Kandara spa in Indonesia with special packages for mothers and daughters. The One and Only Le Saint Geran Spa in Mauritius does the same, but also offers packages to boys (Coutinho, 2012).

There is an organic kids' spa called Pretty in Pink in Oakville, USA, which marked their first anniversary 'with all things pink, pretty and Paraben-free'..Pretty in Pink Spa is for girls between the ages of five and 18 and offers camps (e.g. during school breaks) with special themes and programmes (and mothers enjoy a 5 per cent discount of spa services!). Themes include:

- Midnight in Paris

- Health Nut

- And the Oscar Goes to . . .

- Going Green

- European Artists

Demand and motivations of health tourists

Götz (2008) raises an interesting idea about why many people like to bathe in waters. He refers to the two theories for evolution. One (the more accepted one) bases its approach on savanna-theory or Darwinism, while the other one assumes that water monkeys were the predecessors of human beings. Some etologists believe that some humanoids had to adapt to a lifestyle that was very much based on sea and sea-life. This would explain the propensity of almost all civilisations and societies, ancient and modern, to engage in some form of water-based activities for health and well-being. Water-based activities have also traditionally been linked to spirituality, especially at times when it was believed that 'magic' spirits lived in thermal waters and were healing the body.

Chapter 4 examined in depth the 'push' and 'pull' factors which are driving the growing interest in health and wellness products and holidays. As a summary, these include the factors listed in Table 5.3.

TABLE 5.3 Push and pull factors for health and wellness tourists

Push factors	Pull factors
• Mental and physical exhaustion	• The wish to be healthier
• Stress because of work and a busy life	• The wish to be happier
• Lack of trust in traditional medical services	• The desire for active ageing and longevity
• Loss of a sense of community and loneliness	• The need to build self-esteem and a positive self-image
• Obsession with self and celebrities	• The longing to be slimmer, more beautiful and to look younger
• Loss of religion and the desire for spirituality	• The need for rehabilitation because of addictions
• Addiction to technology and the inability to switch off (literally!)	• The desire to lead a simpler life and slow down
• Not enough time spent outside or in nature	• The desire for self-development

Euromonitor (2012) begins its report about health and wellness consumers by saying that 'Global wellness is no longer just about looking good'. This signifies a move beyond just beauty products and trying to look younger (although these are still very important to the majority of consumers, especially women) towards holistic and preventative health.

Life stage is an important determinant of consumer and tourist behaviour. Younger people, single and childless people may have very different needs to those who are in a relationship or married, who have families or who are in the later stages of their life. According to the findings of the Wellness Lifestyle Insights study (Hartman Group, 2007), the key life stages and situations that make people in the USA interested and motivated in wellness were the following:

- high school athletics;
- going to college;
- pregnancy/having kids;
- ageing/milestone birthdays;
- personal/vicarious health experience.

Clearly, one's education can affect the propensity to be interested in sports or fitness in later life. Leaving home and going to college represents an independent stage in one's life, when it is often possible to engage in more activities in and around a study programme. Pregnancy makes women more aware of their bodies and many tend to eat more healthily, give up smoking, alcohol and caffeine and to begin a programme of specialised exercise (e.g. yoga, pilates, swimming). Turning 40 or 50 can make people aware of the need to look after themselves as they reach middle age, and so-called mid-life crises are not uncommon, often resulting in the desire to retreat for a while. Many people also have a kind of epiphany if they have a serious illness and start to look after themselves better and to value every moment of their life.

According to Younis (2011) most Middle Eastern patients usually travel for factors unrelated to cost:

- quality of health care;
- skills and reputations of the health-care providers;
- technology and availability of advanced medical services (e.g. heart transplant).

Tourism Australia's (2007) research shows that well-being travel is growing, with the motivations listed in Table 5.4.

TABLE 5.4 Well-being travel motivations in Australia		
Emotional triggers	Trip focus	Take home result
'My life lacks meaning'	Learning and finding the direction	Renewed self through awareness of direction
'I know the goal, but I'm stuck'	The goal: to detox, get fit/ healthy, enhance spirituality	Renewed self through progress towards the goal
'I am worn down by everyday life'	To replenish their own needs	Renewed self through enhanced well-being
'My relationship with my partner is worn down by everyday life'	One another and the relationship	Renewed relationship
'I need a reward/ to celebrate'	Indulging themselves	Renewed self
Source: Adapted from Tourism Australia, 2007.		

Alison van den Eynde and Adrian Fisher discuss the concept of well-being and well-being travel in Australia in more detail in Part III of this book. This shows that many people reach a stage where they feel stuck or stagnant in their life and want to improve one or several aspects of it. It may be a desire to find themselves again after looking after others, to re-connect with another person or people, to reward themselves for their hard work, to escape routine, to learn some new good habits, or simply to relax and recharge. Voigt et al. (2011) identified three different types of wellness tourists in Australia: beauty spa, lifestyle resort and spiritual retreat visitors. Six benefit factors emerged from their factor analysis. These were:

- transcendence;
- physical health and appearance;
- escape and relaxation;
- important others and novelty;
- re-establish self-esteem;
- indulgence.

Although all participants in the study were seeking transformation of the self, each group of tourists placed different emphasis on physical, psychological or spiritual transformations. Each group also differed significantly in terms of their demographic and travel behaviour characteristics.

GSS (2010) reminds us that it is important to distinguish between the so-called 'sickness' and the 'wellness' industries, quoting Paul Zane Pilzer's book *The Wellness Revolution* (2002):

- The sickness industry is reactive, providing products and services for people with disease and therefore people are customers by necessity.
- The wellness industry is proactive, providing products and services to healthy people with the goal of making them feel even healthier, look better and prevent sickness from developing. They are voluntary customers.

Euromonitor (2011b) listed the main motivational drivers and challenges of medical tourism:

- *Drivers:*
  - lack of insurance;
  - lower cost;
  - better quality care;
  - procedure unavailable at home;
  - shorter waiting periods.
- *Challenges:*
  - concerns about quality;
  - logistical issues;
  - lack of follow-up support and care;

- ○ uncertainty over malpractice issues;
- ○ crowding out of domestic patients.

Segmenting health and wellness consumers

Segments for health and wellness tourism tend to be related to segments for health and wellness products and services more generally. The National Marketing Institute in the USA has specialised in market research for wellness and sustainability since 1990 and develops segmentation models. For example, 'Well-beings' who tend to be the most health proactive and use many health modalities, take supplements and consume green and organic products. For some years the NMI's LOHAS segment has been considered to be important, especially in the United States. This stands for lifestyles of health and sustainability and refers to a wide range of industries, corporate activities and products/services that are designed to be environmentally conscious, sustainable, socially responsible, and/or healthier – both for people and the planet. Lohas.com (2013) estimates that there is a $290 billion US marketplace for goods and services focused on health, the environment, social justice, personal development and sustainable living, and that approximately 13–19 per cent of the adults in the US are currently considered LOHAS consumers. LOHAS identifies different sectors: personal health; green building; ecotourism; natural lifestyles; alternative transport; alternative energy. Personal health is estimated to be worth $117 billion and includes natural, organic and nutritional products, integrative health care, dietary supplements and mind/body/spirit products. From the same segmentation group, NATURALITES are also considered a top-tier segment. They are committed to their own personal health, and consume many healthy and natural goods. They are also highly attracted to mind/body/spirit philosophies, including prayer and meditation. Their view of health includes not just their physical health, but their mental and spiritual health as well.

Cohen (2008: 13) describes this range of consumer trends under the banner of 'conshumanism', which could be defined as 'conscious and humane consumption' or 'consumption with maximal awareness, efficiency and enjoyment and minimal pain, energy, waste and pollution'. However, he suggests that it might be difficult for spas to attract or engage the LOHAS consumer, as spas may be seen as embracing 'wasteful luxury rather than sustainable health and wellness' (p. 14).

The NMI segments Baby Boomers aged 45 and over, emphasising which members of this group are most likely to be focused on their physical body, their 'higher consciousness' or spirituality, intellectual challenges, as well as those with a mental attitude which does not see age as a barrier or limitation. This segmentation model is especially useful as the average age of most health tourists (including medical, wellness and spa) is around 45. GSS (2010) also emphasises the importance of the baby-boomer generation (aged 40–70). This age group is the most likely to use complementary and alternative medicine (CAM), although there is also a growing number of younger people aged 18–39 becoming more interested. However, the report shows that CAM use in the USA was growing fastest amongst the 70–85+ age groups between 2002–7. CAM is also more likely to be used by women. The study included chiropractic or osteopathic manipulation, massage, acupuncture, naturopathy, Ayurveda, meditation, yoga, Chi Kung, deep breathing exercises and guided imagery.

Deloitte (2012a) produced a report which identified six segments of health-care consumer segments in the USA:

- The '*content and compliant*' (22 per cent) and '*sick and savvy*' segments (14 per cent) tend to behave like 'patients', not particularly inclined to challenge a professional's recommendation and query clinicians.
- The '*casual and cautious*' are simply not engaged because they don't see the need (34 per cent).
- '*Out and about*' consumers actively seek and use alternative, non-Western medicine, often without the knowledge of their clinicians (9 per cent).
- '*Online and onboard*' (17 per cent) use online tools and mobile applications to assess providers and compare treatment options and provider competence.
- '*Shop and save*' (4 per cent) is the value purchaser who is not content with paying more than necessary under any non-emergency scenario.

Only 6–8 per cent of consumers across all age segments fall into the 'out and about' category, which would arguably be the one most likely to be receptive to wellness products. However, a further 14–18 per cent are 'online and onboard' so would look independently for alternative health-care treatments or services in addition to taking advice from a medical practitioner. 46 per cent of 'out and about' consumers prefer alternative/holistic approaches to standard medical care compared to only 1 per cent of 'content and compliant' consumers.

According to a study by Konesens (2010) approximately 2 per cent of the US population have already travelled abroad for medical services, most of whom had cosmetic, orthopaedic or bariatric/weight loss surgeries. Some 55 per cent of respondents mentioned concerns about safety and quality of care as reasons why they would not consider travelling abroad for medical services. Interestingly, only 16 per cent mentioned that they were not familiar with the concept!

As another special segment, the Muslim populations are not homogeneous in their lifestyle and daily life. However, in general, health-care providers should consider some of the following expectations when treating Muslim patients:

- special diet;
- gender issues;
- availability of the information regarding the location;
- direction to Mecca;
- hygiene issues for prayer and cleaning;
- social issues.

(after Younis, 2011)

GSS (2010) identifies three segments of health and wellness consumers, which have been developed from ISPA's (2006) categorisation of spa-goers:

- Periphery – sickness reactors, not active spa-goers (not proactive in looking after their health or not yet engaging in a healthier lifestyle, although the aspiration is there).
- Mid-level – moderately involved in a health and wellness lifestyle and purchase large amounts of conventional and health and wellness-specified products.
- Core – most involved in a health and wellness lifestyle and serve as trendsetters for other consumers. Health and wellness is a major life focus for them.

Over time, many consumers in the periphery group are likely to move towards more holistic and proactive lifestyles.

The global market research company GfK started a socio-lifestyle research project a few years ago. The objective of data collection was to identify the main types of lifestyle and the corresponding characteristics. Although questions about health tourism demand were not included in the survey, these lifestyle categories could give us some directions as to who may become a customer and why for the different forms of health tourism. (Note that market studies on motivations and drivers are more regular in other industries than in tourism, i.e. travel and tourism can learn a lot from segmentation-oriented studies carried out in the service industries.) This information can also provide the necessary links to and with accompanying industries, such as cosmetics, travel gear, transportation. The GFK Roper (2010) lifestyles distinguish eight groups based on lifestyles and attitudes (see Figure 5.1).

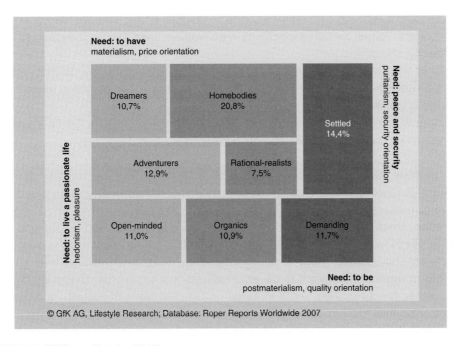

FIGURE 5.1 GFK Roper lifestyles (2010)
Source: GFK AG, Lifestyle Research; Database: Roper Reports Worldwide (2007).

We might assume from this model that the most likely consumers to engage in health and wellness tourism would be 'Adventurers', 'Open-minded' and 'Organics'. The tendency towards more organic or green buying behaviour is increasingly rapidly as the earlier section on the LOHAS segment explained.

Lifestyle segmentation may also draw on the geography, topography or culture of a country or region. For example, for wellness tourism in Eastern Finland where there are many lakes and forests and the emphasis is on outdoor recreation. Kangas and Tuohino (2008) suggest the following segmentation:

- *Careless of holistic well-being*: mostly men, under 35 years old, little interest in mental well-being, sport or fitness. They enjoy sleeping and sauna (note that saunas are an integral part of life for most Finns and not a luxury spa activity!).
- *Work and health-orientated nature people*: over 85 per cent women mainly 35–44 years old, interested in sport, fitness, health and nature, as well as mental well-being and balance. Tend to eat healthy food, go to the gym and do Nordic walking.
- *Seekers of mental well-being*: A third of respondents were men, a third of respondents had children. Over 60 per cent are aged 25–44. They are most interested in domestic life, mental well-being and balance.
- *Cultural appreciators who exercise in nature*: Interested in nature, health and sport rather than domestic life. Almost 75 per cent were women mostly aged 45–65. One third lived alone, one third has children, and 25 per cent were empty nester couples. They tend to enjoy cross-country skiing and winter swimming.
- *Family-orientated*: Love and family are the most important things in life, but nature, sport and health are also rather important. Spiritual and mental well-being are less important. 75 per cent of respondents were women, aged 18–44. They tend to enjoy downhill skiing.
- *Home-orientated*: enjoy domestic activities, cooking and handicrafts. Mostly 45–54-year-olds and empty nesters if they had children. Less interest in gyms than in walking or outdoor recreation.
- *Spirituality and nature appreciators*: 72 per cent women, mainly 55–65 years old, many of whose children have left home. Walking is a popular activity.

Many of these segments could be used in other contexts, but the wellness activities chosen by the participants such as cross-country skiing, Nordic walking and winter swimming (e.g. in lakes) are very typical of the region and would not be relevant elsewhere (e.g. the Mediterranean, Asia). While this is an excellent cluster analysis and the methodology could be used in a more international context, the factors will vary according to geographical and cultural context. There is clearly a need for research at national level in most countries or regions which want to develop wellness tourism in order to identify clusters or segments. It may also be useful to focus on different types of tourism, such as spa tourism or spiritual tourism.

The Institut für Freizeitwissenschaften published a report in 2008 about the health tourism trends until 2020 in Germany (Sydow, 2011). According to the forecasts on target segments, these were the factors influencing holiday choice:

- leisure time: time to recover, recharge batteries to maintain health status, possibility to compensate daily deficits;
- demographic change:
  ○ strong increase of leisure time of the elderly until 2020: women + 9 per cent, men: + 18 per cent
  ○ risk of having chronic diseases increases
  ○ elderly people have to adapt to increasing physical weakness
- wish to spend leisure time appropriately:
  ○ you can only enjoy your leisure time when you are in a good physical condition
- employment:
  ○ increasing retirement age, increasing stress
  ○ feeling under pressure
  ○ maintaining good physical condition is a must
- general lifestyle:
  ○ living at high speed
  ○ unhealthy nutrition
  ○ physical inactivity
  ○ being overweight
  ○ subject to stress
  ○ alcohol and cigarette consumption.

Spa tourists

Coyle Hospitality Group's (2011) research on spa-going respondents from 34 countries showed the following as the primary reasons for visiting a spa:

- relaxation/stress management (88 per cent);
- hair/nail/waxing maintenance (59 per cent);
- improve appearance (47 per cent);
- skin care (37 per cent);
- gift (31 per cent);
- pain management (22 per cent);
- social experience (19 per cent);
- other (3 per cent);
- medical reasons (3 per cent).

ISPA (2013c) also states that the number one reason that people go to spas is to reduce or relieve stress and relax. McCarthy (2013) describes how spas offer a precious refuge and safe space in which to disconnect from the world and technology, to be touched and cared for by another person, and to bring the mind, body and spirit back into alignment.

The National Tourism Development Authority in Ireland (2007) produced a Health and Wellness Strategy in which they note that in the UK and Ireland indulgence is one of the main reasons people visit a spa. Research shows that there is an increased need for consumers to feel better. This desire is driven by a hectic commuter culture, stress-related health problems and a tiring pace of life. Irish spa-goers have two main reasons for visiting spas: to pamper and indulge themselves and to escape. They also identified six discrete segments for health and wellness:

- *fun seekers* (going away with friends and enjoying themselves – not spa regulars or experts);
- *occasional pamperers* (taking time out from a busy, stressful schedule – spas are a rare treat);
- *relaxers* (seeking rest and time out – spas as escapism);
- *serenity seekers* (seeking peace, understanding and self-acceptance – wellness as lifestyle);
- *beauty queens* (interest in looking good and being glamorous);
- *help seekers* (looking for change in their lives).

Azara et al. (2007) showed that the average age of typical visitors to the Devonshire Spa in the UK was 41 for men and 45 for women. Most people were looking for relaxation, escape, a new experience and personal/individual fulfilment. Many liked to be alone there, especially women. Men in particular emphasised the stress-relief aspect.

Mak et al. (2009) examined the factors that motivate people to search for spa experiences while travelling. Their study of Hong Kong spa-goers revealed that the top five motivations for Hong Kong spa-goers were:

- to seek physical relaxation;
- to pamper oneself;
- to reward oneself for working hard;
- to seek mental peacefulness;
- to get away from the pressures of work and social life.

Koh et al. (2010) segmented spa-goers using benefit segmentation. They identified four motivation factors:

- social;
- relaxing;
- healthy;
- rejuvenating.

They also grouped spa-goers into three clusters:

- escapists – interested in improving their health;
- neutralists – interested in rejuvenating themselves;
- hedonists – interested in relaxing and rejuvenating.

GSS (2010) segments the wellness consumer in the context of the spa industry as follows:

- *Wellness-focused, moderate-to-active spa-goers* – people who live a healthy lifestyle and have a personal interest in fitness, health or wellness. These consumers are relatively affluent and educated. Spas and wellness services are not necessarily seen as luxuries.
- *Sickness reactors, not active spa-goers* – people who are suffering from disease or medical conditions and may seek new and alternative approaches to treatment as they are frustrated with the conventional medical system. These consumers may not be regular or even casual spa-goers, although spas can help them to discover new and alternative approaches to wellness.

The medical benefits of spas could be growing in importance. GSS (2010) notes that 71 per cent of consumers in their research said that they would be more likely to visit a spa if they learned that a series of research studies had demonstrated that the spa treatments would deliver measurable benefits. However, it is generally recognised that it is not the best idea to mix sickness and wellness guests within the same space. The profile and motivations of medical spa visitors, for example in Central and Eastern Europe, may be radically different from recreational, day or beauty spas. Here, guests tend to be older (55+) and there are likely to be more equal numbers of men and women.

Spa data demonstrates that the majority of spa-goers still tend to be women. ISPA (2011) shows that around 78 per cent are women in USA spas, but special packages can be used to target other segments such as men, teenagers, seniors or children. McCarthy (2012) and many other spa practitioners (e.g. GSWS, 2012) urge that spas should be made accessible to a wider range of lower-income consumers. Already many spas have reduced the length and therefore the cost of their treatments (ISPA, 2011). The cost of spas is prohibitive to many people, as well as lack of knowledge about what might happen there. Voigt et al.'s research (2010) show that Australian respondents do not visit spas because they do not know what spas offer (29 per cent), they think that spas are not for people like them or that spas are too self-indulgent (both 19 per cent), they do not have time for the spa (29 per cent), there is no spa in a convenient location (18 per cent). The rest were uncomfortable in spas because of the 'hard sell' approach or about having treatments such as massage by a man (both 13 per cent). Positive and trustworthy experiences need to be created for first-timers so that they become repeat consumers, and non-goers should be offered incentives such as discounts or free samples of products. Budget spas should also be created.

CASE STUDY 5.2
Spas and camping in France
Véronique Campion

There is this idea that spas are expensive and only for wealthy travellers, but this need not be the case.

New three-star spa hotels, self-catering rentals in spa resorts and upmarket campsites with spas are offering real comfort and authenticity in the most beautiful regions of France, as well as affordable spa services and treatments. This is a new generation of high-quality campsites with spa facilities and upmarket accommodation in chalets or Tree Houses.

For spa breaks or spa holidays, the Resort des Alicourts has a large indoor lagoon surrounded by beaches and a terrace. Large bay windows give an expansive view of the lake and stream fed by a waterfall. The hydrotherapy centre is dedicated to water in all its forms: jacuzzi, hydro-massage pebble corridor with peripheral water jets, anatomic benches, hydro-tubs, water cannons, water bell, water-jet cabins, large beaches, relaxation terraces and outdoor solarium. The accommodation includes a wide choice of rentals including chalets, cottages, villas and tree houses. The tree houses are eco-friendly (e.g. ecological toilets and garden furniture) and do not have water, heating or electricity.

This example shows that it is possible to combine spas with economy *and* ecology.

Whilst it is desirable for most spas to attract more visitors, they should not fall into the trap of trying to attract all markets simultaneously (a common mistake in under-visited spas, for example). Elderly medical visitors would not appreciate being disturbed by young people or children amusing themselves in 'fun waters'; many women find it difficult to share bathing, relaxation or sauna areas with men, especially where nudity is enforced (e.g. Germany and Austria); visitors looking for relaxation, pampering and beauty do not want to be surrounded by sick people or feel like they are visiting a hospital; those who are interested in healing the physical body will have little interest in psychological or spiritual practices; straight men may not be comfortable sharing the same space with openly gay men, and so forth. Common sense should prevail when developing, managing and promoting spas.

CASE STUDY 5.3
Spas for men

The importance of men in the spa market is demonstrated by research about the increase in the European men's grooming market (e.g. Mintel, 2011) with an increase of 45 per cent

since 2005, with the greatest growth in Germany and Spain. Euromonitor's (2011) data also shows that this market is growing. Some of the leading spa brands (e.g. Clarins, Thalgo, Germaine de Capuccini, Murad, Refinery, Sothys, Pevonia) now have ranges which are specifically designed for men's skin which has a thicker epidermis and intense cellular activity. Treatments such as manicures are being synthesised with facials.

The spa industry is therefore becoming increasingly focused on men and spas as it is usually assumed that all spas attract mainly females. However, in urban hotels and those that cater for business travellers, the gender split is closer to 50/50, and male spa clients may even outnumber women. Nevertheless, it is acknowledged that the needs of male spa guests are very different to those of women. Lowman (2013: 98) lists the following from the Hilton Hotels and Resorts research:

- Men prefer a 'no-nonsense' approach. They want to know that a certain treatment will be effective and to reach a specific goal through a treatment. Being pampered is less important.

- Men are starting to place more importance on their skin and men's skin-care products are developing twice as quickly as women's globally.

- Men's skin is biologically different from women's and therefore they need a different approach to their skin-care routine.

- Men are increasingly willing to experiment with products and services to find out the ones that will best meet their needs.

Spas ideally need to have separate male treatments menus with simple packages, such as facials, massages and hand/feet treatments. Men may also show an interest in nutrition products such as vitamins for health, fitness and well-being. The design and interior of the spa also needs to appeal to men as much as to women or there needs to be an area which is dedicated specifically to men. Décor ideally needs to be neutral and even the colour of the robes, slippers or towels are important. Men will generally need larger couches than women too to be really comfortable. According to several studies, around 60 per cent of men go to the spa to have a massage and 40 per cent go because they are stressed.

(Smith, 2012; Lowman, 2013)

The Hilton Blue Paper (Hilton, 2012) states that if spas wanted to attract men they should apply a no-nonsense approach, should introduce products created for them specially and should use clear, concise and specific communication.

CASE STUDY 5.4
Gay spas

The first question that may be asked is why is a gay spa needed. Barr (2005) answered this question well by quoting one client who said 'Because I don't want raised eyebrows if I check in with another man and I don't want the masseur to make small talk with me about my non-existent wife and children. I totally relax here because I know everyone else is gay. I don't have to deal with anybody else's issues about my sexuality.' It is more comfortable if gay couples want to check into accommodation in hotels or resorts together. It is also problematic sometimes to mix men's spas when some men are straight and others want to be openly gay.

One of the main gay-oriented websites (gay.com) compiled a Guide to Spa Travel for gay men including gay-friendly spas. There are only a limited number of exclusively gay spas, therefore they warn visitors to check what a spa may offer. Passport Online (2013) magazine lists numerous spas which are seen to be gay friendly but few of the descriptions suggest that they are exclusively gay.

However, popular gay and lesbian destinations like Bali, Las Vegas, Barcelona and Thailand tend to provide more and more gay-only spas. Turtle Cove in Australia is located between Cairns and Port Douglas (North Queensland) and has been serving gay and lesbian travellers for more than 15 years. This makes Turtle Cove one of the very first gay and lesbian-only resorts in the world. It is described as 'A piece of gay and lesbian paradise'. The Adonis Tulum in Mexico promotes itself as 'Gay, Lesbian and "Straight Friendly"'. They promote the gay-friendly bars in Playa del Carmen nearby. 241 out of 450 reviews on TripAdvisor describe it as 'excellent', including heterosexual couples enjoying the 'straight-friendly' atmosphere!

Medical tourists

Medical tourists usually tend to be patients from richer more developed nations travelling to less developed countries to access health services. This is driven by low-cost treatments, cheap flights and internet sources of information. Connell (2012), Glinos (2012) and Lunt et al. (2012) suggest that medical patients can fall into one of several categories:

- Temporary visitors abroad (incidental): Munro (2012) suggests that international patients can be considered to be 'incidental' or 'accidental' medical tourists (the latter refers to unplanned medical conditions or treatments whilst on holiday).
- Long-term residents (this can include expatriates, foreign students, soldiers or people who retired to another country): However, Lunt et al. (2012) and Munro (2012) argue that expatriates living in a country and using national or local services are *not* medical tourists, even if they are covered by international medical insurance policies paid for by corporations (therefore they should not be counted in medical tourism statistics!).

- Tourists who decide to have medical treatment (e.g. cosmetic surgery or dentistry) once in a country even though they may not have planned it.
- Border-crossing patients (e.g. those within the EU or those who go to a neighbouring country).
- Diasporic patients (e.g. emigrants or migrant workers who go back to their own countries for treatment).
- Outsourced patients (those who opt to be sent abroad by their national or local health agencies for special treatments or because their governments have bilateral agreements with another country).
- Patients with rare diseases or who travel for treatment not available in their own countries.
- Relatively wealthy people for whom waiting lists in their own country are too long.
- People with no health cover in their own country (e.g. USA) for whom going abroad may be cheaper.

The flows of visitors from certain countries are also important to consider. For example, those accessing dental treatment in Hungary tend to be from Western Europe; many UK patients go to Malta or Cyprus as the relationship with the countries has always been very close; the colonial connection between the UK and India is still an influencing factor; Korean immigrants from Australia, the USA and New Zealand often go home for treatments. American medical tourists might prefer to fly to the Caribbean or South America because of the geographical proximity. Middle Eastern tourists are only a short flight from India, and so on. The development of the Dubai Health Care City (DHCC) was partly established to attract the vast number of Middle Eastern medical tourists to stay within the Middle East rather than travel to Asia. Japan is also trying to reverse the flow of outbound medical tourism (Lunt et al., 2012).

The motivations of medical tourists may be very simple, but further research could reveal some more complex motivations, especially reasons for choosing certain destinations over others. Here is a summary of the main motivations for medical travel or tourism:

- to undergo a treatment or procedure which is not available or is too expensive at home;
- to go elsewhere because the patient's hospital or clinic outsources or has a bilateral agreement with that country or medical facility;
- to avoid long waiting lists in one's own country;
- to go back home for medical treatments because the patient feels more comfortable culturally or linguistically in his or her own country;
- to have cosmetic surgery away from home so that it can be kept a secret from friends or family;
- to recover in a setting which is more beautiful or tranquil than home and to enjoy the tourism attractions there.

There are several factors that drive international medical tourism. The most important ones are the price differences, the availability of services in another country and shorter waiting lists, and image and acceptance of medical professionals and interventions. Apart from the key drivers, many other factors should also be mentioned (after EIU, 2011):

- Developments in information technology. The internet has enabled patients to research options beyond national borders, and has expanded international marketing opportunities. It has also broken down cultural barriers and helped to calm fears about the quality of foreign medical services.
- Lower air fares. The advent of budget airlines and a drop in airline fares have made foreign travel – and therefore medical tourism – more affordable. This has also chipped away at prejudices about foreign countries and cultures.
- Trade liberalisation. Consumers have become increasingly familiar with the idea of buying goods internationally, a trend that is shifting into services. The General Agreement on Trade in Services, agreed by the World Trade Organization (WTO) in 1996, paved the way for trade in medical and other services. The EU has taken this one step further, with its 2011 Directive on cross-border medical services.
- Increasing foreign investment. The relaxation of restrictions on foreign ownership in many emerging-market economies has helped to finance the building and running of modern hospitals.
- Internationalisation of the medical workforce and medical training. As health-care systems have expanded, developed countries have recruited more immigrant health-care workers. As their home countries' economies have improved, some health-care workers have returned home, seizing the opportunities offered by medical tourism.
- The rise of facilitator firms. Thousands of agencies now offer medical tourism services to healthcare travellers, such as arranging accommodation and acting as a mediator with the hospitals. Their presence has made the job of researching and comparing treatment costs much easier for patients. These agencies also act as a channel for governments and hospitals to promote medical services.

Segmentation for medical tourists needs to understand that most of the target segment will be first time buyers (FTB) and any segmentation effort should look at all three elements of the market, namely customer, competitor and the business itself.

- What will family say if one wanted to be treated in a foreign country?
- Concerns that the doctor/consultant picked would not be the best.
- Doubts that the hospital selected would not be up to expected standards.
- Worries about privacy laws and the transfer of the patients' records to the home country.
- What if prices changed after it was quoted?
- Whatever else one may worry about?

(After Geva, 2012)

Holistic, spiritual and new age tourists

Throughout history the motivation of those who went to retreat was to withdraw from modern living and to nourish their spirit. The Good Retreat Guide (2013) describes how, 'All the great spiritual traditions are about discovering ourselves in ways that help us to grow in happiness and love. For many people a retreat will be an awakening to the presence of God in their lives.' Chiladakis (2010) states that, 'Once considered "New Age-y", holistic retreats have evolved into much needed havens for those of us who are overworked and stressed. In our hectic world, even perfectly stable people find that their spiritual life is in need of attention.' However, modern retreats focus on more than just spirituality and offer the chance to take time out of ordinary life, to give oneself peace and calm, to take a break from the responsibilities of caring for children or others, to escape a difficult emotional situation, or just to find out who you are for a while. As discussed in Chapter 4, there has perhaps never been a greater need to escape from and/or to find the means of coping with the political, economic, environmental and social crises that have hit many countries in the world today. Zega (2010) suggests that:

> Retreats offer the benefit of physical, emotional and psychological withdrawal from the stresses and strains of everyday life: a chance to escape from the toxic effects of noise, information overload, unrealistic demands and the frantic busy-ness of 21st century living; to enjoy a safe haven in which to start to recover from trauma and to heal on all levels.

The Retreat Company (2013) represent 500 retreat centres in the UK and Europe. They report that currently their most popular requests are for yoga holidays, followed by 'getting away into nature and doing nothing at all' and, third, detox programmes. The company's founder Jo Pickering describes why there is more demand for retreats these days: 'To be with yourself is the most important thing you can do because it is there that you find all the answers. We so often look outside ourselves for life's meaning and we forget that we are human beings, not human doings.' Black (2011) suggests that some people like retreat holidays because they can go alone without it being a 'singles' holiday. She states that the motivation can be to retreat from everyday life, to attend to one's spirituality, to go on a journey of self-discovery, or simply to rest and relax. Living in harmony with the natural environment is also an important dimension.

There are several categorisations of retreat which gives a good indication of the motivations of people to go there. Retreat Finder (2013) lists at least 20 categories of retreat, including those for all different religious faiths; for men, women and gays and lesbians; for those interested in specific therapies such as aromatherapy, Ayurveda, reiki, reflexology; nature, wildlife, outdoor and adventure retreats; relationship retreats; counselling retreats; nutritional retreats, including vegetarianism, veganism, raw foods, fasting. The list below is a selection of some of the most common types of retreat.

Categorisations of retreats

- *Mind/body/spirit retreats*: an approach to self-growth which draws on many alternative and ancient healing traditions but not usually religious practices.
- *Spiritual retreats*: for people who are open to and want to explore all types of spirituality and religious belief. This can include silence and meditation.
- *Yoga retreats*: for those who want to learn and practise yoga, including postures, breathing and meditation.
- *Meditation retreats*: for those who want to learn and practise meditation techniques, sometimes of a specific kind (e.g. transcendental, Vipassana silent meditation).
- *Health and detox*: for those who want to lose weight, get fitter, eat more healthily.
- *Personal development retreats*: for those wanting life coaching, stress management, emotional or psychological help.
- *Creative and arts retreats*: for those who want to learn or practise creative skills and to express themselves through the arts (e.g. painting, dance, music, writing).
- *Eco-retreats*: for those looking for a greener lifestyle, sustainable travel, organic and vegetarian food.
- *Women's retreats*: focusing on women's issues, health and empowerment.

(The Good Retreat Guide, 2013; The Retreat Company, 2013; Alternatives for Healing, 2013; Retreat Finder, 2013)

The Good Retreat Guide (2013) suggests that, 'At a retreat centre you will meet people of all ages and from every kind of background – factory workers, unemployed, students, housewives, grandparents, business people, millionaires and famous celebrities'. Voigt et al. (2010) show that spiritual retreats in Australia tend to attract the highest proportion of visitors over the age of 55 (38 per cent) and the highest percentage of males (26 per cent) of all wellness facilities in Australia. Mia Mackman shows in her case study of holistic wellness tourism in Sedona, Arizona in Part III of this book that the typical visitor is 56 years old with one-half of all visitors (53 per cent) falling between 50 and 64 years old and seven out of ten (71 per cent) are 50 or older. Baby boomers over 45 generally dominate the lifestyle resort and spiritual retreat experience. Cortijo-Romero, one of the best-known holistic retreat centres in Europe, describes its guests as follows:

Ages range from the early twenties to the retirement years. (The holidays are not suitable for children.) Most come on their own, whether or not they have a partner. An average week has two couples out of a maximum 30 guests. Usually, about 55% of the participants in any week have been before (some many times) and they help newcomers settle in easily. Occupations vary widely but professionals and service-givers are well represented. 70% of our guests come on recommendation from others – and most return.

Building on Smith and Kelly's (2006) and Kelly and Smith's (2008) work on holistic and retreat tourism, Kelly's (2012) research based on several retreats showed that 88 per cent of retreat visitors were female. The age range varied, but a higher number tend to be older (35–55). 58 per cent had never been on a retreat holiday before whereas 32 per cent were repeat visitors at the retreat where they were questioned. Respondents were asked about typical retreat activities like yoga, Tai Chi and meditation, and although 14 per cent practised every day, 20 per cent had never done them before. The most important motivations were cited as being:

- to unwind and de-stress;
- to improve health;
- to improve a specific practice (e.g. yoga);
- for social reasons;
- for spiritual reasons.

Kelly (2012) also developed a retreat visitor typology which consisted of the following:

- refuge seekers (seeking peace, rest, quietness and respite from everyday pressures);
- learners (those wishing to learn a new practice like yoga or to be part of a programme led by a well-known teacher);
- exploratory dabblers (visitors who have never tried retreat activities but who have always wanted to);
- reinforcers (often repeat visitors who want to deepen their practice and have a clear idea of their goals);
- spiritualists (visitors looking for personal development of a spiritual nature who may be more likely to choose ashrams or pilgrimage centres).

The following quotations selected from the internet sites of various holistic centres also gives some idea of tourists' experiences of a holistic holiday and the motivations that led them there or might encourage them to book a holistic holiday in the future. For many, the location is an integral part of the experience; for others it is the presence of a charismatic group leader or teacher; some enjoy the relaxation or social elements; and others take parts of the experience back home into their everyday lives.

> A very special experience in an idyllic, nurturing setting.
> As close to paradise as I can imagine.
> (Cortijo-Romero, Spain)

> I'd recommend this to anyone. A truly outstanding and life-changing experience.
> (Skyros, Greece)

> Yoga Plus is a true retreat from my urban pace of life. It provides nourishment both for the body and soul in the most tranquil and beautiful surroundings.
> (Yoga Plus, Crete)

The atmosphere, the food, the people, the treatments were all perfect, and the organic wine excellent!

(Oxon Hoath, UK)

From arriving on Friday night to leaving on Sunday night I feel there has been a transformation of the old to the new – a realisation of potential – a growth, knowledge and deeper understanding. The meeting of like-minded people in safe surroundings – each with a very special part to play and message to give.

(Wellbeing Retreats, worldwide)

I practised meditation, learnt breathing techniques that now rescue me from stress on a daily basis and made some great friends in an inspirational setting.

(Sunflower Retreats, Italy)

After a tough year and some decisions to make I booked into bliss for a week. With the personal care, nurturing massages, natural food and perfect calming space I reunited with the person I had lost in my busy life.

(Bliss Sanctuary for Women, Bali)

Here it can be seen that there are many reasons to go to a retreat and that the impacts or benefits can be the same or different from what was expected. For example, the desire for stress relief, escape, calm and rest are sought by everyone to an extent, but many find the experience truly transformative, even life-changing, with the added bonus of making new, like-minded friends.

Yoga is currently the most popular activity in retreats. Yoga tourists are a sub-sector of holistic tourists in that true yoga enthusiasts do not see yoga as a fitness or exercise programme rather as a spiritual path which aims to balance body, mind and soul. The kind of visitors who choose yoga holidays are those who already tend to practise yoga at home, although some beginners are also attracted to yoga holidays because of positive press and promotions. Although more women than men tend to practise yoga, there are large numbers of male yoga teachers and spiritual gurus. Gerritsma (2008) analysed yoga in the Netherlands and showed that on average yoga practitioners are about 80 per cent women and 20 per cent men, where more dynamic forms of yoga (e.g. Ashtanga) attract a higher percentage of men. Men are perhaps more likely to get involved in martial arts and practices that are perceived to be more 'masculine' such as Tai Chi and Chi Kung. Interestingly, women-only classes are a rarity in Tai Chi and it is generally beneficial to have a mix of yin (female) and yang (male) energy within a class (Tai Chi Finder, 2007). Retreats exist which focus just on Tai Chi and Chi Kung, but these practices are also included in many holistic holidays.

Gerritsma (2008) quotes research conducted amongst 101 yoga and pilates students: 75 per cent joined the classes for relaxation reasons, 42 per cent to get more energy, 24 per cent for better respiration and 9 per cent to meditate. The respondents consider yoga/pilates mainly as a way of taking care of their body (marked 68 times) and less for their mind (marked 43 times). Ali-Knight (2009) showed that yoga tourists are a distinctive

segment who are motivated primarily (sometimes only) by their interest in yoga. Yoga tourists tend to be mainly female, professional, well-educated and aged 35–54 (Lehto et al., 2006). Ivett Sziva and Noémi Kulcsár's case study in Part III shows that those yoga enthusiasts who participate in yoga holidays tend to be those aged 30–49. Their main motivations are to improve self-understanding (82 per cent), to have a spiritual experience (61 per cent), to be part of a community (51 per cent) and to get fit (45 per cent). The yoga teacher and being in a natural setting were also key motivations. Aggarwal (2008) researched the experiences of yoga tourists in Rishikesh which is seen to be the yoga capital of India. They showed that yoga tourists were motivated by the spiritual nature of the destination. They were not looking for luxury but to make life simpler and to meet spiritual goals and gain peace of mind.

CASE STUDY 5.5
Yoga in Rishikesh, India

Rishikesh lies at the foothills of the Himalayas along the banks of the river Ganges, the first town that the river reaches on its descent from the Himalayas. Rishikesh is home to many yoga centres and ashrams, such as Sivananda, Osho, Vivekenanda and Bihar school of yoga. It is world-famous as a place to study classical Indian yoga, and has a spiritual atmosphere which attracts many Western visitors. Although class instruction in India often tends to be less precise and directive than in Western countries, it is expected that the students will not be beginners in yoga. Rishikesh is also a pilgrimage centre for Hindus and wandering sadhus (holy men). Many people come to bathe in the sacred waters of the Ganges, as Hindus believe this can remove layers of karma. There is live temple chanting and religious ceremonies or pujas on the river, especially at night time. As a holy city, it is fully vegetarian.

Rishikesh hosts an International Yoga Festival, which is held every year in the first week of March. In addition to daily yoga sessions led by expert teachers, visitors to the festival can learn more about yoga through a programme of workshops, lectures and live demonstrations. With 350+ attendees from over 30 countries it has grown to become one of the largest yoga events in the world.

To stay in some of the ashrams students need to commit to 15 days or more and attendance at the morning and evening yoga and meditation classes is compulsory. Some of the centres offer three intensive courses a year and each course is of about three weeks duration. Asana (postures), Pranayama (breathing techniques) and basic yoga philosophy are taught. Besides these three-week courses, there are short workshops and on-going 'general-classes'.

Cross-cultural differences in guests' expectations and preferences

There ideally needs to be more research about guests of different nationalities, as their understandings, perceptions and expectations of health and wellness experiences are likely to differ considerably as described in Chapter 1. Many cultural preferences can be linked to Hofstede's (1984), Trompenaars' (1993) or other similar cultural indices. In more 'masculine' countries, men and women may not be mixed in the spas and they would almost certainly not be naked if they were. This might be different in more 'feminine' countries like Scandinavia or Germany. Mixed nudity may also not be acceptable for religious reasons (e.g. in Muslim countries). Individualistic cultures may prefer to visit the spa alone and in silence. On the other hand, more collective cultures may prefer to be in groups or with friends. This is true of many Mediterranean visitors for example and Russian visitors sometimes like to drink and party in spas. In Asian cultures, it might be expected that employees socialise with their boss or senior colleagues in the spa. There may also be food preferences depending on religion or culture (e.g. kosher, halal, vegetarian). This means that providing suitable services to meet all customer expectations in health tourism destinations, resorts and hotels can be extremely challenging.

Grove and Fisk's (1997) research analyses the negative effects that other customers' presence and behaviour can have on satisfaction levels. They note that this is especially exacerbated by differences in nationality or age. Spas and wellness facilities need to manage inter-client relations, but this may be difficult if the exact nature of the conflict is not known or understood (e.g. the different needs, expectations and perceptions of guests). Spas and wellness facilities are fairly intimate spaces where interpersonal interaction occurs in close proximity. Although Grove and Fisk (1997) conclude that satisfying all customers simultaneously is virtually impossible, it may be possible to devise ways of harmonising social interaction. This could include better observation of or research on the compatibility of customers, not mixing groups which are known to be incompatible in the same spaces, and providing codes of appropriate conduct to guests. Many older people with medical needs do not want to be disturbed by young people and children enjoying leisure, and, conversely, healthy young people do not want to be surrounded by sick people. Even on retreat holidays, there can be conflicts, as stated by The Good Retreat Guide (2013):

> It is true to say that you may meet people you like at once, those you do not want to know better and those who may make a nuisance of themselves. There are people who will hammer away about God and salvation or the greening of the planet or why vegetarianism or raw juice or deep breathing is the secret key to good living. This is apt to annoy even the nicest person. If cornered by this sort of person, just excuse yourself go away at once to your room or for a walk. You are there to listen to another voice – your inner spiritual one.

CASE STUDY 5.6
Different nationality guests in Pärnu, Estonia

Research was undertaken in a number of spas in Pärnu, Estonia in order to find out the needs of different nationality guests. Interviews were organised with spa managers and marketing managers from the following Pärnu spas: Tervis Medical Spa, Tervise Paradiis Spa Hotel and Water Park, Viiking Spa Hotel, Medical Spa Hotel Estonia, Strand Spa and Conference Hotel between 15 January and 15 February 2012.

The main objectives of the research were:

*   to find out the main target groups of the visitors to Pärnu spas;

*   to define the behaviour of the spa guests and differences according to their cultural background;

*   to analyse the results and show the importance of these issues and the impact on the overall satisfaction of visitors using the spa services.

The following key findings were identified:

*   The main visitors come from Finland, Sweden, Norway, Latvia and Russia.

*   Finnish, Swedish and Norwegian numbers are declining, but the numbers of Russians and Latvians are growing and there are some new markets (e.g. China, USA).

*   Finns (the biggest market) are generally aged 60+, need medical care, packages including three treatments a day, socialising, cultural evenings. The Finnish like to be spoken to in Finnish, are price sensitive and do not like change.

*   Swedish often travel alone or in couples, they demand high quality and comfort, prefer Swedish to be spoken, like culture and nature programmes in addition to massage, baths and medical services.

*   Russians tend to come for a weekend only, prefer beauty and relaxation, spend a lot of money, and like parties, alcohol and loud music.

*   Latvians prefer wellness to medical treatments, are happy to speak English, and like detailed explanations of treatments and services.

*   Young people (regardless of nationality) prefer wellness, leisure, healthy food and fitness, and want high quality.

The managers interviewed indicated their awareness of the cultural background, language, needs and expectations of the biggest group of spa guests (Finns), and stated that their staff are trained accordingly. The spas organise regular training courses for staff to improve their level of Finnish but also English, Swedish and Russian. However, the research shows that there are new visitors coming to Pärnu and there is a need for languages such as German and French, maybe even Mandarin in the future, as the traditional therapeutic mud is gaining exotic fame among Chinese visitors.

Overall, the pilot research in Estonia clearly shows that there is a need for further research into cross cultural issues in spas. Flexibility, excellent customer service, a high level of foreign-language knowledge, sensitivity to and understanding of cultural differences may be a strong advantage for a spa in order to remain competitive and attract new visitors. It is important to design services and promote them to different markets, work with guests' needs, arrange cultural evenings and other events in spa areas. However, the needs of different nationality guests staying at the same time may not be compatible (e.g. Russians and Finns in this case), so measures need to be taken to manage and improve compatibility (Grove and Fisk, 1997).

(Tooman et al., 2013)

Ormond (2013) suggests that cultural issues can also be important in medical tourism, especially for those tourists who decide to go back to their country of origin because they feel more comfortable, or for those who have specific religious preferences and needs. Ormond presents a case study of Malaysia which is seen as having considerable 'cultural expertise' or 'cultural competence' in catering for the diverse lifestyles of medical tourists, for example linguistic needs, religious practices and dietary requirements.

Conclusion

It is clear that more research is needed on the various sub-sectors of health tourism to identify which segments or clusters should be targeted. Increasingly, lifestyle factors are becoming the most important determinants of segmentation, but these are complex and specific to different age groups, genders, even societies and cultures. As discussed in Chapter 4, there is a clear link between the way people conduct their everyday lives (e.g. their propensity to integrate health practices or not) and their travel behaviour. The growth of customised service and the experience economy also means that visitors are becoming more discerning and demanding, so destinations and attractions have to focus on tailoring their products not only to segments but to individuals. This is challenging, especially when visitors also expect to experience something indigenous or local to a destination. Thus, health tourism needs to become even more diverse and unique in its product development, targeting new markets at the same time as satisfying ever more demanding existing ones.

6

Targeting and branding

Humans are not trapped in time, squeezed into the volume of a body and the span of a lifetime. We are voyagers on the infinite river of life.

(Chopra, 1993: 314)

Introduction

The marketing of health and wellness tourism is almost like any service industry's marketing, with one exception: it involves some kind of health element, which is one of the most personal, therefore sensitive aspects. This has an impact on the demand, the supply and the intermediary side, too. This chapter does not follow the textbook marketing approach; for example it does not necessarily follow strictly the logic of Ps or Ss. The major characteristics of demand were already introduced in Chapter 5 (e.g. lifestyle).

As we could see many times earlier, health tourism specifically builds on trust. Guests trust the healing natural asset. Participants trust the guru. Patients trust the surgeon. And all of them expect a little more than just nice experiences and memories. They want better health, nicer teeth, nicer curves or a more stable frame of mind. The real and perceived risks associated with health services during the trip, therefore, can be much higher than in the case of other types of trips. This results in a wide range of techniques and approaches which service providers and marketers use to reassure existing and prospective visitors.

Based on the above mentioned qualities of health tourism it is crucial for any facility, operator or organisation to apply quite different marketing approaches. This is certainly new to those facilities that intentionally or unintentionally started to receive tourists from other parts of the country or of the world, such as clinics, medical spas or small-scale retreats. The whole concept of marketing can be very new to those spas and spa hotels that were operating in a market-free environment in Central and Eastern Europe or in Russia or to hospitals that now want to open to foreign patients. Facing the same market challenges that all other entities do, and adapting to a new situation is not easy (especially given that most of the medical spas still rely on substantial amounts of state or local

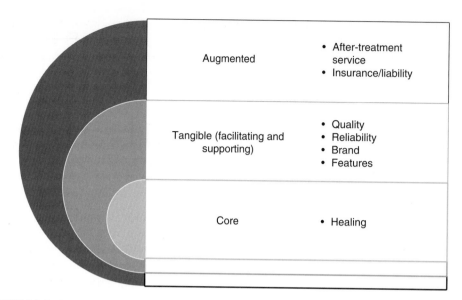

FIGURE 6.1 Product levels in health and wellness tourism

government subsidy every year). This highlights another aspect of health tourism marketing and marketing communication. Many facilities are two-faceted: on the one hand they provide health care; on the other hand, they want to attract visitors who pay the market price for the treatments and services. These two major types of demand make marketing complicated, since in the first case we cannot even talk about a 'market' as such, whereas tourism is one of the most competitive sectors.

Before entering into the complexity of communication and branding we must re-address a very simple, but often overlooked, issue, namely the several levels of the product.

As we can see in Figure 6.1, the core of the product is the benefit the customers gain by purchasing and using the service or product. It is essential in modern marketing regardless of which approach, for example experience, enchanting or transactional, one may use. The facilitating and supporting product levels provide the customers with the opportunity to purchase, such as a shuttle service or child care for the period of the treatment or operation. Augmented health tourism products are necessary to be considered for any service provider if they want to create and cater for loyal customers (e.g. online, seasonal health juice, suggestions from spa hotels).

Marketing communications

Holloway (2004) and others (e.g. Kotler et al., 2005) summarised the determinants for marketing communication strategies and tactics as follows:

- *The nature of the product.* Tourism products are not homogeneous and this is particularly true in the case of health and wellness tourism. Products are not well

known and even similar labels may mean something rather different. Brochures, websites, blogs, mobile applications, fairs make attempts to introduce services and facilities, but to understand the complexity, more and more attach a guide or manual to their products facilitating better understanding (e.g. Spa Week Media Group (2013) created a video library that was 'designed to promote the spa lifestyle to a new generation of spa-goers'. The library under the brand name of Spadcast introduces procedures, treatments and products. The categories from which customers can view short films are: Non-Invasive Cosmetic Procedures, Plastic Surgery, Beauty, Anti-Ageing, Male Grooming, Teen and Ween, and Wellness).

- *The target at which the communication is aimed.* Both 'push' or distribution channel-oriented; and 'pull' or final customer oriented communications are heavily used in health and wellness tourism. In many countries, based on the relative novelty of the product, dealers, retailers or doctors still can be motivated (push), and customers can also be relatively easily attracted by buzzwords such as 'experience', 'ritual', 'self-realisation', 'escape', 'sanctuary' or more lately ''vital'', 'refuge' or 'hideaway' (pull).

- *The stage in the life cycle in which the product is to be found.* This determinant has very close links with the 'nature of the product'. It is almost impossible to create a global promotion mix for health and wellness tourism, since the products are at very different stages in their respective life cycles. We could see before that luxury spa resorts and medical services can face similar life cycle positions, but at different times everywhere. Therapeutic medical tourism, however, is relatively new to North America, while it is one of the fundamental forms in Central and Eastern Europe, or Asia.

- *The situation in which the marketer finds him or herself in the marketplace.* Health and wellness tourism, especially those forms that are not site-specific, are highly competitive and the market, especially in the luxury or the relatively easily standardised medical tourism segment, is the whole world. In this case price/quality ratios, surgeons ('brand names'), personal and personalised services, attractive and unique architecture, the location or a ritual, etc. can become the focus of communication (or USP).

Not only well-known sites with global coverage, but country- or region-specific ones can also be popular. Arizona SpaGirls (2008), for example, claimed in 2008 that they were 'combining yellow page practicality with insider information'. The site positioned itself as an information site for women almost exclusively and this is also manifested in the style of language they use, for example: 'Simply put, Arizona SpaGirls is your little pink book to looking and feeling your best!' By 2013 the girls extended their activities to cover men as well! 'Arizona Spa Girls is a business dedicated to supporting the local spa and salon community while empowering women (and men!) to live a healthy, fulfilling lifestyle.'

As we will see in the various cases we refer to, the messages can come at three different levels. Discussing the regional and thematic similarities and differences of health and wellness products and related communication it seems that at all level marketers have to face challenges.

TABLE 6.1 Multi-level marketing messages	
Levels	Challenges for health and wellness tourism
Cognitive level (i.e. making customers aware of the products and services)	**Fading labels** The proliferation of use and the erosion of the term wellness or spa devalues original products and confuses customers (e.g. Car Spa Weekend)
Affective level (i.e. creating an emotional response to messages)	**Demolishing barriers** A significant part of the market takes with a pinch of salt anything that is called wellness and believes that it is not for him or her, but for the rich and famous (and often they are right, too)
Behavioural level (i.e. making customers act in the aspired way: to make a purchase)	**Compound segmentation** Segmentation takes place based on numerous factors; from basic factors such as age or gender (e.g. men or young people), to a very complex one such as lifestyle
Adapted from Holloway, 2004.	

The world's largest search engine, Google, listed (in March 2008) spas under 'Speciality Travel'. Interestingly the geographical and thematic coverage is not complete, since Africa (with two), Asia (with six), Europe (with 35), North America (with 56) and Oceania (with three links) listed, but South America is not. In 2013 Google shows over 1.3 billion results for the search-word 'spa' only, and some 125 million for 'medical tourism'. Certainly, social media forms (e.g. Facebook, Twitter, Pinterest, Instagram) all provide communication opportunities to health and wellness tourism providers (see Secret Surgery Ltd on Facebook). This opportunity, however, can easily become overwhelming since in terms of staff and costs social media can be a burden, often with not so clear results and benefits. As a report by PWC states, 'Social media likes healthcare' (2012).

CASE STUDY 6.1
Royal Spas of Europe

Eight historic spa towns (previously nine with Loutraki in Greece) with very different, but still somehow similar characteristics joined together and started the Royal Spas of Europe partnership. The members are:

- Archena (Spain);

- Baden-Baden (Germany);

- Bad Neuenahr (Germany);

- Bayreuth (Germany);

- Budapest (Hungary);

- Marienbad (Czech Republic);

- Naantali (Finland);

- Sárvár (Hungary).

These European spas and health resorts are rich in tradition: emperors, kings, members of the high nobility and famous heads of state were among their guests, making them famous. The Royal Spas return visitors to a time when European spas were to enjoy wellness in sublime elegance. The initiative's aim is to promote both the long tradition as well as the modern facilities of baths and thermal centres. The communication highlights health services and facilities that are complemented by attractive packages of cultural and historical heritage.

The Royal Spas of Europe initiative aims to meet the highest quality requirements. For this reason a set of criteria were set, which has to be met by any member, e.g. health, wellness and fitness services, thermal facilities, medical care, infrastructure, standards of hotels and cultural events.

Interestingly the alliance refers to spas, but the members are spa towns, except Finland, where a spa hotel became member. This may leave little room for misunderstanding for anyone who visits the website or reads the brochure. The information provision of the alliance does not really go further than providing one platform from where the individual members can be reached.

(Royal Spas, 2013)

There are a great number of sources from which visitors can find out more about health and wellness services and destinations. The printed and online sources, such as SpaFinder Wellness, Beautifulbreak, Relax-Guide, SpaIndex, Beauty24.de and Wahanda, use very extensive lists of categories introducing their partners (and advertisers). These categories represent the given source's segmenting and targeting strategy as well as the listed partners' positioning strategy. From the compilation of these categories, it is quite clear that as the market saturates, new segments and categories are emerging continuously. The lists are very long and items often do not really represent clear differences from other items. These clarifications are, of course, provided by the given supplier (e.g. the Connoisseur Spas are 'The crème de la crème of spas, this elite collection was chosen using strict criteria such as extraordinary ambience, luxurious accommodation, high staff-to-guest ratio, exceptional spa services, outstanding cuisine, and industry awards and recognition'). Beyond the already rather long list of possible service categories, lately, communication is being stretched and now includes 'Spa Lifestyles' (incorporating cuisine, shopping, home or living).

TABLE 6.2 Online sources of spa and wellness information

spaindex.com (2008)	spaindex.com (2013)	beauty24.de (2013)
Adventure Spas	African American Owned Day	Wellness Services
African American Owned Day	Spas	Sauna
Spas	Airport Spas and Spa Kiosks	Pleasure pools
Airport Spas and Spa Kiosks	Spas Honoring our Armed	Steambath
Bed and Breakfast Spas	Forces	Whirlpool
Casino Spas	Spas for Babymoons	Infrared cabine
Cruise Ships with Spa	Spa Programs after Bariatric	Thermal pools
Facilities	Surgery	Outdoor pools
Dental Spa Centers	Bed and Breakfast Spas	Themes
Detox Programs	Spas Offering Chinese Medicine	Wellness packages
Eco-Friendly/Holistic Spa	Spas with Cooking Classes	5-star lux
Facilities	Cruise Ships with Spa Facilities	Bath
Family Oriented Spa Facilities	Spas with Culinary Programs	For Two
For Armed Forces	Spas offering Detox Programs	Hamam
For Breast Cancer Patients	Family Oriented Spa Facilities	Family and Wellness
For Cancer Patients	Fly In Spa Resorts	Ski and Wellness
For Sportsmen	Green Spas	Outdoor Wellness
For Teenagers	Maternity/Pregnancy Programs	Private Spa Suites
Juicing, Fasting, Colonics, and	Spas with Hot Springs and	Day Spa
Cleansing Programs	Mineral Springs	Ayurveda
Maternity/Pregnancy Programs	Pet-Friendly Spas	Corporate Groups
Medi-Spas	Ranch Style Spas/Dude Ranch	and Group of
Mobile Spa Services and	Spas	Friends
Mobile Spa Parties	RV Parks/Spa Resorts with RV	Medical Wellness
Pet-Friendly Spas	Access	For Men
Ranch Style Spas/Dude	Spas with Smoking Cessation	Wellness and Horse
Ranch Spas	Programs	Riding
Smoking Cessation Programs	Spa Programs for Teenagers	Honeymoons
Vinotherapy	Spas/Salons offering Threading	Touring/hiking and
Wedding and Honeymoon	Spas Offering Traditional Chinese	Wellness
Spa Packages	Medicine	
Weight Management Programs	Vegan Spas	
Wine Spas	Spas Offering Vinotherapy	
Women Only	Wedding and Honeymoon Spa	
Yoga Programs and Retreats	Packages	
	Weight Loss Retreats and Spas	
	Spa Programs after Bariatric	
	WLS	
	Spas for Women Only	
	Yoga Retreats	

	Destination Spa Group (2008)	Destination Spa Group (2013) Spa Vacation Types	spasofamerica.com (2008)

Types of Services and Programmes	Aquatics
	Biking
	Canoe and Kayak
	Cooking School
	Creative Arts
	Cultural Activities
	Dance Instruction
	Educational Workshops
	Fitness Programs
	Gardening
	Golf Programs
	Guided Hiking
	Health Assessments
	Labyrinth
	Nutrition Education and
	  Counselling
	Outdoor Adventure
	Personal Training
	Skiing
	Specialty Cuisine
	Tai Chi and Pilates
	Tennis Programs
	Walking
		Aquatics
		Biking
		Canoe and Kayak
		Cooking School
		Corporate Retreats
		Creative Arts
		Cultural Activities
		Dance Instruction
		Detox
		Educational Workshops
		Fitness Programs
		Gardening
		Golf Programs
		Guided Hiking
		Health Assessments
		Labyrinth
		Luxury Vacation
		Medical Packages
		Nutrition Education and
		  Counselling
		Outdoor Adventure
		Personal Coaching
		Personal Training
		Skiing
		Specialty Cuisine
		Spiritual
		  Retreats
		Stress Management
		Tai Chi and Pilates
		Tennis Programs
		Walking
		Weight Loss
		Women Only
		Yoga
			Resort
			Beach and Spa
			Ski and Spa
			Ayveda
			Weight Loss
			Urban Spa
			Golf and Spa
			Thalassotherapy
			Medical Spa
			Anti Aging

(Continued)

TABLE 6.2 Continued

	spasofamerica.com (2013) Spa Experiences	Spa Finder (2008)	Spa Finder Wellness (2013)

Types of Services and Programmes	Adventure Spas
	Beach Spas
	Casino Spas
	City Spas
	Country Spas
	Desert Spas
	Destination Spas
	Green Spas
	Historic Spas
	Luxury Spas
	Medical Spas
	Mineral Spas
	Mountain Spas
	Ocean Spas
	Pet-Friendly Spas
	Wine Spas
		Affordable Spa Vacations
		Detoxification Programs
		Inclusive-pricing Vacation
		Kids/Family-Friendly Vacations
		Luxury Spa Vacations
		Male-oriented Vacation
		   Programs
		Mommy and Baby Programs
		Mother and Daughter
		   Programs
		Nudist Spa Vacations
		Pet Friendly Spa Vacations
		Pre and Post Natal Programs
		Romantic/Honeymoon
		Senior Friendly Spa Vacations
		Sleep-Health Consultation
		Smoking Cessation Programs
		Spirituality Programs
		Stress Management Programs
		Teen Spa Vacation Programs
		Wedding/Event Programs
		Weight-management Programs
		Winter-sport Spas
		Yoga Programs
			Spa and Beauty
			   Day Spas
			   Medical Spas
			   Salons
			   Spa services (e.g.
			massage, facial)
			Yoga
			Pilates
			Fitness
			   Gyms and Health Clubs
			   Personal training
			   Barre classes
			   Bootcamps
			Travel
			   Hotel and Resort Spas
			   Destination Spas
			   Family Spas
			   Ski Spas
			   Weight Loss Spas
			   Yoga Travel
			Acupuncture
			Alternative Medicine
			Reflexology
			Weight loss
			Spa Types
			   Resort/Hotel Spa
			   Destination Spa
			   Connoisseur Spa
			   Spa Lifestyle Real Estate
			   Casino Spa
			   Day Spa
			   Medical Spa: Cosmetic
			   Medical Spa: Wellness
			   Dental Spa
			   Mobile Spa
			   Airport Spa
			   Cruise Ship Spa

Sources: Destination Spa Group, 2005 and 2013; Beautiful Break, 2008; Spas of America, 2008 and 2013; Spa Finder, 2008 and 2013; Spa Index, 2008 and 2013

Operators are also aware of the quick proliferation and sometimes misleading use of the terms, so those that find informing their customers important often create lists, glossaries, A–Zs, 101s, and so on, of wellness and health services.

In addition, almost all printed and online magazines (e.g. IMTJ.com, medialtourismtoday. com, Spa Australasia, SpaAsia India, European Spa Magazine, American Spa Magazine, AVIDA Magazin, Professional Spa and Wellness, medicaltourismmagazine.com), association publications and websites (e.g. australianspaassociation.com, federterme.it, leading-spasofcanada.com or visitspas.eu) or distribution and destination portals for communication (e.g. medeguide.com, traveltowellness.com; spasofamerica.com) and communication and sales (e.g. wahanda.com, spafinderwellness.com or mednetasia.com) provide help and guidance for their readers or visitors about what certain treatments and forms of health, wellness and spa tourism and various services may mean.

CASE STUDY 6.2
Healing Hotels of the World

Health is not only a physical state but also concerns the mind and the emotions. Keywords such as a successful work/life balance are important factors in our time. We are living in a time that is characterized by blurred boundaries between work and private life, by a constant increase of speed and the dissolution of securities. At the same time more and more people are gaining an understanding of health, which goes beyond the treatment of symptoms and acknowledges the interconnectedness of body and mind. This is the reason that CAM (Complementary and Alternative Medicine) therapies are becoming increasingly popular. It also implies that we are responsible for our health and that we can stay healthy by maintaining a healthy lifestyle, which includes healthy eating habits and sufficient movement. Today the leading experts of holistic health can be found in Healing Hotels, in an environment that allows regaining emotional balance and joy of life. Healing Hotels of the World collects the leading hotels and resorts in this field and is a trusted source for all those who are seeking the ideal location for their health vacation.

All HHoW partners embrace a holistic spa and health concept. Holistic wellness goes beyond pampering: holistic spas create wellbeing and educate their guests about their constitution and health. In order to do so, a personal consultation is a must. Treatments are specially designed for the guests' individual needs to obtain the most benefit. When leaving, guests should be thoroughly informed about different aspects of their health and should be able to use this knowledge at home for a better lifestyle. Every partner hotel offers the following:

Diagnosis and personal consultation
Holistic spa treatments
Healthy cuisine
Activities with professional guidance
Lifestyle coaching
Action plan to take home

The concept of HHoW is based on many years of experience in international tourism as well as a deep knowledge about holistic health and holistic lifestyle. This expertise allows selecting new partner hotels according to their holistic health offers and the quality of the venue itself. Holistic health means to understand the body/mind relationship in respect to health and healing. It also includes the notion that we are responsible for our health and wellbeing and that we can be proactive to improve our health and to stay healthy in the future. Further, holistic in regards to hotels and resorts refers to the location, the atmosphere of the place, how nature is included, sustainability and cultural as well as social sensibility. This understanding of holistic health is reflected in the comprehensive set of the HHoW criteria, which form the foundation in accepting new partner hotels.

With more than 70 partner hotels worldwide, Healing Hotels of the World is an authentic and trusted source for holistic health. Healing Hotels of the World offers individual consultation for all those who want to improve their health and lifestyle during a high quality health vacation in beautiful surroundings.

(Healing Hotels of the World, 2013)

There are many beautifully presented books on the market using amazing images, for example Spa Style series that can lure even those who have never been in a spa before.

Branding

Branding is seen as essential to any operator or organisation in making their product different from others. It is not uncommon in health and wellness tourism that brands are seen as only logos or simply as a term. Whereas a brand can be a name, symbol, term or combination of all these and brands should reflect the product or service and the benefit customers may have from the consumption. Brands with strong and well-managed personalities and pillars can give better returns. Still, we have to agree with Geva (2012) that 90 per cent of branding is internal and only 10 per cent is external. Whatever any organisation or company promises the delivery of that is very much dependent on how staff members deliver it.

Anybody considering branding activities should consider some key elements in brand positioning. This may seem to be easy but it has to be noted that there are not too many brands with high brand equity (i.e. for which customers are ready to pay high prices) in health and wellness tourism. Major international brands, especially hotel chains (e.g. Four Seasons, Marriott, Hilton) all stretch their existing and well-established brands over new products, i.e. spas and wellness centres.

Rocco Forte Hotels has unveiled Vita Health – a new approach to preventative health care, in partnership with integrated medicine physician Dr Nyjon Eccles. On offer are four tailored programmes based on Eccles' specialities of nutritional, non-invasive and anti-ageing medicine as well as natural therapies. The programmes are available

TABLE 6.3 Branding considerations in health and wellness tourism

Key elements	Meaning	Examples from health and wellness tourism
Benefits	What can it offer?	'Healing' (functional benefit) 'Escaping' (emotional benefit)
Values	What does it stand for?	'To create innovative and enriching experiences in a sustainable environment' (Six Senses)
Personality	The behaviour of the brand	'We touch life' (Kientalerhof, Switzerland)
Reason to believe	Evidence – why this is better?	'Professional dental care for reasonable price' (Indexmedica, Poland)
Brand essence	What is it about – in one line	'A Better state of Health' (Bavaria, Germany)

in one- and two-week sessions and will focus on the core health issues of stress management, detoxification, weight loss and better ageing (SpaBusiness, 2012).

Branding, such as planning or management, can take place at national, regional, local and site level, too.

Branding at national and regional level

As was mentioned earlier, many countries have entered the competition in health and wellness tourism at national or regional level. Countries such as Thailand, South Korea, the Philippines or Colombia, the UAE or Hungary, Estonia or Lithuania are all trying to position themselves as medical or wellness destinations. National tourist offices and non-governmental organisations (NGOs) publish promotional leaflets, operate websites and various social media, and participate in health-oriented fairs and exhibitions to promote the service providers of their respective countries. They run campaigns and themed years in which special attention is given to health and wellness, plus the complementary services and products, for example:

- 2011 was the 'Year of Health Tourism' themed year by the Hungarian National Tourist Office
- 2011 was the 'Health and Fitness Holidays in Germany' theme year by the German Tourist Board (Kunhardt, 2011)
- 2013 was a 'Wellness Tourism' themed year in the Estonian Tourist Board's communication to foreign markets.

Krisztina Priszinger and Katalin Formádi analyse spa and wellness hotel marketing in Hungary in their case study in Part III of this book. The best way to compare national and regional branding efforts is to compile the most typical examples. We collected communication (and positioning) messages from many countries all around the world. Some of them have been communicating their health services for many years, so we show the changes where this was possible. Interestingly, many countries that really are strong in health tourism, such as the Czech Republic, Ireland or New Zealand, do not provide separate communication for this product. In these countries health and wellness tourism related information are available about the existing services and locations under the country brand, and no special 'health' oriented brand is communicated.

We can see that most of these messages revolve around the same words: wellness, health, life, feeling good. This generalisation leaves prospective travellers with the problem of not being able to identify and link the messages to and with the given countries (i.e. try to name the countries reading the messages only).

CASE STUDY 6.3
Switzerland's marketing of wellness and spa tourism

Switzerland has changed its label, and also changed the health tourism approach. As of 2013 mySwitzerland's website categorised the country's wellness offers as follows:

- wellness destinations;

- wellness and spa hotels:
  - active wellness
  - city wellness
  - day spa
  - design spa
  - gourmet wellness
  - private spa
  - wellness with mountain air
  - hotels with thermal water

- water stories – a rather inspiring approach since it introduces the country's different natural water bodies and approaches under one umbrella:
  - thermal baths and treatment: well-being in its purest form
  - bathing, one of the joys of summer
  - water and construction: a perfect partnership (innovation in building design)
  - good for the legs . . . and the mind (wandering around lakes, etc.)
  - the fabulous world of waterfalls
  - sustainable development to preserve our resources
  - water for all (establishments allocating a proportion of the price for water to mutual aid organisations)
  - spring water: pure and refreshing

(MySwitzerland, 2013)

TABLE 6.4 Country communication and positioning messages for health and wellness tourism

Country	Messages	Year
Argentina	Wellness tourism: 'The pleasure of absolute relax.'	2013
Armenia	'Nature's healing power'	2013
Austria	'Europe's No. 1 Spa Destination'	2008
	'Feel good in Austria' (or 'Schlank und Schön') (for non-German speakers)	
	'Wohlfühlen. Lebenselixier' ('Well-feeling. The Elixir of life') and 'Kuren. Entspannungen'('Cures. Relaxation') (for German speaking countries)	2011
	Ayurveda: 'Wir berühren Sie. Ayurveda berührt Körper, Geist und Seele.' (We touch you – Ayurveda touch the body, mind and soul) (Ayurveda Rhyner)	
	'Arrive and revive'	2013
Bulgaria	'Waters of Wellness-Refreshing. Bulgarian Spas.'	2007
	'Open doors open hearts. Balneology and SPA Tourism'	2008
	'A discovery to Share'	2013
Canada	'All aboard! Take a seat on the Route to well-being' (Central Canada, Canadian Tourism Commission)	2013
Chile	'A journey through the senses'	2013
Croatia	'To Croatia for Strength and Health' (iconised by a red apple)	2000
	'The Way of Life'	2008
	'Croatia, the strength of a new morning' (Wellness)	2013
Egypt	Spirituality: Soul Searching in Egypt	2013
Estonia	'A Source of Vital Energy' (Wellness Holidays in Estonia Brochure)	2010
France	'Harmony and Well-being. Are you looking for de-stress or feel revitalised?'	2008, 2013
Germany	'Everything but Stress'	2000
	'Germany has everything your heart and soul could desire. Here you'll discover new meanings of happiness. Welcome to a world of well-being.'	2008

(Continued overleaf)

TABLE 6.4 Continued

Country	Messages	Year
	Better state of health (Bavaria)	2012
	'Germany does you good: health and Wellness'	2013
Greece	Spa: 'The energy of the mind is the essence of life' (Aristotle)	2013
Hungary	'Hungary Keeps the World Healthy'	2002
	'Hungary – The Land of spas'	2008
India (wellness)	Wellness:	2008
	• Ayurveda: 'A gateway to Indian Medical Heritage'	
	• Yoga: 'Communion of soul with the universal soul or God'	
	• Well-being: 'Nature's gift for well-being'	2011
Ireland	Immerse yourself in a Destination Spa	2010
Italy	Wellness: 'In search of wellness'	2008
	Treatments: 'Salutary effects'	
	Spas/treatments: 'Naturally Regenerated"	
	Well-being and Health: 'Italy, Territory of Wellness and Beauty'	2013
Jordan	Leisure and Wellness: 'A Place to Rejuvenate and Restore Your Mind, Body and Soul"	2008
	Leisure and Wellness: 'Nature's Healing Power"	2010
Malaysia	Quality care for your peace of mind	2013
Morocco	'A paradise of well-being'	2013
Poland	'Natural Choice (for Health and Beauty)'	2013
	'Poland For Health and Beauty'	2012
Portugal	Relax: 'Where all else is forgotten'	2008
	Spa: 'Healthy minds and bodies'	2008
	Treatments: "Rest your body and invigorate your soul" (Thalassotherapy)	2008
Serbia	'Spas and Health Resorts in Serbia'	1999
	'Legendary Mineral Springs and Mountain Air. Since the Roman Empire travelers have sought the rejuvenating effects of the region's forests and waters' (wellness)	2008

Country	Slogan	Year
Serbia (contd)	'Springs of Life and Vitality' (health resorts)	2013
	'Oases of greenery and tranquillity' (Spas and Health Resorts)	
Slovenia	'With Nature to Health'	1999
	'Wellness – tailor-made for you.' 'Wellness is not a remedy, but a healthy way of life.'	2008
	"HEALTHY: The country of well-being"	2013
South Africa	'Spiritual: The Sacred South'	2008
	'Leave ordinary behind'	2012
Spain	'Looking after yourself'	2013
	'Relax, look great, spoil yourself'	2013
St. Lucia	'Health and Fitness: A holiday on St. Lucia is a total refreshment for your mind, your body and your spirit.'	2008, 2013
Sweden	Treatments: 'Being. To "be" is a richer, more fulfilling state than simply to "do". We believe in the value of nurturing your being.'	2011
	Spas: 'At one with nature'	2013
Switzerland	'Health Destination'	2008
	'Oases of relaxation'	2013
Thailand	'Health Tourism Hub of Asia'	2003
The Philippines	'Island of Wellness'	2007
Turkey	Health and Wellness: 'Do something good for your body.'	2010
	Healing Generations for Centuries	2013
UK	Spa: 'Go with the flow'	2010

Sources: National Tourist Offices and Spa Associations' brochures and websites.

Branding can take place at regional level, too, which can either mean cooperation between countries or branding for a region or country of a single country. For example, the See Wellness (Lake Wellness) is a trademark of the Carinthia region of Austria. This initiative is a perfect example of product development at regional level. The member hotels build on the natural energies of Carinthia's lakes. See Wellness is actually a research project that aims at identifying the beneficial impacts of the natural energy flows of lakes and the sub-Mediterranean climate. These energies should improve the well-being of visitors (See Wellness, 2008). There is also the lake wellness concept being developed in Finland, and the Nordic well-being concept for the Scandinavian countries.

Regional initiatives, especially the ones that cross borders as well, may not continue for ever or change significantly over a relatively short period of time.

CASE STUDY 6.4
Alpine Wellness

What once was a leading regional initiative promising 'Breathe again – Recharge your batteries – Move mountains', and had partners in Bavaria (Germany), Austria, Switzerland and South Tyrol (Italy), now seems to be a loose cooperation between three regions, since South Tyrol left the initiative.

The founding idea behind Alpine Wellness was that medical studies showed that the simple fact of being over 1,500 metres above sea level has a positive effect on bodily health. Visitors are invited to treat themselves to a bit of good: whether gently relaxing, taking part in physical fitness or partaking of medically supervised health care – member hotels, quality certified by independent auditors, are categorised into different specialist areas and are ready and prepared to welcome you with an individually tailored programme to meet personal relaxation requirements.

Alpine Wellness Philosophy meant a return to grass roots, and rediscovering the knowledge associated with the nature, culture and quality of life in the region. The effect of natural displays and the original charm of the alpine environment do their bit to make the special sensuality of the Alps a unique and exclusive experience. The specialist areas or sub-brands of Alpine Wellness were:

- *Alpine relaxing*: Topping up on vitality, feeling the sensuality of the mountain landscape, taking refuge in nature (saunas with a view, purifying whey baths and aromatic hay baths, natural resources for treatments and food).

- *Alpine fitness*: Nature provides inspiration through its spiritual power and Alpine Fitness means outdoor activities.

- *Alpine health*: Tailor-made medical wellness packages for preventative health, alleviation of symptoms, healing using natural resources of the Alps (for spinal trouble, burnout syndrome, asthma or allergies).

- *Alpine character*: It is reflected in the hotel architecture, as well as in the room furnishings and the decor in the relaxation areas, establishments are characterised by free access to nature, a particularly peaceful and idyllic location, as well as the use of healthy home produce in the kitchen and cellar.

Alpine Wellness as it used to be does not exist anymore. The Bavarian part is now called WellVital (the regional brand), in Switzerland the links goes directly to mySwitzerland and Austria is the only region that still follows the original idea of the initiative.

(Alpine Wellness, 2008; Alpine Wellness, 2013; Bayern Wellvital, 2013; MySwitzerland, 2013)

Theming, i.e. creating and developing a brand based on a theme, is a well-known technique in branding. Themed attractions, such as parks, restaurants, hotels or routes, can be found everywhere. Visitors can enjoy many themed spas or spa hotels, and even cruises. Health tourism oriented routes, however, are very rare, and only in a handful of cases were developed so far. One example is the Wellness Route 'Salz und Sole' in Germany, which links salt flats between Neckar, Hohenlohe and the Swabian hills. The thematic route includes hotels and wellness hotels, pools and sunbathing areas, cities and attractions. Salt and sunshine are used to offer a rich diversity of sporting activities, accommodation and pampering treatments for body and soul (Salz und Sole, 2008).

Health destinations often have their own organisation responsible for destination management and marketing. If not in an exclusive resort, guests (and accompanying visitors) can easily find it a little claustrophobic to stay in the same facility all day (i.e. between treatments that are rather short), therefore destination management organisations' (DMOs) main objective is to offer and introduce the available additional services and attractions in the area. In Europe, mainly historic spa towns or towns with an established clinic or major spa tend to label themselves as health or wellness destinations (e.g. Baden-Baden, Germany). In other parts of the world, the health element typically is only one of the many image making elements or strengths.

Branding at local and operator level

It seems to be a little easier to create and maintain a brand for a site or for an operator. It only seems that way though. We can see that customers are not yet that experienced in health and wellness vocabulary and do not yet know as much about destinations either, as they may know of sun and sea destinations. This can cause a lot of problems for operators or for local organisations.

International spa and hotel chains, however, have made progress in creating their own brands, based on health services, for example:

- Hilton identified the brand love curve of the guests based on four stages:
  - Indifferent
  - Like it (satisfies guest needs)
  - Love it (guests crave it)
  - My loved brand for life (as means of self-expression)

  The Hilton group launched eforea, its first branded spa concept in 2010, and there are now 50 eforea spas planned for development around the world. The Conrad Spa, the second in-house brand from Hilton, in line with Conrad's philosophy of the 'luxury of being yourself', has the ethos of the hotel and spa of quality and customer experience (Hilton Branding, 2012).

- One&Only Spas are blissful sanctuaries of tranquillity, where the body is restored and the soul is soothed. Just as each One&Only resort is individually designed and inspired by its local surroundings, so too, is each One&Only Spa. Within each unique spa environment, the highest levels of personalised care and pampering are consistently lavished upon guests with indulgent blends of contemporary treatments and authentic rituals (One&Only Resorts, 2013).

- Mandarin Oriental Holistic Spas: relaxation and rejuvenation. The multi-award winning Spas at Mandarin Oriental are havens for contemplation and discovery. Guided by our oriental heritage but influenced by local cultural diversity, we provide world-class treatments in luxuriously serene surroundings. From signature therapies to locally inspired treatments, our expert therapists offer a completely holistic experience that goes well beyond simply delivering massages to tired bodies. Each spa also provides a variety of other disciplines that include: fitness options, nutrition counselling, yoga, tai-chi, meditation, beauty and relaxation (Mandarin Oriental, 2013).

CASE STUDY 6.5
Starwood Hotels and Resorts

Starwood Hotels and Resorts manages nine hotel brands and most of their brands have their own in-house spa brands, too:

- Shine Spa for Sheraton

- Iridium Spa for St. Regis

- Explore Spa by Le Meridien

- Heavenly Spa by Westin (with Heavenly Bed and Bath brands)

- Away Spa by W Hotels

- Bliss and Remede Spa brands (for W and St. Regis, respectively) owned by Steiner Leisure exclusively for Starwood, and

- Spas for The Luxury Collection

'Like pools in the 1980s and fitness centers in the 1990s, the increased presence of spas at hotels has been fueled by both demand and the perceived quality of hotels with spa facilities', Mia Kyricos of Starwood said in 2010. 'Spas are no longer considered an amenity; guests expect them. And they're no longer viewed as an indulgence, but an essential part of the balance and wellness guests seek while on the road' (Asiatraveltrips, 2010).

The wellness and well-being buzz, however, can result in such word-stretching that we can see in the case of Ibis hotels (from Accor Hotels). Ibis has taken the concept-stretching to another level when on the room-card holder they put: 'The Key to Your Well-being.'

Not only traditional hotel facilities, but newcomers from different industries, also enter the wellness market. Water brand evian has created a new licensed spa concept (evianSpa) set for roll-out around the world in luxury hotels. The story takes its inspiration from the 15-year journey that the spring water makes before emerging at the source in the heart of the Alps. The evianSpa menu has 16 signature therapies themed around the water journey – four for each of the stages. First is celestial, the start of the water cycle in the sky, which is represented by 'let go moment' treatments; second is mineral, the journey the water takes through the rocks, that lends itself to detox treatments; third is precious, where the water gathers in a reserve, which is linked to anti-ageing; and fourth is vital, the flow at the source of the water, which includes rejuvenating treatments (Houel, 2012).

There are thousands of hotel and resort spas and most international hotel brands have already or soon will launch their in-house spa or wellness brands, but there are only a handful of organisations that specialise in the chain operation of these facilities (e.g. WTS International, American Leisure, VAMED, Steiner Leisure, GOCO Hospitality). One of the very few specialist chains is the Danubius Hotels group.

CASE STUDY 6.6
Danubius Hotels

Danubius Hotels Group, the largest hotel chain in Europe specialising mainly in health-oriented hotels, rebranded some of its hotels. Members of that hotel chain which are located primarily in medical tourism-oriented destinations in Hungary, Czech Republic, Slovakia and Romania, were labelled as 'Danubius thermal' hotels in Hungary and 'hotel balnea' in Slovakia. The new brand (for nine properties in four countries), 'Danubius Health Spa Resorts' or DHSRs, following the upgrading and diversifying of the on-site health facilities in the hotels, fits more the expectations of the demand and can represent the brand assets of the hotel chain. The six elements of the brand are: Natural Resources, Medical Expertise,

Therapeutic Treatments, Well-being and Relaxation, Fitness and Beauty, and Spa Cuisine. The hotel chain has opened its membership based on fitness centres under the brand of Danubius Premier Fitness (ten properties in two countries), whereas the beauty and cosmetic unit is branded with The Emporium Wellness and Beauty label (four properties only in Hungary).

(Danubius Hotels, 2008)

Interestingly, individual facilities, especially in the spa and wellness arena, have shown a shift from standard approaches and techniques. Here are some rather unusual or standalone branding examples: Kamalaya Wellness Sanctuary and Holistic Spa Resort (2013): www.kamalaya.com.

CASE STUDY 6.7
Lanserhof Health Spa

At Lanserhof Health Spa (Lanserhof, Austria), a signature health product, the so-called Lans Med Concept was developed and represents the essence of this unique facility and brand. The concept which aims at Innovative Vital Aging contains the following elements:

- detox and aesthetics (body, face and charisma);
- diet and exercise (energy cuisine and body-awareness);
- energy and information medicine (energetic and spiritual balance);
- life-coaching and philosophy (self-optimization and change of daily habits);
- sleep medicine and biorhythm (regeneration and well-being);
- check-up.

(Lanserhof, 2013)

We can conclude that focusing on emotional elements of the brand really is the most often applied strategy of operators and marketers, regardless of which part of the world the given attraction happens to be in, for example:

- 'The power of nature' (Lanserhof, Austria)
- 'The Source of Healing' (Healing Hotels of the World)
- 'The Power of Contrast' (AquaDome, Langenfelden, Austria)
- 'S.O.S. Package. Transform a hectic life into a good life.' (Stay Overnight and Spa, Vintage Hotels, Ontario, USA)

- 'The Crossings offers their guests moments of welcome, focus, discovery, meditation, surprise and delight' (Austin, USA)
- 'Soulful Sanctuaries' (The Golden Door, California, USA)
- 'We've Spent 40,000 Years Creating the Day Spa of your Dreams.' (Li'tya Spa Dreaming, St Kilda, The Caribbean)
- 'Enjoy a Whipped Cocoa Bath, a Chocolate Fondue Wrap or a Mojito Sugar Scrub' (The Spa at Hotel Hershey, USA)
- 'Thermal Village' with thermal walks, geyser or dipping in the communal bath (Whakarewarewa, Rotorua, New Zealand).

We can see a somewhat different branding approach in holistic and spiritual tourism. As was mentioned before, these forms of health tourism heavily build on either the spiritual leader or a key person (e.g. a yogi or guru), or a site-specific quality (e.g. Earth Chakra). Since these operators do not compete with each other as, for example, spa resorts do, and since the business orientation is often missing from the operation itself, the branding, in whatever form it takes place, can differ significantly from other forms of health tourism. The same very selected branding and communication can be observed in the surgical form of medical tourism, too.

Mass communication is very typical of spas, hotels and cruises; however, festivals, clinics or ashrams use very well selected and much more focused channels of communication. The internet and social media is certainly the ever growing channel to inform customers and web surfers, and most service providers and destinations publish brochures, too. Holistic and spiritual destinations tend to be marketed via special interest groups (e.g. yoga groups), specialised magazines or direct mail.

Medical tourism has its own special characteristics in branding, although the services are more standardised than in wellness for example (consider the international protocol of a hip-replacement surgery). Any brand audit in medical tourism should look at all of these 'touchpoints' (After Geva, 2012):

- doctor referral;
- equipment;
- English/foreign-language speaking;
- advertising;
- follow-up treatments;
- accommodation;
- air carrier;
- word-of mouth;
- ground transportation;
- patient experience management;
- billing;
- facility appearance;
- sales force;
- medical tourism conferences;
- customer service;
- facilitator story;

- website;
- interviews and testimonials;
- tours and sightseeing;
- billing;
- twitter post.

In medical tourism, if it was based on natural resources, the key branding consideration is the natural quality of the healing resource and its healing benefits. In surgical tourism the branding consideration can be the following:

1 price;
2 quality;
3 reputation of (hospital/clinic);
4 a specific surgeon;
5 technology available;
6 faster access;
7 services provided;
8 good location;
9 government exchange programme;
10 non-FDA approved therapies.

Stackpole (2012) lists the ten most important marketing mistakes everybody should avoid when marketing medical tourism, such as:

- not clearly defining the benefits of the product or service;
- not understanding the lifetime value of a customer;
- not selling more services to the customer.

Branding of health and wellness tourism services should keep in mind that especially members of Generation Z (and Y) are looking for augmented realities, mobile or virtual try-outs and brands and should consider the ways in which they can build on emotional intelligence.

Cultural and language differences make marketers' life even more complicated since certain terminologies may not exist or mean something different in other languages.

CASE STUDY 6.8
Speaking health German

In German-speaking countries, branding (and product development) in health and wellness tourism has developed in much wider directions than we can see in, for example, English-speaking countries. The deeply rooted *bad* or bathing tradition in German-speaking countries is not only supported by the wide choice of available services, but also by the names

of settlements. One can find well over a hundred places called 'Bad *something*', many of which have become very famous and popular. Interestingly, in all three countries there is a place, i.e. Baden (Switzerland), Baden-Baden (Germany) and Baden-bei-Wien (Austria) that actually represents the historic spa concept and tradition itself in the respective countries. Visitors may either think that every 'Bad *something*' has something similar to offer, for example a bath (spa), or may think that this is just one-of-a-dozen. These assumptions and perceptions, of course, mean challenges to marketers.

The market is very much segmented nowadays, so the service providers also position and brand themselves more diversely. There are a handful of expressions or labels that cannot even be translated into English (or they would just be called 'spa'). Introducing some of the sophisticated labels from German:

- *Medical tourism*:
    - *Kurpark* (cure park) – historic spas and spa towns tend to have a so-called *Kurpark*, which provides resting and walking opportunities for guests before or after the treatments in the spa (e.g. Königlichen Kristall-Therme am Kurpark in Schwangau)
    - *Kurzentrum, Kurhotel* or *Kurhaus* (clinic or medical hotel)
    - *Gesundhotel* (health hotel)
    - *Kompetenzzentrum* (medical centre)
    - *Heilbad* (medical bath), *heilklima* (climatic resort), *heilstollen* (medical cave)

- *Wellness tourism*:
    - *Wohlfühlen*, or *Wohlsein-Oase* (well-being oasis or hotel)
    - *Wohlbefinden* (well-feeling)
    - *Vitalhotel* or *vitalbad* (vitality hotel, bath)

- *Leisure and recreation*:
    - *Thermenhotel* (spahotel)
    - *Bad, Warmbad*, (*Römer*), *Therme* or *Quelle* (bath or spring).

We have to refer briefly to the branding practices for the upcoming market of *men*. Both straight and gay men visit more and more health and wellness service providers, but the communication they accept is certainly different. Every destination and attraction wanting to increase the number of men in their facilities should bear in mind that it is very easy to send misleading or unclear messages to these segments. Just compare these slogans. It is sometimes difficult to distinguish between the promotion of gay compared to straight facilities, which could lead to either embrassment or disappointment. Some select branding messages from straight spas:

- 'Men's only – To be selfish is good!' (Beautiful Break, 2008)
- 'Achieve a higher state of happy' at Bliss promoting 'He-wax' services (Bliss, 2013)

- 'Get a golfer's massage. If this spa doesn't rejuvenate you, the entertainment in the Lobby will!' See the game of the day, with Keep Your Shorts on Day package. (You'll get a t-shirt and shorts instead of the typical robe.) Wow! sign up for your Sports Massage! (Sonwai Spa at The Hyatt Regency, Scottsdale, USA, 2008)

Hilton has revisited its spa strategy and identified several key areas for development such as treatment experiences, to be result focused, to provide relaxation (quick and urban as well) and to create experiences for men. They also change the language they use referring to services, such as calling them 'Guest Journeys', which are prescribed journeys such as thermal or express.

Considering the gay market, the branding messages are often much more direct and suggestive than those of straight counterparts:

- 'A spa with men in mind' (Hiranyikara Spa, 2013)
- 'House of Male' (House of Male, 2013)
- 'Welcome to Singapore's Most Exciting, Versatile and Complete Men's Spa! Unwind after a day's work, or rewind after a night out – Club One Seven is the place to refresh, renew and release! Catch up with old friends or make a few new ones!' (Club One Seven, 2013)

12 Marketing Tips (for reaching men)

There's more to marketing to men than extra-large robes and tacking the word 'executive' onto your basic facial. The International Spa Association (ISPA) collected some helpful tips on marketing to potential male clients.

1   Advertise in men's magazines.
2   Create special golf/spa and tennis/spa packages.
3   Offer bachelor parties.
4   Reward double "referral points" to customers who refer new male clients.
5   Create special promotions encouraging women to bring in their spouses and boyfriends.
6   Host a men's-only night.
7   Highlight men's treatments on the service menu.
8   Develop signature treatments for men.
9   Use warm, earthy colors throughout your spa.
10 Offer more athletic-type fitness classes.
11 Choose different color robes for the sexes.
12 Hire a mix of male and female therapists.

(American Spa Magazine, 2008)

Packaging, distribution and pricing

The advertisement of health and wellness tourism services, destination or brands does not really differ from the practices of any other form of tourism. However, we can see some typical and product-specific advertisement and distribution approaches:

- Hotel and resort spas, destination spas and spa lifestyle communities are featured in upmarket (both for women and men) lifestyle, on-board flight and spa-oriented magazines (and their respective on-line versions) and in TV programmes (e.g. see 'Stars and spas' at TravelChannel).
- Medical tourism advertisement uses healthy or luxury lifestyle-oriented magazines and websites, and doctors' waiting rooms (e.g. cosmetic surgery ads can be found in luxury lifestyle, while medical wellness treatments in healthy living magazines). On the other hand, many medical tourism services, such as dental and plastic surgery offers, tend to prefer online platforms and distributions sites, such as Treatmentabroad.com, Medeguide.com or Placidway.com. Therapeutic medical services based on natural healing assets are not featured that often on these sites. This is mainly due to the relatively unknown nature of evidence based medicine. Patients Beyond Borders was the path-making information source (both in printed and online form) that collected medical tourism information from 20 countries and introduced the whole concept of travelling abroad for medical reasons.
- Holistic and spiritual tourism is not mass advertised, but more likely to use direct mailing (e.g. newsletters), specialist magazines and via special interest classes, clubs and societies or marketed under a tour operator's umbrella, like Skyros.com.

As an example of how specific one market can be it is recommended that websites hoping to attract Russian clients are advised to have a .ru version as well and should have cross-browser compatibility.

The way in which, or even the extent to which, wellness tourism products are packaged depends very much on the typology of wellness tourism and the intended target market. As a general rule, wellness tourists seem relatively happy to purchase pre-selected packages within which there is some flexibility and freedom of choice. For example, spa visitors may select a pampering and relaxation package to which they can add further treatments or fitness activities. Holistic tourists may opt for a week in which certain courses are offered, but usually they select only a small number of those or can even choose to do something else (e.g. relax on the beach or go on an excursion).

Insurance companies can play very complex roles in the management and distribution of travelling for health as can be observed in how Techniker Krankenkasse (TK, Germany) has been doing it. It is a non-profit company under public law and eight million insurants who pay 8.2 per cent compulsory contribution (of income) completed with 7.3 per cent contribution by the employer. TK has service contracts with over 130 hospitals in eight EU member countries, cure contracts with some 40 cure hotels in six countries, dental clinic contracts. TK has over 20,000 planned and over 10,000 unplanned interventions every year and just over half of TK clients are retirees. TK assumes that the cross-border care initiative can provide impetus for making new and rare treatments and has opportunities for insurers with a wide network (both in terms of geographical and specialty coverage (Wagner, 2012).

Most packages seem as if they are customised to the visitor's needs and take into consideration individual needs. Even if the transport and accommodation and food provision is the same for everyone, few health and wellness tourists like to travel in groups or feel as if they are being treated *en masse*. For this reason, health and wellness holidays (with the exception of state-subsidised medical tourism) tend to be more expensive than average holidays, and are more in line with other special interest tourism trips where groups are small or individuals are offered tailor-made packages.

Quality is another issue that is of extreme importance to most health and wellness tourists, especially if they are receiving treatments which are physical or psychological. Although the qualifications of the practitioners may not be known to them, they need to feel cared for and safe. Therefore, the packages may need to include some pre-care (e.g. advice about treatments or preparation for treatments) and some after-care (e.g. the means to ask questions about recovery, or the chance to be part of an online community in the case of holistic retreats). One of the most sophisticated systems would require the potential visitor to give details of their profiles and needs and for a package to be recommended. Even if the operator or hotel only has two or three packages available, visitors would feel special and catered for as individuals. AccorThalassa Sea and Spa, for example, pre-packaged its services in the following ways, which have changed significantly in the last five years (Accor Thalassa, 2008):

2008:
- Vitality
- Fitness La Cure by Accor Thalassa
- Slimming
- Anti-stress
- Young mother
- Refreshed Legs

- Marine Beauty
- Men's Tonic

2013:
- Vitality
- Harmony
- Slimming
- Health
- Discovery Stopover

A typical spa package from a wellness or spa hotel tends to offer visitors their accommodation, full or half board, a welcome drink (either fruit juice or champagne, or fruit basket), use of all facilities on site or the adjacent spa (e.g. pools, saunas, fitness programmes), and maybe one or two treatments (e.g. a massage, facial, manicure). Transport is not usually included and other treatments have to be booked on arrival or in advance and paid for as extras. Holistic centres also include accommodation, full or half board, and two–three courses or workshops per day. Within a typical package, there would be some freedom of movement everyday and time for rest and relaxation (e.g. two–three hours in the afternoon). Too much programming or a tightly timed schedule can make a wellness visitor feel as stressed as he or she would at home!

It has been estimated that there are over 100 different forms of yoga (*Yoga Magazine*, 2013), so the choice of holidays and activities can be somewhat overwhelming for the beginner. However, for more experienced yoga enthusiasts there are growing numbers of exciting new products and combined packages. As well as offering specific types of yoga such as Astanga or Kundalini, many yoga holidays or retreat centres combine yoga with meditation, dance, creative activities, nutrition, music and mantras. In terms of packaging, yoga can be combined with skiing, wildlife safaris, dancing, surfing, diving, and so on. Combined packages are appealing to those people who are not 'hard-core' yoga aficionados but may want to use yoga to warm up for other sports or to use yoga to relax at the end of the day. For more dedicated yogis and yoginis, there are numerous deep and spiritual yoga-based retreats being offered all over the world. Holidays for yoga practitioners and teachers are increasing all the time too, and numerous centres offer the chance to intensify knowledge of one form of yoga or to acquire knowledge of a new form. Some yoga teachers may want to increase their repertoire and introduce some massage, dance or martial arts to their practice. Yoga festivals are also becoming popular, as are fairs and trade shows which are open to the general public.

Medical tourism services are well defined since the treatment plan, especially in the case of invasive treatments should be agreed before the actual travel. Often the medical service provider has a representative or partner located in the home country of the medical tourist. This representative helps the patient with the initial tests and agreeing on the treatment plan and the costs. Buying a dental package, very likely will contain everything from organising a check-up at home, through transferring existing medical data and X-rays between the dentists back home and the destination, to leisure and cultural programmes in the location. The medical tourism facilitator organises the whole stay including doctor appointments, transfers and accommodation.

Medical packages tend to be very complex and all inclusive, even providing services for the accompanying passengers, especially for ill guests who may require door-to-door transport. In some cases, accommodation could be booked separately, but this is not appropriate if visitors are having operations or medical treatments which require extensive supervised rest.

Not only facilitators but insurance companies, the ones that actually finance the medical services, also have an impact on packaging and the delivery process. Boucher (2011) from Companion Global Healthcare listed the key questions companies ask from insurance companies as they contemplate a global option for their employees:

- Where in the world are these facilities?
- What is the level of care provided?
- Are the cost savings significant?
- What types of procedures allow for travel?
- How would I design my benefit plan?
- What if something goes wrong?

Boucher (2011) also lists employee benefit plan incentives that American employers are using:

- Waive out of pocket costs for select procedures.
- Cover travel costs for patient and companion.
- Share Savings with employees.
- Time off not counted as PTO or sick leave.

Whereas benefits of an international medical travel benefit for self-funded employers are:

- each procedure yields direct savings;
- potential for reduced stop-loss premiums;
- improved competitiveness nationally and internationally.

The US-based MedRetreat, for example, provides services for corporate employers, which can include medical trips in the health insurance packages they offer for their employees (MedRetreat gives a hint: consider a medical trip only if the costs in the USA were higher than 6,000 US dollars (MedRetreat, 2008). Another example is GlobalChoice Healthcare, which provides all medical travel-related services for patients from the USA from scheduling clients' procedures, transferring medical records, arranging travel and accommodations, and providing access to on-the-ground local assistance for the duration of clients' stay (GlobalChoice Healthcare, 2008).

Tour operators and health insurance companies tend to have a varying role in the packaging and distribution of health and wellness tourism products and services. Travellers can find information about health and wellness offers via the following distribution channels:

- General tour operators that diversify their existing product portfolio with mainstream spa-type services.

- Some independent and smaller tour operators/facilitators specialised in wellness tourism or medical tourism (e.g. FIT Reisen, Skyros Holidays, Mondial or Thermalia Travel in Europe, Virtus Tours and Travels in Arabia or travelshanti.com or IndiaHeals. com in Asia).
- Specialist operators that are often linked to the service provider itself (e.g. retreat) and offer additional products (e.g. essential oils or books), package holistic and spiritual trips (e.g. Skyros).
- Health insurance companies, because of better prices, more efficient or faster treatments, may cover treatments that are not at the home place of the insured. This can encourage people to take both domestic and foreign trips. Of course, medical doctors can also act as part of the distribution channel recommending a site for a certain set of treatments.
- Both general travel search engines (e.g. Yahoo!Travel) and specialised ones (e.g. SpasofAmerica.com, SpaFinderWellness.com, Wahanda.co.uk) offer, promote and introduce destinations and operators.
- General and specialised fairs and exhibitions.
- Lifestyle clubs and societies of the trainer or leader can be a source of information about where-and-what to do.

Major or international tour operators (e.g. Thomas Cook/Neckermann and TUI in Europe, Classic Vacations or Pleasant Holidays in the USA) with many brands can either programme health services into the 'standard' packages or have one that is specialised in health and wellness (e.g. Spa Vacations and Retreats from Classic Vacations). General tour operators, as part of diversifying their package portfolio may publish a brochure or create a link on their website for health and wellness offers. Certainly, the titles of these brochures and websites follow the global trend: TUI calls it 'Vital' or 'FitandGesund', Thomas Cook/Neckermann labels it with 'Care/Wellness Holidays' or 'Wellnesswelten' by DERTOUR, online agent (OTA) Kayak.com labels its services under 'Resort and Spa'. Since the various forms of health and wellness tourism do not tend to enjoy similar market position in all countries managed by the tour-operator, these special publications may be available for certain markets only.

The following example from Kuoni shows the kind of language that is used by general operators in their promotion. It is obvious that the spa services are merely an add-on benefit to the mass tourism product, and very little specialised vocabulary is used.

CASE STUDY 6.10
Spa holidays by Kuoni

Recharge your batteries at a luxury spa resort! Over 60 per cent of the people we surveyed for our 'It's Official: Holidays Change Your Life' report said they desperately needed to recharge their batteries, and 70 per cent go on holiday to escape from work. We've put together a selection of breaks designed to relax, rejuvenate and revitalise, leaving you glowing inside and out.

Indulge with one of Kuoni's specially-selected spa holidays and experience a wide range of luxurious treatments. Discover the unique underwater treatment rooms in the Maldives or book a short-haul pampering break in Europe. Treat yourself.

As spa holidays become ever more popular, the range of treatments on offer continues to grow. From Aerobics to Zen treatments, our guide to spa treatments will help you decipher some of the confusing spa terminology.

(Kuoni, 2013)

We can consider what the MICE (Meeting, Incentives, Conferences and Exhibitions) industry tends to apply more and more as a special packaging approach. In an application for a MICE bid, organisers and destinations incorporate health and wellness services as well and they consider it as an added bonus, and competitive advantage. It is quite interesting to follow up what happens to the marriage of MICE and spas, since congress, conference or corporate meeting delegates' time is often completely full with the official programme. When will they have time to use the spa, in that case?

In health and wellness tourism various pricing strategies can be observed. We can estimate that at least one third of spa operators transmit the 'we-are-not-for-everybody' message to prospective visitors. Associations and cooperation with other luxury brands, the way in which they promote themselves and the language they use in the communication, all support the upmarket pricing (and vice versa). This is one way to select visitors and to create the necessary image. There can be, however, a huge gap between the prices of wellness and medical services. Surgical trips to Asia, Central America or Central Europe become competitive because of the relatively low costs of medical and tourist services there. Some might argue that this is a risky and short-term strategy to base competition on price levels, though, but both intra-regional, for example within the Middle East, or global tourism can also be boosted by better prices.

In many countries medical tourism or medical services offered during trips form a close part of national health services, and prices are, at least partially, subsidised, that is consumers receive standard medical services (e.g. balneotherapeutic treatments) for free or at very low prices. This form of tourism can constitute a significant part of domestic tourism in numerous Central and Eastern European countries.

We can see some atypical pricing practices as well. For example, in the Alpine region, winter is the main season. That is when most of the guests arrive to ski. The summer is the second most important season, that is for hiking and trekking. Autumn and spring are considered as low seasons. This situation leaves hotel operators with no other option than to apply lower prices in summer than they can do during winter. Visitors can find very good deals in four–five-star spa hotels for trips in the summer, which is their main holiday-taking period. This pricing can make mountainous areas with high-quality spas very competitive with the seaside.

Conclusions

Reaching for health and wellness tourists can differ a little bit from standard approaches in tourism. The very personal and sometimes very risky nature of the services makes the selection of applicable communication strategies and tactics challenging. While in North America both segmentation and product development seem to have been reaching very sophisticated levels (e.g. Dude Ranch Spas!), other parts of the world have not yet applied similar approaches. Although consider what the following title may mean to an average customer: 'Optiwell-Fitbalance', as the marketers labelled a lifestyle and fitness day sponsored by a global breakfast cereal brand.

Destinations and service providers tend to build on emotional brand elements and benefit-focused positioning themes. Still, this means limits to marketers (maybe that is why there are so many new words and expressions in the German language). It really is very difficult to brand and communicate a whole country as some type of health destination, especially globally. We can see that the understanding of terms and messages can vary country by country. This may slow down the globalisation of marketing in this field (i.e. the simple copying and not adapting of what marketers say about health and wellness tourism may become less standard than in other types of tourism).

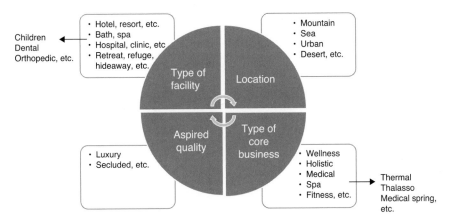

FIGURE 6.2 Positioning health and wellness tourism facilities

7

Planning and management

If we are open to renewal and change we are alive, whatever stage we are at.

(Luft, 2003: 93)

Introduction

This chapter analyses the way in which health and wellness tourism is planned and managed. It is important to consider why it is necessary to plan and manage health and wellness tourism. First, a destination, resort or facility must be economically viable and make good business sense. It should be high quality and designed with the right target markets in mind. Second, it is important to consider the impacts that any tourism development may have on the environment and local communities' lives. This should be done in accordance with the principles of sustainable and 'green' development, which are becoming essential to the future of the planet and its people. Third, it is being argued more and more (e.g. GSS, 2011) that health and wellness tourism destinations or resorts need to be unique in some way in order to survive in a very competitive market.

The need to plan and manage health and wellness tourism

Like all forms of tourism, health and wellness tourism needs to be carefully planned and managed. Although there are some destinations which seem to have developed fairly successfully in an organic way (i.e. without formal planning), sustainable examples are few and far between. We could name Byron Bay in Australia, Goa in India or Chiang Mai in Thailand, but these were mainly 'alternative' backpacker enclaves which have gradually evolved into more mainstream wellness tourism destinations. Planning is needed in order to have a holistic overview of a place and its attractions and facilities. There ideally needs to be complementarity rather than competition, which is why the development of Destination Management Organisations or Health Tourism Clusters and Health Cities starts to become more popular. By working together, health and wellness providers can help each other to create the best possible business environment for themselves and the best experiences for visitors, not to mention stronger (joint) promotion of the destination. Planning is needed in order to have a strategic view of a destination or site and to think about its long-term future. This is one of the basic principles of sustainability, which also requires the balance of economic development (i.e. profitability, income for the destination and its inhabitants), with the minimisation of environmental impacts (e.g. on nature, wildlife) and the involvement of local people (e.g. education, training, entrepreneurship, employment). Planning is also needed in order to create or enforce regulations for safety or quality control. This may be done by governments, industry or supra-national organisations (e.g. the EU, World Tourism Organization). Lack of planning can result in unsustainable, unprofitable developments which exploit the local environment and fail to involve local people. Ultimately, these destinations tend to become unpopular with visitors even if they were attractive to begin with. Degraded environments, unhappy locals, and unregulated facilities are not appealing to tourists.

The list below provides a summary of the main planning and management challenges in health and wellness tourism, all of which will be addressed in this chapter:

- to manage the economic, environmental and social impacts of health and wellness tourism in order to be sustainable, green and ethical;
- to maintain historic spa destinations where the buildings need maintenance renovation and adaptation to modern services in old or heritage facilities;
- to make water-based facilities profitable (it is notoriously expensive to run spas, especially those which do not have a natural source of thermal water);
- to avoid too much standardisation and generic development (i.e. uniqueness and place distinctiveness are important in tourism in order to be competitive);
- to regulate the health and wellness industries so that they are safe for tourists (this is especially essential for medical tourism);
- to provide adequate quality control systems for health and wellness tourism facilities and attractions;
- to employ fully qualified staff and to ensure the best customer service possible (health and wellness tourism are centred around personal and individual service);
- to create the best possible design, atmosphere and experience for visitors.

Impacts of health and wellness tourism

This section summarises some of the main economic, environmental, social and cultural impacts which can be caused by health and wellness tourism. Bringing these into balance is one of the main aims of sustainable development and can only be done through effective, responsible and ethical planning and management.

Economic impacts

Health and wellness tourism can bring significant economic benefits to a country so it is not surprising that many governments of the world have placed considerable emphasis on attracting health, wellness or medical tourists to their country. Chapter 3 shows that there are very few countries in the world which are not promoting some form of health tourism, even if development usually focuses on one type of tourism or another. Only countries like Thailand and India are successfully managing to combine all types of health tourism (i.e. spas, wellness, medical and spiritual).

In economic terms, health and wellness tourism is especially desirable because it is non- or less seasonal, guests tend to stay longer than other tourists (e.g. two or three weeks in therapeutic medical resorts), they are higher spending than average, and usually stay in hotels at the higher end (at least three star quality) and pay for medical services (many of which are rather pricey). However, it should still be noted that seasonality can be a problem, for example, STR SpaSTAR estimates that in the US luxury hotel market one spa treatment costs approximately US$137, and treatment room utilisation dips in the summer by some 20 per cent compared to winter months (Freitag, 2012). The services health and wellness tourists use are very human resource intensive, such as personal services (e.g. treatments or high-quality accommodation). This can mean a higher employment multiplier than other forms of tourism (i.e. it creates non-seasonal employment at a relatively high level for which training is needed). The only problem may be if local people cannot easily be employed because they do not have adequate education and training and this is unavailable in the local area. Some health and wellness facilities struggle to find good staff and high wages may need to be offered to attract the right people to work. Hutchinson (2012) writes about the problem of finding people with the right qualifications to work in spas and Sokolova (2012: 49) also mentions the lack of appropriate education of spa and wellness staff. In Part III of this book, Kathryn Dowthwaite and Sarah Rawlinson analyse the challenges of providing educational courses for students wanting to work in the spa industry, and Marion Joppe talks about the issue of compensation of employees.

CASE STUDY 7.1
Operational issues: retaining staff in a seasonal environment
Su Gibson

Background

The European Spa was one of the first spas to open on Hilton Head Island just off the southeastern coast of South Carolina, USA in the 1990s. The spa's original location was in a small business centre on the south end of the island, and over time, it expanded to several other locations because of its success. The spa quickly gained a reputation in the area for its high-quality experiences and, most importantly, the great care provided by its dedicated staff of spa therapists and other employees. This was generally attributed to the influence of the spa's owners, Elizabeth and Liz McGinnes, a mother and daughter team.

Situation

One of the spa's additional locations was in a timeshare development which had high occupancy during the summer months and low occupancy during the winter months. As a consequence, spa therapists were booked with services heavily during summer months, but were frequently sent home from their shift during winter months without appointments. Since spa therapists' primary income was a commission on services performed, this resulted in lower pay during slower seasons.

Employees were sometimes forced to find additional employment to supplement their income or leave the area to find temporary work elsewhere during winter months. This led to higher staff turnover, since workers that did this would sometimes not return the following spring.

Solution

In an effort to instill a sense of reward, belonging and team motivation amongst the therapists, and to guarantee that the best staff members remained with the spa year after year, Liz spent much time working on the compensation model for spa therapists in addition to other team building and company culture activities. Instead of the set commission rates, fee per service and flat hourly wages that were commonly used in the industry, Liz created an adjustable hybrid 'tips-plus' model that included the therapists' tips plus either a flat percentage commission on services or an hourly rate based on the hours worked in the spa for that pay period. The spa therapist received whichever combination was greater for the pay period in question.

This guaranteed employees a certain amount of pay each week based on the hours they worked regardless of the season, and still offered an incentive for spa therapists to take appointments and upgrade the services performed. It also encouraged them to do support duties such as training, inventory, laundry, or product stocking during 'down-time', since they were paid for their time if they were not busy with treatments.

Although the labour expense was higher during the first winter season this new compensation strategy was in effect, it paid off in the spring with reduced recruitment and training-related costs given the lower employee attrition rate. It also increased employee satisfaction, transferring into even better customer care for spa clients.

Conclusions

Many spas and resorts face staffing issues such as the one experienced by The European Spa. Since there is not one standard compensation model used by the spa industry, spa owners and directors have the ability to create a model that fits best with their spa's environment, situation, and goals. In this case, reducing staff turnover and creating a consistent and happy spa team was of utmost importance to the business's reputation, operations and mission. Therefore, the manipulation of the therapist compensation to ensure financial stability for the staff was a successful solution.

Economic recessions can have a big impact on the health and wellness industries, as spas are often perceived as luxuries and may be the first activity to go if people have to decide how to save their money. Recessions also mean that governments have to make savings and social tourism or state-supported health tourism (i.e. to medical thermal spas in Central and Eastern Europe) may be the first to suffer. For example, the German government cut its *kur* treatments from four to three weeks in 1997 and allowed its prescription only every four years instead of three (Pforr and Locher, 2013). Many Central and Eastern European countries like Hungary or the Czech Republic have an over-supply of thermal baths which are state-supported and publicly owned. If state support should be withdrawn or decreased, most of these facilities could not afford to survive and would close down as they would not attract international (i.e. non-domestic) and self-financing tourists in the same numbers. In recent years, the inverse travel has been growing in medical tourism, that is the medical specialist travel to the patients and not the patients to the service provider. This shift in direction of travel can have serious and not too positive impacts to medical destinations.

Environmental impacts

Environmental impacts can come in two major groups, on the natural and the built environment. Health and wellness tourism can have impacts on both groups and are especially significant if tourism was built on a local natural asset, for example a thermal lake, cave or mud. The impacts on wildlife need to be considered as these healing assets are

TABLE 7.1 Economic impacts of health and wellness tourism

Impacts on ...	Positive aspects	Negative aspects
Employment	Skilled workforce	Imported workforce (from other cities or even countries)
	Limited seasonal fluctuation of employees	Migration (both ways)
Economy	Multiplier effects (especially employment multiplier)	Formation of dependence
	Higher than average per capita spending	Spending concentrated in health and wellness facilities
	Complex spending structure	Increase of regional inequalities
	Imported technology and products	Imported technology and products
Living conditions	Proliferation of services offered	Mono-cultural supply
	Image of settlement develops	Prices may increase
	Infrastructure developments	Differences between the tourist and non-tourist areas

part of a habitat, therefore any development and use has a direct impact. Any modification of the natural environment can even create detrimental impacts to the assets themselves. For example, the Tapolca medical cave (Hungary) lost its water due to a nearby bauxite mine. When mining was discontinued, the water level rose slowly again. The water levels in the Dead Sea are being significantly diminished because of diversion of water and mining industries (see Dalit Gasul's case study in Part III of this book).

CASE STUDY 7.2
Therapeutic tourism on the Dead Sea of Jordan is in danger
Salem Harahsheh

Therapeutic tourism in Jordan dates back more than 3000 years since the time of the Greeks and Romans as evidenced by the Madaba map of the fifth century AD that shows the Dead Sea, Ma'in Hot Springs, Jordan River and the Baptism Site of Jordan and the Holy Land (JTB, 2012). The Dead Sea is the world's largest, lowest, saltiest natural spa known for its healing powers for thousands of years. The sea is located between Jordan, Israel and Palestine around 462 metres below sea level (*Science Daily*, 2012). Jordan started to invest in therapeutic tourism on the Dead Sea in the 1980s. However, it also developed other therapeutic hot and mineral springs such as Alhimmah in the 1960s, Ma'in and Alshouna at the beginning of the 1980s, Afra in the 1990s and Albarbaitah in the 2000s.

The Dead Sea is one of the best health destinations in the world as it has a hot dry climate with a mean temperature of 24°C all year round and 335 days of sunlight. Because it is located more than 420 metres below sea level, it has ten times more oxygen than any other place on earth as well, as it holds a lot of black volcanic mud and salts accumulated over millions of years, which are useful for healing many skin diseases and body ailments as well as for wellness purposes. The north eastern shore of the Dead Sea of Jordan is now developed as a destination for health tourism as well as for conferences. There are five hotels (one four-star and four five-star hotels) belonging to international hotel and spa chains such as the Mövenpick, the Marriot, the Holiday Inn, the Kempinski and the first spa that was built in 1989, known as the German Spa (now the Dead Sea Spa Hotel) as it was based on German and Austrian patients-tourists (JTB 2012). Jordan has invested in MICE tourism on the Dead Sea through the King Hussein Bin Talal Convention Centre that hosts Economic Forum 'Davos' nearly every year in May (KHBTCC, 2012).

The above characteristics of the Dead Sea are under threat as the sea is losing around half a metre of its water level annually due to many factors such as little water flowing in (*Science Daily*, 2012), Israel diverting many sources of the River Jordan north of Tiberias Lake to the Negev District, high evaporation rates and the mining industries extracting minerals on the southern edge of the sea (Lean, 2012). Jordan, Israel and the Palestine are aware of the problem of the Dead Sea and they are trying to solve it by seeking international support since 1995 to build a canal from the Red Sea to the Dead Sea (Red–Dead Canal) despite its high cost. It is argued therefore, that if nothing is done to solve the problem of the Dead Sea,

then the consequences will be huge and destructive for the eco-system of the sea, therapeutic tourism services and the mining industry. Consequently, Jordan as well as Israel and Palestine will lose their magnificent natural gift and the curative healing spot will vanish in the coming hundred years.

The most significant impact of thermal spas is the excess water. Water used in spas can be hot and full of minerals. These waters, theoretically, should all be treated, since warm water rich in minerals means an unnecessary load to natural waters. The rise of temperature results in the disappearance of species and the minerals are deposited in the waterbeds. Water-based facilities have to face the risk of high running, maintenance, renewal and replacement costs. Thermal or medical waters can quickly plug up pipes, which then need either regular cleaning or frequent replacement. Excess waters also mean hazardous waste (because of temperature and mineral content) that needs special treatment.

Water wastage is also a major environmental issue. The environmental impacts of spas and wellness hotels can be significant, especially luxury hotels which use vast amounts of water in destinations where water is scarce (e.g. swimming pools, golf courses). Sloan et al. (2013) show that luxury hotel guests are estimated to consume up to a staggering 880 litres per day. On a per capita basis, hotel guests and tourist activities demand more water than local residents.

CASE STUDY 7.3
Management challenges in Pamukkale, Turkey

The health-giving properties of Turkey's natural hot springs have been well known since antiquity. The ancient city of Hierapolis was built on the site of the rich mineral waters of Pamukkale, where the hot waters created enormous circular basins in the earth as it flowed down the mountainside, resulting in dazzling white calcareous rock. For thousands of years visitors, including pilgrims, have enjoyed the healing powers of Pamukkale's calcium-rich hot springs and bathed in the white terraced pools, as well as swimming in the Sacred Pool. The Sacred Pool is where the springs that feed Pamukkale's mineral pools originate in a depression among the cultural artifacts of the ancient Romans, and columns and capitals can therefore be found under the water.

In the 1970s and 1980s visitors could still come to the little town outside Denizli, take a cheap room, walk to the springs and enjoy the pool. However, larger hotels built at the site of the spring to service increasing numbers of tourists and irresponsible tourism itself caused the spring to almost stop producing water, and the originally white pools started to turn grey. Visitors walked with their shoes on and even bathed using soaps and shampoos. Locals also disregarded the site and rode motor bikes up and down the slopes causing destruction. UNESCO was called in and Pamukkale was given World Heritage Site status in 1988 and the additional protection this requires. Hotels that diverted the spring water were torn down. Trails were set up through the pools, and bathing in them was not allowed. Some replica pools were built for tourists to enjoy themselves in with water pumped in at certain times of day. As a consequence, the pools have returned to their pristine whiteness, and are once again a worthwhile tourist destination.

(CTG Heathcare, 2008)

Many retreats are located in environmentally fragile locations and access can be difficult. Transporting large groups of people can cause significant impacts to the environment so it is best if retreats cater for small groups. As researched by Smith and Kelly (2006) the average number of participants in one retreat holiday is 10–15.

Medical services may produce hazardous waste (e.g. needles, waste from operation theatre or radioactive waste). Waste disposal requires special impacts management practices and the collection and treatment of hazardous waste are provided by specialist companies.

TABLE 7.2 Environmental impacts of health and wellness tourism

Impacts on . . .	Positive aspects	Negative aspects
Vegetation and wildlife	Conservation of habitat	Pollution
	Parks and gardens	Introduction of new species
Elements	Infrastructure developments	Waste (solid and water) and hazardous waste management
		Change of landscape
		Emissions (gas, vapour, fumes)
		Thermal, healing water (drilling)
Land use	Change in land use	Growth of built up area
		Change in hydrological and other natural systems
Buildings and milieu	New architectural styles	Growth of built up area
	Conserving local styles	Wear and tear
		Introduction of new styles

Social and cultural impacts

There are also social and cultural impacts of health and wellness tourism. Many visitors, after enjoying their stay in a spa or retreat home, may decide to buy a summer or holiday home there. Owners of holistic retreat or yoga holiday facilities may even move there permanently. In small settlements the appearance of new locals can mean revitalisation; on the other hand, holiday-home owners do not necessarily understand the everyday problems of the community. Many traditional spa towns, for example, have a whole new part with holiday homes and hotels. The municipality is left with the obligatory tasks, for example street cleaning and lighting or litter collection for twelve months, whereas home owners come for only a couple of weekends per year. It also radically changes the composition of the local community, who may not even want to share their home with foreigners.

Local people may find it difficult to understand and absorb new developments because of religion, tradition or lifestyle issues (e.g. the locals of the Greek island to where Skyros organised its first holistic trips in the 1970s thought that those visitors were simply mad!). Indigenous or tribal people may be living in areas (e.g. jungles, rainforests, deserts, small villages) which are used for holistic retreats or eco-spas. The people should be consulted about their needs and even their involvement. The use of tribal medicines or indigenous healing treatments can be very attractive for tourists. On the extreme side, in relatively poor countries, such as India more and more people illegally sell their kidneys for hospitals that take foreign medical patients. Surrogacy is estimated to be a USD 445 million a year

TABLE 7.3 Social and cultural impacts of health and wellness tourism		
Impacts on . . .	Positive aspects	Negative aspects
Cultural heritage	Revitalisation and protection of traditional architecture	Mismatch in style and overuse
Population	Growth of population	Imported workforce (from other cities or even countries)
	Presence of holiday home owners	Facility and holiday home owners do not consider the destination as their permanent home
Employment	Generation of new jobs and income opportunities	Competition with workforce outside the settlement
	Skills developed	
Community	Revitalisation of social, cultural life	Costs of impact management
	Increase of the community's pride in their settlement	Growth of the proportion of seasonal residents
	Transformation of social stratification	Demonstration effect
	Learning languages, education	Suppression of local language

business in India earning USD 6,000 to 10,000. Some fear commercial surrogacy could change from a medical necessity for infertile women to convenience for the rich (Malik, 2012).

Sustainable planning and management for health and wellness tourism

Sustainability has become a necessity rather than an option in all businesses. Commitment is needed from governments, societies and individuals too. The health and wellness tourism sectors are no exception. The carbon footprint from flying alone is quite considerable (although surprisingly not as significant as that of other large industries). Sustainability is not just about protecting the environment and being greener; it is also about making responsible social decisions, treating people ethically, but all whilst continuing to make a profit. Cohen (2008: 15) suggests that the current model for healthcare may not be sustainable in itself: 'Western medicine is based on an illness model with most money or effort being spent on developing drugs and therapies to treat disease rather than enhance well-being.' He goes on to state that 'the current illness-based medical model is not sustainable and will never be able to meet the needs of the global population'. Therefore sustainability is also about investing in wellness and preventative health care and increasing public education.

The majority of health, wellness and spa operators have very quickly become aware of the need for sustainable practices in their businesses. Hotels and all forms of accommodation comprise the largest sector of the travel and tourism industry and have been shown to have the highest negative influence on the environment of all commercial buildings (Sloan et al., 2013). Many hotel chains have therefore already committed to sustainability schemes which run throughout all of their operations, including their spas (e.g. Accor, Mariott, Hyatt). ISPA (2013b) also gives guidelines on how spas can be greener:

To grow this industry toward a deeper connection with the natural laws of nature, the spa embraces the three pillars of sustainability: planet, people and prosperity.

- *Planet*: It is the spa's purpose and responsibility to work with the natural world to promote its healing properties while conducting business in a way that sustains the life of the planet and thus humanity.
- *People*: To serve others, the spa staff members must keep themselves physically, mentally and spiritually healthy by maintaining their overall health and well-being.
- *Prosperity*: Member spa supports sustainability through education on more efficient uses of energy and resources, thus lowering the cost of operations.

These are some of the guidelines they give for spas to become more sustainable:

- LED light bulbs;
- filtered water instead of bottled water;

- corn-based cups rather than plastic cups;
- organic detergents and cleaning products;
- organic treatment products;
- re-usable implements that can be washed and sanitised;
- purchase in bulk rather than small containers;
- turning off lights in rooms that are not in use;
- turning off all electronics, such as computers, at night;
- natural chlorine generators or saline systems for pools and whirlpools;
- bamboo or other sustainable-based elements used in towels and linens.

Sloan et al. (2013) suggest that the ultimate aim of all hospitality (and ideally all businesses) would be to develop zero-energy buildings that have zero net energy consumption and zero carbon emissions. This means using less non-renewable materials by building more simply, using more local and plentiful (i.e. sustainable and renewable) materials and with less waste. The social and environmental impacts of development should be considered, including the materials used for construction procured from elsewhere. Old buildings should be renovated where possible. The chain of people involved in the development, including architects, civil servants, developers and designers may all need training in the fundamentals of environmental protection, and the tools to design and construct more sustainably. Businesses can become more profitable in the long term by saving energy and water. They can save heating costs by insulating better, lighting costs by having more natural sunlight and water costs by re-using grey water or collecting rainwater.

The Green Spa Network was established officially in 2006; however, the seed of the idea came from the 2002 International Spa Association conference, when Rancho La Puerta founder Deborah Szekely urged spas to become more actively involved in the burgeoning environmental movement. Following her inspirational keynote address, a small group of individuals joined together in an informal task force, initially called 'Healing the Waters', to explore the connections between personal and planetary wellness. Organisations like LOHAS (Lifestyles of Health and Sustainability) and Green America helped this early group by offering conference and networking opportunities for like-minded individuals to connect and share ideas. In 2006, a dozen leading spas from all parts of North America came together and devoted time and financial resources to developing an initial sustainability assessment process. The Green Spa Network was officially incorporated as a not-for-profit trade association in 2007, and opened the door for spas and resource partners to become members. In 2008, the Horst Rechelbacher Foundation provided a generous contribution that enabled the organization to continue to develop educational materials and survive the recession. Since its inception, Green Spa Network has grown to include more than 140 members, representing all facets of the spa industry. Since 2008, there has been an Annual Congress for members to share research, best practice and implement actions. The assessment system called GreenGain developed by the group allows companies to evaluate their own environmental and social performance. The assessment takes 45–60 minutes and each question highlights an initiative – a concrete and operational action that a company can take or has already accomplished in three broad areas: environmental sustainability, social justice and accountability.

CASE STUDY 7.4
The Green Spa Network

Green spas not only benefit the natural environment, but also offer a number of health and wellness benefits to their clients:

- **Green spas are naturally healthy**: By eliminating toxins in their skin care products and in their spa's environment, green spas provide a healthier experience.

- **Green spas are more relaxing**: By putting aside the stressors of modern life – including noise, pollution, toxins and waste – green spas are able to offer a more balanced and relaxing experience.

- **Green spa treatments are more effective**: Synthetically derived skin-care products may produce quick results, but they might also cause damage. Natural treatments are gentler and help ensure long-term health and beauty.

- **Green spas put the body in harmony with nature**: Green spas are attuned to the rhythms of nature as well as the rhythms of the human body. When nature and body are in harmony humans feel healthier, stronger and more attractive.

- **Green spas are good business**: Although up-front costs for some greening programmes may be high, they usually pay for themselves and start to provide savings within one to two years. For example: investing in low-flow shower heads and toilets will cost up front, but the savings in water use will continue well into the future.

(Green Spa Network, 2013)

It is also important to manage other types of health and wellness destination, especially natural resources. One of the best examples of the sustainable management of a natural resource is the Blue Lagoon in Iceland.

CASE STUDY 7.5
A sustainably managed natural resource: the Blue Lagoon, Iceland

Mynatour (2013) describes Iceland as one of the most sustainable countries in the world with a government committed to sustainable development and sustainable tourism. Due to its natural sources of hydro and geothermal energy, Iceland is the cleanest energy consumer in the world, with 75 per cent of its total energy consumption coming from these natural sources. Iceland is a world leader in pollution control, natural resource management, environmental public health, greenhouse gas emissions and reforestation.

The Blue Lagoon is one of Iceland's most famous attractions. It is a natural geothermal spa outside Reykjavik, and offers unique spa and wellness experiences in a natural, sustainable wilderness setting. It has been awarded an Environmental Award by the Icelandic Tourist Board.

Blue Lagoon describes itself as 'a leading company in terms of green thinking' which is 100 per cent powered by clean thermal energy. The Blue Lagoon is seen to be part of a so-called ecocycle, where nature and science work in harmony, with as little environmental impact as possible. The Blue Lagoon is part of the Svartsengi Resource Park, which is a concept based on ecological balance, economic prosperity and social progress. The Blue Lagoon has a Blue Flag award meaning that the waters meet stringent quality standards and are monitored regularly. Architecture and design are also harmonised with nature. The Blue Lagoon's facilities, including the Blue Lagoon spa and Blue Lagoon Clinic, were designed by Sigríður SigÞórsdóttir from Basalt architects. The aim of the design was, she says, to 'protect the environment and respect its geological history. Pure Icelandic materials from moss and stones characterize the design. We wanted to emphasize the relationship between nature and the man-made' (Blue Lagoon, 2013).

Retreat centres tend to be small scale by nature and one of the major selling points may be the proximity to nature, the low-scale operations, and the use of local or home grown foods. However, Smith and Kelly's (2006) research showed that only about one fifth of holistic retreats out of a sample of 500 actually employed local people used local transport or promoted products or services from the local area. Retreat Finder (2013) includes a category for so-called Eco Retreats which are described as 'Environmentally sustainable retreats and retreat centers employing a wide variety of tactics to help the planet including: solar power, rain barrels, organic farming, recycling, and much more!' The Retreat Company (2013) lists over 80 Eco Retreats around the world, which shows the growing importance of sustainability in the holistic sector as well as in spas (it should perhaps be noted that many retreats started out with the express intention of being sustainable and eco-friendly, unlike spas and wellness hotels which were often obliged at a later stage to adopt these principles). Marinus Gisolf provides examples of Costan Rican eco-friendly retreats in his case study in Part III (it is worth remembering that Costa Rica was the highest rated country in the New Economics Foundation's Happy Planet Index in 2012).

In terms of sustainability medical tourism facilities count as high risk, since a purpose-built hospital cannot be turned into serviced apartments, whereas hotels and resorts could actually be reused as condominiums, should the original (tourism) plan not work out as expected. The technology used in hospitals (e.g. digital screening or operations such as the CyberKnife) can cost as much as 3–4 million euros, so sustainability requires very careful planning, management and sound financial background.

Standardisation versus unique experiences

The proliferation of spa and wellness hotel and resort developments around the world means that it is possible to experience a large number of health and wellness products almost anywhere where there is a reasonable infrastructure for tourism (and leisure provision). Products can include national and regional assets and resources, such as mineral waters, mountain chains, seas or rivers, indigenous and local traditions and treatments, or site-level facilities and packages. Although many countries do not have natural sources of medical or thermal waters, swimming pools, saunas, steam rooms, massage and fitness facilities can be created anywhere. This is unproblematic if health is the secondary motivation of tourists (i.e. they are business or conference tourists who may just use the facilities if they have time or sightseers for whom spa facilities are an added bonus). Leisure and day visitors also do not care much if their main motivation is relaxation rather than having a cultural experience. However, for more dedicated health tourists, the expectation is likely to be higher and the search for some form of uniqueness or local features may lead to disappointment if it is unfulfilled.

There needs to be some differentiation of destinations on a national level, especially if they are trying to market themselves specifically as health, spa or wellness destinations. This might mean promoting their unique physical resources (e.g. hot springs, mineral waters, lakes, mountains), or even claiming to have the 'largest', 'longest', 'highest', and so on, of these. Signature treatments can be promoted in hotels around the world, but it is debatable as to whether tourists would travel specifically for a massage. More likely they would pay for a long, leisurely package of several hours or days which is unique and makes use of local traditions or indigenous ingredients. It is clear that the majority of wellness and spa hotels and centres are including more and more ancient traditions as selling points. This can range from the design of the hotel (e.g. using principles of Feng Shui or Vasati) to the range of massages and treatments offered. The most common include yoga, Tai Chi, Thai massage and Ayurveda. However, it would arguably make more sense (and be more sustainable) to focus on traditions, products or treatments which are local to the area in which the hotel or spa is situated.

In terms of experience management and monitoring mystery shopping often seems to be an attractive tool. SpaAudit.com (2013) for example, has developed a checklist for spa performances comprising the following key sections checking over a hundred competencies, including:

- the reservation process;
- the confirmation process;
- the arrival and pre-treatment;
- the treatment experience;
- retailing;
- the departure;
- the overall experience.

CASE STUDY 7.6
A unique cultural experience: Botanique Hotel and Spa, Brazil

Botanique Hotel and Spa opened in Brazil in 2012. The aim of the spa is to set a new benchmark in luxury hospitality by focusing on all that it is local and indigenous to Brazil. It has been built by regional architects and designers using local slate, stone and wood. It has a 'farm to fork' philosophy with national cuisines and wines, and a library with over 400 titles by Brazilian authors. The spa is referred to as 'the world's first 100 per cent Brazilian spa'. The founders stated that:

> To make an experience that was totally local and avoiding the comfort zone of Asian, Indian or European treatments and techniques. We consulted with native Brazilian practitioners, local shamans of sort, and carried out extensive work with universities to develop authentic treatments.

The spa includes a rainforest sauna, an indigenous-inspired treatment menu, including Afro-Brazilian massage techniques and native American movements, a bath filled with fresh milk and ground brazil nuts, and Brazilian martial arts like capoeira. A geologist from a nearby University advised on a water menu of 15 sparkling and still waters from around the country. Another professor specialising in aromatherapy helped to create 28 essential spa oils from ingredients in the surrounding mountains. Extensive research has also been carried out by 19 professors and scientists to prove the benefits of the treatments.

Guests seem to appreciate the unique experience and the founders have the sense that they have also contributed positively to Brazilian self-esteem.

(Barnes, 2013)

Among several hotel and hospitality trends, Euromonitor (2011a) stated that regarding hotel wellness services a stronger focus on experiences rather than hotel stays is impacting on the way hotels market themselves and their relationship with suppliers as they incorporate more spa elements and food items into day-to-day operations. The forecast also suggests that hotels would pay more attention to their in-house spa brands (at the expense of outsourced spas at the premises). Hotels are expected to provide healthier food choices (e.g. SuperFoodsRx in Westin Hotels) and 'anti-energy' rinks supporting their holistic image.

According to Georgeson (2011) the key architectural trends that are relevant to the spa and wellness industry are:

- jaw-dropping views;
- sustainability and applying energy saving techniques;
- bio-inspired design;
- incorporation of local architectural designs;
- bringing nature and culture in;

- development of medical rooms;
- special attention to outdoor thermal experiences.

The location for holistic retreat tourism is largely incidental, although centres are likely to be in a beautiful mountain village or beside the sea as an added attraction. However, the experiences gained within a holistic centre could just as easily be created elsewhere. Many holistic practitioners such as yoga teachers or life coaches work in different locations throughout the year offering the same workshops and courses. Skyros Centres in Greece and Thailand attempt to create some local experiences, such as language or cookery lessons, but these are fairly limited and most of the experience is global or placeless. On the other hand, spiritual or New Age tourists often visit very specific landscapes or choose pilgrimage destinations which have a special significance. Some holistic/spiritual tourists are keen to go to Rishikesh in India for yoga, to experience Ayurveda in Kerala, or to learn Thai massage in Thailand. Visits to ashrams or meditation retreats also tend to take place in countries of perceived heightened spirituality, but it is now perfectly possible to visit such centres in the UK, USA or most other Western countries. Ironically, in many cases, it suits foreign visitors better as the forms of yoga or meditation are adapted to Western bodies and lifestyles. Holistic or New Age festivals can technically take place anywhere, although the experience is no doubt enhanced if the destination has some kind of spiritual significance.

Medical tourism is somewhat different in that most visitors require a stay of several days or weeks to recover, rehabilitate or rest. Their choice of destination may be more influenced by their doctor's prescription or fame and the favourable price levels than their own personal travel motivations in the case of state-supported medical thermal tourism. They may also be limited by where natural healing resources are located or where specific treatments are available. Those opting for private surgery may have far more independence in their selection of destination, hospital, even surgeon. This may depend less on cultural factors (although language, religion and feeling socially comfortable are important factors), and be based more on price, reputation, quality and safety. Tourist attractions may be an added bonus rather than a primary motivation. Although the tourism industry provision can make a difference for accompanying person(s) who would not want to spend every day indoors.

The complex management issues and the wide range of health and wellness tourism facilities in several cases created large organisations. Complex travel conglomerates emerge, where every aspect of the travel is available, such as in the case of the American Marketing Group, Inc., which has both traditional and speciality tour operation and travel agent brands (e.g. Travelsavers or The Affluent Traveler Collection), media brands (e.g. Travelmarket Report) and medical tourism brand as well (Well-being Travel, Inc.).

Planning and managing national, regional and local destinations

Although multi-level planning is usually recommended in tourism, it is not always possible to harmonise national, regional, local and site level developments. Ideally, the government should agree on a health tourism strategy, identifying regions which will focus on health

tourism (e.g. Kerala for Ayurveda in India, or Victoria for spas and wellness in Australia). Towns and resorts should then develop their health tourism resources and attractions in accordance with the regional priorities.

The German Bundesministerium für Wirtschaft and Technologie published a study entitled Innovative Health Tourism in Germany aiming at the development of medical baths and medical destinations (BMWI, 2012). The study lists the key drivers of health tourism:

- new demand and new needs due to changes in demography (e.g. ageing populations);
- health becomes the lifestyle;
- new frameworks via opening up traditional market structures, such as health insurance;
- innovation and cooperation.

The Dubai Government adopted a five-year strategy to promote medical tourism in Dubai (Abdullah, 2012):

- Increase integration and coordination with governmental bodies.
- Increase government and private healthcare investment.
- Establish a medical tourism board for required legislations.
- Develop and strengthen existing medical wellbeing services and elective procedures.
- Grant medical visit visas.
- Forge contracts between healthcare providers and airlines.

UAE's medical tourism market was worth close to USD 1.7 billion in 2010 and was projected to grow 15 per cent annually.

The Croatian government labelled its health tourism development plan as 'intelligent development', since it involves not only the public and the private sector but defines development objectives based on academic achievements, too.

A rather complex approach is applied by KHIDI (Korean Health Industries Development Institute). The South Korean government selected medical tourism as one of the key industries for South Korea and in 2009 they changed the legislation. The law established a 'medical visa' and permitted hospitals to treat foreign patients. Medical Korea is the specialised agency of KHIDI that provides supporting and marketing services to healthcare providers, such as organising industry events and fairs, running information services for patients (e.g. Medical Call Center) and supporting medical care providers and facilitators (Medical Korea, 2013).

In reality, many regions or resorts in a country may be in competition; the same is true of sites and attractions. However, cooperation is increasing which can help to harmonise development. Some examples are given below:

- *Supra-national initiatives such as Alpine Wellness or Nordic Wellbeing, or the EU Cross-Border Healthcare Directive*: Initiatives have been developed which involve several countries with similar resources (e.g. the Alps, Nordic climate and landscape). These collaborations focus on research, joint promotion and branding, sharing of good practice, and quality management.

- *Regional collaboration/complementarity*: Burgenland (Austria) provides an interesting case of coordination of developments at regional level. The region (or 'land') has four major spa destinations and all four have a different specialisation. The Sonnentherme specialises in families with young children, Therme Stegerbach offers services for older children and their parents, Bad Tatzmannsdorf is a destination for leisure and recreation, while Sauerbrunn specialises for men and Jennersdorf for women. Altogether these form an integrated destination with complementary rather than competing facilities.
- *Medical tourism clusters*: The Medical Tourism Association (2013) describes a Medical Tourism Cluster as 'an independent organization of hospitals, clinics, medical professionals and the government in a specific city, state, or region'. The main purpose is to promote the members of the Healthcare Cluster and to build a reputation as having extremely high quality health care. Germany has four medical tourism clusters attracting foreign patients in Berlin, Bonn, Hamburg and Munich, and South Korea also has (in Daejeon or Jeju) and the Turkish Healthcare Tourism Development Council (THTDC) has been working as a medical tourism cluster in Turkey since 2008, and so does the Malaysia Healthcare Travel Council (MHTC) for Malaysia.

CASE STUDY 7.7
Health-care cluster: Medellin Health City (Colombia)

Several destinations in South America have created some form of cooperation or partnership for medical tourism development. One of the leading networks is in the city of Medellín. They defined the motivation for creating the cluster as follows: 'Members working together to establish a standard of high quality care, in order to attract a larger share of the international market carefully targeting specific goals to achieve results otherwise impossible to attain by individual members acting independently' (Medellin Healthcare Cluster, 2011).

Based on the clusters' activities they expect:

- to be more competitive;

- to create employment;

- to increase capacity for more institutional services;

- to have more revenues and increased profitability;

- to have better integration via enterprise networking.

The cluster has more than 2,000 partners (health-care and dental service providers and medical schools). They defined the Healthcare Tourism Configuration with the following parameters:

1   greeting and orientation services;
2   transportation services;
3   accommodation services;
4   health-care services;
5   entertainment and other services;
6   comprehensive release support services.

The cluster anticipated that the cluster companies with an investment for 2009–12 of about US$ 250 million would result in an increase of 45 surgical rooms and 850 hospital beds. This would generate approximately 10,500 jobs (direct and indirect).

- *Destination Management Organisations*: Destination Management Organisations may be established in destinations which have a focus on health and wellness tourism in order to help co-ordinate management and marketing and to share good practice (one good example of this is Baden-Baden Kur and Tourismus GmbH/Cure and Tourism Ltd, Germany).
- *Healthcare cities*: Some destinations have marketed themselves as healthcare cities or Biomedical Cities such as Singapore or Dubai Healthcare City (DHCC). Such cities attract some of the best healthcare specialists and brands. For example, DHCC currently has over 120 medical facilities and 3,700 healthcare professionals (Dubai Healthcare City, 2013).

Dubai Healthcare City while treating 75,000 medical tourists in 2011 pays special attention to quality healthcare through (Abdullah, 2012):

- physicians' credentials (3,500+)
- CPQ accreditation
- international affiliations
- medical malpractice insurance
- 86+ specialties
- 40+ spoken languages
- clinically master planned and commercialised land
- anchor projects and strategic partnerships.

The Turkish government announced a support scheme for medical tourism, which probably cannot be met by any other destination (THTC, 2013). The government provides the following incentives:

- 50 per cent cover of flight tickets of international medical patients (flying any airline!);
- 70 per cent support for Turkish medical tourism providers, facilitators attenting at exhibitions, fairs and conferences;
- 50 per cent co-financing of related websites;
- 50 per cent cover of accreditations and certifications (e.g. JCI, TEMOS);

- 50 per cent co-financing for advertisements (e.g. in magazines);
- 50 per cent support for advertisement materials (i.e. prints);
- 50 per cent cover of the cost of running representative offices in foreign markets for up to four years.

CASE STUDY 7.8
South Korea: Healience Zen Town
Timothy Jeonglyeol Lee and Ji-Sook Han

In 2005, the first wellness resort in South Korea, 'Healience Zen Town', was built providing preventative medicine regimens. It is located at an altitude of 250 meters at Hongcheon in Gangwon Province. This was the vision of Dr Shi-Hyeong Lee, who is a psychiatrist, brain scientist and best-selling author, and realised through investments from several corporations. The vision of Healience zen town is to make people live a life like 9988234, which means to live to 99 years of age in 88 condition (88 has same pronunciation as spry, rejuvenated in Korean), and suffering for only two or three days and four (die) (four has same pronunciation as die in Korean).

The point is that spry (healthy) living is important until death rather than spending time in hospital, dependent on medicine or suffering an illness. Since opening, the number of visitors to the town has rapidly grown, with 20,000 people visiting in 2010. The number of patient visitors (that is, medical/health tourists) is over 6,000 people annually. The data demonstrate how many people pay attention to their health and wellness issues in today's world.

Healience focuses on prevention rather than treatment, and the most important issue for prevention is to reform bad living habits. Through the processes adopted at the centre, the natural healing power is activated and this results in a healthy mind and body. Part of the process is to check food intake, stress, exercise habits and physical body condition through professional consultation, and diagnosis followed by advice. After that, visitors learn how to change their bad habits and practice good habits when they return home.

Characteristics of Healience Zen Town

- Intended inconvenience: no television, no refrigerator, blocked mobile phone, no smoking, no drinking.

- Wonderful natural environment: great views of forest, an altitude of 250 meters (longevity known to be associated with heights), 8 walking tracks, valley, and mountain streams.

- Environment-friendly facilities: Environment-friendly energy system (ground heat, solar heat, environment-friendly building materials (wallpapers, paint, ceiling, etc).

Facilities information

- Total 70,000 square meters, ten buildings.

- The concept of architecture and design: four seasons co-existing with the aesthetic of a poor man.

- Facilities: Customer service center, six complexes of rooms (far-infrared radiation, yellow soil stone, star-watching ceiling), spa, fitness centre, lecture room, walking tracks, yellow soil *jjimjilbang* (Korean dry sauna), farm, gardening experience zone, baking experience zone, horticultural experience zone, and so on.

Major programmes

- *High life*: Providing lectures on natural medicine and the serotonin hormone, meditation therapy, meditation in the forest, meditation in the lying back programme, serotonin walking, walking for living for 100 years, eating habit reform programme (Total of two days and three nights).

- *Reforming living habits*: Eating habit improvement programme (unpolished rice food therapy), having a consultation with professional mind and body counsellor, self-healing programme, anti-stress meditation, mediation in lying back programme, music medication, detox spa, medical examination, body composition analysis, exercise prescription and guide, daily yoga, tracking (Total of six days and seven nights).

- *Cancer conquest living school*: Meditation therapy, music meditation, nature meditation, exercise prescription, natural healing power enhancing yoga, serotonin walking, eating habit reforming program, healthy sleeping habit, mediation in lying back program (Total four days and five nights).

More programmes

	Title
Regular programme	High Life, Mind studying, Reforming living habits, Cancer conquest living school, Married couple camp, Romantic courtship, Young healing camp, Healing diet camp.
Short-term programme	Zen town stay, Staying a day in forest, Health workshop.

Local destinations where listed or ancient buildings host the health and wellness facilities, for example historic spas, need special management. Architectural styles and milieux can be destroyed by the introduction of new building styles and keeping balance between the needs of conservation and expectation of visitors and operators can be hard. For example the Colonnades in the historic Czech spa towns of Marianske Lazne or

Karlovy Vary mainly serve as tourist attractions of architectural beauty and not as facilities for drinking cures. Health and wellness developments may mean significant change in land use, such as building new and large buildings. These developments can mean the introduction of new styles and can make a destination densely built up. The responsibility of developers and authorities are especially important in natural settings, where any building can change the whole atmosphere. Almost all historic spa towns and facilities struggle to keep the harmony alive, which can easily be lost with only one wrong decision (e.g. permitting a non-matching architectural design).

The BMWI study (BMWI, 2012) made recommendations for the likely typologies medical destinations and baths can follow in their development:

- Type 1: high quality, specialised services, innovative products supported with a strong brand and focused segmentation.
- Type 2: good supply composition and quality but with limited health tourism focus, located mainly in mountains and by the sea. Often health services are developed to complement existing provision and to overcome seasonality.
- Type 3: facilities and destinations with average service quality, products and infrastructure, often achieving limited or no profits. They have certain natural attractions but their geographical locations are not unique or exceptional. Destinations face serious decisions on the type and direction for future development.

Chapter 2 discussed briefly the history of historic spa destinations and showed that many of them were struggling to remain operational. This was true of Spa in Belgium, for example, where it was considered more desirable and no doubt more profitable to build a new modern spa complex than to renovate and operate the historic one. In the UK, almost all of the historic spas are no longer in use except Bath, which has tried (successfully) to combine its historic features with new developments.

CASE STUDY 7.9
Bath: regeneration of a historic spa

In Bath (or Aquae Sulis as it was known by the Romans) there was archaeological proof of human activity around the hot springs as far back as 8,000 BC. This was followed by evidence of Celtic shrines around the springs, as the waters were deemed sacred. It was the Roman invasion in AD 43 which transformed them into a series of baths and bathing facilities. Following the withdrawal of the Romans, the early Christians largely rejected the idea of regular bathing, so the baths fell to ruin. This was also attributed to a possible earthquake. It was not until AD 973 that Bath's position as a centre for religion and healing was reconfirmed and pilgrims and invalids alike flocked to its waters, as well as travellers and writers. Various monarchs, including Queen Elizabeth I in the sixteenth century, made the baths available to the public as well as royalty and nobility (although facilities were often separated). It was noted that men and women bathed naked together, as well as animals of all kinds! In subsequent centuries (i.e. 1700s onwards) it became a more sophisticated and

glamorous resort for royalty and aristocracy with pumps rooms to drink water in, assembly rooms in which to gamble, dance and socialise, as well as parades, parks and promenades. It was thought that Bath influenced the development of many other European spa towns and resorts. By the late 1700s, however, the spa declined again because of economic recession.

The nineteenth century saw a new revival of the spa culture, this time with the creation of the complex called the Royal Baths complete with treatment centre and ladies' swimming pool. However, Bacon (1998) describes how Bath already began to go out of fashion in the mid-nineteenth century, having been a pioneer for other European spas decades earlier. Patronage was largely transferred to seaside towns. The New Private Baths opened as a medical facility in 1889, and during and after the First and Second World Wars, many soldiers were treated there and National Health Service funding was provided. However, its withdrawal in 1976 meant the beginning of another decline.

Following a 25-year closure, Bath's new spa opened in 2006. For years, visitors could enjoy the buildings and the view of the hot springs, but they could not bathe. Like other UK historic spa towns, most visitors came to enjoy the heritage buildings and the town centre, but were not able to experience what the buildings were designed to achieve. A spa revival scheme was developed in the late 1990s based on National Lottery money via a Millennium Commission grant. This represents the seventh reinvention of the spa in its history. Five listed buildings were regenerated and a new modern spa – the Minerva Bath – was created. Although the architecture and facilities are completely contemporary (and maybe a contro-versial juxtaposition with the traditional buildings), the rooftop view from the pool over the whole World Heritage Site city demonstrates that the new can represent the multi-layering of history and heritage and not just its replacement.

(White, 2003)

Baden-Baden in Germany has also managed to retain its appeal and the town is especi-ally proud of its heritage and traditions. Product developments kept a very close eye on the combination of the preservation of what made the town unique as well as the diversi-fication expected by the market. Friedrichsbad, or the Römerbad (Roman Bath) repre-sents history and tradition, while Caracalla Therme is for the new demand, with pleasure and wellness services (e.g. sauna world). The two facilities are located separately and not linked with each other. The town management and planning has proved to be successful, since it could keep the historic charm as well as develop.

Managing health and wellness facilities

In addition to addressing issues of sustainability and creating unique experiences as discussed earlier, spas, wellness hotels, medical facilities and retreats need to be planned according to a development concept and designed accordingly. There are then many operational factors which need to be considered, such as human resources management, financial management, marketing and promotion. There are several books devoted to spa management (e.g. Cohen and Bodeker, 2008), hot springs (Erfurt-Cooper and Cooper, 2009), medical tourism (Connell, 2011; Hall, 2013), destination management in wellness tourism (Voigt and Pforr, 2013), and health and wellness services (Kandampully, 2013). This section will therefore not aim to repeat what is already available, but merely to analyse the main issues and challenges.

Development concept and design

Most spas and wellness facilities should start with a development concept, which may relate to the theme(s), experiences to be created, uniqueness, design and/or sustainability. Architecture and design can make a significant (first and often lasting) impression, for example asking a 'starchitect' like Frank Gehry to design the Marques de Riscal City of Wine and spa in Elciego near to Bilbao in Spain or the collaboration between Rogner and the Austrian architect Hundertwasser in Bad Blumau. At the Backstage Hotel Vernissage in Zermatt, the artist/architect/hotelier Heinz Julen has crafted a narrative spa experience with seven room treatments, called therapy cubes, themed after each of the days of Creation. The cubes blend visceral and visual components, utilising lights, images, temperatures and sensations meant to cleanse and relax the body and soul (Gayot, 2013).

Marguiles (2013) summarises ten elements that any design should consider:

1 light;
2 scents;
3 colours;
4 natural versus synthetic;
5 retail boutique;
6 corridors;
7 relaxation space;
8 music;
9 locker room;
10 temperature.

The concept of Experience Mapping (created by the Experience Gym of The Tourism Observatory for Health, Wellness and Spa) can allow developers and managers to plot their facility on an 'Experience Grid' which gives a good indication of areas that need enhancement and improvement. The four key factors of the grid visually introduce how the health and wellness facilities perform from the visitor experience point of view:

- How beneficial: the complexity of the benefit structure (rejuvenation, learning, relaxation, social interaction, etc.)
- How accessible: ambiance, safety, etc.
- How valuable: value for money, personal service, customer involvement, etc.
- How authentic: what elements of the experience had roots in local traditions or materials, the relationship of the service to the spa's theme, etc.

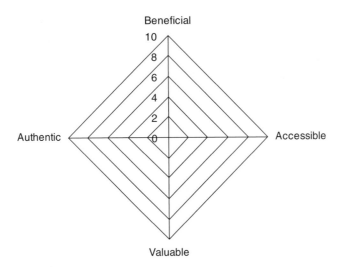

FIGURE 7.1 Experience mapping
Source: The Tourism Observatory for Health, Wellness and Spa, 2013.

It is important to consider the way in which design varies from country to country. Many buildings in China would not be designed without considering the Feng Shui concept, the same may be true in India with Vasati. Although energy flows are intangible, they can be greatly influenced by physical design. The location of certain features is important. This allows the maximum amount of energy or 'chi' to flow freely, balancing yin and yang or masculine and feminine energies; using lighting to enhance dark corners, and strategic placement of objects to break up long corridors. Thompson (2007) suggests ways in which the principles of Feng Shui can be implemented in a design context (see Table 7.4).

A well-designed facility should be aesthetically pleasing, comfortable, and functional (D'Angelo, 2005). Japanese designers tend towards a Zen approach, and this may be similar to Scandinavians who favour simple, clean designs, natural materials and neutral colours. Nordic Well (2007) states that design is one of the key factors in inducing a feeling of wellness:

> Modern, simple, unassuming, clean, airy, light, calm, uncluttered, in harmony with nature, inviting, functional, inclusive. These are the values and senses that Scandinavian designs have emphasized over time. They are the combined result of three influences: a Zen-like belief in the power of nature; a tradition of linking design to the wellbeing of all people; and a skill for choosing appropriate technology . . . An idea of design that promotes creativity, intimacy, personal calm and sense of meaning.

On the other hand, Middle Eastern cultures may prefer more opulent décor. Muslim guests may even request that the whole facility corresponds to halal specifications (e.g. some of the new spa developments in the United Arab Emirates). The trend in many spas and wellness facilities at present tends to be towards Asian style, often with warm colours,

TABLE 7.4 Feng Shui colour basics

Colour	Theme	Good for . . .
Red	Energizing	the dining room to keep guests energized and excited.
Orange	Joy	family rooms, playrooms, use softer shades for more relaxed fun.
Yellow	Happy	dens, kitchens, offices, wherever creativity is needed.
Green	Balance, Renewal	living rooms, bedrooms, halls.
Blue	Healing, Calming	wherever you want to relax.
Indigo	Healing, Relaxing	children's rooms, healing rooms.
Purple	Richness, Transformation	spiritual rooms, feelings of abundance.

Feng Shui elemental decor				
Strive for balance between the five elements. Are any of the elements below missing from the room?				
Water	Wood	Fire	Earth	Metal
fountains glass	wood furniture	fireplace red accents	browns earthtones stone	chrome mirrors stainless
Are any of the elements above dominating the room? Balance it with the complementary element below.				
Earth	Metal	Water	Wood	Fire
browns earthtones stone	chrome mirrors stainless	fountains glass	wood furniture	fireplace red accents

Source: Adapted from Thompson, 2007.

Buddha statues, incense burning and ambient music. However, such a style may not be to all guests' tastes and it is not always culturally appropriate for the location, especially if guests are seeking a local experience. Cross-cultural considerations arguably need to be combined with environmental psychology (Mehrabian and Russell, 1974) in order to create the ideal wellness experience. Puczkó (2011) suggests that more research is needed on questions of interpretation, experience creation and applied psychology in spa demand, as customers can react very differently to the same servicescape. He makes the important point that interior designers are not psychologists and that interior design does not equal experience creation.

Environmental consciousness should pervade spas and wellness facilities. Many spas and hotels already use natural resources such as thermal or spring waters, geysers, sea-water, waterfalls or caves. Naturally textured woods, bamboos or cork are popular as they are eco-friendly and also sustain moisture. Many designers try to use features that are in keeping with the local architecture and cultural styles so that the spa or wellness centre is integrated into the environment in which it is located. Sometimes design needs to be adapted to different markets; for example, men may prefer less feminine environments and prefer minimalist styles. Spas that want to attract families with children tend to use brighter colours and motifs that capture the imagination.

Noise control is important especially if some areas are open-plan. Ease of transition is also a major consideration so that the flow from one facility to another does not involve long walks in cold or draughty corridors or the climbing of numerous stairs. There should be a centrally located reception with information provision and a welcome desk, in addition to well-placed relaxation areas with reading materials, herbal teas, small snacks and perhaps chill-out music or nice scents from oil burners or incense.

Atmosphere can be created by other means than architectural design. However, it is difficult to ascertain what should be an ideal atmosphere, especially one which is acceptable or attractive to multiple visitors. Colour, lighting, music, olfaction and temperature are all key to creating the optimum servicescape. However, colours have different symbolisms in different cultures (e.g. white in Western spas may seem to be calm and relaxing, whereas white is the colour of death and mourning in Asia). Creating a relaxing, clean and pleasant environment is of paramount importance for all wellness facilities, but most especially for spas and spa or wellness hotels, which may also need a touch of luxury (spiritual or holistic tourists may accept more basic facilities).

In medical tourism, it might be thought that facilities just need to be clean, clinical and functional. However, there is an increasing realisation that many medical tourists may prefer to be offered 'less hospital and more hospitality'. The bedside manner of the staff can make a real difference to their experience too, and it is possible that tourists may already choose medical destinations because of the friendliness of the people or the relaxing atmosphere of a particular place. Bumrungrad International Hospital (Bangkok, Thailand), for example, has its own residences and suites. One of the trends we can observe is the H2H Converions, i.e. Hospital-2-Hotel or Hotel-2-Hospital conversions creating facilities that are somewhere between the two ends of the spectrum.

Staff, service and revenues

As discussed earlier, skilled, qualified people in health and wellness tourism are of paramount importance. However, staff are sometimes lacking proper qualifications in the field of wellness tourism. The Global Spa and Wellness Summit report (2012a: i) states that, 'People are a spa's greatest asset and are essential to its success, but people are also typically a spa's greatest expense and challenge'. GSWS research shows that 95 per cent of spa industry leaders have problems hiring managers or directors with the right combination of qualifications and experience because a huge mix of hard and soft skills are needed. One of the problems is that there are relatively few spa management degree programmes. GSWS (2012) estimates that there are around 64 spa management-related degree programmes in universities, colleges and schools around the world, and about 41 providers of continuing education (e.g. short courses, workshops). Kathryn Dowthwaite and Sarah Rawlinson analyse the challenges of providing spa education in their case study in Part III of this book.

Lyon (2013) compiled an extensive list of reactions from spa therapists and staff which they should never use. Some of these are really spot on (and not only for spas):

1   Oh yes, now I remember you.
2   If you don't see it we're probably sold out.
3   Oh, you found it. No, the sale ended yesterday.
4   What service would I suggest? What about a make-over?
5   We can take two of you at 10.00 and one at 11.00.
6   I think I'm getting something . . . sniff.
7   That might bruise.
8   Did I burn you?
9   Oh, those were old prices.
10   Yes, we take an automatic 20 per cent gratuity, I'm sorry you also tipped.

The above listed selection highlights the role of front-line staff since therapists and other health-care staff are seen as brand ambassadors!

It is often difficult to identify the relevant qualifications for a 'spa therapist' as they may specialise in one service only (e.g. massage, beauty), but it is becoming more common for therapists to multi-task as this is more economical for spas and wellness centres. Thus beauticians might extend skin-care and make-up expertise to manicures and pedicures. Many massage therapists become aromatherapists or learn different massage techniques. Yoga teachers can offer meditation or Thai massage (sometimes dubbed 'the lazy man's yoga'). New accreditations and qualifications may be needed to accommodate the cross-over skills that are being developed, as many require a separate diploma and licence.

As in all tourism businesses, service in wellness centres or spas should be professional, friendly, welcoming and helpful. Service approach is especially essential in any health operation, since most visitors (or patients) hand themselves over to the staff (either physic-ally or mentally). Tourists also expect a certain level of knowledge or expertise about the treatments that they are paying to receive. Receptionists and support staff should be able to inform visitors about treatments available and advise them what might be suitable. Equally, staff working in restaurants and catering should be able to help guests make healthy food choices according to their individual dietary requirements. The increasing customisation of health services means that every individual should be made to feel special and cared for. They should not be neglected or made to wait for long periods in a reception area, or be left feeling uncertain about spa etiquette (i.e. what should be done once in the spa). This might be difficult to achieve in a large, chain hotel, so most wellness (and medical) hotels tend to be small(er) and run by the owner (family). One of the key management challenges in resort and hotel environments is the cooperation between the

often outsourced spa or medical unit and the hotel front office. Hotel staff tends to have very little information (and knowledge) about the spa, the spa menus and treatments, therefore the cross-selling cannot provide the expected benefits to either parties.

A certain level of sensitivity is required on the part of those people administering services, treatments or courses. Therapists and medical staff should preserve the modesty of clients at all times, as many people feel very vulnerable before and during a massage, especially one that requires nudity. Help may also be needed to guide visitors around, as it could be their first visit or rituals and traditions may differ from those in their home country. Language may be a barrier where there is little or no translation, especially in countries where language can seem completely unfamiliar (e.g. Hungary, Finland, Japan, China or South Korea).

More and more emphasis is put on revenue management in every health and wellness tourism facility and company (Patrizia Modica and Elisa Scanu analyse revenue management in their case study in Part III). Nowadays not only the sales force is expected to take part in selling and revenue improvement, but the same is expected from health professionals, too. Revenue management at spa and wellness facilities (after Kimes and Singh, 2009) are often influenced by the following instruments:

- relatively fixed capacities;
- perishable inventory;
- predictability of demand;
- cost structure challenges;
- varying customer price sensitivity;
- time-variable demand;
- dependency on human resources (skills, motivation and attitudes).

A clear understanding of how well a health and wellness (tourism) facility could operate with every member of staff playing their part could do wonders not only to guest experiences but to financial performance too.

Safety, regulations and ethics

Crebbin-Bailey et al. (2005) discuss some of the most important health and safety aspects for spas, which are equally important in other health facilities, too. These include the health and safety of employees and guests alike, and they need to comply with the different laws and regulations of a given country. There is a need to assess the risk of injury or illness, hygiene issues are paramount, filtration, purification and disinfection of waters and facilities are crucial, and chemicals need to be stored safely. Food provision also needs to be given health and safety considerations. Spa employees should be trained in first aid and know what to do if a guest has a problem or injury. Typical accidents may be caused by slipping on wet floors, poor or non-swimmers getting out of their depth in pools, diving in shallow waters, drinking alcohol before treatments, misuse of equipment, illnesses caused by overexposure to hot temperatures, infections from under-sterilised waters, long hair or body parts being caught in water outlets, amongst others. Some hot springs carry health warnings because of the high temperature of the water or potentially dangerous bacteria or organisms in the water. Toxic fumes or gases can also be lethal (Erfurt-Cooper and Cooper, 2009).

Psychological counsellors need to ensure that clients do not go away feeling too exposed and emotional. Yoga and meditation teachers need to recognise the sometimes powerful spiritual impact of their work and ensure participants do not feel confused or upset. Spiritual leaders and gurus especially in India have often been criticised for preying on the vulnerability of tourists who are drawn to charismatic practices without really understanding them (Brown, 1998). In some cases, certain medical processes or fitness programmes could result in pain or injury, therefore practitioners need to deal with both the practical (first aid elements) and any personal distress caused. Some holistic centres (e.g. Skyros) recommend that visitors do not make any major life-changing decisions when they return home (e.g. leaving their jobs or partners or going to start a new life) for at least two months. This means that the potential impact of some wellness holidays can be extremely powerful.

It is actually possible to 'qualify' as a yoga teacher, massage therapist or life coach after a series of short training programmes, sometimes lasting only a month or a few weekends. The British Wheel of Yoga in the UK now only accredits yoga teachers who have completed a two-year intensive training programme approved by the Sports Council of Britain. The government of India insists that true Ayurvedic practitioners train for three years. These are, however, rare examples. Some practitioners have no training whatsoever, for example those individuals who set themselves up in destinations like Goa as yoga or meditation teachers or retreat owners. It seems that many tourists neither know nor care about the lack of qualifications or regulations. Kelly's (2012) research shows that 60 per cent of retreat visitors did not even think about asking whether their instructors were accredited and 52 per cent thought it was not an important criterion of a retreat holiday anyway. This is quite a dangerous pattern, as irreparable damage can be done to body, mind or spirit through neglectful or uninformed practice. As stated by Kelly (2012) 'rogue traders' in wellness tourism can do a lot more damage than in other types of tourism.

There is an ongoing discussion about the role and different scope and regulation of activities of travel agents and medical travel facilitators. In theory, a facilitator does rather similar activities to a travel agent: it organises a trip during which travellers receive certain medical treatments. However, there are several qualities of medical tourism which mean that a standard travel agent may not qualify as a facilitator, such as:

- certain liability issues since travel agents are not responsible for the products they sell;
- lack of expertise in medical services (e.g. understanding the requirements of ill patients who may need medically equipped transportation or special airline seating arrangements;
- probable lack of certification but that is not as common as it is in the case of medical service providers (e.g. hospitals and clinics);
- lack of medical training of staff.

In many countries, the regulation is lagging behind practice, since authorities cannot categorise new (cross-over) facilities such as H2H Conversions. These facilities are not fully equipped hospitals but they are not typical hotels either.

Quality management systems

At present, although there is no global regulation of the medical tourism industry (Hall, 2013) there are certification and accreditation systems, for example by the Medical Tourism Association, JCI, ISQA, TEMOS, TRENT, ESPA-EHV, Accreditation Canada International, ACHS or by national accreditation boards or certifications. More and more accreditation and certification initiatives emerge but one may ask the question: for whom? If they were to certify service quality and internal processes then the general public would not understand or care too much about it. It they were to create trust and to support brands, then the prospective customers would need more understandable information about the scope, the processes and the benefits of these systems.

Joint Commission International (JCI) defines accreditation as a voluntary process by which a government or non-government agency grants recognition to health-care institutions which meet certain standards that require continuous improvement in structures, processes and outcomes (Ramponi, 2012). According to JCI's experiences of 450+ accredited organizations in over 50 countries:

- Accreditation is the most comprehensive and powerful tool for quality improvement.
- Accreditation has been found to be effective in many cultures and countries with very different systems.
- International accreditation is the appropriate answer to increasing needs of quality and safety in a global society.

TEMOS provides certification services which are different from that of JCI, and so on, since it looks at medical services from the 'International Patients' Care Cycle' perspective (Mika, 2012):

- validates existing Quality Management Systems combining it with medical tourism relevant parts when national or international QMS is a precondition;
- Temos Quality Criteria have to be met complementary to existing QMS;
- (travel) health insurance and assistance perspective;
- emphasis on non-medical services.

Probably the hottest topic at the time of the writing of this book is the patient data safety and management. Patient and treatment information are very sensitive and the protection of their privacy is one of the most important expectations of international medical travellers. Patient flows require rigorous, encrypted and safe patient data management often eHR (electronic Health Record) since data flows must ensure that (Lanyi, 2011):

- sufficient information provided to every party involved;
- the right information is available for the right person/party;
- always available information to every party;
- it ensures better and the right preparation for the treatment team;
- it avoids unnecessary and repeated diagnosis procedures (MRT, ECG, Lab, etc.).

It does not make data safety any easier the fact that data safety and management should comply with rather different legislation in different countries, such as:

- USA: Health Insurance Portability and Accountability Act (HIPAA);
- Germany: Federal Data Protection Act;
- UK: Data Protection Act 1998;
- Canada: Personal Information Protection and Electronic Documents Act (PIPEDA) and Privacy Act.

There are some examples of quality systems that have been put in place in Europe, for example the Alpine Wellness label (covering more than 40 hotels in Austria, Germany and Switzerland), and the possibility to use existing quality models such as ISO (International Organisation for Standardisation) or the European Foundation for Quality Management (EFQM). These operate more as management systems focusing on organisational and operational processes. Customers often have to know about the system to appreciate the wellness operator's achievement, but arguably such schemes give wellness centres, spas and hotels something to aspire to, clear guidelines for good practice, and enhances their competitive advantage (e.g. Rheinland TÜV of Germany has developed a quality assurance system for wellness hotels and ESPA-EHV has created a similar system for medical spas).

Service quality and regular monitoring of service quality in health tourism is the focus of many organisations all around the world. Andrea Vermesi discusses how Hungarian wellness and spa hotels could be professionally benchmarked and assessed in her case study in Part III of this book. Various, mainly voluntary quality assurance initiatives are available for use, for example:

- Spaaudit.com recommends the ways in which owners or managers can do quality checks on their own. The Do-It-Yourself Secret Shopper is a self administrated system that overcomes a common challenge faced by spas; how to accurately assess team performance when most of the service delivery happens behind closed doors (Spa Audit, 2008).
- The European Spas Association (ESPA) has started its own international quality seal, the so-called EUROPESPA. These criteria '. . . focus on safety, hygiene and the therapy infrastructure. Aspects such as service, therapy, wellness, accommodation as well as kitchen and food safety are addressed in around 400 audit questions' (European Spas Association, 2007). A mystery shopper assigned by ESPA carries the audit out, which then will be awarded for three years (and the seal costs the site 1,250 euros per year).

Visitors, besides the various seals of quality, can learn about sites and destinations from various sources, for example from:

- The many 'World's Best Spas by Readers Awards' by SpaFinder Wellness Magazine, Concierge.com, World Wellness and Spa awards from Professional Spa and Wellness, European Health and Spa Awards, or Condé Nast Traveller, etc.
- Travel diaries by previous guests which they share in online virtual communities (e.g. Facebook groups, Pinterest.com, Instagram.com, tripadvisor.com, lonelyplanet. com, etc.).

- Facilities either owned or franchised to a well established brand, e.g. in medical tourism: Fortis, Apollo, Fresenius, Johns Hopkins, Cleveland Clinic or in spa and wellness tourism general providers: one of the several Starwood Hotels and Resorts brands, Mandarin Oriental, or specialist brands, such as Danubius Hotels, Accor Thalassa or Skyros Holidays.

In terms of quality management Geva (2012) provides a very good summary of the key issues through the example of the Mayo Clinic. Quality can be defined in many ways. At Mayo Clinic:

- Quality is not just a simple measure. Quality is a comprehensive look at all aspects of a patient's experience.
- Patients seek excellence in care, the best medical knowledge and experience, the best technology available and the kindness and hope offered by our staff.
- Quality can be measured in the outcomes achieved such as mortality rates and surgical infections; in the compliance with evidence-based processes known to enhance care; in the volume of patients successfully treated who have complex diagnoses and procedures; and in the safety record of the institution.
- Quality and service can also be measured in other ways as the amount of time spent with each patient; making sure each patient is treated with respect; kindness and dignity by every member of the Mayo team; making sure appointments are on time and that all test results and other patient information are available to every doctor whenever needed.

Quality at Mayo Clinic involves the totality of a patient's experience – from the first phone call to the last appointment.

Conclusions

This chapter has shown clearly that the most successful developments are those which are planned or regulated in some way, ideally combining national government intervention and support of private-sector creativity and vision. Although some 'organic' resorts can flourish, these usually have a relatively long history of alternative and holistic lifestyles which would be disturbed by the imposition of too much structured development or regulation. However, the same is not true of spas and resorts which make use of fragile natural or cultural resources. These developments need to be monitored for adverse impacts and controlled to avoid despoliation of the environment or local traditions and lifestyles. In addition, some attention must also be paid to the provision and presentation of facilities for visitors down to the smallest detail. This includes not only services but experiences too. In medical tourism, regulation, ethics and safety are paramount considerations. However, the idea of creating better hospitality and customer service in medical facilities is an increasingly important issue, especially if people see themselves primarily as visitors, tourists or guests rather than mere patients. More research is perhaps needed to see how important these issues really are to medical tourists.

CHAPTER

Future trends and predictions

> Spas and wellness resorts may be conceptualised in cultural/sociological terms as modern day temples where people can experience rituals, learn to deepen their personal wellness practices, raise their consciousness, become open to enhanced ways of being and deepen their experience of being alive.
>
> (Cohen, 2008: 8)

This chapter provides a summary of some of the main issues discussed in Parts I and II of the book, including some of the definitional challenges. It also looks at the changing relationship between the spa, wellness and medical sectors. There is an analysis of current developments, as well as new trends as identified partly by spa and wellness experts around the world (e.g. from the Global Spa and Wellness Summit 2012 Industry Briefing Papers), and others from research which was undertaken by the authors over the past three years, both in conjunction with GSWS (e.g. 2011), Xellum Ltd. and the Hungarian National Tourism Office, as well as The Tourism Observatory for Health, Wellness and Spa (established by the authors in 2012). The final part of this chapter makes some predictions for the future of spa, wellness and medical tourism.

Ongoing definitional challenges

This book has shown that it is not necessarily becoming easier to define terms like wellness or medical tourism; sometimes just the opposite in fact. This is especially true of the medical tourism sector, where debates are raging about whether or not a separation should be made between medical tourists, medical travellers and international patients, for example. There is unfortunately a limited amount of reliable data which can tell us how patients who travel abroad for treatments see themselves. If they are sent by their hospital or referred by their doctor or there was no appropriate treatment available in their own country, then they are more likely to see themselves as patients who are merely travelling for medical treatment out of necessity. If, on the other hand, they have made an individual decision to go abroad for treatment and have chosen their own destination, then there is more chance that they may be thinking about the tourism dimension. However, we have little idea about whether medical tourists choose destinations or simply treatments. It is undoubtedly much more pleasant to receive treatment and recover in a beautiful, sunny environment than in a cold, dark, rainy one! It is nicer to be cared for by smiling, hospitable people than by unfriendly, brusque, dour ones. It is surely better to find oneself in an environment that resembles a hotel rather than a hospital. Factors such as local culture, climate, hospitality traditions, aesthetics, or calmness of the location may play a major role in decision making beyond price, quality or diversity of treatments. But this must be researched further to make any stronger statements. Of course, it is difficult to collect reliable statistics because of patient confidentiality agreements and many operators may not want to risk competitors finding out about their patient lists. Working directly with hospitals, clinics or medical tourism facilitators could be an option when collecting data of this kind. It is also in their own interest to have reliable statistics.

The GSS (2011) already indicated that it was not really appropriate to talk about spa tourism, but instead to analyse the role that spas can play in wellness tourism or medical tourism industries. The first chapter showed that only certain types of spas attract tourists (i.e. those involving a stay of over 24 hours, although airport spas are clearly used by tourists too). It is sometimes difficult to know if those tourists who stay in spa and wellness hotels can really be counted as wellness tourists. Many of them may have come with a completely different motivation in mind, such as business, a conference, cultural tourism or shopping. Many of them may not even use the hotel spa, yet in many countries, all visitors to spa and wellness hotels are being counted as health tourists (one rule of thumb in the hotel industry is that hotel spas cannot really expect more than 15–20 per cent of the hotel guests actually to use their facilities). Those who go to a destination or resort spa or go on a spa cruise are much more likely to have had wellness as a primary motivation. There are also still definitional challenges in countries which have healing water traditions and promote their medical thermal baths as 'spas'. As we could see from the discussions of cultural expectations, this may be misleading for many tourists who have a very different understanding of what a spa should be. It also raises the question about whether definitions of medical tourism should include thermal medical tourism. Bjurstam (2012: 51) suggests that the convergence of spas, wellness and the medical domain will be reflected in the health industry of the future, which will 'become less spa-orientated and more wellness-orientated, with the integration of fitness, nutrition, advanced beauty and alternative health care and, later, the merging of all of the above with medical practices'.

The term wellness has perhaps not been debated so hotly, but it has definitely grown in popularity in recent years. This is reflected in the Global Spa Summit change of name to the Global Spa and Wellness Summit, for example. Even languages which never really recognised this term have adopted it for want of a better word. Well-being is still used in many countries, especially those where it is a direct translation of a foreign word; however, it is also popular in English-speaking countries like Australia. This is maybe not surprising, as wellness was not originally an English word, merely an invented one. Well-being is perhaps more related to happiness and satisfaction, whereas wellness deals with all dimensions of life. Glover (2012: 81) describes wellness as 'the bridge between medical

and well-being'. It is important in wellness and wellness tourism that a deliberate and proactive approach is taken to improving the different domains of one's life to bring them into balance. The history chapter in this book showed us that all cultures' approach to optimum health has been about balance and harmony, whether it is body, mind, spirit, yin and yang, the four elements or the four humours. Wellness is about learning how to create balance in one's life and maintaining that as far as possible.

It is also an interesting debate as to how wellness can be optimised. Often wellness is depicted in a circular form where all elements are necessary to complete the circle. However, other models put spirituality at the centre. Some models are multi-layered and build on each other. For example, according to some gurus, even the Dalai Lama, it is only possible to attain higher levels of happiness or spirituality once certain material conditions have been fulfilled (much like Maslow's hierarchy of needs). Chakra balancing usually starts with work on the lower chakras which are based on grounding or roots before moving up to the higher, more spiritual ones. In reality, many people may cling to their spiritual beliefs or practices even when they are in the most abject circumstances (e.g. poverty or serious physical illness) and it is this which gives them strength. All elements of wellness are inter-related but even when equally weighted, it is unlikely that all domains can be balanced simultaneously at all times. Wellness therefore can mean different things to different people at different times of their life.

Terms like spirituality are used less liberally, especially in the spa industry, even though they are central to wellness. The GSS (2010) research showed that whereas the industry sees and promotes the benefits of treatments which enhance a sense of spirituality, customers are less keen on seeing this label applied to their treatments. As stated by Chaudhari (2012: 5) 'industry ranks holistic health and spiritual health significantly higher than consumers do. The difference in perceptions of holistic health may indicate that consumers have less of a grasp on this concept.' Of course, one could argue that industry practitioners technically know better what is good for people, but they may need to find ways of introducing and promoting these benefits which require different terminology. There are fewer psychological barriers for retreat tourists, who may be actively seeking a spiritual experience, or at least a holistic one which balances body, mind and spirit.

The links between leisure, lifestyle and tourism

There are important developments in people's attitudes to ageing. The World Health Organization's predictions mean that there is going to be an even more significant number of older people in the future, most of whom will want to stay fit, active and youthful. The emphasis on quality of life and happiness is likely to become more important than looking young(er). Bogacheva (2012: 21) suggests that, 'There has also been a shift in the understanding of what is important – better living rather than looking younger is gradually becoming the focus'. Of course, both is likely to be important, and many older people, especially women will no doubt partake of the burgeoning cosmetic surgery industry especially if/as it becomes cheaper, more available and more socially acceptable or normalised (e.g. as it is becoming in Central and South America). Biging (2012: 40) suggests that, 'The focus isn't about reducing wrinkles but about disease prevention and health enhancement. We like the idea that 'it's not the years in your life, but the life in your years that count'. Of course, there will need to be a close cooperation with the medical industries in this case to combat some of the problems experienced by the physical body as people age. It is a good question as to how important tourism will be in the quest for 'active ageing', but as many older people retire and have more time, they may also be keen to travel more and see the places they did not see when they were younger – maybe with some wellness treatments along the way. The only major barrier could be the problem of public pensions being eroded in many countries and the decrease in government-supported medical thermal tourism.

Tourism used to be about escapism and getting away from it all. Unfortunately, now much of 'it' comes with us in the form of emails, mobile phones, laptops, and such like. Several spa experts from the GSWS (2012b) Briefing Papers share their views about people's relationships to technology. We are rarely unplugged which can be disruptive to a healthy lifestyle (McNees, 2012: 101–2). There are positive but also negative sides of technology, such as the way we socialise (Glover, 2012). Social media means that we communicate with people at a more superficial level, leaving little time for deeper friend-ship: 'we become overstimulated by media yet remain undeveloped physically and spiritu-ality. Our mental development is heavily influenced' (Wiedemann, 2012: 53). Brepohl (2012) suggests that we are hostages to gadgets, wonderful tools but which cause a lack of balance. Matthews (2012: 3) is also right to conclude that, 'When we replace a recep-tionist with an iPad we miss out on simple conversations and the warmth of a smile'. It was discussed in Chapter 4 that people who are forced to live without their gadgets for even 24 hours display similar symptoms to cigarette addicts. The fact that the concept of a 'Digital Detox Retreat' has even been coined tells us something!

Aside from technology, other stresses and strains have become endemic in most socie-ties, especially those where people work long hours. Williams (2012: 123–4) suggests that burnout is one of the top diseases nowadays. Chapter 4 discussed the regrets of the dying and one of the main ones was that people (especially men) wished that they had not worked so hard all their lives. Companies are starting to realise the economic benefits of trying to reduce workplace stress and cut down absenteeism and sickness. This might simply be by offering their employees a massage or a place to have a power nap in the afternoon, or it could include spa visits and wellness weekends as incentives or team building. The role that tourism plays here is that it takes people away from their normal environment, which is often needed in order to rest or recover properly. This is especially important for people who have experienced burnout and may not want to face their workplace for a long time.

Lifestyle-related illnesses have become much more common, especially when people do not have time to exercise, socialise or eat healthily because of their focus on work or because of a lack of public education. Iida (2012: 15) writes about 'the increasing size of mentally unbalanced or unstable population (whether because of a stressful social system or because of the decline in face-to-face communication)'. Glover (2012: 81) describes how the spas of the future will focus on 'the world's pandemic maladies, such as obesity, stress-related ailments, and sexual disfunctions' and Lampers (2012: 94) states that

'internal health through nutrition, exercise, spirituality, mental challenges, and physical self-contentment is our greatest opportunity and our greatest challenge in the spa market'. There is no doubt that many people need to slow down and re-discover the joy of living. This might be achieved through learning yoga, meditation or Tai Chi. Hutchinson (2012) says that the slow movement reminds people of mindfulness in the moment and McCarthy (2012) predicts that mindfulness will be the next big health trend. One of the most important aspects of tourism is that wellness and spa guests learn how to improve their lifestyles over a period of several days and then continue their self-healing process back home (Zake, 2012: 125). As stated by Bartura (2012: 23), 'To play a part in empowering people to take stock and control of their own health and well-being and reconstruct the image of wellness-holidays from a self-pampering luxury to a balanced lifestyle choice.'

Product development and trends

One of the major concerns in the future for many destinations is that all products and services will be available everywhere. Although more and more spa hotels and resort chains make an effort to include signature, indigenous and local traditions or to reflect local architectural styles, many of them could be located anywhere. If they are based on natural resources and assets (e.g. a Blue Lagoon, a Héviz or a Dead Sea), this will give them a unique selling point, but if they are offering the whole spectrum of global wellness products, their lifespan and appeal may be limited. For leisure visitors (i.e. those from the local area) it can be a great bonus to receive Thai massage or Ayurvedic treatments in their home town. But for tourism destinations which are trying to compete in terms of their unique selling propositions, this should not include culturally displaced treatments at the expense of local or indigenous ones. The Global Spa Summit (2011) report noted that there is a new trend of consumers looking for local, traditional and unique experiences, and recommended that there should subsequently be an emphasis on national or regional specialisms and signature treatments. In the GSWS (2012) Briefing Papers, several spa experts re-emphasised this idea, for example McDonald (2012: 99) advocated that there should be, 'A shift to an indigenous and local community approach, where spa and wellness facilities can tap into the strengths of their location, geography or people that make their area unique'. Chaudhari (2012) writes about ancient, culturally based healing and wellness traditions, unique options that reflect the country or region. Voit (2012) suggested that this is already starting to happen, at least in design: 'Designers have learned to create spas based on, and rooted in, the culture they are meant to serve.' This was seen in the case study of a Brazilian spa in Chapter 7, where the whole development concept from design to completion was based on Brazilian culture and nature.

In North America, Australia and Western Europe, there is something of an emphasis on holistic and spiritual activities; for example, the largest growth sector in the UK appears to be holistic retreats rather than luxury spas. However, most of these are not indigenous to the countries in which they take place (with the exception perhaps of Australian Aboriginal or Native American Indian traditions in a small number of spas or retreats). Most Western people, especially big city dwellers, are now used to a diversity of cultures and multiple faiths. It is therefore not that usual for them to partake of Buddhist meditation, to do Tai Chi in the park, to have a Thai massage or chant in Sanskrit during their yoga class. Retreat centres therefore offer a range of activities which may be fairly familiar to the majority of participants and they may be open-minded to trying even more. One of the wonderful aspects of the globalisation of health and wellness is that people can select from the world's richest healing traditions, often on their own doorstep. The downside is that the practices are de-contextualised, displaced and may even be diluted. For example, many Western yoga classes have omitted the spiritual dimension altogether. Going to the home of those practices or experiencing wellness traditions in an authentic context can be one of the greatest joys of health and wellness tourism.

It is becoming clear that you can even have too much of a good thing in wellness. This has already started to happen in Germany and Austria where there is an over-supply of top-quality wellness hotels and spas. Visitors have started to lose interest and are already searching for alternatives. The spa sector is growing exponentially in Asia, but this is perhaps at the expense of more 'organic' holistic or spiritual developments; for example, Thai islands which were once backpacker havens and retreats are now becoming over-developed with more standardised spa hotels for package tourists. Kelly and Smith's (2008) research showed that most holistic practitioners in Goa in India thought that too much regulation would be detrimental to the diversity of activities and atmosphere of the destination. There is also likely to be resistance to the growing number of spa and well-ness hotel resorts. Byron Bay in Australia has also grown organically and although new destination spas and luxury retreats have been developed, they have not replaced the alternative, holistic centres which pre-dated them and gave the destination its unique atmosphere and appeal.

There are few countries in the world that do *not* wish to develop some form of wellness or medical tourism. However, we have already started to see that some countries are developing facilities deliberately to encourage their patients to stay at home for medical treatments (e.g. Dubai, Japan) or to provide services for the diaspora (e.g. South Korea for the USA West Coast patients with Korean origin). If there is also more and more emphasis on preventative wellness in everyday life (e.g. public health campaigns, local longevity centres, global treatments available locally), this may decrease the need or desire to travel for wellness. As people's lifestyles become healthier, life expectancy increases and the rate of serious illness decreases, it is also more likely that wellness facilities will be visited for enjoyment and entertainment, rather than medical reasons. This has started to be the case in many traditional thermal medical spas in Europe (e.g. Italy, Portugal, Slovenia), which are shifting their emphasis from medical to wellness activities. Whereas medical thermal tourism usually requires stays of two or three weeks to be fully effective, wellness breaks tend to be only two or three days.

There is a definite shift towards more sustainable, eco-friendly, natural operations. This is reflected in some spa cuisine, slow food, the development of eco-spas, adventure spas and even farm retreats. An education for guests may also be necessary, as stated by Sethi (2012: 13): 'Educating spa-users on counting carbons not calories.' Hougaard (2012: 9) describes wellness as the challenge of 'how to spend our lives well and avoid wastage,

whether in time, calories, fossil fuel or water'. He goes on to say that 'Life is simple and all we do most of the time is complicate it; the spa and wellness industry constantly reminds us of our roots because wellness is not about the latest fad or trend; it's about being natural, back to nature, so to speak' (ibid.: 10).

CASE STUDY 8.1
Wellness in the countryside
Corné de Regt

The company Rode Wangen which was established by Corné de Regt, a farmer's son who was also a manager for major companies, embodies many of the newest trends in wellness discussed in this book: focusing on local specialities; sustainable operations; organic fresh food; corporate wellness. Corné and his company run retreats on a farm, using a 'country-side or farmer's philosophy'. They organise team-building and training days, which involve active participation in the life of the farm, but also thinking and talking about new ideas.

The retreat has attracted the attention of media all around the world, including the *Guardian* in the UK, which mentions stressed Dutch businessmen lying on a bed of straw and medi-tating with cows! Corné's idea is that businessmen should benefit from the fresh air and have red cheeks before they leave ('Rode Wangen' means red cheeks in Dutch).

- The body can be scrubbed with clay, sand or salt from the local area (Well-beauty).

- Fitness is done outside instead of in a dark hotel basement. Sometimes they walk through a river in wintertime, learn to milk cows or chop wood (Well-fit).

- Meditation takes place in silence, darkness, or indeed, with cows (Well-spirit).

- Food comes directly from the farm (Well-food).

As a child with his parents on the farm, Corné and his siblings would ask why they had to eat their vegetables again, to which his father would reply that he took care of them, saw them grow, took them from the ground, especially for them, healthy and ready to eat. This he sees as another kind of energy when this story and those vegetables are on the plate. Food directly from the garden is fresh, tasty and gives a special kind of satisfaction.

Corné's idea is that the value of life can improve with more green and light. He advocates that homes could be built on farmers' estates. He works in cooperation with the Twents Office of Tourism (Twents Buro voor Toerisme). Their project 'Wellness in Twente' investi-gated how hotels, restaurants and wellness centres could act differently and show aspects of the region or surroundings they are part of in their products and services. When they do so, each company has a unique proposition and the region offers consumers a totally unique selling point compared to other regions.

Many spas and wellness hotels are using technology to create unique but also 'natural' effects and experiences. Kapur (2012: 11) outlines some of the new trends as being organic products, de-stress therapies (e.g. hot stone therapy, lava shell massage), and capsules (e.g. naturopathy, steam, water, colours, smells, sounds of nature). The need to create experiences is becoming more and more important. As stated by Chipalkatti (2012: 7) spas should aim to 'transform the "treatment" to an "experience" and go beyond the "physical" realm'. Chaudhari (2012: 5) also outlines some of the new trends:

- multi-sense spas (e.g. sound, light, technology);
- wow factor (e.g. spa suites, pre-pampering areas, post-relaxation deck).

However, the simplification of spas has also become a major point of discussion in recent years with many spas cutting down the number of treatment options on their menus. It is not an exaggeration to say that many clients can be stressed out or over-whelmed by too many choices (McCarthy, 2012; Zake, 2012). There is also a debate about how far spas should continue to offer pampering to their guests. Of course, this is often cited as one of the most popular motivations for going to spas, and Matthews (2012: 3) argues that, 'The pampering component of spas should always exist'. On the other hand, spas perhaps need to be about much more if they are to attract new markets (e.g. men) or to be taken more seriously by the medical industry. De Gabriac (2012: 38) suggests that they need 'to prove that they go beyond pampering fluff, that they offer ways to impact positively the human physiology, and that they can deliver reliable solutions to improve the lives of their clients' and Bramham (2012: 73) predicts that, 'Spas will be an expression of our emotional and physical landscape. It will be an experience of re-discovery and personal empowerment'. Spas must also become more democratised if they are to serve societies better. The dream of many spa experts is that budget spas and cheaper services are provided, such as Thai massage, Chinese medicine or Korean spas (Griffin, 2012: 83). Egger (2012: 41–2) advocates that spas should not just be for the rich and beautiful but for everyone who would like to stay healthy. The description of a spa by Mestre (2012: 65) is perhaps the most comprehensive and holistic, and also the most beautiful:

> I see the spa as a new human development and resource center, a unique space that can be enjoyed on a physical, spiritual or mental level. A synergy between people connected by the touch and warmth of another human being; but also a space where we can find our inner silence, inviting us to reflect, to think, to feel, to listen, to appre-ciate and preserve life's vital energy. A retreat from everyday wear-and-tear where we can appreciate nature, discover ancient and meaningful healing rituals, develop new expressions, talents and dormant abilities, through reading, painting, meditation, music, learning how to cook healthy meals, hiking, sporting endeavors, meeting new friends. A spa can be anything we want it to be, as long as it caters to a higher spirit, a stronger, healthier body and a visionary mind where imagination has no limits.

In addition to the growth of spas and wellness hotels, there is also a development of wellness treatments in the transport industry to make travellers more comfortable and

recover from their journey more quickly. This service is most likely to be used by business travellers or those who can afford business or first class travel. However, some of the airport spas are becoming more affordable (i.e. they are not just in exclusive lounges, e.g. Xpress). Some airports have a reasonably priced massage service which is available to anyone and massage chairs can now be used in many airports for as little as two EUROs. Qatar Airways has worked closely with the (Deepak) Chopra Center to develop flight tips for passengers. These are mainly based on Ayurvedic principles and recommend that passengers practise relaxing breathing, use self-massage, do meditation, as well as eating lightly, avoiding alcohol and drinking adequate water. Many airports now have spas, such as JFK, Amsterdam Schipol and Singapore, to name but a few. They offer various treatments such as massage, oxygen therapy (sometimes with scented oils), manicures and pedicures, foot reflexology, facials, and waxing. Munich Airport even introduced a relaxation and sleeping (Napcab) capsule for those waiting for (intercontinental) connection.

CASE STUDY 8.2
Helsinki Airport Spa

In terms of size Finnair's full-service spa concept is currently found nowhere else in the world. The services are designed specifically with passenger needs in mind. The spa is open 10 a.m.–10 p.m. Facilities include a steam room, four saunas, a stone bath (like a normal steam room except hot stones are plunged into cold water to create the steam), Rasul for mud skin peels, a mineral water pool, and loungers facing the runway – the lower parts of the windows are blacked out so people cannot see in. It costs €45 for entry to the spa area, while treatments range from €51 to €141, but the €45 is subtracted from the treatment cost. All spa products are purely organic.

Treatments are designed to combat the side effects of flying. For example, passengers on long flights are sitting for a long time so they might have problems with circulation, such as heavy legs, so special treatments have been designed for them. One special package is called 'Finnish Delight' and includes a Finnish sauna, footbath to increase blood circulation in the feet, Magic Legs and Jet Lag treatments, using herbal bundles, steam and mint oil to revive tired legs.

There are also specially designed services for passengers making connecting flights. These include short treatments, which last from ten minutes to a half an hour. For example, the 15-minute neck and head jet lag massage and traditional hamam bath.

The spa and lounge have been developed jointly by Finnair, Finavia, which maintains Finland's network of airports, and airport catering company SSP Finland. Samuli Haapasalo, president and CEO of Finavia, said: 'When planning the new extension, we focused on experiential services and travel efficiency, and a high level of expertise has been the hallmark of its construction.'

There were a few debates about whether the spa could be profitable, as it was promoted to economy class travellers but at first-class prices according to one TripAdvisor page. Unfortunately, as a result it closed. However, with a better model, airport spas could perhaps become more widespread in the future.

(Business Traveller, 2009; Finnair, 2013)

Medical tourism has been showing an incredible development during the last couple of years. More and more countries, destinations and service providers enter what they hope is a global market. Having very little data available on real patient flows, any forecast can be rather difficult. Most medical services are standard (and standardised, certified and/or accredited). Many depend very much on one physician or surgeon or a certain treatment. More and more companies try to link the patients with the doctors and/or the hospitals. Still, we can see an opposite turn, that is more and more doctors go to the patients, or the given hospital (brand) opens a new facility closer to (prospective) markets. E-health and telemedicine may also decrease international patient flows. Health and healing, however, cannot be and should not be considered as short term concepts. Integrative medicine and active-ageing, if practitioners (and governments) started to educate young generations (e.g. Gen Z) can provide attractive alternatives for the tourism industry for many decades!

Liability issues are certainly key to any medical service, since the latest scandal of PIP implants raised concern (and costs). Women who had had breast augmentation with PIP implants became concerned that the leaking implant can cause infection and illness and demanded to take them out. But that was left to be done by the National Health Service providers and women would not go back to the foreign plastic surgeon who initially put the implant in.

Future predictions

A research project was undertaken by the authors with and on behalf of the Global Spa Summit (2011) about the role of spas in wellness and medical tourism. Forty interviews were undertaken with health, wellness, spa and tourism practitioners. A few quotations have been selected to show some of their predications for the future of health and wellness tourism in their countries and the rest of the world:

- Spas might link themselves to medical facilities, to provide more holistic health offerings (Australia): Australia has been starting to develop medical tourism, although the main emphasis is still on wellness spas and retreats. However, as a general comment, this is certainly true as many spas either use new medical technology (e.g. for cosmetic treatments) or are looking for more scientific and medical evidence to prove the benefits of their treatments.

- Especially plastic surgery will grow (Brazil): This comment is certainly true of Brazil and most of Central and South America. The active ageing trend will fuel this further all around the world and treatments will become more available and probably cheaper.

- People will see spas as part of lifestyle (Canada): Spa lifestyle compounds have become popular in North America, and many new accommodation buildings come complete with a gym, fitness and spa facilities. Of course, in Finland and some other countries, it is not uncommon to have a sauna in your own home, but this is not a new trend.

- Ageing, retirement, active lifestyle, living compounds (Thailand): Once again, living compounds are mentioned. The active ageing trend is an extremely important one and spas are likely to play a major role in helping people to stay physically healthy, fit and youthful, in body, mind and appearance.

- Traditional treatments remain important (India): This book has emphasised the importance of historical, local and indigenous traditions, not only in or from India but all over the world. This is especially important when developing unique selling propositions for tourism and destination marketing.

- The spa and the thermal verticum will converge (Hungary): This means that thermal medical spas will gradually make the crossover to become more like wellness spas or a combination of the two. Of course, it is difficult to mix the medical thermal and leisure spa segments, but the two can be offered in different parts of a complex. It is also clear that the reduction in government support for domestic thermal medical tourism (e.g. in Central and Eastern Europe) is going to mean the need to shift towards international wellness tourism in the future if not already.

- Evolution of hot spring spa culture (Australia): Hot spring healing traditions exist in many countries (as discussed in more detail by Erfurt-Cooper and Cooper, 2009). Many of these have been developed for tourists, but in some countries they have not yet (e.g. Uganda). Even South Africa which has a large number of hot springs which could be used for healing purposes are still only used for leisure, if at all (see Mark Boekstein's case study in Part III). Some of the springs are too hot or are dangerous for visitors, but with careful management in the future and the right infrastructure, they could represent an important growth sector.

- Spiritualising the experience. Location and environment play a huge role (Finland): In many countries, especially the Nordic and Baltic countries of Europe, landscape plays an extremely important role in well-being (see Edward Huijbens' and Henna Konu et al.'s case studies in Part III). Even though the climate is cold and dark, outdoor recreation is popular, ice swimming is not uncommon, and many people walk regularly in the woods or forests picking mushrooms or berries. The sense of spirituality can be something close to animism. For many city or town dwelling people, 'nature deficit disorder' may be a real problem and they could head to natural landscapes for eco-therapy.

- Sustainability and authentic marketing (Austria): Sustainability has become a big part of the spa and wellness industry as it has in the tourism industry. The growth of the Green Spas Network is proof of this, as well as the significant measures being taken even by chain spa and wellness hotels. The need for authentic marketing refers to the need to use labels properly, for example, 'eco labels', but also to move towards an industry where there are more authentic products to promote. For example, Austria is part of the Alpine Wellness brand, which is a seal of quality and authenticity for local and regional products.

- Not just relaxation: but prevention and rehabilitation (Philippines): Many countries have a tradition of rehabilitation and cure, but most of these are less focused on prevention. The spas, wellness and medical centres of the future will need to provide for those people who think they only want leisure and relaxation, but at the same time, they could (or should) be educated to lead a healthier lifestyle to prevent future illness or health problems. Rehabilitation can also be offered to those people who have suffered from physical illnesses, mental or psychological problems, even addictions. As stated by Maruyama (2012: 20) spas are starting to manage services for after illness/medical treatment, such as cancer patients, as 'they are keener to stay physically and psychologically well after surviving their illness than healthy people are'.

It seems clear from the GSS (2010) research that many clients would be far more willing to visit spas if there were more medical evidence that treatments have health benefits. However, the relationship between spas, wellness and medical sectors is a complex one. Tompkins (2012) suggests that a true integrated model of the medical, spa and wellness industries is needed, but there is still resistance to this process. For example, Nemer (2012: 103) says of spas that 'the medical community sees us as witch doctors as opposed to bona fide healers'. On the other hand, in some countries, those who work in spas have some medical training. Bogacheva (2012: 21) writes that most spa therapists in Russia have to have basic medical education, so are setting a good example for an evidence-based approach. Ironically, the placebo effect in medicine has been researched extensively in the medical field and is generally accepted by practitioners. In the spa sector, this is not yet the case, but Bjurstam (2012) and McCarthy (2012) amongst others are already discussing its significance.

However, Shivdasani (2012: 31) believes, 'There will come a time when destination spas and alternative healing centers will have as much credibility as Western medicine', and Schweder (2012: 30) discusses the fact that more and more people are questioning the validity of conventional Western medicine, and that substantial academic and scientific research is going into ancient wellness traditions. From the other side, there is no doubt that scientific evidence and research can benefit the spa and wellness industries and the guidance of medical experts will be increasingly important. Even spa-goers are starting to demand this. Yap (2012: 57–8) suggests that, 'Well-versed spa and wellness customers are increasingly going back to holistic methods to maintain their health and fitness but they demand technology to diagnose their condition before they embark on their program of treatments, and to demonstrate the results afterwards'. Chaturongkul (2012: 27) writes about, 'The use of science to refine and create new products and services, e.g. anti-aging, mind-body work, and disease prevention and management'. Gibson (2012: 1) suggests that, 'Some of the biggest game changers in our industry are innovations and discoveries in medical procedures and products that influence the beauty industry'. In terms of

hospitality and tourism, Ullrick (2012) thinks that hotels and hospitals will share ideas with each other, especially when it comes to hospitality in medical spas. Nevertheless, Jordan (2012: 87–8) is perhaps right to urge that we should resist over-medicalising the spa experience otherwise people will need a vacation from their vacation! This goes back to the debate about how far patients are medical tourists.

BMWI (2012) suggests that the 'new' health or medical tourism and services could be described as:

- a product that becomes a fundamental part of the supply in every destination, due to the growing proportion of ageing travellers;
- more and more differentiated services, e.g. by indications;
- growing expectation of results and evidence which may result in the increasing importance of medication (i.e. pills);
- primary prevention is losing importance, while secondary and tertiary prevention may prevail (primary prevention protects healthy people from developing a disease or experiencing an injury in the first place; secondary prevention halts or slows the progress of a disease (if possible) in its earliest stages; tertiary prevention includes preventing further physical deterioration and maximizing quality of life (IWH, 2013));
- becoming more sustainable since it includes longevity, checkups and coaching, too;
- new forms and new packages incorporating services which go beyond the actual stay bringing the health benefits home;
- built on strong and complex networks comprising professional health-care providers, hotels, fitness services, doctors, etc.;
- focused segmentation and targeting beyond traditional tourism channels due to changes in motivations, communication behaviour and platforms.

The Tourism Observatory for Health, Wellness and Spa's (2012) (a global initiative from Xellum Ltd.) research entitled *4WR: Wellness for Whom, Where and What? Wellness Tourism 2020* collected opinions from 140 stakeholders from wellness, tourism, spa and health-care industries in over 50 countries worldwide. The research aimed to provide an analysis of the greatest opportunities over the next ten years for policy-makers and practitioners and to better define new product development strategies. The research aimed to be as representative as possible of what is happening worldwide in wellness, spa and medical tourism. The interviewees were chosen to reflect a diverse range of countries, organisations and initiatives.

Wellness hotels and resort spas are forecasted to remain the most popular wellness tourism product in several continents and regions by 2020. It is suggested, however, that products that are available globally will lose their differentiating qualities including beauty treatments, massage of any kind, saunas, day-spas, and some spiritual practices (e.g. yoga or meditation).

Fifty-eight per cent of respondents consider traditional medical tourism services (i.e. travelling primarily for surgical interventions, dental services, rehabilitation) to be popular or very popular in the industry. There is a growing trend, especially in medical tourism towards 'evidence-based' services which have been extensively researched and are

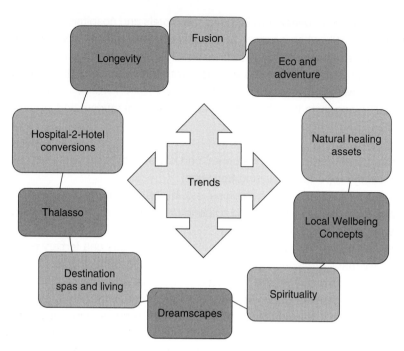

FIGURE 8.1 Some new trends in health and wellness travel

proven to have health benefits (e.g. healing waters, muds). In Central and Eastern Europe, therapeutic services and treatments are mainly based on the availability of natural assets (e.g. thermal waters) and will stay/or become the most important. In terms of wellness tourism services, the research showed that beauty treatments (89 per cent), sport and fitness services (89 per cent), leisure and recreational spas (85 per cent), and spa and wellness resorts (83 per cent) are the most popular within the industry. Spirituality remains important in countries where there is a strong spiritual tradition (e.g. Asia). However, the growing interest in non-religious spiritual practices in increasingly secular societies (e.g. Europe) means that such products and services need to become more widely available. For example, many European monasteries or nunneries are offering spiritual retreats.

Summarising the key trends we can predict that:

- In *Africa* there will be an increased leisure and recreational segment, based on wellness products. At present, Africa has limited medical tourism development (e.g. South Africa, Kenya). There is some potential for hot springs (which are often used extensively by local people for healing), but this will require considerable infrastructural development.
- In *Australia, New Zealand* and the *South-Pacific* leisure and recreational spas, as well as wellness hotels and spas seem to be the most important in 2020, while lifestyle based services (e.g. the combination of physical fitness, nutrition etc.) will gain ground.

Although Australia has started to develop some medical tourism, the growth of holistic retreats and spas in this region is much more likely to be the dominant growth trend. The South Pacific is likely to stay focused on spa and wellness hotels.

- In the *Far East* holistic and spiritual approaches/services will still be the most important services, with a strong wellness base. The historic spa or hot spring tradition can be quite strong in this region and may be developed further for international tourism (they are already popular with residents and domestic tourists).

- *South-East Asia* will still be the main centre for holistic and spiritual tourism. The number of resort and destination spas and wellness hotels is growing fast in this region. Many of them draw on local traditions in their design and treatments rather than being too generic or standardised in their offer.

- In the Middle East wellness as well as medical tourism will determine the market. Many Middle Eastern destinations are competing to become the 'mecca' of medical tourism. In addition, more and more top luxury spa hotels and resorts are being developed.

- *South America* and *Central America* remain strong in wellness tourism, as well as in leisure and recreational spas. Cosmetic surgery is likely to remain a major selling point for this region where a high number of local residents are also undergoing surgery. The diverse wilderness landscapes and the focus on sustainability (e.g. in Costa Rica) is also likely to give rise to growing numbers of adventure or eco-spas.

- In *North America*, wellness and lifestyle-based services will gain importance, based on leisure and recreational spas, and wellness hotels. The USA and Canada mainly focus on spas and wellness. Medical tourism is predominantly outbound. Occupational wellness may be more of a priority in this region because of long working hours and relatively short holidays.

- *Southern Europe* seems to be the most dominant in leisure and recreational spas (with the highest rating in the world), but wellness hotels and spas will dominate the market. There are also a growing number of holistic retreats in this region as the climate, lifestyle and landscape is popular with entrepreneurs (i.e. retreat owners) and tourists alike.

- In *Central* and *Eastern Europe*, therapeutic medical services still dominate the market, but wellness and lifestyle-based services will become important. The likely future decrease in government subsidies for medical thermal tourism will mean a certain shift towards more wellness developments.

- The *Western European* health tourism market will be dominated by wellness hotels, but leisure and recreational spas remain popular. Holistic and spiritual retreats seem to be growing in this region, possibly even faster than spas.

- *Northern Europe* will be the most important hub for wellness and lifestyle-based services, with leisure and recreational spas. Nordic countries have close links to landscape and outdoor recreation with combinations of hot and cold therapies. Baltic countries have more of a medical thermal tradition like Russia. Medical (thermal) wellness may be more of a growth trend in the Baltic countries than in Scandinavia, where preventative, lifestyle-based wellness will be more popular.

Overall, the product-base analysis of the 4WR research showed that:

- No clear emerging megatrends are expected before 2020.
- Wellness destinations and hotel spas will remain as dominant products (having 18.5 per cent of the answers), while leisure and recreational programmes and services will be the second most popular service (16.7 per cent).
- The new trend of wellness and lifestyle-based services will increase dynamically, and reach third place on the popularity list of wellness products.
- Leisure and recreational spas will be particularly popular in Southern Europe and in Africa. Wellness hotels and spas will be especially important in Southern Europe, Central and South America as well as in Africa, while wellness and lifestyle-based services will dominate the Northern European as well as the North American market.
- Holistic services as well as medical services will show an average popularity.

In terms of demand, four segments were chosen for the research, which were *men, singles, GenY* (those currently aged approximately 20–34) and *families*. Wellness tourism preferences were analysed against ten tourism products (leisure and recreational facilities, therapeutic services, medical services, wellness hotels/spa resorts, wellness/lifestyle-based services, holistic services, spiritual services, adventure and eco facilities and spas, and wellness and spa cruises). The results were that:

- *Singles* will prefer wellness and lifestyle-based services as well as leisure and recreational facilities and spas.
- *Families* will show a continued interest in leisure and recreational services, but wellness hotels and spas will also be popular.
- *Generation Y* will show growing demand for adventure and eco facilities and spas.
- The popularity of wellness and lifestyle-based services, as well as adventure facilities and spas will grow among *men*.

Conclusions from the 4WR research were as follows:

1 Wellness goes beyond relaxation and is a key element of lifestyle, which is a significant opportunity for the travel and tourism industry, since people following a wellness lifestyle will look for similar services when they are travelling. Wellness tourism is more than spa tourism and includes healthy cuisine, specific fitness or body/mind/spirit regimes, active-ageing or longevity programmes, learning, adventure, spiritual enlightenment, personal growth and has the ability to enhance lives.
2 The industry appears to be dominated by wellness destinations and hotel spas, however other attractions and facilities are becoming more popular with consumers (e.g. wellness retreats, outdoor recreational activities, lifestyle centres, thermal treatment centres, etc.).
3 There will be a proliferation of new, cross-over and fusion services and products which will support the development of wellness tourism in countries and regions that are not yet on the global map of wellness tourism. These need to position themselves

in a distinctive way so as not to 'disappear' in a competitive environment. Unique and signature products and services need to be developed.

4 Spirituality remains important in countries where there is a strong spiritual tradition (e.g. Asia). However, the growing interest in non-religious spiritual practices in increasingly secular societies (e.g. Europe) means that such products and services need to become more widely available.

5 Consumers are becoming more attuned to the importance and value of green, eco, sustainable and organic practices and products. These should become more of a norm than an exception in wellness facilities, and the products and services should merit the 'label'.

6 A health-focused region has the ability to provide enough variety of services to meet the needs of multiple target segments. One facility cannot be all things to all people.

7 There is significant potential in targeting the growth segments identified in this report, namely men, singles, families and youth (Gen Y). Men have different needs and expectations from women. Single people may feel uncomfortable surrounded by families and need tailor-made programmes. Young people have few physical health problems compared to the elderly. Parents with children need relaxation but can rarely achieve this.

8 Evidence-based wellness is becoming more important, i.e. consumers need to know that the treatments or rituals that they are receiving have been adequately researched and are safe and beneficial. This could include healing waters, muds, cosmetics, nutrition, etc. Similarly, wellness practices and practitioners should be regulated properly.

9 Wellness tourism tends to be fairly exclusive, especially when it is based on wellness hotels and spas. In the future, there is likely to be a democratisation of wellness (especially if young people are being targeted), for example, budget spas, basic retreats, nature-based activities.

10 Wellness tourism is likely to be seen as contributing to long-term well-being and quality of life, especially if there is a focus on the whole person and their entire life-span in the form of active ageing and longevity.

11 Travel often affords the opportunity to learn about culture, history and other ways of life which contribute to the overall understanding of human nature and one's place in the world, thus corresponding to intellectual and social well-being.

Several recommendations could be made to those who are developing spa, wellness or medical tourism based on this research. These could be summarised as follows:

1 There is a very likely risk that the supply of wellness tourism products and services becomes too standardised. However, most regions have a number of unique assets which can and should be developed for wellness tourism. This will help to create unique selling propositions, distinctive brands and competitive destinations.

2 Several ubiquitous wellness services (e.g. saunas, massage) may lose their differentiating power and become entry-level services without which no wellness provider can (or should) operate. However, they are not enough to guarantee an appealing

attraction and other newer or unusual services should be offered in parallel (e.g. rituals, traditions).

3   Operators also need to consider the significance of alternative and complementary medical treatments, especially those which enhance mental and social well-being as well as physical health.

4   Natural assets, as the most critical component to wellness tourism product development should be utilized in a sustainable manner, protected by legal arrangements and supported by private and public enterprises.

5   Natural healing assets (e.g. healing waters) will (re)gain popularity as evidenced by the growing interest in CAM, Ayurveda, Traditional Chinese Medicine and other non invasive approaches to healing and wellness.

6   There is an opportunity to better serve and create specialised products and programmes for the ageing, for those with chronic conditions and/or disability (e.g. therapeutic recreation, rehabilitation).

In March 2013, the Global Spa and Wellness Summit asked its members to imagine the spa of the future and quoted some comments from Spa 2020, a special report for spa and hospitality professionals published by The Hotel Yearbook. For example, Alison Howland, president of Spa Success Consultants, Inc., in Palm Beach, Florida, looked at the unique characteristics of four demographic groups: baby boomers, now aged 47–65, who do not want to admit they are ageing but need a 'subtle safety vibe'; highly educated, sophisticated

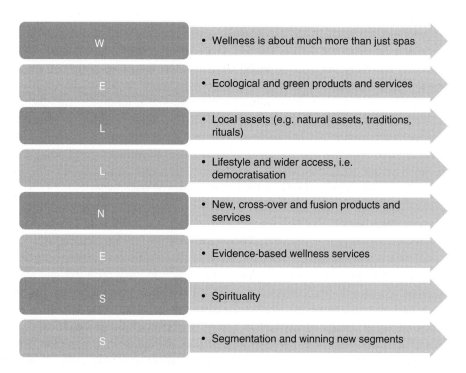

W	• Wellness is about much more than just spas
E	• Ecological and green products and services
L	• Local assets (e.g. natural assets, traditions, rituals)
L	• Lifestyle and wider access, i.e. democratisation
N	• New, cross-over and fusion products and services
E	• Evidence-based wellness services
S	• Spirituality
S	• Segmentation and winning new segments

FIGURE 8.2 Characterising wellness tourism

GenXers, 27–47, who will demand the best – but remember the recession – and expect exceptional value; complex Gen Yers, 24–34, looking for authenticity, ecology and technology; and Generation Z, 14–24, who will make fast decisions and look for brands that can keep up with their demands. Ingo Schweider, CEO of the Bangkok-based spa consulting firm GOCO (and a contributor to this book), predicts that over the next ten years the global spa industry will be deeply influenced by trends from Asia – and a growing number of tourists from Asia will dramatically impact on both the spa and hospitality industries. GSWS Chairman and CEO Susie Ellis (also a contributor to this book) looks into the future and imagines 'Lisa', aged 36, who is trapped in a cycle of unhealthy food, bad sleep and incredible stress, checks into a 'wellness everywhere' hotel and leaves four days later rested, energised and happy. And of course Lisa will be able to stay on track when she returns home, thanks to her new apps and her online fitness/diet coaches and psychologist.

Plessier (2013) reported on the results of the sixth annual State of Spa Travel survey, which suggested that people are now more interested in travelling to spas specifically for programmes like stress-reduction, fitness and weight loss. Sixty-seven per cent of agents reported that their clients were more interested in spa vacations with a strong health-wellness focus in 2012. The baby-boomer generation remains the core demographic, with 67 per cent of agents reporting that they were the age group most likely to book spa travel in 2012, but a significant 31 per cent of agents also mentioned the younger, 26–45 age group as now most likely to book spa vacations. GSWS (2013) states that 'wellness tourism is no longer an exotic concept, but is becoming a powerful, mainstream trend that will influence where people go, and what they choose to do, on their increasingly precious time off'.

The Observatory for Health, Wellness and Spa in 2012 launched a global monitoring initiative called The Global Spa and Wellness Tourism Monitor (TOHWS, 2013). The GSWTM endorsed and supported by over 60 industry associations, organisations and leading companies collected over 430 opinions from over 45 countries. The key findings of the global study were as follows:

- There are over 15 different forms and types of spa and wellness service providers available (from resort spas to lifestyle oriented hotels/spas and centres) which make the marketing of products and services globally very challenging.
- The role of tourism is significant in wellness and spa facilities, since every second customer was a tourist (either domestic or foreign).
- There are significant differences between what can be attractive for tourists travelling within their home countries for health reasons and those who are ready to travel abroad. Foreign health and wellness trips are influenced by the special offers and concepts of destination spas (and similar facilities), facilities based on natural healing resources, eco-spa and wellness facilities. Domestic travellers will be looking for family spas and wellness facilities, eco-spa and wellness facilities, wellness hotels and facilities based on natural healing resources.
- Segments will differ according to the distance they are happy to travel for health and wellness. Almost every second international health tourist will fall into the 'core' segment, i.e. those who live a health-conscious life and look for healthy services during their holidays. Most (67 per cent) of domestic tourists, however, qualify as

'mid-level' customers, who are interested in healthy alternatives during holidays as well, but do not necessarily pursue a health-conscious lifestyle.

- The most popular therapies are based on natural resources with proven benefits (e.g. thermal water, mud).
- Couples took over the number one segment from women travelling for spa and wellness, and travelling with friends (in groups) and families with kids and single men show significant increase in demand.

Figure 8.3 gives an indication of the authors' understanding of medical tourism development trends and what it entails.

Medical or health-care services are already and certainly will change dramatically in the coming years. Here are two cases representing leading development and management concepts:

- Cancer Treatment Centres of America has introduced a new medical approach (the centres serve intra-country patients in the USA). They redefined the whole service and experience creation and they involved their patients and colleagues in the re-design and re-definition of their services and facilities, which are now not tumour but patient focused. For example, a whole team of specialists deal with the patient holistically (e.g. nutrition, fitness, psychology, therapy, in addition to medical treatments).
- Golden Horses Health Sanctuary in Malaysia opened a full service spa on their premises to provide relaxation to their patients as an integral part of the preventative healthcare services.

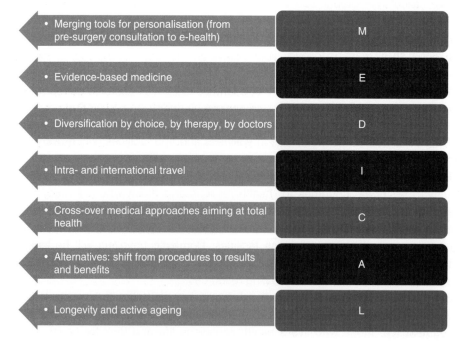

- Merging tools for personalisation (from pre-surgery consultation to e-health)   M
- Evidence-based medicine   E
- Diversification by choice, by therapy, by doctors   D
- Intra- and international travel   I
- Cross-over medical approaches aiming at total health   C
- Alternatives: shift from procedures to results and benefits   A
- Longevity and active ageing   L

FIGURE 8.3 Characterising medical tourism

Woodman (2013) also highlighted that medical services have to change the existing paradigm and should apply integrative approaches where the patient is the core and not the doctors or the treatments. The integrative health approach especially in the short term is expected to influence private health-care providers since public health-care organisations and facilities may have other problems to solve (e.g. finances, shortage of skilled staff).

Medical tourism will shift from focusing on medical interventions (e.g. surgery) and will understand more the role of longevity, active-ageing, alternative therapies and evidence-based medicine. Services and treatments need to be (more) personalised and individual (i.e. using consultations, diagnostics and supervision), both face-to-face and online (e-health), before, during and after procedures. The concept of total health, which is basically the application of the WHO definition of health to practise, will influence health-care services and patient flows and mobility. Cross-border and international initiatives (the likes of the European Union's cross-border health-care directive) can also change international patient mobility but we have to note some challenges. Kunhardt (2011) estimated that the EU cross-border healthcare can be 1 per cent of the total health-care market achieving up to 10 billion euros. As noted by Glinos (2012) the tension between EU member states may accelerate since the patient flows would also bring in the migration of medical staff and most certainly can cause financial challenges, too.

The future of health, wellness and medical tourism

This book provides an overview of health, wellness and medical tourism with a considerable emphasis on the role of spas within these forms of tourism. It attempts to provide a wide and comprehensive geographical coverage with a focus on all of the major regions of the world. Of course, it is impossible to provide an in-depth analysis of all of these forms of tourism in all countries of the world. Even the authors' previous research for the GSS (2011) only focused on a small number of countries which were seen to be representative of their regions. However, the history and geography chapters showed that the traditions which exist in many countries of the world can be fairly typical of their region, especially in countries which have similar natural resources (e.g. the Alps, the Mediterranean Sea) or which had a similar cultural background for a period of their history (e.g. the Russian influence in CEE or the Baltic States).

Figure 8.4 shows the key trends that are likely to direct tourism in general, such as dreamscapes, which represent architecturally unique even fantastical spas, hotels or wellness facilities, or 'wellpitals' which is a combination of a hotel and a hospital.

Part III of this book is devoted to case studies by a number of authors, academics and practitioners from around the world. Some of them focus on one country and usually only one form of tourism (e.g. spas, medical, holistic, wellness or well-being). For example, Mark Boekstein's case study is a short extract from his PhD about hot springs in South Africa. This indicates that whole books could be devoted to one form of tourism in one country or even one region of a country. Other authors look at one facility or attraction, which may or may not be typical of others. There is so much to say about development,

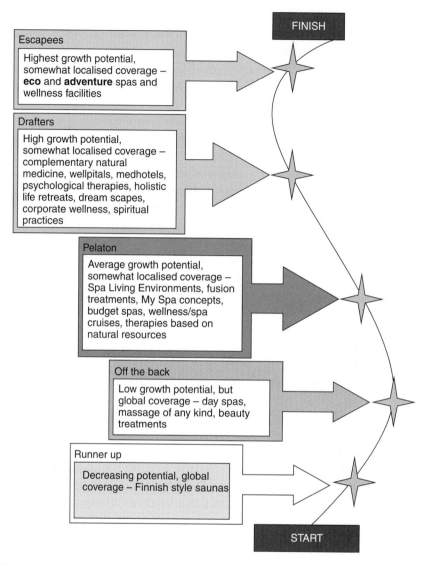

FIGURE 8.4 Tour of wellness and spa
Source: TOHWS (2012).

management, marketing, demand and regulation. The health tourism sector is already attracting studies of so-called 'micro-niches', for example Erfurt-Cooper and Cooper (2009) on hot springs; Connell (2011) on medical tourism; Voigt and Pforr (2013) on wellness tourism. There are several books already on spa management (e.g. Cohen and Bodeker, 2008). Hall's (2013) edited book is focused on the ethics and regulation of the medical tourism sector. Whole books could easily be devoted to holistic and spiritual retreats, the subject of a growing number of journal articles (e.g. Voigt et al., 2011; Kelly, 2012).

This book concentrates on defining what wellness and medical tourism are, but it is also important to consider what they are *not*. This is important for delineating the academic field of study, but it is also essential when collecting statistics, and when marketing destinations and services. Care must be taken that existing forms of tourism are not simply re-packaged as wellness in order to attract more tourists because wellness has become such a 'trendy' term. For example, the Canary Islands and the Caribbean are now claiming to have the world's 'biggest natural outdoor spa' based on sun, sea and sand. This is arguably a re-packaging of an existing product which is not technically a wellness-orientated product. We contended in the first chapter of this book that wellness tourism must be based on a conscious and proactive approach to wanting to improve health and well-being, ideally in the long term. Wellness should not merely be a by-product of all holidays and there is the risk that these terms (wellness, medical and health) will be overused and stretched (as already happened with 'spa'). Wellness or medical tourism should be:

- active or proactive;
- a conscious decision or prescribed by a medical professional;
- based on individual or personal commitment;
- a primary motivation for the trip;
- a long-term aim (e.g. prevention, rehabilitation);
- a balanced approach (e.g. body, mind, spirit; all dimensions of wellness).

CASE STUDY 8.3
Product development: smart and intelligent versus plain unappealing!

Information technology has not left health tourism products untouched. One very interesting and rather smart project idea is from the Island of Mget (Croatia), which has a national park status. Developers plan to create a small-scale health tourism facility (something like a destination spa). What makes the plan exciting is that it would have a mobile application which would be used by prospective tourists. The app (via a medical practitioner) would collect information about their state of health (e.g. stress level and heart condition), which would be sent to the centre. Based on the collected information every guest would be provided with a personal programme and treatment plan for their one–two-week stay.

On the other hand, some destinations hear but do not listen and the result can be a rather surreal and unappealing idea such as the 'Hoe Fitness' concept. A traditional (thermal) medical destination (Gyula, Hungary), which has been enjoying the benefits of the well-established historic spa town brand, decided to be innovative. The idea was that hoe fitness participants would be picked up from their hotels at around 6.30 a.m., then would be taken to the fields to do three hours of hoeing (when the weather can easily be over 30°C). During that time they would be given some bacon lard which they could then wash down with some strong spirits (e.g. local 'pálinka', which can be as much as 70 per cent alcohol content). Not that surprisingly, the destination management organisation could not really sell many tickets!

It could be argued that medical tourism is only about the physical body in many cases, but the widely researched placebo effect shows that the role of the mind or psychology is significant. Positive thinking and belief that one can get better is often an essential part of the healing process. Many cosmetic surgery procedures are not based on necessity but on low self-esteem or poor body image which might be better treated with psychology or counselling than with surgery. Furthermore, patients going through invasive treatments would most certainly benefit from more pre- and post-operative treatments. The preparation process can include several holistic approaches or skin treatments and the rehabilitation and recuperation stage should also incorporate those. The results of a more complex approach can be multiple, such as faster and better healing of wounds, better state of mind of the patient and higher spending and longer length of stay.

TABLE 8.1 What is wellness and medical tourism and what is not

Wellness and medical tourism	NOT wellness and medical tourism
• Wellness is a primary motivation for a trip (a conscious choice) • An active or pro-active approach to improving health • A long-term commitment to one's health and wellness • Visiting a spa purely for wellness or medical reasons • Travelling away from home to have medical treatment • Visiting a thermal medical spa because it has special healing waters • Booking a spa or resort specialising in sports and fitness • Choosing a retreat in a rural or natural landscape	• Wellness or well-being is a by-product of a holiday (e.g. feeling better during or afterwards) • A passive approach (e.g. sunbathing or relaxing in a destination) • A short-term desire to improve well-being or happiness • Staying in a spa and wellness hotel but with a different motivation than health (e.g. business, culture) • Having medical treatment in a destination because of illness or an accident • Visiting an historic thermal bath because it has beautiful architecture and it is nice to sit in warm waters! • Doing some sports or fitness activities while on holiday • Going to the countryside on holiday

In many countries, medical thermal baths do not have the same credibility that they do in Central and Eastern Europe, Russia and the Baltic States. There is not a universal belief in the healing powers of waters. In some countries (e.g. Africa) many local people still believe that magic spirits or Gods live in the waters but know nothing of evidence-based research. Elsewhere, people are not convinced at all of their effectiveness in healing.

Table 8.1 summarises what wellness and medical tourism is and is not since having some wellness, spa or medical treatment while on holiday or during leisure time without some pre-planning does not qualify as health tourism.

The tourism industry is more and more focused on creating experiences and memories, the spa, wellness and medical industries too. As stated by Kurtz-Ahlers (2012: 90), 'A treatment can be as much of a souvenir of a place or time as a painting or souvenir purchased during a trip'. Of course, some medical tourists may prefer to forget the medical part of their trip, but perhaps the beauty or other characteristics of the destination may lessen the pain or discomfort of having a medical procedure in a way which would not happen at home. Unlike other forms of tourism where memories and photos may be the only souvenir, many forms of health tourism offer more than just magical, unforgettable experiences and can have the capacity to change lives for ever.

The international context for health, wellness and medical tourism
Case studies

This section contains many diverse case studies from around the world which have been written by academics, researchers, practitioners and entrepreneurs in health, wellness, spas, medical and tourism sectors. There are case studies from over 25 countries from more than 50 authors. Some of their work can be found in Parts I and II of the book, but this section contains more detailed work and, in many cases, primary research too.

This part is divided into four sections:

- Spa developments
- Health tourism destinations
- Well-being, holistic and spiritual tourism
- Medical tourism and medical wellness

The first section on *Spa developments* starts with an overview of recent trends courtesy of Susie Ellis, Chairman of the Global Spa and Wellness Summit. We are grateful to Susie for sharing these trends with us, as it is well known in the spa industry that these are the most influential annual predictions in the industry. Recently, GSWS has been focusing more on the importance of wellness tourism, it therefore seemed appropriate that Susie should both begin and close this section with the final case study about GSWS itself. The other authors provide interesting analyses of what is happening in spa destinations around the world. For example, Ingo Schweder emphasises the importance of Asia and the Middle East, where lifestyles start to emulate those in the West so wellness practices need to follow suit, but still with a strong connection to cultural context. Elena Bogacheva focuses on Russia, where there is a slow but sure shift towards wellness practices, but still rooted in medical traditions. The role of spas in lifestyle is discussed by Mick Matheusik, especially resort communities. Sonia Ferrari looks at developments in Italy where wellness practices are also becoming more common in spas. Geradine Parisi focuses on the Trentino region of Italy, where she states that it is important to create a new spa tourism that is between medical and wellness tourism. Some authors focus on complex management issues which affect spas, such as revenue management (Patrizia Modica and Elisa Scanu), and employee compensation (Marion Joppe). Managing demand can also be challenging. Yechezkel Israeli gives a positive example from Israel where multiple segments are managed simultaneously and with some success. Krisztina Priszinger and Katalin Formádi look at the degree of success in spa and wellness hotel marketing in Hungary, and Andrea Vermesi questions how Hungarian wellness and spa hotels can be professionally benchmarked and assessed. Kathryn Dowthwaite and Sarah Rawlinson analyse the challenges of providing educational courses for students wanting to work in the spa industry, noting the importance of industry links and a practical focus. Several of the authors mention innovative spa treatments, and Inna Bentsalo provides details of a particularly important growth area in spas, that of sleep therapy.

The second section on *Health tourism destinations* shows how health, wellness and spa tourism are developing in different countries. Some historic destinations and resorts declined in popularity for a while and therefore needed regeneration or diversification. This is true in the case of Domburg in The Netherlands, as described by Peter Kruizinga. In others, it may simply be a case of marketing better what is already well known by domestic tourists, for example Te Aroha in New Zealand as discussed by Maria Hyde-Smith and John Hull. In some cases, there is a strong thermal medical tradition which has remained, but which also requires upgrading in terms of quality of services or facilities, or which needs to shift to wellness in the face of government cuts to support for domestic medical tourism. This is particularly true of Slovenia, as discussed by Sonia Sibila Lebe. The Czech Republic as outlined by Alexey Kondrashov still maintains its traditions, especially in the world famous historic spa towns, but there is nevertheless a move towards more wellness products too. Poland has also retained it historic medical traditions well, but it is noted that domestic visitors' expectations of services and facilities may not be as high as those of international visitors. The authors Andrzej Hadzik, Dorota Ujma and Sean Gammon therefore recommend the need to build on quality of preventative treatments and wellness products. Portugal also has strong thermal medical traditions, but here the shift towards holistic concepts of health and wellness rather than medical therapeutic ones is becoming more evident, as discussed by Nuno Gustavo and Fernando Completo.

By contrast, as Mark Simon Boekstein shows, many of the thermal springs in South Africa have the potential to be used as medical thermal tourism resources, but they have not yet been developed as such. Instead, they have started with leisure and wellness, but the healing potential could be significant too. Some medical traditions are especially unusual, and could be used as an extremely unique selling proposition, such as horse milk therapy in Kyrgyzstan as described by Ingeborg Nordbø and Elvira Sagyntay Kyzy. Other unique selling propositions may come from gastronomy, as seen in Nico Dingemans' analysis of several health cuisine destinations around the world. He also emphasises sustainability and the importance of the local, indigenous and organic. Many destinations make use of their natural landscapes to promote health and wellness, so environmental considerations are especially important here. Nowhere is this more true than in Finland, where Henna Konu, Anja Tuohino and Peter Björk analyse the Nordic well-being concept and its connection to nature as well as other typical Finnish attributes. The Dead Sea is the

ultimate natural resource and unique selling proposition, but as outlined by Dalit Gasul, it is under threat because of a lack of sustainable development. Lóránt Dávid, Bulcsú Remenyik and Csaba Szücs provide an overview of the diversity of wellness experiences that can be gained in the mountain areas of Hungary, including climate tourism, medicinal herbal tourism and spiritual tourism. Thousands of kilometres away, Parikshat Singh Manhas similarly discusses the range of wellness activities in the Himalayas, which can also be climate-based, herbal or spiritual (amongst others).

The third section on *Well-being, holistic and spiritual tourism* looks at the concept of well-being, as well as holistic and spiritual practices. Alison van den Eynde and Adrian Fisher begin with a very honest look at what Australian respondents considered to be well-being and whether well-being travel was for them or just 'mumbo jumbo' (well-being tourism is clearly not for everyone, although it could arguably benefit everyone if they engaged in it). Heather Hartwell, Ann Hemingway, Alan Fyall, Viachaslau Filimonau, Stacy Wall and Neil Short look at the ways in which destinations could be developed or promoted as healthy or well-being destinations. They give examples from the UK, especially of seaside towns which have a long history of providing healthy holidays as well as being seen as healthy places to live or retire to. Other governments have long been involved in the concept of social tourism, where it provides support for under-privileged members of society to have holidays. Riikka Ilves and Raija Komppula discuss holidays which have a well-being or active dimension to them. It would clearly make sense for governments to support those forms of tourism which benefit the recipients physically and mentally. This is more typical of CEE countries, the Baltic States, Russia or even Germany, where state-supported tourism was (and is) largely medical. Jacques Vork and Angelique Lombarts provide a summary of their detailed research on preventative wellness in the Netherlands, where it seems that there is a national shift in this direction. Although this 'trend' does not yet benefit the whole population, it is arguably most effective if governments and public education can address a whole nation in its developments and promotion, not just an elite segment. Hence, the move in other countries too towards a democratisation of wellness and spas.

In India, the Ayurvedic tradition goes back thousands of years, but is being re-packaged for tourists so that they can enjoy authentic experiences. Ramesh Unnikrishnan analyses the development of Ayurvedic tourism in Kerala, for example. Edward Huijbens discusses the importance of landscape not only for physical health but also mental and spiritual health too. Landscapes can be healing or therapeutic, he argues, especially those that are devoid of human habitation. It could be argued that the 'meditative' dimension of landscape can seem more accessible to ordinary people than retreat centres or meditation classes. On the other hand, there is a definite growth in retreat and spiritual tourism which focuses on the balance of mind, body and spirit. Marinus Gisolf talks about the continuing interest in so-called New Age tourism and retreat centres in Costa Rica and elsewhere, and Mia Mackman describes the experience of holistic wellness in Sedona, Arizona, one of the world's most famous 'energy centres'. Tzuhui Tseng and Ching-Cheng Shen present their research on the importance of meditation in Taiwan for well-being, balance and flow, and Ivett Sziva, Noémi Kulcsár and Melanie Smith discuss their research findings about yoga practitioners in Budapest. The latter case study proves the growing popularity of yoga, even in countries where the practice is relatively 'new', and the increasing propensity of practitioners to become tourists with the primary motivation of doing yoga (as discussed earlier in the book, yoga retreats are the fastest growing type of retreat).

The fourth section concentrates on *Medical tourism and medical wellness*. As discussed earlier in the book, the boundaries between medical and wellness are becoming increasingly blurred. It could be argued, for example, that ancient healing traditions like Ayurveda should be included in this section, or thermal medical tourism, which is 'evidence based' in many regions of the world. However, it was decided that this section would only focus on those case studies which have a clear aim of providing medical tourism or wellness services which are strongly supported by medical practitioners. Anita Medhekar looks at one of the most famous hospital groups in the world offering medical tourism. Despite their fame and relative success, there is still a need to keep an eye on quality, regulation and competition. This is arguably true of most medical destinations in the world. Neil Lunt, Johanna Hanefeld, Daniel Horsfall and Richard D. Smith present a slightly uncharacteristic case study, which is the National Health Service in the UK. Many sources about medical tourism focus on the flows of tourists away from Western developed countries with perceived failing health services, high costs or long waiting lists (like the UK), but here, top-end procedures are being requested by Middle Eastern patients, for example. The UK also has a diverse population and numerous nationalities working in the medical sector, especially in London, so the chances of being able to match patients to practitioners who speak their language and understand their culture is high (e.g. Greek Cypriots are mentioned).

Victoria Winter highlights one of the fastest growing new trends, which is longevity centres and lifestyle centres which focus on providing clients with a detailed analysis of their state of health and lifestyle and giving them a comprehensive programme also based on education to take away. However, this arguably needs to be fully supported by medical services to be fully effective and trustworthy. Cornelia Voigt addresses some of the problems when 'alternative' approaches are taken to serious illnesses like cancer. Although the medical benefits of a specific technique may be proven time and again, especially by word-of-mouth or anecdotal evidence, if there is no scientific evidence, it is difficult to convince the somewhat sceptical medical profession of its validity. On the other hand, as discussed earlier in the book, the placebo effect is a widely accepted phenomenon and should not be under-estimated, especially in medicine, but why not also in wellness and especially medical wellness? Cornelia Voigt's example of a foundation which provides incredible support for those with life-threatening and even terminal illnesses is a truly positive one, whether it is scientifically accepted or not. It is also important to reiterate that it is often the human touch, 'bedside manner' or hospitality dimension which is driving medical tourists to leave their own country in search of something else. Islam Elgammal and Heba Elakras discuss another problem, which is that of destinations which have medically proven therapies (e.g. balneotherapy in Egypt in this case), but which lack the government support or industry investment to develop fully as a tourism destination. This was also true of thermal medical tourism in Iran, as seen in the case study of Sarein in Chapter 3.

Overall, the case studies highlight many of the themes which have been discussed in Parts I and II of the book. As a summary, these include:

- the concern that decreasing government support for thermal medical tourism or social tourism will force the closure of many baths or force diversification and a shift towards wellness tourism (e.g. Central and Eastern Europe, Russia, Baltic States);
- the fast growing shift towards wellness products and activities (e.g. in Italy, Portugal) because of changing lifestyle habits and increasing longevity (i.e. young people now are less likely to require medical services as they grow older, especially if they engage in preventative wellness programmes while they are still young);
- the decline of some historic thermal bath towns which need to improve quality of service and facilities to attract international visitors (e.g. Poland, Hungary);
- the need for infrastructural developments and investment in those countries which have considerable healing resources but not enough funds or expertise to develop them (e.g. South Africa, Uganda, Iran, Egypt);
- the cross-over between medical and wellness tourism, especially in the case of thermal medical tourism, ancient healing traditions and cosmetic surgery (e.g. Central and Eastern Europe, India, Brazil, Thailand);
- convincing the medical profession of the important role of spas, retreats and other wellness facilities in improving health or treating lifestyle-related conditions (it is accepted that serious and life-threatening illnesses may require a more 'scientific' approach);
- the need to manage natural resources sustainably (e.g. the Blue Lagoon is managed very sustainably but the Dead Sea is not);
- the need to create unique selling propositions ideally through the development and promotion of products and activities which are rooted in historical traditions, indigenous practices or locally available materials and ingredients;
- the growing popularity of retreat holidays away from the stress of everyday life, work and technology; this includes more spiritual practices, especially in countries where traditional religion is declining (e.g. the UK, the Netherlands,Germany, Scandinavia);
- the lack of educational programmes for spa, wellness and medical tourism, especially those which are recognised or welcomed by the industry; on the other hand, industry practitioners are lamenting the lack of qualified employees;
- the challenges of trying to develop and market facilities and services to different target segments simultaneously.

Spa developments

CHAPTER

9

SpaFinder Wellness trends
What they teach us and why they are important

Susie Ellis

SpaFinder Wellness publishes an annual forecast of global spa and wellness trends that has become known around the world and is widely anticipated when it is introduced each January. In fact, many have said that they look to this Trend Report for its thought-leadership role.

The Trend Report is based on ongoing surveys with the SpaFinder Wellness Network, which consists of over 20,000 spa, wellness, fitness and beauty providers, thousands of travel agents and hundreds of thousands of consumers. We also conduct ongoing interviews with top industry stakeholders and review current research, articles and case studies, and our team of editors and experts visits spa and wellness establishments regularly.

A review of these trends that have informed and changed the industry in recent years is a useful case study. It is important to know what consumers have embraced, and understanding the trends others in the industry have adopted – or see on the horizon – is essential to good planning. It doesn't mean you will necessarily adopt a trend. In fact, sometimes you will decide to look at a 'counter-trend'. But ultimately trend tracking can lead to making wiser decisions for your business.

Significant trends: a look at the past – and a glimpse of what lies ahead

Wellness

By far, the shift from 'pampering' to wellness offerings at spas around the globe is the most significant trend of the past decade. The term 'high-level wellness' was originated in the 1950s in lectures given by physician Halbert L. Dunn. In 1961 he published a book on the same topic, and the phrase gained momentum after the millennium when skyrocketing health-care costs around the world made it important to look at prevention and not just focus on curing ailments with drugs and surgery. Wellness was a term with a positive connotation, and because it aptly described what spas and other establishments offered, such as fitness, massage, alternative medicine and healthy nutrition, 'wellness' was embraced by the industry and beyond. There has since been an explosion of wellness offerings at spas, and the term has become mainstream. In fact, many stores now have 'wellness aisles' filled with products that promise to make us healthy.

Since SpaFinder predicted in 2008 that wellness might end up becoming the next trillion-dollar revolution, it has become increasingly central to the spa experience, with education, as well as alternative practices such as energy medicine, reiki, and Traditional Chinese Medicine (TCM), all becoming important aspects of 'spa'. And in subsequent years, as we tracked the rise of numerous wellness trends and the important connection between stress and health, wellness coaching, corporate wellness programmes and the development of wellness tourism all played important new roles.

Online spa

It's hard to imagine, but at the turn of the millennium, there were many spas that didn't even have websites. Today, almost every spa, fitness and wellness business – and even therapists and practitioners – have their own site. But that's just the beginning of the SpaWellness.com revolution: today consumers can find and learn about spa and fitness offerings, book appointments in real-time, buy products, review businesses and fully engage in new forms of wellness-related social networking – all online.

And with the internet so well matched for wellness coaching, and new technology enabling online medical diagnosis and virtual health records, unprecedented aspects of the spa/wellness experience are becoming available through the internet. SpaFinder Wellness recently predicted the rise of online wellness gaming and technology that tracks and interprets lifestyle data, and we are starting to see spas offering even more innovative technology, such as the ability to check in with no front desk. Only the therapists' hands haven't been brought online – yet.

Indigenous treatments

While one would see the use of local ingredients and local customs on occasion at spas decades ago, during the past years this became an almost unspoken rule. Culturally grounded ingredients, treatments and customs deliver a healthy native flavour, and they also represent the unearthing of special, often centuries-old experiences that could not be easily replicated. From a lomi lomi massage in Hawaii to the Royal Javanese Lular wedding ritual in Indonesia, indigenous treatments gave spas a grounded 'sense of place' that has made each spa-going experience around the world truly unique.

With spa-goers increasingly seeking authenticity, tradition and that magical spa experience that also offers true results, the Middle Eastern hammam (hamam in Turkey) represented one of the hottest trends for 2010. And 2013 promised to be the year for aggressively authentic and comprehensively executed global wellness experiences at spas with a distinctly ancient look, feel and language. One excellent example was the shift from just

one or two Ayurvedic treatments on a spa menu to a more authentic Ayurveda that honoured the 3,500-year-old Indian-born Ayurveda and more awareness of doshas and, in general, a more holistic approach with diet, mental well-being and yoga, and so on.

Medicine and spa

In the early 1990s there was very little overlap between medicine and spas. That has changed dramatically over the last decade. More doctors have discovered that spa and wellness establishments can be allies in helping their patients make long-term lifestyle changes. Then, when botox arrived in 2002, a new type of aesthetic/medical spa was born and the spa and medicine connection was solidified not only through health but also through beauty.

Holding alternative therapies up to scientific scrutiny became a top trend in 2012, and the wealth of positive results found at SpaEvidence.com encouraged the medical community to adopt spa approaches, while providing an opportunity for the spa industry to link their menu of treatments to medical evidence.

Organic

Organic was the headline story in spa products for the past decade. The popularity of all things 'green' helped several obscure organic lines make it big, and nearly all spa product companies launched their own branded organic lines. The organic product trend also helped open the door for a more far-reaching eco-friendly, environmentally conscious zeitgeist throughout the spa arena – from spa building and design – to healthy, organic cuisine.

In 2005 SpaFinder Wellness also predicted the idea of the eco-spa. By 2009 that trend had become 'Eco 2.0' and the industry was turning green. In 2013 'earthing' was a hot trend (the movement promoting direct contact with the earth's electron-rich surface, walking barefoot, etc.), but we expect to see far more 'nature grounding' in a wider sense. Think less background music with nature sounds and more *real* nature to help combat 'Nature Deficit Disorder' (Louv, 2005).

Spa comes home

The influence of spas on the home has its humble beginnings at the start of the decade (2000) with spa-inspired consumers, say, purchasing a candle to use in the bath, or maybe a loofah sponge. In the years since, it's blossomed into a booming industry of spa and wellness products, design, furniture, home amenities (like spa bathrooms), even clothing and cuisine. The trend reached its most bold expression with the birth of spa or wellness living real estate, where consumers could actually 'live at the spa', purchasing residences with spectacular spa/wellness offerings in new luxury high-rises or special communities. We've not only seen spa-ing burst the confines of its traditional walls – but a new term, 'spa and wellness lifestyle', has emerged to describe a whole healthier way of living, thinking and being.

Gift certificates, vouchers, cards

The explosion of spa and wellness gift cards was a development that evolved so gradually it never made any of SpaFinder Wellness' annual trends lists. And yet it probably has had more to do with the expansion of spas and spa-goers around the world than any other trend – or even all of them combined.

The emergence and popularity of the spa gift certificate, card and voucher has introduced so many new people to the spa experience. (In fact, research shows that approximately one-third of all spa visits are generated by the redemption of certificates and vouchers.) Spa gifting has been galvanised by their near-universal availability at almost every individual spa and via third-party programmes – and they've not only given people permission to take care of themselves; they've ushered in a new era where gifting 'spa and wellness' represents an expression of true thoughtfulness and care.

To put it in perspective: while SpaFinder Wellness is now the largest retailer of spa gift certificates, cards and vouchers in the world, the company didn't make its first certificate sale until 1999. Today, over 20,000 spa and wellness providers worldwide are part of the company's gift card programme, and the cards/vouchers are available at over 70,000 retail locations.

And in 2012 SpaFinder Wellness noted an emerging trend, the growth of corporate wellness programmes. This is a new opportunity for spas and wellness businesses to accept 'wellness vouchers', which are powerful incentives and rewards given to employees for healthy behaviours.

Yin of luxury, yang of discount

While the last few tough economic years have put more industry emphasis on the 'yang' of discount, and in recent years we've seen the trend of 'deals gone wild' turn out to be very true, the wider 'spa decade' definitely spent quite a bit of time on the 'yin' of luxury. The reality is, that with more than 80,000 spas across the world, there's plenty of 'yin' and plenty of 'yang' to go around. In almost every country across the globe consumers can find bargain-priced spas/treatments and online technologies that let them pick exactly where and when they want their deals served up. But right alongside are sky-high-priced options (with their bejewelled massage oils and exotic, over-the-top settings). As spa going has become totally mainstream, there's a spa now to suit every taste and budget.

Men

While the decade saw a range of new demographics rush into the spa arena (from teens to pre-teens to babies and seniors), it was the steady stream of men making spa-going a regular part of their lives that's had the most profound impact. While it took some doing to get men to try a spa for the first time, this 'first time', typically, resulted in a second and third, and so on. Men discovered there was more to this 'spa thing' than just idle pampering: it was, in fact, the quickest way for them to reduce stress (something there was plenty of), and it helped improve their sports performance.

SpaFinder Wellness trends 241

And a more recent Trend Report predicts dramatically more men – from Beverly Hills, to Berlin, to Beijing – are having more serious 'work' done at medspas and plastic surgery offices, as injectables, 'love handle' remedies and advanced new surgery technologies make for little downtime and tell-tale scars. So look for far more spas to build out comprehensive, for-men 'beauty' menus – with male waxing and threading services and man-geared cosmetic procedures.

What lies ahead?

More wellness offerings and unimagined technologies are on the horizon, but the hottest trends will include an explosion of new 'wellness everywhere' hotel chains and environments; an emphasis on ways to reduce stress quickly with mindfulness or meditation; spas embracing a new age of predictive, personalised medicine grounded in each person's unique genetic profile; and a future where bodies welcomed at spas will look more like bodies in the real world, thanks to a massively greying global population and the recognition that at some point in our lives all of us will have a disability.

But perhaps no genomic breakthrough holds such profound implications for the spa industry than genetic testing, specifically for telomeres: the only malleable part of DNA, which some studies are showing can be repaired by stress-reduction, exercise, sleep, healthier food and meditation. It's easy to see how this could change the reasons we go to spa, galvanise more participation in healthy activities and in general become the foundation of a healthier – and longer – life.

(Sidebar: About SpaFinder Wellness) In the late 1980s, at the dawn of the spa boom, SpaFinder Wellness was founded as a travel agency dedicated solely to spa. It also published a catalogue by the same name that eventually became a magazine. Today SpaFinder Wellness is the world's largest spa and wellness media and marketing company, and every year it connects millions of people seeking access to a healthier, happier lifestyle with its worldwide network of over 20,000 wellness providers. The company is also the largest retailer and wholesaler of gift cards for the spa and wellness industry and offers SpaFinder Wellness currency to support corporate wellness programs that help employees maintain healthy productive lifestyles.

CHAPTER 10

Spa lifestyle resort communities and staycations

Mick Matheusik

Introduction

First it was golf-based communities, next came speciality recreation-based resort communities such as ski, marina or equestrian based, with each generating their own appeal to somewhat limited recreational real estate market niches. Now, a growing trend is integrated resort communities and residential developments which have established spas and wellness centres as their key focus. Their appeal is much wider demographic segments than single-based activity real estate developments. Plus, on top of selling traditional recreation experiences, healthy lifestyles and wellness are the new 'fountains of youth' behind these new resort products, enabling purchasers to 'live younger longer'. This chapter outlines the key trends and characteristics of the spa and wellness industry that underlie this development evolution, who has already embraced these trends from a real estate development perspective and what is needed for their success. Lastly, it reveals that some developers are now examining how to create a multi-faceted town centre using spas and wellness as the core of both their residential and commercial facilities.

Overall trends affecting the spa/wellness movement

The spa industry has solidified itself as a major player in the hospitality and leisure sector. According to Price Waterhouse Coopers, the revenue associated with the US spa industry has rebounded to pre-recession levels and has increased significantly since 1999 from approximately $4.2 billion to about $13.4 billion in 2011.

Wellness within the context of creating a spa lifestyle community is seen as contributing to long-term well-being and quality of life, especially if there is a focus on the whole person and their entire life-span in the form of active ageing and longevity. Increasingly with more problems facing our public health system (i.e. crowded hospitals, virus outbreaks,

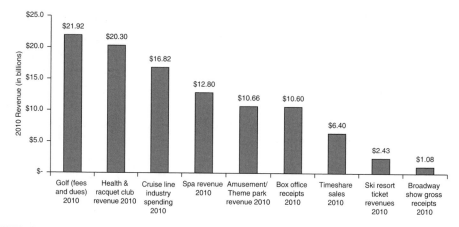

FIGURE 10.1 Comparative size of US spa industry
Source: Adapted from Price Waterhouse Coopers (2010).

spending cutbacks, etc.), more consumer segments are realising they need to be more proactive. Accordingly, they are taking active interest and embracing preventive medicine/ health practices many of which are now offered by the spa and wellness industry.

Rather than being an 'amenity' offered at hotels and resorts, spas are becoming the deciding factor or primary draw as hotels with spas now represent the fastest growing hospitality segment. Approximately three quarters (73 per cent) of Canadian spa travellers and 81 per cent of US travellers went to a resort/hotel spa when taking a spa vacation. Further, the CTC/ISPA study revealed that a spa vacation also appears to be an excellent opportunity to go shopping, take in some cultural attractions and indulge in culinary delights.

The majority of the spa market is being driven by the baby boomers, many of them seeking it as a requisite to staying healthy, looking good and as an integral foundation to their daily/weekly lifestyle. As the leading edge of the baby boomers are now buying spa lifestyle real estate, Pat Corbett, the Chairman of the CTC task force on Spa and Wellness Tourism, predicts that the longevity of this trend will continue for the next 15 to 20 years following the ageing baby boomers' desire for healthy and active lifestyles. This prediction is reinforced with independent research conducted for Canyon Ranch (North America's premier integrated wellness destination resort operator) by American LIVES; a market research firm in the US that has estimated one third of North Americans are seeking a healthy lifestyle which is predicted to increase by to two-thirds by 2025.

During vacations and now increasingly as part of their daily living or resort experience, people see spa visits as a form of self-improvement and relief from the pressures of work and social life. As more projects become developed, this is becoming increasingly entrenched in their lifestyles both in urban and vacation settings. According to Spa Finder's President, Susie Ellis, spas are rapidly becoming an essential amenity, providing ageing baby boomers with their most important lifestyle requirements, namely health, wellness and fitness, pursued in a spa setting. Sixty-one per cent of respondents in an

extensive survey of *Luxury Spa Finder Magazine* readers and Spafinder.com visitors indicated they would be interested in living in a community built around a spa facility offering spa programmes and services to community members. Fifty-three per cent classified a spa as a 'very important' residential amenity, while another 18 per cent indicated a spa is a 'decisive' buying requirement. (In contrast, only 9 per cent indicated golf was a 'very important' amenity and only 2 per cent designated it a 'decisive' buying factor.) Overall, nearly half of the Spa Finder customers surveyed (48%) said they considered the idea of purchasing a second home or vacation home, with about 10 per cent indicating a 'very serious' interest (i.e. they've contacted a broker/owner, researched properties, etc.).

According to ISPA, medical spas are the fastest growing type of spas as spa-goers are interested more than just being pampered, a historically important reason behind spa visits. Now many spa consumers are realising rather than just looking good, they are addressing the underlying reasons of how to feel good and maintain an energetic lifestyle. Thus, increasingly spas are now offering some form of integrative or complementary and alternative medicine (CAM) as part of their spa menu of services and programmes. This includes preventative health treatments and regimens, nutrition and fitness, as well as health and wellness education. Two of the North American pioneers in this field are Canyon Ranch based in Tucson, Arizona, and the Hills Health Ranch in British Columbia, Canada which have been practising 'integrated wellness' since early 1980s and early 1990s, respectively.

What is a Spa Residential Community?

According to *Spa Finder*, a Spa Residential Community is a spa lifestyle dream come true. It encapsulates the following attributes:

- a community where both residents and its patrons share their enthusiasms in health and wellness;
- where they can enjoy activities such as walking and biking trails, take fitness classes and work out in the gym;
- where the spa offers an extensive menu of spa and beauty services, water plus other therapies, and a relaxation area or central club to lounge in;
- where spa cuisine meals and healthy snacks are readily available;
- where patrons and residents can find wellness-oriented education opportunities and possibly even avail themselves of medical options.

Generally, spa lifestyle real estate can be classified according to one of three types as follows:

1   urban and resort hotels (either popular branded or non-branded operators) with residential and spa components;
2   master planned communities with spa and often other recreational facilities (e.g. golf, skiing, equestrian, hiking);

3   a diversity of spa lifestyle real estate projects, with various levels of integration with spa/wellness programmes and services.

Each type places different emphasis on the spa component and, in most cases, it is an 'appendage' to the main real estate component and typically does not address the more comprehensive needs that the wellness market is seeking. While progressive companies such as Canyon Ranch and Miraval have adopted their brands into the 'living' environment, most other operators have not catered specifically to this market.

Historically, companies such as Canyon Ranch, Miraval and Golden Door are among the first branded spa operations that have added a residential component to one or more locations. This largely resulted from responding to regular or core spa-goers' request where repeat guests found that their typical one to three week staycations at their operations often resulted in reverting back to their old lifestyle habits when they returned home. Thus, they requested whether they could purchase a unit(s) and receive the full services and amenities offered at the subject operations to stay longer and come back more frequently. This was similar to five-star resort hotel chains such as Hyatt Regency, Ritz Carleton, Four Seasons and Fairmont selling residences and condos in their complexes which typically are developed by independent developers and investment companies. At these operations, purchasers typically have full access to the hotel's services and amenities (including the spa), sometimes as part of a club concept such as Club Intrawest, which may also provide them with VIP privileges and discounts.

It is important to note that this trend is not solely based in the USA and Canada. In the Caribbean, many new development projects have a residential component and are becoming integral components in countries as far afield as Dubai and in Turkey with a multi-faceted spa town.

Key success factors

- *Round out the healthy and active lifestyle appeal.* People expect more than just a spa facility from spa lifestyle real estate. Both residents and long-term guests indicated they want programmes, healthy cuisine, classes and education. In addition, they value both privacy and opportunities for interaction with others through a social community.
- *Quality of experience and environment is pivotal.* Recognising many people want to escape the pressures of urban life, the spa environment must be soothing to a person's senses, offering serene and tranquil environments. Of course, there will be varying degrees of providing this in both urban and rural setting as well as having different meaning to market segments (see next point).
- *In tune with spa market 'psyche' and needs.* The product that spa real estate purchasers are buying is significantly more than just recreational real estate; it is a healthy lifestyle preferably within a 'community of shared values', and 'places of discovery' or learning.
- *Sustainability and integration with nature.* A strong regard for preservation, ecological sustainability, resource renewal, personal interaction with nature have become key ways for non-urban spa lifestyle communities to differentiate themselves from others.

- *Get away appeal and environmental experience promotes remoteness.* Accessibility is not such an issue as other recreational resort communities given the wellness/health amenities and consumers' desire to escape into a secure, safe and serene environment to receive the health and stress deduction benefits. Many consumers also find that the drive through the countryside en route to/from the resort can be a time to unwind and connect.
- *Branding a successful spa operation and location.* A recent survey by TREC International of resort owners and real estate executives revealed that the majority of purchasers of spa lifestyle real estate are avid spa-goers and typically have been to the subject resort property at least a six or more times; thus they are well aware of what the destination spa and surrounding environment has to offer plus the associated experiences.
- *Partnering with developers who share the same philosophy.*

Back to the future

Similar to historic spa towns such as Baden-Baden in Germany and planned spa-based towns in Turkey, master-planned communities in North America are starting to broaden the spa residential concept to also incorporate retail, offices, business parks, recreation centres, sports and cultural facilities. The developers are recognising that the spa and wellness consumers desire to not only live this lifestyle but corporations are beginning to see the value of wellness for attracting and retaining their employees by rounding out their appeal with these other facilities.

11

The rise of destination spas in emerging economies

A case study of GOCO Hospitality's Qatar and China destination spa projects

Ingo Schweder

Introduction

Since the first destination spa, Rancho La Puerta, opened its doors in Tecate, Baja California, Mexico in 1940, destination spas have gained in popularity as their benefits became increasingly recognised, especially in the Western world where the lifestyle was faster-paced and more stressful than that in the East. Globalisation and cultural imperialism has changed the lifestyle of the East to ever more resemble the Western lifestyle. The shift in the global economy from West to East has resulted in increased spending power of the population in the East. This as well resulted in changing lifestyle trends and consumer behaviours, mirroring those of the West, leading to a higher consumption of Western products and services. These factors have led to a growing number of health problems that were not previously apparent in Eastern societies. The need to address these issues combined with the demand for products and services that are unique and offer more than just a foreign brand name have led to the growing development of destination spas in regions such as Asia and the Middle East. In this chapter I will explore this development using as examples two wellness hospitality developments, one in Qatar and the other in the People's Republic of China.

What is a destination spa?

From early beginnings as places where more affluent individuals retreated to 'take the waters' of natural mineral or hot springs, the evolution of destination spas began when these locations began offering activities in addition to bathing and health treatments, thus becoming known as resort spas.

It was in 1940 when Rancho La Puerta opened in Tecate, Mexico that the destination spa as we know it today emerged, focusing on body and mind health through diet, meditation, exercise and mind–body connection rather than the traditional hydrotherapy aspect (Tabacchi, 2008).

Today, a destination spa is defined by the International Spa Association (ISPA) as 'places devoted to enhancing overall wellbeing through a variety of professional services that encourage the renewal of mind, body, and spirit' (Types of Spas, 2007). Some key characteristics of destination spas opposed to resorts/hotels with spas are:

- Destination spas tend to be smaller and offer guests a more nurturing and personalised environment.
- Destination spas sell wellness programmes, not rooms.
- Food and beverage is included in the programmes sold by destination spas.
- At resorts, food and beverage concepts try to be innovative, are design-driven, and sensory engaging. As a result, resorts often lose control of the food quality. Destination spas offer fewer food and beverage outlets, focus on the quality of the food, and encourage guest interaction throughout the meal.
- Destination spas focus on a particular wellness tradition or bring together wellness traditions such as traditional Chinese medicine (TCM), Ayurveda, naturopathy, emotional healing and healthy cuisine offerings.
- Destination spas typically discourage or disallow short stays below three nights.
- At destination spas, the 'spa' is the entire experience. The guest lives the spa experience throughout their entire stay at a destination spa. At a resort, the spa experience occurs only in the spa.

Destination spa guests can be categorised into three segments, as follows:

- Conscious well-being seekers looking for integrated health, personal growth and optimal well-being.
- Burnt-out business professionals looking to escape from stress, personal attention, and tangible solution.
- A-listers of the world looking for privacy and an escape, lasting solutions and personal attention.

Shift from West to East and emerging economies

A significant change in the world today is manifested in the inevitable shift of power and influence from the West to the East. Antonio Fatas and Ilian Mihov stated in their article 'Global economic balance shifting east' in the *Financial Times*, 'the economic centre of gravity of the world is now over the Middle East'. The growing economies of the Gulf Cooperation Council (GCC), particularly that of Qatar which is currently the fastest growing economy in the GCC and the world (Qatar National Bank, 2013, quoted in

Emirates 24/7), have become major players in the international business world, steadily replacing Western powers.

The Asia-Pacific region is also expanding its influence, evident in the fact that the global economy recovery depends in many aspects on the growth engines of India and China, the two largest emerging economies. In 2010 China's GDP (PPP) per capita was USD 10,600, India's was USD 8,000, while Central and Eastern Europe combined was at USD 4,300 and the US was at USD 1,800 (*The Economist*, 2011). In 2011, China's economy grew 9.2 per cent (Kalish, 2012). Today, China is the second largest economy in the world. The IMF forecasts that in 2012 and 2013 emerging markets will grow by around 4 per cent more than the 'rich' Western world, which could mean that by 2013 emerging markets will produce more than half of global output (*The Economist*, 2011).

The demand for destination spas in emerging economies

Due to the rapid growth of their economies, the population of these emerging markets now enjoy greater wealth that enable them to indulge in Western values and luxuries that they adopted to an even greater extent. This has led to significant lifestyle changes, many of which have led to lifestyle habits that contribute to serious health concerns such as cardiovascular diseases, diabetes, cancer and respiratory diseases. The World Health Organization (WHO) categorises these health concerns as non-communicable diseases (NCDs) and has identified this category as the largest contributor to morbidity (WHO, 2011).

According to WHO, NCDs are driven by forces such as ageing, rapid unplanned urbanisation, and 'the globalization of unhealthy lifestyles' such as unhealthy diets, which result in raised blood pressure, higher blood glucose and lipids, and obesity, which in turn can lead to cardiovascular diseases. Tobacco use, physical inactivity, unhealthy diet and harmful use of alcohol are the main factors that cause NCDs.

With growing awareness and concern about the pitfalls modern lifestyles present to their health and well-being, a shift from the materialistic to the holistic has begun to emerge. An increasing number of individuals are becoming more concerned with their physical, mental and emotional well-being than with their material possessions. To them, services or products from high-end or well-known brands are of less importance than how services or products could help them maintain or achieve well-being. Destination spas, seen as places of retreat, relaxation and rejuvenation, have thusly increased in popularity.

GOCO Hospitality, a Bangkok-based consultant and management company specialising in developing and operating wellness hospitality projects, was instrumental in the development of destination spas in two of the largest emerging economies – Qatar and China – to help address the issue of non-communicable diseases and well-being in these countries. Both destination spas developed by GOCO Hospitality and its partners are set to be the first in their respective countries, thus setting a benchmark for the wellness industry in both.

Qatar destination spa – Doha, GCC

GOCO Hospitality is working with the Qatar Foundation and Msheireb Properties to develop the first destination spa in Qatar and the Middle East, creating a lasting legacy of wellness for the Islamic world in the form of a multi-faceted lifestyle brand rooted in comprehensive research, cutting-edge design and extensive hospitality offering.

The concept developed by GOCO Hospitality for the Qatar destination spa is one that is created around core values that are inspired by values inherent in Islam. These values are categorised into inner values – values that relate to oneself – such as self-purification and personal discipline, and outer values – values that relate to the external environment – such as tolerance and diversity.

The inner core values will be manifested in the wellness programmes of the Qatar destination spa, addressing issues such as vitality, ageing well, balance, detox and weight-loss. The wellness programmes will combine research findings on traditional wellness in Islamic regions and modern-day therapies to create wellness solutions specifically designed to address the health concerns prevalent in the Middle Eastern region.

The outer core values will be manifested in the approach, atmosphere and ambience of the Qatar destination spa, such as an open and welcoming environment for guests from all cultures, a diversity of treatments and activities, celebrating and educating on arts, crafts and traditions from different Islamic regions, and architecture and interiors that evoke the principles of Islamic design evolved through modern interpretation into a style that is distinctive and luxurious.

GOCO Hospitality has worked closely with a team of researchers led by Professor Gerry Bodeker of the Global Initiative for Traditional Systems of Health (GIFTs of Health) to compile a comprehensive 'living library' of culture and wellness from the Islamic world. The research identified traditional Islamic approaches to purification, beauty, water, aromatherapy, movement, vitality, balance, and food and nutrition. Research findings went through an extensive peer-review process to ensure accuracy. Knowledge gleaned from the research will be incorporated into the wellness programmes and treatments offered at the Qatar destination spa.

Octave Living Destination Retreat – Suzhou, China

In 2011 GOCO Hospitality also began working with its partner, IMC Octave, on developing China's first destination spa, the Octave Living Destination Retreat, which will also feature high-end residential real estate and a cultural village in addition to the spa and wellness facilities and hotel.

Octave Living Destination Retreat aims to encourage the discovery of wellness by a blend of Chinese traditions and ideologies with today's foremost medical and wellness practices, a meeting of East and West. Octave Living's concept is based on the Chinese five dimensions of wellness – health, world-view, work, expression of inner-self and relationship with the community – encouraging the learning and discovery of wellness that will

lead to a 'wellness way of life', transforming its guests' lives by turning old destructive habits into new productive ones.

Octave Living Destination Retreat advocates a proactive approach to improving an individual's holistic wellness and emphasises education and prevention. The concept's ethos encourages self-development where a guest is given the freedom to explore the most effective and efficient way to improve their personal well-being. By guiding a guest to new physical limits and understanding, Octave Living Destination Retreat awakens personal potential and supports guests in realizing the true meaning of health while providing the inspiration for a lifelong journey to an improved self.

The wellness programmes and treatments at the Octave Living Destination Retreat are focused on balancing and rejuvenating the mind, body, and spirit. The programmes are customised and focused on an individual's lifestyle improvement through the integration of dietary change, traditional Chinese medicine (TCM) and conventional medicines. Primary programmes address ageing well, detox, weight-loss and de-stressing.

Treatments offered at the Octave Living Destination Retreat are created around Eastern wellness regimes being offered in a Western physical context and environment, time-honoured, based on proven benefits and results, has breadth of choice and depth of quality, and are for both female and male guests.

Moving forward

Destination spas are no longer simply 'fat farms' for the rich elite to retreat to and lose weight, albeit temporarily, but are now more universal in terms of programmes and services that appeal to a wider audience as well as providing longer-lasting, if not life transformative, results. The need for destination spas has grown immensely in the past decade and will continue to do so exponentially as the awareness of personal well-being and the pursuit of such continues to increase in populations across the world, no longer limited to the privileged few in the Western world. Holistic healing will work hand in hand with modern medical science in the fight to prevent against and relieve non-communicable or chronic diseases that are a result of the sedentary, stressed lifestyle of today. It is imperative that as we move forward into the future, we rely both on contemporary science as well as the wisdom of ancient wellness traditions to ensure the well-being of mind, body and soul. Based on current developments, including the Qatar destination spa and the Octave Living Destination Retreat, it is more than likely that nations will also put increased efforts behind the creation of wellness communities where a wide span of wellness services, hospitality, and real estate combine and celebrate the cultural symbiosis of the respective country.

The Russian spa market
Diverse and maturing

Elena Bogacheva

For the longest part of its history the Russian spa industry was dominated by a huge segment of institutions (the Russian term for those being 'sanatorium') that belonged to the governmental health-care system and before the 1990s were accessible to the country's population, whenever rehabilitation or prevention measures were considered necessary by physicians. The majority of 'sanatoriums' would be located on the sea coasts, close to mineral springs, or in favourable climatic zones. The rehabilitation and medical wellness treatments offered to the patients (who were considered as 'patients', not 'clients') would include a wide range of naturopathic methods, such as balneotherapy, thalassotherapy, hydrotherapy, and so on, backed by strong medical and scientific evidence. The character of treatments, as well as the location of 'sanatoriums', means they could be called 'spas', although the term 'spa' had never been applied by either Russian professionals or by their patients to those traditional health resorts. Working under the rule of the Ministry of Health, 'sanatoriums' would specialise in particular rehabilitation goals (i.e. vertebral dysfunction, lung diseases, cardio-vascular diseases, etc.). Logically, their staff would be a hundred percent medical, and the patients would have to go through detailed diagnostics before receiving any treatments. Besides, the accommodation level was never that of comfort and indulgence, and in an average 'sanatorium' would rather resemble a hospital.

Independently and apart from the medical wellness institutions, another segment of wellness had been popular with the Russian population – the age-long traditions of 'banya' – a form of private public baths including heat therapy, soap bathing and massage with birch twigs (*venick*). The public baths that had nothing in common with modern spas were accessible to the population, and a lot of Russians would visit them weekly as part of individual hygienic practice. Therefore, the culture of rehabilitation and wellness through spa treatments was historically inherent in the Russian society.

Following the political, economic and social changes (*perestroika*) in the early 1990s, the autonomy of the ex-Soviet republics and the access to international tourism, a huge part of resorts and 'sanatoriums' turned to be located in the newly founded states, and the official system of preventive health care was shaken. The lack of finance from the state, alongside with the new demands of the new generation of Russian clients, very quickly made Russian 'sanatoriums' unattractive and outdated. Russian tourists gained the possibility of travelling abroad, where they could see higher standards of hospitality and catering, as well as new types of facilities – modern spas. The 'nouveaux riches' were so much attracted by the new health and leisure destinations that some of them were determined to copy the foreign experience and create 'spas' in Russia.

With the first few fitness clubs, rehabilitation clinics and day spas emerging mainly in Moscow and a few big cities of Russia, the private segment of the Russian health and wellness market started to develop in the late 1990s. Strange as it might seem, the Russian spa business did not stem from either medical traditions of 'sanatoriums', or the popular traditions of 'banya'. The first Russian spa facilities were salons (day spas) combining eclectic design and latest western equipment, providing sophisticated cosmetological treatments and oriental massages. The high prices in the new segment of the beauty and health market made it inaccessible to the majority of the Russian population, and the notion of 'spa' for quite a long time was perceived as a synonym to 'bourgeois luxury'. At the same time, the beauty market was in a continuous growth.

Alongside the low demand for spa services, the key challenge for the Russian spa market was the medical licensing, obligatory for practically all spa therapies. The national standards of water treatments (including baths and showers) were absolutely inapplicable in modern spa facilities. The above-mentioned conditions, as well as a very slow development of the hospitality market, created a serious obstacle for the segment of hotel and resort spas that started to appear in Russia much later than the day spas. However, today the number of hotel/resort spas is constantly growing. The hotels belonging to international chains have either spa salons or wellness centres in their structure. Some of them are international brands.

The 'sanatorium' segment and the health resort industry had been experiencing a serious decline until 2003 when the Ministry of Health adopted the unprecedented concept of 'Protecting the Health of the Healthy', which was aimed at creating a national wellness industry. The programme of development of preventive medicine, rehabilitation and wellness stimulated a large number of institutions to start modernisation and integrate the modern concepts of spa and wellness in their facilities. Adding extensive spa treatments to their medical services the redeveloped 'sanatoria' still lack comfortable accommodation and proper customer service.

One of the popular trends in Russian medical wellness institutions is 'endo-ecological rehabilitation' – an innovative method of detoxification on the cellular level, which is a perfect match of medical treatments with spa therapies. The method has gained popularity recently and is being used in a large number of former 'sanatoria', rebranded these days as 'medical spa hotels'.

Today there are almost all of the internationally recognised categories of spa and wellness institutions in Russia. With city spa salons (day spas) still leading in number, there are about 2,000 facilities belonging to 'sanatoria' and waiting for serious investments. Some of them have already been modernised and turned into 'spa hotels'. One of the current trends is the creation of relatively small (no more than 100 rooms) spa hotels in suburban areas, far from resorts or ecological environment. Country spa/wellness hotels offer a

variety of services, including outdoor leisure activities, depending on the season. The occupancy of country spa hotels is amazingly high, the target clientele being urban residents, who for different reasons prefer to spend their vacation close to their homes.

Sochi will be the host city for the Winter Olympic Games in 2014, therefore spa hotel projects are being developed to be operated internationally. Other significant investment projects are being planned in the South of Russia, either through reconstruction of old 'sanatorium' facilities, or created in popular resort areas. However, the infrastructure in the majority of regions is still undeveloped to become future spa resorts as destinations for international tourists. The price range (both for accommodation and spa treatments) would be high, with the service standards still remaining below the European level.

In some regions of Russia (i.e. Altai Mountains) the concept of 'eco-spa-resorts' is actively promoted, based on both local healing methods and modern sustainable technologies. The proximity of the new eco-resorts and eco-spas to natural curative sources (mineral springs, mud lakes, etc.) is definitely an advantage that could make them popular tourist destinations.

The traditional Russian healing methods currently employed in modern spa and wellness institutions include:

- the Russian banya (authentic heat therapy rituals in a steam sauna);
- traditional cryotherapy (ice-water bathing after 'banya', snow applications, cold water dousing);
- apitherapy (use of honeybee products for massage, wraps);
- use of natural ingredients in different spa treatments: buckwheat, honey, birch leaves, 'pantotherapy' (extracts from antlers of young Siberian stags), local herbs and berries, etc.;
- the Russian massage.

The strengths of the modern spa and wellness industry in Russia are rich curative resources (the Black Sea, the Altai mountains, mineral springs of the Caucasus, etc.), the revived traditions of health maintenance, the profound medical evidence of spa treatments, highly qualified staff with a medical background. The main weaknesses and threats of the Russian health and wellness market are: absence of standards and regulations for the new type of business; high cost of imported equipment and cosmetic products resulting in high prices for spa treatments; obligatory medical licensing for the majority of spa treatments and wellness services; undeveloped infrastructure in the traditional health resort areas.

The opportunities for further development of the wellness industry in Russia are linked to the introduction of a federal standard for non-medical spa services, as well as the growing interest of foreign investors in the Russian hospitality and wellness market. Increase of awareness and interest of international tourists in Russian national curative methods might be a strong stimulus to the industry development. The support of the young and developing spa and wellness market from the state alongside investments in the health resorts segment could make Russia one of the most attractive destinations for international tourists.

CHAPTER **13**

Italian spas today
Demand and offer evolution and trends

Sonia Ferrari

Introduction

In Italy today the wellness market is growing and no longer involves only the higher-income classes but also middle-income segments, and is thus growing markedly in terms of quantity. All this is not the result of some passing fashionable phenomenon, but rather of a profound change in the lifestyle of many Italians (Gregori and Cardinale, 2009), which has led postmodern consumers to be more careful about their look, physique and mental and physical well-being, and sees them looking for opportunities to relax in harmony with nature, and to demand accommodation facilities that increasingly act as wellness services.

The development of the wellness and spa market in Italy

The situation described above has caused significant growth in the offer, which has risen in terms of both quantity and quality, involving widely differing companies in the sector, which offer services aimed at tourists and/or residents, as well as products. These include beauty centres, thermal spas, fitness centres, beauty farms, gyms, beauty products, swimming-pools, bathing establishments, and so on.

The wellness sector thus consists of numerous segments which are independent but complementary, in which the degree of specialisation is very high and currently involves around 31,000 companies, with 56,000 workers and turnover of around 16 billion euros, with forecast worth in 2010 of 25 billion euros (ISTAT, 2008). It is increasingly common to try to create an integrated offer, by putting together packages of goods and services and, in particular, thermal treatments enhanced by fitness, relaxation and beauty services (AICEB, 2010), and thermal spas that are turning into beauty farms.

In recent decades tourism demand has shifted towards complex wellness products, which, besides fitness and beauty services, also include diets, exercise and other elements relating to health, relaxation, and meditation for mental wellness (Le Cardane, 2011). Consequently, accommodation structures, especially those in the middle to high category which are located in important tourism destinations, are increasingly investing in wellness and seeking to offer their customers multi-sensory experiences linked to wellness and relaxation.

In 2009 Italians took over one million wellness and/or thermal spa holidays in Italy. The favourite destinations for this type of holidays are those in the following regions: Veneto, Tuscany, Campania and Emilia Romagna (AICEB, 2010). The greatest focus on providing accommodation for thermal spa and wellness holidays, on the other hand, is found in Trentino Alto Adige, Campania, Emilia Romagna and Tuscany (ONT, 2011a). The number of tourists in these destinations is over 15 million per annum, or 4.2 per cent of all tourists in Italy. These are foreign (4.4 per cent) and Italian (4.1 per cent) tourists. The latter decide to spend a holiday in thermal spa and wellness destinations in Italy for one of the following reasons: desire for wellness and fitness (46 per cent), wish to have a relaxing holiday (35 per cent) in a luxury natural environment (30 per cent), and for gastronomic reasons (21 per cent). During their holidays one in two tourists visits spas and wellness centres; 37 per cent undertake sporting activities (AICEB, 2010).

These destinations are home to 3.2 per cent of all sleeping accommodation in Italy and 5.1 per cent of sleeping accommodation in hotels, for a total of 148,918 beds, of which 111,884 are in hotels, with a high ratio of four–five star hotels (34 per cent compared to the national average of 29 per cent). The ratio of Italian tourists is high, especially for the leading destinations (AICEB, 2010).

The wellness offer between tradition and innovation

In recent years in Italy there has been an increase in demand for forms of *special interest tourism*.[1] In particular, in 2010 tourists often turned their backs on traditional destinations to try more *authentic*[2] locations on a liveable scale (ONT, 2011b). Italy has a strong tradition in thermal spas and has always been a leading country in the sector. In the twentieth century some famous thermal resorts, in which great importance was also attached to recreational and social aspects besides the medical treatment, such as Salsomaggiore, Abano and Montecatini, helped the development of the whole sector; this positive stage continued until the major crisis at the start of the 1990s, which still today affects the more traditional forms of tourism on offer.

While throughout Europe, in order to withstand the crisis, thermal spa destinations have shifted from a purely therapeutic positioning to a more diversified offer, also in order to address new market segments (the young and families) and to satisfy other types of tourists (tourism for meetings, sport, culture, etc.), in Italy the thermal spa companies have been somewhat slow in appreciating the growth of the sector and only started to address the wellness market in the last two decades of the twentieth century. All this has caused a loss of competitiveness compared to facilities, such as beauty farms and wellness centres, which launched wellness holidays in the 1980s, the period in which the first packages for thermal spa holidays were created. Often wellness companies would state that they also offered thermal services, which in reality were not (such as saunas, Turkish baths, etc.). These structures used to target middle to high market niches, satisfying a need which at that time was not considered as primary.

This slowness in reacting to the development of consumers' needs was mainly caused by the fear of compromising the image of the thermal sector as a supplier of health-care services, by contaminating it with other elements in the offer that were not strictly part of the treatment and consequently also losing public funding. In that period, thermal spas, in keeping with their image, promoted their product offer above all through family doctors, the best communication channel for that type of product at that time, and by *word of mouth* (Becheri and Quirino, 2011).

All this meant that thermal spas, which continued to offer only health-care treatments aimed above all at the elderly with undifferentiated marketing policies, started their repositioning policies towards thermal wellness only in the 1990s; in this period, however, many of the market competitors had consolidated their position and market shares, making the process of transformation very difficult and the market very competitive. This was true above all for those thermal centres in which the offer was centred on treatment structures, while in thermal spa towns where treatments were offered in hotels it was easier to make the investments needed to expand the range of services provided, above all in the better-quality hotels (Becheri and Quirino, 2011).

Italian spas and spa towns as tourist destinations

Therefore, only at the start of the new millennium did thermal spas manage to expand their role and become places for mental and physical rest and regeneration, thus coming into direct competition with beauty farms, many of which now have a well-established image and represent a kind of evolution of thermal spa tourism. Today the majority of thermal centres (85 per cent) have space dedicated to wellness (Becheri and Quirino, 2012), which sometimes operates independently and, in other cases, together with the thermal structure.

In 2009, 378 Italian thermal spas offered their services to 1.5 million people. The number of customers seeking traditional treatments begins to fall from the start of 2000, with an average annual drop of 1.2 per cent. The demand for wellness increases, on the other hand, at an average annual rate of 18.3 per cent. Arrivals at thermal destinations in 2009 numbered 2,950,727 and overnight stays 11,614,947. Overnight stays too show a decreasing trend as from 2000, especially in exclusively thermal localities which do not have other significant tourism resources. Customers are mainly Italian (61.1 per cent of arrivals) (Becheri and Quirino, 2012).

The transformation of the thermal offer towards a broader concept of health is helped by numerous phenomena, such as growth in the segment of senior tourists (many of whom enjoy early retirement programmes and have a good level of disposable income), greater attention to health problems, greater flexibility in the timing of holidays, an increase in demand for single person tourism (Santuari, 2010) and special interest tourism, the advent of Web 2.0, which increases the interest in thermal spa holidays from new targets. Another element which has favoured the repositioning of Italian thermal spa companies towards wellness has been the ongoing reduction in the funds destined by the state to purchase of thermal spa services, which are still today paid for by the National Health Service, and the consequent need to increase flows of private customers.

This new concept of thermal spa tourism has also been taken up by law-makers with the Law Reordering the Thermal Spa Sector (Law no. 323/2000). In addition, Italian law establishes that the word 'spa' may refer only to thermal spa companies, thus seeking to reduce the widespread confusion over terminology.

Thermal spas then, which until a few decades ago were part of the medical health-care sector, are gradually becoming independent and increasingly integrating into the tourism sector (Faroldi et al., 2007). They represent increasingly important tourism attractions and the centres in which they are built are destinations which today are home to around 4,500 hotels with 240,000 beds, or 13 per cent of the national total (Becheri and Quirino, 2012).

The future: threats and opportunities

Today numerous elements offer important opportunities for Italian thermal spas. First, as already mentioned, the significant ageing of the population and the growing interest in sophisticated wellness, as well as the new and broader conception of health.

In addition, the continuous growth in demand for natural therapies, for non-pharmaceutical and non-invasive products and the ability of thermal spas to offer pack-ages which include not only treatments but also other elements such as physiotherapy, diet, beauty and thermal cosmetic products, increase the value of a sector which could be termed the *tourism of thermal wellness*.

All this could enable a repositioning of the sector, also through the rediscovery of thermal destinations as places in which to experience more complete holidays, thanks to unique elements linked to the specific characteristics of the place, to the uncontaminated natural environment, to the recreational aspects which were part of spa holidays in the Belle Époque and which could now be offered once again. Objectives of this type can be achieved by investing in the local area to create a true thermal wellness tourism sector, to add innovative services to the traditional ones and to focus on the unique and authentic aspects of destinations (such as gastronomy, nature, culture, events) in order to differen-tiate the offer, also by supporting the offer with other types of tourism, such as meetings, green tourism or seaside holidays.

In this way it could be possible to re-launch the image of Italian spas internationally, creating value from the know-how and individual features of the thermal localities, and radically innovating their image which, in any case, requires significant investment by the whole sector both in renewing the offer and in communication. These investments, which have largely already been started, should address in terms of the offer, as is happening in some localities, a redefinition both in conceptual terms (with a broader and more complex view of the role of thermal spas) and in structural terms (focusing on themes which can differentiate a locality from the competition, such as that of wellness through the senses or that of the thermal oasis or that of socialisation) (Faroldi et al., 2007).

Notes

1 The special interest tourism segment includes different types of tourists (Zeppel and Hall, 1992: 62); all, however, are looking for new experiences, linked to gastronomy, wellness, history, sport, events, lifestyles, nature, etc.

2 The *authenticity* of the tourist experience refers to primitive, natural environments that are untainted by modernity, and preserved thanks to geographical separation (MacCannell, 1976).

14

Traditional spas – between health and wellness tourism
The Trentino strategy to face the challenge of the market

Geradine Parisi

A short history of Trentino spas

Trentino is an Italian alpine destination that has developed a traditional double-season tourism offer: hiking and outdoor in the summer and snow and ski in the winter.

Since the late nineteenth century, Trentino has been famous for its mountains, the Dolomites and its spas, which were born under the influence of the mitteleuropean *kurorte*. Trentino's spas were famous all over Europe for the medicinal properties of their water. In the sixteenth century it was possible to buy the green bottle of Pejo's spa water in a lot of pharmacies, not only in Italy but also in the Austro-Hungarian Empire. In the eighteenth century the spa of Rabbi was chosen as a holiday destination from a lot of European nobles. In the nineteenth century Levico and Roncegno were two important spas too and were quite famous all over Europe. Trentino was famous not only for its thermal water, but also for the property of its particular grass and still today it is possible to experience the grass bath in the spa of Garniga. Slowly Trentino's spas lost their importance and were replaced by other tourist attractions and by alpine mass tourism. Spas became gradually places chosen by people affected by some diseases where it was possible to recover and spa buildings became more similar to clinics than to touristic facilities.

Trentino spas today

Nowadays in Trentino there are eight spas. Every structure has its specific identity and specialisation. All the spas are well developed, but they still have a significant growth potential. In 2010, seven of the eight spas attracted a total of 40,000 visitors.

FIGURE 14.1 Location of Trentino spas
Source: Adapted from a Trentino marketing map.

All are alpine spas, but they are located in different areas of the region: there are mountain spas, mid-altitude spas, lake spas, and some of them are in the valley. The main thermal resource of all spas except one – Garniga, which has a grass bath – is water, which has specific and unique features in every spa. The facilities have different dimensions: Levico and Comano are the biggest and Garniga is the smallest, but all of them have a quite similar governance model with a spa director, sometimes a manager and sometimes a doctor, and a team of specialised employees. Usually the organisation chart is very simple and there is not a functional division of tasks.

Trentino spas: an opportunity to complete the tourism offer of an alpine destination

Traditionally, Italian spas differ from other European ones. They were places where people with diseases – most of them elderly or children – went for a period of recovery, taking advantage of the refund guaranteed by the national health system. This image is deeply rooted in the mind of the Italian population, so that it is necessary to give – especially to the domestic market – a different view of spas, making them more oriented to wellness and to the holistic well-being of the person.

Today, in fact, traditional spa tourism is over. There are new and important trends that have strongly changed the spa industry. Health and wellness, experience, authenticity,

TABLE 14.1 Resources and specialisations of Trentino spas			
Spa	Location	Resource	Principle specialisation
Rabbi	Mountain	Acidic, ferruginous water containing sodium, bicarbonate and rich in minerals	Vascular and diseases
Pejo	Mountain	Three types of water: Oligomineral water Medium mineral, ferruginous, bicarbonated, carbonic water Mineral, natural sparkling, bicarbonated, ferruginous, water containing calcium and bicarbonate	Rheumatic diseases
Val Rendena	Mountain	Oligomineral water	Respiratory diseases
Comano	Mid mountain	Calcium-magnesium bicarbonated water	Dermatological diseases
Garniga	Mountain	Grass	Rheumatic diseases
Linfano	Lake	Oligomineral water rich in calcium and bicarbonate	Dermatological diseases
Levico	Lake	Arsenical, acid, highly mineralised, sulphate, ferruginous water	Rheumatic diseases
Casa di salute Raphael	Valley	Antroposophic medicine Use of Levico's water	General diseases
Dolomia	Mountain	Sulfur, calcium, magnesium fluoride water	Gastrointestinal diseases

personalisation and short breaks are some trends that suggest how today it is important to create a new spa tourism that is in between medical[1] and wellness tourism.[2]

Trentino local government is aware of the strategic importance that spa tourism can have for this sector, especially in order to replace the decrease of demand for traditional alpine tourism activities (such as skiing). For this reason in 2011 a new law was approved (legge provinciale 4 aprile 2011 n. 6 'Sviluppo del settore termale trentino e modificazioni della legge provinciale sulla ricettività turistica') that regulates the future development of spas.

The law was studied to increase the attractiveness of Trentino spas and its main pillars are the following:

- *Valorise thermal resources*: The thermal resource is strategic for the whole Trentino province and not just for the individual areas where there is a hot spring or other thermal opportunity. Spas are recognised as an economic resource and could be a key element to develop some area of the region. To reach this goal the local government will define some thermal areas where spas will foster local development. All the thermal initiatives and the general strategy will be described in one specific document called 'strategic guidelines', which will be the point of reference for the development of the entire sector.

- *Renew thermal station*: All the structural action to renew buildings and plants must be part of an integrated project, and not viewed as single initiatives. Investments should not only be directed to structural plants, but have to be planned referring to the territory to create a reciprocal process of valorisation between the spa and other resources.
- *Coordinate the thermal offer and all the marketing activities*: The spas of Trentino are relatively small economic actors therefore it is necessary to start cooperation among spas in order to create an integrated offer and a coordinate image where it is clear that all the spas belong to a unique territory, but at the same time that they have different characteristics and features. The companies owned by the local government in charge of promoting local development will guide the entire sector and will create a coordinated image promoting a clear development strategy for Trentino's spas.
- *Promote the full use of the thermal resource*: Nowadays not all spas use the total amount of thermal resources that they have at disposal. The law wants to create a compensation system where if the resource is not totally exploited, the concession can be divided between a number of subjects and not reserved only to one subject as it is now. This measure is proposed to foster the best use of the thermal resources.

The new spa law is a first step of a general strategy that has the aim to increase the competitiveness of all the spas of Trentino. The law has an important goal: it was proposed to foster a long-term planning approach that will be able to guarantee a continuous update in accordance with the new market trends. The law will be implemented through a specific policy and especially through the guidelines of the sector that will be a strategic and operative document. The guidelines will promote the development of the sector – as a whole and as a sum of the eight different spas located in the Province – and the creation of a strong territorial system, a cluster. The law and the guidelines will define a context, but the success will depend on the commitment and the collaboration between all stakeholders of Trentino's spas industry.

Notes

1 Medical tourism: the main motivation of the trip is health with the aim to cure or prevent a disease.
2 Well-being tourism: the main motivation is to maintain physical and mental health and well-being.

CHAPTER 15

Day spa revenue management
Some examples from Italy

Patrizia Modica and Elisa Scanu

Revenue management in the day spa sector

In Italy day spas represent a relevant part of the wellness sector and are expected to grow in the next decades. Day spas, as many other industries in the service sector, are characterised by operational and management difficulties, linked to the features of demand and supply. These can compromise long-term economic results. The study considers revenue management as a method that can contribute to maintain and improve the day-spa economic performance and analyses the existence of the conditions for its use in the Italian day-spa segment. The investigation was conducted in summer 2012, through questionnaires and interviews directed to owners and managers of a selected sample of Italian day spas.

Revenue management or yield management is a managerial system that maximises revenues and profits and also increases customer satisfaction. Revenue management is effectively applied to those industries characterised by fixed capacity, perishable inventory, specific cost structure, predictable and time variable demand, and price sensitive/insensitive customers. The method is utilised in the tourism industry, for example hotels, cruise lines, airlines and car rental firms, but less frequently in the spa segment. Literature and case study research have recently emphasised the possibility to apply revenue management to spas and its potential in improving spa profitability.

Spa operation and hotel operation are very similar. The spa capacity is fixed and is measured by the number of treatment rooms. The time during which rooms and therapists are available can be considered the spa inventory. If rooms or therapists are not occupied for a period of time, spa available services perish. The spa cost structure is also consistent to the appliance of revenue management. Spas are characterised by low variable costs and a high level of fixed costs, often originated by amortisation and cost of labour. This cost structure impacts significantly on the efficiency and performance of the spa business. For this reason it is crucial to optimise the spa cost structure and, in many cases, like in Italy, when labour cost is generally fixed, the cost of therapists.

Spa demand is variable during time and is characterised by different features. Customer demand should be predicted and classified with respect to a series of variables, like residence, gender, age, booking patterns, treatments and preferred treatment times. This information can be easily collected by an opportune computerised reservation system. Spa customers have different behaviours towards treatment price. Some are price sensitive, are attracted by discounted prices and are willing to make use of spa services at an unusual time of the day or the week. Other customers are price insensitive and are not willing to move from their preferred treatment time in order to benefit from lower prices.

To successfully apply revenue management to spas, two levers should be managed: time and price. Spa managers should control duration of treatment, the amount of time between treatments, and attempt to reduce the uncertainty of arrivals and duration. The management of price can be considered one of the most efficient strategies to maximise profits and improve customer satisfaction. Traditionally pricing policies are considered as discounting policy, but, in the context of the revenue management system, managers adopt differential prices, discounting or increasing prices based on the predicted demand trend. Discounts are only a part of pricing strategies. For example, those customers that have treatments on Saturday should pay a higher price than those that reserve the same treatment on Tuesday. Price of treatments can vary based on type of treatment, treatment room location or type, characteristic of therapist, time of day or week, attendances, timing of reservation, treatment duration and different prices can be applied to customers who are members of groups. It is important that different prices are associated with a logical and real reason otherwise customers would not accept having the same treatment for different prices. The purpose of differential prices is to attract potential demand and also shift customer demand from peak periods to non-peak periods, obtaining the highest profit both at busy and at slow times.

Revenue per available treatment hour (RevPATH) represents the measure of spa performance. It can be calculated by dividing revenues by the number of available treatment rooms in a time period or by multiplying treatment room occupancy rate by the average treatment expenditure per person. The indicator captures average customer expenditure and treatment room occupation and their trade-off. Generally, a high level of occupation is obtained by sacrificing average customer expenditure and, the opposite, a high level of average customer expenditure is gained by sacrificing occupancy. Through revenue management this trade-off does not occur. In fact, revenue management is able to increase both indices simultaneously and spa managers, in order to maximise revenues, by selecting the appropriate combination of the two variables.

Spa operators, who intend to develop a revenue management system, should follow these steps:

1   collect detailed information about treatment room occupation, treatment times, customer preferences, reservation patterns and average treatment cost structure;
2   identify causes that affect occupancy performance and RevPATH, analysing the variation of these two indicators;
3   develop strategies to increase RevPATH for busy and slow periods;

4   apply revenue management practices, defining exactly criteria, behaviours and goals;

5   measure results, by monitoring occupancy rate, revenues and RevPATH.

As regards the third point, managers can increase RevPATH in busy periods encouraging price insensitive customers, limiting discounts and reducing treatment duration. Alternatively, during slow periods managers can attract price-sensitive customers with promotions and discounts, proposing two for one, alternative treatments and the like.

Revenue management for day spas: the case study

A case-study approach was used to investigate the application of revenue management to day spas in Italy. A representative sample of Italian day spas located in North Italy, Central Italy and Sardinia was selected, and questionnaires and semi-structured interviews were employed. The questionnaire to complete was delivered to the head receptionists of the selected spas. The questionnaire was focused on gaining general data and information on Italian day-spa operating management. Questions concerned three aspects: general information about the day spa, methods used to collect data regarding characteristics of demand and number of treatments purchased during specified periods of the year. With regard to this last point, four months of 2011 were selected – February, April, July and October – and respondents were asked to indicate how many treatments were purchased on a Tuesday and Friday in one week during these months. The question allowed the researchers to determine the current occupancy level of Italian day spas in peak and off-peak periods of the year.

The semi-structured interviews, carried out by telephone, were addressed to owners and managers of the selected day spas. They were divided into two sections. The first section was focused on ascertaining the existence of the conditions for the method applicability. The second section was focused on obtaining opinions about the efficiency of discounting policies and the possibility to apply revenue management in Italian day spas.

The day spas considered in the case study are characterised by different dimensions, with diverse number of treatment rooms, but they are all affected by not satisfying the occupancy rate of treatment rooms. The occupancy rate fluctuates on average from 21 per cent in February and 25 per cent in October that can be considered the off-peak months, to 34 per cent in April and 36 per cent in July that can be considered the peak months. Only in a few cases the occupancy rate improves to 60–65 per cent in the peak period and 34–38 per cent in the off-peak period, but these are amazing situations. Causes of these occupation levels are different. Therapists present in the spas are less than those needed to occupy all treatment rooms during all the opening time. Therapists work on shifts and for this reason treatment rooms cannot be all utilised jointly. Furthermore, spa owners and managers say that the recent world financial crisis and recession have had a negative impact on their businesses. In fact, in the last few years they have observed a decrease of demand and more attention to the price of treatments.

Owners and managers say that they are capable of qualifying clients on the basis of their characteristics – age, residence, price sensitivity, typology of treatment demanded, booking patterns – but prevalently the knowledge of demand is intuitive and not based on a periodic annotation of the different characteristics. When the annotation is recorded, it is made in a paper form and not computerised. Only in a few cases data is collected through the use of information systems. Also reservations are frequently recorded through paper daily forms and not through computerised forms.

In order to stimulate clients to purchase more or different treatments, diverse discounting strategies are applied. Frequently managers and owners apply discounts for regular clients or to all customers during particular periods of the year, month and week. Some day spas offer discounts for new clients, for the customers' birthday or for those clients who involve a friend. Only in a few cases a discount is applied for customers who make a reservation in advance. The discount generally consists of a reduction of treatment price; other typologies of promotions like gifts are rarely utilised. All spa owners and managers are in agreement considering discounting policies as a managerial instrument difficult to manage, because an inappropriate utilisation of discounts can negatively affect the reputation of the spa.

Furthermore, owners and managers are aware that a great part of their clients are price sensitive and believe that discounting policies can increase the number of clients or the number of treatments demanded. They are also uninformed about the positive or negative impacts on revenues derived by discounted policies and they are not able to indicate if discounts can shift spa customers from peak periods to off-peak periods.

Owners and managers do not have knowledge of the revenue management system as a method suitable for spa industries, but they believe that, in the context of the Italian day spas, it could be applied successfully. In fact, they are interested in improving economic performances through the management of customer demand, occupancy rate and revenues. Especially younger entrepreneurs are well disposed to adopt new managerial systems that could help the business to reach their aims.

On the other hand, the low utilisation of information systems, the imprecise knowledge of the characteristics of spa demand and spa economic performance, and the employment of discounting policies not based on demand trend and characteristics represent an obstacle to adopt revenue management in the Italian day-spa segment.

Conclusion

The study reveals that Italian day spas, characterised by low treatment-room occupancy rate, high fixed costs, and variable and instable demand, could take advantage of the managerial system considered and investigated in the field research. Some aspects of Italian day-spa management, in particular the widespread use of discounting policies, the attention to the characteristics of customer demand and the interest of day-spa owners/managers in improving performances and solving operational and management difficulties can be considered positive and significant conditions for the development of the method in the future. But other aspects, like the limited use of information systems to register reservations, the intuitive knowledge of the different characteristics of customer

demand and the consequent impossibility of predicting demand represent a limitation for its implementation. An adequate information and training of the spa operators, linked to the propensity of owners towards improvement, can stimulate the application of the method which represents an important instrument for the economic growth of the whole sector of beauty and wellness.

CHAPTER 16

A multipurpose wellness park
The case study of Hamat Gader, Israel

Yechezkel Israeli

Introduction

Hamat Gader is Israel's largest and oldest spa complex. It is one of the most popular tourism and recreation sites in Israel that combines recreational experiences, attractions and activities for families, groups and couples. The site is considered to be the fifth largest tourism site in Israel with annual visitor numbers of 450,000 (Dun and Bradstreet, 2012). Hamat Gader is located at the Yarmuk River gorge (flowing to the Jordan River), some 7 km east of the Sea of Galilee, one of the leading tourism regions in Israel, and near the triangle border of Israel, Jordan and Syria. The site is 160 metres above sea level, so the average daytime temperatures in winter are 15 centigrade and in summer 38 centigrade (while quite often it exceeds 40 degrees) (CBS, 2011).

There are five springs which come up from the ground with varied temperatures: 51 centigrade which was used for the Ancient Roman baths, 42 and 25 centigrade which are both used today for bathing (they are mixed so as to have varied temperatures between 37 and 42 degrees). The other two springs are of 34 and 28 degrees. Hamat Gader Park was opened to the public in 1977. It spreads over an area of 40 acres, includes covered outdoor settings, restaurants, lawns, ancient Roman baths and the thermo mineral pool area. Furthermore Hamat Gader boasts one of the largest crocodile farms in the Middle East with approximately 200 crocodiles of various species. The park can accommodate in open areas up to 4,000 people.

The thermo mineral water, which was researched quite extensively (Levitte et al., 1981; Shalev et al., 2008), has two important properties: heat and mineral-rich content. The water gushes at a steady temperature of 42°C, 500–700 cubic metres per hour. It contains sulfur at a concentration of 4.7 per cent as well as other important minerals which has potent medicinal and curative qualities. The therapeutic effect contributes to accelerated metabolism, cell renewal and relief of joint pains. Due to the large capacity of the hot springs, the water circulates every four hours, ensuring it remains clean and fresh.

The Ancient Roman Baths

Hamat Gader (literally, 'Hot Springs of Gadara') is named after the ancient Hellenic city of Gadara, which is situated about 4 km away on the heights. Gadara was a prosperous city and Hamat Gader was one of its suburbs. Sacred springs with curative properties combined with luxurious baths and a ritual theatre attracted many visitors to the area, making it an international centre even in ancient times. The baths were built by the Romans as early as the second century, and were regarded as the second most beautiful in the Roman Empire. Evidence from historical sources shows that it was a favourite place for many emperors and other prominent figures. The importance of the place for the Christians stemmed from the Miracle of the Swine made by Jesus in the land of Gadarenes (Mark 5:20). The springs were used also in the Byzantine and the Muslim periods, until a serious earthquake in 749 ruined most of the baths. The Roman baths were abandoned and forgotten.

The building complex, which is exceptionally well preserved to a height of 8–12 metres, covers an area of over 500 sq. m. It offered six pools, of different shapes and sizes, each in a separate hall. These were connected to one another by passageways which enabled the bathers to pass from one pool to another, gradually adjusting to the differences in water temperature. The pools were filled from the spring and drained to the river by a sophisticated complex system (Hirschfeld, 1994, 1997; Bagatti, 2001).

The Roman baths complex, which has been restored, is an attractive place to visit for various market segments. As much of the old plumbing is intact, there are future plans to operate a part of the Roman baths, in the same way as in the old days, by running thermal water from the spring.

The structure of the modern site

The vast area of the site enables the visitors to be spread in different spaces according to their interests. The diversification of tourist attractions responds different market segments and their necessities. With relation to the scale of health tourism, suggested by Smith and Puczkó (2009), Hamat Gader site positions itself between medical wellness and wellness tourism (leisure and recreation and holistic tourism).

There are five distinguishing areas in the park:

- Central Bath Complex: This is the centre of the park. Two pools of thermo mineral water are available: a large one with water varying between 42 and 37 degrees (depends on the location in the pool), including a waterfall and Jacuzzi beds, and a pool of 42 degrees located on top of the spring. About 1,500 visitors can be accommodated near these pools. This place is the most visited in the park.
- SPA and treatment centre: Hamat Gader offers a full range of water treatments and massages of various kinds. The Spa has 17 treatment rooms with a professional team of masseurs. Some of them are located in the central bath complex, but most are located in an intimate zone named Spa Village which is open to guests over 16 years old. At the centre of the spa there are intimate thermo mineral pools, used for bathing

and for water treatments. They are also equipped with Jacuzzi beds and a waterfall. The atmosphere is peaceful as the village is a bit isolated and surrounded by tropical vegetation and enjoys some spectacular scenery. Towards evening torches around the pools are lit and give a romantic atmosphere. The treatment rooms are located in wooden chalets. Among the treatments are Swedish massage, shiatsu, Thai massage, aromatic massage, hot stones, Ayurveda, crystal therapy, water therapy, Tibetan bowls and reflexology. For those who are interested to stay over, there is a possibility in the Spa Village Hotel. This boutique hotel comprises 29 luxurious suites that are situated around the centre of the spa.

- Animal farm: The compound, which is mainly visited by families, includes a crocodile farm, a well-known site in Israel. Also there are performing parrots, snakes, an animal petting corner and mini wildlife reserve.
- Antiquities: Visiting the archaeological sites includes the Ancient Roman Baths and the Roman Theatre.
- Open areas for activities: These areas fit more to activities during warm seasons such as spring or summer. It includes a mini water-park which comprises a cold water pool with slides and geysers, mainly for the young, sport yards and a large area of lawns, mainly for groups. So as to capitalise on the organised market, workshops and fun days are suggested for groups. Among them are: awareness workshop, water therapy workshop, meditation workshop, power of touch and many more holistic workshops. This approach fits well the category of 'Occupational Wellness' or 'Workplace Wellness' (see Smith and Puczkó, 2009; Global Spa Summit, 2010).

In addition, the park contains restaurants, shops and inner transportation vehicles.

Visitors' behaviour and perceptions

Analysing the patterns of visits and perceptions shows clearly how Hamat Gader functions as a multi-purpose site with highly diverse market segments. The following analysis is based on observations, administrative documents and two surveys, all from the years 2008–12. One survey investigated 500 visitors in the site, while the other investigated the perception about the site, using 1,000 households.

Analysis of seasonality illustrates differences between market segments in the open park:

- Daily seasonality (working days): Early morning is the time for retirees. Late morning and noon are the periods for domestic groups. It should be noted that the organised market holds almost half of the total visits. Individual domestic visitors arrive mainly around noon time, while late afternoon and evening are the favourite times for young people and local residents.
- Weekly seasonality (working weeks): The beginning of the week is a low period; hence the first day is kept for a religious and conservative population who need separations

between genders. Weekdays are characterised by an organised market (domestic and incoming groups) and individuals coming from short distances (the north of the country). During weekends domestic tourism comprises mainly individuals and families from other parts of the country, daily tourism and stay-over visitors in hotels around the Sea of Galilee.

- Annual seasonality: This seasonality is contrary to other recreation sites in Israel, as the winter is the peak season while the summer is off season. Looking at the figures, 77 per cent of the visitors arrive between October and April. These visitors are coming mainly for bathing in the thermo mineral water. The majority of the individuals are from the north of the country (while organised groups are from other parts). In the summer, despite the high temperature, many families can be found (on summer holidays) coming from other parts of the country, mainly for the crocodile farm. The survey shows that the perception of northern citizens who have a short distance to the site, is as a 'one-season site' (means winter), mainly for spa, while the others who live far away see it as a 'multi-season site' (winter and summer), for spa and recreation.

The hotel does not accommodate families, so the off-season (summer) shows a low occupancy. In winter, daily and weekly seasonality of the hotel and the spa centre (Spa Village) does not show differences in market segments' arrivals, as all are individual couples and friends.

The spatial distribution of visitors shows the diversification of purposes in the park. The Central Bath Complex attracts almost all market segments, including groups and individuals, domestic and general incoming tourism (mainly from Russian-speaking countries). Their purpose is bathing and recreation. As this place is noisy and not intimate, for those who are interested in well-being and treatments, the Spa Village is a legitimate destination. It attracts mainly couples and individuals. The Animal Farm attracts mostly families whose purpose is purely recreation. Also some individual adults can be found for the same purpose. The cold water pool is targeted only at families for the summer period, obviously for recreation. The antiquities attract domestic tourists who are interested in culture and heritage tourism (mainly adults individually or in groups) and incoming pilgrimage tourism who are interested in the story of Gadara and the first era of Christianity. Sport yards, large areas of lawns and varied workshops are used by the organised market, mainly as part of an occupational wellness/health incentive for reaching inner balance, motivation and performance.

The surveys clarify the distinction between market segments. While 93 per cent use the baths (main pools), and 38 per cent visit the animal farm, only 10 per cent were interested in spa treatment. (It should be remembered that 10 per cent of 450,000 visitors is still a significant figure.) Although the level of satisfaction with the Animal Farm is very high, the main attraction is still the pools (73 per cent). The perception of households about the site shows that 60 per cent perceive the park as a place of thermo mineral water, 30 per cent as a crocodile farm and only 10 per cent as a place of well-being and treatment. Despite the results, most people perceive Hamat Gader as a park for family recreation (63 per cent), while 29 per cent see it as a place for romantic leisure. The last figure explains the decision of having a limited isolated place for spa and treatment. It is worth noting that a

relatively low percentage (36 per cent) perceives the park as a destination for medical treatment. This finding strengthens the aforementioned insight, that on the scale of health tourism Hamat Gader is located on the 'soft side' of medical wellness. When two concepts were presented to the interviewees, a site for adults with no kids or a site for families, most of the respondents preferred the family concept (63 per cent), although those who preferred the adult concept still remained significant (53 per cent). Many interviewees preferred both concepts (overlapping responses) as they do not feel any contradiction.

The conclusion is that there is no one predominant concept for Hamat Gader. The park is perceived as a multi-purpose site which needs to respond the diverse market segments.

CHAPTER **17**

Benchmarking pilot study for Hungarian wellness and spa hotels

Andrea Vermesi

Introduction

Management skills and tools are necessary to run a spa profitably at a high-quality level. In Hungary, the country of thermal spas and springs and numerous wellness and spa hotels, the general perception is that one can operate a spa with a very small margin, and the return on investment takes a very long time. The wellness hotels in Hungary usually have a spa or wellness department operating within the hotel for their in-house guests and in many cases they are open for the public as well. According to the interview results received from the hotel directors the spa is often quoted as the 'money-burning' department, where no profit or in the very best case a low profit can be generated.

The International Wellness Institute (IWI), having a wellness and spa manager training programme consisting of benchmarking techniques in its training curriculum, was often questioned by its students about which is the best wellness hotel in Hungary. How can hotels be professionally and equally assessed? We could not give an adequate response, since the classification based on the proper benchmarking techniques was not available, therefore we decided to develop a questionnaire and assess the Hungarian wellness and spa market. The study was completed in the second quarter of 2010.

Scope of the study

There is no industrial related market size and technical information on the spa and wellness sector in Hungary; therefore we had multiple aims when completing the study, which were the following:

- defining the benchmarking standard questionnaire for the wellness and spa industry;
- acquiring industry related performance data, if possible stratified by type of service providers;
- providing feedback and information for the wellness and spa market stakeholders on possible areas of improvement and development;
- mapping the deficiencies of Hungarian wellness and spa industry compared to other countries where the health, wellness and spa tourism is prospering.

Method

The survey consisted of 58 questions and was available for completion online. The survey link was sent by e-mail to all wellness and spa hotels, wellness and fitness centres and day spas in Hungary accompanied by instructions on how to complete the survey and what kind of data should be prepared in advance in order to adequately complete the questionnaire. The e-mail was monitored for receipt and reading rate. Simple statistical calculation methods were used such as pareto ranking, percentage calculations and ratio calculations.

The questionnaire was designed according to the BISA and ISPA recommendations, key performance indicators of the spa sector and similar questionnaires of an Austrian spa benchmarking study.

Results

- The total number of addressed institutions = 350
- The number of completed surveys = 52 (15 per cent)

Due to the low number of returned questionnaires the 2010 Hungarian Wellness and Spa Benchmarking Study was reclassified as a pilot study only.

Stratified results per service provider (spa hotel, day spa, wellness hotel spa, wellness centre spa, healing spa) could not be obtained based on returned data; therefore the conclusions and data should be interpreted as Hungarian spa industry average data.

The question groups of the survey were the following:

- geographical, location and environment related;
- personnel related;
- institution – physical parameters;
- financial key performance indicators;
- effectiveness and capacity related key performance indicators;
- target group and guest related;
- business operation methods, tools related.

The survey was completed by 4-star wellness hotels with spa departments (42 per cent), 4-star health and wellness hotels with spa and medical departments (19 per cent), 3-star

wellness, health and wellness hotels with spa and/or medical department (12 per cent), 5-star health and medical wellness hotels (4 per cent) and other service providers – day spas, wellness centres, aqua parks with wellness services (23 per cent). The responses were received from Budapest and Pest county (26 per cent), Balaton region (51 per cent) and North-East Hungary (23 per cent).

Regarding the employment type of the personnel working in the wellness and spa industry based on the study the results indicates that 63 per cent of the labour force is working eight hours a day as full-time employees, 24 per cent as part-time and 13 per cent on a contractual basis.

The survey included questions concerning relevant wellness and spa-related qualifications in various positions. Forty-eight per cent of the respondents employ personnel with relevant wellness and health tourism related qualifications, while the remaining 52 per cent of the spa and wellness personnel has no adequate qualification in the field of wellness and health tourism. Where the personnel has wellness or health tourism-related qualifications, the level of their qualification is: 55 per cent college or university degree; 11 per cent high-school or vocational certification; 34 per cent other adult learning course qualification, such as sales training and conference workshops. The following wellness-related positions were given by the employers: receptionist, masseur, spa manager, beauty therapist, manicurist, hair-dresser, physiotherapist, medic, animator, personal trainer, physiotherapist nurse, manager assistant, aqua trainer and children animator. The survey asked about the employee benefits received included in the remuneration package. The following benefits are provided by the employers: continued education and training, free in-house service usage, flexible work time, cafeteria and time in lieu.

In terms of tipping customs of the service providers, 67 per cent of the respondents said that tipping is allowed at their premises and 44 per cent offers commission as bonus payment after the sales activity of their employees.

The profitability of the wellness and spa departments is one of the key factors of the long-term operation and maintaining a high-quality-level service. The survey asked if there is any finance planning for the wellness and spa department. Fifty-nine per cent of the respondents have a detailed financial and business plan for the department, while 41 per cent do not. Only 63 per cent of the respondents have any product or accessory sales activity within the wellness and spa department. Nineteen per cent of the respondents have signature products available for sales at their facility. We asked the participants what factor would influence the most their profitability in the near future. Forty-one per cent cited the status of the national economy; 11 per cent employing the right people; 11 per cent application of a competitive pricing policy; 4 per cent proper cash-flow management; 4 per cent increasing competition activity; 4 per cent management training; 4 per cent none of the above; 22 per cent don't know.

Regarding the effectiveness and key performance indicators the results received were worse than expected. Most of the service providers responding to the survey (54 per cent) do not use any key performance indicators other than daily/monthly revenue data. Rarely capacity utilisation data are used for their facilities within the wellness and spa department. There is data collection available for utilisation rate of the services provided where the most popular are: massage (12 per cent), body treatments (11 per cent),

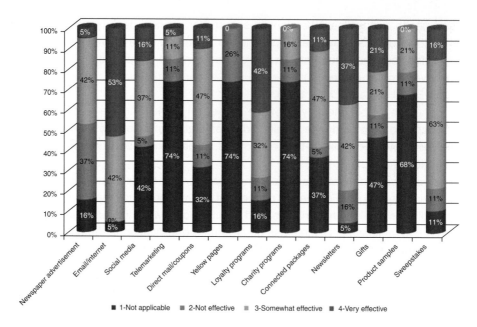

FIGURE 17.1 Effectiveness of marketing channels

manicure/pedicure (10 per cent), fitness services (9 per cent), children's animation (8 per cent), beauty treatments (8 per cent).

The survey's intention was to map the effectiveness of the marketing channels used in relation to returning guests. The data is exhibited in Figure 17.1. The percentage of returning guests is 41 per cent and the most loyal age group is 31–40-year-old guests (30 per cent of the returning visitors).

Questions were available to map the purchasing channels within the wellness and spa sector. The most popular purchasing method is the direct sales of the manufacturer's sales agent where the second purchasing place is the wholesale store. The products purchased are selected based on the following preference list: price, manufacturers' brand name, availability, warranty and liability.

The study aimed to detect computer utilisation within the spa and wellness sector. Based on the returned surveys only 41 per cent of the respondents use any spa software within their spa department, 15 per cent use paper-based registers, 4 per cent use paper and software parallel and 7 per cent have no adequate register method within their facility.

Conclusion

The results of the pilot benchmarking study clearly demonstrated, that there is plenty of room for improvement for Hungarian wellness and spa service providers. The biggest deficiency is the management and business attitude that should be improved at a fast pace to meet the expected customer service level and profitability with the wellness and spa service providers of developed countries.

CHAPTER **18**

Comparative analysis of health tourism products and online communication of selected Hungarian spas and hotels

Krisztina Priszinger and Katalin Formádi

Introduction

Health tourism in Hungary can be marked as the leading tourism sector: the government highlighted the so-called health industry as the most prominent growth sector. This means that the health industry is earmarked for improving employment and economic growth, further improving the competitiveness of the country.

Hungary's health tourism supply is based mostly on its significant geothermal facilities (medical and thermal water); however, other natural resources are notable as well (medical mud, medical climate, medical caves). It is important to mention that since the beginning of the twenty-first century the preventive sector (wellness) of health tourism has been more and more prominent, and even medical wellness has appeared.

Similar to international trends, health tourism products are categorised according to four types of suppliers:

1   spas;
2   wellness hotels;
3   health resorts/institutes;
4   day-spa suppliers/wellness/health centres.

The first two groups are measured: according to statistics there are around 243 different spas in Hungary (that means that every thirteenth Hungarian settlement has some sort of spa); and every fifth room is in a health or wellness hotel. However there is no exact statistical information on the latter two groups; that is the number of health resorts and day spas are hard to estimate.

Methodology

This case study focuses only on the first two groups: spa and wellness hotel services and their online communication activity related to product development.

Wellness hotels can be found all over Hungary, but half of them and the biggest capacity are concentrated on the Western-Danubian region and in Budapest. Except in the Northern-Plain region, in all Hungarian regions there is at least one wellness hotel with a capacity of minimum 400 guests (Ács and Laczkó, 2008).

The sampling method was based on non-probability method and we selected the suppliers according to their importance in Hungarian demand. All of them are at the top of the Hungarian health tourism supply; the researched hotels have their own wellness centre and are forerunners in new offers and packages. We analysed five important Hungarian wellness hotels and five spas (as shown in Table 18.1).

The research was based on small-scale internet-based document analysis. Besides the examined hotels and spas' own web pages, we collected information on the offered products provided by the www.termalfurdo.net spa collecting web page; furthermore the health and wellness hotels' supply were analysed on the www.wellneshetvege.hu, www.wellness.co.hu web pages, as well.

The main research questions were the following:

1   Who are the target groups? Are they clearly identifiable by the online activity?
2   What are the highlighted products of the supplier? Are there any niche-products?
3   How do the examined hotels and spas use social media in their online communication process?

Findings

Target groups

Hungarian spas usually target a wide range of segments. The National Health Tourism Development Strategy (2007) summarises the main target of health tourism as the 25–50-old market who are travelling with friends and families. Single visitors or spa-goers without

TABLE 18.1 Analysis of Hungarian spas and wellness hotels	
Spas	Hotels
Spa of Sárvár	Spirit Hotel *****
Spa of Bükfürdő	Lotus Therme Hotel & Spa *****
Hévíz	Saliris Resort Spa & Conference Hotel ****superior
Spa of Debrecen (Aquaticum)	Thermal Hotel Visegrád ****superior
Spa of Hajdúszoboszló (Hungarospa)	Velence Resort & Spa ****superior

children are more common in health tourism. The National Health Tourism Development Strategy identified that the younger generation are seeking entertainment or regenerating water elements (using beauty and fitness services as well), while the older segment are using the healing water services and the complex health and/or wellness packages. They identified eight target groups in the strategy as follows:

- active young people who spend their holidays actively: they prefer entertaining and sport services, not necessary to have thermal baths;
- young people searching for entertainment: they prefer entertaining services, aqua parks, water slides, etc.;
- health-conscious young people: they are interested in beauty or relaxing packages, not only fitness programmes;
- middle-aged families searching for entertainment;
- middle-aged people focusing on health prevention;
- health-conscious older generation: seeking healthy packages;
- visitors needing rehabilitation after a medical surgery or treatment;
- sick people having medical treatments.

Nevertheless these groups can disturb each other if they are in the same area, for example families with small children (who want to have a good time), regenerating and recuperating guests and recovering seniors. Many spas realised the different needs of various target groups, therefore product diversification is necessary. In order to accomplish it, they are making important investments to enable guests to have the best time possible.

Products and packages

Our aim was to identify which type(s) of health tourism are reflected in the examined hotels and spas' offers and whether these products and packages are segmented according to the target groups.

1   Spirit Hotel covers much of the spectrum of health tourism: The supply is based on the hotels' own medical water spring that is used in medical therapies and medical wellness as well. Leisure and recreation services cover beauty treatments, sport and fitness facilities and pampering services. Guests can choose from 13 packages that are composed either from different services (like Spirit Winter Magic or Spirit Love) or focused on one point (like Spirit Derm or Spirit Stress-free Days).

2   Lotus Therme Hotel & Spa is the most exclusive hotel in Hévíz. The services of the hotel pamper all of the senses of the guests to balance body and soul. There are 24 different massages, from 'simple' body massage to massage rituals. The beauty services are highlighted as well. The hotel offers packages for the guests mostly in the field of therapies (like Lotus to Discover), (medical) wellness (like Lotus Wellness) and sport activities (Like Golf).

3   Saliris Resort Spa & Conference Hotel offers mostly leisure and recreation packages and some medical therapy packages. A speciality of the hotel is the wine from the area, but it is used as a gastronomic service, not for wellness treatments. The hotel offers mostly two–four-night packages with different focuses (like salt or wine) and offering fitness facilities in all of them. Packages with longer (7/14/21 nights) stay are medical therapies alone.

4   Thermal Hotel Visegrád is connected to Lepence Spa and offers the services of the spa as well; it is hard to make a distinction. Only a few classic packages (accommodation + other service(s)) are available in the hotel: guests can choose from four packages with different conditions – the difference is in the nights (from two to seven nights). The packages combine the pool, sauna and fitness facilities of the spa, plus a defined pampering service (mostly a type of massage).

5   Velence Resort & Spa offers a wide range of services with a day spa and services 'for him' as well. Guests can choose from many medical wellness treatments, like Reiki massage or Ayurvedic massages. The fitness activities have the trendiest services, like squash or speed fitness. The hotel is family-friendly, so some packages focus more on kids than wellness services.

Table 18.2 summarises the products and packages offered by the examined hotels. The numbers next to the hotels in brackets relate to the number of available packages, showing the diversity of offers.

The situation is a bit different in the case of the spas. The spas offer individual services and in some cases day packages (entrance tickets combined with health and wellness services and food and beverages).

1   The spa of Sárvár is one of the biggest and most famous spas of Hungary, targeting all generations and motivations but offering separate facilities. There are some pre-composed packages in the spa's offer, but guests can match the wide range (massages, medical therapies, beauty therapies and fitness facilities) of services according to their needs.

Bükfürdő is the geographically closest competitor of Sárvár and has more or less the same supply. In this spa the focus is rather on medical wellness services. Guests

TABLE 18.2 The spectrum of health tourism in the examined hotels

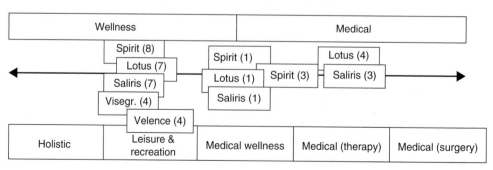

TABLE 18.3 The spectrum of health tourism in the examined spas

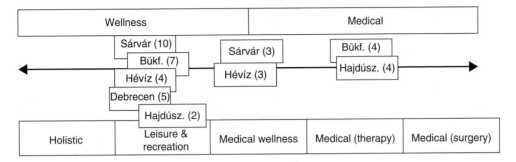

	Wellness		Medical	
	Sárvár (10)	Sárvár (3)	Bükf. (4)	
	Bükf. (7)	Hévíz (3)	Hajdúsz. (4)	
	Hévíz (4)			
	Debrecen (5)			
	Hajdúsz. (2)			
Holistic	Leisure & recreation	Medical wellness	Medical (therapy)	Medical (surgery)

can combine services according to their needs, but they can buy medical treatment packages (one/two/three weeks long) or leisure and recreation packages as well.

2 The spa of Hévíz is the most prominent spa of Hungary, with an unusual situation: it is a traditional medical spa, a modern wellness supplier, a hospital and a hotel together. In this case study we research the so-called *tófürd* (medical spa) part. Here, guests can purchase a separate ticket to the spa (lake) plus traditional medical (physiotherapy) treatments and medical examination (as part of medical wellness). The spa offers combined packages also, where entrance ticket and relaxing services (like massage and sauna world) are combined.

Aquaticum in Debrecen is a complex supplier as well. The Aquaticum does not offer packages for the guests; they are allowed to mix services. However, the hotel connected to the spa combines accommodation mostly with the relaxing and leisure services. As a free possibility, (only) hotel guests can buy the packages of the spa, like luxury or 'for him' packages.

3 The Hungarospa is called the biggest spa-complex in Europe. In the traditional spa part Hungarospa offers a very wide spectrum of traditional therapeutic services as well as four medical therapy packages. The Aqua Palace offers many individual services in fitness, beauty, massages, as well as some relaxing facilities as well, but as a complex product, the suppliers provide only two packages.

In the case of spas, the keywords and values in the online communication are fairly similar, though hotels seem to vary more. The formerly mentioned product-developing strategy of the spas is highlighted in values and keywords, for example trustworthiness and tradition in the case of medical treatments, recreation and rejuvenation in wellness, family-friendly and family-centred services, multi-generational offer.

Languages

All researched websites are available at least in English and German, while many suppliers include Russian, Czech and Polish, as well. This is important, as many Central and Eastern Europe guests are not able to communicate in English or German. Unfortunately the content of foreign language websites are superficial: mostly only the opening-hours and the price-list are available on spas' web pages, while hotels communicate more content (some of the services, packages, hotel facilities).

Photos

In the case of spas we can find mostly photos of an empty pool or guests using treatments and other services. Hotel websites show on one hand generic hotel rooms, treatment rooms or check-in desk with models, but on the other hand the occurrence of uplifting photos is higher.

Social media

Most of the hotels and spas have a Facebook profile, but the use of it differs among spas and hotels. Hotels are in closer contact with guests than spas and they are more active – they post more times weekly and respond more often to the comments of guests. We can determine that all suppliers use this facility as a direct communication channel to the potential and existing guests: they share actual news, actions, games, or even the time-table of trainings or treatments.

Unfortunately, suppliers use YouTube rarely and sporadically, although there are some image-films or shorter advertisements, and many guests upload their own film on YouTube as well.

Summary

In our pilot research based on the content analysis of the chosen wellness supplier's web pages and online appearance we attempted to identify if the whole spectrum of health tourism is covered. Generally the examined hotels and spas are strong in their wellness offers; however, medical products are less common.

CHAPTER 19

Sleep therapy
A case study from Tervis Medical Spa, Estonia

Inna Bentsalo

According to the Better Sleep Council's third annual stress and sleep survey from 2005, women identify getting a good night's sleep as their priority for personal wellness. Twenty-seven per cent of them believe that sleep is more important to wellness than eating a balanced diet (24 per cent) and exercising 30 minutes a day (19 per cent). The poll shows that women are failing to get the sleep they need and for them sleep is also a priority to ensure the optimal health and happiness which shows that the quality of sleep and health is related to quality of life (Better Sleep Council, 2011). Sleep experts point out that good health means good sleep and high alertness. Sleep loss takes its toll on mood, energy, efficiency and ability to handle stress. Too little sleep can affect the ability to think properly and respond quickly, also compromise health, energy balance and ability to fight infections. Not only is the quantity of sleep important but also the quality of sleep. Some people sleep eight or nine hours a night but do not feel well rested when they wake up because the quality of their sleep is poor.

Most people do not get enough sleep. Nowadays people have lives where they stay up long nights working or having fun. However, going without adequate sleep carries with it both short- and long-term consequences. In the short term, a lack of adequate sleep can affect judgement, mood, ability to learn and retain information, and may increase the risk of serious accidents and injuries. In the long term, chronic sleep deprivation may lead to a host of health problems including obesity, diabetes, cardiovascular disease and even early mortality. The most damaging effects of sleep deprivation are from inadequate deep sleep. Deep sleep is a time when the body repairs itself and builds up energy for the day ahead. It plays a major role in maintaining health, stimulating growth and development, repairing muscles and tissues and boosting the immune system in order to wake up energised and refreshed.

The diagnosis of sleep disorders (e.g. insomnia) is based on a thorough history, physical examination and the results of several tests. A polysonmogram monitors the client's electrophysical responses during sleep. It includes such measurements as brain wave activity, muscle movement and extraocular eye movements (Valfre, 2001).

Sleep therapy

The term sleep therapy is related to a treatment that induces sleep in order to treat various medical disorders. In its simplest form, sleep therapy can be viewed as a treatment by rest required by situations that promote fatigue. Sleep therapy may also involve the inducement of sleep by medications and drugs, the use of hypnosis, or the application of electrical current, which has been termed electrosleep, electronarcosis or electroanesthesia (Thorpy and Yager, 2001).

There are several ways to treat sleep disorders; it depends how serious they are and how much medical care is needed. In serious sleep disorders such as OSA, narcolepsy and insomnia, people should find help from the sleep specialist just to know what kind of therapy is necessary. Other sleep disorders that are not so serious and do not disturb a person's everyday life are easier to treat – people can find help on the internet, books or they also have the opportunity to visit a special sleep centre or a spa hotel that has a sleep specialist on site. More and more medical spa hotels are providing services that help to reduce sleep disorders and are specialised in promoting the quality of sleep.

Sleep therapy at the Tervis Medical Spa, Estonia

Sleep study has existed in the world for about 40 years and in Estonia for the last ten years. During the Soviet period sleep diagnosis in Estonia was absent and it was only mentioned in medical or physiological fields and subjects. The first sleep study was performed in Tartu University Sleep Clinic in 1998.

Tervis Medical Spa has provided professional spa treatments for more than 37 years and is a three-star medical spa, the biggest spa in Estonia. Tervis Medical Spa has a Sleep Centre, but it is not owned by the spa hotel. Instead, the rooms for the Sleep Centre are rented by a senior researcher of sleep medicine. Therefore Tervis Medical Spa has no information about the Sleep Centre on the web page or in its brochures.

I collected data from questionnaires of 429 Estonian and foreign (e.g. Russian, Finnish, Swedish, Latvian and Norwegian) guests to Tervis Medical Spa who visited the spa for health or cure reasons. Most of the respondents were 51 to 61 years old (43 per cent), 32 per cent were 62 to 72 years, 15 per cent 40 to 50 years old, 6 per cent 73 years or older, 3 per cent were between 29 to 39 years old and 1 per cent aged 18 to 28 years. She also carried out interviews with the senior sleep therapy doctor and her assistant in the Sleep Centre of Tervis Medical Spa, a sleep therapy specialist in Kubija Nature Spa, sales and marketing director, chief doctor and spa manager of Tervis Medical Spa.

In the first part of the questionnaire the enquiry about the quality of sleep showed that most of the responders (28 per cent) in Tervis Medical Spa who came to the spa for cure or treatment evaluated their quality of sleep as good, which means that usually they have no problems with sleep but sometimes have trouble falling asleep. Twenty-two per cent of the respondents evaluated their sleep quality as very good, which means they have no problems with falling asleep and sleeping. Twenty-one per cent were of the

opinion that their sleep quality is sufficient but sometimes they have repeated waking during sleep. Twenty per cent chose the answer 'from time to time I sleep badly' and 9 per cent marked the answer 'I have suffered from sleep disorders for a long time'. Twenty-seven per cent answered they feel sleepiness during the daytime less than once a month, 25 per cent chose 'never or not more often once a month', 17 per cent were of the opinion that they feel daytime sleepiness every day or almost every day, 16 per cent feel it one–two days a week and 15 per cent feel sleepiness during the daytime three–five days a week.

I wanted to know if the customers knew about the existence of the Sleep Centre in the spa mentioned above. Most of the respondents, 60 per cent, answered 'no', 18 per cent chose the answer 'yes, I have heard about it but I would like to get more information', 12 per cent answered they know about the Sleep Centre in Tervis Medical Spa and they have also done a sleep study there and 10 per cent know about it but have never been there. Most of the respondents – 54 per cent had not participated in sleep studies but they would be interested in doing so, 29 per cent were of the opinion that they have no reason to do it, 12 per cent had participated in a sleep study in the Sleep Centre of Tervis Medical Spa, and 5 per cent had participated in a sleep study in other Sleep Clinics or Centres.

I wanted to know how successful the Tervis Medical Spa Sleep Centre has been so far. In the sleep therapy doctor's opinion the Sleep Centre has been successful because it was available in a health spa and the convenience of it being in a spa environment has significantly raised its popularity.

I also wanted to find out what a sleep package would look like or what kind of spa treatments should it contain. The feedback revealed the possibility of having a spa package consisting of a sleep study with sleep conducive spa services in Tervis Medical Spa. This kind of package can definitely have potential; however, also depends on the creation of the package and logistics of it as well as the final price.

The doctors could help sufferers of conditions which affect sleep quality by recommending a sleep promoting spa service. For example, patients could benefit from a physiotherapist who has knowledge of restless legs syndrome and incorporates it in a therapy. It is very important to know what suits the patient or client best as some people need more stimulating baths on the other hand others need relaxing baths. Another significant element is to offer quality nourishment and it should consist of special vitamins, juices, and so on. Music therapy in a spa would also be good. The rooms of the spa could have special bed and sheets that help the guest sleep better (special material that warms the body and helps to promote falling asleep). The specialists agreed that the sleep package should consist of spa services such as massage (head, body, legs, and arms), baths, light therapy, salt chamber, music therapy (blues), acupuncture and different water procedures. I would suggest the following example of a four-night sleep package.

First, obtain a consultation and good recommendations from the senior researcher of sleep medicine or sleep specialist. Try up to three different sleep-improving procedures and spa treatments per night of stay from the following list as recommended by the senior researcher of sleep medicine (according to experts' opinions the customer should not take more than three spa treatments a day):

- music therapy such as blues or other calming music tones, light therapy, salt chamber;
- relaxing or stimulating bath (according to senior researcher of sleep medicine recommendation), underwater shower massage, mud therapy, warming ozocerite paraffin for shoulders, neck or feet;
- Swedish massage (all body massage, head massage, leg massage or hand massage);
- Nordic walk, stimulating morning exercise, training activities or workouts in the gym;
- spa and sauna centre (aroma sauna, salt sauna, infrared sauna, steam sauna, Japanese bath, swimming pool);
- healthy and delicious breakfast, lunch, dinner and a relaxing good night's tea in the evenings;
- accommodation in a comfortable single room (or double room if preferred).

In future Tervis Medical Spa will be a spa specialising in different disorders, therefore specialists are interested in developing new services or packages and sleep therapy would be a good opportunity to look into. On the other hand, there are some points that would need to be discussed with the Sleep Centre senior researcher of sleep medicine. The sleep specialists are considering combining sleep study or sleep therapy with spa services to see if it would be interesting, but it is also important to have the right equipment, professional staff and capabilities to ensure the security and quality for the client. Also a booklet about sleep study, sleep therapy and cure in Tervis Medical Spa would be necessary to develop because there is no information about it at all.

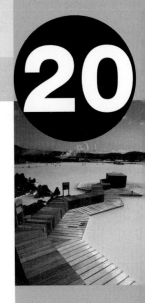

Benefits of higher education to the international spa industry
A UK perspective

Kathryn Dowthwaite and Sarah Rawlinson

This case study outlines the curriculum design model used by the University of Derby that places equal emphasis on learning that takes place in the workplace and learning that takes place in the university, which includes learning in specialist spa facilities. Research at the University of Derby (Rawlinson, 2012) found that students on spa management degree programmes are better prepared for industry when their degree programme teaches them how to apply their knowledge in a spa context. The dominant logic of the model is that learning must be contextually focused and the teaching and learning strategy must include teaching students to transfer concepts and theories into practice. This then dictates that the teachers need to provide the strategies to affect that process. The central concept of the curriculum model is a sharing of knowledge between the university and industry.

The spa industry has experienced considerable growth in recent years. Indeed the Global Spa Summit (2010) stated that the spa industry was worth $60.3 billion annually. The future of the spa industry is predicted to develop and expand; research from Global Industry Analysts (GIA) forecast that the global spa market will be worth US$77.2bn by 2015 (Professional Beauty, 2012). More specifically the United Kingdom's spa industry is worth $15.3 million. Alongside this exponential growth is the perception that there is a lack of skilled, experienced managers available within the spa industry to meet the growth in demand. This shortage of spa managers, and a lack of management training, were reported as the main obstacles to the successful growth of spa businesses worldwide (GSS, 2008, 2011). Moreover, the spa industries evolution, growth and globalisation has fragmented and complicated the skills required of spa managers. Dependent upon the location, type and size of the spa the skills required of spa managers/directors vary considerably. Dowthwaite (2012) discovered that the nature of the skills gaps for these global spa managers included business acumen, leadership, financial understanding, people connection, experience and practical practitioner skill and an understanding of spa philosophy.

The development of spa management in higher education started at the University of Derby in 2001 with the validation of the BSc in International Spa Management. This was the first programme of its kind in the world and was developed to meet the growing demand for spa managers in a sector where a specialist graduate labour market did not exist. Today there are approximately 4,000 spa degree students worldwide, with an estimated 130,000–180,000 spa management jobs available (GSWS, 2012a). The numbers of spa graduates is, therefore, not keeping pace with the demands of the spa industry which already poses a challenge for the sustained growth of the spa industry.

The challenge in understanding the expectations and capabilities of spa graduates could be due to a lack of communication between the spa industry and universities (Dowthwaite, 2012). Many spa degrees are under-resourced and are perhaps undervalued by the industry (GSWS, 2012a). The majority of spa employees 'work their way up' in the industry, which poses challenges with some current managers understanding and accepting spa degree graduates. Less than 20 per cent of spa industry leaders are able to name a university that provides a spa degree (GSWS, 2012a). Whilst the academic benefits of higher education are often acknowledged, employers seek a combination of skills and attributes that include generic management skills, alongside specific vocational skills (Little et al., 2003). According to Rowley (2000, cited in Little et al., 2003: 27) the hospitality sector, for example, are 'suspicious of "college learning" and have a clear preference for work-based training and relevant experience rather than formal education'. This approach could also apply to the spa industry where employers value experience over qualifications (Dowthwaite, 2012). Degrees offered at universities that have an emphasis on concepts and theories that are not sufficiently contextualised are therefore challenged for not providing the kind of graduates sought by industry. Brown and Hesketh (2004) and Kember and Leung (2005) suggest that employers are concerned that young people leaving colleges and universities often lack the knowledge, commitment and business awareness. Crebert et al. (2004) argue that the transition from university to employment can bring insecurity and unease which can be misinterpreted by the employer as a lack of, or poor preparation for, the workplace by the university. Crebert et al. (2004: 48) suggest that there is an

> assumption that universities are responsible for equipping graduates with all the skills and knowledge necessary for the work-place and ignore, for the most part, the employer's responsibility to enculturate and even train the new graduate for the demands of postgraduation employment.

It is evident that the key principle for the success of spa management degrees appears to be the notion of a shared responsibility between the university and the workplace. The model proposes a new structure for vocational degrees in partnership with industry where the dominant logic is focused on the context where knowledge is applied. The recommendation from research conducted at the University of Derby (Rawlinson, 2012) was that curriculum developers should consider ways to share the epistemology of work-based learning and learning at university and bring together work-based and procedural knowledge used in work with the concepts and theories learnt within the university. This sharing

of knowledge between the workplace and the university can be scrutinised and provides the student with the opportunity to analyse their learning outside its context in classes with academic staff and to re-contextualise their independent learning back in the workplace. This shared epistemology provides students with the opportunity to engage in active learning (Moore, 1998; Boreham, 2004) and what Portwood (2007: 16) refers to as 'pragmatic philosophy' and develops a culture of learning that values knowledge gained from active engagement in the workplace (Teare, 1998).

Smith et al. (2007) established that students found the challenges of transferring their knowledge considerable. The transferability of concepts, theories and generic skills is particularly interesting in the context of spa graduate employment. Star and Hammer (2008) highlight that to truly master knowledge the emphasis on what is taught and how it is taught in universities must shift from the traditional focus on 'content' to one which emphasises 'process': what graduates can do with knowledge.

The capabilities needed for a knowledge-based society are best developed through active engagement in learning, though Kember and Leung (2005) argue that this type of learning is not commonly found in higher education. A number of universities, however, have sought to achieve this through 'realistic working environments' providing students with spa facilities within which to gain and develop procedural knowledge. Increasingly, universities have moved away from this model, which is resource intensive and expensive to operate. However, according to research conducted at the University of Derby (Dowthwaite, 2012) the spa industry requires spa managers to have prior experience of business concepts combined with practical skills.

The future success of spa degrees in universities will rely on curriculum development that includes work-based learning and can demonstrate that graduates have the procedural knowledge required by employers. This will only be achieved when the whole curriculum is based within a framework of 'real world' learning and includes an integrated approach from the stakeholders, namely academics, students and employers.

The curriculum model used at the University of Derby is focused around a £1.2 million commercial spa facility that students manage and the time spent learning in the spa allows students to apply the concepts and theories learnt in the classroom with the procedural knowledge used in a work context. Students can consider and reflect on the practices learnt in the context of the spa in the classroom and re-apply new ideas back into the spa context. This sharing of knowledge between the classroom and the spa, and the re-contextualising of knowledge in different situations teaches students how to transfer their knowledge from the classroom to the workplace. Research conducted with spa graduates at the University of Derby (Rawlinson, 2012) evidences that they have the necessary commercial awareness and business acumen for a successful career in the spa industry including a combination of good procedural skills and management and leadership qualities.

In examining the perceived value of the knowledge gained in the University of Derby International Spa Management degree, employers participating in the research reported that they measure the benefits of higher education by the quality of the graduates they employ. They also measured the content of the degree programme by the knowledge and skills graduates bring to the workplace. Employers and graduates participating in the research placed a great deal of value on work process knowledge and the ability of graduates to bring together their academic and procedural knowledge in the workplace. Graduates participating in the research also had a good understanding of how knowledge relates to practice and the whole work process. The research concluded that the spa management degree produces graduates that have a good personal knowledge and can make a contribution to new knowledge in the workplace because their degree provides them with a good insight into the whole work process and develops dispositions of inquiry, critical thinking and problem solving. Although employers attached less importance to academic credentials and an increasing importance to personal attributes, enthusiasm, skills, competencies, self-confidence, and the knowledge needed in the workplace, the spa management degree provided graduates with these attributes. The balance between developing competence and developing capability meant that spa graduates were making a difference to businesses. The research found that spa graduates are demonstrating graduate employment skills recognised by employers and that employers consider these graduates have a positive impact on their business (Rawlinson, 2012).

The research concluded that vocational degrees that develop the concepts of the discipline within the context where they are to be applied are better prepared graduates that can make value judgements in the workplace. The research also concluded that, where spa degrees provide opportunities for students to learn how to transfer propositional knowledge in context, they provide better-prepared graduates for industry.

The fundamental principle of the model is the combination of the following:

- gaining concepts, theories and procedural knowledge within the university and learning to apply it in context in the spa facility;
- gaining concepts, theories and procedural knowledge within the university and learning to apply it within an organisation;
- gaining procedural knowledge within an organisation and re-contextualising it within the university;
- gaining work-based knowledge through an organisation, contextualising the knowledge in the workplace and re-contextualising the knowledge within the university.

CHAPTER 21

Labour and compensation structure of the spa industry in Canada

Marion Joppe

Introduction

Labour is generally paid in the form of wages, salaries, commissions and bonuses, or a combination thereof. In addition, workers may receive any variety of benefits – ranging from health/dental insurance and pension plans to employee and dependent life insurance to long and/or short term disability – and perquisites, which are particularly prevalent in the different branches of the tourism industry. Some employees are actually independent contractors, paid a fee for services, even though they may only work for one company. In the spa sector, we can actually find all of these work arrangements, sometimes even in the same business!

This chapter will provide a detailed look at the spa sector in Canada's most populous province, Ontario, based on the information provided by the 25 members of Premier Spas of Ontario. This association is committed to creating a superior standard of spa service through member accreditation, professional development, industry advocacy, and public education. The accreditation process covers a 200+ item inspection of facilities, treatments and personnel certification. Annual revenues for these spas range from a low of $153,000 to a high of $9.3 million with a mean of $2,032,147 and a median of $1.5 million. Permanent full-time staff to operate the spa businesses ranges from a low of 2 to a high of 115, with a mean number of employees of 25 and a median of 13. Permanent part-time employees range from a low of two to a high of 74 with a mean of 12 and a median of seven. Lastly, seven spas reported taking on between two and 20 seasonal staff. To provide a more meaningful comparison of annual revenue between large and small operators, part-time and seasonal employees were converted to permanent full-time equivalents at the rate of 2:1. Thus, on a per employee basis, annual revenues ranged from a low of $33,682 to a high of $164,705 with a mean of $73,106 and a median of $69,924.

Salaries, hourly wages and gratuities

Spa workers fall into four different categories of position, most with a fairly large number of sub-categories: front line, professional/service staff, supervisory/management and executive. Full-time employees work anywhere between 25 and 60 hours per week, while part-time employees work less than 25 hours per week. In addition, many spas also call on registered dieticians, nutritionists and medical doctors, but it is relatively rare for these professions to be permanently attached to the business.

There is a great range in the type of compensation used for various positions, from hourly to annual, commission only, fee for service only or a combination of any of these. Indeed, the complexity of some of the compensation arrangements is such that it is very difficult to provide a comprehensive understanding of total earnings by job category. In some instances, the same occupation may even be remunerated in several different ways, for instance some on hourly wages and others on commission.

The majority of front-line positions receives hourly wages, although spa concierges/receptionists, host/hostess and cooks may also be salaried. Where spa concierges or receptionists receive commission in addition to their wage, this is 10 per cent on products/retail sales, whereas commission in addition to salary ranges from 2–9 per cent on sales.

Registered Massage Therapists (RMTs), Alternative/holistic therapists and aestheticians see the greatest range of types of compensation and combination of remunerative packages. Where RMTs are on commission, this can range from 40 to 60 per cent on services, generally speaking after the cost of products has been deducted, depending on experience and length of tenure. In some cases, RMTs may also receive from 10 per cent to 20 per cent on product sold. RMTs remunerated on a fee for service basis receive $32–$50/service or 30–50 per cent of the cost of service after a service fee or product costs have been deducted. Where the remuneration includes an hourly wage or annual salary, the commission is often limited to 8–10 per cent of products sold. Alternative/holistic therapists have similar arrangements, although generally speaking their commission or fee for service is significantly less than that of RMTs. Where aestheticians are on commission, this can range from 30 to 45 per cent on services, generally after the cost of products has been deducted. If commission is paid in addition to a wage or salary, it tends to be in the range of 8–20 per cent on products. Very few spas will also pay a modest percentage of the treatment cost. In a number of instances, commission on retail is not paid until a minimum monthly amount has been sold by the employee.

Typically, supervisory/management staff are paid an annual salary, but in some instances, particularly if the employee is on an hourly pay basis, they may also receive a commission in the range of 10–20 per cent on products and/or services for spa managers/team leaders and up to 40 per cent for salon managers/team leaders. Only in the smallest spas do executive directors receive hourly pay, however the salary drawn depends on whether the spa director is also the owner or has an ownership stake in the operation.

TABLE 21.1 Hours and salaries of spa employees

Front line		Mean # of hours/week	Mean salary	Mean hourly wage
	Spa Concierge/Receptionist – full-time	38.8	$26,500	$12.71
	Spa Concierge/Receptionist – part-time	17.5		$12.71
	Host/Hostess – full-time	37.5	$38,250	$11.41
	Host/Hostess – part-time	17		$11.41
	Cook	N/A	$37,250	$11.00
	Bartender/Barrista	35		$10.58
	Food & Beverage Server	36.5		$10.45
Professional/ service staff		**Mean # of hours/week**		**Mean hourly wage**
	Registered Massage Therapist – full-time	33.1		$22.30
	Registered Massage Therapist – part-time	17.9		
	Alternative/holistic Therapist – full-time	36.3		$14.33
	Alternative/holistic Therapist – part-time	21.3		
	Esthetician	31.1		$13.26
	Hair Stylist	39.5		$11.06
	Assistant	37.0		$9.35
Supervisory/ management		**Mean # of hours/week**	**Mean salary**	**Mean hourly wage**
	Spa Manager/Team Leader	40.7	$48,639	$19.02
	Assistant Spa Manager/ Team Leader	36.0		
	Salon Manager/Team Leader	45.0	$47,250	
	Food & Beverage Supervisor		$36,000	
Executive/ owner		**Mean # of hours/week**	**Mean salary**	
	Spa Director	44.9	$71,460	

Many of the workers, particularly some of the professional/service staff, also receive gratuities. Since these are at the discretion of the client and given directly to the employee, it is not possible to know to what extent incomes are supplemented in this way. Gratuity splitting is not a common practice in the spa sector. Hours worked per week and wages or salaries earned have been averaged out to allow for a more meaningful comparison between the levels and the sub-categories.

Bonus, incentive and benefit programmes and work arrangements

For the most part, only larger spas and/or those attached to a larger hotel or resort are able to offer extensive bonus, incentive and benefit programmes. Professional/service staff followed by supervisory/management employees tend to have the best bonus and incentive programmes. Particularly popular are those incentives that impact directly on sales and the quality of the services rendered. Some bonuses are linked to meeting or exceeding budget projections, particularly at the executive or management level.

Thirty-nine of Canadian tourism businesses offer no bonus or incentive programmes to their staff, a level that reaches 60 per cent for front-line workers. This is in stark contrast to the spa sector where only about 16 per cent do not offer such programs. Only at the executive/owner level do we see 60% not providing performance bonuses. Sales bonuses and commissions as well as professional development opportunities or advanced training are the most prevalent at all levels of the organisations. About 40 per cent of the spas also distinguish between short- and long-term incentives. Short-term incentives are designed to reward an individual for performance over a period of one year or less, for example, performance or merit bonuses. Long-term incentives are for performance over a period of more than one year, for example stock options.

Only 28 per cent of spas do not offer any benefits. This, too, compares favourably with other businesses in the tourism industry where 38 per cent of organisations do not provide any benefits. The larger the spa, or where the spa is associated with a larger property such as a hotel or resort, the better the benefit package tends to be. Extended health/dental care and life insurance are the most prevalent benefits. However, where benefit programmes are provided, these are not necessarily fully paid for by the spa business. The percentage covered ranges from 50–100 per cent with a mean of 84.6 per cent and a median of 90 per cent.

As in other sectors of the tourism industry, attraction and retention of qualified staff is a constant challenge. Therefore, many organisations make a concerted effort to provide an attractive work environment. Treating all employees fairly and providing a safe workplace are considered the most important human resource practices overall. Due to the nature of the spa business, allowing flexible work hours is the practice that received the lowest rating, although some spas are creative in providing increased flexibility to staff, for instance by allowing its salaried staff to devise their own schedule, taking into account the business' needs and a full 50-hour work week. However, many businesses will offer

additional perquisites, and by far the most popular one is employee discounts on services. Executives and management level employees tend to benefit from a greater assortment of perquisites than do either the professional staff or front-line employees. Where spas are located within or in proximity to a hotel or resort, more perquisites are offered, especially the use of onsite fitness centres, or participating in social evenings.

CHAPTER

Joining together and shaping the future of the global spa and wellness industry

Susie Ellis

Background

A defining moment in the development of the modern spa industry was the launch of the Global Spa Summit (GSS) in 2007 and its subsequent name change to the Global Spa and Wellness Summit (GSWS) in 2012. Until that time there was no global entity – or gathering – for those interested in spa, wellness and tourism – but this Summit changed that.

The gathering that has become known as the GSWS was started by a group of ten industry visionaries who found themselves at a spa conference together in Singapore in 2005. Lamenting that there was no gathering for senior executives and no gathering for a global focus on spa and wellness, they decided that it would be a worthwhile effort to start one. This group used, in part, the very successful format of the World Economic Forum as a model to develop its own conference. When it came to funding the first event, entrepreneur Pete Ellis, Chairman and CEO of SpaFinder Wellness, stepped up to declare that he would take the risk and front the money for the first gathering. They organised themselves with Peter as CEO and Chairman of the board and the others from the initial group of ten becoming board members. While the initial vision was simply to create a once-a-year global event, in time the success of the GSWS allowed it to consider branching out into other areas of contribution.

It was decided to hold the first Summit in New York in May 2007. The idea from the beginning was for the Summit to tackle issues that could be better accomplished together than by any one individual person or company. The motto of 'Joining Together. Shaping the Future' was adopted. Everyone who attended was asked to 'take off their competitive hat' and contribute ideas on how to make progress for the industry in general.

The landmark 'global spa economy report'

One of the first orders of business that became obvious at this first gathering was to engage a respected research firm to take on the daunting task of looking at the entire spa market globally and estimating figures that could give a solid picture of what the industry looked like. SRI International (founded as Stanford Research Institute) was engaged to take on the challenge. They were asked to define the industry and give us figures that could help stakeholders understand the market. The resulting report delivered that – and more. It became a landmark study that suggested a very broad definition for the term *spa*. Having taken an inclusive approach, their definition allowed for other categories and segmentation by type, cultural traditions and such, underneath this broader definition: 'Establishments that promote wellness through the provision of therapeutic and other professional services aimed at renewing the body, mind and spirit.' The report estimated the number of spas in different countries as well as their annual revenues and estimated numbers of people employed. It also identified core spa industries, spa enabled industries as well as associated industries and attached revenue figures to each. This spa industry cluster became known as the 'Global Spa Economy'. This is the chart that was published in 2008 that became the first global picture of the spa economy worldwide.

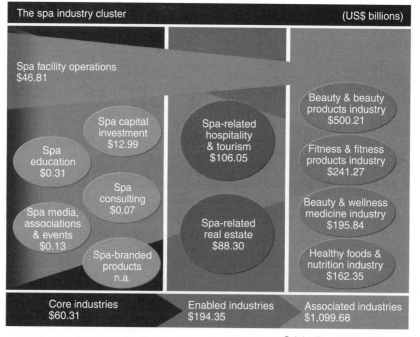

Originally published in 2007

FIGURE 22.1 The spa industry cluster

Source: Global Spa and Wellness Summit (2008).

GSS Summits

In 2009 the Summit was held in Switzerland including a student competition titled 'The Spa of the Future'. This Summit proved to be a useful framework for subsequent Summits as all would be held in different parts of the world, include pre and post-Summit excursion options as well as student competitions. The GSS started becoming known by various governments showing interest in hosting a future Summit in their country. The 2010 Summit location was decided based on an invitation by the government of Turkey. That year's Summit theme, 'Bridges Worth Building', put a spotlight on the value of reaching out to other industries, countries and businesses to strengthen the spa industry. This Summit attracted the largest delegation to date with 40 different countries represented.

'Spas and the Global Wellness Market: Synergies and Opportunities' research report

The research presented that year was once again conducted by SRI International. It sought to examine the spa industry in light of the burgeoning arena of wellness that was increasingly being discussed around the world. The research report quickly became

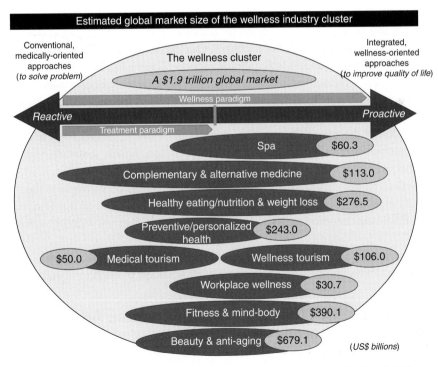

Originally Published in 2010

FIGURE 22.2 The wellness cluster

Source: Global Spa and Wellness Summit (2008).

known as the definitive work that traced the term *wellness* from its early roots – the first study to do so. The following chart explains what SRI International introduced as the Wellness Industry Cluster.

The Summit was held for the first time in Asia in 2011 with the theme of 'Engage the Change: The Customer. The Money. The Future.' It explored new ways to engage with consumers, enter new markets and embrace new technologies. The world's first online portal dedicated to the medical evidence that exists for spa and wellness therapies, Spaevidence.com, was unveiled. Dr Ken Pelletier, Dr Daniel Friedland and Dr Marc Cohen. Nader Vasseghi and his company, SelfOptima, designed a portal that made it possible for a lay person to easily find the actual medical studies that supported – and in some cases didn't support – many of the spa and wellness therapies on spa menus around the world.

In addition, a landmark research report exploring the differences between wellness tourism and medical tourism and where spas fit was also presented.

'Wellness Tourism and Medical Tourism: Where Do Spas Fit?' research report

This first rigorous exploration of *wellness tourism* and *medical tourism* as two distinct concepts and markets was presented in this study. It included information from the results of a survey of consumers and industry professionals, case studies from 12 countries around the world, and recommendations for governments and businesses. The research report was a joint effort between four parties: Katherine Johnston, a senior economist who had worked on the previous SRI International reports, Susie Ellis, President of SpaFinder, Inc., László Puczkó, managing director and head of the tourism section at Xellum Ltd, and Melanie Smith (PhD) a lecturer, researcher and consultant from Corvinus University of Budapest. Dr Puczkó and Dr Smith were authors of the book *Health and Wellness Tourism* (the first edition of the current book). The diagram in Figure 22.3 presented a visual way to look at various entities in this market spectrum of spa, health, wellness and medical establishments.

As a result of its own research and the increasing emphasis on wellness in the industry and marketplace, the Summit board decided to modify the name of the Summit. As a result, the GSS was renamed the Global Spa and Wellness Summit (GSWS) at the beginning of 2012.

The Summit that year was held for the first time in collaboration with another organisation, the Aspen Institute. The event's theme was 'Innovation through Imagination'.

'Spa Management Workforce and Education: Addressing Market Gaps' research report

That year's research addressed an issue that delegates had been saying was one of their top challenges year after year – a shortage of well-trained management and staff. The industry's robust growth year after year had necessitated a look at possible solutions. The research was once again conducted by SRI International.

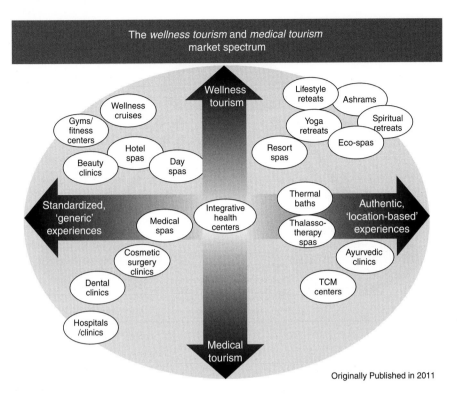

FIGURE 22.3 The wellness tourism and medical tourism market spectrum
Source: Global Spa and Wellness Summit (2008).

Not only did the report examine reasons behind a worldwide lack of qualified management; it also provided some very useful recommendations to close the talent gap. The diagram in Figure 22.4 shows the three key stakeholders identified and summarises suggested interactions.

The 2013 Global Spa and Wellness Summit took place in New Delhi, India under the theme 'A Defining Moment'. This Summit, for the first time, dedicated its first day to a Global Wellness Tourism Congress as well as speciality forums that made it possible for groups with specific interests to gather and discuss topics uniquely of interest to them. These forums have expert leaders who shape their own agenda. The idea is to give various interest groups a chance to look more closely at what they might be able to accomplish together that would not be easily accomplished individually. Forums on the agenda for 2013 included: Ancient Healing Traditions Forum, a Global Destination Spa Forum, a Global Corporate Responsibility Forum, a Global HydroThermal Forum, a Global Spa Education Forum and a Global Spa Retail Forum.

In addition the 2013 gathering hosted, for the first time, a Global Wellness Tourism Congress that brought together thought leaders, government officials as well as private entities to collaborate on a definitive direction for wellness tourism. In addition SRI produced a global wellness tourism economy study that sought to define the wellness

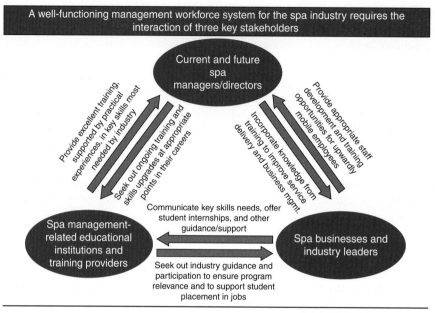

Originally Published in 2012

FIGURE 22.4 Spa industry stakeholders
Source: Global Spa and Wellness Summit (2008).

tourism cluster and industry segments; identify the size of the various markets; look at the share of the overall tourism industry that wellness tourism plays; explore the economic impacts of wellness tourism including multiplier impacts and job-creation impacts; as well as project future growth of the global wellness tourism market.

Final thoughts and future vision

From its debut in 2007 the Global Spa and Wellness Summit has been a tireless contributor to the growth of the modern spa and wellness industry. Over time it has more formally developed its mission statement and objectives as follows: the Global Spa and Wellness Summit endeavours to live up to its mission as an international organisation that brings together leaders and visionaries to positively impact and shape the future of the global spa and wellness industries.

Objectives:

- to establish a forum for dialogue among global industry leaders;
- to create community by fostering friendly relationships among stakeholders;
- to inspire a spirit of collaboration to solve shared problems;
- to facilitate healthy growth for the industry and its individual businesses;

- to initiate and support quality research;
- to encourage innovation;
- to cultivate leaders for tomorrow.

Along the way some principles have emerged as key contributors to its broadening reach and impact.

Transparency and accessibility have been two key developments. While the Summit is invitation-only so that it attracts top executives who want to meet with peers, it was soon decided that the speeches, presentations, panel discussions and especially its research was simply too valuable to limit its access. Thus over time it was decided that with the support of sponsors everything would be made available to everyone – for free.

The GSWS website, www.globalspaandwellnesssummit.org, has become a popular hub of information designed to make myriad resources available that help strengthen the industry. These resources include: a comprehensive list of and links to all the research commissioned by the Summit; links to various spa and wellness research conducted by others around the world; a listing of spa and wellness associations globally; a listing of spa management education programs around the world; a list of spa and wellness publications for both consumers as well as trade; and an aggregation of country specific briefing papers written each year by delegates attending the Summit that give a grass-roots look at the industry in their country that year.

On the drawing board are additional website sections that will include an aggregation of standards and practices documents from various organisations and countries around the world; the development of a section on metrics that will eventually be useable for benchmarking; as well as a section dedicated to the various philanthropic endeavours in which spas and wellness establishments are engaged.

Involvement in social media is continual and ongoing and includes a blog, regular posts on Twitter and Facebook as well as a private Facebook group for use by alumni with likely additions in the future. In 2012 the GSWS launched a weekly newsletter called the GSWS Weekender. Its purpose was to reach more people than just delegates who participate in the Summit.

The amount of energy and support behind the Global Spa and Wellness Summit since its inception has been tremendous. It is likely, therefore, that its growth and influence will continue. In addition new opportunities are anticipated that will help it carry out its commitment to 'Joining Together. Shaping the Future.'

Health tourism destinations

CHAPTER **23**

Wellness tourism development in Slovenia in the last two decades

Sonja Sibila Lebe

Introduction

Slovenia is rich in thermal water sources. Some of them had already been discovered in Roman times. Healing based on thermal water has remained the core theme for millennia. This chapter will present the development in the last two decades, since political changes in Central Europe replaced the communist economy system with the market economy.

Research question and methodology

This chapter aims to analyse five topics regarding the development in three chosen Slovenian thermal spas during the last two decades. The research is based on semi-structured interviews undertaken with general managers in autumn 2012. All three organisations have in the past been classical thermal spas. The majority of visitors (about 80 per cent) were patients/convalescents, sent to the spa by the medical insurance company. After 1991 they started renewing their programmes by adding wellness elements into their range of services.

The same four questions were put to all three managers and they were asked to briefly elaborate on them. These questions were:

1. What has changed for your enterprise during the process of the core business transformation (health spa to wellness)?
2. How has the share regarding domestic and foreign visitors developed in the last two decades, and what is the present ratio between medical patients (convalescents) and wellness/leisure guests?
3. What do you consider your main unique selling proposition (hereafter USP)?
4. What are your future plans in the field of wellness development?

Case study from Slovenia: health spa resort development in the last two decades

Slovenia has 20 thermal sources that are commercially used by thermal spas. Until 1990, 80 per cent of guests were coming automatically as direct referrals (insurance company contact). After that, thermal spas had to find the major part of their business on the free market. This meant a complete re-thinking and re-designing of their businesses. They had to start thinking like entrepreneurs, and had to establish marketing departments that were in charge of researching the market trends and attracting leisure visitors.

Looking for alternative business challenges, they have decided to add wellness to their existing orientation. Thermal spas seemed to be the ideal place for developing such an offer: thermal water, one of the basic elements of pampering in the wellness offer was available on the spot in all health spas, as well as medical services. To become successful in this regard, a lot had to be changed in Slovenian health spas, beginning with infrastructure.

Between 1995 and 2010 all Slovenian spas renewed their swimming pools, upgraded and sometimes enlarged their accommodation facilities, and added wellness programmes to their classical health spa (and thus medicine based) offer. Consequently new segments of guests joined the traditional convalescent ones. Soon it became clear that the expectations of these two segments were usually diametrically contradictory. Convalescents were searching for peace and quiet and excellent medical services. Wellness guests on the contrary were looking primarily for pleasure, leisure and enjoyment, and only secondarily for medical support. Hotel managers recognised that the two segments needed to be spatially separated, as neither of them felt good if mixed. Insurance guests on the one side were often using crutches to get into the dining room, dressed in a bathrobe. They were often feeling uneasy when looking at how, on the other side, wellness guests seemed to be overdressed, wearing nice evening clothes and expecting to have fun dancing and socialising with other wellness guests – without being reminded of illness (by looking at convalescents).

Today all Slovenian thermal spas have a segmented offer. The vast majority of guests (60 up to 100 per cent) are wellness guests, living in supreme quality hotels (4 star, 4 star superior and 5 star). Medical insurance guests are accommodated in lower graded hotels (3 star). Both segments still have one common denominator: they all wish to consult a doctor to be sure to get the most convenient and individually fitted treatment.

Radenci Health Resort

Everything in the Radenci Health Resort is based on its thermo-mineral water, being the most popular one in Slovenia. Having a gentle taste, the water is ideal for preparing refreshing beverages. It is being exported to all continents – this being known far beyond national borders is a mighty selling support for the enterprise.

In the last two decades, the ratio between convalescent and individually paying guests has radically changed. From the traditional share of 80 per cent on convalescent and

20 per cent on free market guests they now have a 15 to 85 ratio. Remaining loyal to its health spa tradition, this resort offers excellent medical services to its guests. They are known for top-level diagnostics, for using predominately non-invasive medical examination methods, and for having top-level medical staff who offer physiotherapeutic and curative medical treatments. All treatments are supported by thermal water programmes and by adding pampering and if possible recreation elements to the individually designed schedule for every guest.

The competitiveness of the Radenci Health Resort is based in their 'going back to the roots' paradigm. They are building their USP on four natural factors available on the spot: first, thermo-mineral water; second, sweet water mud; third climate and environment, consisting of (a) friendly people, (b) local heritage, including great gastronomy and wines, and (c) green and well preserved nature (the Radenci Health Resort is also known as a bioclimatic spa, with more than 250 sunny days a year); and fourth, highly skilled and technically perfectly equipped medical personnel.

The national backgrounds of the guests are very diverse, showing a clear prevalence of international guests. The resort management intends to foster this trend by penetrating new international markets (especially the Middle East). Their vision is clear: offering their rich experience and high professionalism in medical wellness to individuals and insurance companies abroad who wish to profit from first-class services by paying for them remarkably less than in West European countries. Their motto for the future is: 'Enable the ageing European society to retain their autonomy even in advanced age by permanently taking part in medical wellness programmes.'

Olimia Thermal Spa

The Olimia Thermal Spa is – by Slovenian standards – a relatively young player, founded in 1960. Located far from any big city, and very close (8 km) to Rogaška Slatina, a well-known thermal spa resort with centuries of tradition, they are aware of their location's disadvantage. They have consequently decided to anchor their USP and their point of differentiation in two elements deriving from local uniqueness. The first one is their unique thermal water, and the second one is the use of herbal treatments; with them, the spa is building on the tradition of the nearby Olimje Monastery, which houses the third oldest pharmacy in Europe (herbal medicines are available there).

Today the Olimia Thermal Spa is known as a fine wellness centre. Besides this principal pillar, they have established a spatially separated offer for youth, young families and sport teams: a popular aqua-park, placed far enough from the core spa facilities not to interfere acoustically with guests who wish to relax in peace and quiet.

As huge investments into enlarged infrastructure (hotels, wellness areas, recreational areas and pools) were not running to capacity, additional programmes have been introduced. Beside services for typical wellness guests, the Olimia Thermal Spa is now inviting sport teams to have training camps there. This was crucial for the low season. The next step was development of conference and congress facilities. Before starting the renewal of their offer, the thermal spa had a ratio 80 to 20 regarding domestic and international visitors. Today's ratio is 45 to 55, with the rapidly growing share of international visitors. Today 40–50 per cent of income derives from wellness business, and only 10 per cent from health programmes. The rest are contributions of sport and congress programmes.

Although the Olimia Thermal Spa is a small player in Slovenia, it is one of two thermal spas that have been successful in transferring knowledge abroad. They have invested in a ruined Tuhelj Health Spa in nearby Croatia, which is now following a similar development concept as its parent company. Being a relatively small player, this spa will never compete with mass tourism programmes therefore they are concentrating on individually created high quality wellness services. In view of the rapidly ageing European population they intend to re-foster their medical programme and develop a new offer aimed at the 60-plus segment.

Sava Rogaška Hotels

Sava Rogaška Hotels are one of three major tourism players in the Rogaška Slatina Health Resort, one of the oldest and once best-known health spas in Europe. Today's providers are building on the place's rich tradition based on more than 400 years of curing and pampering visitors with their unique magnesium-rich thermo-mineral water. Drinking this water (exported to practically every country in the world) is the core of any cure in Rogaška Slatina.

The Sava Rogaška Spa was one of the first ones in Slovenia that developed a wellness centre (2000/2001). It was a wise decision that let the enterprise enter the international spa market. The first guests to discover their enriched offer were guests from Austria, followed by guests from Italy that constituted 80 per cent of all foreign guests in 2008. Today, feeling the consequences of the financial crisis on the Italian market, the most important group of international tourists are guests from Russia (45 per cent), followed by Italians (25 per cent) and Israelis. The rapid changing of markets was connected with intense investments into the knowledge and skills of their employees: they had to learn the culture and at least some basics of the Italian and Russian languages.

They are lucky regarding the demand, as all major nationality groups are asking for similar types of services: medically researched beauty wellness. The motivation is clear: anti-ageing using high-tech devices. Massages – their main product still five years ago – have become a secondary product. These mechanical anti-ageing treatments are often combined with non-invasive aesthetic surgery, for example botox and minor cosmetic surgery. The nearby Medical Centre Rogaška is their crucial business partner, offering first-class diagnostics and excellent medical treatments thanks to their top-level staff and equipment. Beauty- and weight-loss programmes under medical surveillance are their two bestsellers. They are intending – like most thermal spas in Slovenia – to build their future competitiveness in the field of medical wellness. Having great results in international markets, they will start sourcing markets in the Middle and Far East (China and remoter parts of Russian Federation).

Conclusion

All Slovenian spas and thermal health resorts presented in this chapter can be seen as wellness services, yet with clearly differentiated programmes. They all intend to compete in the future with services based on natural resources (thermal or thermo-mineral water and natural environment) and in training their staff to be able to deliver the highest quality in highly specialised services. All of them intend to stick to their medical tradition but to combine it with their wellness services – some of them even intend to convert back to the status of a health resort resulting in a predominantly medical orientation of their services.

Sources

Interviews (all in November 2012) with:

- Mr Mladen Kučiš, general manager of the Radenci Health Resort
- Mr Zdravko Počivalšek, general manager of the Thermal Spa Olimia
- Mrs Nataša Pšeničnik-Goričan, general manager of the Sava Rogaška Hotels in the Rogaška Health Resort

CHAPTER 24

Wellness and spa provision in the Silesian health resorts of Poland

Andrzej Hadzik, Dorota Ujma and Sean Gammon

Health tourism has been researched in Poland for a number of years. Forty-five places in Poland have approved status of a health resort, 70 others may potentially join the group in the future (Stowarzyszenie Gmin Uzdrowiskowych RP (Association of Health-related Communities in Poland) website, 2013). The health and wellness tourism industry is represented by 160 destination spas compared to 146 in 2010, with value sales increased by 9 per cent to PLN 2.0 billion in 2011 (Passport GMID, 2012).

This case study focuses on some of relationships between wellness, spa and health and travel to health resorts. It focuses on the Polish region of Silesia (Polish: Śląsk), a region of Central Europe located mostly in the south-west of Poland, with smaller parts in the Czech Republic and Germany. It presents two of the Silesian health resorts, Ustronie and Goczałkowice, and reports on the findings of a short research project undertaken there. The aim of the project is to establish the importance and perception of preventative pro-health services offered and their quality as seen by the visitors in the two selected Silesian spas.

The history of health tourism in Poland

Ciszewski (1988) points out that the history of 'travelling to the waters' in the area of Poland as it is today is obviously not as long as in the Roman Empire, but nevertheless it is many centuries old. For example, the Slavs utilised the power of nature and 'folk medicine' to cure many ailments, and similarly to their Mediterranean counterparts, often observed the behaviour of fauna to guide them in their treatments. One of the legends mentions the Polish King Bolesław Kędzierzawy (Bolesław the Curly Haired, ruling c. 1125–73) who when encountering a wounded deer whilst hunting observed the animal bathing in a thermal spring in the wilderness to heal itself.

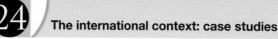

A description of one of the first curative therapies in Poland is mentioned in relation to Judyta, the wife of the Polish Duke Władysław Herman in the eleventh century. Judyta used mineral baths as a fertility treatment – apparently an effective one, as the following King Bolesław Wrymouth (Polish: Bolesław Krzywousty, 1086–1138) was born soon after (Ciszewski, 1988).

The first written confirmation of the existence of thermal springs (Polish term *cieplice*) dates back to the twelfth century and is linked to the Polish Sudety Mountains. Cieplice Śląskie (Silesian Cieplice) are briefly mentioned in 1137. Later on health resorts of Cieplice-Zdrój and Lądek-Zdrój (where the add-on 'Zdrój' means 'spa'), Szczawno and Lądek are also listed. The location of these resorts indicate that in the thirteenth and fourteenth centuries the Polish villages which developed health-related functions originated in today's region of Lower Silesia (Kowalczyk, 2001).

In the sixteenth and seventeenth centuries the list of better known spas, specialising in 'healthy waters' in Poland, grew. Later, in the nineteenth century the most popular spas became Busko-Zdrój, Krynica, and a number of seaside resorts, including Kołobrzeg, Świnoujście and Sopot also became popular (Kowalczyk, 2001; Dryglas, 2005).

However, it is in the twentieth century that the on-going scientific development of balneology and medical treatments in the Polish health resorts truly flourishes. It is at this time that the dynamic of spa development changes, with more emphasis placed upon the destinations with a better climate and bathing facilities. It became fashionable to get involved in thalassotherapy (a therapeutic treatment that involves bathing in sea water) which was combined with various forms of active recreation and sport activities. This trend introduces another change in the nature of the health resorts; the curative services became more limited, whilst the recreational services and sport activities started to develop quickly.

At the end of the twentieth century quite a few spas actively marketed their health-enhancing services, targeting not only the 'patients' paid for by the Narodowy Fundusz Zdrowia (the National Health Fund, the Polish national health insurance organisation), but also customers buying these services independently and privately. Krasiński (1998) identified that the paying customers' needs differed from the regular patients in that they were searching for a holistic set of preventative offerings, leading to an improvement of a 'psychophysical condition' as well as their beauty and overall well-being.

Preventative health services offered in the Silesian resorts of Ustronie and Goczałkowice

In the Silesian region, Ustroń and Goczałkowice-Zdrój are examples of health-resorts with a state-approved status. Both belong to a category of the 'mud poultice spa'. The natural medicinal resources that Ustroń boasts include thermal waters (chloride-sodium-calcium; bromide and iodine of 28°C) and medicinal moor (peat). Based on the natural resources, treatments are directed at orthopaedic ailments and traumas, rheumatism, problems with nervous system, upper respiratory tract, cardiac, blood peripheral system and obesity.

The visitors hope to benefit from climate therapy, heliotherapy (sun therapy), aerotherapy (air therapy) and kinesiotherapy (movement therapy).

Goczałkowice-Zdrój is located in one of the warmest regions in Poland. The health resort is known a 'mud spa', where the salt waters are predominantly used in treatments that rely on a host of differing elements such as chloride – sodium, bromide, iodine, iron-based (ferruginous) and boric. The quality of local deposits of mud is claimed to be the best in Poland. Medicinal treatments are recommended to visitors with movement problems, rheumatism, respiratory illnesses, neurological problems in adults and children, orthopaedic and gynaecological diseases.

Customer perceptions of preventative health services in Ustronie and Goczałkowice

In June and July 2011, a random sample of 200 visitors in these health resorts were contacted in a diagnostic poll. The respondents were there either as tourists on holidays (leisure motives), or as patients/health tourists (health motive). The questionnaire consisted of 14 questions related to the services offered in the health resorts and an additional seven questions about the respondents themselves. This case study only focuses on the questions related to the perceived expectations of the pro-health offerings and their assessment after the services have been received. In both cases the scale used varied from 0 (lowest importance/assessment) to 5 (highest importance/assessment). Table 24.1 shows results of a statistical analysis based on 150 fully completed questionnaires.

The offerings of the Silesian health resorts were presented in 17 groups, as suggested by the list of standardised health-resorts treatments (Wykaz Standardowych Procedur Uzdrowiskowych, e-kurorty website 2012), and covering a wide spectrum of services – from health treatments, through sporting activities to wellness and beauty offerings. Initial findings indicate that the visitors to Goczałkowice and Ustroń rated highly kinesiotherapy (4.62), massages, balneotherapy (mineral water treatments) (both at 4.05), whilst herbalism, psychotherapy, pharmacological treatment and health education were rated the lowest (range 1.6–2.4).

It is interesting to note that the initial expectations/importance of the majority of categories seem much lower than the actual post-delivery assessments of received treatments. Low importance of the leisure and wellness treatments may be connected with the 'newness' of these types of offerings in the Polish health resorts, where the curative system had dominated the scene for a number of years (Szromek, 2011). Whilst in the past mainly the medical/curative aim was addressed in these health resorts, the current richer sporting and leisure offerings may have moved the balance towards other forms of health tourism, such as beauty treatments, longevity through active lifestyle and relaxation techniques. So far, the visitors are still focusing on the core health-restoring services of spas, rather than active lifestyle and leisure activities. Visitors also know that national sanatoria have specialised in health-related services for centuries in some cases, so the assumption is that their quality must be higher, than in the newer, leisure-based offerings.

TABLE 24.1 Pre-delivery importance and post-delivery assessment of the quality of the health-resort tourism services offered in the Silesian health resorts of Ustroń and Goczałkowice

No.	Type of the provision/service/therapy	Importance	Post-delivery assessment
		0 (Lowest importance/assessment) – 5 (Highest importance/ assessment)	
1.	**Balneotherapy with mineral water-based treatments**	2.13	4.05
	salt water baths	3.79	4.45
	carbonic acid baths	3.00	4.11
	sulphide baths	2.74	4.00
	radon baths	1.28	4.00
	aromatic baths	1.77	4.13
	inhalations of mineral water	2.16	4.13
	irrigation of body cavities	0.80	4.00
	mouth rinse	1.48	3.60
2.	**Balneological treatments using therapeutic mud**	2.23	3.45
	mud baths	3.34	3.89
	mud poultice treatment	3.43	3.89
	sitz baths	1.38	3.25
	peat suspension baths	1.98	3.13
	peat poultice	2.03	3.38
	mud tampons	0.98	3.17
	ionophoresis peat bath	2.47	3.50
3.	**Balneotherapy with medicinal gases**	1.98	3.11
	CO_2 baths (carbon dioxide baths)	1.85	3.14
	oxygen-ozone baths	1.81	3.00
	hydrogen sulphide baths	2.29	3.20
4.	**Climatotherapy**	2.48	3.05
	thalassotherapy	2.51	3.20
	thermotherapy	3.29	4.20
	sub terrain treatments (treatments received in ex-mines chamber after the excavation of salt and uranium ore)	2.02	1.80
	aerozol inhalations	2.12	3.00

5.	**Hydrotherapy**	2.30	3.25
	full overheating baths	1.44	3.00
	varied temperature baths for legs	2.24	3.13
	constant temperature baths for legs	2.40	3.13
	warm baths	1.42	2.88
	sitz baths	1.31	2.86
	kinesitherapy baths	1.71	3.14
	under water massage	3.40	3.60
	bubble bath	3.75	3.83
	whirlpool	3.37	3.78
	showers/douche	3.01	3.56
	crenotherapy/rinsing	1.29	2.83
6.	**Thermotherapy**	2.80	3.35
	warmth therapy	2.52	2.86
	Finnish sauna	2.37	3.38
	cryotherapy	3.52	3.82
7.	**Phototherapy**	2.25	3.22
	irradiation with visible light/exposure to	2.20	3.11
	UV exposure	2.40	3.55
	polarised light irradiation	2.14	3.00
8.	**Ultrasonoteraphy**	2.88	3.75
	ultrasound	3.08	3.67
	phonophoresis	2.68	3.83
9.	**Electrotherapy**	2.53	3.74
	galvanisation	2.29	2.83
	iontophoresis	3.13	3.75
	baths with electricity	1.61	3.86
	electrodiagnostics	2.08	3.80
	electric treatments/shock treatments	2.93	3.86
	magnetotherapy	3.15	4.33
10.	**Massage**	2.47	4.05
	partial	3.49	4.40
	classic	3.49	4.60
	segments of the body	2.61	4.11
	pneumatic	2.19	4.00
	lymphatic massage	2.32	4.00

(Continued overleaf)

TABLE 24.1 Continued

No.	Type of the provision/service/therapy	Importance	Post-delivery assessment
		0 (Lowest importance/assessment) – 5 (Highest importance/assessment)	
	Chinese massage	1.88	4.00
	Hawaian lomi-lomi	1.74	3.75
	Thai massage	2.00	3.50
11.	**Kinesiotherapy (therapy by movement)**	3.73	4.62
	individual exercises in sport halls	3.75	4.40
	individual exercises in water	3.81	4.70
	group exercises in sports halls	3.58	4.60
	group exercises in water	3.77	4.78
12.	**Diets**	2.21	2.77
	low fat	3.18	3.20
	low carbohydrate	2.05	3.10
	vegetarian	1.41	2.00
13.	**Leisure, sport and beauty treatments/ offerings (wellness)**	2.04	2.58
	outdoor thermal swimming pool	2.77	3.71
	indoor thermal swimming pool	3.49	4.20
	outdoor swimming pool	2.87	3.29
	indoor swimming pool	3.57	4.00
	sauna	2.62	3.38
	Jacuzzi	3.01	3.50
	solarium	1.30	3.13
	tennis courts	1.58	3.00
	golf	1.28	3.33
	indoor fitness activities	2.60	3.71
	bowling alley	1.73	2.80
	salt chamber	3.11	4.86
	a beauty parlour – face treatments	1.46	2.67
	a beauty parlour – body treatments	1.20	1.50
	dancing	2.56	2.63
	pool table	1.62	2.00
	darts	1.36	2.00

	aerobics	2.06	3.14
	yoga	1.67	2.50
	other relaxation techniques	1.51	2.80
	acupuncture	1.42	1.00
	Ayurweda	1.40	0.50
	shiatsu	1.23	1.00
	tai chi	1.57	1.33
	volleyball	1.82	3.00
	football	1.15	1.00
	lowland hiking	3.00	4.38
	mountain hiking	2.48	3.78
	sailing	1.14	1.67
	kayaking	1.31	0.00
	Nordic walking	2.92	4.00
	walks	3.83	4.54
	bicycle tours	2.93	2.60
	cross-country skiing	1.27	0.33
	downhill skiing	1.39	0.33
	horse riding	1.32	1.25
14.	**Phytotherapy research/herbalism**	1.48	1.60
15.	**Psychotherapy**	1.75	2.17
16.	**Pharmacotherapy/pharmacological treatment**	1.60	2.14
17.	**Health education**	2.41	2.43

Summary of wellness services and spas in Poland

It appears that Polish literature views spas and health resorts as popular destinations with a number of protected natural on-site sources (e.g. mineral or thermal water), offering contact with nature resulting in some improvements in health and well-being. Polish spas tend to be functional, utilitarian and regimented in their delivery; where 'improving health' is achieved through basic, traditional treatments, connected with a specific locale. Moreover, there is a belief that just staying within the spa environment is beneficial; that improvements to health and well-being occur simply by 'being there'.

In contrast to Western facilities both the quality of facilities together with customer orientated service is not expected to be of a high standard. In Western Europe the connection with nature and natural resources, along with its perceived effectiveness of related treatments, is less prevalent and so is of less importance. The philosophy and customer approach of Western 'spas' are often founded in gentle encouragement towards healthy living through often exotic and luxury treatments which take place in random premium settings (Hadzik et al., 2010). At the moment the visitors to Goczałkowice and Ustroń are relatively satisfied with the services on offer, but the health resorts researched in this case study need to build on the quality of their preventative treatments and extend the wellness products.

History, traditions and the recent trends in the spa industry in the Czech Republic

Alexey Kondrashov

Today the spa industry is considered to be one of the fastest growing industries in the Czech Republic. The recent economic downturn had a significant impact on the tourism sector; however, it lasted a relatively short period and the upturn started in 2010 and sustained through 2011 and 2012. In 2012, 37 spa towns or health destinations with more than 88 balneological care facilities and 108 spa hotels existed in the Czech Republic. In 2011 spa tourism indicators in the Czech Republic continued to improve reaching 5.4 per cent growth in tourist arrivals (711,000) and more than 48 per cent were foreigners. The most visited was the Karlovy Vary region with 427,000 spa guests (Statistical Office of the Czech Republic, Spa Statistics, 2012).

Traditionally Czech spa facilities offer balneotherapy, which involves complex drinking and bathing therapies based on the use of mineral spring waters, peloids and natural gases. The country possesses a great number of healing assets: spa mineral and thermal waters, mud, gas, and climatic resources. These curative agents have been used for therapeutic treatment for centuries and gave rise to the foundation and development of towns around these springs.

Mineral waters have been used for therapeutic purposes since the beginning the twelfth century, as the oldest spa city of Teplice was established on the north-western part of the Czech Republic. Carlsbad (Karlovy Vary), the second oldest and the world famous spa town, was established in the mid-fourteenth century by the Bohemian King Charles IV, when the healing properties of thermal water springs located in this area was made known to him (Burachovič and Wieser, 2001).

In the sixteenth century doctors started to advise patients to drink mineral waters as a so-called drinking cure. The increase in popularity of drinking cures during the sixteenth and seventeenth centuries may be considered as a turning point in the development of Czech spa medicine. This is due to the specifics of geological characteristics of the terrain of the Czech Republic, where the most predominant are cold mineral water springs and only the north-western part of the country possesses hot thermal waters that could be found only in Teplice and Carlsbad. The lack of other thermal water sources was an obstacle in the development of the spa industry. The success of drinking cures in the treatment of various disorders attracted great interest in investigating the healing properties of mineral waters too. Since the eighteenth century mineral waters underwent chemical analysis in order to justify their healing properties.

During the nineteenth and the beginning of the twentieth centuries most of the well-known spas and spa cities were built. The spa town of Frantiskovy Lazne was established in 1793 and the Marianske lazne spa resort was established in 1808 (Burachovi and Wieser, 2001). Czech spa towns have distinctive architecture, beautiful colonnades in Carlsbad and Marianske Lazne, and the splendid spa buildings and hotels are surrounded by gardens and parks. These became world famous spa destinations that attract tourists for both spa treatments and entertainment. Carlsbad become famous for its 12 thermal springs used in the treatment of gastroenterological disorders as well as joint and back pain. Marianske Lazne with its 40 springs of cold mineral water has became a destination spa offering a wide range treatments such as urological illnesses, locomotive system disorders, respiratory and metabolic disorders (Czech Spas and Balneology, 2007).

In 1822 Doctor Priessnitz built up the first hydrotherapeutic sanatoria in the world. Today it is known as Priessnitzovy Lazne and is located in the north-east of the Czech Republic. Priessnitz is generally considered as the founder of modern hydrotherapy and he also introduced climatotherapy. He also proposed water-cures. In 1906 a new spa town of Jachymov was developed in the Western Bohemia region, which was the first spa in the world to offer treatments with radioactive radon waters.

During the nineteenth and the beginning of the twentieth century, spa stays were no longer considered as just a form of treatment, but became a hallmark of social status. Spa towns became centres of social and cultural life due to numerous visitor attractions such as casinos, theatres and colonnades. Nature as an indispensable component of spa towns was also recognised as a healing agent (e.g. parks, walking paths). By the beginning of the twentieth century more than two hundred healing mineral water springs were found in the Czech Republic (Křížek, 2002). Even in Prague there were four mineral water springs that today are no longer in use.

Fortunately most spa towns were not destroyed during the two World Wars. From the late 1940s a new period began in the spa industry in the Czech Republic. Most spa facilities were nationalised and the state governed their development. The function of spas was changed. State social and health policy was focused on offering stays in spas to the masses and considered spa complexes as an important factor for restoring the ability of citizens to work (Speier, 2011). The spa complexes were expanded and modernised, as well as new spa complexes including spa hotels being built in many spa towns. Accommodation facilities in spas offered the standard set of services in order to satisfy the basic needs of visitors. The stays in spa facilities were funded by the state by means of trade unions, and national medical insurance.

Spa medicine became a central branch of rehabilitative medicine with the key role of the Ministry of Health, which regulated therapies, indications and duration of stay for the patients as well as the quality of water at mineral springs. During that period spa complexes

in the Czech Republic become highly specialised on medical treatments and rehabilitation of certain types of disorders with efforts to provide their services to the greatest number of visitors (Jandova, 2009). Before the 1990s there were few foreign visitors in Czech spas and they visited mainly Western Bohemian spas.

The development of balneology and the specialisation of spas was also backed by the Balneology Research Institute, located in Marianske Lazne, which more than forty years (from 1952 until 1993) was focused on studying the nature and effects of healing assets used in spas. Today, the importance of such research institutes has been revived and the Balneology research institute opened in 2011 in the spa of Msene Lazne. State regulation and planning of spa facility development lasted until the end of the 1980s.

Recent trends in the Czech spa industry

The shift to a market environment in the early 1990s brought major changes in the spa industry. In 1990, the Czech Republic had 22 spa operators. In the beginning of the 1990s, spa complexes were privatised, and became joint stock companies. Several big spa complexes were divided into smaller independent facilities.

Today, 37 spa towns or health destinations exist in the Czech Republic. As a result of the Spa Act in 2001, spa town status is granted to settlements, where proven natural healing assets exist. The quality of mineral waters, their healing properties and hygienic conditions of spa facilities are regulated by the Ministry of Health, using a set of standards and they are regularly examined.

Opening the state borders brought hundreds of thousand of foreign clients per year into Czech spa facilities. The Czech spa industry became a new emerging spa destination for foreign visitors, who arrived to enjoy a new destination and combine the advantage of travelling with the benefits of cheaper spa therapies with the same quality as in Germany (Speier, 2011). The competitive advantage of Czech spas is mainly due to their value for money combined with advanced therapeutic and rehabilitative methods and a long tradition of use of natural mineral waters, peloids, natural gas and climate. Good accessibility by different transportation means adds to the popularity among tourists, for example. Carlsbad as the biggest spa town and also as the capital of the Karlovy Vary region has its own international airport, train and bus connection with Prague and other big cities.

The spa industry plays an important role in the tourist industry of the Czech Republic, being a significant source of revenues in foreign currency. For example, according to the Czech National Bank statistics, tourism generated 5.4 billion euros in 2011. According to the Czech Statistical Office, more than 6.8 million tourists visited the Czech Republic in 2011, and more than 711,000 of them visited spas. The numbers of spa visitors are steadily increasing. Destination spas in Western Bohemia (Karlovy Vary region) such as Carlsbad, Marianske Lazne and Frantiskovy Lazne attracted 60 per cent of all spa guests to the Czech Republic. This made Western Bohemia spas the second most popular tourist destination after the capital Prague.

Traditionally in the Czech Republic spa therapy has been recognised as an essential part of the therapeutic process, which is covered by health insurance companies under specific terms. Today, there are two main types of spa therapeutic programmes: complex or contributory spa care. Complex spa care means that health insurance companies cover spa therapy, accommodation and meals. During contributory spa care a health insurance company covers only the costs of spa therapies. Both types of programme last at least three weeks.

During the past two decades spa complexes have adapted to the market conditions and changes in their clients. Today, Czech spa towns offer spa-rehabilitation and wellness complexes most of which were completely renovated, and new wellness centres including swimming pools were built in order to launch new treatments and wellness procedures that meet the growing demands of their clients. The high quality of Czech spa medicine is recognised by the European Spas Association, which awarded several spa facilities with EuropespaMed certificates that insures the high-quality standards of spa premises, management and treatments.

The quality of accommodation in spa hotels adds to the overall image of the destination. From 2004 the Czech Republic participated in Hotelstars an official standard classification of the accommodation facilities that sets uniform quality standards for accommodation facilities in 13 European countries. During the past decade from 2000 to 2012 significant changes occurred in the spa accommodation sector. According to the Czech statistical office in 2000 there were 61 spa hotels in the Czech Republic; among them were no five-star hotels, but there were 21 four-star hotels. By the beginning of 2012 there were 108 spa hotels in total, four five-star hotels and 62 four-star hotels. This development reflects the growing popularity of spa destinations for the luxury segment. The growth in upper-scale spa accommodation was almost 300 per cent (Statistical Office of the Czech Republic, Spa Statistics, 2012).

These trends in the spa accommodation sector are consistent with the dramatic changes in spa clients. During the past 12 years the number of spa visitors has nearly doubled, from 437,000 in 2000 to 711,000 in 2011. The share of foreign spa guests has grown from 26 per cent to 48 per cent for the same period (Statistical Office of the Czech Republic, Spa Statistics, 2012).

Simultaneously during this period, there was a reduction in the spa trips paid for by health insurance companies. In 2011 the situation of spa patients was as follows: private paying foreign patients 37 per cent, health insurance patients 32 per cent and private paying domestic patients 31 per cent (TLT Benchmark Study, KPMG Czech Republic). Despite this, cooperation with the health insurance companies remains important for the spa complexes' positive financial performances for the coming years.

The coordination of activities of spa destinations and spa complexes is carried out by two major associations: the Union of Czech Spa Resorts and the Association of Czech Spa Towns and Municipalities. The Union of Czech Spa Resorts is an interest group of spa resorts and other enterprises without distinction of ownership. Its mission is to develop contemporary methods in balneology as well as utilise the natural curative sources. It represents the interests of the Czech spa operators and the other enterprises engaged in spa business in international organizations such as spa and resort associations (e.g. European Spa Association).

Conclusions

Reflecting recent global trends, Czech spa complexes have gradually shifted their focus from purely medical treatments to generalised relaxing, anti-stress, beauty and anti-ageing packages of therapies. The Czech health tourism industry has managed to retain certain competitive advantages and has developed positively over the past decade. In 2008, the Czech Republic was selected as one of the top ten destinations for health tourism in the world by Forbes magazine. Among the spa destinations in the Czech Republic, Carlsbad remains the most developed and popular spa town. Recently, a World Travel Award in the nomination of the Czech Republic's leading spa resort 2012 was granted to Sanssouci spa resort located in Carlsbad.

CHAPTER 26

Special health tourism products in the Bükk and Mátra regions

Lóránt Dávid, Bulcsú Remenyik and Csaba Szűcs

Introduction

The two largest mountains of the North Hungarian Mountain Range are the Mátra and the Bükk. The Bükk and the Mátra regions have become famous not only for active tourism but also for developing special health tourism products. Special health tourism products include climate tourism, herb tourism and spiritual tourism. The origins of all three tourism products can be traced back to the cultures of the ancient East, and the story matrix attached to them has always had an important role in the development of the products. Their special characteristics stem from the fact that they are designed for a well-defined target group who believe in the healing power of the products and their number is rising year by year in North Hungary.

The development of health tourism in the mountains

In addition to mountain tourism (e.g. skiing, hiking, adventure) health tourism products have also been developed. The large spa and wellness hotels in the Mátra Mountains recommend the Parádfürdő Rehabilitation Hospital as a complementary product for those who intend to improve their health. In Parádfürdő as a result of post-volcanic activities there are chalybeate-aluminous and sulphureted hydrogen acidulous water springs whose consumption help the treatment of metabolic disturbances. Further curative effects of chalybeate-aluminous water in gynaecological treatments have also been proved (chronic inflammation, sterility, pre- and post-treatment of surgical interventions). The treatments provided at the Thermotherapy Health Centre in Feldebrő (A feldebrői Termoterápiás Egészség Központban) aim to re-establish healthy enjoyment of life.

The medicinal gas in the Mofetta in Mátraderecske is a unique treasure of Hungarian balneology as it is suitable for curing vascular and certain rheumatology symptoms. Its radon content is especially effective for the treatment of high blood pressure, the vascular complication caused by diabetes, auto-immune diseases that cause serious vascular symptoms, arthritis, osteoporosis, certain gynaecological diseases, sterility and impotency problems, internal medicine problems originating from the autonomic nervous system.

The hotels situated in the Bükk Mountains expressly recommend the medicinal caves found in the Bükk and in the Aggtelek-karst Mountains, for example the István-cave (length: 350 m, greatest depth: 55 m) in Lillafüred which is situated near Hotel Palota. The microclimate of the Black-chamber of the Szent István-cave in Lillafüred as well as the low environmental stimuli have extremely beneficial effects on people suffering from respiratory diseases (Molnár, 2010). The treatment room, which is suitable for cave therapy, is situated in the Black-chamber and it is closed to tourists. According to measurements the temperature in the chamber is around 10°C but the relative humidity exceeds 80 per cent, the calcium and magnesium content of the aerosol is significant. The dust content as well as the number of bacteria and fungi of the air in the cave is negligible, its radon content is low. The natural ventilation of the chamber is provided by a huge natural funnel.

Climate tourism in the Mátra Mountains

The healing power of mountain climate was recognised even in ancient times and it was used to cure a number of diseases. Currently the most widely known centre for Alpine climate is Davos, the 'Mecca of people with pulmonary diseases' (Dávid et al., 2007). According to the decree of the National Directorate of Curative Places and Spas curative places are the ones that have a recognised natural medicinal factor, the institutional conditions for using these medicinal factors are provided, the environmental conditions for the continuous healing activities and the tranquillity of the patients are guaranteed and infrastructure for relaxation is developed. In Hungary the healing effects of high mountain climate have been utilised for hundreds of years. In the Austro-Hungarian Monarchy the most famous climatic curative place was developed in the Tátra Mountains. After the Treaty of Trianon (when Hungary lost 70 per cent of its territory) only the Mátra Mountains had the right conditions (altitude over 900 m) for medicinal institutions. The effects of the favourable mountain climate can be observed at the Alpine Foothills in the Sopron-Kőszeg-Mountains and in the Bükk Mountain near Lillafüred, which are also climatic curative places.

The healing effect of the Alpine climate manifests itself in the fact that over 900 metres above sea level the air becomes extremely clean (the dust and pollen content of the air drops, even house dust mites cannot thrive at this altitude) and thus it may cure respiratory diseases (asthma, trachitis, dust allergy, coniosis, etc.). In Kékestető atmospheric pressure is 10 per cent less than in lower altitude flat areas and as a result ventilation in the lungs improves by 10 per cent, the number of red blood cells and the haemoglobin content increase, the viscosity of the blood improves which contributes to the successful treatment of anaemia, haemophilia, nervous exhaustion, neurological irritations, neurotic restlessness, Grave's disease, etc.) (Goodrich, 1987). At high-altitude climates the temperature fluctuation is low, relative humidity content, the area, the number of sunny hours,

and the oxygen content of the air are all high, which together will result in increased appetite, which facilitates the curing of metabolic disturbances.

The Mátra Health Resort in Kékestető is situated at 1,000 metres above sea level where patients with respiratory problems and thyroid gland problems are treated. Currently the health resort has 385 beds and a 100-seat conference hall; the number of tourists aiming to improve their health is continuously growing. Recuperation, however, requires substantial changes in one's lifestyle and participation in active and nature tourism has an important role in achieving such goals, therefore the health resort has tennis courts, mini-golf and ski tracks, as well as an ice rink.

The beneficial effects of the climate of the medium height mountain range mountain climate are provable even at the altitude of Mátraháza; this settlement situated at 710 metres above sea level is the home of Hungary's first sanatorium, built in 1932, where people with tuberculosis, one of the dreaded illnesses of the era, were treated. Currently patients with lung cancer and allergy are treated there.

Medicinal herbal tourism in the Bükk

Medicinal herbs are plants which have been used for thousands of years all around the world, their leaves, flowers, fruit, stem and root can be used for embrocation, as well as for making tea, ointment, tincture, dream pillow, ointment, either externally or internally and they can be found easily (Babulka and Kósa, 2003). Hippocrates taught that people can be healed with the help of medicinal herbs, which can play a role in disease prevention as well as in the treatment of heart diseases, blood pressure problems, digestive and metabolic problems, joint diseases and allergy.

Most tourists who are interested in herbal gathering arrive in Bükkszentkereszt in summer though all seasons have their particular medicinal herbs. In winter, roots and mistletoe (*Viscum album*) can be collected; the beginning of the spring is the time to gather barks and rinds as well as medicinal herbs of early flowers (violet, wild garlic, chervil, etc.). Naturally the main season is summer when the following plants are available:

- yarrow (*Achillea*);
- milk rennet (*Galium verum L.*);
- silver-weed (*Potentilla anserina L.*);
- centaury, erythreae (*Centaurii herba*);
- eyebright (*Euphrasiae herba*).

Around Saint Stephen's day (20 August) St John's wort (*Hypericum perforatum L.*), which can be used for a large number of illnesses, can be collected and at the beginning of autumn there are plants like goldenrod (*Solidago gigantea*), tansy (*Tanacetum vulgare*) and mullein (*Verbascum*) (Szendrei-Csupor, 2009). The end of the autumn is the time to collect leaves as well as haw, blackthorn and rosehips.

Even in the middle ages it was the Kingdom of Hungary that provided medicinal plants for Europe; the introduction of these plants can be linked to Benedictine monks therefore its centre at the beginning was Pannonhalma, Tihany and Halimba. In medieval Benedictine monasteries monks carried out not only sacral and secular tasks but also medical activities since the earliest times for which they used their own medicinal plants grown in their gardens. Bükkszentkereszt has by now become the centre of medicinal herb tourism in Northern Hungary. György Szabó, the medicinal herb expert of the Bükk, created his medicinal plant garden at the turn of the second millennia and medicinal herb tourism followed it in 2005 (Szabó, 2004: 79).

Travel agencies advertise three–four-day programmes, and during a 1.5–2 km hike one can become familiar with 120–180 types of different herbs. In 2012 tours were offered seven times a year for a maximum of 25 participants among whom were physicians, pharmacists, and health professionals (Lakatos, 2012). The walking distance is between 2–5 km but further habitats can be reached by car as well. In the teahouse which is situated in the garden guests can also taste the teas and different lavender drinks made according to century-old recipes. One of the most important medicinal herbs in Bükkszentkereszt is the lavender, nevertheless sage, lemon-balm, thyme and peppermint are also grown in the village. Visitors will get an insight into the medicinal herb culture of the past in the teahouse with the help of traditional recipe books and leaflets. Many also visit the lavender-distillery situated next to the medicinal plant greenhouse where visitors are introduced to the know-how of lavender oil making.

It is a long-established common practice of popular piety that on the day of the celebration of Our Lady medicinal herbs are blessed at the end of the holy mass. The medicinal herb days of Bükkszentkereszt are connected to this tradition, and a significant number of tourists visit the village for the medicinal herb week (in 2011 the number of visitors reached 25,000) during which food and drink specialities made with medicinal herbs can also be purchased (Szabó, 2004). A so-called medicinal wine, the Néró red wine, is also sold there; it is made from red grapes and has an outstandingly high resveratrol content and has an anti-inflammatory effect.

Spiritual tourism in the Bükk and Mátra area

In medieval times the relics of saints or a pilgrimage to their shrine triggered miraculous healings (that is how the shrine of Saint Ladislaus became a place of pilgrimage). The link between faith and recuperation is so strong that even nowadays thanksgiving plaques are being placed in the churches situated along the Mary trail (Máriagyűd, Máriapócs) in order to express gratitude for recovery for illnesses.

In Egerszalók, situated in the Bükk Mountain, there are peculiar beliefs about the local medicinal water, namely that the surfacing water created a salt hill. As a matter of fact the 'salt hill' is limestone and the calcium carbonate content of the water is deposited. The Valley of Egerszalók is crossed by energy lines which are thought to activate breathing and have curative effects for gynaecological problems, and is believed to be suitable for the treatment of chronic inflammations and dermatological illnesses.

There are similar energy lines in the Mátra region as well along which miraculous recoveries have been recorded. These recoveries have been explained by individuals

interested in esotericism by the intersection of these energy lines and they think the illnesses themselves are caused by low energy conditions. The links between faith and recuperation are accepted by medical science as well since spiritualism has a psychological effect on people, they believe that they can regain their health which induces favourable processes.

Miraculous recoveries, supernatural occurrences, and visions can often be experienced in these energy centres. The visualisation of the energy lines (by means of boards and descriptions) are widespread in neighbouring countries (Slovenia, Austria) and in Nagyatád, Hungary, an Energy park has also been established.

There is a stupa, a Buddhist religious monument, in Becske, North Hungary. Its popularity has been rising continuously since 2008 (30,000 people visit it annually including the meditation sessions) and this attraction attracts a significant number of (mainly Buddhist) visitors from abroad. The stupa established on an energy line is a cult structure, a symbol of Buddha's teachings and that of the universe. When near the stupa one may just enjoy its presence, one can meditate or walk around it clockwise according to tradition. It is believed that the merits accumulated by walking round the stupa are the equivalent of presenting gifts to Buddha himself. Buddhists believe that the good wishes thought of near the stupa may become reality. Whichever religion one belongs to the stupa reminds people of the possibilities of personal development. During this development our own inner perfection, inherent traits and abilities with which we can do good for ourselves and others unfold and as result we can control our body and recover from illnesses.

CHAPTER 27

Health tourism and horse milk therapy in Kyrgyzstan

Ingeborg Nordbø and Elvira Sagyntay Kyzy

Introduction

The Kyrgyz Republic is located in the north eastern section of Central Asia bordering Kazakhstan, Uzbekistan, Tajikistan and China. Kyrgyzstan is a mountainous country and the Tien Shan (Heavenly Mountains) range occupies the greater part of the area. Tourism has played a central role in Kyrgyzstan since ancient times and the country's vast regions have been hosts to travellers for thousands of years. Kyrgyzstan was a central node on the Silk Road functioning as a kind of 'mountain gatekeeper' of the route. The ancient caravan route took three directions crossing the country's territory in the north, south and through the Fergana valley. These routes connected the East and the West for 15 centuries. The directions of the Silk Road were constantly changing, but the routes through Kyrgyzstan have always remained the same.

In modern times the tourism industry in Kyrgyzstan has been increasing rapidly and has become one of the priority areas of the republic's economy (Yesiltas, 2009). Kyrgyzstan's natural mountains and lakes and its culture based on nomadic traditions reflecting the days of the Mongol hordes are attractive to tourists from all over the world. Although factors such as political unrest have led to fluctuations in tourist arrivals and limited investments in necessary infrastructure, there has been an exceptional growth of 950 per cent in tourist arrivals during the last decade from 100,000 visitors in 2001 (ibid.: 242) to 2 million in 2011, and with a turnover of $US 3.2 million (Marchenko, 2012). Furthermore, by the end of August 2012 2.5 million tourists had already visited the country (Kazakov, 2012). The majority of tourists travelling to Kyrgyzstan are from former republics of the Soviet Union, mainly Russia, Kazakhstan and Uzbekistan, but year by year the number of tourists from the USA and Europe is also increasing: specifically Germany, Switzerland, France and Czech Republic. Kyrgyzstan provides different types of tourism activities such as mountain tourism, adventure tourism, skiing, trekking and alpine tourism, fishing, hunting, car-tourism, ecological tourism, and health and wellness tourism.

Health and wellness tourism in Kyrgyzstan

One of the oldest forms of tourism in Kyrgyzstan is health and wellness tourism, due to the country's vast natural resources such as hot springs, mineral waters, thermal waters and therapeutic mud. Kyrgyzstan has more than 100 fields of mineral waters with a wide variety of contents, components and temperature (Alymkulov et al., 2005). There are 40 types of mineral waters available for balneology treatment in the world; 30 of them can be found in Kyrgyz balneology divided into the following groups (ibid.):

- water without 'specific' components and properties;
- salty and bitter-salty waters;
- carbonated waters;
- siliceous thermal waters;
- radon waters;
- sulphide waters;
- iodine-bromine waters.

All these types of waters are used by resorts in distinct regions of the country, with examples including: the area of Issyk-Kul in the east, Jalal-Abad in the southwest and Chui in the north. Jalal-Abad is known for its mineral springs in the near surroundings, while the water from the nearby Azreti-Ayup-Paygambar spa was long believed to cure lepers. Kyrgyzstan was a republic of great importance for health tourism within the Soviet Union. Most of the country's resorts were built during that time and were very popular due to their mineral water treatment programmes for people with various chronic diseases. Several of the resorts have great potential for further development. Today the use of balneology mud has grown in popularity: here too there is substantial potential in the future of health tourism in Kyrgyzstan. Therapeutic muds are of two types: silt and peat-silt and most of these resources are located near the Issyk-Kul Lake. Tourists to the resorts are mainly from Kyrgyzstan, Russia, Kazakhstan and Uzbekstan.

The Kyrgyz people have numerous traditions for health treatments. Natural resources and cultural traditions have created some innovations in health tourism services, and a number of resorts, sanatorias and jurt camps provide climatotherapy, horse milk therapy (*kumyz*) and shilajit (mumijo) therapy for tourists. After the collapse of the Soviet Union, health and wellness tourism has been partly self-financed and partly with government subsidies, with the unfortunate result of declining quality of service. There is a need to develop the infrastructure and installations, and add an activity and adventure element in addition to the medical treatment in order to spur further development.

Horse milk therapy

Kumyz is a national Kyrgyz drink produced from horse milk. Kumyz is made by fermenting raw unpasteurized mare's milk at a temperature between 26 and 28°C and over the course of hours or days, often while stirring or churning. Ready kumyz is a foaming effervescent

beverage with an alcohol taste and smell. Kumyz is an ancient beverage and the historical origins of the drink can be traced back to the nomadic traditions of the local population – the Kygyzs. Herodotus, in his fifth-century BC *Histories*, describes for instance how the Scythians processed the mare's milk. Archaeological investigations of the Botai culture of ancient Kazakhstan have revealed traces of milk in bowls from the site of Botai, suggesting the domestication of the animal (Outram et al., 2009). In the USSR in 1982 230,000 horses were kept specifically for producing milk to make into *kumyz* (Steinkraus, 1995). Today, kumyz remains important to the nomadic populations of the Central Asian steppes of Huno-Bulgar, Turkic and Mongol origin: Bashkirs, Kalmyks, Kazakhs, Kyrgyz, Mongols, Uyghurs, and Yakuts (Zeder, 2006: 264).

Kumyz is used both as a national soft drink, a substitute for breast feeding and as a main component of infant food. Furthermore, it is widely used in preventive and therapeutic medicine. *Kumyz* is believed to be a good diuretic and choleric agent. It is believed to be easily assimilated by weak and emaciated human organisms. It is said to improve the appetite, improve processes of food digestion and to increase enteral absorption. Studies show that the content of vitamin C in *kumyz* is more than three times that of cow milk. In addition, *kumyz* lowers the level of cholesterol while the abundant iron content increases haemoglobin levels in the blood and improves white blood cell structure (Kuskov and Lysikova, 2004). The *kumyz* chemical compound includes fibres, fats, carbohydrates, group vitamins B, PP, A, E, C (Manshina, 2003). Kumyz therapy is being used to treat emaciation, anaemia, gastric and duodenal ulcer, dysentery and typhoid fever. It is also used for therapeutic purposes in tuberculosis of the lungs or lymph nodes and to cure exhaustion.

Kumyz is also used and believed to have great effect for washing fistulas, bladder instillations, douches, vaginal swabs, and a number of other diseases; drinking *kumyz* also increases digestibility of protein and fat (ibid.). *Kumyz* is also used in the treatment of diseases or disorders in the nervous system and benign neuroses, reportedly with good results. It is promoted to be especially beneficial to city dwellers. The high nutritional value of *kumyz* can be explained not only by the composition of the milk but also by the process of fermentation. Fermentation kumis fat remains unchanged, but the protein becomes digestible and the milk sugar is transformed into lactic acid, ethyl alcohol, carbonic acid and a number of aromatic substances (ibid.). Doctors who prescribe *kumyz* recommend to start drinking *kumyz* in small doses, up to 50 ml, gradually increasing the dose to 250 ml or more, bringing the daily intake of *kumyz* to three liters. *Kumyz* needs to be drunk six times a day, and should be taken one and half hours before eating. There are no side effects when using *kumyz*; the only restriction is for patients with gastritis or with high acidity of gastric juice. Strong natural mare's milk contains 4.5 per cent alcohol and is not recommended for medicinal purposes. Patients undergoing kumyz treatment receive a *kumyz* in which the alcohol is low (1–1.75 per cent) (ibid.).

There are many resorts and private organisations which provide services for *kumyz* therapy, and even tour operators, like Sankurtour, specialise only in horse milk therapy tours. The size of many of the resorts and sanatoria is quite impressive and they have their own horse farms and pastures, implying that they in most cases are located in natural surroundings. The most popular resorts in Kyrgyzstan are located in the regions of

Issyk-Kul, Naryn and Chui. One of the most famous *kumyz* resorts in Kyrgyzstan is Baytur in Suusamyr, a high mountain area 2,200 m above sea level and approximately 160 km from the capital Bishkek. *Kumyz* and mare's milk from Suusamyr valley were from ancient times famous in Kyrgyzstan for their healing properties. In Baytur *kumyz* is a much used substance in the therapy of such diseases as:

- gastric and duodenal ulcer;
- chronic gastritis;
- chronic cholecystitis;
- chronic enterocolitis;
- functional disorder of gall bladder and large intestine;
- chronic nonspecific lungs diseases;
- atherosclerosis;
- essential hypertension;
- diseases of central nervous system and hemopoietic organs;
- liver diseases, hepatitis and initial stage of cirrhosis.

A milk therapy treatment in Baytur normally lasts for a minimum of ten days; the mare should be milked about five times a day, and it is recommended to undergo the mare's milk therapy every year. Baytur market their facilities as providing healthy and comfortable accommodation for the guests surrounded by gorgeous jailoos (high mountain pastures). There are comfortable rooms for three persons with all facilities, deluxe and suites and also spacious guest yurts (Kyrgyz traditional houses), other facilities are saunas and play-grounds for children all designed and thought of in order to make the guest have the best results from their horse milk therapy. Another famous *kumyz* resort in Kyrgyzstan is Karkyra, located in the Issyk-Kul region. There are also, as mentioned, many tour opera-tors which provide tours for those who desire *kumyz* therapy; for example Asia Mountains, Ecotrek, Sayakat tourism and Kyrgyzstan travel. In Kyrgyzstan people flock to the resorts because *kumyz* is believed to be a panacea for any diseases or ills.

CHAPTER 28

Well-being tourism in Finland

Henna Konu, Anja Tuohino and Peter Björk

The first discussions on wellness and well-being tourism in the Finnish tourism industry started in 2002 when the Finnish Tourist Board (FTB) recognised the importance of developing well-being tourism (Hentinen, 2002). The Finnish Tourism Board has since decided to include well-being tourism as one focus area in the Finnish tourism strategy document, alongside snow and Christmas tourism, water related tourism, and event tourism (Suomen matkailustrategia vuoteen, 2020). In January 2009 the new Finnish well-being tourism strategy was launched for the period 2009–13, and is based on operational goals (e.g. terminology, developing core products), image goals (e.g. strengthening the country brand) and quantitative goals (e.g. increasing overnight stays).

In the Finnish language the words roughly equivalent to English wellness and well-being are complex, especially in the tourism context. Wellness tourism is usually connected to luxury products and five-star hotels. Well-being tourism may include products and services from a wider scale; possibly pampering, activities and experiences of luxury, but this is not necessarily available only from first-class hotels. In the Finnish context, but also in the wider Nordic context, the well-being tourism concept is more suitable because the wider description highlights better the Finnish and Nordic understanding (see e.g. Konu et al., 2010; Hjalager et al., 2011).

At present the wellness segment of the travel industry in Finland is booming and is one of the main themes in the Finnish tourism strategy. However, the profile of Finland's well-being tourism can still be described as vague and inaccurate despite the systematic work of the Finnish Tourism Board in recent years (Tuohino, 2012). Challenges have been encountered, for instance, in product development and in targeting products at particular customer segments. Many of the core resources of Finnish well-being tourism are to be found in nature, including forests, lakes and other waterways, hills and vast wilderness areas, therefore Finnish well-being tourism companies concentrate mainly on (nature-based) activities and sauna (Kangas and Tuohino, 2008). Finnish sauna and Nordic walking in particular have strengthened their standing in general knowledge as Finnish products (FTB, 2009). In Finland the problem is that sauna and Nordic walking products and offerings are not easy for international tourists to find or buy.

According to the Finnish Tourist Board (2008) a basic well-being holiday offering includes elements such as getting away from everyday routines, enjoying peace and nature, relaxing and 'recharging your batteries'; outdoor recreation, exploring nature, events related to Finnish culture and retreats; traditional Finnish forms of sauna bathing; a pleasant, aesthetically pleasing and authentic environment; personal service; healthy, preferably locally produced food with information available to the customer on the origin and nutritional content of the food; attention to the environment and sustainable development in the offering; consideration for the ageing customer base and people with impaired mobility; and an aesthetically pleasing, well-maintained environment.

In addition to the basic offering, there are two targeted customer and product groups – health and fitness exercise, and pampering. The characteristics of a health and fitness holiday are: activities such as Nordic walking, hiking, walking, snowshoeing, skiing, swimming, winter swimming and golf). Pampering includes several diverse spa and beauty treatments and hence the offering is the closest to the international understanding of wellness (FTB, 2009).

The following three examples illustrate how the elements and contents of Finnish and Nordic well-being are used in product development, place branding, and concept development in Finland. Nordic well-being is oriented towards nature, outdoor experiences and enjoyment combined with healthy local gastronomy, local culture and cleanliness of air, nature and water (Hjalager et al., 2011).

Case 1: natural well-being as a lifestyle in brand development and in social media (Case SaimaaLife)

The Nordic well-being project was one main source of inspiration for the establishment of a blog about finding balance and happiness in a woman's life on the shorelines of Lake Saimaa in Finland. SaimaaLife (www.saimaalife.com) is a novel lifestyle blog with a strong local attachment to Lake Saimaa. The main aim of the blogger is to harvest the unique selling points of Lake Saimaa by creating opportunities for viewing and gazing at relaxing and meaningful life on Lake Saimaa through her family life. By using storytelling in English she conveys her own experiences and interactions with nature and lake landscape. SaimaaLife is all about quality of life, relaxed attitude, real food, creating one's own way of life, deriving well-being from nature and from all things natural. She has defined her own natural well-being as:

- finding balance in work, family life and yourself;
- well-being of body, spirit and mind;
- quality before quantity, relaxed attitude not stressed attitude, positivity over pessimism;
- life where you have time for your passions and creativity;
- being in nature and drawing vitality from its beauty and tranquillity;
- real food and listening to yourself;
- everyday luxury and life according to your natural rhythm;
- courage to be yourself, courage to be a beautiful and happy woman.

SaimaaLife since its inception has entered into concrete co-operation relationships with both the public and private sectors. Extensive networking makes it possible to use the partners in the SaimaaLife development process. Further partners may utilise the services of the blogger. The SaimaaLife blog content with its marketing value can also be widely used in Finland's international brand marketing. The themes of the blog also fit well with the Nordic well-being concept. The identification of a set of unique selling points and the development a blog site has been done and the main themes of the blog are defined as follows:

- nature – be well in nature;
- handmade – enjoy creativity: I find this strange but dare not intervene;
- family – love;
- roots – be yourself;
- food – at well;
- beauty – enjoy womanhood.

Case 2: development of new well-being (tourism) products based on traditional Finnish sauna

One Finnish well-being innovation – Finnish sauna – is well known all over the world. In Finland the sauna is a part of everyday life and almost every Finn has a sauna. Thus it is challenging to offer sauna as a well-being product that people are willing to buy, especially in domestic markets. 'Just going to a sauna' might not be appealing to a Finn, but if it offers a person added value it becomes interesting. In addition, for foreigners and tourists going into a sauna as such may well be a new experience. However, the opportunity to go to the sauna (because saunas are available not only in spas or hotels but are also located outdoors, with the added exotica of the traditional smoke sauna) needs to be made as easy as possible and guidelines on how to go and how to act in sauna need to be provided.

In the Jyväskylä region in Central Finland a network and a concept of Sauna from Finland was set up. The concept aims to create new types of business activity in Finland, and to profile Central Finland as the Sauna Province. The goal of the Sauna from Finland Association is to promote Finnish sauna culture, support the development of services connected to sauna and support and inspire new entrepreneurial activities. It also brings together actors from different business sectors (e.g. the sauna manufacturing industry, tourism, wellness/well-being, service sector), which makes it possible to create new types of business activity and innovations. One of the aims of Sauna from Finland is to create new memorable service innovations connected to sauna. To do this diverse types of customer involvement methods are used. For instance, a competition to collect different sauna stories and pictures from local people was set up.

One of the well-being services created is Saunayoga, a half-hour exercise consisting of poses all done seated on a sauna bench in a temperature of about 50–55 degrees Centigrade. There are already 100 certified instructors in Finland, Sweden and Germany.

Case 3: well-being in South Ostrobothnia

'Wellbeing in South Ostrobothnia', defined as a bundle of services for the purpose of maintaining and enhancing an individual's well-being in body, mind and soul, which are influenced by natural, cultural and social conditions of the countryside, is presented as a tourism brand (available at www.epmatkailu.fi/wellbeing_in_south_ostrobothnia.html also in English).

TABLE 28.1 Finnish well-being tourism characteristics and well-being in South Ostrobothnia	
Characteristics of Finnish well-being tourism	Well-being in the South Ostrobothnia case, illustrative descriptions from the website
The environment – Aesthetically pleasing – Authentic – Clean and relaxing – Preferably close to water	'The region is famous for its entrepreneurship, the fertile countryside and the wide variety of culture and events. Original in its culture, independent and proud in its attitude and colourful in its history. The vast flatlands are awe-inspiring and easy on the eye, and the peace and quiet of nature surrounds the traveller everywhere. The Ostrobothnian milieu is traditional and idyllic.'
The Services – Personal – High quality – Indoor and Outdoor	The hostess's traditional buffet awaits the guests in a cosy atmosphere. Quality services are offered, in excellent surroundings and with know-how. Outdoor activities can be combined with relaxing peat poultice treatment for the shoulders and back.
The Activities – Sauna bathing – Water activities and exercise – Treatments and pampering – Year-round activities – Food and eating	Nice relaxing experience of the Finnish sauna. On leaving the saunas, step to the verandas to cool off and for a swim in the lake, or try ice hole swimming in winter. Exercise is an opportunity, not an obligation. Fitness Formula, testing and Feel-good stretching for those who want an active holiday. Relax in the aquatic therapy pools and hot tubs, or enjoy a therapeutic peat treatment. Once we're clean as a whistle, we'll enjoy a taste of liqueur-marinated fish, functional salads, hodge-podge dishes and brawn, 'blue' casseroles and steamed vegetables, potatoes, sauce and meat on a plank (in thin slivers or huge slabs).
Vision Well-being tourism has become part of the Finnish Tourism brand. Finland is known as a country that can offer well-being, rest and relaxation.	Well-being in South Ostrobothnian is a relaxing holiday in the peace of the countryside or amidst of vibrant events, a break from everyday life.

Source: Development Strategy for Finnish Wellbeing Tourism, 2009; www.epmatkailu.fi/wellbeing_in_south_ostrobothnia.html.

Tourists' perceptions of the well-being in South Ostrobothnia are still to be analysed. Tourism firms and organisations aiming at an international market can obtain support from the Finnish Tourism Board if they meet specified quality standards. A next step for the well-being in South Ostrobothnia project would be to initiate a quality assurance process.

Conclusions

Three cases were presented in this chapter to illustrate how the elements and contents of Finnish and Nordic Wellbeing are currently used in product development, place branding and communication. The well-being in South Ostrobothnia case illustrates how regional tourism development projects in Finland are based on the available local resources, which are upgraded to comply with national and international quality standards, and amalgamated in service offerings to be marketed. Innovations for service development are sought in all directions. The Saunayoga case is illustrative of how cross-sector service combinations can be used to come up with new service offerings that can also be used as a part of a well-being tourism product. The SaimaaLife blog, which is probably at present the only lifestyle blog produced in English, with clearly defined business objectives and strategic plan, presents the cultural values of Finland in a new way.

To summarise, there are strong arguments why Finland should accelerate its well-being tourism development projects and branding processes. Existing resources resonate well with the essence of well-being tourism and there is documented interest among Finnish tourism actors to host the growing number of tourists searching for high-quality well-being tourism services.

CHAPTER 29

Health leisure market
The evolution in Portugal
Nuno Gustavo and Fernando Completo

Introduction

Leisure and health practices associated with hot springs have a unique place in Portuguese history and society. The occupation of the Portuguese territory by Greeks and Romans left a significant thermal legacy. The use of thermal springs by Portuguese monarchs, as well as the legends and myths associated with them, have made them popular in Portuguese culture throughout the centuries. However, it was in the first decades of the twentieth century that thermal centres became truly established and reached their height in Portugal. They were legally institutionalised through a decree in 1892 and thus had new financing and investment from the government, as well as becoming fashionable places for leisure and vacations. The Portuguese thermal facilities were transformed and given a new dimension through the construction of hotels, casinos and recreational facilities. The new railroad was also a determining factor in the developing process of the spa, bearing in mind the fact that they were usually located in rural areas, outside city centres such as Lisbon, Coimbra and Oporto.

The 1950s and 1960s were a turning point in the use and profile of the Portuguese thermal centre clients. The decline of the 'Estado Novo'[1] in Portugal (which later led to the establishment of a democratic state) and the subsequent occupation of the thermal facilities by many people who returned to the country from the African colonies,[2] along with a set of structural reforms of the Portuguese health system,[3] meant there was a period of democratisation which attracted new customers from lower classes who mainly had therapeutic motivations (healing and treatment). The prevalence of an essentially healing and hospital model perspective led the Portuguese thermal centres to a new social representation, devoid of elitism, inaugurating a model of popular inclusion aimed at an ageing population.

Besides state financing, new legislation was published in 1976 in order to match thermal treatments to other primary health care treatments and thus allowing state co-payments

TABLE 29.1 Evolution of thermal facilities offer, 1926–2010

Years	Thermal facilities
1926	48
1930	65
1935	71
1940	75
1946	79
1958	45
1965	45
1970	41
1975	42
1980	39
1985	39
1990	38
2000	32
2005	37
2010	36

Sources: DGMSG/IGM, Boletim de Minas (several years), Acciaiouli (1942, 1947), Portugal. País de Turismo (1958),Turismo de Portugal (several years) 2005.

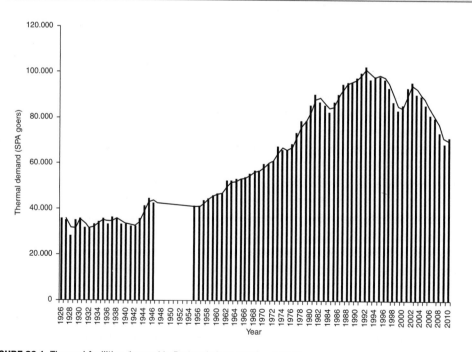

FIGURE 29.1 Thermal facilities demand in Portugal since 1927 – evolution

Sources: DGMSG/IGM, Boletim de Minas (several years), Acciaiouli (1942, 1947), DGT (1958), Turismo de Portugal (several years).

to cover accommodation, travel and food costs. This measure which lasted until 1981 meant that spa demand peaked in that year, after which the abolishment of such measures greatly affected demand. The investments made in the Portuguese thermal centres during the 1990s according to the National Plan of Tourism (1989–92) relaunched the spa concept and allowed a significant increase in demand. It is also noteworthy that this Plan considered the promotion and development of a significant number of spas as a priority, according to the Government Resolution (Mangorrinha, 2000).

SPA demand in Portugal in the twenty-first century

According to a set of studies carried out in the present century in Portugal (Ramos, 2005; Alpoim, 2010) and with reference to the research done by Gustavo (2006) – comprising a sample of 285 individuals – specially focused on the spa town of São Pedro do Sul (the most important in Portugal), it is possible to identify a set of general and transversal characteristics of the Portuguese thermal centres demand and thus establish a means for understanding the profile of its users. In this spa town, 61.4 per cent of the hot spring SPA goers are female. Their age distribution is clearly asymmetric (84.5 per cent are aged 65 or over) and those aged 34 or less represent 8 per cent of the total.

When asked about the reason why they use the thermal facilities, 94 per cent of the spa-goers say they use it for therapeutic purposes and 99.3 per cent of the individuals stated that going to a spa is important for the quality of their health throughout the year. The decision of going to the spa town of São Pedro do Sul was especially influenced by doctors (71 per cent) and friends (26 per cent). On the other hand, the characteristics of the hot spring waters of São Pedro do Sul are considered by 74.7 per cent as very important in their decision. It is also noteworthy that 95 per cent of the spa users consider thermal treatment more effective than medicines. The presence of family and/or friends was also very important in the decision process, a phenomenon which explains the importance of the social and cultural dynamics that affect the representation of the spa towns. Generally speaking, thermal visitation is not something recent, as 69 per cent stated that they have used thermal spas for five or more years. It is also significant that the thermal spa use is annual in periods of 15 consecutive days, which tells us that it is a leisure as well as a therapeutic activity.

The socioeconomic identity of the thermal centre goers is characterised by their low level of education, as the majority (56 per cent) only holds primary education and just 15 per cent have higher education. Regarding their occupation, only 48 per cent are gainfully employed. From those without income, 36 per cent are retired. These situations are reflected in the household incomes (average monthly income of 1.180 euros), although 48 per cent of the spa-goers belong to a group which does not earn a monthly income above 1.000 euros, and thus affects the accommodation choices (especially renting houses or bedrooms in private homes instead of more expensive hotels).

A hot springs Act was published in 2004 aimed at creating the necessary legal conditions to adjust the thermal facilities activity to the new challenges and opportunities of the health leisure market. This Act was based on the new concept of wellness and tries to mitigate the declining tendency of the last decades. It recognises the potential of thermal centres and widens its scope of action as well as trying to attract new customers with other motivations beyond therapeutic ones.

The new dimension of the health leisure market: from traditional thermal spa to the modern urban spa

In the past few years there has been a rediscovery of some of the most charming spa towns in Portugal. New spaces are being developed around more holistic concepts of health and wellness rather than the medical/therapeutic paradigm.

These new places are targets for high investments and provide a new and more versatile offer in accordance with the new aesthetic and wellness demands of post-modern societies. It is now possible to find medical techniques (whether or not of high technology) side by side with more natural techniques developed from popular knowledge, thus combining tradition and innovation, old and modern, sacred and profane, and creating a new holistic perspective of body and health.

The National Strategy Plan for Portuguese Tourism presented in 2007[4] has identified health tourism as one of the ten strategic products of the Portuguese tourism, thus highlighting the potential and relevance of this business area (TP, 2007). The reconversion and reinvention of spa towns in Portugal is not the only priority, but also the development of a new spa offers, especially those of hotels whether in urban areas (e.g. Lisbon and Oporto) or in tourist areas like the Algarve, outside the traditional spa towns.

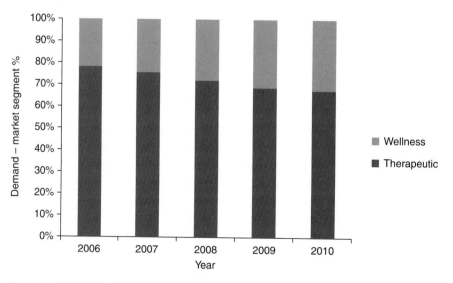

FIGURE 29.2 Motivations for thermal facilities demand in Portugal, 2006–10
Source: Turismo de Portugal (several years) based on the data collected by DGED and ATP.

Spa-goers: new facilities, new motivations and leisure consumers in Portugal

The profile of the new consumer of spas in Portugal was researched in 2009 through a survey[5] carried out at national level. The questionnaire was given to 824 spa-goers and measured not only consumerism and motivations, but also health care and practices in general. Based on the sample it was possible to define a sociocultural profile of the current spa customer. Regarding age, they are on average 38.5 years old (38 per cent of the individuals are aged between 30 and 39). As for gender, spa-goers are mainly female (69.8 per cent). Most of them reside in Portugal (73 per cent) and the remaining 27 per cent live in other countries. Concerning education, the majority (73.9 per cent) has higher education and 91.7 per cent are employed. Most of the respondents are working in the tertiary sector (89.1 per cent), in senior executive management (28.0 per cent) and professionals (37.0 per cent). As for their average monthly income, 48.9 per cent of the spa-goers earn more than 3.000 euros, and the remaining percentage between 2.000 and 2.999 euros.

Regarding the uses and frequency of spas, it can be defined as an emerging practice, but 31.2 per cent refer to it as a monthly routine/frequency. 40.7 per cent of spa customers state that it is not something they do everyday but however with some regularity. Underlining this situation is the fact that 44.4 per cent choose in their daily leisure time to engage in spa practices. Holidays are also spent in spas for 41.3 per cent of the individuals. Seventy-five per cent of the clients in the sample state that they consider the existence of spas as a determining factor for their holiday accommodation and destination. The main reason that individuals go to spas is linked to *stress relief and/or relaxation*, with 74.3 per cent saying this is a very important reason to go to a spa. Concerning motivation, it should be noted that *improving mental health* and *improving physical health* were determining reasons for over 50 per cent of these spa-goers. In terms of the most popular services available in spas, spa-goers prefer massage (90.9 per cent) and body treatments (including balneotherapy). Regarding services used in spas it should be noted that about 50 per cent did not use hydrotherapy (*vichy* shower, immersion bath, hydro massage) in their last visit to a spa.

Spa-goers are individuals who engage actively in their health management. 71.2 per cent regard sport as a vital part of their lifestyle. 70.2 per cent eats healthily and 70.1 per cent takes or has taken food supplements whereas 34.1 per cent takes or has taken weight control products (natural or synthetic) in order to control their weight. These two types of care are reflected in the body mass index (BMI) of the clients interviewed (23.2 kg/m^2). In our overall sample, 69.5 per cent of spa-goers have an average or below average BMI. 51.3 per cent do not drink alcohol apart from at meal times or only do it very seldom; and only 18.1 per cent are frequent smokers. Weight control is common among 59.5 per cent and 80.4 per cent have medical exams/check-ups.[6] These practices and habits are supported by a regular use of information sources like *the internet* (63.5 per cent) and frequent reading of magazines and books specialised in health (40.4 per cent). Despite the fact that the overwhelming majority (84.2 per cent) of the individuals are beneficiaries of the national health service, 65.7 per cent also have health insurance.

Finally, regarding special beauty care, 78.1 per cent of the sample usually uses beauty products and 21.0 per cent uses or has used the latest technologies to have surgery (e.g. lifting, liposuction) and weight loss treatments, among other treatments.

Final remarks

Today the health market in Portugal is distinguished by its increasing diversification. If, on the one hand, the spa towns are a living heritage representing ancient health and leisure practices in Portugal, on the other hand, the health tourism offer has also partly reinvented itself and developed new areas and customers. As a result of this proactive approach, modern spas have started to acquire a place of their own within Portuguese society in response to the new reality and demands of twenty-first-century societies.

Notes

1 Dictatorship, 1933–74.
2 After the decolonisation process of the African colonies, half a million people returned to Portugal and had to be accommodated in leisure facilities such as hotels and spa resorts, where they stayed for more than two years.
3 Expressed in social benefits associated to SPA practices and materialised in allowances and co-payments of SPA treatments.
4 Currently under revision.
5 Carried out as part of the Doctoral Research by Nuno Gustavo (2011).
6 56.7 per cent do it by their own accord.

CHAPTER 30

The holy Himalayas
An adobe to wellness

Parikshat Singh Manhas

The Indian subcontinent is lined by the Great Himalayas on its northern side, which is considered the home of spirituality. More and more people are flocking here to the lush green meadows, pastures and forests away from the busy life of the congested cities. The Himalayan peaks are an adobe where people come from different continents and stay because of the calmness, air, water and natural purity. Many faiths across the religious spectrum consider the Himalayan Mountains to be an epicentre of spirituality, and Hindus, Buddhists and other religions find spiritual guidance and divine inspiration there. The most visited places of pilgrimage in India are located in the Himalayas. Mata Vaishno Devi is a very important adobe in the foot hills of the Himalayas where approximately 11 million people visit every year to find solace and blessings of the goddess. This is one of the most visited sites in the Himalayas where people come to be healed of physical and mental problems. It has been a pilgrimage site since ancient times.

In India it has been observed that people prefer to visit places like Kerala for health treatments like spa and Ayurveda whereas the Himalayas itself is enriched with such natural treatments in the form of fresh air, hot springs and natural herbs as well, as they form the basis of Ayurvedic treatments. In terms of wellness tourism the Himalayas offers the best retreat for tourists in all respects.

The Himalayas and medical tourism

India was projected to capture 2.5 per cent of the international medical tourism market by the year 2012, with concurrent revenue projects of $2.3 billion. It was estimated that the medical tourism industry in India would attract over 1.1 million patients from across the globe, by the end of 2012. Ayurveda in India has been around since 5000 BC. Ayurvedic clinics and hospital clinics can be linked to medical tourism. Various Himalayan regions or destinations such as Nepal and Sikkim are the home of about 3,500 species of herbs and aromatic plants which have high medicinal, culinary and cosmetic values and can be used for Ayurveda. They are exported abroad for various treatments, but could also be used more to attract tourists to the region for healing. The traditional medicine concept known as Sowa Rigpa dating back to the seventeenth century involving the usage of herbal plants for the treatment of various health diseases can also be considered part of wellness tourism in the Himalayan region.

The Himalayas and spa/yoga tourism and meditation

The Himalayan regions have an abundance of hot springs such as the Gasa hot springs which is one of the most popular hot springs in Bhutan. These hot springs offer healing properties for all kinds of ailments such as body aches and skin diseases. The therapies provided in Himalayan spas such as Uttrakhand and Sikkim include body massage using natural herbs and various other treatments such as aromatherapy and thermal mud. However, such destinations have still not been widely promoted, so tourists tend to go to other places like Kerala, for spas and also for yoga. Yoga is the best method for improving mental health and the Himalayas offers the best environment for this, as it could be considered the birth place of yoga. The history of meditation and yoga in the Himalayas goes back more than 2,500 years. Places like Vaishno Devi, Rishikesh, Dharamshala, Kaidarnath and Amaranth Ji shrine lie in the foothills of the Himalayas. These places are the base for pilgrimage tourism but could also be a part of meditation and yoga tourism attractions.

The Himalayas and escapism and relaxation

Escape tourism is the concept of being away from the various social and other daily activities that make individuals mentally or psychologically sick. Escape and relaxation activities include adventure, mountaineering, or being close to nature, finding calm and a fresh environment. The various regions in India such as Ladakh, Himachal Pradesh, Uttrakhand, Jammu and Kashmir are blessed with such aspects.

The Himalayas and hedonistic/experiential wellness

This definition of wellness focuses on experiences and being a part of various activities related to fun and enjoyment. The Himalayan regions are enriched with various religious festivals and special events. Visiting various Himalayan regions and taking part in such activities can contribute to a sense of experiential or hedonistic wellness.

The Himalayas, existential and psychological wellness

Self- or psychological development has become important in this contemporary and hectic world. The Himalayas offers an ideal place for such development, inspiring the

individual to understand his/her existence and enjoying the closeness to nature. Even having a long walk in nature can be one of the best forms of psychological retreat.

The Himalayas and spiritual tourism

Spiritual techniques such as Vipassana meditation are offered in the Himalayas. Such teaching is offered in Gyuto Monastery, for example. Various religious monasteries, temples and shrines are located in the Himalayan regions of Tibet, Ladakh, Kashmir, and Uttrakhand. Pilgrimages can be taken to places like Vaishno devi shrine, Amarnath shrine, Kedarnath, Mansarovar and Badrinath.

The Himalayas and community well-being

The Himalayan region offers a good place for community well-being, which includes charity treks and campsite programmes which make the tourists or participants aware of eco-friendly tourism.

The role of the Himalayas in global wellness tourism

Wellness tourism in the Himalayas should not be limited only to Indian regions. It should also include other countries as Bhutan, China, Tibet and Nepal which offer equally significant natural wellness resources. For example, the concept of spa and meditation as well as spiritual tourism is very well defined in Tibetan religious and medical practices known as Kum Nye and sKu-m-Nye which means massage of the subtle body. Such treatments are similar to yoga and massage treatments available in modern spas. Chinese traditional practices of medicine focus on three basic elements i.e. Chi (energy), Jing (governing force of vitality and longevity), and Shen (the mind). Such practices in China are performed in the monasteries and other traditional institutes situated in the high altitudes of Himalayan ranges of China.

Conclusion

Wellness tourism includes medical, spiritual, even adventure tourism which can add fun and fitness to an individual's life. The Himalayas are enriched with so many natural well-being resources which can have long-term effects on health. However, there needs to be some product development linked to pilgrimage tourism, medical tourism, spa tourism, adventure tourism, and so on. The development of wellness tourism in the Himalayas could help to attract more tourists, especially foreigners, and to expand the products for health and medical tourism in India, as it is currently limited only to a few destinations such as Kerala. The wellness resources offered in Himalayan destinations have the potential to be affordable to a wide range of visitors.

The natural environment with its herbal treatments and Ayurveda could be promoted as part of authentic wellness and ecotourism with a focus on sustainability. The purity of nature in the Himalayas is such an important part of human health and well-being. Urbanisation has made the human environment polluted and stressful. Nature can create a positive and calming effect on the individual's health and spirit thus encouraging mental relaxation.

Wellness is not merely about the relaxation; it has a broader dimension covering the fundamental aspects of complete mental and physical well-being of the individual. Wellness tourism has formed a prominent place among other tourism forms in countries like China, Thailand and USA, but it is more limited at present in the Himalayan regions, which lack basic services and facilities.

The Indian government has considered the concept of wellness tourism in the tourism development framework but no special consideration is given to Himalayan tourism. However, in the future, Himalayan wellness tourism could help to expand considerably the number of tourists to India.

31

Te Aroha wellness tourism
Yesterday and today

Maria Hyde-Smith and John S. Hull

The Global Spa Summit Report (2010) referred to a seven-dimensional model for the spa industry that includes mental, emotional, physical, occupational, environmental, social and spiritual wellness. The following case study from Te Aroha, New Zealand, provides a context for considering the various dimensions of a wellness spa from the nineteenth century.

Te Aroha wellness spa

In the late nineteenth century, the government of New Zealand, realising the potential of the country's mineral waters, initiated a series of spa-development initiatives modelled on the great resorts of Europe (Rockel, 1986). The intention was to create a globally recognised South Seas Spa experience. The first spa facility was initiated with the construction of Te Aroha's Cadman Baths in 1898. Te Aroha, a small township in the North Island of New Zealand, was identified as having natural resources in the form of 22 geothermal springs that offered a range of temperatures and minerals that had the potential to satisfy the European spa market (Rockel, 1986). Seventeen of the springs vary in temperature from 86 to 150 degrees Fahrenheit while the remaining springs are cold. Thomas Cooks Guide to New Zealand (1905) reports four kinds of springs – alkaline, acidic, sulphur and magnesia – offering treatment for a number of ailments including gout, rheumatism, skin diseases, as well as urinary, kidney, liver and spleen disorders.

Te Aroha's setting was as important as its geothermal water resources. The spa was located on the side of Mount Te Aroha, rising up to 952 meters with an average annual rainfall of 55 inches and a mean temperature of 56 degrees Fahrenheit, naturally beautiful and healthful (Thomas Cook, 1905). Historically, the springs were highly valued by the local Marutuahu people. Formal development of the springs began in the late nineteenth century. In 1882, a reserve of 8 hectares was gazetted and the Hot Springs Hotel was built. By 1884 the Te Aroha Hot Springs Domain Board was formed and three original bathhouses constructed along with fencing and formal gardens. From 1885 the spa was marketed through newspapers and travel literature to domestic and international markets (Thomas Cook, 1905; Rockel, 1986).

Due to the discovery of gold in the area, the spa was easily accessible from Auckland by boat, coach service and railway and during the first six months of 1886 there were 18,686 baths recorded, making Te Aroha the most visited spa town in New Zealand at the time (Rockel, 1986). There were seven bathhouses with one reserved for women, two shallow baths for children, one for 'natives' and one with eight private baths. In 1886, Dr Alfred Wright was appointed as a physician to the Thermal Springs Domain. The spa offered daily and weekly bathing courses as well as a digestion guide for invalids and visitors. The mineral waters were also bottled and sold (Rockel, 1986).

By the 1880s a booming spa tourism industry was established. A number of new hotels were built offering dances, concerts, billiards, reading rooms, and verandahs with views of the Waihou River. Walks along the river, through the Domain and up Mount Te Aroha were offered in addition to golf, picnics, gipsy parties in the ravines and buggy trips to Lake Waikare. Rowing boats and roads for riding were also available (Thomas Cook, 1905). In 1894, a library, reading room and waiting room was added to the spa facilities. In 1898, the largest development of Te Aroha spa was completed – the Cadman Baths, with 19 tiled private bathrooms containing porcelain baths. Both male and female attendants provided services to clients. The spa was acknowledged at the most attractive bathhouse in the country at the time (Rockel, 1986; Thomas Cook, 1905).

The construction of the Cadman Baths succeeded in attracting wealthy tourists who helped to make the spa a financial success with bath fees generating £954 in 1898. The financial success of the baths resulted in the replacement of the bathhouses over time and the development of new spa services for visitors including massage therapy (Rockel, 1986). By 1903, the Domain Board ceased to exist and the Government Department of Tourist and Health Resorts took over control of the spa. The Domain at Te Aroha was further expanded to 60 acres and developed with tennis courts, bowling and croquet greens. A rotunda provided a venue for brass bands and concerts while walkways were lit with Chinese lanterns for summer evening outings. A library and teahouse were also constructed. Tours for botanists, geologists, entomologists, ornithologists and other natural history enthusiasts were also promoted (Thomas Cook, 1905).

Even with 22 springs in the domain area, Te Aroha's greatest challenge was a lack of water. Limited hot water supply and insufficient cold water restricted spa development. A series of bores were attempted in the early twentieth century to increase water supply but these largely failed. Eventually, the Cadman Baths were closed. Rotorua and Hanmer Springs, other New Zealand spa towns, soon surpassed Te Aroha as New Zealand's leading spa destination. The Te Aroha mineral spa continued to be managed by the local council and remained open to the public but did not enjoy the notoriety it once had.

In 2006 the local council made a decision to restore the historical spa buildings and build additional spa facilities with the view to possibly making Te Aroha a more wellness-focused spa destination. Today the Te Aroha Hot Springs domain is unique in that it is the only complete Edwardian domain in New Zealand. The mineral spa baths have retained their historic charm and this has resulted in a resurgence in visitation. Not only are the spa facilities experiencing greater demand, the township is also enjoying growth in the form of

new cafés, additional accommodation and development of other tourist attractions such as the Hauraki national cycle trail.

Te Aroha is currently frequented by mainly domestic visitors (80 per cent). The main target groups are couples (40+ years old) who wish to experience the pools, spa facilities, walking tracks, heritage, arts and craft, cafés and rail cycle network. Family groups are targeted for the pools, cycle trails and walking tracks. Future target markets include campervan visitors (aged 55+) and wellness orientated visitors. Future development plans for Te Aroha includes increasing visitor accommodation, further development of the cycle trails, improved infrastructure of visitors and additional guided walks (Te Aroha Information Centre, 2012).

The Te Aroha Spa Pool facilities do not currently market themselves as a wellness spa destination. To be considered as a legitimate wellness spa destination, the town would need to offer products and services that could contribute to multiple dimensions that form a wellness spa experience. Table 31.1 shows some of the products and services Te Aroha currently offers that contribute to the wellness experience.

The table recognises that many of the above products and services contribute to more than one wellness dimension at any one time. According to the seven dimensions proposed by SRI (2010), Te Aroha spa does not currently offer products and services that cover all the dimensions related to a wellness spa destination. While it is strongly represented in the physical and social dimensions, it is weak in the occupational and spiritual dimensions.

If Te Aroha wishes to become a true wellness spa destination in the twenty-first century it is evident that the following steps are needed to move the spa industry forward at Te Aroha (SRI, 2007):

1   to communicate the importance of the spa industry to government to classify local establishments for consumer protection, and to leverage public sector resources to advance wellness dimensions such as occupational and spiritual wellness;
2   to link Te Aroha with the growth in the larger wellness and lifestyle industries to increase consumer awareness through such attractions as the rail cycle trail and walking tracks;
3   to reach out to consumers by offering a more inclusive approach that appeals to broader target markets domestically and internationally;
4   to attract qualified professionals, such as spa therapists and spa managers, to meet the demand of the growing spa industry in the area;
5   to adopt a holistic definition of wellness which incorporates the seven dimensions of wellness and acknowledges wellness as an active process through which people become more aware of, and make choices towards, a more successful existence (NWI, 1977).

TABLE 31.1 Wellness dimensions

Mental	Emotional	Physical	Occupational	Environmental	Social	Spiritual
Practitioners are qualified to a recognised standard (e.g. spa therapists, hospitality staff)	Practitioners are qualified to a recognised standard (e.g. spa therapists, hospitality staff)	Practitioners are qualified to a recognised standard (e.g. spa therapists, hospitality staff)	Practitioners are qualified to a recognised standard (e.g. spa therapists, hospitality staff)	Practitioners are qualified to a recognised standard (e.g. spa therapists, hospitality staff)	Practitioners are qualified to a recognised standard (e.g. spa therapists, hospitality staff)	Practitioners are qualified to a recognised standard (e.g. spa therapists, hospitality staff)
There is healthy food available in accordance with recognised guidelines (e.g. health food shop, local café and restaurants)	There is healthy food available in accordance with recognised guidelines (e.g. health food shop, local café and restaurants)	There is healthy food available in accordance with recognised guidelines (e.g. health food shop, local café and restaurants)		There is healthy food available in accordance with recognised guidelines (e.g. health food shop, local café and restaurants)	There is healthy food available in accordance with recognised guidelines (e.g. health food shop, local café and restaurants)	There are spiritual classes available (e.g. Yoga, Tai Chi)
There is access to counselling service	The natural environment is an integral part of the experience (e.g. mineral spas, gardens, mountain tracks)	There are spiritual classes available (e.g. yoga, Tai Chi)		The natural environment is an integral part of the experience (e.g. mineral spas, gardens, mountain tracks)	The natural environment is an integral part of the experience (e.g. mineral spas, gardens, mountain tracks)	There is access to counselling services

Educational classes are available (e.g. swimming, museum tours)	A variety of therapeutic water based treatments are available (e.g. mineral spas, Green health and wellness club)	There is organic food and beverages available (e.g. local cafés and restaurants, health food shop)	There is evidence of social responsibility
A variety of therapeutic water based treatments are available (e.g. mineral spas, Green health and wellness club)	There is a high standard of presentation throughout facilities and environment	There is a high standard of presentation throughout facilities and environment	There are opportunities for social interaction (e.g. bathing, cycling, walking, eating, group classes, tours, family bbq areas)
There are opportunities for social interaction (e.g. bathing, cycling, walking, eating, group classes, tours, family barbecue areas)	There is access to counselling services	The local culture is emphasised in the tourists experience (e.g. food, Edwardian buildings, beauty and body treatments)	There is access to counselling services
	There are opportunities for social interaction (e.g. bathing, cycling, walking, eating, group classes, tours, family barbecue areas)		

(Continued overleaf)

TABLE 31.1 Continued

Mental	Emotional	Physical	Occupational	Environmental	Social	Spiritual
	A variety of physical activity options are available (e.g. walking, cycling, bathing, aquacise classes, croquet, bowling)	There is organic food and beverages available (e.g. local cafés and restaurants, health food shop)		Historical features are maintained and protected (e.g. Edwardian spa buildings)	Overnight accommodation available (e.g. hotels, motels, camping)	
	A variety of hands on body and face treatments (e.g. massage, facials, waxing, manicures)	Overnight accommodation available (e.g. hotels, motels, camping)		Environmentally friendly skin-care products available (e.g. Pure Fiji)	A variety of physical activity options are available (e.g. walking, cycling, bathing, aquacise classes, croquet, bowling)	

A variety of physical activity options are available (e.g. *walking, cycling, bathing, aquacise classes, croquet, bowling)*	Environmentally friendly skin-care products available (e.g. *Pure Fiji)*
A variety of hands on body and face treatments (e.g. *massage, facials, waxing, manicures)*	

CHAPTER 32

Revitalising the healing tradition
Thermal springs in the Western Cape

Mark Simon Boekstein

> South Africa has in its medicinal springs a potential national asset which is capable of considerable development.
>
> (Rindl, 1936: 7)

South Africa has some 87 documented thermal springs (Tshibalo et al., 2010), although only about one-third of these have been developed into resorts of various sizes. Most of South Africa's thermal springs, particularly those in the Western Cape, have been used at some time in the past for medicinal purposes, both by European settlers after they arrived in the seventeenth century, and by indigenous tribes before them (Booyens, 1981).

The health spa tourism industry in South Africa is dominated by day spas, resort spas and destination spas (Global Spa Summit, 2011). There are currently very few links between South Africa's health spa industry and its thermal springs. While there are numerous thermal spring resorts in South Africa, only a few offer health or wellness treatments.

The Western Cape has all four of what Niv (1989) describes as the basic characteristics which can transform a destination into a leading centre for health tourism, namely:

1 thermal mineral springs;
2 a stable, comfortable climate all year round;
3 a good medical system;
4 attractive scenic locations.

There are 11 thermal springs in the Western Cape, seven of which have been developed into eight resorts. Only one of these resorts has a focus on health and wellness, with appropriate facilities, with the others functioning primarily as family leisure resorts. Internationally there has been a move by traditional thermal spring resorts to begin offering a combination of health (medical and wellness) services in combination with leisure activities. In light of current international trends, as well as perceived domestic needs, it appears that the Western Cape's thermal spring resources are not being optimally utilised as tourist attractions, neither for domestic nor for international tourist markets.

TABLE 32.1 Distribution of thermal spring resorts among the provinces of South Africa	
Western Cape	Caledon Spa, Goudini Spa, Avalon Springs, Baden Klub, Warmwaterberg Spa, Calitzdorp Spa, Uhuru Guest Farm, The Baths
Eastern Cape	Aliwal Spa, Cradock Spa, Fish Eagle Spa, Badfontein Guest Farm
Northern Cape	Riemvasmaak Hot Springs
North-West	Nkolo Spa
Free State	Florisbad
Kwazulu-Natal	Natal Spa, Thangami Safari Spa, Shu-Shu Hot Springs, Lilani Hot Springs
Mpumalanga	Badplaas
Limpopo	Warmbaths, Tshipise, Zimthabi Resort, Die Oog Hot Spring Resort, Rhemardo Holiday Resort, Eiland Spa, Makutsi Spa, Mphephu Hot Spring Resort, Sagole Spa

Eight different types of 'medicinal' thermal waters have been distinguished in South Africa, three of which occur in the Western Cape, each of which has specific therapeutic uses (Kent, 1952), and stories abound of amazing 'cures' that have taken place over the years (Proctor, 1948; Booyens, 1981). In the words of Wilmot (1914: 23), 'It is quite unnecessary to go to Baden-Baden or Carlsbad when we possess waters superior in efficacy'. However, medical treatments are not offered at any of the Western Cape's thermal spring resorts, despite the fact that domestic leisure visitors believe in the apparent healing powers of the water, report considerable health benefits from their visits, and express a desire for information on the health benefits of the water (Boekstein, 2001).

There was therefore a need to research and evaluate the development potential of these springs. This will undoubtedly assist in the positioning and marketing of the thermal spring tourism product in the Western Cape, so as to, first, better satisfy the needs of domestic leisure tourists who have an inherent belief in the healing qualities of the water and, second, to attract the growing international health (medical and wellness) tourism market. It contributes to revitalising a centuries-old healing tradition that is in danger of being lost altogether.

The mineral contents of the thermal springs in the Western Cape present some interesting opportunities for the development of balneotherapy/medicinal products. All of the springs contain radon gas, which has well-known medicinal properties, as well as various combinations of minerals with known medicinal/healing properties (e.g. sodium, magnesium, potassium, calcium, chloride, fluoride, sulphate, silicon, iron, lithium and arsenic). In addition, the presence of relatively rare trace elements, such as nickel, rubidium, selenium, strontium and zinc, which are thought to have medicinal properties, but about which very little if any research in a thermal spring context exists, could also present opportunities for further research and product development.

While the mineral and gas content of thermal waters in the Western Cape are an indication of considerable potential for the development of water-based medical and wellness products, the actual viability of such products would depend, to a large extent, on the

motivations and activity preferences of visitors. A visitor survey was thus carried out, involving 383 respondents at six thermal spring resorts in the Western Cape. The questionnaire included a section comprising 32 activities to provide data for activity-based market segmentation, together with questions designed to elicit trip-related data, respondents' opinions on the health and healing aspects of the water, and limited demographic information. A combination of closed-ended and open-ended questions was included, with the final question inviting respondents to add any comments they wished to make.

Almost all of the respondents (97 per cent) were domestic tourists, with only 3 per cent from outside South Africa. Respondents were fairly equally divided between male (47 per cent) and female (53 per cent), and also fairly equally spread in age, with about half (51 per cent) between 31 and 50 years old, almost one-third (30 per cent) over 50, and 19 per cent being 30 years old or younger. Nearly half of the respondents (41 per cent) were travelling as a group of three–four, a good indication of their being family units. Almost one-third (29 per cent) were travelling in groups of six or more. A similar number (28 per cent) were travelling as couples, with 23 per cent of these aged 61 or older. Almost half of the respondents (46 per cent) indicated that they visited a thermal spring resort more than once a year, with one-third (34 per cent) visiting once a year. Some 99 per cent of respondents were overnight visitors. More than half (58 per cent) of respondents were staying from one–three nights, with a further 28 per cent staying four–six nights, and the remaining 14 per cent staying longer than six nights.

A range of activity groups was identified. Two of the three activity groups with an average of more than 50 per cent 'Strong interest' are 'Water-based leisure activities' and 'Wellness activities'. In the first group, almost all the respondents (91 per cent) attach importance to being able to swim in a hot pool. The availability of hot water for swimming is, of course, the *raison d'être* of thermal spring resorts. However, the majority of respondents (65 per cent) also attach importance to having a cold swimming pool available. These would seem to be essential components of any thermal spring resort that wants to attract both summer and winter markets.

The second group, 'Wellness activities', has four activities with more than 50 per cent 'Strong interest'. Having a quiet pool available for relaxing is important to most respondents (77 per cent), as is swimming in mineral water (72 per cent). While both of these activities are essentially passive wellness activities, support for them does indicate a general desire for respondents to use their visits to thermal spring resorts to improve their health in some way. Many (60 per cent) would prefer to cook and/or eat healthy food, and more than half (53 per cent) would enjoy sitting in a jacuzzi/sauna/steam room, with another 35 per cent showing some interest. Wellness treatments and activities, such as massage and yoga, would be welcomed by 39 per cent of all respondents, with slightly more (42 per cent) showing some interest. While only 28 per cent have strong interest in beauty treatments, such as skin care, manicures and pedicures, a further 35 per cent have at least some interest. While the last two figures seem comparatively low, it still indicates that at least one-third to half of the respondents would be interested in these types of treatments and activities if they were available. It is, however, interesting to note that as many as 43 per cent of respondents express an interest in water-based medical treatments for diseases such as rheumatism, arthritis and psoriasis.

Respondents were asked their most important reasons for visiting the thermal spring resort where they completed the questionnaire. The most common reasons for visiting are for relaxation (29 per cent), and for the hot swimming pools (27 per cent), followed by the peaceful, tranquil atmosphere (11 per cent), the scenery and natural environment (8 per cent), to rest and do nothing (6 per cent), a holiday, vacation or break (5 per cent) and to have family time/be together as a family (4 per cent). Almost all respondents (95 per cent) were aware that bathing in thermal mineral water is reputed to be healthy, and 80 per cent felt that it was good for their own health, or that of members of their family or group. Some 5 per cent felt that the water did not help in any way, and 15 per cent were not sure. Those respondents who did feel that the water was good for their health were asked if there was anything specific that the water helped with. Out of 268 answers, some 34 different ways in which the water was found to be good for respondents' health were given.

Respondents found that the water helps them to relax and unwind (20 per cent), that it soothes, relaxes, heals or reduces stiffness in muscles and joints (14 per cent), it alleviates back pain (8 per cent), it helps with arthritis and rheumatism (6 per cent), it reduces stress and relieves tension (6 per cent), it moisturises and softens the skin, and is good for the eczema and psoriasis (6 per cent), it relieves general aches and pains (5 per cent), it relieves tiredness and leaves one feeling rested, refreshed, or invigorated (4 per cent), it helps one to sleep better (2 per cent), it helps to relieve painful legs and hips (2 per cent), it detoxifies and cleanses the system (2 per cent), it is good for the mind and makes one feel clear-minded (1 per cent), it improves blood circulation (1 per cent) and is good for overall well-being (1 per cent).

While thermal spring resorts in the Western Cape function primarily as family leisure resorts, it would seem that health, albeit indirectly, is still a strong motivation to visit. The resorts differ considerably from each other in terms of a number of factors, including water type and mineral content, range of facilities and services offered, number of visitors that can be accommodated, distance from Cape Town (the principal tourist-generating city), and location in relation to tourist attractions and scenic drives. Furthermore, each resort receives different types of visitors with different combinations of interests. It is doubtful, given the diversity outlined above, if any single framework could be designed to facilitate optimal health tourism development for all the resorts and undeveloped springs.

Nevertheless, there appears to be considerable potential for the development of thermal spring health (medical and wellness) tourism products in the Western Cape, based on available resources. It would, however, be unrealistic to expect thermal spring resorts in the province to produce the types of facilities and services that are offered by large international thermal spring resorts. The results of the survey suggest that the types of products that may appeal to international health tourism markets, particularly the wellness and beauty treatment markets, might only appeal to a relatively small segment of current, almost exclusively domestic, visitors.

CHAPTER 33

Opportunities and barriers to sustainable health tourism development in the Israeli Dead Sea region

Dalit Gasul

Introduction

This study aims to explore and map opportunities for and barriers to sustainable tourism development (STD) at the Israeli Dead Sea region and the implications for health tourism. The Dead Sea region is one of the most distinguished and important tourism areas in Israel, it is also extremely sensitive to various kinds of development pressures. The opportunities for STD are based on the region's physical characteristics and its attractiveness for tourism. The Dead Sea is the lowest point on earth, currently located 426 metres below sea level. It is the saltiest body of water in the world, rich with therapeutic minerals and is famous world wide as a health tourism destination. Lying in the heart of the Syrian-African Rift Valley at the southern outlet of the Jordan River, the Dead Sea region has an arid micro-climate: sunny all year round, with dry oxygen-rich air. The region itself contains pristine nature reserves with desert landscapes dotted with springs and lush ravines and is a home to unique flora and fauna. In the region are also famous heritage sites such as the baptism site of Jesus, Masada fortress (declared a UNESCO World Heritage Site), Qumran home of the Dead Sea Scrolls, among many more.

Dead Sea's natural health resources

The Dead Sea is one of the oldest thermal health resort regions in human history, as referred to by many historians and researchers. The curing properties are mentioned in the Bible and were acknowledged by King Herod who built a spectacular spa in his palace on top of Masada fortress over 2,000 years ago.

The fundamental curative assets are:

- Unique sun rays: The unique filtering reduces the intensity of the more harmful lower wavelength rays. Climatic treatment has therefore become a well-established treatment of Psoriasis, Psoriasis-Arthritis, Atopic Dermatitis, Ecsema, etc. For more than 35 years, climatotherapy has been used at the Dead Sea in Israel.
- High salt concentration: The Dead Sea contains a greater amount of dissolved salts than any other body of water on the earth. Compared to the 3 per cent salt content of ordinary sea water, Dead Sea water contains 32 per cent salts with a relatively high concentration of minerals such as magnesium, calcium, bromide and potassium (www.deadsea-health.org/new_html/general_main.html – Table 2). Exposure to Dead Sea water is acclaimed for nourishing the skin, easing rheumatic discomfort, activating the circulatory system, and relaxing the nerves. It's very high density enables the body to float effortlessly. This special feature permits free a relaxed and easier movement in the water thus enhancing the effects of physiotherapy.
- Thermo-mineral springs: Mineral water emanates from more than a dozen underground springs near the Dead Sea. The temperature of the water in these springs ranges from 28° to 30°C. The amount of minerals dissolved in the waters of these springs is much less than that of the Dead Sea, but still much more than that of all other health springs in the world. Their high hydrogen sulphide content, strong salinity and mineral rich waters are effective in the Balneotherapy treatment of various joint disorders, and have a remarkably relaxing effect on the nervous system.
- Medicinal mud: Mud used for therapy at the Dead Sea health resort is mined at specific sites along the shore of the sea. The medicinal natural black mud is a homogeneous mixture of Dead Sea minerals, organic elements retrieved from the shoreline as well as mixed with earth. When applied to the skin, the Dead Sea mud improves and stimulates blood circulation in affected areas of many types of joint diseases, due to its thermopexic properties. Medicinal black mud is also useful for cleansing and softening the skin. Mud therapy is called Pelotherapy.
- Extraordinary air: Located 426 metres below sea level, the Dead Sea area has the world's highest terrestrial barometric pressure resulting in 3.3–4.8 per cent (maximum in winter and minimum in summer) higher oxygen density than the air at sea level. The air along the shores of the Dead Sea is rich in magnesium and bromine, the relaxing effects of which help to reduce nervous tension. Together with unpolluted air which is virtually free of allergens, a comfortable temperature and low rainfall, in many cases the Dead Sea area provides a simple way of improving chronic Pulmonary diseases (asthma, cystic and chronic obstructive lung disease) (Sukenik, 2008; D.S.R.C., website).

The Dead Sea health tourism industry

Following the creation of the state of Israel, scientists and physicians from all over the world began to show interest in the unique healing properties of Dead Sea water and since

then have written and published hundreds of studies proving the importance of the region as a unique therapeutic site (Sukenik, 2008).

In the early 1980s the Israeli government established the first health resorts in the Dead Sea and in other hot springs along the Great Rift Valley at Tiberius. The government recognised the promotion of health tourism as an issue of national importance and established a Health Spa Authority that was responsible for research, planning, development and promotion of health and spa infrastructures and tourism marketing (Niv, 1989). By this initiative a health tourism hub was established in Ein Bokek including 1,500 hotel rooms; beaches along the Dead Sea shores, a solarium and medical treatment centre. The Germans' and the Scandinavians' national health insurance plans cover the medical expenses for psoriasis and rheumatic conditions and thousands of cure seeking tourists demanded rooms, frequently exceeding the room supply available.

The Dead Sea tourism industry is mostly associated with the Ein Bokek hotels zone, a clear example of a 'tourism ghetto', with its congested building of urban style high-rise hotels detached from the natural desert surroundings and from the socio-cultural environment. Ein Bokek, the geographical centre of the local tourism system, houses 14 of the area's 15 hotels and most of the tourism services. However, in terms of tourist attractions the geographical centre is situated in the heart of the region, around Ein Gedi and Masada.

The Dead Sea region is one of Israel's major tourism areas. Its strength as a leading tourist destination is apparent from the number of visitors and hotel nights as shown in Table 33.1. Until the end of the 1990s there were approximately 1,500 hotel rooms in the Dead Sea. Supply was small and met demand. The distribution was 50 per cent inbound tourism (all of them pure health tourists) and 50 per cent domestic tourists. In the years 1997–2000 new hotels were constructed, some 2,500 rooms – all with state-of-the-art spas. Following this the oldest hotels developed spa centres too.

Since the end of 2000, Israel has been suffering from its worst tourism crises ever, but demonstrated an amazing recovery. In 2005, national figures had not yet reached pre-crisis statistics, but 2011 showed an increase in hotel nights and high occupancy, actually the highest occupancy rates throughout Israel. Even though its share of the national total hotel beds is less than 8 per cent, the Dead Sea region is ranked third as the most desirable domestic and inbound holiday destination (State of Israel Ministry of Tourism, 2010).

Table 33.1 summarises tourism statistics for the year 2000 (this refers to the period before the crisis) compared to year 2005 and current figures for 2011.

Most of the tourism in the Dead Sea can be categorised under the heading of 'wellness' – health cures and rejuvenation. Approximately 70 per cent of inbound tourists staying 10–14 days take health and SPA treatments. In the past, 90 per cent of tourists were German and Danish (payment by health insurance companies). Today the Russian market accounts for about 50 per cent of incoming tourists. For domestic tourists, about 15 per cent are pure health tourists (IDF disabled veterans as well as skin diseases patients), the other 85 per cent are recreation and wellness tourists. Seventy per cent of Israelis during the week are retirees – in fact it is the most significant market segment for the Dead Sea Hotel. At the weekends mainly families and couples are coming.

TABLE 33.1 Tourism statistics for the Dead Sea region (2000, 2005, 2011)			
Year	2000	2005	2011
Accommodation units – hotels	3,765	3,638	4,004
Accommodation units – rural tourism	525	525	550
Total beds	~ 12,500	~ 12,300	~13,300
Hotel nights (inbound and domestic tourists)	1,565,500	2,000,820	2,301,4000
Percents of inbound hotel nights out of total nights	27%	15.5%	25.5%
Occupancy rates (%)	70.6%	70.5%	76.9%
Source: State of Israel Central Bureau of Statistics, 2001, 2006, 2012.			

Environmental pressures

The Dead Sea region is an ecosystem that is sensitive to changes. The entire range of environmental problems in the Dead Sea can be classified into four main source groups:

- an extreme decline in sea level that has resulted in the last 20 years in a drop of over 1m a year causing the shoreline to recede;
- evolvement of sinkholes as a result of the sea level falling, which prevents any further development in certain areas – currently over 4,000 sinkholes has been counted at the Israel Dead Sea's shore, and it has been estimated that over 400 new sinkholes are evolving every year;
- the Dead Sea Works factories whose location at the south-west bank of the Dead Sea facilitate an industrial pond for the purpose of evaporation and extraction of sea minerals – the Ein Bokek hotels area is actually located on the shores of this evaporation pond; in the processes of mineral extraction, the ponds water level is constantly rising and creates a danger of flooding the foundations of the nearby hotels;
- infrastructure and development hazards as well as environmental sensitivity resulting from the unique natural properties (the Rift, a junction between bio-geographical zones, desert, floods, etc.).

These sources cause different risks to and effects on the tourism industry, which can be generally summarised into three main issues: damaging the ecological system, landscape pollution and undermining infrastructures. These harm the tourist image of the Dead Sea and generate uncertainty regarding future planning.

Tourism development plans

The Ministry of Finance and the Ministry of Tourism have extensive tourism development plans for the Dead Sea region, at least 2,000–3,000 new hotel rooms in the next decade.

Hotels are supposed to be built in new tourist zones that require considerable infrastructural development, which constitutes serious danger to the sensitive ecological system of this area. In view of this, it is crucial to produce a strategy for developing sustainable tourism that will moderate these threats.

The geo-political environment

Alongside the above mentioned challenges the region is a cross point of three borders: Israel, Jordan and the Palestinian Authority. Management of water, environment and tourism cross-border resources constitutes a significant challenge anywhere, but a bigger challenge when the borders are in dispute. The Dead Sea region is an important tourism destination to the Hashemite Kingdom of Jordan as well and they are dealing with similar challenges at their shore as in the Israeli shore. Although the challenges are mutual, little cooperation regarding overcoming those challenges has been made so far. The obstacles to overcome with the Palestinian Authority originated mainly from the need to share water resources and from the fact that non-treated sewage from the upper drainage basin is flowing to the Dead Sea.

Summary and conclusions

The local municipal councils were engaged in a sustainable tourism development strategic plan for the Dead Sea Region between 2002–2004 (Gasul and Mansfeld, 2004). This planning process involved in-depth community participation processes (Gasul, 2006). Following the assimilation of the plan some evidence of sustainability can by indicated:

- It is clear that there has been an awareness raising at local, regional and international level regarding Dead Sea development processes.
- An environmental education programme for the entire education system in the Dead Sea region has been implemented in the last eight years (Gasul et al., 2005).
- A new national master plan for the Dead Sea shore has been in the planning process over the last two years, involving a broad planning team including community, environment and heritage expertise.
- Increasing cross-border cooperation and planning processes in many areas (e.g. the comprehensive Kidron basin Master Plan).

The continuous declining of the sea level has necessitated dramatic rehabilitation programmes such as the Red Sea–Dead Sea canal. The project's goals are to stabilise the shrinking Dead Sea, supply water and electricity to countries in the area, especially Jordan, and engender regional cooperation that would promote peace. After almost a decade of pre-planning feasibility studies of a proposed pipeline between the Red Sea and the Dead Sea, the World Bank released a series of reports on January 2013 that declare the project feasible from an engineering, economic and environmental standpoint. The World Bank concluded that without the pipeline, the Dead Sea would shrink by about 10 per cent over the next 50 years, which would do major harm to tourism, local industries and the environment. On the other hand, environmental groups are concerned that the transfer of mass volumes of water from one sea to another can create drastic consequences; for example, damage to the unique natural system of the Dead Sea, due to mixing its water with Red Sea water which has a different chemical composition. This includes changes in water salinity, formation of gypsum, change in water evaporation rates and loss of unique health benefits that account for much of the tourist attraction to the Dead Sea area.

Heritage and the renaissance of Domburg as a health resort

Peter Kruizinga

Health and wellness in the Netherlands

With regards to health and wellness tourism the Netherlands is a white spot on the European map. A tradition of using spas for medical reasons is totally absent in the country. Unlike in Germany and other European countries there has never been any recognition of the effect of mineral waters or sea-water upon one's health. It is even being denied by the Dutch Association Against Quackery (Vereniging tegen Kwakzalverij), which is strongly opposed to every form of complementary and alternative medicine. In an article about water therapies on its website this Association states that 'after a century little is known about the effectiveness of Kneipp therapy' (Kwakzalverij.nl, 2012), thus denying the health effects that are obtained from treatment by water therapies throughout the world.

The point of view of this Association, however, does not correspond with the general opinion in the Netherlands, where an increasing part of the population is using complementary and alternative medicine (CBS, 2008). This does not imply the use of spas and health resorts, or perhaps we should say not yet. The increasing popularity of wellness (Rabobank, 2011) could well cause the development of health tourism in the country.

Since the end of the twentieth century there are some resorts in the Netherlands where bathing in warm water is used for medical treatment. All of them use mineral sources, located near the German border, where geothermal activity is much higher than in the west part of the country. Fontana in Nieuweschans (since 2009 Bad Nieuweschans) opened in 1985, Thermaalbad Arcen and Thermae 2000 (Valkenburg) in 1989 and Sanadome in Nijmegen in 1995. The latter started as a medical health centre, but soon had to focus on the wellness market. None of them could exist from medical tourism alone. The range of cure programmes is restricted to rheumatism and other complaints of the joints, skin diseases such as psoriasis, physiotherapeutic treatment, Parkinson's disease and anti-ageing. It is only because of the wellness boom that took place in the last decennia that they are still there, but the medical part plays a very minor role.

The case of Domburg

The south-western part of the country, the province of Zeeland, wants to develop into a nationally and internationally known region for health tourism. Touristic entrepreneurs and the communities of Veere and Sluis (each about 20,000 inhabitants) want to develop the villages of Domburg and Cadzand into a health and wellness destination of international standing, which will attract German, Dutch and Belgian tourists, seeking relaxation and improvement for their health. An important tool for achieving this goal is the quest for the official acknowledgement as health resorts (in Dutch: *badstatus*) for both villages (Bad Domburg, 2011). Both are situated on the North Sea coast. The same goes for many other places at the coast, like Zandvoort, Katwijk, Noordwijk and Scheveningen. All of them have nice beaches and are receiving a large number of tourists every year, but the coast of Zeeland and Domburg especially is by far the most popular among German tourists (Kustvakanties im Holland, 2008).

What makes Domburg and Cadzand such unique places that they think they can achieve the official status as a health destination? The case of Domburg is interesting for its historical background, which shows that once there used to be a tradition in health tourism, not only regional or national, but also international.

Domburg as an early bathing resort

The village, lying in the dunes, has always been surrounded by an attractive countryside. In the seventeenth and eighteenth centuries the bourgeois from the city of Middelburg came to the coast to relax and enjoy themselves. They built summer houses and country estates with beautiful gardens (Warners, 1984).

The history of Domburg as a bathing resort starts in 1834, when two bourgeois families from Middelburg decided to take baths in the sea with bath carriages. They were the first health tourists, most likely inspired by a visit to Scheveningen, where since 1818 sea baths were offered by the owner of the first bath house, Jan Pronk (Canon van Zuid-Holland). It is most likely that the idea of taking sea baths spread from Great Britain, where the later Dutch Royal Family lived during the French occupation of the country (1795–1813).

These health tourists *avant la lettre* had close contact with the Lord of Domburg, Mr. J.J. Slicher, and with circles of the Dutch king, Willem I. With fundraising amongst the elite of Walcheren, and a donation from the king, in 1837 the first *badpaviljoen* (bathing pavilion) was erected, with which the growth as a bathing resort was initiated. In 1866 the *badhotel* (bathing hotel) was opened. The circle of bathing guests however was restricted to the small circle of elite from Zeeland, mainly from Middelburg (Warners, 1984). It was the appearance of doctor Mezger that changed the landscape.

Johan Georg Mezger (1838–1909) was the son of a German butcher, who came from Wiesbaden to Amsterdam. He worked in his father's business and at the same time studied gymnastics. Because of his talent in kinesiology he was stimulated to do medical studies. He became one of the founders of physiotherapy. He tapped and rubbed and

recommended movement, where up till then parts of the body were tightly bandaged and absolute rest was prescribed. His speciality was friction. He squeezed, rubbed and tapped the limbs of his patients with his 'golden' thumbs. He invented four of the five now known strokes of massage: *effleurage* (stroke), friction, *petrissage* (kneading) and *tapotement*. The fifth stroke used today is vibration (*lagrasse*). He was the founder of classical massage, in the US named Swedish massage, because it was – erroneously – attributed to Per Henrik Ling (Calvert, 2002).

The career of Mezger started in Amsterdam, and was an instant success. After treating the son of the Dutch king Willem III in 1870 and curing the Swedish crown prince Gustav from invalidity in 1871, his career was booming and he became famous in the world of European royalty. Next to fame it brought him fortune. He also worked in Bonn, Wiesbaden and Paris. He learned to know the province of Zeeland by his wife, who came from Middelburg, the capital of the province, about 12 kilometres from Domburg.

Until 1870 Domburg was hardly accessible, because of its remote laying on the island of Walcheren. This changed radically in the 1870s, when the main islands of Zeeland were connected and a railway was opened, which meant the end of isolation, because it connected the region with the rest of the country and Europe. There was a direct connection with Amsterdam, but also with Berlin. Endpoint was Vlissingen (Flushing), from where in 1875 the Steamship Company Zeeland (Stoomvaartmaatschappij Zeeland) opened a daily mail boat connection with Sheerness, later with Queenborough and Folkestone, in the UK.

In 1880 a committee was established to promote the interests of Domburg as a bathing resort. Together with the local authorities a doctor was appointed to take care of the well-being of bathing guests (who still used bathing carriages). From 1883 this committee published the weekly *Domburgsch Badnieuws* during the summer months, with lists of all arriving guests, so we have an accurate impression of all the visitors. Among them were wealthy and royal guests from Germany, Belgium, the UK, other European countries and the United States. Many of them built villas in the dunes and returned every summer.

One of them was Dr Mezger, who came to Domburg for the first time in 1886 and came back every year. Domburg was by then emerging as a seaside resort and was also popular amongst painters. In 1887 Mezger built his own villa, where he treated European Royal patients, but also local farmers. Domburg became the place to be, not only for the royal and well-to-be, but also for artists. Attracted by the still untouched country life, but especially the quality of the light, Dutch painters such as Jan Toorop, and Piet Mondriaan came to stay in the village during the summers. The sea-water which almost surrounded them, which plays an important role in the reflection of sunlight, also the relatively high salinity of the air, which can make the light almost transparent, gave birth to a new movement in painting: luminism (Van Vloten, 2004). A small exhibition hall was erected in 1911, where exhibitions were held, until a storm demolished the building in 1921.

During the Second World War many villas were destroyed and the village lost its position as a bathing resort for the well-to-do. As mass tourism emerged, during the 1960s and later, Domburg became a mass tourism spot, with nothing special but a nice beach, an old village, fish and chips, and some remnants of past glory times. The old *badhotel* from 1866 gradually fell into decay, but was rebuilt in 1994, while the *badpaviljoen* from

1889 was narrowly saved from demolition, but was restored with subvention in 2008. With these restorations Domburg had regained some of its grandeur. In the last 20 years the village has grown in popularity, driving up prices of real estate to one of the highest in the country. The capacity grew up to more than 1,000 beds, in some 20 hotels, several camping parks and bed & breakfasts (Kenniscentrum Kusttoerisme, 2012). The whole community of Veere is receiving about 4 million overnight stays per year, in which Domburg plays a major role (Veere, 2012). For some years the numbers of overnight stays have been falling; the main reason for this is that guests stay for a shorter time. This trend is a threat to business. With the help of the wellness trend touristic entrepreneurs hope to be able to lengthen the season and the average stay of guests and to get them to return more often, as wellness is not vulnerable to the influence of the weather (Janzen, 2012).

Well-being in Domburg: a SWOT analysis

The community of Veere developed a DNA-picture for the village of Domburg. Keywords in this DNA are: luxury, bon-vivant, mondain, culinary, art and tourism. With the wellness boom the community and some innovative touristic entrepreneurs became aware of the unique features of Domburg: the natural environment (sea, beach, dunes, park-like forests), heritage (Badpaviljoen, villas from the nineteenth century, the rebuilt exhibition hall), gastronomy (seafood), history and folklore. With a subsidy from the province, the project 'Vitality and Wellness, a Sea of Chances' was carried out. The project resulted in the definition of market chances for the region and in plans for regaining a position for Domburg as a wellness resort by obtaining an official status as a health resort (bath status). The heritage of the village certainly provides a solid base for this, but more is needed. A weak point is the lack of knowledge in the field of health tourism, especially the absence of medical provisions, focused on health tourism. There is no experience with therapies or wellness programmes that make use of the qualities of the sea, such as thalasso. The opening of European borders for health-care provision from January 2013 is an opportunity. Hotel managers see a panache in offering health programmes, in order to achieve year round exploitation, and thus getting profits from their investments in wellness. I think that to reach this market a clear vision should be formulated, programmes have to be developed and knowledge and experience will have to be imported. The bath status certainly is a good label for achieving distinctiveness and to position Domburg as a bathing resort with quality. Whether it will lead to the desired goals will be a matter of planned action, and of cooperation of entrepreneurs.

35

Health cuisine
A new health destination marketing tool

Nico Dingemans

Introduction

After Spain, Thailand and Hong Kong . . . Twente? Twente is a relatively low-key rural region in the east of the Netherlands. For Dutch insiders it is fondly known as the country estate of the Netherlands. 'Why not search closer to home?' officials at the local Chamber of Commerce asked when I became curious because I am in the process of writing a book about health cuisine, featuring 12 top chefs in 12 destinations around the world, and I wondered if the Twente region would fit in such a global book. But what started with some hesitation, turned into a rediscovery of my own green region and an unexpected destination marketing tool, full of healthy gastronomy.

Modern macrobiotics in Alicante

Our first culinary health travel brought us to modern macrobiotics chef Pablo Montoro, who was handpicked directly from the kitchen of celebrity chef Ferran Adrià. Pablo's task was to cook healthy gourmet food at the ultra luxury SHA Wellness Clinic in Alicante, Spain. The philosophy of SHA is based on the ideas of macrobiotics guru Michio Kushi who stood by SHA owner Alfredo Bataller during his recovery process. Macrobiotics is a universal philosophy and way of life based on nutritional and health-based values developed by the Japanese George Ohsawa. Kushi was one of his pupils. Macrobiotics comes from the Greek word 'macros', meaning *long* or *great*, and 'bios', meaning *life*. Grounded in the traditional teachings of East and West, macrobiotics originates from the yin and yang philosophy, a combination of 5,000-year-old experience with incorporated knowledge about Japanese Zen, Buddhism and Western science. In Western Europe, in the 1960s, it was known as 'hippie-food' and considered boring and not very tasteful. To chef Pablo the SHA owners said: 'We would like you to apply the presentation techniques you learned at El Bulli to the ingredients we use in Kushi's teachings.' From a nutritional point of view, chef Pablo is supported by a team of medical, alternative (Eastern) medicine and macrobiotic experts. One of those experts is Ms Virginia Harper (a pupil of Kushi), with whom I had an interesting interview about how she learned to cope with Crohn's disease and Takayasu arthritis thanks to macrobiotics, as she explained how essential proper nutrition is for your bowel function and how simple it can be to combine 'tasteful' and 'delicious' food. Interestingly, Japanese Cuisine has a lot of macrobiotic components, such as sushi, miso, edama beans, tofu and sencha tea.

Health and wellness in Thailand

After Spain, we travelled to the famous Chiva-Som International Health Resort in Hua Hin, for decades the retreat town of the Royal Thai family. General Manager Paul Linder advised us to first undergo the 'guest experience' with therapeutic massages and a health scan, which includes a 'mental and emotional health' consultation. Only afterwards were we able to taste and photograph all the tasteful dishes that Thai spa cuisine has to offer. We were told: 'You had a long journey, and if you are going to write about us, then you first need to experience our approach to Wellness. Then work.' Needless to say we enjoyed and learned from every moment of our stay. Upon our departure chef Paisarn Cheewinsiriwat quickly highlighted his signature dish with a cheeky smile: 'Khun Nico, look up the Latin description of my special flower when you're home.' I didn't get the hint back then, but when I was back in the Netherlands I looked it up: '*Clitoria ternatea*, or butterfly pea.' I took a closer look at the purple/blue flower again on the picture we shot of the monkfish and spinach terrine with Madras curry emulsion and Dijon mustard. Then I realised why he had smiled: butterfly pea is one of four herbs traditionally used as Shanka Pushpi, an Ayurvedic medicine used to promote neurological health and proven to have memory enhancing effects. That is something you don't forget. Back home, Studio Paf graphic designer translated our Thai and Spanish culinary travels into beautiful mood-boards and the design of the book, as well as the culinary story we wanted to convey to our readership, began to take shape.

TCM in Hong Kong

In China we visited design hotel Mira Hong Kong, located in the middle of trendy Tsimshatsui, to write a chapter about delicious Cantonese Cuisine in this super modern five-star hotel, and about the influence of traditional Chinese medicine (TMC) and Chinese food therapy with master-chef Ken Yu. Chef Ken does not speak English but he has a Michelin star. We ate of good food, including special dishes with sea cucumber, chocolate-infused tofu with goji berries, sea star soup and black hen. Healthy and tasteful eating is embedded almost religiously in Chinese cuisine. TCM is all around you, in herbs and spices shops around every corner, in restaurants and supermarkets, and so on. We knew this before we arrived, but when you eat and drink amongst Hong Kong residents, you become more deeply immersed into their food culture and that makes a big difference.

Because, within that diverse Chinese Cuisine, Cantonese cooking (i.e. thanks to the many special spices used and slow cooking) is regarded as healthy haute cuisine. And this is exactly what health cuisine is all about; healthy gastronomy with top chefs such as chef Pablo, Chef Paisarn and Chef Ken Yu, who incorporate ancient and tried-and-tested knowledge (which has been passed on from generation-to-generation) into modern tasteful dishes. These top chefs did not reinvent the wheel. Rather they recognise that the knowledge has been amongst us for centuries. They just preserve that knowledge in a very appealing manner; they improve where needed and present their dishes in a highly attractive and modern way. They keep our interest warm.

Inspiration: what is healthy food?

Other health cuisine destinations include India, Jordan, Italy, Poland and Indonesia, all countries with traditional cuisines where 'healthy' and 'tasteful' food go hand-in-hand, grounded in culture and in authentic lifestyle. As a personal touch, for instance, I want to write about traditional 'djamus', those smelly herbal medicinal potions and lotions from Java which I still recall my Indonesian grandmother used to make and which are nowadays being used in the most luxury five-star resorts on Bali and Java, simply because they work. During my research for my book *Health Cuisine* a homeopath drew my attention to the late Dr David Servan-Schreiber, author of *Anticancer: a New Way of Life*, who, despite a brain tumour, managed to prolong his life 19 years by eating more consciously. I lost my father to cancer at 58, far too young to die. During times like those you also asked yourself several essential life questions. My photographer advised me to read Michael Pollan's *In Defense of Food*, about how we have collectively forgotten how to eat well; mainly because of mono-culture, eating too much of the same type of food and our reduced sense of taste. I became inspired by Ayurveda and Dr Vandana Shiva from India, author of *Monocultures of the Mind* and in 2010 pronounced by Forbes as one of the seven most influential women in the world. Dr Vandana is a strong advocate for Indian farmers and fights for the preservation of seed banks through her Navdanya programme, which means nine seeds and stands for the protection of biodiversity. Because without seeds, there can be no life. I began to recognise touch points and common ground and a connectedness between the stories of chefs, farmers, gourmet lovers, culinarians, spa and wellness experts and bon vivants who spoke to me about the rediscovery of culture-based knowledge of our food: a culinary heritage of core values.

From Farm to Fork

Based on those core values, local farming and eating what nature has to offer in our close vicinity, became one of *Health Cuisine*'s 12 themes. 'Let the story of the farmer, the chef and biodiversity do its work.' That is how the Dutch-themed *From Farm to Fork* was born. I began to tickle the interest of chefs in the west and south-west of the Netherlands, those with Michelin stars and who are listed in the top 100 of Dutch fine-dining restaurants. But

I could not quite find what I was looking for. Then that tip came in from the local Chamber of Commerce. The article they gave me read: 'Country Estate hotel De Bloemenbeek, awarded with a Michelin star, has a long established tradition within the world of international top sports, thanks to the specialized knowledge of SVH Masterchef Michel van Riswijk about healthy and delicious dishes. Chef Michel enhances sports accomplishments of athletes and sports professionals.' That very same day I drove through the countryside of Twente to the famed Country Estate hotel, which decided to participate.

Healthy gastronomy in Twente

One month later we held the first health cuisine event, which led us to a presentation to the Twente Association of Artisan Chefs (Twentse AAK). There we were in rural Bornerbroek, a place very few people ever heard of, standing between Dutch cows on the left and farming tractors on the right, talking about exotic destinations like Thailand and Hong Kong and Spain. The artisan chefs were slightly confused at first, but the more we engaged in conversation about healthy cooking, organic farming, pure food and culture-based knowledge about food, the more they understood that their story is essentially the same as those top chefs and farmers abroad, but just in a different cultural context. It triggered a sense of connectivity – connected through healthy gastronomy.

Things moved fast since then. Harry's Farm called to ask if an authentic organic cattle farm, 200 years in the family, could be suitable for the book. A few days later, we were walking in the countryside again between Black and Red Angus cattle in Wierden, the first in the region: 80 pedigree cows on 40 hectares of farmland, 100 per cent free range, purely organically raised, hormone-free and no antibiotics. The result: 'stress-less' tasteful meat with intra-muscular fats (or marbled meat as we know it), full of omega-3. My 'Twente-tour' took me further to other organic farmers, local top chefs and artisan entrepreneurs from north to south, and from east to west of the Twente region. Chef Willem Dankers of Dorset Restaurant and Chef Jelle Wagenaar of Restaurant Het Seminar joined as well, and in September 2012 we finished our photo-sessions. It turned out that we had more material than we needed for the Dutch health cuisine chapter, so we decided to publish a separate book, a sort of prelude to Health Cuisine. Soon enough three students of the Cas Spijkers Academie Twente (the best culinary school in the Netherlands), Dr Frank van Berkum (author on diets and nutrition, who graded the students' dishes), chef Rob Fiselier of award-winning spa resort De Holtweijde and even the Regional Tourism Office of Twente participated in the book which we titled *From Farm to Fork in Twente*, a book about health cuisine in the country estate of the Netherlands. The book was symbolically released on 12/12/2012 and in January 2013 the book was being sold by the Twente Regional Tourism Office during the 'Vakantiebeurs', the largest annual international Tourism and Travel Trade fair in the Netherlands.

What the Twente story has taught us, is that health cuisine (linked with wellness and spas), has strong destination marketing value. Food tourism is a growing worldwide trend. Wellness and health travel is a growing trend. And when we combine and build on the two, placing it in a cultural holistic context, and where possible supported by evidence-based

material about health benefits, then you have a powerful health destination marketing tool. The main challenge here is to connect private with public, farmers with hoteliers, trade associations with entrepreneurs, educators with the work field, young talent with professionals, and more importantly to recognise that healthy food is universal and culturally binding. However, once packaged and presented in the right manner, be it a book or a magazine or other media, you have a formula in your hands for a successful addition to your health travel portfolio.

Sources and acknowledgements

SHA Wellness Clinic, Alicante
Michio Kushi, Japan
George Ohsawa foundation
Chiva-Som Health Resort
Chiva-Som Academy, Bangkok
Mira Hong Kong
Dr David Servan-Schreiber
In Defense of Food
Dr Vandana Shiva
Twente Tourism Office
Hotel De Bloemenbeek
Dorset Restaurant
Het Seminar Restaurant
Wellness Resort De Holtweijde
Cas Spijkers Academy
Slow Food Netherlands
Slow Food International
Dr Frank van Berkum

Well-being, holistic and spiritual tourism

36

The social construction of travelling for well-being in Australia

Alison van den Eynde and Adrian Fisher

There has been significant recent industry and consumer interest for well-being tourism in Australia. It is reported that the demand for well-being tourism has grown considerably in the last ten years with spa visitation increasing 13.8 per cent annually during the period 2001–4 and with an annual growth rate of 1.6 per cent (Tourism Victoria, 2011). Responding to this demand over the last five years, both the Australian Tourism Export Council (ATEC) (ATEC, 2010) and Tourism Victoria in particular have paid attention to well-being tourism for potential expansion opportunities through strategic plans, such as 'Victoria's Spa and Wellness Tourism Action Plan, 2005–2010' (Tourism Victoria, 2010). However, a fundamental question to be addressed is: what drives this interest in well-being travel participation?

To investigate the driving forces of well-being travellers and non-travellers in Australia, it is suggested by Lean (2012: 153) that travel can no longer be understood as a binary action: '. . . as bodily movement from a static "home" environment to "away", with eventual return to home'. Lean suggests people are motivated to travel based upon the construction of their social reality which occurs before, during and after travel. It is because social realities and social practice are constructed by discourses (Pernecky, 2012) that the motivation or prelude to travelling can be grounded in a discourse of well-being. This research investigated this discourse of well-being in a qualitative study of well-being travellers and non-travellers with the emergence of three key themes.

Theme 1: defining well-being, 'doing health' and 'well-being as a feeling'

Both well-being travellers and non-travellers unequivocally associate the term 'well-being' with 'health'. The terms are used interchangeably and synonymously when defining well-being. Descriptors of health and well-being were used in conjunction with grounding well-being into two main categories: (1) Well-being is health, and health is an action; and (2) Well-being is a state of being or a feeling.

The achievement of health was described as activities predominately related to physical health, such as nutrition or exercise. Alternatively, as a state of being or feeling, well-being is achieved by connections with family or community, with an emphasis upon making the best of life by self contentment and less stress.

For well-being travellers, the main responses for how to achieve well-being as a state of being or feeling were by 'doing what feels good' and maintaining 'social connections'. Religion and spirituality were foremost in this theme. For example:

> By listening to what your body needs, e.g.: sleep, nourishment, rest, activity. Important for the survival of this system of things, in a physical way, and in a spiritual way, to be on God's side, be his friend. Because his time will come to deal with mankind his way.

The well-being travellers exhibit a heartening, positive attitude toward achieving well-being. However, conversely within the 'doing health' theme a frequent and dual understanding of 'hard work' featured. Financial stability and maintaining a work and life balance with 'thrifty saving' and 'financial stability' were described by some well-being travellers as their primary method of achieving well-being.

A slightly different account of 'hard work' also featured. The requirement of stringent regular and sustained effort, such as 'being strict with diet and exercise, very important'. Alternatively, a participant used the word 'disciplined' to describe the condition under which it could be achieved: 'This happens when I am being disciplined with a combination of exercise, prayer, rest and diet.' Therefore, achieving well-being was described as a struggle and perhaps not enjoyable.

Well-being non-travellers primarily defined well-being as physical health and happiness/personal contentment. Nutrition and exercise featured in their definitions as a means to achieving well-being, with a focus upon outward appearances including fitness and 'looking your best'.

Following from this understanding emerged a notable theme for the non-well-being travellers, the attitude of health/well-being and relativity. A number of participants articulated that in comparison to the rest of the world, Australia is a 'lucky country' with comparatively good health systems and standard of living. 'I think Australians don't realise how good we really have it here in this country and have to adjust our attitude to appreciate what we have.' Therefore, non-well-being travellers thought access to services which assist well-being was a privilege rather than a right, while well-being travellers mostly expressed well-being was the result of hard work. Well-being is primarily a self-responsibility, for example: '. . . some believe others should carry the burden of their failure to follow a path to "well-being" and refuse to help themselves believing society owes them a better life' (well-being traveller). While non-well-being travellers shared this view to a lesser extent, they were more inclined to be sceptical of the financial gain by some in creating the well-being industry, 'It has become a mega dollar industry. From self help books, to the acceptance of counselling, to the growth of the fitness industry.'

Theme 2: reflective well-being: the potentially unachievable journey

The driving forces prompting well-being travel participation are also grounded in the extent to which participants feel they have achieved well-being. Approximately half of well-being travellers had not reached their ideal state of well-being at any point in their life, compared to two thirds of non-well-being travellers. Although making a concerted effort to be well, both by travelling and regular well-being activities, well-being travellers still have not reached their goals. For them, well-being is important but somewhat elusive, thus the need for effort and perseverance.

Those who did reach an ideal state of well-being, expressed that it occurred at another stage of life. Reflections for the well-being traveller included a time when participants were younger and fitter. They were either single without children, or newly married without children, were more financially stable, independent and in control of their own time. This group's focus upon work and financial stability as an important element also appears as a component of well-being achievement upon reflection: '. . . in a previous position [work] where all of my hard work paid off and I had achieved all I wanted to achieve and I had taken the organisation as far as I could possibly do so. Then I got bored . . .'

In stark contrast, the non-traveller group cited marriage and the birth of children as the cause of their well-being. Both male and female participants demonstrated this perspective:

> A number of years ago when I was working, earning money and looking after myself and my family.
>
> (Male well-being non-traveller)

> When I was in my 30s I had two beautiful children, a loving husband, a house . . .
>
> (Female well-being non-traveller)

It is clear that although not expressing well-being as a state of being or feeling to the same extent as the well-being travellers, they understand well-being to be grounded in their family in a way the well-being travellers do not. The reflection theme informs the well-being participation discourse by demonstrating the striving to achieve a past ideal state, or perhaps well-being as the never ending journey.

Theme 3: the increased public consciousness of well-being and the importance of participation

Overwhelmingly, the well-being participation discourse is informed by a perceived increase of well-being knowledge in the public realm. The majority of the sample stated that an increase of information is occurring in the media, particularly television in the form of reality shows, news reporting upon the unhealthy masses, and advertising selling well-being products. In addition, there is easier access to information on the internet, where there is a plethora of well-being knowledge (and misinformation) to be had. The increased awareness of Australians is not without criticism or scepticism. It is perceived by some as overwhelming in volume and nature:

> Constant bombardment of TV/news articles citing figures on obesity/diabetes/cancer.
> (Non-well-being traveller)

> [M]edia pressure, especially TV . . .
> (Well-being traveller)

The participants presented a picture of continual presence of well-being knowledge from a variety of sources in the public realm. Clearly, for some the continual presence is not entirely welcome and experiences as undesirable pressure. Nevertheless, despite criticisms, well-being travellers expressed that increased knowledge is contributing to the well-being travel participation discourse.

As a part of the public consciousness of well-being, both groups articulated that society was the antithesis to well-being, that we are living in a 'bad society' because of the perceived ruthless conditions of current living. This includes stress and a sense of being overwhelmed and over-stimulated: 'the world is moving too quickly'. The stress felt by participants is related to work and financial pressures, technology and materialism, and a direct response to their perceived state of society.

> [M]ost people are under too much stress, as there is always a quota to fill, a time limit, a budget to fill, bad transport, traffic problems, so by the end of the week they are totally stressed out, then its time for domestic duties, shopping etc.

For the well-being traveller, society was a direct insult to the state of being: 'the body, mind and spirit can become disconnected from self if left too long within a materialistic, consumerism, superficial environment' (well-being traveller).

Well-being travel participation and non-participation discourse

Well-being travellers and non-travellers seemed to engage with a well-being discourse based upon the perceived increase of information in the public realm and the conditions of society today as the antithesis of well-being – the bad society. For well-being travellers, achieving well-being has become more important, yet the majority of the sample has never achieved well-being.

The well-being discourse was carried out, or performed, in well-being travel participation. When talking about the well-being travel experience, participants expressed their escape from the 'fast paced' society by isolation and being in control of their own time: 'Being alone and isolated from all outside influences . . . The feeling of being in total control

while going where I want to go.' The persistence of the bad society was demonstrated with well-being as the never ending journey and the need to persevere with further well-being participation: 'I went to Sydney, stayed at the Shangri la with my mum and had a spa day, it was good for that day but the next day I felt stressed again.'

While engagement with the well-being discourse seems a prelude to participation in well-being travel, factors that constrain participation were largely, but not limited to, socio-economics. More than half of the non-well-being travellers stated that finances were the determining factor as to why they wouldn't participate: 'too expensive' and 'sometimes wish to have more money for that'. Further circumstances included simply not being interested. Asked if they would participate if it was affordable, more than half of the non-travellers stated they would still choose not to participate. They were either uncomfortable with it, or it was not a holiday preference for them: 'Not particularly, I am past redemption'. A good portion of the sample simply considered it 'a waste of time'; it was a holiday they did not revere: 'Please don't be offended but well-being travel is starting (really started some time ago now) to sound like a piece of mumbo-jumbo!'

Returning to the key question, what is the driving force of well-being travel, overall a similar well-being discourse is constructed by both well-being travellers and non-travellers. It is suggested that this well-being discourse is carried out in well-being travel participation. However, there are several points of deviation between those who do and do not travel for well-being. For instance, attitudes towards well-being; the level of spirituality/religion between the groups; whether well-being is hard work and self-responsibility (well-being travellers), or a privilege (non-well-being travellers); that well-being was achieved before family and responsibility or for non-travellers, family and connections increase feelings of well-being. Finally, the non-well-being travellers scepticism ('mumbo jumbo') towards the industry of well-being and well-being travel and financial ability to participate are areas to be addressed in the marketing and services of well-being travel.

37

Building tourism and well-being policy
Engaging with the public health agenda in the UK

Heather Hartwell, Ann Hemingway, Alan Fyall,
Viachaslau Filimonau, Stacy Wall and Neil Short

Introduction

In part driven by the economic climate in the United Kingdom (UK) and in part driven by a belief in the prevention of ill health, and the wider benefits and economies that such an approach brings to society, the UK government is currently pursuing a 'localised' policy whereby health improvement functions are being relocated from health funded regional to local authority control (Hartwell, 2011). Underpinning such an approach is the view that the relocation of health improvement functions, and perhaps more significantly budgets, to local authorities across the UK will enable decision makers at the local level, where knowledge and expertise is more cognisant of local conditions, to prove more effective in enhancing the general levels of health and well-being of the local population than has proved achievable in the past. One of the interesting and more innovative opportunities arising from such a shift in policy at a national level, is the potential in many parts of the country to bring together health and tourism policies as a vehicle to promote physical and mental well-being for both residents and visitors. Not only can such a fusion of policies bring health benefits to resident and tourist communities but the adoption of health-friendly tourism strategies can help differentiate tourist destinations, serve as the essence of brand and brand-repositioning strategies, and at the same time generate economic benefit to the destination (Fyall, 2011). Notwithstanding, the primary rationale for the co-development of a tourism and public health policy is in the knowledge that the promotion of mental and physical health for residents and visitors alike is a socially desirable and economically-beneficial outcome.

To achieve such a desired state through a marriage of policies, collaboration between all key stakeholders is a necessity. Although with quite distinct agendas when looked at in isolation, the potential for tourism and health to be 'natural' partners is very real with considerable opportunity for the development of a sustainable symbiotic relationship; this despite the fact that historically neither have been intuitively connected (Hartwell, 2011). A strategic, policy-driven framework for planning and development of a destination with increased well-being as the intended outcome promotes a potentially competitive and sustainable avenue and is consistent with the wider sustainable and collaborative approach to the development of destinations advocated by Ritchie and Crouch (2003). They go on to add that such a policy will dictate the direction for strategic focus and will in turn form a clear statement of intent from a local government perspective. Not only will a combined health and tourism policy communicate the goals and intended footprint for a long-term vision for a destination but it will also put in place the mechanics for policy to be achieved. In this regard, the specific role of tourism policy is to establish a social, economic and infrastructural environment that enables the sector to develop and prosper in a sustainable manner where opportunities for policy synergy with health are evident, transparent, realistic and implementable.

Building tourism and well-being policy

The aforementioned reorganisation of public health in the UK supports the World Health Organization's (WHO) 'Healthy Cities' initiative which seeks to engage local governments in European towns and cities in health development through a process of political commitment, institutional change, capacity-building, partnership-based planning and innovative projects (WHO, 2012). To date, there are 14 cities in the UK participating with numbers expected to grow exponentially in the future once dissemination and implementation of the recently-emerged public health agenda is more widespread. The key change in emphasis is on prevention rather than cure, an approach which reflects a 'salutogenic' or health-creation focus with a public health emphasis on factors which support and enhance well-being, rather than on factors which aim at merely preventing disease (Lindstrom and Ericsson, 2006).

Such an approach, quite naturally, will lead to a focus on societal quality of life (QoL) and well-being with both increasingly being recognised by the UK's central and local governments as an area for potential policy enhancement (Hartwell et al., 2012). While the primary responsibility of local government within the localism agenda on health is to provide quality services that maintain or enhance QoL and well-being of communities (Baker and Palmer, 2006), the local tourism agenda is a particularly complex one concerned with the development and management of the public realm (i.e. beaches, parks, lakes and rivers) that is integral to the visitors' experience at the tourist destination (Fyall, 2011). Although not recent bedfellows in the context of policy formation, it is important to note that the origins of tourism development in many countries were in fact underpinned by either religious pilgrimage, which many would argue as integral to mental well-being, and the perceived (and often real) healthy properties of sea-water, spa waters and the

generally good quality of air in early tourist destinations (Walton, 1983; Middleton, 2005). These destinations served as a suitable escape from unhealthy, overcrowded and fast expanding industrial cities.

Well-being

It is no coincidence then that well-being and QoL are increasingly being reflected in both tourism and public health academic and government planning agendas (Fayers and Machin, 2007; McCabe, 2010); with tourism and public health policy, planning and practice moving towards a new paradigm considering overall societal health, rooted in the well-being and QoL of individuals and communities (Local Government Improvement and Development, 2010). This is consistent with a recent study by Rodrigues et al. (2010) who argue that promoting the well-being of tourists should be integrated into all tourism destination management and marketing strategies! One of the drivers behind such a viewpoint is the current imbalance of tourism policies on the economics of 'hedonic', rather than 'eudaimonic' paradigms of health and wellness. At the current moment in time, the debate anchors on the two general perspectives: the hedonic approach, which focuses on happiness and defines well-being in terms of pleasure attainment; and the eudaimonic approach, which focuses on meaning and self-realisation. Pleasure is the hallmark of hedonism, and engagement serves as the core feeling of eudaimonia. Clearly, engagement with a well-being agenda is central to a public health strategy but could also form the basis for a well-being concept of tourism. A hedonistic product development approach that, for example, highlights the night time economy, drinking and eating to excess would sit uncomfortably within a health paradigm, and arguably often within local communities. Alternatively a eudaimonic product fit which emphasises human flourishing could be more contemporary and acceptable. Within the new reorganisation and localisation of public health in the UK, this provides an excellent opportunity for other key strategic and synergistic directions to come together for the benefit of the population at large.

Central to the co-location of public health and tourism strategies is the need to create an inclusive community culture where the tourist destination serves to enhance and promote the advancement of physical and mental well-being for both residents of and visitors to the destination. An emerging conceptualisation of public health practice is thus to reject the model of ourselves as 'mechanics' that diagnose and fix what is wrong to organic metaphors where we understand ourselves as 'gardeners', enabling the growth of what nourishes human life and spirit (Hemingway, 2012). For example the measures applied by UK local government to encourage people to walk or cycle could serve as an example of synergy between tourism development, destination improvement, slow travel and public health, achieving a mutual goal of sustainable tourism enhancement and healthier communities (Dickinson and Lumsdon, 2011). For, not only does greater active participation in walking or cycling improve physical and mental health (a public health goal) but it also reduces carbon impact (a tourism development goal) and creates a more favourable image of the destination (a destination marketing goal).

The case of Rockley Park: policy and product integration

One area within the UK actively exploring the benefits to be derived from a unified tourism and well-being policy are the adjoining destinations of Bournemouth and Poole on the south coast of England. Although not without its challenges, with the pressure to fill thousands of hotel beds every night driving the economic agenda, both destinations are open to innovation as a vehicle to differentiate their respective propositions in the marketplace. Consistent with the historical development of tourism in many coastal resorts around the UK, the history of positioning Bournemouth, Poole and the surrounding area towards well-being has its roots in the natural habitat and geographical location of being near the sea and being surrounded by pine trees. Heraldry in England is held to express some leading facts in the history of an individual or locality and, in the case of the latter, to display some distinctive features which help form the identity of an individual or place. In accordance with these principles, the Arms of Bournemouth (which were constructed in 1891) depicts pine trees, sandy cliffs and clear blue seas which collectively indicate the salubrity of the climate. In addition, the local authority in Bournemouth adopted 'beautiful and healthy' as the town's motto positioning the area as a destination for health and pleasure; this reflecting that the fusion of tourism and well-being is not in fact new at all, but merely represents a rejuvenated opportunity from the reorganisation of health and local authority policy!

Although with a healthy history, as evidenced above, it is interesting to note that local levels of physical activity among adults in Bournemouth and Poole were both below the England average (Bournemouth Borough Council, 2011) and therefore the synergy of agendas for both residents and visitors commenced. One such example of an already successful case study that integrates both tourism and well-being policy and product development is that of Rockley Park, a local attraction within the area which has nurtured the development of cycling opportunities for both residents and visitors alike. In this particular instance, tourism development is guided by the promotion of 'wise growth' which sees the value in tourism that promotes well-being. The Local Transport Plan (2011) identifies the correlation between cycling and better health and well-being where cycling is cited as a cost effective method of tackling health issues and inequalities.

The Rockley Park cycle route expansion project is an example of how the integration of product development (cycle hire) and local policy (cycling infrastructure/public realm) can achieve well-being outcomes for both residents and visitors. One stratagem is the railway 'trail way' which developed an extended cycling route from Rockley Park to the nearby coast which, in turn, offers a healthy option for residents and visitors as well as economic benefits to the related local business of cycle hire. The Rockley Park case study provides an example of the local implementation of a tourism strategy that supports wider well-being and sustainability goals. In this case, infrastructure development simultaneously met goals contained within Bournemouth's health, low carbon travel and accessibility strategies. As shown in Figure 37.1, this case study reveals the practical application of each concept level (macro to micro) which can contribute to sustainable well-being for all.

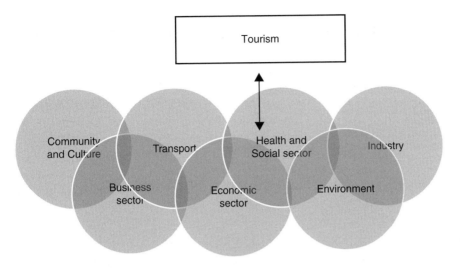

FIGURE 37.1 The policy determinants of well-being at tourist destinations

Conclusion

This chapter and the case study of Rockley Park in the UK captures the essence of an innovative multidisciplinary policy direction which builds on the emerging trend for wellness tourism. The added value of this cohesive approach will ensure that novel, and participative research and development opportunities can be exploited further with an overriding ambition to build on the already well-established literature and political focus on healthy cities. The output will clearly be of interest to those responsible for policy, strategy and operational practice within the tourism industry and will lead to a greater understanding of the considerable opportunities to be derived from the fusion of both well-being and tourism agendas. Consequently, the societal impact of this orientation brings with it the potential to extend beyond a public health perspective to impact more fully the ability of tourist destinations to leverage health creation through re-positioning and re-branding of their destination proposition, a potential synergy that can contribute to both sustainable health and well-being and economic gain.

   In conclusion, policy that addresses both tourism and public health goals must surely demonstrate more potential than focusing on either one unilaterally. In addition, the potential to integrate carbon-reducing efforts and inequalities in health reduction into a local tourism strategy will contribute much to the gradual migration to a well-being-focused tourism industry which over time becomes the norm for both the supply and demand perspectives of tourism. Not only will such an approach be one that destinations can deliver but so too will it be an approach driven by demand from healthy residents and visitors seeking a more balanced approach to their own quality of life.

38

Activities as a component of a social tourism holiday experience

Riikka Ilves and Raija Komppula

Social tourism

Holidays are an important part of our lives in Western societies, but still a distant dream for a large number of people. The mission of social tourism is to promote access to holidays, leisure and tourism for all (Belanger and Jolin, 2011). Social tourism started in 1936, when the International Labour Organization (ILO) agreed on the Holiday with Pay Convention (Convention no. 52). Later on this convention has also been mentioned in the Universal Declaration of Human Rights in 1948, where it is stated that 'everyone has the right to rest and leisure, including reasonable limitation of working hours and periodic holidays with pay' (International Social Tourism Organisation ISTO, 2011).

As the concept of social tourism is versatile and complex, there is not one single definition for it. Hunzicker (1951) describes the term as 'the relationships and phenomena in the field of tourism resulting from participation in travel by economically weak or otherwise disadvantaged elements in society' (in Minnaert et al., 2011). Later Minnaert et al. (2007, 2009) described social tourism as 'tourism with an added moral value, of which the primary aim is to benefit either the host or the visitor in the tourism exchange'. This recent definition acknowledges how the aims of social tourism can be applied to both visitors and hosts. Current objectives and challenges of social tourism can be defined on three levels: tourism for all, solidarity tourism and the lack of resources. 'Tourism for all' is a priority for ISTO and the social tourism sector (national governments and states, social organisations and tourism operators). The main current target segments for a social tourism policy are young people, families, senior citizens and persons with a disability (Belanger and Jolin, 2011).

In Finland, social tourism is financed mainly by Finland's Slot Machine Association (RAY), the main purpose of which is to raise funds through gaming operations to promote Finnish health and welfare. The fund allocation is guided by and agreed with the Ministry of Social Affairs and Health. In Finland funding for social tourism is distributed to social

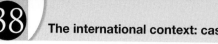

holiday associations, through which individual people or families of limited means, or with disabilities may apply for a supported holiday, which in most cases is a five days full-board holiday with daily activities run by instructors. The most important reasons for applying a supported holiday in Finland are economic and health related reasons. Illnesses such as allergies, asthma, high blood pressure, cardio vascular diseases, thyroid disorders, depression, stress and burnout are often mentioned reasons for the need for a social holiday. Senior applicants may be tired caused by age, and younger ones may have been wearing themselves out at work (Kinnunen and Puhakka, 2005). Similar reasons for a social holiday were found in McCabe's (2009) study in the UK: an opportunity to spend time together as a family, having fun and good times, escaping from a violent atmosphere, cementing the family ties, breaking from daily life, a chance for children to play outside in a safe environment and having good childhood memories.

Social holiday applicants in Finland have several expectations for the supported holiday. Among other things they anticipate gaining new relationships and experiences, enjoyable activities, professional guides, friendly staff, tasty food, clean rooms, beautiful environment, good weather and the possibility to exercise outdoors as well as indoors (Kinnunen and Puhakka, 2005). The social tourism beneficiaries themselves also expect to improve their health conditions during the holiday (McCabe, 2009). Gilbert and Abdullah (2004) found out that holiday-taking has a positive impact on the subjective sense of well-being of holidaymakers. Several studies also show a range of benefits to children and families (Hazel, 2005; McCabe, 2009; Minnaert et al., 2009), and social tourism may bring concrete changes in people lives (McCabe, 2009; Minnaert et al., 2009; McCabe et al., 2010). The importance of new relationships was emphasized in the results of Kinnunen and Puhakka (2005: 48–51) based on Finnish data.

As in other countries, in Finland social tourism is seen as part of the social policy, but not as a part of health tourism. Nevertheless, most of those businesses that are involved in wellness and well-being tourism in Finland are more or less dependent on the demand for supported holidays. One special phenomenon in Finland is the rehabilitation centres that were originally established to treat the Second World War veterans. As this target group is now ageing and declining, a remarkable number of these businesses are trying to attract other social tourism target groups as well as self paying customers. Often the quality of these facilities is not luxurious but characterised by a hospital-like atmosphere. Another group of well-being businesses are holiday centres that have been established by social holiday associations. The following case description represents this type of well-being businesses.

Social holiday for Huhmari

Holiday centre Huhmari in Eastern Finland describes itself as a holiday centre providing well-being experiences (www.lomakeskushuhmari.com/en). The offering is organised according to supported holiday weekly themes promoting health and well-being (i.e. recreation week, feel good week, well-being week for unemployed people). Huhmari is a typical Finnish holiday centre specialising in social tourism, located by a lake in the country side of North Karelia, Eastern Finland. Accommodation is organised in cottages suitable

for families. The main building contains dining hall, restaurant, auditorium, spa, gym and a playground for children. There are also two tennis courts, two saunas, lakeside café, bonfire hut and shelter on the outdoor area, and a network of hiking trails. In the winter time ski tracks and skating rink are available.

The goal of this case study was to capture the meaning and essence of different leisure activities for a successful holiday experience in the context of social tourism. An ethnographic approach was applied: the researcher spent a whole week with the group of 77 customers taking part in everything that was offered. As previous studies on social tourism have focused mainly on families, a group of elderly people was chosen for the target group of this study. Most of the customers in the group suffered from different kinds of heart illnesses and hence applied for the holiday through the Finnish Heart Association, a public health and patient organisation promoting heart health. The theme of the study 'heart week' combined the case with medical and health tourism.

The material was collected using three methods: participant observation, survey and group interviews. The case week is an example of a typical supported holiday in Huhmari, comprising three meals and five to six activities per day. During the week e.g. lectures about nutrition and pilates technique were offered as well as physical activities, comprising regular and water aerobics, orienteering and hiking. Games, such as memory games and 'olympic games', were designed especially for this segment. Additionally, relaxation classes, stretching classes, cooking over bonfire, and an excursion to the nearby town were offered. A typical day of the week (Wednesday) starts at 7.30 a.m. with a 2 km hike, followed by a breakfast at 7.30–9.30 a.m., quiz in the auditorium at 10 a.m., aerobics outdoors at 11 a.m., lunch at 12 a.m.–2 p.m. In the afternoon olympic games at 1.30 p.m., water aerobics starting at 3 p.m., and dinner at 5–7 p.m. The organised itinerary finished with a coffee by the bonfire at 6.30 p.m.

Most people in this group saw different kinds of organised activities as a determining part of their holiday experience. Activities were seen as the thread of the week. If one took part in all of them, only a little free time was available around mealtimes. Some aspects of the activities made them special. One of the most important things was socialising with other customers and a chance to spend time with a group of people with similar age and interest. Instructors were also seen to play an important role in creating the experience: according to the informants they were appreciated due to their good sense of humour, professionalism and enthusiasm. They were also fun to be around. Also the lectures were seen among the best things in the week. Holiday takers also enjoyed playful activities, which gave them an opportunity to compete and challenge themselves with others.

Activities had several different effects on customers' well-being holiday experience. Mainly they were seen as a socialising tool providing a friendly environment and good atmosphere for connecting with others both during and after the activity. Second, these pre-planned activities motivated people to take part in sport, play and exercises, which they do not normally do at home. They also provided a learning environment by giving new information mainly during the lectures, brought new perspectives of life, gave some new ideas for the future and gave an impression of improved health condition.

The activities were important for everyone, but the findings also stated that customers participated in the activities depending on their health condition. The meaning and role of activities in the well-being holiday experience differed between customers. Based on the results five different subgroups could be distinguished in terms of activeness of the customer in participating in the activities. The first group 'actives' included those in an excellent physical condition. They participated in almost every activity, were mainly women and appreciated activities for their physical challenges. The second and the biggest group 'average movers' included people from different age groups. They participated in many activities but not all, were in medium shape and exercised quite a lot. Some of the men had a rather strong competitive spirit, but did not reach the active level due to their health. The third group 'unfit participants' was either in poor health or old. They took part in some activities depending on their health conditions. The fourth group 'sick ones' participated mainly in lectures or other light activities requiring only a little physical effort. The fifth group 'independent ones' spent time on their own or with their spouses or friends rather than participating in organised programmes.

The main result of this study indicates that activities together with other components of the tourist product such as meals, accommodation and hospitality have a positive effect on holiday takers' perceived mental and physical health. This is in accordance with several earlier studies in social tourism context (Kinnunen and Puhakka, 2005; Minnaert et. al., 2009; McCabe et al., 2010). Hence, we suggest that social tourism could be regarded as one type of well-being tourism.

39

Research on preventive wellness in the Netherlands

Jacques Vork and Angelique Lombarts

Wellness may be regarded as a global, broad social phenomenon whereby an increasing number of people are assuming responsibility for their own health and well-being. Three megatrends guarantee the continued growth in demand for wellness, namely: (1) the ageing of the world's population, (2) failing and disintegrating health-care systems and (3) increasing globalisation and awareness of various health treatments. These (health) trends are also discernible in the Netherlands and people wish to remain healthy and continue to be active in society.

In the Netherlands there are approximately 60 large wellness centres, hot baths and saunas. However, a broad offering of preventive wellness, aimed at promoting lifestyles within wellness centres, is lacking. Preventive wellness focuses on activities involving the mind and body to ensure that a balance is achieved and maintained and that one can function in society in a way which is happier and healthier. Preventive wellness takes advantage of the trend in which citizens acquire individual responsibility for their own well-being.

Elsewhere in Europe, in the so-called wellness model countries, namely Germany, Austria and Switzerland, the barriers between *cure, care* and *wellness* have been removed. *Cure* and *care* emanate from the health-care sector; wellness originates rather from the recreation sector. All three encompass aspects of well-being. In the Netherlands, the demand for preventive wellness and its provision in wellness centres is also changing. This has been signalled by companies in the SME sector active in the wellness branch and they wish to take advantage of this by developing innovative preventive wellness concepts within Dutch wellness centres. This is the focus of the research into 'Preventive wellness, also in the Netherlands'.

Table 39.1, which includes strengths, weaknesses, threats and opportunities, provides a concise summary of the most important characteristics, trends and developments of (preventive) wellness.

TABLE 39.1 Strengths and weaknesses of the wellness sector in the Netherlands

Strengths	Weaknesses
The wellness sector is growing and becoming more professional. The wellness sector is taking advantage of demand for sustainable operations.	The Netherlands does not have a tradition of spas: this is a relatively new phenomenon here and is positioned, in particular, as 'pampering'. Supply threatens to exceed demand due to an excess of one-sided supply. The image of wellness in the eyes of many is still 'unnecessary luxury'. Unclear positioning: small and large centres, hotels with facilities, fitness clubs, etc. The many discounts offered on admittance to and treatments of wellness centres have the effect that consumers 'wait' for discounts to be offered and are no longer willing to pay the full amount. The effects of preventive wellness receive little attention and are hardly linked at all to chronic illnesses and other ailments. The term 'preventive wellness' is unknown. Little use is made of social media.
Opportunities	**Threats**
The further interweaving of the wellness sector and the hospitality, fitness and healthcare sectors will result in the launch of new products and services. The use of wellness centres by inhabitants of the Netherlands is increasing. Inhabitants of the Netherlands are more aware of and their attention is drawn more often to the importance of a healthy and sustainable lifestyle. New target groups are being attracted or approached in other ways, such as the chronically ill, men, sports people and people suffering from stress. Opportunities exist for joint branding of preventive wellness in the Netherlands. (There are no or hardly any total concepts in the area of preventive wellness in the Netherlands.) Cooperation is also possible with new partners, such as fitness centres or hotels. Technological developments, such as tests and e-coaching, may make a contribution to the lifestyle programme. The government and health insurers are increasingly assigning responsibility and financial consequences for good health to citizens. The government and health-care insurers must be convinced of the effects of preventive wellness. The lifestyle professional can be embraced, an active contribution can be made to the development of this profession and these professionals can be deployed in implementing preventive wellness.	The economic crisis is putting a brake on the willingness to invest and investment opportunities, technological developments and consumer spending. Consumer confidence in the economy is low and consumers are saving on expenditure. Leisure wellness is being combined with preventive wellness. Do consumers see the value of preventive wellness and are they willing to invest time and money in this? There is a shortage of qualified staff (for instance, in relation to the interpretation and supervision of tests, carrying out treatments and coaching).

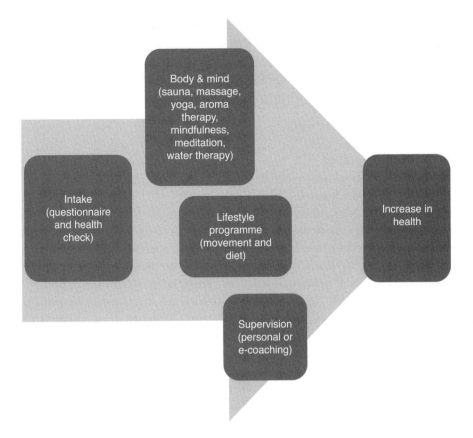

FIGURE 39.1 Preventative wellness model

A total wellness concept consists of an intake procedure (questionnaire, health check) followed by an action plan (activities in the wellness centre and a lifestyle programme outside the wellness centre), with supervision (either personal or through e-coaching). It is important that the programme consists of various elements (within and outside the wellness centre) which can be compiled depending on preferences, the outcome of the intake and opportunities. The diagram in Figure 39.1 was drawn up on the basis of the literature. Justice is perhaps best done to the total concept if a selection is made for the programme from each category. Massages, saunas, hot water baths, meditation and water therapy are the basis for the total wellness concept.

As part of the Preventive Wellness Project, a study trip was made to the so-called wellness model countries, Austria and Germany. The visits to the wellness centres of Lanserhof in Austria and Bad Buchau, Bad Wurzach and Baden-Baden in Germany, provided important insights. The success factors are, for instance, a strong concept, a link to the environment and the staff.

A strong concept is essential. People are willing to travel further for a special concept. The concept must be clear to the customer – expectations must be fulfilled. The guests do not need to be educated in what they require, but must decide for themselves what they do and do not require. Follow-up after six months provides an additional motivation to continue working to achieve a healthy lifestyle.

Making use of nature or facilities in the environment may strengthen the concept, without additional investments. This cooperation also produces added value in relation to the marketing of the destination. The latter is only important for guests who indicate that they wish to be involved actively in the wellness centre.

The staff play an important role in this. If they are well aware of the concept, they can keep each other on their toes. The implementation of the health component requires specialised and professional staff, such as doctors, physiotherapists, dieticians, and so on. Additional attention must be given to internal training of staff and interaction between the hospitality and health teams.

On the basis of 11 interviews with health-care providers, employers, a marketing specialist and a health insurer, research was carried out to ascertain whether employers in the Netherlands are open to investment in wellness as a means of promoting the health of their employees. Partly due to the economic crisis, promoting health is not a priority for a number of employers at present. Employers already offer employees opportunities to work on their health. Examples of this are health checks, company fitness and bicycle schemes. Wellness, however, is not a component which has been integrated by all employers in relation to the health of employees.

The most important reason for employers not to invest in wellness is a lack of evidence of its effectiveness. If making use of wellness programmes can contribute to improving the labour process and reintegration by accelerating recovery and reducing absenteeism, employers may possibly be interested. Preferably, the wellness offering should focus on specific (long-term) ailments and should be offered in combination with other health programmes and from a medical perspective. If health insurers include wellness in their reimbursement packages, it would be an indication to employers that it does in fact work. However, it is unlikely that insurers will do so in the short term.

Extensive research was carried out amongst visitors of sauna and wellness centres. Data pertaining to the motives, search behaviour and activities of more than 9,400 visitors were collected. The results can be used for product development and the optimisation of marketing. By linking the results to the seven lifestyle groups for daytime recreation in the BSR model,[1] it is possible to describe the target groups not only in terms of socio-demographic, but also in terms of socio-psychological criteria. Compared to the average person seeking a day's recreation, visitors to wellness centres pay more attention to the activity and less to the company, and seek activities which are a combination of being active and making an effort, and relaxation and rest. There are also visitors of wellness centres on the other side of the model, where the emphasis lies on relaxing together and seeking a release from obligations, but this applies less to people seeking a day's recreation.

For each of the seven lifestyle groups, a fact sheet was drawn up with a description of the wishes, needs and behaviour of these people in relation to saunas and wellness. It is possible not only to adjust the offering, but also the marketing communication to the target group.

A number of additional questions on preventive wellness were included in the research amongst customers of wellness centres. Almost a quarter of them were (very) interested

in preventive wellness. Their reservations in relation to a financial contribution through employers and/or health insurance was striking. The greatest potential lies in the target groups in the upper half of the model. They are particularly interested in a healthy body and a healthy mind in combination with a moment for themselves.

A number of recommendations and conclusions were formulated on the basis of the research. The Netherlands is only interested in prevention to a limited extent and even then only in relation to parts of the health experience. An holistic lifestyle, in which movement, diet and relaxation are in balance and receive equal attention, is perhaps in the ascendancy, but only few people are very consciously involved in this. Nevertheless this development appears to be unstoppable. The number of *communities* which are involved in this in one way or another is growing rapidly. When we started our research two years ago, the term 'preventive wellness' was unknown to the vast majority of the population. The term now enjoys increasing familiarity. A shift in thinking from curative (curing/problem-solving) wellness to preventive wellness is under way. This also applies to a number of our research partners.

A clearer presentation of wellness centres is essential. The collective promotion of Sauna and Wellness in the Netherlands may perhaps contribute to this. However, a quality mark, such as that of our German partner, Wellness Stars, may be a solution in this regard. In addition, professionalisation of the branch is still an area requiring attention. This relates not only to specialist knowledge in the area of health, but also knowledge and expertise in the area of hospitality. Apart from on-the-job training, professional education in both secondary vocational education and at universities of applied sciences may contribute to this professionalisation. Co-ordination between and intensive consultation with employers and educational institutions is necessary for this. The further broadening of its knowledge and expertise will also assist the branch with its professionalisation. This is certainly the case with regard to the health claim. In short, there is a long way to go from preventive wellness in the Netherlands to preventive wellness for all inhabitants of the Netherlands.

Acknowledgements

Besides Angelique Lombarts and Jacques Vork, Roos Gerritsma, Afke Kerkstra, Remy de Boer, Martijn Mesman and Kiem, who are all lecturers from InHolland, made a contribution to the research into preventive wellness in the Netherlands.

Note

1   A SmartAgent model which describes the experiential world of a leisure seeker.

CHAPTER 40

Natural wellness

The case of Icelandic wilderness landscapes for health and wellness tourism

Edward H. Huijbens

Introduction and conceptual grounding

This short case study comes from Iceland which, along with the Nordic countries more generally, builds its tourism on the role of nature and natural phenomena (Hall et al., 2009; Jóhannesson et al., 2010; Jóhannesson and Huijbens, 2010; Sæþórsdóttir, 2010). The natural variations specific to Iceland are the country's abundant geothermal resources and vast tracks of land devoid of signs of human habitation, or what has been termed wilderness (Sæþórsdóttir et al., 2011). With most people coming to Iceland to experience nature (Icelandic Tourist Board, 2012) and varying degrees of wilderness, my focus in this case study is on how these can be perceived as delivering well-being.

The experience of rejuvenation afforded to us by a holiday is well known, at least in Europe, to the extent that governments will support people in being able to holiday, recognising the opportunities represented by tourism to 'social and personal growth' (McCabe, 2009: 668; see also Gilbert and Abdullah, 2004). The perceived importance lies in changing one's place from the everyday. To a person coming from Iceland's source markets in the cities of West Europe and North America, this change involves getting away to nature or whatever is perceived as such. As MacCannell (2012: 187) argues: 'Landscapes seen as "picturesque" symbolize peaceful calm and soothing solace along with the bedrock physical challenges of human existence and endurance. They are sought out by tourists seeking relief from the artifice, jangled nerves and insults of urban existence.' Indeed this, perhaps somewhat clichéd, idea is being worked with in tourism product development worldwide. As Smith and Puczkó (2009: 252) demonstrate:

> [n]ature plays a significant role in health and wellness in many countries, especially those which have a sea coast and can offer products like thalassotherapy (common in Europe). Mountains are another feature which have always attracted health visitors, especially the Alps in Europe. Jungles and national parks (e.g. in Central and South

America, Africa) make ideal locations for adventure and ecospas, which is a growing trend. To a lesser (but increasing extent) deserts (e.g. in the Middle East or North Africa) are being used as locations for yoga and meditation holidays.

My emphasis on the role of nature and the picturesque means in the Icelandic context focus on landscapes devoid of signs of human habitation. To understand how health and well-being can be drawn from these I rely on understanding landscapes as therapeutic. Therein 'the sensorial experience of places and the therapeutic virtues of the landscape' (Fleuret and Atkinson, 2007: 107) are highlighted as healing places (see Kearns and Gesler, 1998) and/or therapeutic landscapes (see Smyth, 2005). These are: 'places, settings, situations, locales, and milieus that encompass both the physical and psychological environments associated with treatment or healing; they are reputed to have an 'enduring reputation for achieving physical, mental, and spiritual healing' (Williams, 1998: 1193, quoting Gesler, 1993: 171; see also Gesler, 1992).

The association with treatment or healing, however, is too narrow for me. I would like to emphasise the way in which Williams (2010: 1633) expands on the notion of therapeutic landscapes and healing places, advocating how 'the therapeutic landscape concept provides a fitting framework into which this challenging research direction can move in order to better elucidate the relationship between spiritual practices/activities, landscapes/places and health, broadly defined'. What Williams (1998, 2010) is thus claiming is how the social and mental aspects of health and wellness can be reflected in therapeutic landscapes and at the same time how therapeutic landscapes 'today can similarly be seen to reflect the values of our societies' (Smyth, 2005: 491). For a person coming to Iceland, drawing benefits from the wilderness landscape is thus about ways to relate. Therapeutic landscapes do not revolve only around places with an 'enduring reputation for achieving physical, mental, and spiritual healing', but must also '[take] seriously post-positivist assumptions about relational selves, healing must of necessity extend beyond individual psyches and biologies. Embedded individuals cannot heal in isolation but must instead transform in and through relationships to and within a range of places' (Willis, 2009: 86–87; see also Conradson, 2005). Therefore through focusing on a range of places that can be perceived as therapeutic, therapeutic landscapes can also revolve around the places that can seem simply void of human habitation or wilderness.

If taken from the point of view of the tourist coming to gain health and/or well-being through experiencing landscapes devoid of human habitation, Thrift (2008) proposes that nature, and wilderness landscapes for that part, form a background within which sensory experiences get constituted and at the same time constitute the landscape. Thrift (2008: 57; see also Wylie, 2007) argues, '. . . immersive body practices account for a large part of what we attend to as "nature"; they define much of what we cleave to as a "natural" experience by setting up a background of expectations'. Thrift (2008) goes so far as to place his argument under the heading of the marketing slogan of the American Wilderness Experience, 'step into the great outdoors', couching his understanding of nature within the terminology of Pine and Gilmore's (1999) 'experience economy'. In this respect tourism is indeed 'tuning our bodies to an economy of naturalized experience' (Thrift, 2008: 74). Focusing on these immersive body practices into the background within which

sensory experiences get constituted, allows for an appreciation of landscapes. Their visual experience is thus meaningful even going so far as to state that the mere glancing at it as the tourist body is moved through the landscape involves a sensuous experience (Larsen, 2001) of potential benefit to health and general well-being (Parsons et al., 1998). Indeed this is not that new, e.g. environmental psychology has for some time recognised the healing powers of being in a natural setting or extensive views (see Kaplan and Kaplan, 1989; Kaplan, 1995). From the psychoanalytical tradition of the fifties the concept agoraphilia (meaning simply the love of open spaces as opposed to agoraphobia), has been used to describe the need to conquer a petrified Mother Nature (p. 703) entailing the rebirth of the individual (Glauben, 1955; see also Carter, 2002).

Working with wilderness

The above argumentation for the role of landscapes in health and well-being is developed from research into the constitution of the Mývatn Nature Baths. This is a spa resort developed in the north-east of Iceland, in the sparsely populated region around Lake Mývatn. The key attraction and main allure of the region are its unique natural environment and easy access to wilderness areas. The Mývatn region is on the volcanically active belt that divides Iceland, lying between the continent of North America and Eurasia. This results in several geological features being visible which, through the interplay of fire and ice from antiquity till the modern day provide for unique vistas. Moreover, the volcanic nature of the region results in numerous hot springs and sulfatara, which formed the main inspiration for wellness service development.

In many ways emulating the success of the Blue Lagoon destination and product line developed in proximity to the main international gateway to Iceland, Keflavík airport in the south-west of the island, the Mývatn Nature Baths (MNB) were set up by local tourism stakeholders in order to diversify their service portfolio and tackle challenges of seasonality. The key service concept is to provide relaxation and well-being to weary hikers and explorers of the surrounding wilderness area, but also all and any that want to reap the benefits of soaking in hot water. Hence the service concept draws on longstanding traditions of hot water bathing in Iceland, where rheumatic pains or joints weary from work were relieved. However, when visited, both the Blue Lagoon and the MNB share a distinctive feature. That is its setting. Both have their pools and bathing spots set within a rugged lava field from nearby volcanoes and as a consequence they become clearly visible from the Earth, so to speak. Another distinctive feature is how the facilities provide for an appreciation of the surrounding wilderness vista. This is more pronounced at the MNB where unbroken lines of sight into the adjacent highland interior of Iceland are allowed for from several spots within the pools. The design of this is no coincidence and is meant to bring out the forces of nature that many of the developers and other regional tourism stakeholders cited as their inspiration when interviewed (see Huijbens, 2011). This sentiment mostly gets side-lined in general accounts of the development of the attractions. The overall rationale of both projects is tourism development for regional benefits and using geothermal water for the alleviation of aches and pains. However with the ideas drawn from the therapeutic landscape literature, this case is meant to put in words the vague notions evident with so many tourism developers drawing on natural resources. It seems that underneath their development ideas simmer earthly powers that arguably can be fronted more in product development.

What this product development could do, and in some ways already does, is to present the value of sensorial experiences received from landscape viewing and being in what is perceived as authentic nature and wilderness, as a health and wellness tourism product. Once complementing this passive nature-based tourism recreation with concepts from the study of therapeutic landscapes, an idea of nature as power emerges, one that people can connect to in the simultaneous co-constitution of self and space. In terms of health and wellness tourism product development what is of key importance is facilitating this experience of co-constitution and this both the Blue Lagoon and MNB in Iceland do.

CHAPTER 41

Global wellness in Sedona, Arizona

Mia Mackman

Introduction

The synergy of life, health and travel occurring in today's global tourism market makes Sedona, Arizona one of the most unique wellness destinations in the United States. Arizona is home to many world-class destination resorts, spas and wellness facilities, and the City of Sedona alone attracts an average of 1.6 to 2 million domestic and international visitors per year. Over the last 15 years, Sedona has gained prominent attention for its reputation as a stunning tourist destination and a progressive environment for holistic healing.

Located in the northern region of Arizona, Sedona sits at 4,326 feet above sea level at the base of the Mogollon Rim, 119 miles south of the Grand Canyon's South Rim and 116 miles north of Phoenix. 'Over time, erosion has gradually eaten away at the Mogollon Rim in Sedona, leaving behind some of the most spectacular and picturesque canyons and buttes found anywhere in the world' (Arizona Ruins, 2012). The awe-inspiring red rock formations found there are mainly made of sandstone and iron oxide (Fe_2O_3), which is what creates the renowned colouring of the red rocks.

Sedona is known for its mild climate and is considered a year-round destination. It is widely recognised for its adventure travel, eco-tourism, heritage, cultural attractions, and its spiritual and energetic eminence. Many people have travelled to Sedona and found it profoundly inspiring and often times, a life-changing journey. The voluminous reports of experiences related to transformational healing and spiritual awakening drive Sedona's community planning to create genuine hospitality and provide services, which support and enhance well-being.

Local attractions include sightseeing, leisure, hiking and wellness. Sedona is a popular destination for groups, tours, and various types of enrichment retreats including: yoga, spirituality, creativity, healing and self-discovery. Sedona hosts several celebrated annual events and festivals including the internationally acclaimed Sedona Film Festival as well as the Sedona Arts Festival, Sedona Marathon, Red Rock Music Festival and many others

(Sedona Film Festival, 2012). Sedona has also become a romantic getaway destination for couples seeking scenic beauty, couples spa treatments and a variety of wellness offerings:

- fitness;
- nutrition;
- energy balancing;
- massage therapy;
- crystal energy healing;
- cranial sacral therapy;
- reiki;
- shiatsu;
- yoga;
- tai chi;
- chakra therapies;
- stress reduction/management;
- acupuncture;
- lymphatic drainage;
- reflexology;
- hypnotherapy;
- life reading and clearing;
- spiritual life coaching;
- herbology;
- aromatherapy;
- electro dermal screening;
- biophoton light therapy;
- anti-ageing and longevity;
- sound and colour therapies.

As domestic and international tourism rates continue to recover, the value of Sedona's unique attractions also continue to grow. 'Sedona has been long regarded as the place where "Mother Earth speaks" and recently has become referred to as the home of mystical vortex energy' (Miller and Lonetree, 2010). 'A vortex is the funnel shape created by a whirling fluid or by the motion of a spiraling energy. A vortex can be made up of anything that flows such as wind, water or electricity. The vortexes in Sedona are swirling centers of subtle energy coming out from the surface of the earth' (Sedona's Energy Vortexes, 2012). Over the years, the vortex locations have become prevalent sites to visit in addition to the wide array of spiritual offerings unique to the region.

With a residential population of only 10,031 (according to the Sedona 2010 Census) Sedona offers an intimate and dynamic experience for today's wellness traveller. Sedona offers multiple world-class, award winning resorts and spas including the Enchantment Resort and Mii amo Spa, L'Auberge de Sedona, Amara Resort and Spa, and Los Abrigados Resort and Spa. These properties are magnificent examples of high-quality accommodations and offer luxury amenities and a versatile selection of spa and wellness services in addition to those which can be found throughout the local community. This combination of environment, experience and attention bolsters Sedona's status as a top destination for personal wellness.

Wellness and energetic sustenance

The dynamic nature of Sedona supports the irrefutable connection of the consciousness of the mind and the vitality of the body with the nourishment of the soul. Whereas the condition of our health is essentially holistic, these three major components (mind, body and soul) play vital parts in increasing our understanding of how these core elements contribute to our paths to wellness.

Michael Persinger, a behavioural neuroscience specialist says, 'All behaviors, including consciousness, are generated by and correlated with brain activity. The activity can be conceived as complex matrices of electromagnetic patterns and their associated chemical changes.' Some of these energetic effects have been described in the 'Sedona Effect' (Miller and Lonetree, 2010). The 'Sedona Effect' defines how these subtle energies correlate geomagnetic anomalies, EEG Brainwaves and Schumann Resonance in Sedona.

'Native Americans consider all of Sedona to be one harmonious field of energy. When we are in it, we can experience geo-magnetically supercharged brainwave entrainment' (Miller and Lonetree, 2010).The new information and mounting energy studies being conducted around the world have brought forth various new types of energy applications to the forefront of the wellness industry. Indigenous treatment rituals, dynamic spa offerings and modern/ancient techniques are all designed to improve health, stability and prevention. The natural environment of Sedona amplifies these unique energies in tandem with each other, supporting the bio-energetic optimisation found within the nature of one's self and true well-being.

The energy of the vortexes found in Sedona has been measured by various methods including the use of fluxgate magnetometers, large induction coils and portable brainwave outcome equipment. The vortex energies of Sedona have been scientifically proven to generate three specific types of energy: electric, magnetic and electromagnetic (Sutphen, 1988). Scientists have conducted various studies on the impact of these energetic currents with regard to cellular health, vitality and a wide spectrum of multiple benefits associated with the resonance of these naturally occurring energies. A 2004 study published by the *British Medical Journal*, quoted by Vital Wonders (2013), reported on the benefits of magnetic energy on arthritis.

'The Sedona Method' (Sedona Method, 2012), established in 1974, held its first class in Sedona, Arizona. Since then, it has built an international audience of hundreds of thousands of people. 'The Sedona Method is a unique, simple, powerful, easy-to-learn and duplicate technique that shows you how to uncover your natural ability to let go of any painful or unwanted feeling, belief or thought in the moment' (World Research Foundation, 2012).

It has made a tremendous impact on the balance, success, effectiveness and wellness of individuals and corporations worldwide including executive teams from: Exxon, AT&T, Merrill Lynch, J.C. Penney, Marriott Hotels, FAA, Bristol Myers, Chemical Bank, Chase Manhattan Bank and Polaroid. According to a study on the Sedona Method, conducted by Dr Richard J. Davidson of the State University of New York in collaboration with Dr David C. McClelland of the Department of Social Relations at Harvard University, there were significant benefits associated with the Sedona Method in regards to the emotional and physical state of the participants in the study. There were notable benefits and improvements to heart rate and blood pressure and reductions in stress and muscle tension.

Sedona offers a wide range of spa and wellness benefits, ranging from quintessential spa treatments to cutting-edge wellness technologies supported by long-standing health and research organisations. The World Research Foundation (2012) founded in 1997, maintains their main library in the Village of Oak Creek located in Sedona. Considered to be the (largest or leading) global resource for alternative health, they bring a wealth of information to the public forum and are committed to creating compilations of vital wellness information with a non-biased approach to alternative health solutions.

Visitor characteristics

These visitor characteristics are in reference to the Sedona Chamber of Commerce, Sedona Visitors Survey, November 2011 (Sedona Chamber of Commerce, 2011):

- The typical visitor is 56 years old with one-half of all visitors (53 per cent) falling between 50 and 64 years old and seven out of ten (71 per cent) being 50 or older.
- Geographically, 95 per cent of visitors were domestic travellers, 28 per cent of all visitors came from the West, while 27 per cent came from the Midwest, 22 per cent the South and 18 per cent the Northeast. Five per cent of visitors were from outside the US (this number is rapidly growing).
- The typical visitor to Sedona spent 2.9 days with 31 per cent staying five or more days.
- Day-trippers comprise about one in four surveyed visitors (24 per cent).
- One-half of visitors (50 per cent) stayed at a hotel (25 per cent full service) while 25 per cent stayed in a timeshare, and 9 per cent a private home.
- Sixty-two per cent of travel parties contained one or two people with 54 per cent of all parties containing two individuals.
- One-half of visitors (49 per cent) arrived in Sedona via rental car while one out of three arrived in a personal car (31 per cent) and 16 per cent arrived by plane. The remaining 4 per cent of visitors arrived by some other mode of surface transportation (RV, tour bus, motorcycle, shuttle).
- The heaviest travel months are September (19 per cent) and October (18 per cent).
- The typical overnight visitor party spent $548 per day while in Sedona with 23 per cent spending over $1,000 per day.
- Nearly two out of three visitors (74 per cent) say their length of stay in Sedona was too short.
- Word of mouth is the most common way (79 per cent) visitors hear about Sedona.
- Seventy-three per cent of visitors used the VisitSedona website prior to their visit, while 58 per cent contacted the Sedona Chamber. Thirty-six per cent visited the Visitor Center when in town.

A new age in tourism
A case study of New Age centres in Costa Rica

Marinus C. Gisolf

Introduction

This case study concerns activities at various organic farms and New Age centres in Costa Rica. Destinations like these have not traditionally been considered a kind of tourism and voluntary work opportunities at these centres have not been typical tourism fare. This study embarks on an exploration of postmodern tourism and its new associated tendencies, especially the New Age movement and its incursion into the world of experiencing as an activity in Costa Rica. Four farms were visited for this study and a link is being made with existing practices on the level of wellness tourism in general.

Tourism infrastructure

With New Age tourism we can see a clear inclination to all that is natural, including clothing or musical instruments made of natural materials, and most New Age tourism destinations are located in rural areas close to nature parks or protected areas. New Age tourism in this sense has very much to do with the search for nature in the broadest sense of the concept. A New Age tourism destination offers lodging and food – generally in a simple and straightforward way. The food is often home-grown and may be vegetarian. Apart from lodging, the site may offer:

- learning skills, such as wood turning, ceramics, candle making, weaving, etc.;
- aesthetic development: art, drama or music;
- agricultural learning, through courses and direct work involving synergy and permaculture techniques among others;
- formal scholarly learning, including courses by spiritual and intellectual 'gurus';

- experiential and personalised self-development: courses on meditation, personal relationships, family constellations or self knowledge;
- alternative approaches to health and wellness: homeopathy, acupuncture, hypnotherapy, shiatsu massage, Ayurveda, yoga, reiki etc.;
- a pastoral setting or environment for feeling the link with the earth and nature.

This can be considered a form of tourism because, of their own free will, people travel to an area that is completely different from their home environment and stay there for at least one night. There are planned attractions for visitors (tourists) at these destinations, such as courses that are given, working in the field, or any other activity as described above. Furthermore, tourists have particular motivations and needs that in turn generate certain expectations. At the destination tourists have a sensory intake from their daily activities and this will create (learning) experiences, and eventually they will evaluate these experiences. The authenticity involved is mainly activity-related (existentialist). Finally, tourists have an economic input, either monetary or with voluntary labour.

With most New Age destinations financial gain does not seem to be particularly important; education and the transmission of alternative ideology are the primary concerns. The financial part seems to be viewed as a way to facilitate an alternative lifestyle, and in this sense New Age tourism differs from traditional forms of tourism. It should also be stressed, that this type of tourism is not related in any way to wealth or poverty. People from all walks of life may participate and some New Age destinations may be suitable for (poor) students, people with addiction problems who want to solve that situation, or people who simply do not care for material wealth; on the other hand, there are also centres where costs may be quite steep indeed. As is the case with other forms of sustainable and responsible tourism, the issue of tourists with a little or a lot of money does not change any argument.

Among the activities available at what are called New Age destinations, community life and living in a commune form the backbone, where the principles of alternative lifestyles can be realised. It is interesting to note that in the New Age centres visited, the tendency has been to turn the 'normal' daily city life routine into an especially meaningful activity, while the exotic is turned into something routine. Most visitors to New Age destinations will have to help with washing up or gardening as part of a community effort and these actions are made attractive on the basis of their self-development potential and for facilitating a new relationship with the environment. At the same time the exotic is introduced through foreign artefacts, native musical instruments, exotic food or indigenous clothing. Quite often one can find a mix of Buddhist, Hindu or Mayan influences at the same time.

Gardening makes up an important part of daily activities at New Age centres, concentrating on synergetic gardening and permaculture, on the one hand, while stressing the link with the earth and healthy eating habits, on the other. One example is an upward herb spiral, whereby the herbs sown in the upper parts need less water than the ones lower down and some herbs are planted on either the north or south side depending on the amount of light they need.

Projects are often started or continued as part of examining human relationships with the landscape, such as building a pond using clay and cow manure to make it watertight. Some of these projects might never be finished, since what is important here is the action

of doing the project in the first place rather than the final result and by executing such a project one's ecological sensitivity is piqued, while the experience of working the earth and using old survival techniques may inspire many people.

Every New Age centre seems to have its own way of demonstrating its uniqueness to its participants, which may range from community chanting and various rituals to simply giving hugs to each other in the morning. The feeling of belonging to a community is strong, but what holds it together is the interest of the participants (including tourists) in self-realisation and their general focus on self as the common denominator. Somehow there seems to be a common goal, although the particulars may be different for each person. While the feeling of 'belonging to' something is an important ingredient, it is never intended as an end result and tourism in this sense is a means and not an end.

Another observation regards the relationship between New Age destinations and their direct social environment; for example, at the farm VerdEnergia Pacifica in Costa Rica they make stoves that burn (used) vegetable oil and distribute them among the poorer population in the countryside as a cheap alternative for cooking as part of their sustainable development initiatives. In general, New Age centres seek contact with the local population, although it is worth mentioning that most participants and tourists come from urban areas.

Post-modernist influences

Many cultural and alternative religious movements from the 1960s onward have been considered New Age, such as the flower power movement, 'Ban the Bomb', mysticism, Indian meditation, yoga and so on. The common denominator is in the way that New Age people attempt to find new ways of living. That is, their goal is self-realisation, liberation and fulfilment, and the means to achieve that end is a socially responsible, ecological approach that facilitates the actualisation of both the individual and the wider community's potential: the desire to transform self and society (Sutton and House, 2000). The loss of a feeling of identity amid un-authentic people, cultural pluralism and time–space compression have created uncertainty about the present day and the future (Giddens, 1991). However, at the same time this has prompted a search for historical roots, an idealistic authenticity, longer lasting values or an eternal truth, often drawing explicitly upon the spiritual traditions of the East (Harvey, 1989; Huyssens, 1990; Sharma, 1992). It is this postmodern nostalgia that has also pushed some people to the re-invention or re-representation of former religions or cultures (Vikings, Mayas), natural healing methods (acupuncture, aromatherapy and herbal medicine, etc.), organic agriculture and self-sufficiency. At the same time, disenchantment with previous modern times has led to a continued push for alternative styles of living.

In New Age tourism the idea is the experience itself being experienced: people draw upon their own inner feelings and emotions, while reality no longer dominates and rather seems to have been transformed into images. This type of tourism is about tourists in their own identity, exploring themselves as their own main tourist attraction. Additionally, New Age tourism usually embraces some form of environmentalism, community values, constructive host–guest interactions and social responsibility. In this sense New Age tourism can be seen as a mix of identity tourism and sustainable tourism and it is definitely a backlash to existing mass tourism (Sutton and House, 2000).

Postmodern tendencies have affected Western societies profoundly and can be noticed increasingly on other continents. In the twenty-first century these tendencies are propelling a growing interest in both New Age and wellness tourism, but both forms date back to pre-modern times. Wellness tourism existed in the eighteenth century (e.g. spa resorts in Belgium and Germany) and during the beginning of the twentieth century there were examples of projects along New Age lines. Wellness tourism has always had a certain clientele, partly because of the wide array of activities the term covers (medical tourism and aesthetic tourism being two examples); throughout history there have always been societal pressures exerted on certain social classes to attend to their personal well-being.

Life in a commune or at a New Age centre has not generally been considered a kind of tourism, nor have voluntary work opportunities at these centres. Along with the proliferation of New Age centres there has also been growing interest from a broader public leading to wider acceptance. In turn it seems that New Age centres are effectively seeking openings through tourism or similar programmes and they want to be heard, even on an international level, through associations and intensive use of the Internet. Tourism destinations have started to 'borrow' elements from New Age tourism and some hotels are now incorporating spiritual elements into the services they offer, though with the important difference that whereas New Age people try to transform self and society, other tourism initiatives offer people support and help for surviving the postmodern world.

Wellness tourism has seen a tremendous increase in popularity as a result of postmodern tendencies in society, whereby cultural pluralism and a growing preoccupation with the self (hence increased consumption patterns) have led to a wider concern about health and well-being (Sutton and House, 2000). Most wellness tourism activities, however, refer to physical health and have much to do with tourists' abilities to put their life–work balance back on track.

Focusing only on mental health and internal well-being has received less attention so far and the New Age centres visited clearly show that interest in physical wellness is increasing, along with a new search for alternative styles of living. In this respect, tourists are tending to mix various types of holidays: some days of wellness holiday alternating with some really adventurous tours, then a bit of culture, while not forgetting one's self through a reiki course. Learning elements are more readily mixed with leisure elements for example. This observation coincides with postmodern tendencies, whereby many people today like to 'channel-surf' the television, dipping in and out of different channels that capture their interest momentarily, without minding that a programme is not watched entirely (Gisolf, 2010).

Costa Rica seems to offer just the kind of environment on an ecological as well as a conscientious level for the successful development of New Age tourism, as witnessed at Finca Verdenergia, Finca Ipe, Finca Rancho Mastatal and Finca Punta Mona.

43

The holistic approach of Ayurveda-based wellness tourism offered in Kerala

Ramesh Unnikrishnan

Introduction

Kerala has been well known for hundreds of years for its practice of *Ayurveda*, a system of medicine that believes in not simply treating the ailment but attending to the whole person. Kerala is one of the few blessed regions in the world that is networked by 44 rivers. These rivers are also known as the 'backwaters of Kerala' and it stretches up to almost 1,900 kilometres. The backwater routes date back over the centuries and have been long used for all transportation needs, in particular trade in coconut, rubber, rice and spices. Today, these waterways link remote villages and islands to the mainland and nerve centres of the coastal area. The most interesting area in the backwaters is the Kuttanad region, called the rice bowl of Kerala. The area is probably the only place in the continent where farming is done below sea level, using a system of dykes and bunds. This state is also the only place in India which practises Ayurveda in its purest form. Being in this geographical wonder; heals the mind, body and soul with the magical touch of Ayurveda.

Ayurveda and its holistic approach

Ayurveda is the traditional Indian system of medicine that has brought true health, happiness and well-being to millions of individuals throughout the ages. This ancient art of healing has been in practice for over 5,000 years, and was also the mainstream medicine in ancient times. Derived from its ancient Sanskrit roots – 'ayus' (life) and 'ved' (knowledge) – and offering a rich, comprehensive outlook to a healthy life, it is the only medical science in this universe which is useful even when one is not ill. Ayurveda is a complete science of health that is applicable in all stages of life starting from birth, neonates, infants, childhood, youth, old age and even life before and after death. For many people, the image of Ayurveda is limited to the use of herbal or home/kitchen remedies and a traditional way of treatment. But in reality, Ayurveda is a serious medical science, which strongly emphasises diagnosis, examination, analysis of disease, diet, medicinal properties, dose, frequency of medicine and the medium with which it should be consumed. This science of medicine operates on the precept that every material object, be it animal or human or even mineral resources, has some medicinal value.

Everything in nature, including human beings, is made from the five elements of space, air, fire, water and earth. These five elements combine to form the three basic body–mind profiles, called *doshas*, that govern the entire physical composition and how each human is uniquely inclined to react and interact with the world around. In Sanskrit, the doshas are called *vata, pitta* and *kapha*. While each dosha plays an individual role in our bodies, overall good health is achieved only when all three are in balance. Knowing the respective unique proportions of vata, pitta and kapha is a prerequisite to understand Ayurvedic diagnosis and treatment.

The medicare in Ayurveda has broadly two parts: one is preservation of health and prevention of diseases; and the second diseases and their treatment. In Ayurvedic terminology, the first is *swasthavritha* and the later is *athuravritha*. Ayurveda follows a totally different way of treating diseases known as *panchakarma*, which means literally 'five therapies' which are the subtly harmonising purification procedures that dissolve metabolic waste products and toxins generated from the environmental ill effects, in a gentle and effective way from the tissues and eliminate them from the body. These five therapeutic means of eliminating toxins from the body are *vamana, virechana, nasya, basti and raktamoskshana*. This series of five therapies help remove deep rooted stress and illness causing toxins from the body while balancing the *doshas* (energies that govern all biological functions). This treatment is advisable to the diseased as well as the healthy. Before the *panchakarma* therapy, certain preliminary preparations are needed. These are called *shamana* therapies. These include massage – *abhyanga* and *snehana* – and fomentation – Svedana. Following the *panchakarma* treatments, a third phase of healing is advocated. This includes diet, exercises, Ayurvedic herbal tea and other preparations, and plant medicines specifically designed for each person. These are essential to sustain the results of previous treatments. Although promising, the procedures described are cumbersome and require trained persons to carry them out. Added to this is a novel way of treating the patients with 'essential oils' which are the fragrant essences distilled from the various parts of the plants, viz. root, stem, leaves, flowers, fruits, bark, or the whole plant. This is also called aromatherapy. Ayurveda also has a comprehensive system of massages and body treatments that gives relief from a wide range of illnesses, from migraine and sinus to arthritis and paralysis; that detoxify and cleans the body through controlled emesis, purgation, making the individual sweat; and that makes the body receptive to further treatment. These therapies are more effective in Kerala due to the almost year round humid climate of the state. Ayurveda extends excellent treatments for ailments like osteo-arthritis, rheumatic arthritis, tennis elbow and carpel tunnel syndrome, spondylosis, intervertibular disc prolapse, frozen shoulder, insomnia, migraine, skin diseases and of course weight management.

For the past two decades, the necessity for a holistic approach in the treatment of diseases had been an active topic for discussion among the scholars of modern

medical sciences. As a system of medicine that completely eliminates disease from the body without causing any side effects, and which ultimately promotes basic health, Ayurveda stands atop the alternative systems of treatments recognised by the World Health Organization. Many foreign countries have already started Kerala Ayurveda treatment centres and the export of Ayurvedic medicines to international markets is increasing at a faster pace day by day. But surprisingly, foreign tourists are often just as keen to visit the origin of the practice to avail treatments and body purification processes. The basic principles emerging from a holistic outlook, the peculiar and unique techniques of treatments, and the health promoting and non-reactive herbal drugs used are the main elements which differentiate Ayurveda from the other prevailing medical systems.

The Kerala government realises that it is of vital importance to offer assurance to its wellness seeking guests and visitors to the state that safety, hygiene, service quality and quality assurance are top priorities. This is to be achieved through the introduction of quality standards, registration, certification and regulation, and legislation. The comprehensive plan also includes guidelines and measures to ensure fair pricing. Beyond a competitive pricing strategy, achieving quality is another key to Kerala's competitiveness. The ability to attain international standards and consistently deliver high-quality products and services are critical success factors in the promotion of Kerala products on the global market. Kerala, as part of its marketing strategy, continuously organises road shows all around the world for the promotion of Ayurveda along with modern medicine. It is vitally important to create confidence in the products Kerala offers. There is much greater awareness and operators have come to realise that delivering quality translates into greater business efficiency, lower operating costs and increased profits.

Current infrastructure

Kerala, the state almost synonymous with the word 'Ayurveda', is now all set to reap the benefits of Ayurveda through health tourism. The reason for this is the popularity of Ayurvedic treatments and the manner in which Kerala is marketing Ayurveda in medical tourism. The promotion of Ayurveda in health tourism started in 1994 and the Kerala Tourism Development Corporation (KTDC) started Ayurvedic health centres in its premium properties like Hotel Samudra, Kovalam, during the same period. KTDC has tied up with the most reputed Ayurveda treatment providers and hence the authority of doctors and the quality of the medicines used are not compromised. While all the hotels and resorts in Kerala have now started including Ayurveda in their services, there are some resorts, which are exclusive for Ayurvedic treatments. With a view to facilitate the wellness tourism industry to achieve the targets and to give a greater momentum for this growth, the Ministry of Tourism, Government of Kerala, in association with the Department of Indian Systems of Medicine (ISM) has identified an urgent need to evaluate the safety and service standards of the prevailing and newly establishing Ayurveda centres and classify them accordingly. Standards have been set in terms of:

- personnel – qualified physicians and masseurs having sufficient degree and training from recognised Ayurveda institutions;
- quality of medicines and health programmes – prior approval by the advisory committee for the levels of treatments, clear exhibition of the treatment programmes offered and usage of medicines manufactured by approved firms with proper labelling;
- equipment – standards are fixed for the size and make of massage tables, facilities for medicated hot water, sterilisation, electric/gas stove and the hygiene;
- facilities – in terms of the number of treatment rooms with prescribed size, proper ventilation and attached bathrooms, quality and finishing of floors and walls, consultation room with proper equipment, separate rest rooms, locality, ambience and the cleanliness of surroundings.

Ayurvedic centres fulfilling all the mentioned essential conditions are awarded a certification named 'Olive Leaf'. In addition, the government has also set some optional conditions in terms of the construction and architectural features of the building, adequate parking space, facilities for steam bath, separate hall for yoga and meditation, herbal garden attached to the centre and the picturesque location. The Ayurveda centres also fulfilling these optional conditions will be awarded 'Green Leaf'. The Department of Tourism does not take responsibility for any centre, which is not classified in either of the above categories.

In the long run, wellness tourism can become an attractive niche for foreign revenue generation as there is an increasing trend in the number of visitors to Kerala as wellness seekers. The study reveals that the most favourable factor for Kerala to emerge as a Global Wellness Hub is its authenticity and rich Ayurvedic heritage with multifaceted attractions.

CHAPTER 44

Meditation tourism

Exploring the meditation flow experience and well-being

Tzuhui A. Tseng and Ching-Cheng Shen

Meditation is also known as contemplation, reflection and rumination. Master Sheng-Yen said the main purpose of meditation is to gain inner peace, and long-term practice allows purification and change both physically and spiritually. The definition of meditation often differs due to the time period, cultural context and practice method. Eastern societies believe meditation can calm one's mind and body, inspire wisdom, help understand the relationship between oneself and the nature, as well as explore the purpose of life. Meditation in Taiwan is often closely related to Buddhism. Buddhism is one of the most popular religions in Taiwan. According to the Taiwan Social Change Survey, in the population over the age of 20, 47 per cent consider themselves as Buddhist, and in the Chinese World Almanac published in Taiwan in 2001, unofficial statistics suggested there are about eight million Buddhists in the Taiwan-Fujian area, accounting for almost one-third of the total population.

However, meditation can exist independently without having anything to do with religion, attracting people from both Eastern and Western culture. In recent years, meditation in Taiwan has also gradually broken through the religious barrier. In addition to Tzu Chi, which mainly focuses on social relief activities, large-scale Buddhist monastery groups including Dharma Drum Mountain, Fo Guang Shan and Chung Tai Chan monastery all focus on meditation activities and, unlike in the past, they are starting to organise activities that are less related to religion. Instead, they apply the wisdom and use of Zen in a diverse way for modern people to release their stress physically and mentally, and experience affirmation, growth, and go beyond their spiritual power, in order to become the master of themselves (for example, the Excellent Youth Chan Camp organised by Dharma Drum Mountain Monastery). This study will explore whether the participants in Fo Guang Shan meditation gain happiness from the programme).

The meditation flow experience

The flow experience is when people are completely involved in one activity, which can cause an individual to be immersed completely and disregard other conditions. This kind of experience brings the greatest joy to people. After the notion of flow was proposed by Csikszentmihalyi, it was widely applied in all kinds of areas which included music, school education, the network, working, sport, volunteering, leisure, cross-culture research, daily life, internet browsing and so on (Csikszentmihalyi, 1990).

The research referred to in this case study uses the meditation flow scale which was applied by Jackson and Marsh (1996) and Cation (2000), and used the characteristics of meditation, and applied the seven aspects they identified, which included 'a clear goal', 'instant reward', 'the balance of skill and challenge', 'the full concentration on the activity', 'the sense of self-control', 'the sense of time change' and 'self-forming experience'.

Well-being

Well-being is a healthy or joyful feeling which generally may divide into Quality Of Life (QOL), mental health and mental development. QOL emphasises life satisfaction level as well as a spiritual dimension (Diener et al., 1999). In order to have mental well-being, a person first needs to have a healthy mind and emotions. If a person experiences more happy emotions and less unhappy emotions, this person could be said to be experiencing well-being. Mental development is not only about happiness; but about reaching one's full personal potential (Ryff, 1995).

Research method

In order to analyse the relationship between flow experience and well-being, this study established a linear structure equation model. Surveys were distributed to collect data and it was broken into three parts, which were flow experience, well-being and an individual's background information. The first and second parts were measured using Likert's five-point scale, and the third part used a categorical scale. This survey was distributed from January 2009 to February 2009 by using purposive selection, and the respondents who participated in the meditation activities hosted at Fo Guang Shan Monasteries in Kaohsiung and Chang Hua. A total of 538 questionnaires were handed out, and 513 of them were valid, with an effective rate of 95 per cent.

Results

Respondents' basic information analysis

The majority was female (71.6 per cent). The majority were 41–50 years old (30.9 per cent), and under 20 years old (20.0 per cent). The education level for the majority was university level (51.7 per cent). 62.0 per cent are single. Most are students (39.5 per cent), and the armed forces accounted for 23.6 per cent.

Flow experience

The flow experience analysis result is shown in Table 44.1. 'The experience coming from participating in meditation is very good' was the highest; the next was 'when facing challenges during participation in meditation, I have the ability to meet the challenge, and overcome it'. The lowest was 'I do not feel myself when I am participating in meditation'.

TABLE 44.1 Meditation flow activity analysis			
	Flow experience factors	Mean	SD
Clear goal	I know that I want to participate in meditation.	3.65	0.87
	When I participate in meditation, I know clearly what I am supposed to do.	3.73	0.83
Instant reward	When I participate in meditation, I feel very good.	3.75	0.80
	When I participate in meditation, I know that I am doing it well.	3.11	0.84
Skill and Challenge balance	When I face challenges when I participate in meditation, I know that I have enough ability to overcome it.	3.88	0.75
	The challenge which meditation brings to me is not beyond my ability.	3.32	0.85
	I do not need to ponder and I can have the right reaction.	2.90	0.93
Full concentration in the activity	I participate in meditation automatically.	3.38	1.00
	I naturally pay full attention when I participate in meditation.	3.49	0.83
	When I participate in meditation, I give it my full attention.	3.60	0.81
Sense of self-control	I can control all the activity easily when I am participating in meditation.	3.10	0.88

(Continued overleaf)

	Flow experience factors	Mean	SD
TABLE 44.1 Continued			
	When I participate in meditation, I have the ability to control all aspects of the situation.	3.23	0.80
The sense of time change	I am not aware of myself when I am participating in meditation.	2.74	0.90
	The time passes fast when I am participating in meditation.	3.51	0.89
	The passing of time feels unusual when I am participating in meditation.	3.62	0.85
	The experience coming from meditation is very good.	3.91	0.79

Well-being analysis

The well-being analysis result of meditation is shown in Table 44.2. 'I always thought that life should be dynamic and created according to my own initiative' is the highest; next is 'I feel very fortunate'. The lowest well-being item is 'My moods are stable'. Meditation will bring more positive feeling for life and it will be helpful in the work concentration.

	Well-being factor	Mean	SD
TABLE 44.2 Well-being analysis of meditation			
Physiology	My body is healthier and I have less illnesses.	3.66	0.78
	I can use my mind to improve my immune system.	3.63	0.83
	I feel more energized and less tired.	3.62	0.89
Psychology	My moods are stable.	3.43	0.87
	My body and mind are always comfortable.	3.73	0.79
	I can handle setbacks and cope with angry and sad emotions.	3.65	0.83
	I can keep my emotions calm when faced with matters which make me angry.	3.66	0.81
Environment	I am satisfied with the environment which surrounds me.	3.84	0.75
	I can make the atmosphere of the working environment peaceful and harmonious.	3.71	0.75

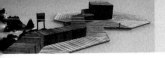

Social relations	I do not argue with people over small things.	3.90	0.73
	I can communicate well with the others, when I live with others.	3.76	0.74
	My co-workers and I often socialise outside work.	3.64	0.80
Self-growth	I can easily focus when I am working.	4.08	0.68
	I can manage my work–life balance.	3.80	0.76
	I try my best to perform well at work.	3.96	0.70
Happy optimistic	I always thought that life should be dynamic and created according to my own initiative.	4.19	0.69
	I am always interested and enthusiastic at work and in everyday life.	3.91	0.74
	I feel hopeful about the future.	3.94	0.81
	I can still be optimistic under adverse circumstances and keep working hard.	3.75	0.7623
Life satisfaction	I can understand life's meaning.	3.90	0.80
	I can get the best from everyday life.	3.99	0.66
	I feel very fortunate.	4.15	0.68

The relationship between meditation flow and well-being

This study developed a linear construction model for meditation flow experience and well-being and used the Lisrel 8.5 software to show a relational path diagram (Figure 44.1). The meditation flow experience and well-being factors reached coefficients between 0.66 and 0.87, which means a good fit. The t-value of each construct is higher than 1.645, and there are no negative error variations. The coefficient of the meditation flow experience to well-being is 0.73 (t-value was 12.85), demonstrating that the meditation flow experience has a positive influence on well-being.

Conclusion

Meditation has the strength to increase people's quality of life both mentally and spiritually, so it is gradually becoming a popular leisure activity for many people. This study examined the relationship between meditation flow experience and well-being, and the findings demonstrated that higher meditation flow experience has higher well-being value. People came from other cities to join these few days' meditation trip, and they thought

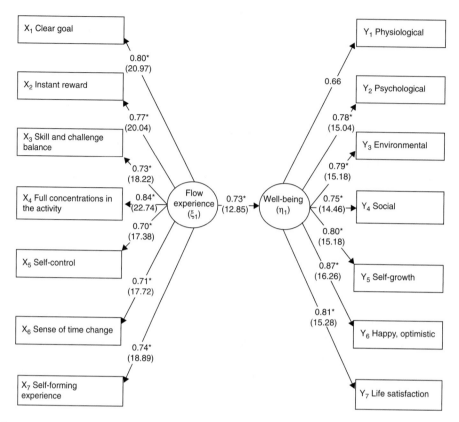

FIGURE 44.1 The causal relationship between meditation flow experience and well-being

that meditation is a very good experience that can bring a more positive outlook to people's life spiritually. The findings also showed that meditation had the ability to reduce the pressure of daily life and increase people's health, and promote intrinsic self-control, so people can enjoy meditation as a leisure activity. It is also can be promoted as a tourism activity in any country.

CHAPTER

45

The propensity for yoga practitioners to become tourists
A case study of Budapest

Ivett Sziva, Noémi Kulcsár and Melanie Smith

Yoga is a relatively new leisure activity in Hungary compared to many other European countries, especially those in Western Europe. However, it is growing rapidly and the number of yoga centres is increasing all the time. This is particularly true of the capital city, Budapest, where most of this research was undertaken. The general state of public health in Hungary is much lower than the EU average and there are a relatively low number of people who are consciously and actively engaged in preventative health care. However, research has shown that 41 per cent of the population perceive body–mind–spirit well-being to be important. Thirty-nine per cent use some kind of alternative therapy service (e.g. bio, energy, or mind-based treatments (e.g. zen). Four per cent of the total population do yoga regularly (several times weekly or monthly) and 6 per cent do meditation. Five per cent take part in personality improvement training, and 5 per cent in mind-control training (GFK, 2012).

There is a lack of research about yoga in Hungary. Most of the articles dealing with the theme can be found in lifestyle magazines, with the emphasis that Hatha yoga (a glossary of yoga terms is presented at the end of this report) is the most popular (as it tends to be elsewhere too). With the objective of mapping the supply side of yoga practice, a content analysis was undertaken of Hungarian yoga centres and wellness hotels which had an accessible website, and 10 per cent of those found were analysed using systematic sampling. The yoga centres were selected from Budapest and the largest cities from six regions of Hungary. Only those yoga centres which had publicly accessible websites were analysed. In addition, wellness hotels which offered yoga classes were also included. The inclusion of wellness hotels in the sample was based on the notion that many hotels also offer yoga classes, not only for guests but for local residents too. Although most wellness hotels mainly offer saunas and massage, the yoga offer seems to be growing. Based on a 10 per cent sample taken from the database of the Hungarian National Tourism Office, it can be seen that 20 per cent of the wellness hotels include yoga classes or meditation.

However, the research showed that yoga holidays tend to be taken in camps or retreat centres, guest houses or apartments rather than wellness hotels.

Ninety yoga centres were identified in Hungary. An online interview was undertaken with 10 per cent of these yoga centres' managers. Based on this research it could be seen that the numbers of members of yoga centres ranged from 40 to 150, of whom 10–20 per cent are men. The average number of members or participants in Budapest is 70, while the rate of men is 12 per cent (but sometimes up to 50 per cent in classes where dynamic yoga is offered, such as Ashtanga or Bikram). A tentative estimate of the total number of yoga practitioners who attend yoga centres (rather than practising at home or with DVDs) is around 6,000.

The most popular kind of yoga in Budapest is Hatha (60 per cent of the analysed centres offer this type of yoga), followed by spinal yoga (55 per cent), pregnancy yoga (50 per cent), mummy–baby yoga (45 per cent), children's yoga (40 per cent), yoga for stress-relief (45 per cent) and women's yoga (50 per cent). Additional services include meditation programmes (50 per cent), classes in English (50 per cent) and 35 per cent organise yoga-camps, or retreat holidays.

A questionnaire with closed-ended questions was distributed to yoga practitioners in Budapest. The sampling approach aimed to analyse as many different kinds of yoga and yoga centres as possible and to gain a representative picture of yoga practitioners in Budapest. Some difficulties arose when attempting to undertake research in yoga centres due to the lack of free access to classes and practitioners and the lack of time before or after classes. Therefore the majority of the questionnaires were undertaken at a Yoga Festival (the Uj Élet Jóga Fesztivál or New Life Yoga Festival) in May 2012. This event which took place in a central city location was a 'showcase' for eight different types of yoga, with the objective of promoting yoga and healthy lifestyle (e.g. nutrition, massage). Around 150 people partici-pated in the festival and the yoga classes offered. To supplement this sample, questionnaires were also distributed electronically using the same questionnaire between May and July 2012. A snowball sampling approach was taken using known yoga practitioners and commu-nity websites. This additional research phase resulted in a total of 201 valid questionnaires.

Eighty-nine per cent of the respondents were female, and according to the qualitative research, the average rate of men participating in yoga classes is 12 per cent. The majority of the respondents (40 per cent) were aged 30–39, and 70 per cent possess a higher education degree, and were permanently employed.

One of the most important motivations for practising yoga is balance, which gained the highest score on the Likert scale of 1–5 (4.44). Following this come calmness and a stress-free life (4.39), and a healthier life (3.99). Another important factor is physical exercise, which is highly important for those practicing Bikram and Hatha (100 per cent of the former, 66 per cent of the latter). The spiritual experience of yoga is important for half of the respondents (reaching an average of 3.5 on the Likert scale), especially for Kundalini yoga practitioners.

Among the impacts of doing yoga being fit and calm are the most important impacts (the former is important or highly important for 75 per cent, the latter for 78 per cent). Self-understanding and improving concentration is important for 65 per cent of the respondents and self-acceptance for 59 per cent. Social connections, community involvement, optimal weight and better sleeping seem to be less important. The spiritual experience is important for 46 per cent of practitioners.

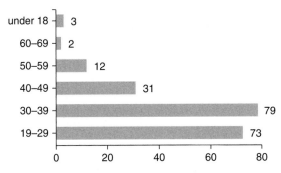

FIGURE 45.1 The distribution of sample by age

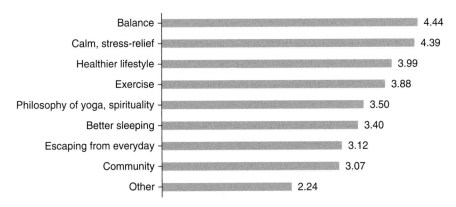

FIGURE 45.2 Evaluation of the motivations for doing yoga

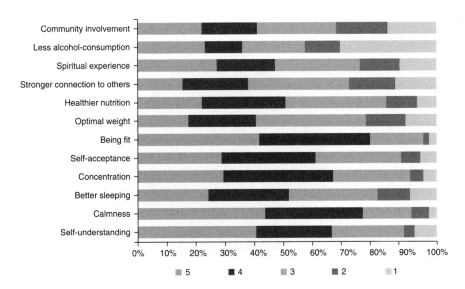

FIGURE 45.3 The benefits of doing yoga

Travelling habits among yoga practitioners

Forty-one per cent of the respondents have already travelled with the objective of doing yoga. All of the Kundalini practitioners have been on yoga holidays, and this rate is high amongst Hatha practitioners (43 per cent), but low amongst Ashtanga as well as Bikram practitioners (for the latter this is not surprising, as a special studio kept at a constant high temperature is needed for this type of yoga). It should be highlighted, that those practising regularly (daily, weekly) are those who tend to participate in yoga holidays, and are mainly in the age group of 30–39, and 40–49. 63.6 per cent of male respondents have participated in yoga holidays (but it should be remembered that the rate of men doing yoga in this sample was only 12 per cent). The tendency to go on a yoga holiday is highest amongst those practitioners for whom self-understanding and spirituality are important, especially Kundalini and Hatha practitioners.

The frequency of travel is highest among those who mentioned self-understanding as a major motivation for doing yoga (81.7 per cent), followed by those for whom a spiritual experience is important (61 per cent). Being part of a community was significant for 51.2 per cent, followed by the desire to get fit for 45.1 per cent.

The characteristics of the trip

Respondents spend an average of five days on a yoga holiday, but with a high variation (one–30 days). 47.2 per cent selected a yoga camp in a forest as the destination for their

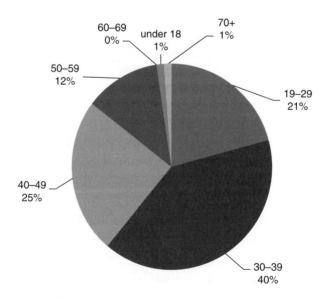

FIGURE 45.4 Yoga travel according to age

yoga holiday, followed by yoga festivals (13.8 per cent) and retreats (10.6 per cent). Domestic destinations (in Hungary) were visited by 61 per cent, while India is the second most frequently chosen destination (10.2 per cent), which is followed by Western European destinations. It should be noted that the salaries in Hungary are much lower than their Western European counterparts (sometimes as little as one fifth), therefore overseas and long-haul travel is relatively expensive for Hungarians. The money spent on yoga holidays (including transportation, full/half board), reached an average of 40,000 HUF (around 140 euros, with a high variation of 6,000–1 million HUF (21–3540 euros)). On domestic trips around 30,000–40,000 HUF (106–140 euros) was estimated, while for foreign trips around 500,000–600,000 HUF (1770–2100 euros) was spent. The most important factor determining the experience was the yoga teacher (4.6 average on a Likert scale of 1–5), the meditation possibilities and the natural environment.

Retreats and silent meditation were popular among Kundalini and Hatha practitioners, while the yoga possibilities in wellness hotels were also sought by Hatha practitioners. In

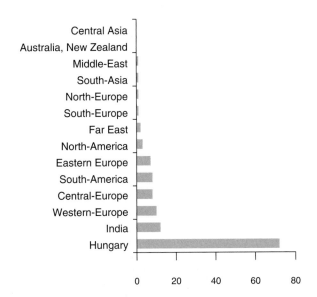

FIGURE 45.5 The destinations for yoga trips

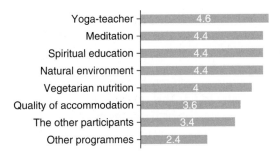

FIGURE 45.6 The factors influencing yoga trips

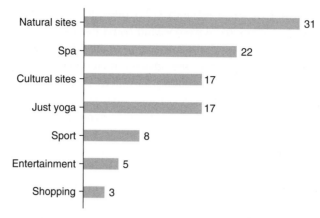

FIGURE 45.7 The importance of other activities

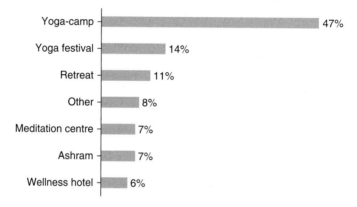

FIGURE 45.8 The preferred locations for yoga trips

terms of doing other activities while on a yoga holiday, visiting natural sites was the most important (30 per cent of the answers), which was followed by spas and cultural sites. However, it is important to note that only doing yoga (i.e. no other activities) was important for many respondents.

Conclusions

Practising yoga is becoming more and more popular in Hungary and seems to be part of a growing wellness or holistic trend. This research shows that for the majority of yoga practitioners it has become a lifestyle with regular practice leading to stress-relief, calmness, self-understanding, as well as many other impacts. Spirituality is also important for many of the respondents, especially Kundalini and Hatha yoga practitioners. Although the development of yoga holidays is in its relative infancy in Hungary, many respondents had

been or were enthusiastic about going on yoga holidays. This includes yoga camps, retreats and also festivals. Although the majority stayed in Hungary, some had been or were keen to go abroad, especially to India. The most important motivations were the yoga teacher, meditation and the natural environment. Supplementary programmes or activities were sometimes deemed unnecessary showing that yoga alone is becoming a primary motivation for travel.

Glossary of terms

The types of yoga mentioned in this report have been defined according to *Yoga Magazine* (February, 2013: 64–71):

Ashtanga: goes back to the ancient principles of yoga sage Pantanjali. Sometimes called power yoga, it was introduced to the West in the 1970s by Sri Krishna Pattabhi Jois. It combines dynamic (*ujjayi*) breathing with a series of strong, fast, flowing movements.

Bikram yoga: consists of a series of 26 energetic postures performed in very high temperatures (around 100C/40F) designed to stretch muscles further and expel toxins. Founder Bikram Choudhoury, who has a college in the USA.

Hatha yoga: although often described as the yoga of physical exercise, hatha follows the classical yoga theory of learning how to control the body so it can absorb the universal life-force energy (*prana*). In Sanskrit 'ha' means sun and 'tha' means moon.

Iyengar yoga: was developed by B.K.S. Iyengar in India. He introduced a systematic, disciplined approach to align mind, body and spirit through *asanas, pranayama* and meditation. Very popular in the West.

Karma yoga: takes the path of selfless action, working for others in the hope of gaining spiritual and healing powers.

Kundalini yoga: is an ancient, mystical branch of yoga. Movement, breathing, sound, chanting and meditation are used to activate the kundalini – a spiritual healing energy – and guide it through seven major energy centres in the body. The kundalini cleanses and purifies the chakras, dispelling negative thoughts, emotions and disease.

Medical tourism and medical wellness

Apollo Hospitals group
A key player in the Indian medical tourism industry

Anita Medhekar

Introduction: medical tourism in India

India is emerging as an attractive health-care destination providing all three holistic wellness choices to international medical tourists such as: (i) alternative spiritual theraphy (yoga and spa), (ii) Ayurveda (herbal medicine) and (iii) complex diagnostic and medical surgeries (heart and hip). India was ranked third after Thailand and Singapore in 2005 (RNCOS, 2007) and in 2009 second only to Thailand as a global medical tourism destination (IMT, 2009). The eight key competitive driving factors and strengths that attract foreign medical tourists to India as a destination for medical treatment are: low surgical and medication cost, no waiting period, Joint Commission International JCI & International Organisation for Standardisation (ISO) accredited quality of medical care, state of the art medical infrastructure facilities and technology, qualified and experienced medical professionals and nurses, affordable Indian pharmaceutical industry, availability of holistic alternative treatment and Ayurvedic medicine (CII and McKinsey, 2002; FICCI, 2008; JCI, 2010; Medhekar and Ali, 2012), and above all provision of personalised health care, English-speaking medical professionals and an attractive tourism destination with rich historical, spiritual and cultural heritage.

A report by the Confederation of Indian Industries CII and McKinsey has forecasted that India's medical tourism market will generate some US$ 2.4 billion in foreign exchange revenue by 2012 by attracting 1.1 million medical tourists from countries such as the UK, USA, Europe, African, Middle East and neighbouring West and South Asia. Many corporate private health-care players (Bortman, 2010) are providing complex surgical procedures and medical treatment to domestic and foreign patients such as Apollo, Wockhardt, Escorts, Fortis, All India Institute of Medical Science, Asian Heart, Max-India, Jaslok, Ranbaxy and Sancheti Institute of Orthopedics & Rehabilitation. Apollo, which has branches in all the major cities of India, has received numerous awards for being the best private-sector super-speciality health-care provider to domestic and foreign patients for over a decade. On 29 February 2012, Ruby-Hall Clinic in Pune was awarded the best private-sector medical tourism provider and facility in India by the President of India, Dr Pratibha Patil, and by the Ministry of Tourism, Government of India in New Delhi (Ruby Hall Clinic, 2012).

Apollo Hospitals Enterprise

The Apollo Hospitals Enterprise Ltd. (AHEL) was founded by Dr Pratap C. Reddy in 1979 with 150 beds to provide low-cost and quality of health care to Indians after returning from the USA. Dr Reddy has many achievements and awards to his credit for Apollo such as in 1991 Padma-Bhushan, 2002 Ernst & Young, Entrepreneur of the Year and in 2006 Modern Medicine Excellence award in the Indian health-care industry. Apollo started its medical tourism operation in 2002 with headquarters on Greams Road, Chennai in the South East of India. It is the largest private-sector integrated health-care provider in India and realised the potential and global opportunity to enter the medical tourism business. It was rated in 2002–3 and 2007–9 as the 'Best Private Sector Hospital' in India. Apollo owns and operates many speciality hospitals, clinics, consultancy services for managing super-speciality hospitals, diagnostic clinics, medical BPO, tele-medicine, health insurance services, clinical research facilities and Apollo pharmacy retail shops. Apollo is the largest private corporate JCI and ISO accredited hospital group in Asia with branches and affiliations in the major cities of India and in other countries, for example in Bangladesh, Sri Lanka, Nepal, UAE, Dubai, Kenya, Ghana, Nigeria, UK and Saudi Arabia (Apollo Hospitals, 2012).

Apollo Hospitals has two key business divisions: (i) provision of health-care services via hospitals, hospital pharmacies and consultancies for super-speciality hospitals and (ii) Apollo Pharmacies which offer a range of services such as medicine, surgical equipments and hospital products. It provides a variety of complex health-care medical surgeries such as cardiology, orthopaedics, neurology, gynaecology, oncology, maternity, radiology, diagnostic, laboratory and emergency services besides general surgery, day care and clinics for diabetes, preventative health, back pain, breast, obesity and adolescent clinic. The Apollo group of medical tourism hospitals provides customised medical packages (covers all costs: airfare, transport, medical, hospital minus vacation cost) and meditour packages (covers all medical costs plus pre-post operative vacation) in partnership with health insurance companies and medical tourism operators. Consultancy services for hospital projects and operations management including pre-commissioning consultancy for super-speciality hospitals, medical infrastructure and feasibility studies (Apollo Hospitals, 2012).

Apollo Hospitals has all the key driving factors to be globally competitive as a medical tourist choice of hospital. Affordable surgical costs which are 50 to 70 per cent lower than in developed countries such as USA, Canada, Australia, Europe and UK, no waiting period, accredited quality of health-care facilities and health professionals. Apollo mainly operates in India and has a total of 50 hospitals with over 8,500 hospital beds in India and overseas (Apollo Hospitals, 2012). The Apollo Hospitals group revenue increased by 26 per cent from 2008–9 to 18,587 million rupees in 2009–10. the key source of revenue

for Apollo was 72 per cent of the overall gross revenue from the health-care services division and the pharmacy division contributed 4846.3 million rupees to gross revenue and 26 per cent share to the total revenue (RNCOS, 2010).

Apollo Hospitals group has demonstrated innovation in health care and sustainable growth in both their business divisions across India and abroad. Apollo plans to open further branches overseas in Africa, West Asia and in the neighbouring South Asian countries and increase the number of beds and income from medical business process outsourcing. It faces a competitive environment from other private sector corporate health-care providers in India as well as from overseas medical tourism destinations in South East Asia, such as Thailand and Singapore.

Some of the key achievements of the Apollo Hospitals Enterprise Ltd. are the following:

- Centre for Advanced Cardiac Care Medical Facility in Hyderabad.
- Provide mobile health space with tie up with telecom operators Aircel to deliver m-health solutions.
- Partnership with British Medical Journal Group, British Medical Association, to provide mobile health applications for patients, medical educators and professionals.
- Partnership with central government health scheme launched a dialysis clinic.
- Apollo Organ Transplant Programme provided 534 transplants in 2010.
- Provision of stem-cell facility in partnership with US StenCyte in Hyderabad.
- Apollo Hospitals Ahmadabad completed 20 successful stem-cell transplants.
- Apollo provides Endovascular (liberation) treatment for Multiple Sclerosis.
- In 2010, Chennai Apollo Speciality Hospital for the first time performed ceramic coated knee replacement.
- Apollo has partnered with CISCO, to provide innovative health care thorough information and telecommunication technology (ICT).

(RNCOS, 2010)

Indian government initiative for the growth of medical tourism industry

The Indian government's successful 'Incredible India' tourism campaign along with world-class medical service provision to international tourists became a government policy in 2003 when the Finance Minister in his budget speech called for India to become a 'global health destination'. The tenth (2002–7) and the 11th (2007–12) five-year plans of the Indian government emphasised the economic importance of the development of medical tourism to India, along with promoting India as a world class high-tech healing destination providing low cost and international quality of medical treatment and procedures (GOI, 2008, 2003). Medical tourism tour operators are now connecting patients with hospitals which are JCI accredited providers of complex medical procedures. The most demanded treatments are heart by-pass surgery, knee and hip replacement, dental care, kidney, IVF-reproductive-gender selection and cosmetic surgery. Table 46.1 provides a cost comparison of selected surgeries between countries, with India having a comparative cost advantage.

TABLE 46.1 Cost comparison for selected surgeries ($US – 2009 prices)

Surgery	USA	Costa Rica	India	Mexico	Singapore	Thailand
Heart bypass	144,000	25,000	8,500	20,000	13,500	24,000
Angioplasty	57,000	13,000	8,500	16,000	7,500	7,000
Heart valve replacement	170,000	30,000	1,200	30,000	13,500	22,000
Hip replacement	50,000	12,500	8,000	13,125	11,100	14,000
Knee replacement	50,000	11,500	7,000	10,660	10.800	12,000
Dental Implants	2,000–10,000	1,000	700	910	2,900	3,000
Breast Implants	10,000	3,500	4,500	8,000	5,400	3,700

Source: Adapted from American Medical Tourism Association, 2009.

Most of the medical tourists who travel to India given the advantage of English language, and commonwealth country are from the developed countries of USA, UK, Europe and Middle East oil-rich countries and the affluent expatriate (diaspora) from the Indian sub-continent, neighbouring South Asia and Africa where the costs of medical surgeries is very high along with long waiting periods and non-availability of certain treatments and facilities.

A study on India's medical tourism sector in 2002 by the Confederation of Indian Industry (CII), in collaboration with international management consultants McKinsey, outlined enormous opportunity and potential growth for this sector. The numbers of foreign patients as medical tourists visiting India are growing at a rate of 30 per cent a year and it is projected that the health-care market in India will be worth around 5.2 per cent of gross domestic product (GDP) by 2010, to between US$ 50 billion and US$ 69 billion, or 6.2 per cent and 8.5 per cent of GDP by 2020 (CII and McKinsey, 2002; Chinai and Goswami, 2007; FICCI, 2008). As an example of public–private partnership approach, the following measures have been taken by the India government to collaborate with key private hospitals not only to support the growth of this industry as a key foreign exchange earner, but also to promote India as a world-class global medical tourism hub and destination overseas (Medhekar, 2010):

- Introduction of medical visa in 2003 (M-Visa) category which is granted to the medical tourists and is valid for one year or for the length of treatment. It is renewable and allows multiple entries for follow-up care with the companion.
- Tourism and Medical Travel-Visa on Arrival (VoA) was introduced in 2011 for selected countries citizens such as: Finland, Japan, Luxembourg, New Zealand and Singapore, to reduce delays and attract tourists. In 2012 under the 12th Five Year Tourism Development Plan, it is extended to Cambodia, Indonesia, Vietnam, Laos, Myanmar and the Philippines. In the near future it may be extended to other countries for

example: Brazil, Brunei, France, Germany, Malaysia, Russia Spain, Sweden, South Africa and Thailand.

- Medical Escort-Visa (MX) was introduced, to family or a friend who are accompanying a patient travelling to India for medical care on a medical visa.
- National Health Policy of the Government of India clearly stated that medical treatment of foreign patients is legally an 'export' and deemed 'eligible' for all fiscal incentives extended to export earnings.
- 100 per cent foreign direct investment (FDI) in medical infrastructure, research and development initiatives.
- Improved air and local road transport service across border for patient mobility.
- Apollo Hospitals Enterprise Ltd in Chennai (Madras-JCI accredited), which was started in 1983 and receives patients from developed and developing countries, has overseas branches in countries such as Sri Lanka, Bangladesh, Ghana, UAE, Nepal, Nigeria, UK, Saudi Arabia, Qatar and Kuwait.
- Joint Commission International accreditation of 17 hospitals in India and medical facilities and professionals.
- Organising international medical tourism trade fairs in developed and developing countries such as Canada, Dubai, Kenya, Oman and UK.

Even though the above reasons help to promote India and Apollo Hospitals group as an attractive choice of destination for medical tourism, the quality of medical treatment provided by the key private hospitals is of major concern for overseas patients. Besides, other key concerns relate to legal medical litigations, safety, country infrastructure facilities, pollution, local transport, poverty and inequality. However, the Apollo group is faced not only with competition from other private hospitals within India but also from abroad who are in the business of medical tourism. It is faced with challenges of franchising and branding to improve the provision of international quality of health care, innovation and research in medical facilities and treatment, country infrastructure, local transport, airport facilities and flight connectivity, safety, clean water and safe food, accommodation and hospitality industry, allied health-care services, interpersonal and communication skills of medical staff and tourism service providers and availability of language interpreters. Finally, not only marketing strategies are needed to promote itself as a safe and trustworthy choice of super-speciality hospital for complex surgeries, but also diversifying their medical tourism products and services and providing Integrated Medical Services (IMS) including alternative spiritual therapy, Ayurvedic medicine and tourism packages.

CHAPTER 47

The UK National Health Service and international patients

Neil Lunt, Johanna Hanefeld, Daniel Horsfall and Richard D. Smith

Background

This case discusses the role of a public health system, the UK National Health Service, in providing medical treatments for inward patients (or international patients as they are known). The NHS is a publicly funded system of health, primarily financed through general taxation. It provides a comprehensive range of health services and treatment, the vast majority of which are available to United Kingdom residents free at the point of use. NHS Hospital trusts (acute trusts) provide services on behalf of the NHS.

For a number of decades the NHS has been providing treatments for international patients. The focus on inward flows is around *the booked and planned admission of international patients treated as private patients within NHS facilities*. This could include outpatient admission, day surgery, as well as overnight stays. Possible payers for these patients include government-sponsored patients, private/employer insurance and those funding treatment out-of-pocket. Data from the International Passenger Survey suggests overall, international patient flows (treated both in private and public facilities) to the UK were in the region of 52,000 in 2010. We estimate that a significant proportion of these are treated annually within the NHS as international patients.

The services provided by the NHS to international patients do not fit popular medical tourist notions of 'bikinis and bandages' (Bell et al., 2011), or 'sun, sea, sand and surgery' (Connell, 2006). Many London-based NHS facilities have longstanding international patient flows, including single-specialty hospitals as well as those offering a broader range of specialities. Countries identified as sending patients to the UK were primarily those from the Middle East (including Kuwait, UAE, Oman, Qatar, and smaller numbers from Saudi Arabia), and strong flows from Cyprus and Greece. Types of treatment centre on complex tertiary including paediatrics, and heart surgery. In a sample of NHS Trusts, the largest numbers of inbound medical tourists were in the large hospitals which are internationally known for their specialism; foremost amongst these is Great Ormond Street Hospital for Sick Children (GOSH) which reported income of over £20 million from 656 patients.

A 2011 report by the Office for Fair Trading investigating the private health care sector in the UK concluded that in 2009 the market was worth £5 billion in total and that 2.4 per cent of this was income generated by foreign patients (i.e. £120 million generated by medical tourists). Based on our calculations medical tourists spend between £192–325 million per annum in the UK, in both the public and the private sector. Data from the 27 Trusts surveyed indicated that spending by private non-UK resident per procedure was much higher than spending by private UK residents. While non-UK patients only constituted 6 per cent of private patients in these facilities they were responsible for 34 per cent of private patient income. These figures suggest that non-UK residents travelling to the UK for medical treatment seek high end specialist expensive procedures.

While this does represent a sizable market and one which obviously could grow, this represents less than 0.5 per cent of projected government spend on health of £130 billion in 2012–13. It is likely the majority of international patients travelling into the UK will visit London and select urban medical centres. Considering the tourism and health expenditure by medical tourists as concentrated more in these locations this may represent a very significant stream of income in specific areas.

The context of NHS international activity

Specialist NHS facilities have a long tradition of treating international patients, and there are established collaborative clinician networks and programmes with regard to training, education and consultancy.

NHS Trusts adopt a range of models and approaches to the organisation and delivery of services to international patients. For example, some Hospital Trusts have entered into partnerships with private commercial interests, typically very large multinational interests. These include the Health Corporation of America (HCA) whose NHS Ventures has a number of partnership arrangements with NHS Trusts, allowing patients to be treated exclusively in private settings. HCA's first such venture was the 2006 partnership arrangement with University College London Hospital (UCH) to develop Harley Street at UCH – a complex cancer centre facility. HCA took over the hospital's private patient wing, leasing space and paying for services, and sharing profits from private patients with the hospital (Timmins, 2007). A 2010 partnership with Christie NHS Foundation Trust in Manchester led to the Christie Clinic, a new Trust/HCA joint venture.

Some specialist London hospitals have opened branches in the Middle East, or partnered with commercial interests and health-care developments in the region. The Gulf region in particular has a significant British and Western expatriate population. Great Ormond Street Hospital opened a regional office at Dubai Health Care City in 2006. The office supports patients and families travelling from the region to London: advice on investigations and pre-treatment; information and assistance with accommodation and transport to the hospital, and information on services and London; and assistance obtaining visas (source GOSH, 2012). Upon return to the Gulf, the office aims to provide medical records and information for the referring hospital/doctor and ongoing contact with families and communication with clinicians at GOSH. In 2007 Moorfields opened a facility in Dubai

Health Care City that operates as an overseas arm of the hospital. The hospital treats around 11,000 patients per year at its purpose built campus with around 70 per cent coming from the Emirati and expat Arab communities (AME, 2012).

Third, within the NHS, private services are offered to patients (including private patients from abroad) within both integrated and standalone facilities. Integrated facilities involve the use of shared theatres and treatments where there is a need to co-locate activities for reasons of intensive care units (ICUs) and specialist support (for example shared theatres but nevertheless with private wards for private maternity patients). For some treatments there may be dedicated facilities with private operating theatre space and ward facilities.

Patient pathways

International patients have distinct processes of referral and patient management. International patients referred to NHS facilities are often highly specialist, where typically it is not possible to treat locally because of relatively small volumes and complex nature of treatment required. Relationships, primarily clinical ones, are paramount in maintaining flows of international patients. Patient flows are perceived to develop from clinical relationships, including training links where overseas referring doctors trained within the UK or spent time alongside receiving consultants. Some Trusts continuously developed and consolidated such links via offering clinical training to overseas consultants and staff exchange and educational programmes. Alongside clinician links there were also cultural preferences that favour specific London hospitals. For example, some Middle East nationals were said to prefer particular London localities for treatment; similarly, a strong connection was identified between some parts of London, and Greek and Cypriot populations.

Embassies and health attachés of sender countries occupy central roles in the market for international patients. Embassies generate 'Letters of Guarantee' to provide reimbursement assurance for a Trust for what may be a very expensive programme of treatment. Detailed patient records may not always accompany the travelling patient and so detailed checks and diagnostics are undertaken upon arrival. Complex cases and lengthy stays will necessarily generate very large bills. (Self-funders are expected to pay up-front for treatments and are seen as financially riskier propositions given they lack institutional surety.)

NHS Trusts offer various forms of patient liaison (which may be 24/7) but not typically hotel-type concierge services. Translation services are either provided through individual patient liaison (for example as fluent Arabic speakers) or sourced externally. There is little door-to-door service – return travel arrangements, for example, are typically made by embassies.

Future developments

The current financial climate for the NHS presents a major challenge, and commercial income, private patient income and international income are seen as possible routes to ameliorating pressure on stretched NHS resources. In launching NHS Global in 2010, David Nicholson, NHS Chief Executive suggested: 'It is now more important than ever to maximise the international potential of the NHS . . .' From 1 October 2012, NHS Trusts have more opportunity to undertake international activities, including securing greater numbers of patients travelling from overseas for treatment as part of wider commercial developments. These non-UK patients will potentially be sponsored by governments, funded by insurers, or paying out of pocket. Whilst critics have pointed to the further privatisation of the NHS, the core legal duty of NHS Trusts remains unchanged – that of caring for NHS patients and delivering authorised services.

In August 2012, the Healthcare UK scheme was launched, supported by the Department of Health and UK Trade and Industry. It aims to further promote and encourage overseas investment and activities from within the NHS which aims to provide profit streams for reinvestment in core NHS services.

Leveraging greater opportunities may require greater attention to marketing and customer care, and these are challenges in the current NHS environment. Traditionally, the NHS orientation was a passive one, whereas private and international activity may involve more marketing and proactivity engaging overseas markets. There is a need to manage both internal and local stakeholder views of such NHS commercial developments. Sometimes these perceptions and misunderstanding are linked to the pejorative notion of 'health tourists'. Local and national political sensitivities of engaging in private patient and international activity are also an obstacle to traverse.

The NHS itself faces competition which is both national (including public and private) and international. Germany and the US compete for Middle Eastern activity, as well as a number of international developments within the Gulf region itself.

Acknowledgement

This project was funded by the National Institute for Health Research Health Services and Delivery Research Programme (project number 09/2001/21).

Disclaimer

The views and opinions expressed therein are those of the authors and do not necessarily reflect those of the HS&DR Programme, NIHR, NHS or the Department of Health.

48

Kurotel – turning a dream into reality
Milestones and keys to success

Victoria Winter

When Dr Luis Carlos Silveira and Neusa Silveira were young, and in university, they dreamed of constructing a place where they could receive clients and help them to regain their well-being and happiness through some of the most modern technological resources aimed at healthcare. Although some of these resources did not yet exist, they were sure that one day it would be possible to diagnose diseases before they appeared, control stress levels, provide weight control and promote the revitalisation of the body as a whole. Neusa and Luis Carlos were what people today classify as 'visionaries', since they dreamed of how the human being could benefit from a longevity centre, at which it would be possible to open up the book of life, DNA, and get a precise assessment of the risk factors and a complete diagnosis.

Their idea was to construct something that could have the sophistication and resources of a hospital, without being a traditional hospital; the comfort of a hotel, without being a traditional hotel; the structure of a beauty clinic and fitness centre, without concentrating solely on weight reduction and external beauty. Moreover, they dreamed of a complete healthcare clinic that would be capable of awakening in its clients the joy of living, while also providing leisure facilities, amusements, shows and other forms of social togetherness.

The idea of a perfect place, in which they would exercise their professional activities and offer their clients the opportunity to transform, renew and improve their lives, became completely entangled with their love story and plans for the future. The dream began ten years before the doors opened for the first time more than 30 years ago in the beautiful mountainside town, Gramado, which is located at the heart of the Hydrangea Region in the interior of the State of Rio Grande do Sul, Brazil.

Neusa and Luis Carlos opened a clinic/hotel that they called the Kurotel. By associating the word *kur* (which in German means 'cure') to the city of Gramado with its clean mountain air and climate, and its European style, they began to give life to all that had taken over their thoughts for such a long time. From the outset, the Kurotel was firm in its policy of not offering a magic formula for problems related solely to physical shape, and it has grown with this policy. Concentrated on ensuring that at the Kurotel, methods and techniques of natural medicine were utilised in association with those of modern medicine, they proposed that each client who entrusted his or her own health to Kurotel should pause to consider how the choices that they make reflect on their consequent quality of life.

The Kurotel has never been considered merely as a spa. On the contrary, they positioned themselves in such a way that it was seen by the public as an integrated centre capable of treating the client in a whole manner and not just on account of his or her physical appearance. Within this philosophy, there are no limits imposed within the services provided. Rather, there are therapeutic indications so that clients can fully exercise their rights in relation to quality, privacy and personal wishes.

A new perspective on life

At the Kurotel Medical Center for Longevity and SPA each client receives individualised treatment that in turn allows him or her to:

- look inside himself/herself;
- reflect on his or her lifestyle;
- leave sedentary life aside;
- repair the damage from unhealthy habits;
- learn to control stress levels;
- prevent diseases;
- take up new healthy habits and attitudes towards lifestyle choices;
- relax;
- adopt healthy and balanced eating habits;
- harmonise body, mind and spirit.

Following the treatment and education received, our clients become great friends with their bodies, improve their health and find their equilibrium in life. It is important to understand that it is never too late to change and no change is for ever. Just like the clients, the interdisciplinary team of over 130 professionals and staff is in a constant process of keeping up-to-date. Our greatest objective is to keep on improving so that we do not just attend to clients, but surprise them with results.

Every client is unique

There is no doubt that the result of a service is a feeling, or an emotion. And the passion that has been dedicated to each client at the Kurotel is based not only on energy and inner strength, but especially on the result of much study and research, always focusing on the health and well-being of the human element. The philosophy implemented at the Kurotel has always had the aim of providing client follow-up 24 hours per day, with the purpose of

gaining greater knowledge of each person for monitoring and attending to him or her through an interdisciplinary team with duties in the fields of clinical health, healthy eating, healthy physical activity and emotional health.

Soon after arriving at the Kurotel complex, the person answers a very detailed question-naire with the purpose of giving information on his or her health problems and expectations. From this point, the person passes through analysis by an interdisciplinary team that will make a diagnosis. With this information, doctors and other professionals prescribe the different therapies within the *kur* method. The attention given to each client is completely individual-ised, with more than two employees to attend to each client. Every day, the client will find there is a programme made especially for him or her, which will be followed up by a duly prepared clinical team. The Kurotel's technical team is made up of doctors who act within general clinical medicine, nutritional science, geriatrics, homeopathy, cardiology, gynae-cology and gastroenterology, as well as physical educators, nutritionists, psychologists, physiotherapists, nurses, biochemists, pharmacists, beauticians and leisure professionals.

Each client is unique and has their own set of values and necessities. Many come to socialise, while others may wish to retreat completely from the attentions of other guests. With this in mind the Kurotel offers restricted access private elevators, exclusive therapy and massage rooms within the restricted access area, and separate dining room and butler service for those who desire total privacy during their stay.

Kur method

The method developed at the Kurotel is based on years of experience built up by its founders, and aims at treatment with concrete results. It is the foundation for everything.

From a therapeutic point of view, this method is based on homeopathy, bioresonance techniques, bioretroalimentation, scientifically proven phytotherapy, diet therapy, physio-therapy techniques, monitored physical activities and Kneipp Kur (an efficacious method for boosting the immune system, activating the circulation and respiration and bringing osteo-muscular benefits).

Healthy longevity

The Healthy Longevity Programme is designed for people who wish to control stress or weight, revitalise their energy, detoxify themselves or change their lifestyle. What's more, the programme is aimed at people who wish to prevent diseases through treatment evaluated by doctors who base their work on a detailed diagnosis of the patient's general physical state.

Advanced Diagnostic Centre

The Advanced Diagnostic Centre provides latest-generation apparatus for use. The results are evaluated by a committee made up of doctors from different specialties, which guarantees an analysis of quality and perfect referral for prevention or cure. The services of the Diagnostic Centre play an integral part in the analysis and consequent treatment of all clients.

The centre counts on latest technology to provide diagnostic evidence that in turn is used to evaluate and treat:

- the level of cellular corrosion in the organism;
- healthy nutrient and mineral levels in the blood stream;
- collagen reserves in the organism, which essentially is the padding for all bodily tissues;
- regulation of hormone levels;
- food and non-food allergies and showing how to treat them;
- dental problems may be producing interference currents in the mouth and thereby causing diseases;
- early diagnoses of tumours;
- lung capacity;
- condition of the heart;
- detection of alterations present in the organism with respect to temperature that indicate possible lesions and or illnesses and diseases.

It is important to highlight that the Kurotel makes use of a technique capable of evaluating some genes for certain illnesses, through analysis of the DNA. In this way, preventive and personalized medicine can be employed.

Kinder Kur: option for mother and baby

The Kinder Kur aims to strengthen the bond and relationship between mother and baby through the use of participative therapies, and at the same time provide controlled slimming and restoration of physical condition for the mother who recently had her baby. While mothers receive a personalised programme, they also participate in physiotherapeutic and feeding advice for their babies.

Through this type of attendance, specialised psychologists are also able to detect unexpressed depression in the mother and treat it appropriately, thereby avoiding future problems for the baby. The Kinder Kur premises have been especially designed to meet the needs of the family, with facilities for the nanny, laundry service, kitchen, playground, and so on.

Kur cuisine

The Kurotel cuisine has the prerequisite of healthy food, without relinquishing the flavour. Here, with the guidance of Kurotel nutrition specialists, the client chooses his/her own menu, and the nutritional properties are adapted according to the needs of each person,

who also receives classes in cooking, in which he or she learns about suitable foods and gets advice on what to do when the period of stay finishes, such as what to buy in the supermarket, what to eat in a restaurant and what to eat at home. The basis for the Kurotel meal programme is a technique developed in Switzerland that has been adapted for Brazilian standards. The ingredients used come from the organic vegetable garden that is cultivated within the grounds of the Kurotel. The nutrition service brings in at the same time not only a rational and well-balanced diet but also functional foods (aliments with medicinal properties), which is considered by scientists to be a great advance in this new era.

Medications and cosmetics

In the line of medications, products such as herbs for teas, ointments and capsules are offered based on clinical recommendation. Brazil has the greatest biodiversity in the world and this marvellous natural laboratory has been put to use the Kurotel for preparing phytotherapeutic medications for external and internal use. Kurotel has also developed a range of cosmetics and home use products are available.

The responsibility that goes with the realisation of the dream

Kurotel client loyalty is important, and this is fostered by making guests understand that they are more than just clients. Kurotel's greatest mission is to guide and contribute to each person's individual health objectives, especially in relation to long-term lifestyle choices and habits learned under the guidance of the professionals at Kurotel. The attention and affection they receive makes them always come back and recommend the Kurotel's work to friends, acquaintances and family. Being a reference point in the field of medicine, it is gratifying to see the continuing increase in the number of people who seek out the Kurotel because they are sent or referred by professionals of a diverse range of medical specialties.

This recognition has been portrayed in specialist publications in Europe, the United States of America and Latin America.

49

The Gawler Foundation in Australia
Wellness and lifestyle-based therapeutic retreats for people with serious illnesses

Cornelia Voigt

Introducing the Yarra Valley Living Centre

This case study is about the therapeutic lifestyle retreat Yarra Valley Living Centre, which is run by the Gawler Foundation established in 1983. Information for this case is derived from interviews with staff employed at the Yarra Valley Living Centre, a site visit and secondary data. The Yarra Valley Living Centre is located on a 15 hectares property, near Yarra Junction, a small settlement with 1740 residents in Victoria, Australia. The township is situated 55 km east of Melbourne's central business district. A broad range of residential lifestyle-based, self-help programmes are conducted at this Centre, primarily designed for people with cancer and their carers. In 1983, the Gawler Foundation was co-founded by Ian Gawler and his first wife Grace. In addition to five and ten-day retreats for people with cancer, Ian Gawler and George Jelinek developed a retreat programme for people with Multiple Sclerosis (MS) in 2002. While the Foundation's main aim is to support people with serious illnesses, it also offers a series of 'wellness' retreats for the 'worried well'; people who are interested in preventative-based lifestyle interventions and want to learn how to lead healthier lives. Additionally, The Gawler Foundation runs annual conferences on integrative health and well-being and is involved in training health professionals.

The Gawler Foundation is a non-profit, registered charity which does not receive any government funding. The Foundation attempts to make the retreats as least costly as possible and bursaries are available for people with limited finances. As the organisation has limited funds, they do not actively advertise the retreats for people with serious illnesses; the demand is solely generated by word of mouth. Cancer and MS retreat participants come from all over Australia, some even from overseas, predominantly from New Zealand. A very small amount of advertising is employed to promote the wellness retreats. Guests who participate in the wellness programs are more likely to be middle-aged women who travel by themselves. The Yarra Valley Living Centre is able to accommodate 40 guests at the same time, in double or twin rooms with private en suites or dormitories with shared bathroom facilities. Since its establishment, more than 10,000 people have participated in one of the retreats offered at the Yarra Valley Living Centre.

The lifestyle-based 'Gawler approach'

At the age of 24, the veterinary Ian Gawler was diagnosed with bone cancer in 1974 which resulted in the amputation of his right leg. Over the next 18 months he was told that the cancer had recurred and the doctors gave him only a few weeks to live. In addition to some radiotherapy and three cycles of palliative chemotherapy, Ian embarked on a self-help regime by adhering to the Gerson diet, later followed by a vegan diet and intense three hour daily meditations. This lifestyle approach together with his strong conviction 'of maintaining hope in the face of apparent hopelessness' (Jelinek and Gawler, 2008: 664), as well as the dedicated and loving care of his first wife, may have influenced Ian's recovery from cancer. Based on this healing experience the Gawlers decided to share what they have learned and founded the Melbourne Cancer Support Group in 1981, developing their first lifestyle-based self-help programme for people with cancer. Since then, based on the feedback of many patients and their families and worldwide research studies, the program has been developed further.

The Gawler Foundation advocates a self-help approach, encouraging and empowering individuals to actively work towards their healing and establish a healthy lifestyle. A typical retreat day consists of a comprehensive schedule focusing on different lifestyle aspects in the form of a variety of sessions, meditation periods and meal times. In the sessions, direct participation is encouraged and there is plenty of room for discussions and questions. Key cornerstones of the Gawler lifestyle approach are meditation and diet. Retreat participants are led through guided sessions to experience mindfulness meditation which takes place in a purpose-built hexagonal meditation sanctuary. The aim is to become 'mindful', to become aware of the here and now and thereby developing the core of effective stress management. The Foundation promotes an organic, no-salt, no-sugar, low-fat and preservative-free vegan diet and participants are educated about nutrition and food preparation. The meals are cooked in a hospital-graded kitchen free of plastic and chemicals. In between meals, retreat participants also receive fresh vegetable juices. Workshops on emotional health and the power of the mind are another key ingredient of the 'Gawler approach'. People learn about the potentially harmful effects of emotions like anger and anxiety on well-being. Faced with the diagnosis of a serious illness, individuals are often confronted with feelings of helplessness and hopelessness. As part of the retreat program they hear about positive thinking, how to use the power of the mind and thereby become empowered to take a more active role in their health. Educational workshops are also given around the topics of pain management and death and dying, that is coming to terms with the real possibility of dying and learn how to die 'well'. Furthermore, gentle exercise, fresh air and sensible exposure to the sunlight in the form of yoga, Qi Gong and

walking is offered and encouraged. Finally, additional services in the form of private coun-selling and a range of body therapies (massage, shiatsu and reflexology) can be utilised by retreat participants. With the exception of the sessions on pain management and dying, the content of the wellness retreat programmes for the 'worried well' is similar to the other retreats, as a good, healthy lifestyle is equally relevant for sick and healthy individuals.

A final aspect of the 'Gawler approach' concerns the importance of a supportive phys-ical and social environment. The staff at the Yarra Valley Living Centre is convinced that the place itself has healing properties that contribute to people's well-being. Concurrently, in blogs and letters available on the Internet, former retreat patients have commented frequently on the beautiful nature that surrounds the Centre which would make them feel more peaceful and relaxed. The Centre is surrounded by a vast area of Australian native bush which hosts an abundance of wildlife. A meditation path leads through the bush, following the Yarra River that runs through the property. Along this path, a labyrinth and a pergola invite quiet meditation. Closer to the buildings are ornamental and biodynamic vegetable gardens which provide the kitchen with organic fresh produce. Former partici-pants have also repeatedly emphasised the friendliness and nurturing care of the staff employed at the Centre and the benefit of meeting others who suffer from similar condi-tions with whom they can share their experiences, fears and doubts. With over 50 staff members, the Centre has quite a high staff-guest ratio. The interviews with the staff made clear that they personally live the lifestyle principles endorsed by the Gawler Foundation.

Controversy surrounding the 'Gawler approach': quackery or paradigm wars?

In Western countries there are two philosophically divergent views of health, the 'wellness paradigm' and the 'illness paradigm'. In the wellness paradigm, health is seen as a posi-tive state, the presence of well-being, not the absence of illness. Consequently, even people who are terminally or chronically ill are able to thrive and be well despite their diag-nosis. While the illness paradigm addresses disease by uncovering and alleviating illness symptoms – mainly by drugs or surgery – the focus on the wellness paradigm is more on proactive self-healing and health promotion. Thus, references to self-responsibility, ongoing lifestyle changes and interdependence of body/mind/spirit dimensions are key ingredients in wellness definitions. Clearly, the 'Gawler approach' can be attributed to the holistic wellness based philosophy of health. In contrast, conventional Western oncology is still mainly grounded in the illness paradigm. While there have been attempts to blend conventional medicine with wellness-based approaches and follow an 'integrative medicine' approach, there are still heated debates and turf wars going on, with propo-nents on both sides highlighting short-comings and questioning effectiveness of the other.

Recent controversies emerging in the Australian media which concerned the 'Gawler approach' and Ian Gawler as a person, can be at least partially ascribed to conflicting philosophical values and paradigmic turf wars. Two Australian oncologists recently published a paper in which they hypothesised that Ian Gawler's secondary cancer that he supposedly cured with the help of 'non-traditional treatments' was in fact advanced tuberculosis (Haines and Lowenthal, 2012). As one motive for publishing this theory, they stated they would see it as their duty to warn other cancer sufferers not to be misled into believing they too could be cured by these treatments. As Gawler is often referred to as 'Australian's most famous cancer survivor', this hypothesis made explosive front-page news in the *Sydney Morning Herald* (Johnston and Medew, 2011) and was followed up by several other Australian news media. In the *Sydney Morning Herald* article one of the authors of the paper was interviewed, saying that he was

> 'distressed' at seeing terminal cancer patients who had chosen alternative therapies over conventional medicine after diagnosis. 'I've seen beautiful young girls with their whole lives ahead of them and they go into these holistic therapies and spend hundreds of thousands of dollars and then in the end we have to look at them. They all eventually go to us.'

More strongly than their academic paper, this quotation reveals the conviction that the 'Gawler approach' is perceived by some orthodox health professionals as 'alternative' with little benefits, or even as outright quackery. Without being equipped with the necessary medical background knowledge to comment on Haines and Lowenthal's medical diagnosis, the following statements are listed to argue that some aspects of their view may be oversimplified: (1) The Gawler Foundation does not aim to discourage people to undertake mainstream medical interventions; they openly promote an integrated approach that includes conventional therapies. Additionally, Ian Gawler has acknowledged that a combination of orthodox treatments and lifestyle interventions may have led to his cancer recovery. (2) The Gawler Foundation does not claim to offer a cure for people with cancer or other serious illnesses. Their aim is to educate, not to treat people, and they are committed to supporting them improve their quality of life. (3) People participating in the Yarra Valley Living Centre retreats do not spend 'hundreds of thousands of dollars'. Moreover, no dubious potions, herbs or crystals are being sold at those retreats, but behavioural lifestyle changes are promoted that are non-patentable and can be followed at home with little costs involved. (4) Haines's observation that 'they all eventually get to us' is biased as it is possible that those people whose conditions improved through holistic therapies did not return to their oncologists. (5) There is the general question to what extent the 'Gawler approach' can be called 'alternative'. Lifestyle interventions, particularly in form of nutrition and exercise and more recently even meditation have become prominent in several frontier branches of health sciences such as behavioural medicine, positive psychology and mind/body medicine. There is also a small body of scientific evidence mounting that lifestyle modification enhances quality of life and may even extend survival rates for people with cancer and MS. Even without this evidence, the question would be to what extent lifestyle interventions could actually be harmful. (6) There are a number of conventional medical professionals who see merit in the 'Gawler approach'. They are comfortable referring their patients to the Foundation or are even involved in research to gather further evidence that lifestyle-based interventions are effective. It is questionable that such support would exist if the 'Gawler approach' were nothing more than a snake-oil sales pitch. (7) Finally, it is too easy to dismiss all valid positive

experiences of former retreat participants as 'anecdotal'. The news articles evoked strong emotional responses in the form of letters to the editors and Ian Gawler's blog where people reported they had survived against the odds because of the strategies they had learned at the Foundation's retreats. There were also many who acknowledged that their disease was not cured, but that they still had experienced a profound life transformation which included greatly enhanced feelings of well-being and happiness, slowed illness progression, and a strong sense of empowerment.

This case study exemplifies the blurry nature and erosion of boundaries between wellness and medical tourism providers as well as the overarching constant shifts between acceptance, dismissal and careful approach between conventional and complementary medicine. The term 'therapeutic medical tourism' has been coined to refer to facilities where a mix of conventional medical diagnosis and treatment is offered alongside water-based or other holistic therapies for people recovering from an illness, accident or surgery. However, this case study is an example of a provider which could be categorised as 'therapeutic wellness tourism' as there is a sole focus on lifestyle-based and holistic intervention without combining it with conventional biomedical therapies at the site, mainly catering to people who are chronically or even terminally ill.

Challenges of balneotherapy development in Oyoun Moussa, Egypt

Islam Elgammal and Heba Elakras

Balneotherapy has been considered one of the effective ways of curing ailments, particularly, skin and bones diseases. It is well known among Bedouin people in Egypt that Oyoun Moussa area (springs of Moses) has a number of characteristics which are useful in curing some disease (e.g. skin and bones). However, this area is not appropriately developed and promoted to attract tourists from different parts of the world. This study aims at exploring the area of Oyoun Moussa and looking at the chances of the area being suitable for balneotherapy. Analysis of the wells' water in the area has been done by researchers in the Chemistry department, Science School in Suez Canal University, to look at the special elements of the water. Additionally, three field visits were conducted to record personal observation about the main obstacles of tourism development in the area. An informal interview with visitors to the area was necessary to investigate reasons behind their visits to this undeveloped area with zero facilities. Results revealed that visitors to Oyoun Moussa are mainly Jewish who know about the area from their religious background and the water analysis showed that Oyoun Moussa has a strong potential of being a balneotherapy destination. The study recommends raising a local and international awareness of the importance of the area and putting the planning and developing of the area as the top priorities of the Egyptian tourism industry.

Background

Balneotherapy is a type of environmental therapy which focuses on the medical uses of special quality water through bathing or immersing completely of an individual in the special quality high temperature water (Foley, 2003; Miller et al., 2010). Balneotherapy comes under the umbrella of hydrotherapy, which include all kind of baths: thermal and cold baths, mineral and hydrobaths and whirlpools, baths at different temperature.

TABLE 50.1 Benefits and effects of balneotherapy/hydrotherapy (includes exercising in water)

Benefits of balneology	Effects
Improves the circulation system by	Altering hearing to develop a stronger heart Increasing circulation Increasing oxygen supply to cells Increasing the nutrients supply to cells Removing of metabolic wastes Decreasing swelling of limbs (May decrease high blood pressure)
Improves the digestive system by	Relaxing the abdominal and intestinal muscles Releasing anxiety (which affects digestion) Stimulating the activity of the liver Removing waste materials
Improves the metabolic system by	Altering the metabolic rate Reducing obesity when combined with proper diet and exercise
Improves the renal system by	Increasing kidney function Stimulating the elimination of water and waste products
Improves the muscular system by	Relaxing muscles Stimulating and strengthening muscles Relieving pain tension and stiffness
Improves the nervous system by	Stimulating sensory nerves Relieving restlessness and stress and insomnia
Improves the lymphatic system by	Stimulating lymphatic drainage in all areas of the body
Improves the immune system by	Stimulating T-Cells lymphocytes and other white cells Acting as if the body had been challenged by an infective agent, such as a bacterium or virus
Improves the skin by	Stimulating the cutaneous circulation to improve tones, elasticity, colour and texture Improving the nutrition of skin cells Encouraging absorption of the trace elements into skin cells
Improves the skeletal system by	Increasing the flexibility of joints Removing excess fluid from joint Exercising to realign correct posture Encouraging better balance reaction
Psychological change	Relax the mind as well as the body Induces a sense of well-being and euphoria Mental and physical fatigue is diminished and energy is promoted

Source: Adapted from Harrington et al., 2005.

However, balneotherapy can also include curing by mud, peat and algae wrap (Harrington et al., 2005). Bathing in special quality warm water has many advantages, as Table 50.1 shows. Additionally, there is a crucial advantage which is avoiding using other medicines which may have side effects; in addition, it has an ability of curing some of the complicated sicknesses that are hard to cure by chemical medicines, such as rheumatology for victims of accidents and rheumatism (Bhowmik and Routh, 1996; Sushant, 2011).

Balneotherapy is considered a legend in the medicinal therapy world (Sushant, 2011) as the high concentration of some mineral salt (i.e. Magnesium-Mg, Calcium-Ca, Sulphur-S, Chloride-Cl) are helping to cure a number of diseases that relate to dermatology (i.e. the branch of medicine that is concerned with the physiology and pathology of the skin) such as, skin diseases, plus joint inflammation and rheumatism. Additionally, these mineral salts are activating system circulation, protecting and renewing the skin cells and reducing pains related to the Loco Motor System (Schempp et al., 2000). Feedback from individuals who tried balneotherapy is positive and always focused on their pleasant experience of using this kind of safe and effective treatment. One of the diseases which are cured rapidly by using balneotherapy is psoriasis. Additionally, it is a great way for an effective pain relief accompanied by all type of arthritis (bacterial arthritis, osteoarthritis, or rheumatoid arthritis) (Sushant, 2011).

Egypt possesses 1256 springs (Omran, 2010) some of them have some curing characteristics and are suitable for all kinds of therapeutic tourism. This study focuses on the area of Oyoun Moussa (springs of Moses) in Egypt, a unique place mentioned in the religious books (i.e. Quraan and Bible and Torah) where Moses is said to have rested after leading the Israelites across the Red Sea and there spring waters started to stream after a miracle happened in which he was instructed by God to throw his branch into it. The site is located approximately 40 km (25 miles) south of Ahmed Hamdi tunnel in Suez. Although the water of the springs is undrinkable, indigenous people along with some visitors believe it has curable characteristics (White, 2011).

Methodology

The study was carried out through conducting three field visits to the area of Oyoun Moussa. In the first visit, a sample of one the spring's water was collected for a water test in the Chemical Department in Suez Canal University in order to look at the water characteristics and determine curable elements. In the other two visits, an informal interview with a total of 39 visitors was necessary to find out their background and awareness of the curable characteristics of the water. In each visit, there were approximately 14 visitors and most of them were Jewish patients who believe that the spring water has curable elements to diseases such as Psoriasis. The aim of the informal interviews was to look at the challenges of the area from the tourists' perspective. Additionally, personnel observation was carried out through the three field visits to record the area's main problems.

Results and discussion

The sample analysis of Oyoun Moussa water collected during the first field visit was showing a number of elements that have great benefits in relation to treating diseases which make Oyoun Moussa area a potential tourist destination for balneotherapy. The results of the water analysis were compared to the Dead Sea water analysis in order to look at the therapeutic properties of Oyoun Moussa water in relation to the main destination of balneotherapy (i.e. Dead Sea) as shown in Table 50.2.

Table 50.2 shows the high concentration of some elements in Oyoun Moussa water compared to the Dead Sea water, such as Sulphur which exists in Oyoun Moussa by 487.355-Mg/L while it's concentration in the Dead Sea water reaches only 2-Mg/L. However, Magnesium (Mg) concentration in the Dead Sea water (45.900-Mg/L) is noticed to be higher than its concentration in Oyoun Moussa (20.460 Mg/L). Oyoun Moussa water analysis was shown to a team of doctors in the Department of Skin diseases, Medical School, Suez Canal University, to look at potential benefits of the water in curing. The team agreed that the high concentration of Sulphur in the water is helpful in treating some skin disease, such as psoriases, oily skin and a number of transferable (infectious) skin disease. Additionally, they indicated that sulphur has a great impact in reducing the oily face spots which commonly appear during the youth phase, particularly among young people in the Middle East.

Magnesium (Mg) is also considered a crucial water component which has a number of benefits in curing skin diseases (i.e. Psoriases) and Tumours (Schempp et al., 2000). Professionals are able to suggest a program for patients with such diseases which may contain only bathing in the water for a number of times determined according to each individual case and the severity of the disease. Unfortunately, Oyoun Moussa area is

TABLE 50.2 A comparison between the components of Oyoun Moussa water and Dead Sea water		
Elements	Dead Sea Mg/L	Oyoun Mousa Mg/L
Chloride (CL) and Bromide (br)	230.400	1065
Tetra sulphur oxide (So_4)	2.000	487.355
Sodium Chloride (Nacl)	36.600	1755
Calcium (ca)	17.600	172.580
Magnesium (Mg)	45.900	20.460
Potassium (k)	7800	–
Iron (Fe)	–	1.520
Sodium (Na)	–	60.293
Cadium (Cd)	–	0.001
PH=8.42 Alkaline		
Sources: Ma'or et al., 2006; Science Faculty, Chemistry department, 2008.		

lacking a Spa or a centre for such purpose. In addition, components such as Chloride (CL), Calcium (ca) are found to be in higher concentration in Oyoun Moussa water, while other components such as Sodium Chloride (Nacl) and Iron are contributing to the richness of the water of Oyoun Moussa.

According to the observation recorded during the field visits, there are 12 springs in the area of Oyoun Moussa, only seven can be seen and the rest are not discovered yet. Out of these seven, only four are known among Bedouins in the area, these four are: Elshiekh (3m deep, 3.5m diameter), Elsaqia (4m deep, 5m diameter), Alshayb (4m deep, 4m diameter), Elzahr (1m deep, 1m diameter). The only spring which is functioning well, is not commonly known by neither tourists nor Egyptians. The spring which is in use is very deep and the temperature of the water is higher than the daily temperature in the area. There are only a few tourists visiting the area and most of them are Jewish; some of them indicated in the questionnaire that they take some of the spring water with them to sick relatives back home. Although the area is famous for its therapeutic properties; none of the previous proposed tourism projects was successfully planned and developed.

Although the area of Oyoun Moussa has a number of properties which is necessary in a therapeutic tourism spa, the area is not developed yet for some reasons. First, the area is suffering from poor facilities (i.e. infrastructure, roads restaurants, shops and supermarkets) and, consequently, it attracted only a few Jewish tourists who visit the area for therapeutic and religious reasons. Second, there is only two resorts close to the area; Alameer and Mousses Oasis villages, these resorts are not specialized spas for therapeutic tourism. Third, the area generally has no recreational facilities, such as, clubs, cinemas, theatres, and so on which affects the stay of the current visitors. Fourth, only limited information about the area is available in the Egyptian governmental records which make it difficult for investors to develop a rich picture of potential tourism spas project. Fifth, lack of trained tour guides and proper road signs made it difficult for visitors to find it.

According to the informal interviews with visitors during the fieldtrips to Oyoun Mousssa, it was clear that the area urgently needs health services/spa with special medical doctors who can provide curing programmes for different diseases. Visitors also indicated that the area needs cafeterias, restaurants and bazaars. It seems that the lack of infrastructure in the area made it difficult for investors to start any projects. Additionally, visitors indicated that the shortage of road signs makes it difficult to find it. Visitors indicated that Bedouins and the local community have limited awareness of the therapeutic importance of Oyoun Moussa.

Recommendations

After looking at the challenges of the area of Oyoun Moussa as a spa and a potential Balneotherapy destination in Egypt, it can be concluded that the area is in need of different stakeholders involvements in order to overcome the area's problems related to tourism development. The study recommends a starting point that includes an invitation from the Egyptian government to investors and stakeholders to visit the area and look at its potential in relation to therapeutic tourism. Additionally, the Egyptian government may consider encouraging tourism development in this area using different strategies (i.e. reducing taxes or facilitating planning permission procedures and developing infrastructures). Raising awareness of the importance of the area is also recommended, especially among local communities and surrounding cities.

References

ABA (2011) www.aba.gv.at/EN/Sectors/WellnessTourism/Health+Tourism.aspx (accessed 4 March 2011).

Abdullah, A. (2012) 'Medical Tourism. The Fastest Growing Industry. A focus on the UAE', EMTC2012, Berlin, 25 April 2012.

Acciaiuoli, L. (1942) *Águas de Portugal: relatório referente à exploração das nascentes de águas minerais e de mesa durante o ano de 1940*. Lisboa: Direcção Geral de Minas e Serviços Geológicos.

Acciaiuoli, L. (1947) *Hidrologia Portuguesa: 1943–1946*. Lisboa: Direcção Geral de Minas e Serviços Geológicos.

Acciaiuoli, L. (1954) *Águas de Portugal Minerais e de Mesa*, Vol. 4. Lisboa: Ministério da Economia – Direcção Geral de Minas e Serviços Geológicos.

Accor Thalassa (2008) www.accorthalassa.com/gb/sejour/bienfaits-eau.shtml (accessed 2 April 2008).

Ács, P. and Laczkó, T. (2008) 'Területi különbségek a hazai egészségturizmus kínálatában', *Területi Statisztika* 11(3), Budapest: Központi Statisztikai Hivatal.

Aggarwal, A. K., Guglani, M. and Goel, R. K. (2008) 'Spiritual and Yoga Tourism: A case study on experience of foreign tourists visiting Rishikesh India', Conference on Tourism in India – Challenges Ahead, IIMK, 15–17 May, http://dspace.iimk.ac.in/bitstream/2259/588/1/457-464.pdf (accessed 3 March 2013).

Aho, S. (2007) 'Spa Rehabilitation of War Veterans: A Finnish speciality of war compensation', ATLAS Spa and Wellness Special Interest Group Meeting, Budapest, 25–28 June.

AICEB (2010) *Il mercato del benessere: imprese e servizi offerti*. Rimini, 14 maggio.

Alexander, J. (2001) *The Holistic Therapy File*. London: Carlton Books.

Al-Hammouri, F. (2010) *Medical Tourism: The fastest growing industry overview with a focus on the Jordanian experience*, http://mitt.ru/downloads/materials/2010/medical/4_Al-Hammori_JordanPHA.pdf (accessed 27 February 2011).

Ali-Knight, J. (2009) 'Yoga Tourism', in R. Bushell and P.J. Sheldon (eds) *Wellness and Tourism: Mind, body, spirit, place*. New York: Cognizant Communication, pp. 84–98.

Alpine Wellness (2008) www.alpinewellness.com (accessed 10 March 2008).

Alpine Wellness (2013) www.alpinewellness.net (accessed 15 March 2013).

Alpoim, M. (2010) *Análise à Procura Termal*. Universidade de Aveiro – Departamento de Economia, Gestão e Engenharia (Master's Thesis).

Alternatives for Healing (2013) *Wellness and Spiritual Retreats*, www.alternativesforhealing.com/cgi_bin/wellness-spiritual-retreats.php (accessed 3 March 2013).

Alymkulov, D.A., Simonenko, T.S. and Alymkulov, R.D. (2005) *Physiotherapy and Balneology*. Bishkek.

AME (2012) *Moorfields Eye Hospital Dubai, Now Health International sign medical services provider agreement*, AME Info, 3 October 2011, www.ameinfo.com/272363.html (accessed 5 December 2012).

American Holistic Health Association (AHHA) (2007) www.heall.com/body/altmed/definitions/holistic.html (accessed 3 October 2007).

American Medical Tourism Association (2009) www.medicaltourismassociation.com/en/index.html (accessed 15 March 2009).

American Spa Magazine (2008) www.americanspamag.com/americanspa/article/articleDetail.jsp?id=30389 (accessed 12 March 2008).

Ananda Retreats (2013) http://ananda.it/en (accessed 22 February 2013).

Anonymous (2011) *1 in 5 Americans Use Social Media for Health Care Information*, http://hcmg.nationalresearch.com/public/News.aspx?ID=9 (accessed 29 October 2012).

Apollo Hospitals (2012) www.apollohospitals.com/about_company.php (accessed 18 March 2013).

Arizona SpaGirls (2008) www.arizonaspagirls.com (accessed 12 March 2008).

Asiatraveltrips (2010) www.asiatraveltips.com/news10/1811-StarwoodSpas.shtml.

Azara, I., Hughes, S., Hunter, G. and Stockdale, I. (2007) 'Profiling Day Spa Visitors and Motivations to Experience Wellness "at Home"', ATLAS Spa and Wellness Special Interest Group Meeting, Budapest, 25–28 June.

Babulka, P. and Kósa, G. (2003) *Képes gyógynövénykalauz*. Budapest: Herbária.

Bacon, W. (1998) 'Economic Systems and Their Impact on Tourist Resort Development: The case of the Spa in Europe', *Tourism Economics*, 4(1), pp. 21–32.

Bagatti, B. (2001) *Ancient Christian Villages of Galilee*. Jerusalem: Franciscan Printing Press.

Baker, D.A. and Palmer, R.J. (2006) 'Examining the Effects of Perceptions of Community and Recreation Participation on Quality of Life', *Social Indicators Research*. February, 75(3), pp. 395–418.

Balch, O. (2006) 'Buenos Aires or Bust', *Guardian Unlimited*, 24 October, www.guardian.com/business/2006/oct/24/argentina.travelnews (accessed 24 November 2007).

Barnes, K. (2013) www.europeanspamagazine.com/experts2.html (accessed 15 March 2013).

Barr, D. (2005) 'Spa: A splash of gay glamour. Homo away from home', *The Times*, 31 December.

Bartura, M. (2012) *Global Spa and Wellness Industry Briefing Papers 2012*. New York: Global Spa and Wellness Summit, Bayern Wellvital (2013) www.bayern.by/wellnessurlaub-in-bayern.

BBC News Online (2006) 'Half of Nation Do No Exercise', 8 December, http://news.bbc.co.uk/2/hi/health/6220358.stm (accessed 26 October 2007).

Becheri, E. and Quirino, N. (2011) *Il benessere termale in Italia*, in E. Becheri and G. Maggiore (eds) *Rapporto sul turismo italiano 2010–2012*. Milano: Franco Angeli, pp. 427–43.

Becheri, E. and Quirino, N. (2012) *Rapporto sul sistema termale in Italia*. Milano: Franco Angeli.

Belanger, C.E. and Jolin, L. (2011) 'Case study: The International Organisation of Social Tourism (ISTO) working towards a right to holidays and tourism for all', *Current Issues in Tourism*, 14(5), pp. 475–82.

Bell, D., Holliday, R., Jones, M., Probyn, E. and Sanchez Taylor, J. (2011) 'Bikinis and Bandages: An itinerary for cosmetic surgery tourism', *Tourist Studies*, 11(2), pp. 137–53.

Better Sleep Council (2011) www.bettersleep.org (accessed 27 February 2011).

Bhowmik, K.R. and Routh, I.B. (1996) 'Basic Tenets of Mineral Water: A glossary of concepts relating to balneaology, mineral water and the spa', *Clinc Dermatol*, 4(6), pp. 549–50.

Biging, A. (2012) *Global Spa and Wellness Industry Briefing Papers 2012*. New York: Global Spa and Wellness Summit, pp. 39–40.

Bjurstam, A. (2012) *Global Spa and Wellness Industry Briefing Papers 2012*. New York: Global Spa and Wellness Summit.

Black, S. (2011) 'Holistic Retreats: Holidays for an Inner Journey', www.positivehealth.com/article/retreats-and-travel/holistic-retreats-holidays-for-an-inner-journey (accessed 3 March 2013).

Bliss (2013) www.blissworld.com/spa/spa-menu/men (accessed 16 March 2013).

Blue Lagoon (2013) *Environmental Focus*, www.bluelagoon.com/about-us/environmental-focus (accessed 4 March 2013).

BMWA (2002) 'Bestandsaufhahme der Entwicklungspotenziale im Gesundheitsturismus', Modul 1. Wien: BMWA.

BMWA (2002) *Health Tourism and Overseas Treatment in England: Analysis of trends and systems*, www.bmwa.gv.at (accessed 7 February 2008).

BMWI (2012) *Innovativer Gesundheitstourismus in Deutschland Branchenreport 'Kurorte und Heilbäder'*, BMWI (www.bmwi.de/BMWi/Redaktion/PDF/Publikationen/innovativer-gesund-heitstourismus-in-deutschland-kurorte-und-heilbaeder,property=pdf,bereich=bmwi2012,sprache=de,rwb=true.pdf (accessed 16 January 2013).

Bodeker, G. and Burford, G. (2008) 'Traditional Knowledge and Spas', in M. Cohen and G. Bodeker (eds) *Understanding the Global Spa Industry: Spa management*. Oxford: Butterworth Heinemann, pp. 414–31.

Boekstein, M. (2001) *The Role of Health in the Motivation to Visit Mineral Spa Resorts in the Western Cape*. Unpublished Master's dissertation. Cape Town: University of the Western Cape.

Bogacheva, E. (2012) *Global Spa and Wellness Industry Briefing Papers 2012*. New York: Global Spa and Wellness Summit, pp. 21–2.

Bolatkale, E. (2012) *Healthcare Tourism Destination Research*, Presentation at 2012 Medical Tourism Research Conference (San Antonio, Texas), 13 February 2012.

Booyens, B. (1981) *Bronwaters van Genesing: Die Tradisionele Warmbronwaterkultuur in Ons Volksgeneeskunde*. Cape Town: Tafelberg.

Boreham, N. (2004) 'Orienting The Work-based Curriculum Towards Work Process Knowledge: A rationale and a German case study', *Studies in Continuing Education*, 26(2), pp. 209–27.

Bortman, B.A. (2010) 'Medical Tourism Private Hospitals: Focus India', *Journal of Health Care Finance*, 37(1): 45–50.

Boucher, D. (2011) 'Have Insurance Coverage, Will Travel! The U.S. Patient', EMTC2011, Barcelona, 28 April.

Bournemouth Borough Council (2011) Bournemouth, Poole and Dorset Local Transport Plan (2011–20), Bournemouth Borough Council, Bournemouth www.dorsetforyou.com/media.jsp?mediaid=163132andfiletype=pdf (accessed 24 January 2013).

Bramham, A. (2012) *Global Spa and Wellness Industry Briefing Papers 2012*. New York: Global Spa and Wellness Summit.

Brepohl, M.N. (2012) *Global Spa and Wellness Industry Briefing Papers 2012*. New York: Global Spa and Wellness Summit, pp. 59–60.

Breuleux, P. (2013) *Medical Wellness. Professional Directory. Resource Guide. Medical Wellness Association*, http://medicalwellnessassociation.com/docs/Medical-Wellness-Professional-Directory-and-Partner-Guide.pdf (accessed 6 January, 2013).

Brown, M. (1998) *The Spiritual Tourist*. London: Bloomsbury.

Brown, P. and Hesketh, A.J. (2004) *The Mismanagement of Talent: Employability and jobs in the knowledge economy*. Oxford: Oxford University Press.

Burachovi , S. and Wieser, S. (2001) *Encyclopedia of Spas and Mineral Springs in Bohemia, Moravia, and Silesia* (in Czech). First edition, Prague.

Bushell, R. and Sheldon, P.J. (2009) *Wellness and Tourism: Mind, body, spirit, place*. New York: Cognizant.

Business Traveller (2009) New Lounge and Spa Open at Helsinki Airport, www.businesstraveller.com/news/new-lounge-and-spa-open-at-helsinki-airport (accessed 22 March 2013).

Calvert, R.N. (2002) *Pages from History: Swedish massage* www.massagemag.com/magazine/2002/issue100/history100.php (accessed 30 October 2012).

Canadian Therapeutic Recreation Association (2007) www.canadian-tr.org (accessed 24 November 2007).

Caribbean Spa and Wellness Association (2013) http://caribbeanspawellness.com/about-us (accessed 26 February 2013).

Carrasco, D. (1996) *Those Who Go on a Sacred Journey: The shapes and diversity of pilgrimages*. London: SCM Press Ltd.

Carroll, J.E. (2004) *Sustainability and Spirituality*. Albany, NY: Sunny Press.

Carter, P. (2002) *Repressed Spaces: The poetics of agoraphobia*. London: Reaktion Books.

CBS (2011) www.cbs.gov.il (accessed 24 March 2013).

Centraal Bureau voor de Statistiek (2008) *Meer Nederlanders naar alternatieve genezer*, www.cbs.nl/nl-NL/menu/themas/gezondheid-welzijn/publicaties/artikelen/archief/2008/2008-90130-wk.htm (accessed 29 October 2012).

Chaturongkul, T. (2012) *Global Spa and Wellness Industry Briefing Papers 2012*. New York: Global Spa and Wellness Summit, pp. 27–8.

Chaudhari, R. (2012) *Global Spa and Wellness Industry Briefing Papers 2012*. New York: Global Spa and Wellness Summit, pp. 5–6.

Chiladakis, A. (2010) *Feeling Restless and Dissatisfied? Holistic Retreats Are Your Answer*, http://ezinearticles.com/?Feeling-Restless-and-Dissatisfied?-Holistic-Retreats-Are-Your-Answerandid=5339023 (accessed 4 January 2013).

Chimenti, S. (2005) *Psoriasis*. Firenze: SEE Editrice.

Chinai, R. and Goswami, R. (2007) 'Medical Visas Mark Growth of Indian Medical Tourism', *Bulletin World Health Organisation*, 85(3), pp. 164–5.

Chipalkatti, S. (2012) *Global Spa and Wellness Industry Briefing Papers 2012*. New York: Global Spa and Wellness Summit.

Chopra, D. (1993) *Ageless Body, Timeless Mind: The Quantum Alternative to Growing Old*. New York: Crown Publishing.

CII and McKinsey (2002) *Healthcare in India: The road ahead. New Delhi*. Confederation of Indian Industries and McKinsey and Company.

Ciszewski, F. (1988) 'Polskie lecznictwo uzdrowiskowe w XIX wieku z uwzglednieniem uzdrowiskowego leczenia chorób reumatycznych. [Treatments in the Polish health resorts in the 19th century, focusing on rheumatologic illnesses]', in: *Rozwój lecznictwa uzdrowiskowego w Polsce [Development of the health tourism in Poland.] Problemy Uzdrowiskowe [Aspects of Health Resorts]*, No. 11–12, pp. 253–4.

Clinebell, H. (1996) *Ecotherapy: Healing Ourselves, Healing the Earth*. London: Routledge.

Club One Seven (2013) www.oneseven.com.sg (accessed 15 March 2013).

Coelho, P. (2011) *Aleph*. London: HarperCollins.

Cohen, E. (2008) 'Medical Tourism in Thailand', in E. Cohen (ed.) *Explorations in Thai tourism*. Bingley: Emerald, pp. 225–55.

Cohen, M. (2008) 'Spas, Wellness and Human Evolution', in M. Cohen and G. Bodeker (eds) *Understanding the Global Spa Industry: Spa management*. Oxford: Butterworth Heinemann, pp. 3–25.

Cohen, M. and Bodeker, G. (2008) (eds) *Understanding the Global Spa Industry: Spa Management*. Oxford: Butterworth Heinemann.

Connell, J. (2011) *Medical Tourism*. Wallingford: CABI.

Connell, J. (2012) 'Contemporary Medical Tourism: Conceptualisation, culture and commodification', *Tourism Management*, 34, pp. 1–13.

Connor, S. (2003) 'Can Buddhists Transcend Mental Reservations?' 22 May, www.biopsychiatry.com/happiness/buddhist.html (accessed 26 November 2006).

Conradson, D. (2005) 'Landscape, Care and the Relational Self: Therapeutic encounters in rural England', *Health and Place*, 11, pp. 337–48.

Cook, P.S., Kendall, G., Michael, M. and Brown, N. (2013) 'Medical Tourism, Xenotourism and Client Expectations: Between Bioscience and Responsibilisation', in C.M. Hall (ed.) *Medical Tourism: The ethics, regulation, and marketing of health mobility*. London: Routledge, pp. 61–74.

Cortijo Romero (2013) www.cortijo-romero.co.uk (accessed 3 March 2013).

Coutinho, N. (2012) 'Big Treats for Little Ones', *Spa Mantra*, July–August, 2(2), pp. 92–4.

Coyle Hospitality Group (2011) *Global Spa Report*, www.discoverspas.com/news/newsstudies41.shtml (accessed 2 March 2013).

Crebbin-Bailey, J., Harcup, J. and Harrington, J. (2005) *The Spa Book*. London: Thomson.

Crebert, G., Bates, M., Bell, B., Patrick, C.J. and Cragnolini, V. (2004) 'Ivory Tower to Concrete Jungle Revisited', *Journal of Education and Work*, 17(1), pp. 47–70.

Crossette, B. (1998) *The Great Hill Stations of Asia*. New York: Westview Press.

Csikszentmihalyi, M. (1990) *Flow: The psychology of optimal experience*. New York: Harper & Row.

CTG Heathcare (2008) www.ctghealthcare.co.uk/?title=health_spa__turkish_bathandmenuid=21279 (accessed 24 March 2008).

D'Angelo, J. (2005) *Spa Business Strategies: A plan for success*. New York: Delmar.

Dalai Lama (1999) *The Art of Happiness: A handbook for living*. London: Hodder.

Danubius Hotels (2008) www.danubiushotels.com/press_room/danubius_hotels_group_general_press_information/danubius_hotels_group_general_press_information?sid=k5tm1302ierihb8h53q9fm8t24and__utma=1.1538222170.1364243765.1364243765.1364243765.1and__utmb=1.1.10.1364243765and__utmc=1and__utmx=-and__utmz=1.1364243765.1.1.utmcsr=google utmccn=(organic) utmcmd=organic utmctr=danubius%20hotels%20dhsr%20brandand__utmv=-and__utmk=142635317 (accessed 16 March 2008).

Dávid, L., Jancsik, A. and Rátz, T. (2007) *Turisztikai er források (Tourism Resources)*, Budapest, p. 287.

Davie, G. (1994) *Religion in Britain since 1945: Believing without Belonging.* Oxford: Blackwell.

Dead Sea Research Center (DSRC) (2013) www.deadsea-health.org/new_html/about_us.html (accessed 27 January 2013).

de Botton, A. (2002) *The Art of Travel*. London: Penguin.

de Gabriac (2010) 'The Evolving Roles of Spas in the Medical, Wellness and Healing Arts Arenas', BISA 2010 Conference, Budapest, 5 June.

De Groote, P. (2008) 'Spa, "the Mother" Spa Resort of Europe', in M. Jansen Verbecke and A. Diekmann (eds) *The Future of Historic Spa Towns: Spa Symposium Workbook*. Belgium: Castermans, pp. 25–34.

Deloitte (2012a) *2012 Survey of U.S. Health Care Consumers*, www.deloitte.com/view/en_US/us/Industries/US-federal-government/center-for-health-solutions/acd450915276c310Vgn-VCM2000003356f70aRCRD.htm (accessed 2 March 2013).

Demetriou, D. (2008) 'Rise of the Spas: Japan is Onsen Country, but Spas are Taking Over', *Japan Times*, 16 December (accessed 22 February 2013).

Destination Spa Group (2005) *Survey on Destination Spa-goers and Vacationers* (A Study by M.H. Tabacchi, Cornell University), www.destinationspagroup.com/cornell.htm (accessed 4 February 2013).

Destination Spa Group (2013) www.destinationspagroup.com (accessed 24 March 2013).

Deutscher Wellness Verband (2008) 'Medical Wellness', www.wellnessverband.de/medical/index.php (accessed 27 March 2008).

Devereux, C. and Carnegie, E. (2006) 'Pilgrimage: Journeying Beyond Self', *Journal of Tourism Recreation Research*, 31(1), pp. 47–56.

Dickinson, J. and Lumsdon, L. (2010) *Slow Travel and Tourism*. London: Routledge.

Dickinson, J. and Lumsdon, L. (2011) 'Slow Travel: European cycle tourism', in B. Garrod and A. Fyall (eds) *Contemporary Cases in Tourism*. Oxford: Goodfellow Publishers Limited, pp. 121–38.

Diener, E., Suh, E.M., Lucas, R.E. and Smith, H.L. (1999) 'Subjective Well-being: Three decades of progress', *Psychological Bulletin*, 125(2), pp. 276–302.

Dingemans, N. (2012) *From Farm to Fork in Twente*, The Hague: Royal Library of the Netherlands.

Discover Medical Tourism (2011) *Medical Tourism Statistics: Brazil*, www.discovermedicaltourism.com/statistics/ (accessed 16 March 2011).

Dixon, R. (2012) 'Top 10 Weird Spa Treatments', *Guardian*, 3 February, www.guardian.co.uk/travel/2012/feb/03/best-weird-spa-treatments (accessed 3 March 2013).

Domburg (2011) *Bad Domburg: Zeeuwse wellness en vitaliteit met internationale allure. Uitvoeringsprogramma badstatus*. Domburg. Middelburg: Economische Impuls Zeeland. www.veere.nl/document.php?m=1&fileid=49161&f=e55d90213120d1199d46aac09e399c5d&attachment=0&c=48233 (accessed 7 July 2013).

Donnolly, L. (2012) 'Facebook and Twitter Feed Anxiety, Study Finds', The Telegraph, July www.telegraph.co.uk/technology/9383609/Facebook-and-Twitter-feed-anxiety-study-finds.html (accessed 17 February 2013).

Dowthwaite, K. (2012) *The Future Modernisation of Spa Education and Training, Bridging the International Management Gap; Response to GSWS Recommendations*. University of Derby, UK.

Dryglas, D. (2005) *Kształtowanie produktu turystycznego uzdrowisk w Polsce. [Shaping the tourism product in health resorts in Poland]*. Kraków: Uniwersytet Jagielloński.

Dubai Healthcare City (2013) www.dhcc.ae (accessed 5 March 2013).

Dun and Bradstreet (2012) *Dunsguide, Israel Business Guide*. Israel, www.dbisrael.co.il/english (accessed 12 December 2013).

Eating Disorders Coalition (2013) *Eating Disorders Coalition Wins Big for Eating Disorders Research!* 18 June, www.eatingdisorderscoalition.org (accessed 17 February 2013).

Economist, The (2004) Medical Tourism to India, 7 October, www.economist.com/node/3276422, (accessed 24 November 2012).

Economist, The (2011) 'A Game of Catch-up', 24 September, www.economist.com/node/21528979 (accessed 15 July 2013).

Edensor, T. (2001) 'Performing Tourism, Staging Tourism: (Re)producing tourist space and practice', *Tourist Studies*, 1(1), pp. 59–81.

Egger, A. (2012) *Global Spa and Wellness Industry Briefing Papers 2012*. New York: Global Spa and Wellness Summit.

EIU (2011) *Travelling for Health, The Potential for Medical Tourism*. London: Economic Intelligence Unit.

Ellis, S. (2008) 'Trends in the Global Spa Industry', in M. Cohen and G. Bodeker (eds) *Understanding the Global Spa Industry: Spa management*. Oxford: Butterworth Heinemann, pp. 66–84.

EMHRSO (2013) *The Role of Contractual Arrangements in Improving Health Sector Performance*, http://gis.emro.who.int/HealthSystemObservatory/PDF/Contracting/Introduction.pdf (accessed 14 March, 2013).

Erfurt-Cooper, P. and Cooper, M. (2009) *Health and Wellness Tourism: Spas and hot springs*. Clevedon: Channel View.

ESPA (2007) European Spa Association, http://espa-ehv.com (accessed 30 March 2008).

ESPA (2013) European Spa Association, www.espa-ehv.eu/association (accessed 18 February 2013).

Estonian Spas (2011) *Tallinn: Estonian Spa Association*. Estonian Spas.

Euromonitor (2011a) *Global Hotels: Reshaping Hotel Experiences*. London: Euromonitor International.

Euromonitor (2011b) *Global Medical Tourism Briefing: A Fast Growing Niche Market*. London: Euromonitor International.

Euromonitor International (2012) *Understanding the Global Consumer for Health and Wellness*, Global Wellness and Spa Summit, Aspen, 4 June, www.globalspaandwellnesssummit.org/index.php/archive/summit-2012/presentations-2012 (accessed 14 February 2013).

European Union (2011) *Directive of the European Parliament and of the Council on the application of patients' rights in cross-border healthcare*, 2008/0142 (COD), http://register.consilium.europa.eu/pdf/en/11/pe00/pe00006.en11.pdf (accessed 12 January 2013).

Faroldi, E., Cipullo, F. and Vettori, M.P. (2007) *Terme e architettura. Progetti, tecnologie, strategie per una moderna cultura termale*. Bologna: Maggioli.

Fayers, P.M. and Machin, D. (2007) *Quality of Life: The assessment, analysis and interpretation of patient-reported outcomes*. Chichester: John Wiley & Sons.

Ferrari, S. (2009) 'The Luigine Thermal Baths: A tool for the deseasonalization of the tourist demand in Calabria (Italy)', in M.K., Smith and L. Puczkó (eds) *Health and Wellness Tourism*, Oxford: Butterworth Heinemann, pp. 307–12.

FICCI (2008) *Fostering Quality Healthcare for All*, New Delhi: Federation of Indian Chamber of Commerce and Ernst & Young.

Filep, S. (2012) 'Positive Psychology and Tourism', in M. Uysal, R. Perdue and J. Sirgy (eds) *The Handbook of Tourism and Quality-of-Life: The Missing Links*. Dordrecht: Springer, pp. 31–50.

Filep, S. and Deery, M. (2010) 'Towards a Picture of Tourists' Happiness', *Tourism Analysis*, 15(4), pp. 399–410.

Findhorn (2013) www.findhorn.org (accessed 22 February 2013).

Findhorn Ecovillage (2013) www.ecovillagefindhorn.com (accessed 22 February 2013).

Finnair (2013) *Finnair Lounge and Spa*, http://media.finnair.com/spa/site (accessed 22 March 2013).

Fleuret, S. and Atkinson, S. (2007) 'Wellbeing, Health and Geography: A critical review and research agenda', *New Zealand Geographer*, 63, pp. 106–18.

Foley, J. (2003) *Great Spa Escapes: The definitive guide to the best spas in the world, and what they have to offer*. London: Dakini Books Ltd.

Fosarelli, P. (2002) 'Fearfully Wonderfully Made: The interconnectedness of body–mind–spirit', *Journal of Religion and Health*, 41(3), pp. 207–29.

Fox, J.T. (2012) *South Pacific Travel on the Rise*, 21 August, Travel Agent Central, http://www.travelagentcentral.com/south-pacific/south-pacific-travel-rise (accessed 25 February 2013).

Freitag, J.D. (2012) 'Data, Dollars and Decisions (presented at the Global Wellness and Spa Summit', 5 June, Aspen, USA, www.globalspaandwellnesssummit.org/index.php/archive/summit-2012/presentations-2012 (accessed 4 January 2013).

FTB (2005) *Hyvinvointi- ja wellness -matkailun peruskartoitus*. MEK A:144. Matkailun edistämiskeskus, Helsinki. www.mek.fi/w5/mekfi/index.nsf/6dbe7db571ccef1cc225678b004e73ed/d86764d4e91dde64c225735b0032a957/$FILE/A144%20Hyvinvointimatkailu_peruskartoitus.pdf (accessed 15 March 2013).

FTB (2009) 'Development Strategy for Finnish Wellbeing Tourism in International Markets 2009–2013'. Finnish Tourist Board. Strategy working group. Helsinki, www.mek.fi/relis/REL_LIB.NSF/%28pages%29/AB7BF278BFC033C0C225751D003149FC?opendocument&ind=w5/mekfi/index.nsf&np=F-50 (accessed 7 July 2013).

Fullagar, S., Markwell, K.W. and Wilson, E. (2012) *Slow Tourism Experiences and Mobilities*. Clevedon: Channel View.

Future Foundation (2007) www.futurefoundation.org (accessed 10 January 2008).

Fyall, A. (2011) 'Destination Management: Challenges and opportunities', in Y. Wang and A. Pizam (eds) *Destination Marketing and Management: Theories and applications*. Oxford: CAB International, pp. 340–57.

Gabriac de, J.G. (2012) *Global Spa and Wellness Industry Briefing Papers 2012*. New York: Global Spa and Wellness Summit, pp. 37–8.

Gasul, D. (2006) 'Community Attitudes towards Sustainable Tourism: The case of the Dead Sea Region', conference proceedings: *International Conference of Trends, Impacts and Policies on Tourism Development*, Heraklion, Crete, GREECE, 15–18 June.

Gasul, D. and Mansfeld, Y. (2004) *Application and Planning of Sustainable Tourism Development Principles in the Dead Sea Region, Israel*. Center for Tourism, Pilgrimage and Recreation Center, University of Haifa, March 2004 (Hebrew).

Gasul, D., Paz, S. and Mansfeld, Y. (2005) 'Curriculum on Environmentalism and Sustainable Tourism in the Dead Sea Region', in Y. Bar-Gal and M. Inbar (eds) *From Region to Environment. Forty Years of Geographical Studies at the University of Haifa*, Department of Geography and Environmental Studies, University of Haifa, Israel, pp. 495–504 (Hebrew).

Gayot (2013) 'Top Ten Health Resorts', www.foxnews.com/travel/2013/01/30/top-10-health-resorts-worldwide, 30 January (accessed 6 March 2013).

Georgeson, A. (2011) 'Innovations in Architecture and Design for Spa', 1st Brazilian Spa Conference, Sao Paolo, 28 August.

Gerritsma, R. (2008) 'The Growing Yoga Community in the Netherlands How Yoga is becoming a Lifestyle Product including Tourism Activities', in M.K. Smith and L. Puczkó (eds) *Health and Wellness Tourism*, Oxford: Butterworth Heinemann, pp. 361–5.

Gesler, W. (1992) 'Therapeutic Landscapes: Medical issues in light of the new cultural geography', *Social Sci. Med.*, 34(7), pp. 735–46.

Gesler, W. (1993) 'Therapeutic Landscapes: Theory and a case study of Epidauros, Greece', *Environment and Planning D: Society and Space*, 11, pp. 171–89.

Geva, I. (2012) EMTC2012, Berlin, 25 April.

GFK (2010) 'Roper lifestyles, another way of looking at your customer', GfK http://news.gfk.be/archives/october-2010/articles/roper-lifestyles-another-way-looking-at-customer (accessed 15 June 2012).

GFK (2012) *Egyre romlik a lakosság saját egészségi állapotának megítélése*, www.gfk.hu/imperia/md/content/gfk_hungaria/pdf/press_2012/press_hun/press_2012_01_11.pdf (accessed 15 June 2012).

Ghafouri, M. (2006) *Recognizing the Spa and Springs in Iran* (unpublished report).

Gibson, A. (2012) *Global Spa and Wellness Industry Briefing Papers 2012*. New York: Global Spa and Wellness Summit.

Giddens, A. (1991) *Modernity and Self-Identity: Self and Society in the Late Modern Age*. Cambridge: Polity.

Gifts of Health (2011) *Zalal: Qatar's Destination Spa*. Qatar: Gifts of Health.

Gilbert, D. (2007) *Stumbling on Happiness*. London: HarperPerennial.

Gilbert, D. and Abdullah, J. (2004) 'Holidaytaking and the Sense of Wellbeing', *Annals of Tourism Research*, 31(1), pp. 103–21.

Gisolf, M.C. (2010) 'Authenticity in Tourism', www.tourismtheories.org/?cat=104 (accessed 7 July 2013).

Glauben, I.P. (1955) 'On the Meaning of Agoraphilia', *Journal of the American Psychoanalytical Association*, 3, pp. 701–10.

Glinos, I. (2012) 'Worrying about the Wrong Thing: Patient Mobility Versus Mobility of Health Care Professionals', *Journal of Health Services Research and Policy*, 17(4), pp. 254–6.

GlobalChoice Healthcare (2008) www.globalchoicehealthcare.com (accessed 17 February 2008).

Global Spa and Wellness Summit (2012a) *Spa Management Workforce and Education: Addressing Market Gaps*. New York: GSWS.

Global Spa and Wellness Summit/GSWS (2012b) *Global Spa and Wellness Industry Briefing Papers 2012*. New York: GSWS.

Global Spa Summit/GSS (2008) *The Global Spa Economy 2007*, www.globalspaandwellness summit.org/images/stories/pdf/gss.spa.economy.report.2008.pdf (accessed 9 December 2011).

Global Spa Summit/GSS (2010) *Spas and the Global Wellness Market: Synergies and Opportunities*, May, New York: Global Spa Summit.

Global Spa Summit/GSS (2011) *Wellness Tourism and Medical Tourism: Where Do Spas Fit?* New York: Global Spa Summit.

Glouberman, D. (2002) *The Joy of Burnout*. London: Hodder & Stoughton.

Glouberman, D. (2004) *Skyros Soul*, www.skyros.com/skyros_soul.html (accessed 20 February 2004).

Glover, L. (2012) *Global Spa and Wellness Industry Briefing Papers 2012*. New York: Global Spa and Wellness Summit.

Goldsmith, M. (2008) 'Spa Trends 2008: the evolved spa' www.healinglifestyles.com/index. php?page=jan2008-insight-spatrends20082 (accessed 12 February 2008).

Goodrich, J.N (1987) 'Health Care Tourism – an Explanatory Study', *Tourism Management*, 8(3), pp. 217–22.

Götz, A. (2008) 'Inkább vízimajmok voltunk', *Index*, http://index.hu/tudomany/tortenelem/vizimaj6108 (accessed 2 April 2008).

Government of India (GOI) (2003) *Health Sector in India*, Government of India (GOI), 2003 Budget Papers, New Delhi.

Government of India (GOI) (2008) *Eleventh Five Year plan 2007–12*, Volume 11: Social Sector, New Delhi Planning Commission, Government of India (GOI), New Delhi: Oxford University Press.

Graburn, N.H. (2002) 'The Ethnographic Tourist', in G.M.S. Dann (ed.) *The Tourist as a Metaphor of the Social World*. Wallingford: CABI, pp. 19–40.

Grainger, L. (2007) 'Sun, sea and . . . psychotherapy', *Telegraph Online*, 8 July, www.telegraph. co.uk/fashion/main.jhtml?view=DETAILSandgrid=andxml=/fashion/2007/07/08/sttherapy08. xml (accessed 2 October 2007).

Gray, J. (2002) *Men Are from Mars, Women Are from Venus: How to Get What You Want in Your Relationships*. London: HarperCollins.

Green, B. and Aldred, L. (2002) '"Money is just spiritual energy": Incorporating the new age', *Journal of Popular Culture*, 35(4).

Green Spa Network (2013) www.greenspanetwork.org/ (accessed 16 February 2013).

Gregori, G.L. and Cardinale, S. (2009) 'Quali "luoghi" per il nuovo consumatore di benessere', *Crescita Turismo*, novembre–dicembre.

Griffin, N. (2012) *Global Spa and Wellness Industry Briefing Papers 2012*. New York: Global Spa and Wellness Summit.

Grove, S.J. and Fisk, R.P. (1997) 'The Impact of Other Customers on Service Experiences: A critical incident examination of "getting along", *Journal of Retailing*, 73(1), 63–85.

Guardian Unlimited (2005) 'Fat to Fit: How Finland did it', 15 January, www.guardian.co.uk/befit/story/0,15652,1385645,00.html (accessed 17 November 2007).

Gustavo, N. (2006) *Representações Sociais dos Aquistas das Termas de São Pedro do Sul*. Dissertação de Mestrado em Lazer e Desenvolvimento Local. Coimbra: Universidade de Coimbra.

Gustavo, N. (2009) 'Sao Pedro do Sul Thermal Centre: Between health and wellness tourism', in M.K. Smith and L. Puczkó (eds) *Health and Wellness Tourism*. Oxford: Butterworth Heinemann, pp. 319–24.

Gustavo, N. (2011) *Novos Espaços de Lazer, Turismo e Saúde em Portugal – o caso dos SPA*. Doutoramento em Turismo (PhD thesis), Lazer e Cultura. Coimbra: Universidade de Coimbra.

Hadzik, A., Gammon, S. and Ujma, D. (2010) 'Polish Spas – in Need of a Polish? Eastern and Western European perspectives on spa and health tourism', TTRA 2010 European Chapter Conference Health, Wellness and Tourism – healthy tourists, healthy business?, 1–3 September, Budapest, Hungary.

Haidt, J. (2006) *The Happiness Hypothesis*. London: Arrow Books.

Haines, I.E. and Lowenthal, R.M. (2012) 'Hypothesis. The importance of a histological diagnosis when diagnosing and treating advanced cancer. Famous patient recovery may not have been from metastatic disease', *Internal Medicine Journal*, 43(2), 212–16.

Hall, C. M. (2013) *Medical Tourism: The ethics, regulation, and marketing of health mobility*. London: Routledge.

Hall, C.M., Müeller, D.K. and Saarinen, J. (2009) *Nordic Tourism: Issues and cases*. Bristol: Channel View Publications.

Hamat Gader official site (2013) www.hamat-gader.com/eng (accessed 10 February 2013).

Harrington, J., Harcup, J. and Crebbin-Bailey, J. (2005) *The Spa book: The official guide to spa therapy*. London: Thomson.

Harrison, E. (2006) 'Divine trash: The psychology of celebrity obsession', *Cosmos*, February, www.cosmosmagazine.com/node/414) (accessed 3 October 2007).

Hartman Group (2007) *Wellness Lifestyle Insights 2007: Emerging trends to shape the future marketplace*. Bellevue, WA: Hartman Group.

Hartwell, H. (2011) 'Can We Bring Tourism and Public Health Strategy Together?', *Guardian Professional*, 28 July.

Hartwell, H., Hemingway, A., Fyall, A., Filimonau, V. and Wall, S. (in press) 'Tourism Engaging with the Public Health Agenda – Can We Promote "Wellville" as a Destination Of Choice?', *Public Health*.

Harvard Health Publications (2009) *The Health Benefits of Tai Chi*, May, www.health.harvard.edu/newsletters/Harvard_Womens_Health_Watch/2009/May/The-health-benefits-of-tai-chi (accessed 21 April 2013).

Harvey, D. (1989) *The Condition of Postmodernity*. Spanish translation: La Condición de la Posmodernidad. Buenos Aires: Amorrortu Editores 1998.

Haw, P. (2011) 'The Longer You Work, the More Productive You Are? Not So, Say Experts'. 20 November, http://pennyhaw.wordpress.com/2011/11/20/the-longer-you-work-the-more-productive-you-are-not-so-say-experts (accessed 15 February 2013).

Hay, L. and Richardson, C. (2011) *You Can Create an Exceptional Life*. Carlsbad: Hayhouse.

Hazel, N. (2005) 'Holidays for Children and Families in Need: An exploration of the research and policy context for social tourism in the UK', *Children & Society*, 19(3), pp. 225–36.

Healing Hotels of the World (2013) www.healinghotelsoftheworld.com/press/press-kit (accessed 23 March 2013).

Heelas, P. (1996) *The New Age Movement: The celebration of the self and the sacralization of modernity*. Oxford: Blackwell.

Heelas, P. and Woodhead, L. (2005) *The Spiritual Revolution*. Oxford: Blackwell.

Hemingway, A. (2012) 'Can Humanisation Theory Contribute to the Philosophical Debate In Public Health?', *Public Health*, 126, pp. 448–53.

Henderson, J.C. (2004) 'Healthcare Tourism in Southeast Asia', *Tourism Review International*, 7(3–4), pp. 111–22.

Hentinen, L. (2002) *Wellness-käsite matkailussa*, www.mek.fi/w5/mekfi/index.nsf/6dbe7db571 ccef1cc225678b004e73ed/b2a27bef4ed2679ac225735a0040aa4d/$FILE/Wellnes-esitys% 20syyskuu2002.pdf (accessed 26 February 2013).

Hilton Branding (2012) *SpaBusiness/digital* 4, http://lei.sr?a=Y1U3k (accessed 23 March 2013).

Hilton Hotels and Resorts (2012) *Hilton Blue Paper. Emerging Global Spa Trends* http://hiltonglobalmediacenter.com/index.cfm/newsroom/category/topic/40 (accessed 26 February, 2012).

Hiranyikara Spa (2013) www.hiranyikara.com (accessed 15 March 2013).

Hirschfeld, Y. (1994) *Hamat Gader and its Baths*. Jerusalem: Israel Antiquities Authority Publications (Hebrew).

Hirschfeld Y. (1997) *The Roman Bath of Hamat Gader: Final Report*. Jerusalem: The Israel Exploration Society.

Hjalager, A.-M., Konu, H., Huijbens, E., Björk, P., Flagestad, A. and Nordin, S. (2011) *Innovating and Re-branding Nordic Wellbeing Tourism*. Nordic Innovation Center, www.nordicinnovation. org/Global/_Publications/Reports/2011/2011_NordicWellbeingTourism_report.pdf (accessed 28 November 2012).

Hofstede, G. (1984) *Culture's Consequences: International differences in work-related values*. London: SAGE Publications.

Hole in the Wall Camps (2008) www.holeinthewallcamps.org (accessed 10 March 2008).

Holloway, J.C. (2004) *Marketing for Tourism*. Harlow: Prentice Hall.

Honoré, C. (2005) *In praise of Slow: How a worldwide movement is challenging the cult of speed*. London: Orion Books.

Hood, A. (2013) 'Lithuanian Largesse', *Spa Business*, 1, pp. 68–72.

Houel, L. (2012) 'evianSpa', *SpaBusiness*, 4, pp. 30–5.

Hougaard, J. (2012) *Global Spa and Wellness Industry Briefing Papers 2012*. New York: Global Spa and Wellness Summit, pp. 9–10.

House of Male (2013) www.houseofmale.com (accessed 17 March 2013).

Huijbens, E. (2011) 'Developing Wellness in Iceland – Theming wellness destinations the Nordic Way', *Scandinavian Journal of Hospitality and Tourism*, 11(1), pp. 20–41.

Humphreys, C. (2007) *Escaping the Rat Race*, ABC News.com, 30 June, www.geocities.com/ RainForest/6783/DalyNewsSimplicity980630øp.html (accessed 24 October 2007).

Hutchinson, L. (2012) *Global Spa and Wellness Industry Briefing Papers 2012*. New York: Global Spa and Wellness Summit, pp. 85–6.

Huyssens, A. (1990) 'Mapping the Postmodern', in J.C. Alexander, J.C. and S. Seidman (eds) *Culture and Contemporary Society Debates*. Cambridge: Cambridge University Press.

Icelandic Tourist Board (2012) *Tourism in Iceland in Figures* (Reykjavík: Icelandic Tourist Board).

Iida, H. (2012) *Global Spa and Wellness Industry Briefing Papers 2012*. New York: Global Spa and Wellness Summit.

IMT (2009) www.imtgt.org (accessed 15 May 2009).

IMTJ (2013) 'Latvia Attracts International Cancer Patients and Develops Health Tourism', *IMTJ*, 18 February, www.imtj.com/news/?entryid82=410192 (accessed 4 March 2013).

Indiatravelite (2007) www.indiatravelite.com/feature/oshocom1.htm (accessed 2 November 2007).

Island Experience (2013) www.theislandexperience.com (accessed 26 February 2013).

Islas Canarias Wellness Delight (2013) www.turismodecanarias.com/canary-islands-spain/products-holiday-travel/wellness-delight/what-is/index.html (accessed 28 February 2013).

ISPA (2003) *The International SPA Association's 2003 Spa-goer Study: Japan*. Lexington: ISPA.

ISPA (2004) *Consumer Trends Report: Variations and trends on the consumer spa experience*. Lexington: ISPA.

ISPA (2006a): *ISPA 2006 Spa-goer Study: U.S. and Canadian consumer attitudes and spa use*. Lexington: ISPA.

ISPA (2006b) *Consumer Report: Spa-goer and non-spa-goer perspectives*. Lexington: ISPA.

ISPA (2007) *2007 ISPA Global Consumer Report*, www.experienceispa.com/ISPA/Media+Room/Press+Releases/ISPAs+13th+Annual+Media+Event.htm (accessed 5 November 2007).

ISPA (2008) 'Key Spa Industry Trends', www.experienceispa.com/ISPA/Media+Room/2008+Trends+Release.htm (accessed 12 February 2008).

ISPA (2010) *U.S. Spa Industry Study*. Lexington: ISPA/PriceWaterhouseCoopers.

ISPA (2011) www.spalietuva.lt/wp-content/uploads/2011/04/ISPA-US-Spa-Industry-Study-2011-FINAL-260911-online.pdf (accessed 2 March 2013).

ISPA (2013a) *Types of Spas*, www.experienceispa.com/spa-goers/spa-101/types-of-spas (accessed 22 February 2013).

ISPA (2013b) *Ten Things You Can Do To Live Well*, www.experienceispa.com/spa-goers/why-spa/ten-things (accessed 16 February 2013).

ISPA (2013c) *Why Spa?* www.experienceispa.com/spa-goers/why-spa (accessed 2 March 2013).

ISTAT (Italian National Statistical Institute) (2008) *The Wellness Sector in Italy*. ISTAT.

ISTO (International Social Tourism Organization) (2011) *Origins of Social Tourism*, www.bits-int.org/en/index.php?menu=1 (accessed 15 February 2013).

IWH (2013) *Primary, Secondary and Tertiary Prevention*, Institute for Work and Health, Canada, www.iwh.on.ca/wrmb/primary-secondary-and-tertiary-prevention (accessed 27 January 2013).

Iyengar, B.K.S. (1989) *Light on Yoga*. London: Unwin Hyman.

Jackson, S.A. and Marsh, H.W. (1996) 'Development and Validation of Scale to Measure Optimal Experience: The flow stats scale', *Journal of Sport and Exercise Psychology*, 18, pp. 17–35.

Jandova, D. (2009) *Balneology* (in Czech). Prague: Grada Publishing.

Jansen-Verbecke, M. and Diekmann, A. (2008) *The Future of Historic Spa Towns: Spa symposium workbook*. Belgium: Castermans.

JCI (2010) *Joint Commission International Accreditation Standards for Hospitals* – 4th Edition, www.jointcommissioninternational.org/ (accessed 3 March 2010).

Jelinek, G.A. and Gawler, R.H. (2008) 'Thirty-Year Follow-up at Pneumonectomy of a 58-year Old Survivor of Disseminated Osteosarcoma', *Medical Journal of Australia*, 189(11–12), pp. 663–5.

Jennings, E. T. (2007) *Curing the Colonizers: Hydrotherapy, Climatology, and French Colonial Spas*. Durham, NC: Duke University Press.

Jóhannesson, G.Þ. and Huijbens, E. (2010) 'Tourism in Times of Crisis: Exploring the discourse of tourism development in Iceland', *Current Issues in Tourism*, 13(5), pp. 419–34.

Jóhannesson, G.Þ., Huijbens, E. and Sharpley, R. (2010) 'Icelandic Tourism: Opportunities and threats', *Tourism Geographies*, 12(2), pp. 278–301.

Johnston, C. and Medew J. (2011) 'Cancer Experts Challenge Gawler's 'Cure' [Electronic Version], *Sydney Morning Herald*, 31 December, www.smh.com.au/national/cancer-experts-challenge-gawlers-cure-20111230-1pfns.html (accessed 8 August 2013).

Johnston, C. and Pernecky, T. (2006) 'Voyage through Numinous Space: Applying the Specialization Concept to New Age Tourism', *Journal of Tourism Recreation Research*, 31(1), pp. 37–46.

Johnstone, C. (2012) 'Czechs Launch Surgical Strike to Boost Medical Tourism', CzechPosition.com, May 11, www.ceskapozice.cz/en/news/society/czechs-launch-surgical-strike-boost-medical-tourism (accessed 29 October 2012).

Jordan, M. (2012) *Global Spa and Wellness Industry Briefing Papers 2012*. New York: Global Spa and Wellness Summit.

Jordan, P. (1999) (ed.) *Atlas of Eastern and Southeastern Europe – International Tourism Attractions 1998*. Vienna: Österreichisches Ost- und Südeuropa Institut.

Jotikasthira, N. (2010) *Salient Factors Influencing Medical Tourism Destination Choice*, DBA thesis, Southern Cross University, Lismore, NSW.

JTB (2012) www.visitjordan.com (accessed 12 February 2013).

Kalish, I. (2012) 'China, Soft Landing Now, Uncertainty Later', *Deloitte Global Economic Outlook*, 2nd Quarter, pp. 20–21, www.deloitte.com/assets/Dcom-Ecuador/Local%20Assets/Documents/General%202012/Estudios/GEO_Q2_2012.pdf (accessed 5 March 2013).

Kamalaya Wellness Sanctuary and Holistic Spa Resort (2013) www.kamalaya.com/index.htm (accessed 12 March 2013).

Kandampully, J. (2013) *Service Management in Health and Wellness Services*. Dubuque: Kendall Hunt Publishers.

Kangas, B. (2010) 'Traveling for Medical Care in a Global World', *Medical Anthropology*, 29, pp. 344–62.

Kangas, H. and Tuohino, A. (2008) Lake Wellness – Uusi itäsuomalainen innovaatio? *Matkailututkimus*, 4(1), pp. 23–41.

Kaplan, R. and Kaplan, S. (1989) *The Experience of Natur: A psychological perspective*. Cambridge: Cambridge University Press.

Kaplan, S. (1995) 'The Restorative Benefits of Nature: Towards an integrative framework', *Journal of Environmental Psychology*, 15, pp. 169–82.

Kapur, J.C. (2012) *Global Spa and Wellness Industry Briefing Papers 2012*. New York: Global Spa and Wellness Summit, pp. 11–12.

Kask, T. (2007) *Pärnu from fortress town to health resort town*. Estonia: Pärnu Town Government.

Kazakov, D. (2012) Kyrgyzstan tourism up 11 percent in 2012, http://english.sina.com/culture/2013/0221/563677.html (accessed 21 February 2013).

Kearns, R. and Gesler, W. (eds) (1998) *Putting Health into Place*. Syracuse: Syracuse University Press.

Kelly, C. (2012) 'Wellness Tourism: Retreat Visitor Motivations and Experiences', *Tourism Recreation Research*, 37(3), pp. 205–13.

Kelly, C. and Smith, M.K. (2008) 'Holistic Tourism: Integrating Body, Mind and Spirit', in R. Bushell and P.J. Sheldon (eds) *Wellness and Tourism: Mind, Body, Spirit, Place*. New York: Cognizant Communication, pp. 69–83.

Kember, D. and Leung, D.Y.P (2005) 'The Influence of the Teaching and Learning Environment on the Development of Generic Capabilities Needed for a Knowledge Based Society', *Learning Environments Research*, 8, pp. 245–66.

Kenniscentrum Kusttoerisme (2012) *Unpublished figures of touristic accommodations in Domburg*.

Kent, L. (1949) 'The Thermal Waters of the Union of South Africa', *Transactions of the Geological Society of South Africa*, pp. 231–41.

Kent, L.E. (1952) *The Medicinal Springs of South Africa*. Pretoria: Publication and Travel Department, South African Railways.

Keyes, R. (1991) *Timelock: How Life Got So Hectic and What You Can Do About It*. London: HarperCollins.

KHBTCC (2012) www.hiltonkinghusseincentre.com (accessed 23 March 2013).

Kimes, E.S. and Singh, S. (2009) 'Spa Revenue Management', *Cornell Hospitality Quarterly*, 50, pp. 82–95.

Kinnunen, K. and Puhakka, S. (2005) *Kun ei ole varaa valita. Tuetulta lomalta toivoa arkeen. Solaris-Lomat Ry*. Helsinki: Cosmoprint.

Koh, S., Yoo, J.J.E. and Boger, C.A. (2010) 'Importance Performance Analysis with Benefit Segmentation of Spa Goers', *International Journal of Contemporary Hospitality Management*, 22(5), pp. 718–35.

Konesens (2010) 'U.S. Consumer Study', *3rd World Medical Tourism and Global Healthcare Congress*, Los Angeles, 22 September, www.medicaltourismcongress.com (accessed 4 January, 2012).

Konu, H., Tuohino, A. and Komppula, R. (2010) 'Lake-Wellness – A practical example of a New Service Development (NSV) concept in tourism industry', *Journal of Vacation Marketing*, 16(2), pp. 125–39.

Kotler, P., Bowen, J.T. and Makens, J.C. (2005) *Marketing for Hospitality and Tourism*. Pearson International.

Kowalczyk, A. (2001) *Geografia turyzmu*. Warszawa: PWN.

Kowalnski, R. (2001) *The Only Way Out is In*. Charlbury: JC Publishing.

Krasiński, Z. (1998) *Zmieniający się świat uzdrowisk*. Poznań: Akademia Ekonomiczna.

Křížek, V. (2002) *Pictures from the history of spas* (in Czech). Second edition, Prague: Libri.

KTM (2006) Suomen matkailustrategia vuoteen 2020 and Toimenpideohjelma vuosille 2007 – 2013. KTM Julkaisuja, Elinkeino-osasto. Helsinki, http://julkaisurekisteri.ktm.fi/ktm_jur/ktmjur. nsf/All/3D61DB118241A034C22571800022FEC4/$file/jul21elo_2006_netti.pdf (accessed 15 December 2012).

Kunhardt, H. (2011) 'Medical Cluster and Complex Germany', *3rd World Medical Tourism and Global Healthcare Congress*, Los Angeles, 22 September, www.medicaltourismcongress. com (accessed 13 December 2012).

Kuoni (2013) www.kuoni.co.uk/spa-holidays (accessed 17 March 2013).

Kurtz-Ahlers, J. (2012) *Global Spa and Wellness Industry Briefing Papers 2012*. New York: Global Spa and Wellness Summit, pp. 89–90.

Kuskov, A.S. and Lysikova, O.V. (2004) *Balneology and Wellness Tourism*. Phoenix: Rostov on Don.

Kustgids.nl (2012) www.kustgids.nl/scheveningen/index.html (accessed 30 October 2012).

Kustvakanties im Holland (2008) *Een onderzoek naar de concurrentiepositie van de Nederlandse kust op de Duitse markt, Nederlands Bureau voor toerisme and congressen*, www. kenniscentrumtoerisme.nl/l/library/download/473 (accessed 30 October 2012).

Kwakzalverij.nl (2012) www.kwakzalverij.nl/1011/Encyclopedie_Watertherapie (accessed 29 October 2012).

Lakatos, M. (2012) 'A gyógynövények turisztikai jelentősége Magyarországon', *XIII. Nemzetközi Tudományos Konferencia. Károly Róbert Főiskola Konferenciakiadványa*, Gyöngyös, pp. 456–67.

Lampers, H. (2012) *Global Spa and Wellness Industry Briefing Papers 2012*. New York: Global Spa and Wellness Summit, pp. 93–4.

Lanserhof (2013) www.lanserhof.com/english/lans-med-concept.html (accessed 15 March 2013).

Lanyi, A. (2011) 'Necessity of the eCare Cycle in Medical Tourism: Quality management and support of telemedicine', *EMTC2011*, Barcelona, 28 April.

Larrinaga, C. (2005) 'A Century of Tourism in Northern Spain: The development of high-quality provision between 1815 and 1914', in J.K. Walton (ed.) *Histories of Tourism: Representation, identity and conflict*. Clevedon: Channel View Publications, pp. 88–103.

Larsen, J. (2001) 'Tourism Mobilities and the Travel Glance: Experiences of being on the move', *Scandinavian Journal of Hospitality and Tourism*, 1(2), pp. 80–98.

Lean, G.L. (2012) 'Transformative Travel: A mobilities perspective', *Tourist Studies*, 12, pp. 151–71.

Le Cardane, G. (2011) 'Wellness Tourism, le dimensioni del mercato: una analisi multidimensional scaling', in *Atti del Convengo, Turisti per caso? . . . il turismo sul territorio: motivazioni e comportamento di spesa*, Catania, 17/06/i2011.

Lee, G. (2004) *Spa Style Europe*. London: Thames & Hudson.

Lehto, X., Brown, S., Chen, Y. and Morrison, A.M. (2006) 'Yoga Tourism as a Niche Within the Wellness Sector', *Journal of Tourism Recreation Research*, 31(1), pp. 25–36.

Levitte, D., Olshina, A. and Wachs, D. (1981) 'The Hot Springs of Hamat Gader: Their geology, geochemistry and geothermal regime', *Proceedings of the Annual Meeting about the Geology of the Golan Heights 15–18 March*. Israel Geological Society.

Lindstrom, B. and Ericsson, M. (2006) 'Contextualizing Salutogenesis and Antonovsky in Public Health Development', *Health Promotion International*, 21(3), pp. 238–44.

Little, B., Connor H., Lebeau, Y., Pierce, D., Sinclair, E., Thomas, L. and Yarrow, K. (2003) *Vocational Higher Education – does it meet employers' need?* London: Learning and Skills Development Agency.

Local Government Improvement and Development (2010) 'The Role of Local Government in Promoting Wellbeing', Healthy Communities Programme. National Mental Health Development Unit. www.idea.gov.uk/idk/aio/23693073 (accessed 10 October 2012).

Loh, M. (2008) 'The Spa Industry in Asia', in M. Cohen and G. Bodeker (eds) *Understanding the Global Spa Industry: Spa management*. Oxford: Butterworth Heinemann, pp. 41–52.

LOHAS (2013) www.lohas.com (accessed 15 February 2013).

Lomine, L. (2005) 'Tourism in Augustan Society (44 BC–AD 69)' in J.K. Walton (ed.) *Histories of Tourism: Representation, identity and conflict*. Clevedon: Channel View Publications, pp. 71–87.

Loszach, F. (2011) 'Improve your ROI with a Wellness Diagnostic', *Corporate Wellness Magazine*, 10 November, www.corporatewellnessmagazine.com/article/imporve -your-roi-with-a-wellness-diagnostic (accessed 15 February 2013).

Louv, R. (2005) *The Last Child in the Woods*, Chapel Hill, NC: Algonquin Books.

Lowman, T. (2013) 'Generation Spa', *European Spa*, December/January, 31, p. 98.

Luft, L. (2003) *Losses and Gains: Reflections on a Life*. Reading: Vermilion.

Lunt, N., Green, S.T., Mannion, R. and Horsfall, D. (2013) 'Quality, Safety and Risk in Medical Tourism', in C.M. Hall (ed.) *Medical Tourism: The ethics, regulation, and marketing of health mobility*. London: Routledge, pp. 31–46.

Lunt, N., Smith, R., Exworthy, M., Green, S.T., Horsfall, D. and Mannion, R. (2012) *Medical Tourism: Treatments, markets and health system implications: A scoping review*, Paris: OECD.

Lyon, L. (2013) '50 Things Your Clients NEVER Want to Hear', www.spatrade.com/spa-business/50-things-your-clients-never-want-hear (accessed 8 March 2013).

Ma'or, Z., Henis, Y., Alon, Y., Orlov, E., Sørensen, K. and Oren, E. (2006) 'Antimicrobial Properties of Dead Sea Black Mineral Mud', *International Journal of Dermatology*, 45(5), pp. 504–11.

MacCannell, D. (1976) *The Tourist: A new theory of the leisure class*, New York: Schocken.

MacCannell, D. (2012) 'On the Ethical Stake in Tourism Research', *Tourism Geographies*, 14(1), pp. 183–94.

MacKenzie, J.M. (2005) 'Empires of Travel: British Guide Books and Cultural Imperialism in the 19th and 20th Centuries', in J.K. Walton (ed.) *Histories of Tourism: Representation, Identity and Conflict*. Clevedon: Channel View Publications, pp. 19–38.

Magyar, R. (2008) 'Hosszú az út a lélektől a lélekig', *Turizmus Trend*, 3.

Mak, A.H.N., Wong, K.K.F. and Chang, R.C.Y. (2009) 'Health or Self-indulgence?', *Journal of Tourism Research*, 11(2), pp. 185–99.

Malik, S. (2012) 'Medical Value Travel – Yesterday, Today and Tomorrow', EMTC2012, 26 April, Berlin.

Mandarin Oriental (2013) www.mandarinoriental.com/experience/luxury-spas/

Mangorrinha, J. (2000) *O Lugar das Termas*. Lisboa: Livros Horizonte.

Manshina, N. (2003) (ed.) 'Kumyz Therapy Resorts', *Guidebook to World Resorts*, Moscow: Medci, pp. 27–30.

Marchenko, I. (2012) В Кыргызстане на 1 сентября озеро Иссык-Куль посетили 1 миллион 104,1 тысячи человек, www.24.kg/community/136566-v-kyrgyzstane-na-1-sentyabrya-ozero-issyk-kul.html (accessed 11 December, 2012).

Marguiles, S. (2013) 'Spa Ambiance Design', *Dermascope*, March, pp. 99–101.

Marks & Spencer (2005) 'Spending Habits of Bridget Jones Generation', 5 September, www6.marksandspencer.com/pressreleases/Press35.pdf (accessed 4 January 2008).

Maruyama, T. (2012) *Global Spa and Wellness Industry Briefing Papers 2012*. New York: Global Spa and Wellness Summit.

Matthews, J. (2012) *Global Spa and Wellness Industry Briefing Papers 2012*. New York: Global Spa and Wellness Summit.

Mayr Centre (2008) www.viva-mayr.at/en (accessed 10 March 2008).

McCabe, S. (2009) 'Who Needs a Holiday? Evaluating social tourism', *Annals of Tourism Research*, 36(4), pp. 667–88.

McCabe, S., Joldersma, T. and Li, C. (2010) 'Understanding the Benefits of Social Tourism: Linking participation to subjective well-being and quality of life', *International Journal of Tourism Research*, 12, pp. 761–73.

McCarthy, J. (2012) *The Psychology or Spas and Wellbeing: A guide to the science of holistic healing*. New York: McCarthy.

McCarthy, J. (2013) 'Consumer, Heal Thyself: Spas and the Psychology of Wellbeing', www.experienceispa.com/includes/media/docs/Consumer-Heal-Thyself.pdf (accessed 16 February 2013).

McDonald, A. (2012) *Global Spa and Wellness Industry Briefing Papers 2012*. New York: Global Spa and Wellness Summit.

McNees, L. (2012) *Global Spa and Wellness Industry Briefing Papers 2012*. New York: Global Spa and Wellness Summit.

Medellin Healthcare Cluster (2011) 'Medical and Dental Care Service Clusters', 4th World Medical Tourism and Global Healthcare Congress, www.medicaltourismcongress.com (accessed 28 March 2012) Chicago, 26 October.

Medhekar, A. (2010) 'Growth of Medical Tourism in India and Public–Private Partnerships', *Proceedings of the Seventh IIDS, International Conference on Development*, Calcutta 13–19 December.

Medhekar, A. and Ali, M.M. (2012) 'A Cross-Border Trade in Healthcare Services: Bangladesh to India', *Business and Management Review*, 2(1), pp 1–13.

Medical Korea (2013) www.medicalkorea.or.kr/eng/why/support.jsp (accessed 22 March 2013).

Medical Tourism Association (2013) 'Healthcare Clusters, Medical Clusters and Healthcare Associations', www.medicaltourismassociation.com/en/healthcare-clusters.html (accessed 5 March 2013).

MedRetreat (2008) www.medretreat.com (accessed 17 March 2008).

Mehrabian, A. and Russell, J.A. (1974) *An Approach to Environmental Psychology*. Cambridge, MA: The MIT Press.

Mestre, D.F. (2012) *Global Spa and Wellness Industry Briefing Papers 2012*. New York: Global Spa and Wellness Summit.

Middleton, J., Lang, S., Ivankovic, D. and Kern, J. (2005) 'A Naturalistic Inquiry on the Impact of Interventions Aiming to Improve Health and the Quality of Life in the Community', *Social Science & Medicine*, January, 60(1), pp. 153–64.

Mika, C. (2012) 'Certification in Medical Tourism Nice to Have or Must-have?', *EMTC2012*, 26 April, Berlin.

Miller, C. (1994) 'People Want to Believe in Something', *Marketing News*, 28 (25), pp. 1–2.

Miller, F., Vandome, A. and McBrewster, J. (2010) *Balenotherapy*. VDM Verlag: Dr. Mueller e.K.

Miller, I. and Lonetree, B. (2010) *The "Sedona Effect": Earth Energies, Schumann, Resonance and Brainwave Resonance* (Scientific Research on Sedona Vortex Sites), http://www.lovesedona.com/01.htm (accessed 12 October 2012).

Mind (2013) www.mind.org.uk (accessed 5 January 2013).

Ministry of Regional Development, the Czech Republic (2007) *Czech Spas and Balneology* (in Czech). Prague: Ministry of Regional Development.

Ministry of Tourism (2010) *Domestic Tourism Survey*. Jerusalem: Ministry of Tourism.

Ministry of Tourism (2011) *Annual Report*. Delhi: Government of India.

Ministry of Tourism (2011) 'Wellness is Generally Used to . . .', *Guidelines for the Ministry of Tourism Support to Promote 'Wellness' as Niche Tourism Product*, Government of India, Ministry of Tourism (AandRT Division), No. 1–4. tourism.gov.in/writereaddata/. . ./Guideline/070620110300530.pdf (accessed 3 November 2012).

Minnaert, L., Maitland, R. and Miller, G. (2007) 'Social Tourism and Its Ethical Foundations', *Tourism, Culture and Communication*, 7, pp. 7–17.

Minnaert, L., Maitland, R. and Miller, G. (2009) 'Tourism and Social Policy. The Value of Social Tourism', *Annals of Tourism Research*, 36(2), pp. 316–34.

Minnaert, L., Maitland, R. and Miller, G. (2011) 'What is Social Tourism?', *Current Issues in Tourism*, 14(5), (July), pp. 403–15.

Mintel (2006) 'Health and Wellness Holidays', www.mintel.com/press_release.php?id=271145 (accessed 28 November 2007).

Mintel (2011) 'Spa Life UK', UK Spa Life Conference, Elveden, 8 November.

Molnár, C. (2010) 'Az egészségturizmus teljesítménye és fejlesztésének hatásai Kelet–Magyarországon [The Performance of Health Tourism and the Effects of its Development in Eastern Hungary]', in Benkő, P. (ed.) *Politikai régió – Régiópolitika*, Budapest: Dr. Deák Bt., pp. 170–89.

Monteson, P.A. and Singer, J. (2004) 'Marketing a Resort-based Spa', *Journal of Vacation Marketing*, 10(3), pp. 282–7.

Moore, C. (1998) 'Process Knowledge', in L. Fischer (ed.) *Excellence in Practice Volume II*, pp. 19–24, www.e-workflow.org/downloads/gue-pro.pdf (accessed 5 April 2009).

Müller, H. and Kaufmann, E.L. (2001) 'Market Analysis of a Special Health Tourism Segment and Implications of the Hotel Industry', *Journal of Vacation Marketing*, 7(1), pp. 5–17.

Mullholland, C. (2005) 'Depression and Suicide in Men', www.netdoctor.co.uk (accessed on 20 September 2005).

Mun, W.K. and Musa, G. (2013) 'Medical tourism in Asia', in C.M. Hall (ed.) *Medical Tourism: The ethics, regulation, and marketing of health mobility*. London: Routledge, pp. 167–86.

Munro, J.W. (2012) *What is Medical Tourism?* Scottsdale: Medical Travel Quality Alliance.

Myers, J.E., Sweeney, T.J. and Witmer, M. (2000) 'A holistic model of wellness', www.mindgarden.com/products/wells.htm (accessed 20 September 2005).

Mynatour (2013) 'Iceland: A Truly Sustainable Destination', www.mynatour.org/destination/iceland-truly-sustainable-destination (accessed 4 March 2013).

MySwitzerland (2013) www.myswitzerland.com/en/suggestions/wellness.html (accessed 23 March 2013).

Nahrstedt, W. (2008) 'From Medical Wellness to Cultural Wellness: New challenges for leisure studies and tourism policies', keynote speech, *The Future of Historic Spa Towns Symposium*, Spa, Belgium, 13–14 March.

National Center for Alternative and Complementary Medicine (2007) http://nccam.nih.gov (accessed 8 October 2007).

National Tourism Development Authority of Ireland (2007) *Health and Wellness Positioning Strategy for Key Markets*. Dublin: Bord Failte Ireland.

National Wellness Institute (NWI) (1977) www.nationalwellness.org (accessed 10 January 2013).

National Wellness Institute (NWI) (2007) www.nationalwellness.org (accessed 29 November 2007).

National Wellness Institute (NWI) (2012) 'Defining Wellness', www.nationalwellness.org/index.php?id=390andid_tier=81 (accessed 10 January 2012).

Nemat, S.N. (2002) *Studying Tourism Condition in Sarein Using the General Electric Model*. Tehran.

Nemer, N. (2012) *Global Spa and Wellness Industry Briefing Papers 2012*. New York: Global Spa and Wellness Summit, p. 103.

New Economics Foundation (NEF) (2004) www.wellbeingmanifesto.net/uk_manifesto.pdf (accessed 4 December 2007).

New Economics Foundation (NEF) (2008) 'Five Ways to Wellbeing', www.neweconomics.org/publications/five-ways-well-being-evidence (accessed February 2013).

New Economics Foundation (NEF) (2012) 'Happy Planet Index', www.happyplanetindex.org/assets/happy-planet-index-report.pdf (accessed 24 February 2013).

New Zealand Tourism (2007) www.nzmaoritourism.com/Home/Hells_Gate___Wai_Ora_Spa_IDL=4_IDT=1375_ID=8268_.html (accessed 20 November 2007).

Niv, A. (1989) 'Health Tourism in Israel: A developing industry', *Tourism Review*, 44(4), pp. 30–2.

Nolen, L. (2012) *Wellness Grows Up: Emerging Trends for 2012 and Beyond*, Dallas: The Radial Group.

Nordic Well (2007) www.nordicwell.com/nordicwell/apps/nordicwell.jsp?pid=380 (accessed 20 November 2007).

O'Sullivan, J. (2011) 'A Game of Catch-up', *The Economist*, www.economist.com/node/21528979 (24 September 2011).

Olte, U. (2013) 'The Hottest Ways to Get through a Cold Winter', *Baltic Outlook*, pp. 46–54, www.airbaltic.com/public/51567.html (accessed 4 March 2013).

Omran, S. (2010) *Geography of Tourism in Egypt*, Cairo.

One&Only Resorts (2013) www.oneandonlyresorts.com/aboutus/spa.aspx (accessed 23 March 2013).

ONTIT (2010) *Indagine sulle prenotazioni/ presenze nelle aree turistiche e sui segmenti di prodotti*, ONTIT, www.ontit.it/opencms/export/sites/default/ont/it/documenti/files/ONT_2010-01-30_02288.pdf (accessed 19 October 2012).

ONTIT (2011) *Impresa turismo 2011*, Unioncamere-Isnart, www.ontit.it/opencms/opencms/ont/it/documenti/02589 (accessed 19 October 2012).

Ormond, M. (2013) 'Claiming "Cultural Competence": The promotion of multi-ethnic Malaysia as a medical tourism destination', in C.M. Hall (ed.) *Medical Tourism: The ethics, regulation, and marketing of health mobility*, London: Routledge, pp. 187–200.

Osho (2008) www.osho.com (accessed 5 March 2008).

Osservatorio Nazionale del Turismo (2011a) *Analisi dei prodotti turistici*, ONTIT, http://www.ontit.it/opencms/export/sites/default/ont/it/documenti/files/ONT_2012-04-10_02810.pdf (accessed 3 February 2013).

Osservatorio Nazionale del Turismo (2011b) *Focus sui prodotti di nicchia del turismo italiano*, ONTIT, www.ontit.it/opencms/opencms/ont/it/documenti/02575 (accessed 3 February 2013).

Osservatorio Turistico Regione Campania (2008) *I prodotti turistici in Campania. Il turismo termale*, ONIT, www.ontit.it/opencms/opencms/ont/it/documenti/archivio/00775 (accessed 3 February 2013).

ØTM (2007) *The National Health Tourism Development Strategy*. Budapest: Budai & Tsa Kft.

Outram, A.K., Stear, N.A., Bendrey, R., Olsen, S., Kasparov, A., Zaibert, V., Thorpe, N. and Evershed, R.P. (2009) 'The Earliest Horse Harnessing and Milking', *Science*, 323, pp. 1332–5.

Parsons, R., Tassinary, L.G., Ulrich, R.S., Hebl, M.R. and Grossman-Alexander, M. (1998) 'The View from the Road: Implications for stress recovery and immunization', *Journal of Environmental Psychology*, 18(2), pp. 113–40.

Pascarella, S. (2008) 'Enjoy Rugged Relaxation at Adventure Spas', www.usatoday.com/travel/deals/inside/2005-10-12-column_x.htm (accessed 24 March 2008).

Passport GMID (2012) *Health and Wellness Tourism in Poland*. London: Euromonitor International Report.

Passport Online (2013) *Gay Travel Spas Directory*, www.passportmagazine.com/spas (accessed 2 March 2013).

Pearce, P.L., Filep, S. and Ross, G.F. (2011) *Tourists, Tourism and the Good Life*. New York: Routledge.

Pernecky, T. (2012) 'Constructionism: Critical pointers for tourism studies', *Annals of Tourism Research*, 39, pp. 1116–37.

Pesonen, J. and Komppula, R. (2010) 'Rural Wellbeing Tourism – Motivation and Expectation', *Journal of hospitality and Tourism Management*, 17, pp. 150–7.

Pforr, C. and Locher, C. (2013) 'Impacts of Health Policy on Medical Tourism in Germany', in C.M. Hall (ed.) *Medical Tourism: The ethics, regulation, and marketing of health mobility*, London: Routledge, pp. 77–94.

Pilzer, P.Z. (2008) *The Wellness Revolution: How to make a fortune in the next trillion dollar industry*. London: John Wiley & Sons, 2nd edition.

Pine, J. and Gilmore, J. (1999) *The Experience Economy*. Boston: Harvard Business School Press.

Plessier, A. (2013) 'A Defining Moment Issue 16: Surprising findings in the state of spa travel survey', *GSWS*, http://blog.globalspaandwellnesssummit.org/2013/03/a-defining-moment-issue-16-surprising-findings-in-the-state-of-spa-travel-survey (accessed 15 April 2013).

Pollard, K. (2011) 'International Patient Streams: Past, present, and future', *EMTC2011*, 28 April, Barcelona.

Portwood, D. (2007) 'Towards an Epistemology of Work-based Learning: Eliciting clues from work-based learning projects', in D. Young and J. Garnett (eds) *Work-based Learning Projects*. Bolton: University Vocational Awards Council, pp. 8–20.

Pritikin (2013) *Longevity Center and Spa*, www.pritikin.com (accessed 20 April 2013).

Proctor, W.A. (1948) 'Cape Argus: Cape's medicine river', *The Argus*, 31 December.

Professional Beauty (2012) European Spa News. GIA Forecast, www.professionalbeauty.co.uk/site/Default.aspx?id=3d408126-8567-482a-97c9-34ed3b63f789andnewsid=8019d0de-3ba7-4bd5-8450-ff2fa9cacc2d (accessed 23 February 2012).

Promises Malibu (2013) *Malibu Luxury Rehab*, www.promises.com/treatment-programs/malibu-luxury-rehab (accessed 17 February 2013).

Puczkó, L. (2011) 'Customer Experiences', *Spa Australasia*, 48, pp. 26–8.

Puczkó, L. and Bacharov, M. (2006) 'Spa, Bath, Thermae: What's behind the labels?', *Journal of Tourism Recreation Research*, 31(1), pp. 83–91.

Puczkó, L. and Smith, M.K. (2012) 'An Analysis of TQoL Domains from the Demand Side', in M. Uysal, R.R. Perdue and M.J. Sirgy (eds) *Handbook of Tourism and Quality-of-Life (QOL) Research: The missing links*. Dordrecht: Springer, pp. 263–77.

Pune Commune (2008) www.osho.com (accessed 15 March 2008).

Price Waterhouse Coopers (2010) *ISPA 2010 U.S. Spa Industry Study*. Lexington: ISPA.

PWC (2012) 'Social Media Likes Healthcare: From marketing to social business', www.pwc.com/us/en/health-industries/publications/health-care-social-media.jhtml, PriceWaterhouseCoopers (accessed 5 February 2013).

Qatar National Bank (2013) www.qnb.com.qa (accessed 10 January 2013).

Quigley, R. (2011) 'Holidays for Tech Addicts? Digital detoxes offer discounts to "unplugged" guests', *Daily Mail*, 6 July, www.dailymail.co.uk/travel/article-2011730/Digital-detox-holidays-offer-discounts-unplugged-guests.html (accessed 17 February 2013).

Rabobank Cijfers en Trends (2011) *Thema-update Wellness*, www.rabobank.nl/images/thema_update_wellness_april_2011_29342093.pdf (accessed 29 October 2012).

Rabobank Wellnesstrend (2011) www.rabobank.nl/images/thema_update_wellness_april_2011_29342093.pdf (accessed 29 October 2012).

Rahman, T., Mittelhammer, R.C. and Wandschneider, P. (2005) 'Measuring the Quality of Life Across Countries. A sensitivity analysis of well-being indices.' Research paper No. 2005/06 in World Institute for Development Economics Research (WIDER) established by United Nations University (UNU).

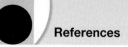

Ramesh, U. and Joseph, K. (2011) 'A Study to Evolve an Effective Marketing Plan to Enhance Wellness Tourism in Kerala', *International Journal of Marketing and Management Research*, 2(9), pp. 193–206.

Ramos, A. (2005) *O Termalismo em Portugal: dos factores de obstrução à revitalização pela dimensão turística*. Departamento de Economia, Gestão e Engenharia Industrial (PhD thesis), Aveiro: Universidade de Aveiro.

Ramponi, C. (2012) 'JCI Worldwide Accreditation', *EMTC2012*, 26 April, Berlin.

Rancho la Puerta (2013) www.rancholapuerta.com (accessed 27 February 2013).

Rawlinson, S. (2012) *Exploring a New Model for Vocational Degrees: A Case Study in Spa Management*. Derby: University of Derby.

Remedios, P. (2008) 'Built Environment-spa Design', in M. Cohen and G. Bodeker (eds) *Understanding the Global Spa Industry: Spa management*. Oxford: Butterworth Heinemann, pp. 281–96.

Retreat Finder (2013) www.retreatfinder.com (accessed 3 March 2013).

Retreats Online (2006) www.retreatsonline.com (accessed 15 November 2006).

Reuters (2006) 'Luxury Rehab Eases Troubles with a Rubdown', 15 December, www.msnbc.msn.com/id/16227377 (accessed 8 October 2007).

Rindl, M. (1936) *The Medicinal Springs of South Africa*. Pretoria: South African Railways Publicity and Travel Department.

Ritchie, J.R.B. and Crouch, G.I. (2003) *The Competitive Destination: A sustainable tourism perspective*. Oxford: CAB International.

RNCOS (2010) *Booming Medical Tourism in India*. New Delhi: Industry Report.

Robinson, R. (1996) 'Spain: Revival of Arab Baths', www.escapeartist.com/efam/63/Baths_In_Spain.html (accessed 20 March 2011).

Rockel, I. (1986) *Taking the Waters: Early spas in New Zealand*. Wellington: Government Printing Office.

Rodrigues, A., Kastenholz, K. and Rodrigues, A. (2010) 'Hiking as a Wellness Activity – an Exploratory Study of Hiking Tourists in Portugal', *Journal of Vacation Marketing*, 16(4), pp. 331–43.

Roth, G. (2010) *Women, Food and God*. London: Simon & Schuster.

Royal Spas (2008) www.royal-spas.net (accessed 2 April 2008).

Royal Spas (2013) www.royal-spas.net (accessed 12 February 2013).

Ruby Hall Clinic (2012) *Ruby Hall Pune*, www.rubyhall.com/news (accessed 14 July 2012).

Ryan, C. (ed.) (1997) *The Tourist Experience: A new introduction*. London: Cassell.

Ryff, C.D. (1995) 'Psychological Well-being in Adult Life', *Current Directions in Psychological Science*, 4, pp. 99–104.

Sacred Sites (2008) *Kumbha Mela*, www.sacredsites.com/asia/india/kumbha_mela.html (accessed 27 March 2008).

Sæþórsdóttir, A. (2010) 'Planning Nature Tourism in Iceland based on Tourist Attitudes', *Tourism Geographies*, 12(1), pp. 25–52.

Sæþórsdóttir, A.D., Hall, C.M. and Saarinen, J. (2011) 'Making Wilderness: Tourism and the history of the wilderness idea in Iceland', *Polar Geography*, 34(4), pp. 249–73.

SaimaaLife (2013) www.saimaalife.com (accessed 15 February 2013).

Salz und Sole (2008) www.openstreetmap.org/browse/relation/38485 (accessed 24 March 2013).

Santuari, A. (2010) *Il termalismo in Europa: un caso di turismo sanitaria*. Padova: Cedam.

Saratoga State Park (2008) 'Park History', www.saratogaspastatepark.org/history.html (accessed 27 March, 2008).

Sauna from Finland (2013) www.saunafromfinland.fi (accessed 15 February 2013).

Saunayoga (2013) www.saunayoga.com (accessed 15 February 2013).

Schempp, C.M., Dittmar, H.C. and Hummler, D. (2000) 'Magnesium ions inhibit the antigen-presenting function of human epidermal Langerhans cells in vivo and in vitro. Involvement of ATPase, HLA-DR, B7 molecules, and cytokines', *Journal of Invest Dermatol*, 115(4), pp. 680–6.

Scher, A. (2013) *Medical Tourism: When push comes to shove, my embryonic stem cell adventure begins*. http://thewip.net/contributors/2013/01/medical_tourism_when_push_come.html (retrieved 14 January 2013).

Schneiders, S. (1989) 'Spirituality in the Academy', *Theological Studies*, 50, pp. 676–97.

Schweder, I. (2008) 'The Emergence of a New Global Luxury Business Model: A case study of the spa at the Mandarin Oriental', in M. Cohen and G. Bodeker (eds) *Understanding the Global Spa Industry: Spa management*. Oxford: Butterworth Heinemann, pp. 171–88.

Schweder, I. (2012) *Global Spa and Wellness Industry Briefing Papers 2012*. New York: Global Spa and Wellness Summit, pp. 29–30.

Science Daily (2012) www.sciencedaily.com/releases/2012/04/120410130849.htm (accessed 22 March 2013).

Sedona Chamber of Commerce (2011) *Sedona Visitors Survey Executive Summary* (accessed 5 November 2012).

Sedona Festival (2012) *Sedona Festival information*, www.sedona-arizona.com/festivals (accessed 13 October 2012).

Sedona Method (2012) www.sedona.com (accessed 11 October 2012).

Sedona's Energy Vortexes (2012) 'John and Micki's Metaphysical Site', www.lovesedona.com/01.htm (accessed 5 November 2012).

See Wellness (2008) www.carinthia.at/en/Articles/View/631 (accessed 23 March 2013).

Seligman, M.E.P. (2003) *Authentic Happiness: Using the New Positive Psychology to Realize Your Potential for Lasting Fulfillment*. New York: Free Press.

Seligman, M.E.P. (2011) *Flourish: A visionary new understanding of happiness and well-being*. New York: Free Press.

Serious Fun (2013) www.seriousfunnetwork.org (accessed 12 February 2013).

Sethi, P. (2012) *Global Spa and Wellness Industry Briefing Papers 2012*. New York: Global Spa and Wellness Summit.

Shalev, E., Levitte, D., Gabay, R. and Zemach, E. (2008) *Assessment of Geothermal Resources in Israel*, Report GSI292008, Geological Survey of Israel, Jerusalem: The Ministry of National Infrastructures.

Sharma, U. (1992) *Complementary Medicine Today: Practioners and patients*. London: Routledge.

Shivdasani, S. (2012) *Global Spa and Wellness Industry Briefing Papers 2012*. New York: Global Spa and Wellness Summit.

Simpson, E. (2012) *Global Spa and Wellness Industry Briefing Papers 2012*. New York: Global Spa and Wellness Summit, pp. 117–18.

Singh, S. and Singh, T.V. (2009) 'Aesthetic Pleasures: Contemplating Spiritual Tourism', in J. Tribe (ed.) *Philosophical Issues in Tourism*. Bristol: Channel View, pp. 135–53.

Skyros (2008) http://skyros.co.uk (accessed 14 March 2008).

Sloan, P., Legrand, W. and Chen, J.S. (2013) *Sustainability in the Hospitality Industry: principles of sustainable operations*. London: Routledge.

Smalley, S.L. and Winston, D. (2010) *Fully Present: The science, art, and practice of mindfulness*. Philadelphia: Da Capo Press.

Smith, K., Clegg, S., Lawrence, E. and Todd, M.J. (2007) 'The Challenges of Reflection: Students learning from work placements', *Innovations in Education and Teaching International*, 44(2), pp. 131–41.

Smith, M.K. (2012) 'It's a Man's World', *European Spa*, October/November, 30, pp. 49–58.

Smith, M.K. (2003) 'Holistic Holidays: Tourism and the reconciliation of body, mind, spirit', *Journal of Tourism Recreation Research*, 28(1), pp. 103–8.

Smith, M.K. (2013) 'Wellness Tourism and Its Transformational Practices', in Y. Reisinger (ed.) *Transformational Tourism Tourist Perspectives*. Wallingford: CABI (forthcoming).

Smith, M.K. and Kelly, C. (2006) 'Holistic Tourism: Journeys of the Self?', *Journal of Tourism Recreation Research*, 31(1), pp. 15–24.

Smith, M.K. and Puczkó, L. (2008) *Health and Wellness Tourism*. Oxford: Butterworth Heinemann.

Smith, M.K. and Puczkó L. (2010) *Egészségturizmus: gyógyászat, wellness, holisztika*. Budapest: Akadémiai Kiadó Zrt.

Smith, M.K. and Puczkó, L. (2010) 'Taking Your Life into Your Own Hands? New trends in European health tourism'. *Tourism Recreation Research*, 35(2), pp. 161–72.

Smyth, F. (2005) 'Medical Geography: Therapeutic places, spaces and networks', *Progress in Human Geography*, 29(4), pp. 488–95.

Softkenya.com (2013) *Medical Tourism in Kenya*, http://softkenya.com/tourism/medical-tourism-in-kenya (accessed 6 March 2013).

Sokolova, A. (2012) *Global Spa and Wellness Industry Briefing Papers 2012*. New York: Global Spa and Wellness Summit.

Sonwai Spa at The Hyatt Regency, Scottsdale, USA (2008) www.insider-scottsdale.com/scottsdalemensspas.htm (accessed 2 March 2008).

South African Tourist Board (2008) www1.southafrica.net/Cultures/en-US/consumer.southafrica.net/Things+to+Do/Attractions/EntertainmentLeisure/African+Spas.htm?SEARCH=%2fcultures%2fen-US%2fconsumer.southafrica.net%2fsearchresults.aspx%3fKeyword%3dspa (accessed 14 February 2008).

Spa Audit (2013) www.spaaudit.com (accessed 23 March 2013).

SpaBusiness (2012) 'Rocco Forte unveils Vita Health wellness concept', www.spabusiness.com/detail1.cfm?pagetype=detailandsubject=newsandcodeID=302568andsite=SBanddom– (accessed 4 September 2012).

SpaFinder (2008) 'Spa Etiquette', www.spafinder.com/spalifestyle/spa101/etiquette.jsp (accessed 20 March 2008).

SpaFinder (2011) 'Top 10 Global Spa Trends to Watch in 2011', www.spafinder.co.uk/about/press_release.jsp?relId=207 (accessed 22 February 2013).

Spa Finder (2013) www.spafinder.co.uk/spaguide/spa-type.htm (accessed 16 February 2013).

Spa Finder Magazine (2005) 'Live at a Spa', www.spafinder.com (accessed 2 February 2008).

SpaFinder Wellness (2013) www.spafinder.com/resort-spas/N=52 (accessed 15 March 2013).

Spagasm (2008) www.spagasm.com (accessed 4 March 2008).

Spa Holidays (2012) 'Official homepage of Pärnu', www.visitparnu.com/en/visitor/spa-holiday (accessed 13 February 2012).

SpaIndex (2008) www.spaindex.com (accessed 12 March 2008).

SpaIndex (2013) www.spaindex.com/Lifestyles.htm (accessed 16 February 2013).

Spas of America (2008) www.spasofamerica.com (accessed 12 March 2008).

Spas of America (2013) www.spasofamerica.com/browse (accessed 15 March 2013).

Spa of Colonial Williamsburg (2013) www.colonialwilliamsburg.com/do/wellness-and-recreation/spa/services/spa-experiences (accessed 24 February 2013).

Spas Research Fellowship (2008) www.thespasdirectory.com/discover_the_spa_research_fell.asp?i=10 (accessed 14 February 2008).

Spa Village (2013) www.spavillage.co.il/eng (accessed 2 February 2013).

Spa Week Media Group (2013) www.spaweek.org/spadcast (accessed 16 March 2013).

Speier, A. (2011) 'Health Tourism in a Czech Health Spa', *Anthropology and Medicine*, 18, pp. 125–36.

Stackpole, I. (2012) '10 Terrible Marketing Mistakes', www.stackpoleassociates.com/resources/presentations/Ten-Terrible-Mistakes%2012-04-26.pdf (accessed 10 March 2013).

Stanford Research Institute (2010) 'Spas and the Global Wellness Market: Synergies and opportunities', www.sri.com/sites/default/files/publications/gss_sri_spasandwellnessreport_rev_82010.pdf, (accessed 7 September 2012).

Stanley, M. (2010) 'Anywhere But Here', *National Underwriter/Life and Health Financial Services*, 114(18), pp. 22–5.

Star, C. and Hammer, S. (2008) 'Teaching Generic Skills: Eroding the higher purpose of universities, or an opportunity for renewal', *Oxford Review of Education*, 34(2), pp. 237–51.

State of Israel Central Bureau of Statistics (2001) *Tourism and Hotel Services Statistics Quarterly*, Jerusalem: Central Bureau of Statistics.

State of Israel Central Bureau of Statistics (2006) *Tourism and Hotel Services Statistics Quarterly*, Jerusalem: Central Bureau of Statistics.

State of Israel Central Bureau of Statistics (2012) *Tourism and Hotel Services Statistics Quarterly*, Jerusalem: Central Bureau of Statistics.

State of Israel Ministry of Tourism (2010) www.goisrael.com/Tourism_Eng/Pages/home.aspx (accessed 17 June 2010).

Statistical Office of the Czech Republic (2011) Spa Statistics 2011. Prague.

Statistical Office of the Czech Republic (2012) Spa Statistics 2012. Prague.

Stefano, R.M. (2010) www.medicaltourismassociation.com/en/press/jordan-to-release-its-health-and-wellness-destinat.html (accessed 15 February 2013).

Steiner, C. and Reisinger, Y. (2006) 'Ringing the Fourfold: A philosophical framework for thinking about wellness tourism', *Journal of Tourism Recreation Research*, 31(1), pp. 5–14.

Steiner, S. (2012) 'Top Five Regrets of the Dying', www.guardian.co.uk/lifeandstyle/2012/feb/01/top-five-regrets-of-the-dying, Wednesday 1st February (accessed 17 February 2013).

Stokowska-Onwugbufor, E. (2011) 'Medical Tourism in Poland', Polishmedic (personal communication).

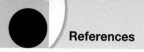

Stowarzyszenie Gmin Uzdrowiskowych RP (2013) *Association of Health-related Communities in Poland*, www.sgurp.pl/index1.htm (accessed 12 March 2013).

Sturebadet (2008) www.sturebadet.se/ (accessed 13 March 2008).

Sukenik, S. (2008) *The Dead Sea: The world's ultimate natural healing resort*. Israel: Hebrew University Magnes Press.

Sunflower Retreat (2013) www.sunflowerretreats.com (accessed 3 March 2013).

Surgeon and Safari (2013) www.surgeon-and-safari.co.za (accessed 12 January 2013).

Sushant (2011) 'Advantages of Balenotherapy, Harmful Effect of Excessive Salt Intake', www.salt.in/advantages-of-balenotherapy.html (accessed 12 March, 2012).

Sutphen, D. (1988) *Sedona: Psychic Energy Vortexes*, Malibu: Valley of the Sun Publishing.

Sutton, P. and House, J. (2000) *The New Age of Tourism: Postmodern Tourism for Postmodern People?* www.arasite.org/pspage2.htm (accessed 6 January 2012).

Swarbrooke, J. and Horner, S. (1999) *Consumer Behaviour in Tourism*. Oxford: Butterworth Heinemann.

Sydow, A. (2011) 'Integration of Medical Wellness Components into Spa Compounds: Markets and Key Success Factors', *EMTC2011*, 28 April, Barcelona.

Sylge, C. (2007) *Body and Soul Escapes*. Bath: Footprint Handbooks Ltd.

Szabó, G. (2004) *Javasasszony unokája [The Grandson of a Wise-woman]*. Bükkszentkereszt.

Szendrei, K. and Csupor, D. (2009) *Gyógynövény tár [Herbal Store]*. Budapest: Medicina Könyvkiadó Zrt., p. 267.

Szromek, A.R. (2011) 'Działalność turystyczno – lecznicza'. *Zakładów Lecznictwa Uzdrowiskowego*. Kraków: Proksenia.

Tabacchi, M. (2008) 'American and European Spas', in M. Cohen and G. Bodeker (eds) *Understanding the Global Spa Industry: Spa management*. Oxford: Butterworth Heinemann, pp. 26–40.

Tai Chi Finder (2007) www.taichifinder.co.uk/article_info.php?articles_id=3 (accessed 8 November 2007).

Taylor, B. (2009) *Dark Green Religion: Nature, spirituality and the planetary future*. Berkeley, CA: University of California Press.

Teare, R. (1998) 'Supporting Managerial Learning in the Workplace', in R. Teare, J.T. Bowen and N. Hing (eds) *New Directions in Hospitality and Tourism: A worldwide review*. London: Cassell, pp. 70–80.

Te Aroha i-Site (2012) http://tearohanz.co.nz (accessed 12 Janary 2013).

Terry, L. (2013) 'Deborah Szekely', *Spa Business*, pp. 32–8.

The Good Retreat Guide (2013) www.thegoodretreatguide.com/grg-front-page (accessed 3 March 2013).

The Retreat Company (2013) www.theretreatcompany.com (accessed 3 March 2013).

Thomas Cook (1905) *New Zealand as a Tourist and Health Resort. 5th edition*. Auckland: Thomas Cook & Son.

Thompson, M. (2007) *Feng Shui*, http://michaelthompson.org/fengshui (accessed 2 January 2008).

Thorpy, M.J. and Yager, J. (2001) *The Encyclopedia of Sleep and Sleep Disorders. 2nd Edition*. New York: Facts on File.

Thrift, N. (2008) *Non-Representational Theory: Space, Politics, Affect*. Abingdon: Routledge.

THTC (2013) 'Turkish Government Support for Medical Tourism', *IMTEC2013*, 22 March, Monaco.

Timmins, N. (2007) 'NHS Trusts Set Up Deals to Avoid Private Income Caps', *Financial Times*, 20 August.

Timothy, D.J. And Olsen, D.H. (2006) *Tourism, Religion and Spiritual Journeys*. London: Routledge.

Tolle, E. (2005) *A New Earth: Awakening to your life's purpose*. New York: Plume.

Tompkins, M. (2012) *Global Spa and Wellness Industry Briefing Papers 2012*. New York: Global Spa and Wellness Summit, pp. 119–20.

Tooman, H., Tomasberg, K. and Smith, M.K (2013) 'Cross-Cultural Issues in Health and Wellness Services in Estonia', in J. Kandampully (ed.) *Service Management in Health and Wellness Services*, Dubuque: Kendall Hunt Publishers.

Tourism Australia (2007) *Wellbeing Factsheet*, www.tourism.australia.com/content/Research/Factsheets/Wellbeing_Experiences.pdf (accessed 24 November 2007).

Tourism Australia (2011) www.tourism.australia.com/en-au/ (accessed 10 March 2011).

Tourism Authority of Thailand News Room (2011) *Thailand as a Centre of Excellent Health of Asia*, www.tatnews.org/emagazine/1983.asp#a (accessed 1 February 2011).

Tourism Observatory for Health, Wellness and Spa/TOHWS (2013) *Global Wellness and Spa Tourism Monitor 2012–2013*. Budapest: TOHWS.

Tourism Victoria (2005) *Victoria's Spa and Wellness Tourism Action Plan 2005–1010*, Tourism Victoria, Melbourne.

Tourism Victoria (2010) www.tourism.vic.gov.au/ (accessed 5 October 2010).

TP (Turismo de Portugal) (2007) *Plano Estratégico Nacional do Turismo – para o desenvolvimento do turismo em Portugal*. Lisboa: Turismo de Portugal.

Trompenaars, F. (1993) *Riding the Waves of Culture: Understanding cultural diversity in business*. Avon: Bath Press.

Tshibalo, A.E., Olivier. J. and Venter, J. (2010) 'South Africa Geothermal Country Update (2005–2009)', *Proceedings World Geothermal Congress* 2010, Bali.

Tuohino, A. (2008) *Nordic Well-being – A health tourism approach to enhance competitiveness of Nordic Tourism enterprises and destinations*, http://mot.joensuu.fi/sivut/in-english/research/nordic-well-being.php (accessed 15 July 2009).

Tuohino, A. (2012) *Löytöretki hyvinvointimatkailuun – Hyvinvointimatkailun nykytilakartoitus ja toimenpide-ehdotukset*. www.prizz.fi/linkkitiedosto.aspx?taso=5andid=477andsid=302 (accessed 22 December 2012).

Tuohino, A. and Kangas, H. (2009) 'Hotel Herttua – Spa and rehabilitation centre in Eastern Finland', in M.K. Smith and L. Puczkó (eds) *Health and Wellness Tourism*. Oxford: Butterworth Heinemann, pp. 312–318.

Uitvoeringsprogramma badstatus Domburg (2011) www.veere.nl/document.php?m=1andfileid=49161andf=e55d90213120d1199d46aac09e399c5dandattachment=0andc=48233 (accessed 30 October 2012).

UK Life Coaching (2007) www.uklifecoaching.org (accessed 8 October 2007).

Ullrick, S. (2012) *Global Spa and Wellness Industry Briefing Papers 2012*. Global Spa and Wellness Summit, pp. 121–2.

Urde, M., Greyser, S.A. and Balmer, J.M.T. (2007) 'Corporate Brands with a Heritage', *Brand Management*, 15(1), pp. 4–19.

USAID (2009) *Market Assessment and Demand Forecast for the Jordan Dead Sea Development Zone*. Amman: Jordan Economic Development Program.

Valfre, M. M. (2001) *Foundations of Mental Health Care*. 2nd edition. London: Mosby.

Van de Broek, J. (2008) Data from the Marketing Department of Les Mills, Netherlands, 31 March.

Van der Meulen, D. and O'Brien, K. (2006) *Spa Style Arabia*. London: Thames & Hudson.

Veere (2012) www.veere.nl/index.php?simaction=contentandmediumid=1andpagid=73 (accessed 30 October 2012).

Veinpalu, E. And Veinpalu, L. (1988) *Pärnu Kuurort 150 (Pärnu Resort 150)*. Tallinn: Valgus.

Vequist, D. (2012) *Medical Tourism and Healthcare Information Technologies (HIT): Enablers or Barriers?* HIMSS Texas Regional Conference, Galveston (Texas), 13 April.

Vequist, D., Guiry, M. and Ipock, B. (2011) 'Controversies in Medical Tourism', in O. Moufakkir and I. Kelly (eds) *Tourism, Progress and Peace*. Oxford: CAB International pp. 73–85.

Virtual Byron (2013) www.virtualbyron.com/visitors/history.php (accessed 24 February 2014).

Vital Wonders (2013) 'The Meaning of Magnetism', www.vitalwonders.com/therapy.htm (accessed 7 July 2013).

Vloten, F. (2004) *Zeeuws Licht*, www.domburgatart.nl/zeeuwslicht/zeeuws_licht.html (accessed 30 October 2012).

Voigt, C. (2010) 'Understanding Wellness Tourism: An analysis of benefits sought, health-promoting behaviors and positive psychological well being', PhD dissertation. Adelaide: University of South Australia.

Voigt, C. and Pforr, C. (2013) *Wellness Tourism*. London: Routledge.

Voigt, C., Brown, G. and Howat, G. (2011) Wellness Tourists: In search of transformation, *Tourism Review*, 66(1/2), pp. 16–30.

Voigt, C., Laing, J., Wray, M., Brown, G., Howat, G., Weiler, B. and Trembath, R. (2010) Health Tourism in Australia: Supply, Demand and Opportunities, www.crctourism.com.au/wms/upload/resources/WellnessTourism_Ind%20Summary%20WEB%20(2).pdf (accessed 22 February 2013).

Voit, M. (2012) *Global Spa and Wellness Industry Briefing Papers 2012*. New York: Global Spa and Wellness Summit, pp. 43–4.

Wagner, C. (2012) 'The Insurer Perspective on Retirees and Provider Networks in EU Cross Border Care', *EMTC2012*, 26 April, Berlin.

Walton, J.K. (1983) *The English Seaside Resort: A social history 1750–1914*, www.cabdirect.org/abstracts/19841813197.html;jsessionid=8F6C9879BB7F401D0AF7F144839192BE (accessed 10 July 2013).

Wang, N. (1999) 'Rethinking Authenticity in Tourism Experience', *Annals of Tourism Research*, 26(2), pp. 349–70.

Warners, J. (1984) *Domburg 150 jaar badplaats*. Domburg: Stichting 150 jaar Badplaats Domburg.

Well+GoodNYC (2012) *Fitness and Wellness Trends of 2013*, www.wellandgoodnyc.com/2012/12/20/wellgoods-14-fitness-and-wellness-trends-of-2013/#wellgoods-14-fitness-and-wellness-trends-of-2013-2 (accessed 12 December 2012).

Wellbeing Retreats (2013) www.wellbeingretreats.com (accessed 3 March 2013).

White, G. (2003) *Hot Bath: The story of the spa*. Bath: Nutbourne Publishing Ltd.

White, M. (2011) The Other Side of the Sinai Ras Sidr, www.touregypt.net/featurestories/rassidr.htm (accessed 3 February 2013).

Whitman, C. and M. Fadra (2007) '15 Keys to Improving Med Spa Efficiences', *MEDIcalSPAS*, July/August, pp. 14–18.

WHO (2011) www.who.int/en (accessed 11 June 2011).

WHO (2012) *Healthy Cities*, www.euro.who.int/en/what-we-do/health-topics/environment-and-health/urban-health/activities/healthy-cities (accessed 10 October 2012).

Wiedemann, M. (2012) *Global Spa and Wellness Industry Briefing Papers 2012*. New York: Global Spa and Wellness Summit.

Wildfitness (2013) www.wildfitness.com (accessed 27 March 2013).

Williams, A. (1998) 'Therapeutic Landscapes and Holistic Medicine', *Social Science and Medicine*, 46(9), pp. 1193–203.

Williams, A. (2010) 'Spiritual Therapeutic Landscapes and Healing: A case study of St. Anne de Beaupre', *Social Science and Medicine*, 70, pp. 1633–40.

Williams, J. (2012) *Global Spa and Wellness Industry Briefing Papers 2012*. New York: Global Spa and Wellness Summit.

Willis, A. (2009) 'Restoring the Self, Restoring Place: Healing through grief in everyday places', *Emotion, Space and Society*, 2, pp. 86–91.

Willson, G.B. (2011) 'The Search for Inner Peace: Considering the spiritual movement in tourism', *Journal of Tourism and Research*, 1(3), pp. 16–26.

Wilmot, A. (1914) 'The Climate of South Africa – the Best in the World', in *South African National Union Report*.

Woodman, J. (2013) 'Future of medical tourism' (personal communication), IMTEC, Monaco, 23 April.

World Health Organization (1984) *Health Promotion: A Discussion Document*. Copenhagen: WHO.

World Health Organization (2005) 'Stop the global epidemic of chronic disease', www.who.int/mediacentre/news/releases/2005/pr47/en/ (accessed 16 September 2012).

World Health Organization (2008) *WHO–China country cooperation strategy, 2008–2013*, www.who.int/countryfocus/cooperation_strategy/ccs_chn_en.pdf (accessed 16 September 2012).

World Health Organization (2011) 'Noncommunicable diseases', www.who.int/mediacentre/factsheets/fs355/en/index.html (accessed 16 September 2012).

World Health Organization (2012) 'Are You Ready? What you need to know about ageing', www.who.int/world-health-day/2012/toolkit/background/en/index.html (accessed 15 February 2013).

World Research Foundation (2012) *Sedona, Arizona*, www.wrf.org (accessed 10 October 2012).

Wray, M., Laing, J. and Voigt, C. (2010) 'Byron Bay: An alternate health and wellness destination', *Journal of Hospitality and Tourism Management*, 17(1), pp. 158–66.

Wykaz Standardowych Procedur Uzdrowiskowych [A list of standardized health resorts treatments] (2012) www.e-kurort.pl/lecznictwo_uzdrowiskowe__zabiegi.htm (accessed 25 November 2012).

Wylie, J. (2007) *Landscape*. London: Routledge.

Yap, C. (2012) *Global Spa and Wellness Industry Briefing Papers 2012*. New York: Global Spa and Wellness Summit.

Yasen, K. A. (2012) 'Statistics of Saudi patients in Germany and Europe', *EMTC2012*, 25 April, Berlin.

Yesiltas, M. (2009) 'Obstacles to the Tourism Development in Kyrgyzstan', Gazi University, Commerce and Tourism Education Faculty, Department of Tourism, Turkey: Ankara.

Yoga Holidays (2008) www.yogaholidays.net/magazine/Rishikesh.htm (accessed 7 February 2008).

Yoga Magazine (2013) 'Variety is the Spice of Yoga', *Yoga Magazine*, February, pp. 64–71.

Yoga Plus (2013) www.yogaplus.co.uk (accessed 3 March).

Yoga Travel (2007) www.yogatravel.co.uk/morocco.htm (accessed 20 November 2007).

Yogi Bajan (2003) 'The Self-Sensory System of the Aquarian Age', in S. Datta (ed.) *Open Your Heart with Kundalini Yoga*, London: Thorsons.

Youngman, I. (2012) 'Those medical tourism numbers . . . revisited', *IMTJ*, www.imtj.com/articles/2012/medical-tourism-statistics-30151 (accessed 15 December 2012).

Younis, M.Z. (2011) 'Muslim Patients', *EMTC2011*, 28 April, Barcelona.

Zake, Y. (2012) *Global Spa and Wellness Industry Briefing Papers 2012*. New York: Global Spa and Wellness Summit.

Zeder, Melinda A. (ed.) (2006) *Documenting Domestication: New Genetic and Archaeological Paradigms*. Berkeley, CA: University of California Press.

Zega, K. (2010) *Holistic Benefits of a Retreat*, 170, May, www.positivehealth.com/article/retreats-and-travel/holistic-benefits-of-a-retreat (accessed 23 March 2013).

Zeppel, H. and Hall, C.M. (1992) 'Arts and Heritage Tourism', in B. Weiler and C.M. Hall (eds) *Special Interest Tourism*. Belhaven: London, pp. 47–68.

Index

aborigine 41, 71, 207
Accor hotels 14
accreditation 187, 196, 199, 299, 449
active ageing i, 10, 81, 82, 114, 206, 212–13, 218–19, 223, 243
adventure spa 74–5, 142, 144, 208
Alpine Wellness 37, 49, 50–1, 152–3, 185, 200, 214
America: Central 43, 73–5, 166, 205, 213, 217–18; Latin 459; North 7, 11, 13, 31, 42, 43; South 17, 43, 73–5, 127, 140, 186, 205, 213, 217–18
Americas 43–4
American Holistic Health Association 22
Ananda 20–1
anti-ageing 47, 52, 82, 103, 139, 146, 155, 318, 379, 418
Arab 33, 37, 77, 453
arabian 37–9
arabic 39, 48, 51, 62
architecture 33, 38, 139, 153, 177, 181, 189, 191–2, 195, 226, 252, 330
Argentina 17, 73, 149
ashram 19, 46, 70, 88, 99–100, 131, 133, 157, 184
Asia 7, 14, 31, 36, 37, 43, 48, 52, 60, 66, 68–70, 77, 80, 88, 120, 127, 134, 139, 140, 166, 195, 208, 216, 219, 221, 229, 249, 251, 308, 341, 447; South East Asia 110, 217, 447
Asia-Pacific 39–42
atmosphere 6, 11, 20, 24–5, 36, 43, 61, 62, 77, 126, 132–3, 146, 170, 190, 195, 208, 252, 277, 348, 372, 404–5, 432
Australia 5, 6, 41, 59, 70–2, 84, 110, 115–16, 123, 126–7, 130, 145, 169, 185, 204, 207–8, 212–13, 217, 231, 391–5, 446, 461–5
Austria 7, 36, 50–51, 89–90, 110, 124, 149, 152–3, 156, 159, 174, 186, 192, 200, 208, 213–14, 282, 318, 339, 407
authenticity 8, 27, 52, 124, 214, 221, 238, 266, 422–3, 428

Baby Boomer 21, 109, 111, 117, 130, 220–1, 244
Baden-Baden 30, 33–4, 140, 153, 159, 187, 191, 247, 370, 409
balance 7, 12, 19, 21–2, 24–5, 27, 35, 38, 40–1, 45, 61, 90–1, 120, 132, 155, 156,180, 194, 205–7, 225, 231, 252, 278, 287, 346, 401, 407, 411, 426, 430–1, 436; balanced diet 291, 456, 459; work-life balance 7, 84, 96, 112, 145, 392, 424, 433
balneotherapy 6, 31, 39, 50, 85, 232, 255, 323, 324, 329, 355, 370, 374, 467–72
Baltic States 6, 15, 49, 50, 57–9, 213, 217, 223, 227, 231, 233
banya 36, 53–4, 255–7
Bath (UK) 30, 33–4, 190–1
bath (bathing) 6, 12, 30–1, 34, 35, 37, 46–7, 73, 84, 85–6, 98, 102, 114, 158–9, 467, 470; Arabic 34, 38, 62, 77; Babylonian 38; Indian 40, 133; Japanese 31, 39, 69; Jewish 38; Korean 70; Maori 42, 72, 361; Mayan 42; Native American Indian 44; Roman 30, 32, 36, 191, 275, 276–9
bathing (sea) 34–7, 322, 379–82
beauty i, 7, 30, 34, 37, 39, 50, 56, 62, 72, 78, 90, 91, 112, 124, 135, 139, 154, 156, 163, 180, 196, 204, 239, 241, 252, 256, 262, 273, 289, 318, 322–3, 333, 346, 347, 356, 455; centres 259; farms 7, 259, 260, 261; clinic 9, 455; industry 214; products 52, 91, 114, 259, 356; providers 237; queens 122; salon 13, 111, 112; services 245, 259, 287; spa 9, 25, 62, 71, 116, 123, 144; therapy 84, 283, 288; treatments 32, 44, 101, 110, 215–16, 227, 237, 284, 287, 323, 346, 371, 372
beer bathing 63
Belgium 30–3, 36, 50, 190, 381, 423,
bio: design 183; energy 419, 435
bioclimatic spa 317
biomedical city 187
Blue Lagoon 58, 180–1, 207, 233, 415, 416
body–mind–spirit 6, 19, 53, 435

branding 137–46; at national and regional level 147–53; at local and operator level 153–9
Brazil 183, 213, 233, 449, 455, 459
Britain 30, 31, 36, 91, 380
Buddhist 4, 99, 339, 357, 422, 429; meditation 208
Bulgaria 49, 50, 55, 149
burnout 61, 95, 152, 206, 404
Byron Bay, Australia 71–2, 169, 208

Canada 7, 43, 63, 72–3, 94, 110, 149, 200, 213, 217, 245–6, 299–303, 446, 449
Caribbean 31, 43, 52, 75–6, 110, 127, 157, 225, 246
Carlsbad see also Karlovy Vary 55, 329, 330–3, 370
Caudalie, France 37, 51–2
caves 6, 36–7, 50, 54–5, 159, 173, 174, 195, 285, 336
Central and Eastern Europe 6, 9, 13, 15, 34, 49, 50, 53–7, 58, 90, 110, 123, 137, 139, 166, 173, 213, 216–17, 227, 233, 251, 289
chakra 38, 63, 157, 205, 418, 441
chi kung see also Qi Gong 25, 41, 72, 118, 132
China 7, 16, 59, 68, 113, 135, 193, 197, 249–53, 318, 341, 359, 360, 384, 448
chinese medicine 23, 30, 41, 48, 70, 84, 142, 210, 220, 238, 250, 253, 384
Chiva Som 70, 384
climate 13, 30, 32, 35–6, 38, 42, 50, 51, 53, 55, 60–2, 65, 85, 96, 152, 174, 185, 204, 213, 217, 231, 285, 317, 322–3, 331, 335, 336–7, 369, 373, 400, 417, 426, 455
climatotherapy 36, 324, 330, 342, 374,
clinic 6, 7, 9, 18, 32, 50, 60, 89, 93, 111, 127, 137, 153, 157, 158–9, 186, 198, 204, 265, 446, 455; ayurvedic 297; Blue Lagoon 181; Christie 452; Cleveland (Abu Dhabi) 63, 201; dental 162; Mayo 201; rehabilitation 256; Ruby Hall 446; SHA Wellness 383; sleep 292
Columbia 73
community 4, 5, 20, 22, 61, 80, 88, 103,105, 177, 246, 252, 310, 359, 392, 399, 423, 436, 438; local 207, 377, 382, 418, 471; loss of 114; medical 214, 239; New Age 23–4, 422; online 162, 436; search for 88, 13; Sedona 417; spa lifestyle 243, 245
complementary 12, 41, 335; and alternative medicine (CAM) 84, 117, 145, 220, 245, 379, 465; and alternative therapy i, 11, 21–2, 27, 84
cosmetics i, 29, 34, 37, 41, 59, 90–1, 119, 219, 257, 262, 357, 459
cosmetic spa 11
cosmetic surgery see also plastic surgery 16, 18, 66, 73, 89, 91, 111, 118, 127, 139, 144, 161, 205, 217, 226, 233, 318, 447
cosmetic treatments see also beauty treatments) 7, 32, 94, 110, 156, 212, 241
Costa Rica 43, 74, 181, 217, 231, 421–4
Croatia 49, 50, 55, 149, 185, 225, 318
cruises 11, 42, 58, 112, 142, 144, 153, 157, 204, 218, 269
cryotherapy 50, 58, 63, 257, 325

curative 5, 6, 10, 13, 16, 27, 33–4, 37, 41–4, 50, 55, 110, 175, 257, 275–6, 317, 322–3, 329, 332, 335–6, 338, 374, 411
cures see also Kur 5, 6, 14, 25, 30, 31–6, 42, 44, 47, 54, 55, 64, 66, 149, 159, 162, 190, 214, 292, 294, 318, 321, 329, 330, 336, 342, 343, 370, 375, 379, 398, 407, 455, 458, 463, 464, 469
customers: branding 146–59; cultural differences 134–6; demand and motivation 113–17; gay 160; men 159–60; profiles 109–13; segmenting 117–21; targeting 137–46
Czech Republic 173, 230, 321, 329–333, 341,

Dea Sea 30, 38, 39, 62, 63, 77, 174–5, 207, 230, 233, 373–8, 470
Definitions: health tourism 9–10; holistic tourism 21–5; medical tourism 15–19; spa tourism 10–15; spiritual tourism 19–21; wellness tourism 25–7
Denmark 95
dental 15, 18, 94, 147, 163, 186, 215, 299, 302, 447, 448, 458; clinic 162; spa 142; surgery 9, 68, 161; tourism 63; tourists 53; treatment 17, 127
desert 37, 42, 62, 63, 65, 144, 177, 373, 375, 376, 414
design 57, 98, 148, 170, 179, 181–3, 189, 190, 191, 192–5, 207, 217, 239, 252, 256
destination xxxii, 8, 15, 18, 19, 20, 30, 33, 34, 36, 45, 51, 52, 53, 265; health tourism 54, 134, 141, 154, 161, 166, 167, 174, 313, 373, 380, 383, 397–401; hot spring 65, 66, 72; medical tourism 19, 60, 63, 70, 84, 102, 147, 155, 173, 279, 445; new age 24, 421–4; pilgrimage 34; spa 10, 12, 42, 44, 47, 65, 73, 74, 86, 111, 143, 149, 161, 170, 247, 249–53, 257, 260, 321, 329, 330–3, 362, 369; spiritual 20, 70, 112, 133, 157; wellness 73, 92, 148, 244, 260, 417
detox(ification) 32, 38, 53, 70, 72, 75, 84, 86–7, 89–90, 93, 112, 115, 129, 130, 142–4, 147, 155, 156, 189, 252–3, 256, 372, 426, 457
diagnostic 54, 96, 223, 255, 317, 318, 325, 445, 446, 453, 457–8
diet 12, 31, 32, 35, 38, 40, 41, 44, 82, 84, 88–91, 98, 101, 118, 156, 189, 239, 250–1, 253, 259, 262, 291, 326, 386, 392, 411, 426, 457, 462, 468; Northern European 50; Mediterranean 6, 60; vegan 462
digital detox retreat 92, 206
disease 4, 5, 9, 10, 15, 17, 30, 35, 37, 42, 55, 58, 64, 81, 82, 90, 96, 110, 112, 116, 121, 123, 127, 174, 178, 206, 214, 215, 251, 253, 255, 265, 266, 267, 291, 323, 336, 337, 342–4, 358, 361, 371, 374, 375, 379, 384, 398, 404, 426–7, 455–8, 463–6, 467–71
dosha (ayurvedic) 40, 239, 426
Dubai 7, 38, 62, 63, 113, 185, 208, 246, 446, 449, 452; Healthcare City 63, 127, 187, 452

earthing 98, 239
eco: friendly 67, 74, 124, 142, 181, 195, 208, 239, 359; psychology 66; retreat 130; spa 174, 208,

217, 221, 239, 257; spirit 22; system 175;
   therapy 66, 213; tourism 417
education 5, 7, 12, 23, 24, 45, 54, 59, 73, 82, 87,
   89, 91–2, 95, 143, 170, 171, 177–9, 196, 206,
   208, 214, 230–1, 233, 238, 245, 246, 253, 283,
   295–8, 309, 311, 323, 327, 353, 355, 365, 377,
   411, 422, 430–1, 436, 452–3, 456, 462
Egypt 20, 24, 40, 62, 63, 65, 149, 232, 233,
   467–72
egyptian (ancient) 29, 30, 35, 37–8
energy 418, 419, 435, 441, 456–7, 468
escapism 7, 8, 36, 89, 94, 112, 116, 122, 129, 132,
   139, 147, 165, 206, 246–7, 250, 358, 394, 399,
   404
ESPA 200
Estonia 50, 58–9, 135–6, 147, 149, 291–4
evidence-based 13, 201, 214, 215, 219, 227, 386

feng shui 41, 48, 95, 182, 193, 194
festival 21, 22, 53, 65, 71, 88, 101, 112, 157, 417;
   holistic 53, 65; Kumbha Mela 40; New Age 88,
   184; religious 358; yoga 133, 163, 436
Finland 6, 7, 30, 35–6, 57–9, 63, 92, 95, 120, 135,
   141, 152, 197, 211, 213, 230, 345–9, 448
fitness 91–2, 143, 147, 151–2, 156, 209
four elements 35, 44, 205
four humours 38, 205
France 6, 13, 14, 31, 35–7, 42, 50, 51–2, 60, 86,
   110, 124, 149, 341, 449

gastronomy 57, 230, 262, 317, 346, 382, 383–7
gay 24, 124, 129, 159, 160; market 160; spa 126
Generation Y 218
Germany 7, 30–1, 33, 34, 36, 50–1, 55, 60, 81, 86,
   110, 112, 120, 124–5, 134, 140–1, 147, 149,
   150, 152–3, 159, 162, 185–7, 191, 200, 208,
   231, 247, 321, 331, 341, 347, 379, 381, 407,
   409, 424, 449, 454
geyser 50, 157, 195, 277
Global Spa and Wellness Summit (GSS, GSWS)
   10, 15, 25, 195, 203, 204, 207, 212, 220–1, 229,
   277, 295, 305–11
Greece 23, 30, 50, 60, 61, 110, 140, 150, 184, 451
guru 19, 20, 22, 83, 95, 99–100, 132, 137, 157,
   198, 205, 383, 421

hammam 34, 37–9, 62, 238
happiness 3, 4, 8, 27, 80, 83, 104, 105, 129, 149,
   204, 205, 226, 291, 346, 392, 399, 425, 429–30,
   455, 465
health tourism: definition 9–10; management
   315–387; demand and marketing 109–167
herbs 35–8, 42–3, 47, 54, 57, 84, 89, 257, 337–8,
   357–8, 384, 422, 459, 464
Heviz (Hungary) 207, 286–7, 289, 459
Hippocrates 30, 38, 337
historic spa town 34, 140, 153, 190–1, 225, 230,
   247
holistic 39, 41, 44, 48, 50, 61, 95, 113, 118–20,
   154, 183, 201, 205, 207–8, 210, 214, 222, 226,
   230, 239, 266, 277, 300, 322, 354, 386, 411,
   418, 440; healing 73, 145, 253, 417; festival 53,
   65, 184; health 5, 19, 27, 103, 111, 114, 145–6;

205, 212; medicine 46; retreat centre 9, 44, 50,
   61, 70–1, 73, 84, 86, 88, 95,110, 162, 163, 177,
   181, 184, 198, 207, 217, 224; spa 12, 70, 86,
   142, 145, 154, 156; system 38; therapy 464–5;
   tourism 21–5, 53, 70, 77, 83, 101, 157, 161,
   165, 184, 217, 229, 231, 276, 389, 425–8; tourists 129–133, 161, 195; wellness 9, 37, 39, 223,
   231, 253, 263, 425, 445, 463
hospital 6, 9, 16, 17, 18, 68, 70, 87, 124, 127–8,
   137, 158, 162, 177, 181, 184–7, 195, 198, 203,
   204, 212, 215, 223, 232, 243, 255, 289, 335,
   357, 404, 445–9, 451–4, 455, 462
hot springs 30, 41, 42, 43, 58, 60, 63–6, 71, 72, 74,
   77, 110, 142, 174, 175, 182, 190–2, 197, 213,
   216, 223–4, 249, 275, 276, 342, 351, 353,
   357–8, 361–2, 370, 375, 415
Hungary 6, 17, 30, 33, 50, 53, 93, 96, 111, 127,
   141, 147, 150, 155–6, 173–4, 197, 213, 225,
   230–1, 233, 281–4, 285–90, 335–9, 435–41
hydrotherapy 6, 12, 31–2, 34, 43, 45–7, 58, 86,
   110, 124, 250, 255, 325, 330, 355, 467–8

Iceland 50, 58, 77, 180–1, 413–16
India 7, 9, 16, 18, 20, 25, 29, 31, 32, 35, 37–8, 40,
   41, 48, 68, 70, 84, 94, 99–100, 110–12, 127,
   133, 150, 169, 171, 177–8, 183–5, 193, 198,
   208, 213, 231, 233, 239, 251, 309, 357–60, 385,
   423, 425, 427, 439, 441, 445–9
indigenous 15, 31, 38, 41, 42, 43, 44, 47, 48, 49,
   62, 65, 66, 71, 73, 79, 136, 177, 182, 183, 207,
   213, 230, 233, 238–9, 369, 419, 422, 469
Indonesia 41, 69, 113, 238, 385, 448
insurance 17, 18, 51, 88, 96, 102, 116, 126, 162,
   164–5, 185, 187, 199–200, 299, 302, 315–17,
   322, 330–2, 355, 375, 411, 446, 451
Iran 63, 64–5, 232–3
Islamic 37, 252
ISPA 10–12, 46, 102, 111
Israel 20, 59, 62–3, 65, 110, 174–5, 230, 275–9,
   373–8
Italy 20, 21, 30–1, 49, 50, 60, 110, 150, 152, 208,
   229, 233, 259–63, 265–8, 269–73, 318, 385

Japan 7, 20, 31, 39, 63, 69, 110, 127, 193, 197,
   208, 294, 383, 384, 448
Jordan 16, 63, 150, 174–5, 215, 275, 373–8, 385

Karlovy Vary see also Carlsbad 30, 55, 190, 329,
   331
Kenya 42, 43, 67, 68, 216, 446, 449
Kneipp 13, 31, 37, 45, 90, 379, 457
kur 6, 15, 37, 51, 149, 159, 173, 187, 265, 455–8
Kyrgyzstan 230, 341–4

landscape 8, 9, 13, 19, 30–1, 57, 61, 74, 97–9,
   111, 152, 176, 184, 185, 210, 213, 217, 226,
   230, 231, 346, 373, 376, 380, 413–16, 422
Latvia 373–8
life-coaching 10, 23, 83–4, 87, 95, 96, 105, 112,
   130, 156, 418
lifestyle 5, 6, 12, 22, 25, 27, 38, 40, 48, 50, 56, 57,
   60–1, 71, 79–105, 109, 111, 114, 117–20, 130,
   136, 139, 140, 145–6, 161, 165, 167, 177, 184,

185, 201, 205–7, 208, 214, 216–18, 221, 222, 229, 232–3, 238–9, 241, 243–7, 249, 251–3, 259, 323, 337, 346, 355, 363, 385, 407–11, 422, 436, 440, 456–7, 459; resorts 71, 116, 130; retreats 461–5; segmentation 119–23; spa 139, 141, 144, 161, 213, 243–7
Lithuania 50, 58, 60, 147
LOHAS 117, 120, 179
Lomi Lomi massage 52, 73, 238, 326
longevity *see also* anti-ageing 10, 41, 60, 81–2, 103, 105, 114, 188, 208, 215, 218–19, 223, 232–3, 243–4, 323, 359, 418, 455–7

macrobiotic 12, 383–4
Malaysia 38, 69, 70, 136, 150, 186, 222, 449
Maori 41, 72
Masai 42
massage 7, 11, 23, 27, 30–2, 35, 36–9, 76, 148, 159, 160–1, 171
Mayan 43, 422
medical tourism: definition 15–19; management 445–472; demand 126–8
Medical Tourism Association 15, 186, 199, 448
Medi-spa 15, 142
meditation 76, 148, 166–9
Middle East 7, 31, 37–9, 48, 62–5, 115, 127, 166, 193, 217, 229, 232, 238, 249–50, 252, 275, 317, 414, 445, 452
mindfulness 4, 27, 83, 207, 241, 462
mindness 6, 50
Morocco 62, 65, 150
mud 6, 30–2, 35–6, 38, 42, 54, 59, 60–1, 72, 85–6, 136, 173, 174, 211, 216, 219, 222, 247, 285, 294, 317, 322–4, 329, 342, 358, 374

Native American Indian 31, 43–4, 46, 73, 183, 207, 419
nature deficit disorder 97, 239
New Age 9, 15, 57–9, 60, 74, 80, 88, 107, 110, 116, 124, 165, 220, 267, 277, 457–60
New Zealand 23, 77, 108, 113, 163, 184, 193, 252, 266, 397–8, 484, 497
Nordic 94, 381; climate 221; countries 43, 93, 94, 249, 253; people 93; Well 93, 94, 229; Wellbeing 85, 93, 188, 221, 266, 382–3; walking 7, 50, 57, 92, 120, 327, 330, 345–6, 363, 381–2, 385, 520
Northern Europe 72, 86, 93, 95, 253–4
Norway 25, 131, 171
nutrition 114, 117–18, 123, 125–6, 132, 137, 147, 153, 157, 161, 165, 179, 182, 190, 199, 240, 243, 252, 255, 258, 274, 281, 288, 336, 379, 382, 419, 420, 422, 428, 441, 454, 472, 493–5, 498, 500, 504

occupational 41, 43, 45, 50, 86, 89, 141, 253, 313, 314, 397, 399, 400, 402
onsen 43, 67, 75, 105, 161
organic 59, 67, 75, 89, 91, 95, 99, 102, 103, 111, 113, 117, 120, 125, 127, 130–1, 135, 138, 149, 179, 181, 201, 208–11, 219, 230, 239, 365, 366, 374, 386, 399, 421, 423, 459, 462, 463
packaging 161, 163–4, 166, 225

pampering 6, 7, 10–11, 52, 72, 74, 112, 124, 145, 153–4, 161, 166, 207, 210, 237, 240, 287–8, 316–18, 345–6, 348, 408
persian 30, 64
Philippines 69, 70, 147, 151, 214, 448
pilates 23, 46, 72, 91, 115, 132, 143, 405
pilgrimage 7, 19, 21, 22, 24, 35, 40, 62, 65, 88, 111, 131, 133, 184, 278, 338, 357, 358–9, 398
plastic surgery *see also* cosmetic surgery 16, 17, 73, 91, 139, 161, 213, 241
Poland 34, 50, 53, 54, 60, 147, 150, 230, 233, 321–7, 385
policy 19, 54, 215, 268, 270, 330, 397–401
Portugal 49, 50, 60, 150, 208, 230, 233, 351–6
positive psychology 4, 83, 464
preventative 5, 9–11, 27, 37, 41, 50, 55, 103, 146, 152, 178, 188, 208, 217, 222, 230–1, 233, 245, 321–3, 328, 409, 435, 446, 461
psychological 4, 6, 8–10, 16, 18, 19, 22, 25, 27, 32, 42, 44, 61, 66–7, 83–4, 86, 88–9, 96, 91, 101, 105, 110–11, 116, 124, 129, 130, 162, 194, 198, 205, 214, 221–22, 226, 339, 358–59, 410, 414–15, 432, 457–58, 464, 468

qi gong *see also* chi kung 84, 462
quality 14, 51, 56, 58, 62, 64, 95, 101, 124, 135, 139, 141, 146, 150, 152, 154, 155, 158, 162, 166, 169, 170, 171, 181, 184–5, 190, 199–201, 204, 208, 214, 232, 246, 250, 259, 281, 291, 292, 327, 328, 330, 332, 348, 349, 353, 404, 411, 418, 427, 428, 447, 449, 458, 467; of care 15, 35, 85, 11, 25, 116, 118, 186, 187, 445–6, 449; of life 3, 4, 8, 27, 31, 73, 79, 82, 83, 91, 94, 96, 97, 105, 154, 205, 215, 219, 243, 253, 291, 346, 401, 430, 433, 456, 464; of service 18, 60, 128, 190, 199, 200–1, 230, 233, 283, 302, 318–9, 321, 323, 342, 348, 398, 427

Rancho la Puerta 44–5, 179, 249, 250
Rasul 38, 211
raw food 89–90, 129
recuperation 16, 43, 50, 102, 226, 337–9
regulation 59, 86, 170, 197–8, 199, 201, 208, 224, 232, 257, 331, 427
rehabilitation 18, 35, 49, 50, 58–9, 72, 86–7, 93, 114, 214–15, 220, 225–6, 255–6, 287, 331–2, 335, 377, 404, 445
reiki 7, 22, 23, 39, 70, 71, 84, 129, 238, 288, 418, 422, 424
relaxation 6–8, 10, 27, 39, 44, 50, 57, 72, 82, 90, 109–12, 116, 121–2, 124, 128, 131–2, 135, 149, 151–6, 160, 161, 163, 182, 192, 195, 211, 214, 218–19, 222, 245, 251, 259–60, 323, 327, 336, 348, 355, 358, 360, 372, 380, 405, 410–11
religion 7, 21, 24, 30, 34, 40, 79, 83, 88–9, 98–9, 112, 114, 134, 177, 184, 190, 233, 339, 357–9, 384, 392, 395, 423, 429
religious 9, 20–21, 40, 50, 65, 79, 96, 99, 111, 129, 130, 133, 134, 136, 216, 219, 277, 339, 357, 359, 398, 423, 467, 469, 471
retreat 9, 10, 19, 21–5, 27, 39, 42–4, 50, 53, 61, 63, 67, 70–5, 83–4, 86, 87–90, 92, 93, 95, 98–9, 101, 105, 110–11, 115–16, 129–34, 137, 142,

143, 162, 163, 165, 176, 177, 181, 184, 191,
198, 205–10, 212, 216–19, 224, 226, 231–3,
249, 251–3, 346, 357, 359, 384, 417, 436, 439,
441, 457, 461–5
revenue 69, 113, 186, 195, 197, 230, 243, 269–73,
283, 299, 306, 331, 357, 428, 445–7
ritual 7, 22, 30, 38, 39, 43, 44, 46–7, 68, 73, 139,
154, 197, 203, 210, 219, 220, 238, 257, 276,
287, 419, 423–4
Roman 30–8, 47, 62, 150, 174, 175, 190–1, 275–7,
315, 321, 351
Romania 50, 55, 155
Russia(n) 9, 15, 31, 36, 49–50, 51, 53–4, 55, 57–60,
134, 135–7, 161, 214, 217, 223, 227, 229, 231,
233, 255–7, 278, 289, 292, 318, 341, 342, 375,
449

safety 4, 18, 118, 170, 184, 192, 197–9, 200–1,
220, 427, 449
sanatorium 59, 255–7, 337
Saudi Arabia 20, 38, 65, 446, 449, 451
sauna 7, 30, 32, 36, 43, 48, 50, 56–9, 73, 77, 110,
112, 120, 124, 142, 152, 163, 182, 183, 189,
191, 211, 213, 215, 219, 257, 260, 288–9, 294,
325–6, 344–6, 347–8, 371, 405, 407, 409–11,
435
sea-water 12, 14, 31, 32, 35–6, 50, 86, 322, 374,
378–9, 381, 398, 470
seaside 6, 13, 14, 30, 31, 34, 36, 42–3, 50, 51, 58,
60, 110, 166, 191, 231, 262, 322, 381
self 8, 19, 21, 79, 88, 114–16, 253, 258, 394, 416,
419, 423–4; development 5, 8, 10, 22, 79, 88,
100, 114, 253, 422; discovery 129, 417; esteem
83, 97–8, 114, 116, 183, 226; healing 90, 189,
207, 463; help 83, 105, 392, 461, 462; image
89, 114; improvement 101, 244; responsibility 5,
7, 27, 45, 392, 395, 463
selfness 6, 50
Serbia 50, 55, 150–1
service quality 190, 199, 200, 427
shiatsu 7, 39, 277, 327, 418, 422, 463
Skyros 23, 61, 88, 95, 101, 131, 165, 177, 184,
198, 201
sleep 27, 30, 38–9, 58, 67, 70, 82, 92, 95, 102,
120, 144, 156, 189, 211, 221, 230, 241, 291–4,
372, 392, 436
Slovenia 6, 50, 53, 55, 151, 208, 230, 315–19,
339
slow movement 59, 95–6, 207
social tourism 9, 13, 54, 102, 173, 231, 233,
403–6
South Africa 18, 42, 65–6, 68, 111, 151, 213, 216,
223, 230, 233, 369–72, 449
South Korea 7, 68, 70, 147, 185, 186, 188–9, 197,
208
spa tourism: definition 10–15; management
237–311; demand 121–126
SpaFinder 11, 31, 46, 51, 68, 141, 165, 200, 237,
238–41
Spain 7, 23, 33, 34, 50, 60–2, 77, 110, 111, 125,
131, 140, 151, 192, 383, 384, 386, 449
spiritual 4, 5, 7, 10, 12, 19, 21–4, 27, 31–2, 35, 38,
39, 40–3, 50, 56, 65, 67, 71–2, 77, 80, 84, 87–8,
91, 95–6, 98–100, 105, 109–12, 114–15, 117,

124, 129, 131–4, 149, 151–2, 156, 157, 165,
171, 178, 184, 194, 198, 205–8, 210, 213,
215–16, 218, 219, 231, 233, 339, 357, 361,
363–4, 366, 392, 395, 414, 417–18, 421, 429,
430, 433–4, 436, 438, 440–1, 445, 449; retreat
9, 10, 23–5, 39, 69, 71, 73, 105, 116, 130, 143,
163, 216–17, 224; tourism 19–21, 24, 65, 70,
120, 129, 157, 161, 184, 195, 217, 229, 231,
335, 338, 359, 389–90
Starwood 154–5, 201
stress 4, 6, 7, 9–11, 23, 27, 50, 62, 67, 71–2,
79–84, 94–7, 105, 112, 114, 121–2, 125, 129,
130–2, 143, 144, 147, 149, 162, 163, 180, 188,
189, 206, 209–10, 221, 225, 233, 238, 240–1,
247, 249, 250, 253, 287, 291, 333, 346, 355,
360, 372, 386, 392, 394–5, 404, 408, 418–19,
422, 426, 429, 436, 440, 455–7, 462, 468
surgery 9–11, 16–18, 66, 68, 70, 73, 89, 91, 111,
127, 139, 140, 142, 157, 161, 184, 205, 213,
217, 223, 226, 233, 238, 241, 287, 318, 356,
446, 447, 448, 451, 463, 465
sustainable 81, 95, 117, 130, 147, 148, 169, 170,
178–81, 208–9, 215, 219, 220, 231, 257, 346,
373–78, 398–9, 400–1, 408, 422–4, 447
sweat lodge 44, 73
Sweden 31, 36, 59, 63, 95, 135, 151, 347, 449
Swedish massage 35, 277, 294, 381
Switzerland 7, 9, 50, 51, 147, 148, 151–3, 159,
200, 307, 341, 407, 459

tai chi 23, 25, 27, 41, 67, 71, 72, 98, 103, 131, 132,
143, 154, 182, 207–8, 327, 364, 418
Taiwan 25, 231, 429–34
technology 47, 53, 57, 79, 88, 92–5, 101, 103,
114–15, 121, 128, 158, 173, 181, 193, 201, 206,
210, 212, 214, 221, 225, 233, 238, 354, 394,
445, 447, 458
temple 22, 30, 35, 98, 133, 203, 359
Thai massage 182, 196, 207–8, 210, 277, 326
Thailand 99, 111, 126, 147, 151, 169, 171, 184,
195, 213, 233, 360, 383–4, 386, 445, 447–9
thalassotherapy 6, 13, 14, 31, 35, 50–1, 60, 62, 77,
86, 110, 143, 150, 255, 322, 324, 413
therapeutic recreation 72, 73, 84, 85, 220
thermal 43, 47, 49, 58, 60, 141, 155, 157, 160, 173,
182–4, 213, 218, 224, 230, 261, 266–8, 275,
316, 326, 351, 353–4, 358; bath 34, 38, 49–51,
62, 148, 173, 204, 226, 227, 233, 287, 467;
resort 33, 42, 260, 319, 373; spa 6, 34, 50, 55,
60, 64, 173, 175, 208, 213, 226, 259, 260, 281,
315–18, 353, 354; springs 9, 30, 31–2, 38, 55,
58, 60, 65, 70, 73, 230, 321, 322, 330, 351, 362,
369–72, 374; tourism 184, 204, 206, 208, 217,
230, 232–3, 261; waters 8, 12, 13, 27, 31, 35,
54, 56, 69, 85, 110, 114, 148, 170, 175, 176,
182, 195, 216, 222, 265, 276, 278, 285, 315,
317–18, 322, 327, 329, 330, 342, 361, 415
therme 30, 31, 33, 159
Tibb 38–9
Tourism Observatory for Health Wellness and Spa
111, 192, 203, 215
tradition 62, 65–6, 68, 69, 70, 72–3, 77–80, 83, 87,
90, 96, 98, 105, 110, 114, 129, 130, 136, 141,
158–9, 177, 182, 184, 191, 192, 193, 197, 201,

204, 207, 208, 211, 213–17, 219–20, 223, 225, 229, 230–3, 250, 255–7, 260–1, 265, 266–7, 289, 306, 316–19, 327, 329, 331, 338–9, 341, 242–3, 346, 347, 354, 358, 369–70, 379, 380, 384–5, 415, 422–3, 425–6, 452, 463

Traditional Chinese Medicine 84, 142, 220, 238, 250, 252–3, 359, 384

treatments 6, 9, 11–14, 17, 22–3, 27, 29, 30–3, 35, 37–8, 41, 43–5, 47, 50, 51, 53–60, 65–6, 68, 70–1, 77, 84, 95, 139, 145, 148, 152–5, 160, 177, 179, 182–3, 196–7, 207, 210–11, 213, 216, 217, 219, 223, 238, 245, 249, 252, 259, 261–2, 270–2, 277–8, 288, 292, 318, 322, 323–30, 332, 337, 348, 351, 355–7, 359, 360, 369, 371, 374, 379, 407, 414, 419, 426, 427, 435; cosmetic 7, 32, 101, 110, 125, 163, 212, 215–16, 256, 284, 323, 346, 371, 372; medical 7, 10, 15–16, 25, 27, 35, 85–90, 102, 111, 118, 123, 126–7, 128, 161–2, 164–6, 173, 184, 198, 203–5, 208, 212, 214, 220, 222, 226–7, 239, 255, 256, 260, 287, 289, 317, 322–3, 331, 333, 335, 338, 342–4, 358, 361, 370, 374–5, 379, 445, 447–9, 451–5, 456–9, 461–5, 467–72; spa 11, 34, 52, 58, 62–3, 74–5, 86, 113, 123–4, 171, 180, 230, 240, 255, 293, 330, 353, 418

Tunisia 62, 65

Turkish bath 7, 30, 77, 260

Uganda 43, 66, 68, 213, 233

unique 25, 29, 37, 41, 46, 47, 54, 58, 62, 65, 72–3, 75, 77, 99, 136, 139, 152, 156, 166, 169, 170, 181–4, 190–2, 207–10, 213, 219–20, 223, 230, 231, 233, 238, 241, 249, 262, 266, 268, 317, 318, 335, 346–7, 351, 362, 374–6, 378, 380, 382, 415, 418–19, 423, 427, 456, 469

United Arab Emirates 62, 63, 193

United States 18, 20, 31, 43, 117, 381, 417, 459

Vasati 7, 182, 193

vegetarian 12, 21, 24, 25, 45, 75, 89, 90, 101, 129, 130, 133, 134, 326, 421

vitality 6, 41, 97, 151–2, 159, 162, 163, 252, 346, 359, 382, 418–19

young people 111–12, 124, 134, 135, 140, 219, 233, 277, 287, 296, 403, 470

well-being 3–6, 8–10, 25, 31–2, 37, 41, 43, 49, 50, 52, 57, 79, 80–1, 83, 98, 103, 105, 111, 114–17, 120, 125, 145–6, 148, 152, 155–6, 159, 178, 185, 193, 204–5, 207, 213, 219, 220, 223, 225–6, 229–31, 239, 243, 250–1, 253, 259, 266, 278, 322, 327, 345–9, 359–60, 372, 381–2, 389, 391–5, 397–401, 404–6, 407, 413–17, 419, 424, 425, 429, 430–4, 435, 455, 456, 461, 462–5

well-being tourism 391–441

wellness tourism: definition 25–7; management 391–441; demand and marketing 109–67

Western Europe 6, 34, 50–3, 127, 207, 217, 327, 383, 435, 439

Yoga 7, 9, 20, 21, 23–5, 27, 31, 36, 40–1, 45, 46, 50, 53, 61, 65, 67, 70–2, 75, 77, 80, 82, 87–8, 90–3, 95, 98, 99, 101, 103, 110, 112–13, 115, 118, 129, 130–3, 142, 154, 157, 163, 177, 182, 184, 196, 198, 207–8, 215, 231–2, 239, 347, 349, 358–9, 371, 414, 417, 422–3, 428, 435–41, 445, 462

Zen 31, 57, 93, 95, 99, 166, 188–9, 193, 383, 429, 435